ATHENS, 403 BC

At the end of the fifth century BC, the Peloponnesian War resulted in Athens' shattering defeat by Sparta. Taking advantage of the debacle, a commission of thirty Athenians abolished the democratic institutions that for a century had governed the political life of the city and precipitated a year-long civil war. By autumn 403 BC, democracy was restored. Inspired by the model of the ancient chorus, this strikingly innovative book interprets a crucial moment in classical history through the prism of ten remarkable individuals and the shifting groups which formed around them. The former include familiar names like the multifaceted Socrates, the oligarch Critias and the rhetorician Lysias, but also lesser-known figures like the scribe Nicomachus, the former slave Gerys and the priestess Lysimache. What leads a community to tear itself apart, even disintegrate, then rebuild itself? This question, explored through profound reflection on the past, echoes our tormented present.

VINCENT AZOULAY is Director of Studies at the École des Hautes Études en Sciences Sociales, Paris. He is a former member of the Institut Universitaire de France and is the current director of the international bilingual journal *Annales. Histoire, Sciences Sociales*. He has been awarded several prizes, including the Prix du livre d'histoire du Sénat (2011). He is the author of several books already translated into English: *Pericles of Athens* (2014), *The Tyrant-Slayers of Ancient Athens* (2017) and *Xenophon and the Graces of Power* (2018).

PAULIN ISMARD is Professor of Ancient Greek History at Aix Marseille University. He is a former member of the Harvard Center for Hellenic Studies and of the Institute for Advanced Study at Princeton. He has received several awards: the Prix du livre d'histoire du Sénat (2014), the Grand Prix des Rendez-Vous de l'Histoire de Blois (2016) and the Prix François Millepierres de l'Académie Française (2016). He is also the author of *La cité des réseaux. Athènes et ses associations* (2010), *L'événement Socrate* (2013), *Democracy's Slaves. A Political History of Ancient Greece* (2017), *La cité et ses esclaves. Institution, fictions, expériences* (2019), *Les mondes de l'esclavage. Une histoire comparée* (2021) and *Le miroir d'Oedipe. Penser l'esclavage* (2023).

In *Athens, 403 BC* Azoulay and Ismard have produced a superb study of the critical period defined by the brief ascendancy and rapid fall of the Thirty in the aftermath of Athens' defeat in 403 BC. This is an original study with a distinctive voice and a compelling thesis.

Jeremy McInerney, Professor of Classical Studies,
University of Pennsylvania

Homonoia (Unanimity) and *Diallage* (Reconciliation) were 5th-century BCE Athenian democratic catchwords but they still resonate today, as perhaps never before. How timely then is this brilliant collaborative investigation of plurality, polyphony and dissonance in the world's first democracy. Let me only add my voice to the chorus of praise that is its due.

Paul Cartledge, Emeritus A.G. Leventis Professor of Greek Culture,
University of Cambridge

CLASSICAL SCHOLARSHIP IN TRANSLATION

Series editors
RENAUD GAGNÉ, UNIVERSITY OF CAMBRIDGE
JONAS GRETHLEIN, RUPRECHT-KARLS-UNIVERSITÄT HEIDELBERG

Classical Scholarship in Translation provides English translations of some particularly notable and significant scholarship on the ancient Greek and Roman worlds and their reception written in other languages in order to make it better known and appreciated. All areas of classical scholarship are considered.

Recent titles in the series:

Mycenaean Civilization
DORA VASSILIKOU

The Roman Republic and Political Culture: German Scholarship in Translation
AMY RUSSELL AND HANS BECK

Choral Tragedy: Greek Poetics and Musical Ritual
CLAUDE CALAME

The Names of the Gods in Ancient Mediterranean Religions
CORINNE BONNET

The Early Christians: From the Beginnings to Constantine
HARTMUT LEPPIN

Platonism: A Concise History from the Early Academy to Late Antiquity
MAURO BONAZZI

The Greeks and Their Histories: Myth, History and Society
HANS-JOACHIM GEHRKE

The Hera of Zeus: Intimate Enemy, Ultimate Spouse
VINCIANE PIRENNE-DELFORGE AND GABRIELLA PIRONTI

ATHENS, 403 BC

A Democracy in Crisis?

VINCENT AZOULAY
École des Hautes Études en Sciences Sociales

PAULIN ISMARD
Université d'Aix-Marseille

Translated by Lorna Coing

Shaftesbury Road, Cambridge CB2 8EA, United Kingdom

One Liberty Plaza, 20th Floor, New York, NY 10006, USA

477 Williamstown Road, Port Melbourne, VIC 3207, Australia

314–321, 3rd Floor, Plot 3, Splendor Forum, Jasola District Centre, New Delhi – 110025, India

103 Penang Road, #05-06/07, Visioncrest Commercial, Singapore 238467

Cambridge University Press is part of Cambridge University Press & Assessment, a department of the University of Cambridge.

We share the University's mission to contribute to society through the pursuit of education, learning and research at the highest international levels of excellence.

www.cambridge.org
Information on this title: www.cambridge.org/9781009490962

DOI: 10.1017/9781009490979

Preface and English translation © Cambridge University Press, 2025

First published in 2020 as *Athènes 403. Une histoire chorale* © Flammarion, 2020

This publication is in copyright. Subject to statutory exception and to the provisions of relevant collective licensing agreements, no reproduction of any part may take place without the written permission of Cambridge University Press & Assessment.

When citing this work, please include a reference to the DOI 10.1017/9781009490979

First published 2025

Printed in the United Kingdom by CPI Group Ltd, Croydon CR0 4YY

A catalogue record for this publication is available from the British Library.

A Cataloging-in-Publication data record for this book is available from the Library of Congress

ISBN 978-1-009-49096-2 Hardback

Cambridge University Press & Assessment has no responsibility for the persistence or accuracy of URLs for external or third-party internet websites referred to in this publication and does not guarantee that any content on such websites is, or will remain, accurate or appropriate.

To the chorus of our children, Alice, Carmen, Ferdinand and Simon

Contents

List of Figures	*page* xii
Foreword	xiii
Acknowledgments	xxvii
Chronology	xxix

Introduction: Toward a Choral History	1
On the Twelfth Day of Boedromion	3
The City in Chorus(es)	7
The Chorus, an 'Absolute Metaphor'	9
At the Heart of Civic Life	10
Chorus and Social Hierarchies	15
The Chorus Put to the Test of Civil War	17
A Choral History: Contemporary Theorization	19
Plurality, Polyphony, Dissonance	21
Dividing Athenian Society Differently	23
Rethinking Collectives through the Chorus' Lens	25
1 Critias and the Oligarchs	31
Incomparable Critias?	32
The Untraceable Leader	33
The Banality of Evil	35
Generation War	37
The Fracture of Exile	41
Critias, Champion of Oligarchic Radicality	45
A Musical Politics	46
Deadly Friendships	49
A Political Praise of Fear	52
The Unified Chorus: A Joyful Purification	55
The Fractured Chorus: Extending the Domain of Fear	62
The Frightened Chorus: The Terrorist Climax	65
After the Thirty	69

x	*Contents*	
2	**Thrasybulus and the Democratic Resistance**	71
	An Illustrious Unknown	72
	Samos, 411: A Political Experiment	73
	Fortunes and Misfortunes of a *Condottiere*	78
	The Hundred Heroes of Phyle	81
	The Enlarged Chorus of Piraeus	86
	To the Slaves: The Promise of Thrasybulus	91
	The City and Its Borders: Back to Order	93
3	**Archinus or the Victory of the 'Moderates'**	96
	Archinus' Reconciled Athens	98
	The Half-Chorus of the Oligarchs Rallied to Democracy	108
	The Half-Chorus of the 'Moderate' Democrats	114
	An Illusory Reconciliation	121
	History Rewritten: The Winner's Version	127
4	**Socrates and the Voices of Neutrality**	138
	Negative Neutrality: In Exile	141
	Positive Neutrality: In the City	145
	Radical Neutrality: Elusive Socrates	151
	The Divided City and Its Backstage	163
5	**Lysimache: The Priestess of Athena and Her Doubles**	166
	The Guardian of an Immutable Ritual?	167
	The Priestess on Stage	171
	Female Chorality: The Servants of Athena	174
	Myrrhine, Athena's Other Priestess	176
	Syeris, the Subordinate Double of Lysimache	180
	'All of the Lysimachai!'	182
	Lysimache's Dream: The Unacknowledged Community	185
6	**Eutherus and the Precarious Workers**	188
	A Scene of Rural Life: The Olive Tree of Discord	189
	Elusive Men: Free Employees	191
	The Intermittent Chorus	196
	The Impossible Union of Wage Workers	199
	Friendship as a Mask for Subjection	201
7	**Hegeso or the Family Torn Asunder**	204
	The Domestic Chorus: The *Oikos* of Ischomachus	205
	A Disputed Heritage	207
	A Political Trial?	210
	The City of the Dead: The Blended Family	212
	Hegeso, the Seated Woman	213

8	Gerys and the World of the Merchant Agora	221
	Slave Names	222
	An Exemplary Greengrocer	224
	If Dying Is a Beautiful Thing …	225
	Men and Women of the Agora	228
	The Thracian Chorus of Mounychia	230
9	Nicomachus and the Servants of the City	235
	Aeschylus in the Underworld: Chorus and Anti-Chorus	237
	Nicomachus, Scribe and Administrator	240
	Politics and Its Borders	242
	A Chorus of Bureaucrats	245
	Beyond Freedom and Slavery	248
10	Lysias, a Multifaceted Man	251
	An Uncertain Date of Birth	253
	A Model Metic?	257
	An Equivocal Democrat	261
	The Paradoxes of Logography	265
	A Family Epic	273
	A Very Small and Rich World	277
	Shared Suffering: A Chorus of Exiles?	282
	The Discreet Charm of the Oligarchy	285
	The Civil War or the Great Simplification	294
	Conclusion: The City in Chorus	297
	The Philosophical Fantasy	298
	Democratic Polyphony	300
	Aristotle, or the Choral City	302
	Back to the Event	307
	Of *Stasis* as Arrythmia	309
	Extension of the Domain of Civil War?	315
	A Change of Pace? Athens after 403	321
	Ariston's Last Dance	327

Bibliography   329
Index   355

Figures

0.1	Map of Attica.	*page* 4
0.2	The Agora, the Pnyx and the Acropolis (view from northwest).	5
0.3	Map of Piraeus.	8
2.1	Map of the Aegean world.	75
3.1	Stele displaying three decrees in honor of the Samians voted in 405/403 BC.	112
3.2	Curse box (photograph and inscription), Kerameikos Cemetery, late fifth century BC.	124
3.3	Cursed figurine (photograph and inscription), Kerameikos Cemetery, late fifth century BC.	124
5.1	Base of Lysimache statue, priestess of Athena Polias.	168
5.2	Funerary lekythos of Myrrhine (420–410 BC).	178
7.1	*Stemma* of the family of Dicaeogenes of Kydathenaion.	209
7.2	The stele of Hegeso.	215
7.3	The enclosure of Coroibos of Melite (Kerameikos, Athens).	216
7.4	Funerary stele of Coroibos of Melite (Kerameikos, Athens).	217
11.1	Chronology of the Athenian civil war according to Canfora.	310
11.2	Chronology of the Athenian civil war according to Krentz.	312

Foreword

How are we to write the history of classical Athens? For most ancient Greek cities the problem of writing their histories is the problem of telling a story when the evidence is so thin. In the Hellenistic period there was a veritable explosion of local history writing,[1] but there is no classical Greek city apart from Athens from which we have extant histories written by members of the city. Even in the case of cities about which we know most, such as Sparta and Thebes, the histories we can write are histories that we put together from the appearances of those cities in general historical narratives and the observations upon how those cities worked offered by members of other cities. By contrast, from classical Athens we have not only histories by Athenians that are, at least in part, focused on Athens, but also a mass of tragic and comic drama composed by Athenians for Athenians, and a slew of speeches written for delivery in the Athenian courts or in political arenas at Athens. Added to this is a much fuller epigraphic record from Athens than from any other classical city, including both public inscriptions recording decrees, laws, accounts, et cetera, and private inscriptions marking dedications or burials. As a result we know in detail how the Athenian constitution worked, and we can name thousands of individuals and reconstruct at least part of the family tree of hundreds of families.

But the comparative abundance of evidence does not make writing the history of classical Athens any easier. For however abundant our Athenian evidence is, it does not begin to match the evidence we have for European countries over the last two centuries. The existence of multiple contemporary accounts of what has been happening in Europe, along with a mountain of financial and statistical records, enables the historian today to establish and discount the selectivity and bias of individual records. Rarely is the order of events or the question of who was responsible for what

---

[1] Clarke 2008; Thomas 2019.

action hard to establish. Quite the contrary is true of Athens. Despite the mass of source material, we frequently end up relying on a single source telling the story from a particular perspective, or, where there are multiple sources, their different interests make it impossible to recover any single correct narrative sequence or establish exactly who did what.

There have been three traditional approaches to dealing with this problem. The first has been to resort to giving an institutional account. This history of Athens is the history of how the constitution worked and how the rules governing the working of individual institutions changed over time. The second has been to concentrate on establishing how to read particular sources. This is less a history of Athens than an explanation for why a single history cannot be written, a separating out of strands of history without commitment to how they should be twisted together or whether twisting them together constitutes anything like a complete story. The third, which has the longest history and remains the most popular, has been to create a narrative by selecting the particular sources to be followed according to the modern scholar's notions of what 'must have been' the case and plugging the gaps with imaginative reconstruction.

Different periods and different national traditions of scholarship lean more towards one of these approaches or more towards another. In the case of the third approach, there are different national traditions as to what the scholar's imagination should feed upon. Within the anglophone tradition the dominant source of models according to which Athenian history might be interpreted and completed has been recent history – life in Athens, and particularly political life in Athens, has been assumed to be like (political) life in the modern world (with disputes following as to, for example, whether modern 'parties' or 'factions' provide better parallels). But within the French tradition the view that the Greeks are not like us has long been strong, and parallels for Greek life have been sought in anthropology rather than in recent history. This is a tradition variously represented by Henri Jeanmaire, by Louis Gernet and by the circle of Jean-Pierre Vernant and Pierre Vidal-Naquet.

The contrasts between French and anglophone scholarly traditions of writing Greek history received classic discussion from John Ma in his 'Black Hunter variations' of 1994, when he offered both a structuralist account in French and a close commentary in English of the story at the opening of Plutarch's *Life of Cimon* and then reflected on the way in which they did not make contact with each other.[2] Ma's own multicultural

---

[2] Ma 1994.

background and education in both francophone and anglophone worlds put him in a good position to understand the academic impulses behind the very different scholarly discussions. But few are in Ma's position, and one of the major incentives behind this series publishing scholarship in translation is to increase familiarity with the different ways of seeing the ancient world that have been developed in different traditions.

Different scholarly approaches show up most clearly not when the ancient evidence is sparse but when it is at its richest. The events following Athens' defeat by Sparta in the Peloponnesian War are events that were so traumatic for Athenians that we are particularly well informed about them. After the disastrous defeat and effective loss of the fleet in the Battle of Aigos Potamos, Athens was starved into submission as Sparta took control of the Hellespont and the Aegean. The Spartans, who generally looked out for their friends in Athens' former allies and chose ten of them to govern their city, oversaw the appointment of thirty men to rule Athens. Those thirty clashed among themselves about exactly how to run the city, and over time became more and more violent. Athenians opposed to the Thirty either left Athens voluntarily or were expelled, and, getting support from other states, mounted a military offensive. This caused the Thirty to summon further help from Sparta, but the opposition to the Thirty quickly achieved enough military success that the Spartan king, Pausanias, brokered a deal to remove the Thirty and restore some form of democratic government in Athens. Part of this deal involved the agreement of the returning Athenians 'not to remember past ills' except with regard to the Thirty themselves.

Notwithstanding this amnesty agreement, the events of 404–3 overshadowed Athenian court cases for the next five years – in some cases the next fifteen years. The condemnation of Socrates, who had remained in Athens under the Thirty, was one of those cases. Many of the cases we know about were cases in which the forensic speech-writer Lysias was involved, and Lysias was himself a man whose wealthy family had fallen victim to the Thirty. The history of the whole period was written up by Xenophon, who seems to have fought in the cavalry under the Thirty and then to have deliberately gone off to join a mercenary army put together by the Persian prince Cyrus in Asia Minor in order to avoid the consequences of his actions. There were other histories written up too, one of which is reflected in the much later account by Diodorus Siculus. Other insights into the life and issues of the period can be derived from the dialogues involving Socrates that Xenophon also wrote, some of which are set in the particular context of the Athens of 403, and later claims about the politics of the period are reflected in the account given by the Aristotelian *Constitution of the Athenians*.

All these literary sources, along with a number of inscriptions from the period, mean that historians can potentially uncover in detail not just the outlines of the political history, but something of what the events of this period meant to different groups and individuals in Athens. But the difficulties of doing this are considerable. Precisely because the period itself was so fraught, the accounts that individuals give of it tend to be heavily shaped by their particular situation. How exactly we discount their bias and how we decide what factors most influenced individuals and groups in these years are difficult matters, and whichever approach historians choose – whether to focus on institutional history, on source problems or on providing an apparently coherent overall narrative – there are many selections to be made and judgements to be passed. This is precisely why *Athens, 403 BC* is so welcome: we see two highly skilled French historians picking their way through the rich evidence by way of a number of striking decisions about what approach to take. In what follows I try to illuminate those decisions and explore their consequences.

Athens, 403 BC is very clearly a product of the French scholarly tradition – or, perhaps better, of French scholarly traditions, since few readers will fail to detect, even in translation, the different scholarly styles of the two authors. Where Vidal-Naquet saw Athenian life as shaped by the imprint of rites of passage and the aetiological myths explaining them, and emphasised the foreignness of ancient Athens in that way, Azoulay and Ismard draw out, instead, the impact on Athenians of the experience of being in a chorus (sometimes itself, indeed, a rite of passage). Athenians sang and danced together as a group, under the direction of a chorus-leader and in costumes paid for by a man obliged by the state to use his riches for the purpose as a form of taxation, in the context of various religious festivals. But whether such choral experience was acquired in the performance of tragedy and comedy, where the chorus interacted with actors, or in contexts, such as the performance of dithyramb, where the chorus was the sole performer, it created a bond between chorus members and between those members and their director and financier that Azoulay and Ismard suggest was a model for social relationships more generally. The chorus, for them, is a metaphor, but also more than that. Having been a member of a chorus was an experience that inclined individuals to network themselves in certain particular ways rather than others. And, they suggest, it was in the interweaving of the dances of the different choruses – the formal ones and the informal ones – that Athenians (and indeed other residents of

Athens) joined that the history of the violent politics, and its dissipation, was shaped.

As reviewers of the French original have already noted, and as the authors themselves anticipate, different readers will find more or less illumination in the notion of choruses. There are, in truth, so many different ways of deploying the image of the chorus – which can be variously thought of as an unchanging group dancing at different times to very different tunes, or as a body that specialises in one particular type of dance, or as a stage of life that metamorphoses into other life stages (from dancing chorus to fighting phalanx) – and indeed so many incompatible ancient uses of the metaphor of the chorus – that it is good for stimulating thought in general rather than offering a particular model. The combination of (homo)sociality with performativity that actual choral dancing involved, the combination of musical, verbal and physical aspects of that performativity and the capacity of the chorus to convey something of its experience not only to its members but also to spectators meant that the chorus itself was a tremendously powerful instrument for 'constructing, experiencing, and projecting a strong sense of civic identity' (to borrow from Prauscello's analysis of chorality in Plato's *Laws*). Exactly how that worked in any particular choral performance is largely unrecoverable, and it is easier to acknowledge in general, as Azoulay and Ismard do in their Introduction, citing Mauss, how choruses transform humans' perception of the world they live in through the universally shared experience of 'rhythm as pleasurable order' than it is to carry this through to particular, and metaphorical, choruses.[3]

The value of the idea of the chorus in *Athens, 403 BC* resides in the excuse that it gives for looking at the oligarchic regime of the Thirty and its overthrow not as simply a set of political events but as a trauma that affected the whole range of different 'choruses' within Athens. What this book vividly reminds us of is the way in which those residing in Athens did not form a single community or interest group. Athens, even at the end of the Peloponnesian War, was a multicultural community – both in the sense of including people from many different origins, but also in the sense that the values of different groups within the city were far from uniform. But whether we think of the Athens of 403 as a place where one tune was replaced by another, or where the music was speeded up or slowed down, or where the direction of the circle dance was reversed, the point is that everyone in Athens was affected by the change of tune, tempo or direction.

[3] Prauscello 2014: 108, 109.

The choral metaphor provides an excuse for moving, between a single set of covers, from studies of the obvious political leaders – Critias, Thrasybulus and Archinus – through studies of the civil servant Nicomachus and the highly atypical 'ordinary citizen' Socrates, to studies of those excluded from normal political participation who nonetheless found themselves more or less actively caught up in events – the Thracian Gerys, the labourer Eutherus, the wealthy and well-bred women Lysimache and Hegeso and the fat cat and smart guy Lysias. The history of Athens in the last five years of the fifth century has never been written like this before.

It is worth pausing to consider what writing a history of Athens' political trauma in this way enables. One of the things that it enables I have already alluded to. The choral metaphor, the emphasis on circles of people, offers a way of authorising a particular set of assumptions about how actions might fit together, a particular interpretative framework. Within this framework personal networks are privileged over links of class, or party, or indeed ideology. Anglophone scholarship has had something of an obsession with the role that 'the ancestral constitution' played in the abolition of democracy in both 411 and 404, both as a protean ideology and as a retrospective justification. In this it was encouraged by the Greek historian whose shadow falls over the late twentieth-century history of the subject even beyond the anglophone world, Moses Finley, who devoted his Cambridge Inaugural Lecture to the topic.[4] Azoulay and Ismard acknowledge what they rather wonderfully – if, in my view, misleadingly – term 'the uniform varnish of the ancestral constitution' but, partly no doubt because they think it uniform, never examine the role of this ideology.

There are significant advantages to removing ideology from the picture. The more the conflict is seen in terms of groups following those they recognise as leaders more because of what they have in common with that leader than because they are attracted by the tune that leader plays, the easier it is to explain how the Athenians came back together at the end of this civil war. Once there are no 'parties' united by a common vision of society but simply factions, formed by individuals who recognise that they have something in common or who simply work together because they always have done, reconciliation becomes a matter of dealing with past wrongdoing, not a matter of political re-education. Yet it was clearly possible to persuade Athenians that political re-education was needed: the trial of Socrates is hard to comprehend unless the education Socrates

---

[4] Finley 1971.

was considered to have delivered was thought to have misled his students into hostility to democracy. Notably Azoulay and Ismard reference the fourth-century view that 'the philosopher had been sentenced for having notoriously trained (*pepaideukōs*) Critias' not in the chapter on Socrates, but in an earlier chapter, enabling them, in their chapter title, to recruit Socrates to 'the voices of neutrality'. Whether or not one is persuaded to buy the possibility of neutrality in the Athens of 404–3 depends to a great extent on whether one is prepared to remove ideology from history.

A second thing that writing the history like this enables is the return of history as the story of individuals. Many of those who take starring roles here would never qualify as conventional 'great men', either because they were women or because they were modest, both in background and in individual qualities (Gerys or Eutherus). But by making them the leaders or representative members of choruses Azoulay and Ismard insist that these individuals need to be recuperated as great figures within their particular worlds. As they point out in their Introduction, choruses were not places of perfect equality. There were a number of potentially leading roles within any chorus, and some roles, like that of the *auletes* who provided the music, were necessarily leading roles. The chorus is therefore the place in which the individual becomes part of a group without losing their individuality. But of course there are some elements of history that become visible only if we do eliminate the distracting details of individuality. For all that Eutherus owes his place here to an anecdote about Socrates' practical wisdom in advising him how to make a living, economic history is not something that can be easily written at the individual level. Economic considerations were intertwined with political decisions, whether in terms of their politicising or depoliticising class relations or of their enabling or disabling political resistance. When, as Xenophon's story goes, Eutherus was persuaded by Socrates to put himself at the service of a rich landowner, he was deciding not simply to swallow citizen pride but to subordinate political independence to economic need. Only once we appreciate what is going on in those terms can we see that Socrates' advice to him to 'avoid those who like to find blame and go after the well-intentioned' (*Memorabilia* 2.8.6) is covertly political.

The bigger economic background really matters here. Azoulay and Ismard comment acutely that the circumstances of Aristarchus' impoverishment, in the story in Xenophon's *Memorabilia* 2.7, highlight political division within the family and the impossibility of getting rent from urban property when the city population has been so reduced. But once we start asking what the city population had been reduced to (nothing in excess of

10,000 would be my guess), we have to ask how an Aristarchus could find a market for the clothing that Socrates persuades him to have his female dependents weave. The dances that could be performed, and who could perform them, were critically affected not simply by the will of chorus-leaders and chorus members but by whether livelihoods could be sustained. Throughout the middle of the fifth century Athens had had access not only to a local market of perhaps 400,000 people and to the whole of the central Mediterranean and beyond, but also to massive income from its silver mines (quite apart from the profits of empire). After Thrasybulus and his 'chorus' took the Peiraeus, Athens was reduced to being a small town without access to any significant outside income or markets. Rather like the Spartans at Tegea in the sixth century, Athenians who had once expected to be able to dance now found themselves heavily fettered (Hdt. 1.66).

Rather more subtly, Azoulay and Ismard's choral metaphor authorises a distinct source preference. Once more, scholarship has spilt much ink on the differences between different accounts of what went on in 404–3, and in particular between the accounts of Xenophon and of the Aristotelian *Constitution of the Athenians* (particularly well laid out in P. J. Rhodes' *Commentary on the Aristotelian* Athenaion Politeia), sewing the vivid vignettes offered by various Lysias speeches onto a fabric woven from these texts. By putting the emphasis on circles of people, Azoulay and Ismard move the focus from either the narrative offered by Xenophon's *Hellenika* or the constitutional analysis offered by Aristotle's researcher to the evidence offered by Lysias and, to a lesser extent, by other orators and by Xenophon's *Memorabilia*. It is not by chance that the chapter on Lysias is made the climax of the book, just as the authors admit that laying out the narrative at the end, not the start, of the book was a deliberate choice.

The selection of individuals to represent different choruses is clearly crucial to the overall picture created by the book. Making space for characters whose stories have never before featured in discussions of the events of and after 403 – men like Gerys or women like Hegeso – necessarily enforces choices as to who, among those centrally involved, features in lights. The very metaphor of the chorus enables chapters to look at the members of the chorus as well as the chosen chorus-leader, but we must still ask what difference it makes looking at the chorus led by Critias rather than that led by Theramenes, or choosing not to represent at all those Athenian citizens who actively served the Thirty: how differently would we understand these events if, instead of looking at Socrates, who left no writings but only a mythology of the citizen who stayed but resisted, they had chosen to focus on Socrates' student Xenophon, a citizen who left copious writings relating to the events of those years, and who had almost certainly himself chosen to assist rather than resist the Thirty?

My point here is not to find fault with the selection representing the different choruses – one can find fault with any selection – but to encourage readers to think critically about what has been selected, for what reason and with what results. In this context one needs also to ask whether it is the choral metaphor alone that has shaped the selection and, indeed, the narrative. It is worth paying some attention to the one modernising allusion (beyond vividly likening the ageing Lysias to the ageing Berlusconi) that Azoulay and Ismard allow themselves (and repeatedly): that is the allusion to the French experience of resistance and liberation in World War II. They invoke the language of 'resistance' (not found in the ancient sources in relation to Athens) throughout, and in Chapter 2 they explicitly highlight the parallel with 'the installation of General de Gaulle's "government" in Algiers in June 1943' when 'a whole section of the administrative and economic elite, who had previously supported the Vichy regime, rallied to the new power'. The parallels are indeed irresistible: the eventual liberation of Paris by the Free French to the liberation of Athens by the 'men of Phyle'; the process of reintegrating collaborators, who turned from the enemy of one day to the compatriots of the next. But this raises the question too of how far we should see the installation by the Sparta general Lysander of the Thirty as a puppet government as parallel to the installation by Hitler of the Vichy government as a puppet government.

One advantage of the parallel is the emphasis it puts on the extent to which the government installed by the victorious enemy was enabled by widespread complaisance. This gives sharp edges to the scrutiny of Socrates, and to his decision not to leave the city but simply to refuse to execute orders from the Thirty with which he disagreed. Another advantage is in drawing attention to how those who were not part of the resistance managed to continue to be active in politics. The valuable analysis here of Lysias' clients and of his willingness to write for those who had stayed in the city under the Thirty is one borne of French experience.

The very attractions of the parallel, and the clear-eyed analysis to which it leads, make it important also to realise its limitations. The differences between Hitler and the Spartans are non-trivial. Although Azoulay and Ismard are tempted to follow those scholars who have seen the Thirty as set up in the image of Sparta and pursuing Laconizing policies, there was no Spartan ideology parallel to Nazi anti-Semitism. Occasional Spartan expulsion of foreigners – itself known more in theory than in practice – does not translate into racism. Nor was there a personality cult, even of Lysander (despite the games instituted on Samos in his honour), in the way that there was a personality cult of Hitler. As events would show, the Spartans were deeply divided over what to do about Athens, and, for all that the Athenians wanted to claim credit for their liberation in 403, as they had claimed credit for removing the tyrant at the end of the sixth century, it was the Spartan king Pausanias who was the real architect of Athens' democratic restoration, just as it was the Spartan king Cleomenes who had got rid of the Peisistratids from Athens. Azoulay and Ismard include no non-Athenian choruses that were dancing with and around Athenian choruses. This makes it all too easy to overlook the extent to which the tunes and dances of the Athenians were the tunes and dances of the Spartans.

Although Azoulay and Ismard themselves draw attention to the fact that the 'process of reconciliation [...] was largely dictated from the outside, according to the divisions between Spartan leaders', and will later talk of 'the Spartans [...] leading the dance', the focus on Athenian choruses means that their focus is elsewhere. So when they quote the Aristotelian *Constitution of the Athenians* 38.3–4, they elide with '[...]' the first sentence of 3.38.4 (I quote P. J. Rhodes' translation): 'The peace settlement and reconciliation were brought to a conclusion by Pausanias, king of Sparta, together with the ten peace commissioners who subsequently came from Sparta at his urgent request.' And when they refer to Xenophon's account of the same events, they emphasise Pausanias' attempt to divide the men of the city (which they ascribe to jealousy of Lysander) in order to get them to seek reconciliation, but ignore the role played by the two ephors accompanying Pausanias. These ephors – unlike the king, elected officials reflecting the recent mood in Sparta – supported Pausanias (*Hellenica* 2.4.35–6). The timeline of events in the Conclusion effaces the Spartans totally.

The downplaying of Pausanias' role, and the role of Spartan initiative more generally, is something that Azoulay and Ismard share with the Aristotelian *Constitution of the Athenians*. But in other ways their account is written against the Aristotelian account. As was his brief, Aristotle's researcher was on the hunt for constitutional changes. He found them in what he claims were the initial actions of the Thirty – repealing the laws of Ephialtes and Archestratus about the Council of the Areopagus and removing from laws qualifications that gave scope for disputes

(*Constitution of the Athenians* 35.2). We are not told who was responsible for these revisions, and so there is no chorus to reconstruct that dances to this tune (the Aristotelian author suggests that the tune was that of 'the ancestral constitution'). But the *Constitution of the Athenians* is the favourite text of institutional historians for a reason. Legislative changes are rarely random; when they are undertaken in revolutionary political situations they tell us something about the underlying arguments behind the personal politics.

Those underlying arguments matter because, for all that it was short-lived, the rule of the Thirty was not an isolated episode of constitutional revision, quickly reversed. In their Conclusion, Azoulay and Ismard rightly explore how we are to read the Thirty in a wider political context. They are quick to resist finding ever earlier precedents for and premonitions of what occurred in 403, but the claims made in antiquity about the degree of overlap between the Thirty and the Four Hundred who had briefly held power in 411–10, even if exaggerated, were not without truth. Not only do we know a lot – rather more than in 404 – about the constitutional arguments that went on in 411, but the decision of the restored democracy to begin revising the laws in 410 indicates how deeply some of these arguments had cut. Azoulay and Ismard's decision to discuss the legal revisions largely in the context of discussing the under-clerk Nicomachus, who was prosecuted by Lysias, have the consequence of somewhat trivialising the revision: of course Lysias was not going to suggest that Nicomachus and his colleagues had tackled serious problems in a serious way, let alone made a good job of what they had done. But the introduction in 403 of the division between decisions that had permanent effect – that is, 'laws' – from decisions that had only a one-off impact – 'decrees' – and the insistence that laws had to be made by a different process indicate that serious jurisprudential work had been done.

But, as Azoulay and Ismard rightly insist, what changed after 403 was not primarily a result of different constitutional rules. It was, however, a result of the Athenians coming to use their constitution differently. As Claire Taylor has shown, the patterns of those politically active in the fourth century differ from the patterns of those politically active in the fifth. The proportion of those politically active known to be wealthy declined from 19 percent in the fifth century to 11 percent in the fourth (even though our knowledge of who was wealthy significantly improves), and whereas the majority of the politically active wealthy in the fifth century came from in or near the city itself, in the fourth century the biggest group of politically active wealthy men came from demes two to four hours' walk away from the city.⁵ However many of those who had stayed in the city in 404–3 re-entered politics, the personnel of politics permanently changed after 403. How far it was the events of 403 that caused these changes is another matter – but to understand the true significance of 403 for Athenian political life, it helps to put it in this bigger context.

If institutional history is effectively excluded from the story that Azoulay and Ismard tell, concerns about how to read the surviving sources are very clearly flagged up in relation to the last of the individuals they discuss – and the one who is least choral – Lysias (Azoulay and Ismard effectively admit that their choral image is tested by Lysias as they talk about the 'shifting choruses' that gravitate 'around this ill-defined man'). Problems of reading can hardly be avoided with Lysias. To start with there is the question of which of the texts ascribed to him he actually wrote. Then there is the problem of what sort of a man it is who wrote them – the difficulty of resolving the discrepant ancient information about his life means we are always given the choice between two Lysiases, one fifteen years older and more life-experienced than the other. But worse than that, Lysias' words are, with perhaps two exceptions, always in the mouths of others. Was Lysias offering us his own views through the other person's mouth? Or were the views those he knew his client to hold? Or simply the views that he thought most likely to help win the argument in court? Was he the sort of writer who was prepared to take on the task of writing a persuasive text for any purpose or any person willing to pay suitably, or was he discriminating, writing only for those with whose politics he had sympathies? We can certainly rule out any narrow definition by Lysias of politically acceptable people to write for, but beyond that it is hard to do more than guess.

By putting the discussion of Lysias the logographer last in the book, after they have made much use of Lysias' texts to discuss others, Azoulay and Ismard might be taken to imply that what we learn in that chapter has no bearing on what they have written earlier. But is that true? The question of how heavily politically coloured Lysias' texts are surely affects how we interpret the information they give. But if that is true of Lysias, it is no less true of other texts. Here again the decision never to discuss Xenophon becomes a marked one. Xenophon himself does his best to make himself invisible in his texts, putting speeches in the mouths of others in *Memorabilia* (and indeed *Apology*), writing of himself in the third

---

⁵ Taylor 2007.

person in *Anabasis*, hiding behind an appearance of objectivity in the earliest books of the *Hellenica*. But should the invisibility of the author not worry us? What exactly is this invisible author doing by selecting *these* historical 'facts', reproducing *these* conversations? These are questions to which the whole architecture of *Athens, 403 BC* offers a particular answer, as I have tried to indicate in this discussion.

As the Conclusion here reveals, 403 stood at a turning point in more ways than simply the political. The culture of fourth-century Athens was quite different from that of fifth-century Athens. Azoulay and Ismard draw attention to the way in which old tragedies begin to be re-performed – and end up taking up all the tragic airtime. Comedy famously changed its nature, ceasing to be closely pointed at individual politicians and gradually transforming itself into the situation comedy of which Menander would be such a master. The end of the fifth century is a break point in Athenian pot painting too, as it is also in the Athenian architectural tradition.

Art and society are linked here. One of Azoulay and Ismard's important innovations is to include within the ten individuals through whom they explore the experience of 403 one Hegeso, a woman known simply from her famous tombstone (though her brother is better known through his appearance in a law court speech about inheritance). The fame of this tombstone tends to obscure how unusual it is. There had been no Athenian tombstones, other than lists of those who had died in war, for at least half a century from the early fifth century onwards, and although some individual tombstones reappear around 420, the number of early tombstones was small. Hegeso heads the list of tombstones of Athenian women, which will come in the fourth century to outnumber tombstones for Athenian men, but at what date her tombstone was carved remains disputed – perhaps as early as c. 410, but for some scholars as late as 390. Whatever the date, it marks a hinge between the male-dominated commemoration of the dead of sixth- and fifth-century monuments and the female-dominated commemoration of the fourth-century monuments – something it is tempting to associate with the reintroduction and then strengthening of Pericles' Citizenship Law limiting Athenian citizenship to those with Athenian mothers as well as Athenian fathers.[6]

Seeing political history as part of cultural history raises a number of questions. Are we correct to emphasise the particularity of a set of events like the establishment and removal of the regime of the Thirty, or should see them within the pattern of wider trends? Is history the consequence of

---

[6] A temptation to which I myself have succumbed; see Osborne 1997.

many individual decisions, the accumulation of many different individual human experiences, or are there bigger changes to a society's outlook and way of experiencing the world?

To take up Azoulay and Ismard's own dancing image (though we need to remember that music and lyrics were as integral to the chorus as was dancing), they not only offer us their own *grand pas de deux*, but as they display their pointe work, moving knowingly around not just the evidence but the methodological issues, they also invite us to judge their dancing. Although the emphasis of this book is on taking part, dancing – and above all choral dancing – is a spectator sport, and the experience of watching choral dances changes one's perceptions of the world. The music and movements of this dance come from a tradition with which anglophone readers have limited familiarity. *Athens, 403 BC* invites us not to join the dance – for this is not a ceilidh – but to watch these performers' moves. Even for those who have heard similar music and seen similar steps before, this is a dance like no other, and those readers will learn most who engage with this dance among the jury panel rather than sit passively among the spectators.

Acknowledgments

This book is the result of a joyful and friendly collaborative project, spread out over more than six years. As in an ancient chorus, it is sometimes difficult to distinguish the two voices that run through it: The introduction and conclusion were conceived of, thought out and written together, and, while each chapter has an identifiable father, they would sound quite different without the intense discussions that fueled them. We hope that the two resulting half-choruses are not too discordant: on one side, Critias, Archinus, Socrates, Lysimache and Lysias; on the other side, Thrasybulus, Eutherus, Hegeso, Gerys and Nicomachus.

We would like to express our deepest gratitude to our editor, colleague and friend, Renaud Gagné. We are also indebted to the person who revised our own translation, Lorna Loing. Last but not least, we want to address our warmest thanks to Claire Taylor, who agreed to proofread the entire manuscript in order to remove, as far as possible, the errors and omissions left, and who polished the expression. It was a real chance to benefit from her eagle (yet benevolent) eye. It's also a pleasure to thank Robin Osborne for his generous preface.

Throughout this adventure, several choruses of friends and colleagues gave us their advice and suggestions. They helped our desire to work together, a notion we dreamt up at a research laboratory – one used by the ANHIMA research centre (Anthropologie and Histoire des Mondes Anciens) – to culminate in a real book.

We would especially like to thank our great mutual friend, Yann Potin, who worked with us on this project from the very outset, as well as Sophie Berlin, who enthusiastically welcomed the choral intuition behind it. Their unfailing support accompanied the progressive transformations of the book until it found its final form.

We are grateful to many colleagues and friends for the exchanges we have had during several colloquia, seminars and editorial committees. It is a great pleasure to be able to thank Etienne Anheim, Patrick Boucheron,

Mirko Canevaro, Françoise Frontisi, Adeline Grand-Clément, Thomas Hirsch, Pierre Judet de La Combe, François Lissarrague, Arnaud Macé, Claudia Moatti, Pascal Montlahuc, Christel Muller, Violaine Sébillotte and Anne Simonin. Some of them have even kindly reread entire chapters: Pierre Chiron agreed to put his rhetorical expertise at the service of the chorus of Lysias; and Anton Powell, a formidable scholar and tireless editor, lent his ear to the chorus of Critias to correct any off-key notes. He is in our thoughts, as he has recently been snatched from us by illness.

The writing of our book took shape during the seminar 'Les figures du politique' at the École des Hautes Études en Sciences Sociales. The chorus that agreed to discuss, week after week, the hypotheses put forward played an essential role in helping our thoughts mature. Our special thanks go to Alexandra Bartzoka, Louise Bruit, Antoine Chabod, Hugo Chausserie-Laprée, Panos Christodoulou, Paul Cournarie, Mathilde Defosse, Charles Delattre, Jocelyn Deseau, Marie Durnerin, Daniele Guasco, Sophie Lalanne, Françoise Legrand, Pierrine Malette, Daria Russo, Nicolas Siron, Alexandre Vlamos and Adrien Zirah.

Finally, this book is a continuation of our previous work on democracy, and we must thank those who, long ago, showed us the new paths of Athenian politics and suggested the relevance of a choral approach: Pauline Schmitt, Claude Calame and, of course, Nicole Loraux, whose intimidating shadow was by our side throughout this adventure.

Chronology

All dates throughout this book are BC unless stated otherwise.

508/7: reforms of Cleisthenes; beginning of Athenian democracy
490: first Persian War (Battle of Marathon)
481–479: second Persian war; naval battle of Salamis
478: creation of the Delian League, instrument of Athenian imperialism
462/1: reform of Ephialtes, reducing the powers of the Areopagus and reinforcing the power of the people
451: law on citizenship (the requirement to have two Athenian parents to be considered a full citizen); institution of the first political allowance (*misthos*) for the members of the popular courts
447–438: construction of the Parthenon
443–429: Pericles reelected as *stratēgos*
431–404: Peloponnesian War between Athens and Sparta (and their respective allies)
429: the 'plague' in Athens; death of Pericles
415: religious scandals in the city (mutilation of the Herms and parody of the Eleusinian Mysteries)
415–413: expedition to Sicily with catastrophic consequences for Athens
411: first oligarchic revolution (known as the Four Hundred); revolt of the Athenian fleet stationed in Samos: Thrasybulus elected *stratēgos* by the rowers
410: end of the first oligarchic revolution and restoration of democracy; beginning of the revision of the city's laws
406: Battle of Arginusai; trial and conviction of Athenian generals
405 (fall): Athenian defeat at Aigos Potamos
404–403: Athenian civil war
    404 (January?): trial of Cleophon; second performance of Aristophanes' *Frogs*

- 404 (April): surrender of Athens; destruction of the Long Walls linking the city to Piraeus
- 404 (September?): establishment of the Thirty; reduction of the civic body to 3,000 citizens
- 404 (December?): capture of Phyle by Thrasybulus and the first resistance fighters
- 403 (Spring?): dissension among the Thirty; trial and execution of Theramenes
- 403 (May–June?): Battle of Mounychia in Piraeus; death of Critias and deposition of the Thirty, replaced by the Ten
- 403 (September or early October): end of the oligarchy and Athenian reconciliation
- 403/2: establishment of the political allowance for the Assembly; distinction between laws and decrees; reinstatement of the law on citizenship; Theozotides' decree in favor of the orphans of the citizens who had died during the *stasis* (or 410?)
- 403–401: multiple trials against former oligarchs (in particular Lysias' lawsuit against Eratosthenes)
- 401: decree granting citizenship to the noncitizen combatants of Phyle
- 401/0: depletion of the last oligarchic stronghold in Eleusis
- 399: trial and acquittal of Andocides; trial and conviction of Socrates

Introduction
Toward a Choral History

> For in a real tragedy, it is not the hero who perishes, it is the chorus.
> Joseph Brodsky, Nobel Lecture, December 8, 1987

On January 11, 2015, millions of people marched in the streets, in Paris and all over France, stunned by the attacks against the editorial staff of *Charlie Hebdo* and French people of Jewish faith. Both a procession of mourning and an expression of national unity and reassurance in the face of terror, these demonstrations resembled a collective exorcism: Many citizens felt compelled to participate, regardless of their political affiliation, as if, after a moment of shock, everyone felt the need to get moving again. For the participants, this was a moment of extraordinary intensity, provoking wild and contradictory emotions, mixing fear, hostility, a spirit of vengeance, solidarity and fraternity – in short, they felt they were experiencing a historic event.

The magnitude of this collective reaction gave rise to the greatest hopes. Many saw in the fervor of these demonstrations the opportunity to renew frayed social ties, as if their mutual trauma had opened a breach in time. This is perhaps characteristic of all historic events: to conjure up other ways of 'building society,' of ordering bodies and minds before being confined to the oblivion of history, swept away by official speeches. But through its very emergence, any authentic event opens up the possibility as much of unification as of radical division.

In fact, just as France was experiencing this moment of fellowship in January 2015, several more or less explicit forms of division appeared. Within hours of the attacks, it was clear that not everyone wanted to take part in these collective marches and moments of shared emotion. While many people joined the demonstrations, many others were absent, to the extent that some saw the mammoth processions of January 11 as an expression of the fear of a middle- and upper-class, ethnically homogeneous France. No, decidedly not everyone was 'Charlie': Social networks offered an exceptional sounding board to the voices breaking with the united song of the chorus. There was a legitimate distrust of the people's holy union, based on principles too general and generous to be honest and instrumentalized by a flagging president and government who had invited known dictators to join them at the head of the parade.

How to 'build society': Such was the question that imposed itself in public debate during the month of January 2015. Begun even before the opening of this sequence of terror and completed while a pandemic was busy reactivating old fears, this book aims to dig deeper into this issue, following a path that leads to the confines of a famous ancient Greek city, Athens. Calling on Athenian society of the fifth century BC to examine the present, our enterprise may at first seem absurd, given how distant the rules that governed this society are from us. Naturally, it is difficult to relate to a system founded on the political exclusion of more than three-quarters of the inhabitants who lived there (i.e. the free women, the foreigners and the slaves). Yet in the face of this quite understandable difficulty, it is advisable to recall that the Athenians of the fifth century instituted the first political regime based on the participation of a considerable proportion of the population, within which distinctions of wealth did not hinder legal equality in any way, and that to this form of unprecedented communal organization they gave the name of democracy, which continues to offer a backdrop – or an *arrière-pays* – to appraise politics today.

Undoubtedly the return to Athens could not offer us the unmediated 'Lessons of History' that our concerns and our helplessness seem to require. Thucydides and Plato cannot re-enchant our present. The Athenian experience may, however, help us to sharpen several decisive questions of our time: In what form do the mechanisms of inclusion and exclusion that run through a group build a true society that is more than the sum of its disparate networks? Conversely, by what processes does a society come to tear itself apart, or even disintegrate? How do heterogeneous social arenas and temporalities coexist within it? Under what conditions should the fervor of exceptional situations be maintained without sinking into totalitarian unity? All these questions unfold with clarity in one quite singular moment of the history of Athens.

The end of the fifth century BC marked the end of 'the greatest movement that had ever stirred the Hellenes, extending also to some of the Barbarians, one might say even to a very large part of humankind.'[1] Conceived as a single, long conflict by Thucydides, the Peloponnesian War (431–404 BC) resulted in the defeat of Athens and the dissolution of its maritime empire. Long marginalized, the Athenian oligarchs took

---

[1] Thucydides, 1.1.2.

advantage of the debacle to exact their revenge in the city: With the support of Spartan troops, a commission of thirty Athenians put an end to the democratic institutions that had governed political life for more than a century. Under the leadership of Critias and Charicles, the Thirty drastically reduced the civic body – henceforth limited to 3,000 citizens – and multiplied the number of extrajudicial executions, arbitrary dispossessions and collective banishments.[2]

In the face of these abuses, democrats did not remain unresponsive: At the end of the year 404, Thrasybulus assembled an army of volunteers, made up of exiled Athenian citizens, metics and even slaves. Departing from Thebes, this heterogeneous troupe first seized the fortress of Phyle in northern Attica, before taking control of the strategic port of Piraeus a few weeks later. Taking advantage of the wait-and-see attitude of the Spartans and the divisions within the oligarchy, 'those of Piraeus' won several resounding victories over 'those from the town (*astu*).' Although the negotiations proved long and difficult, a truce was concluded in the early fall of 403.

On the Twelfth Day of Boedromion

Nearly fifty years later, the Athenians could date Thrasybulus' army's victory precisely: Each year, on the twelfth day of the month of Boedromion, they celebrated; more than a simple restoration of democratic institutions, this was the refoundation of the regime inaugurated nearly a century earlier by Cleisthenes in 508/7 BC. On this occasion, the Athenians celebrated their newfound freedom, 'for on that day the exiles returned from Phyle'[3] by making a sacrifice to Athena, allowing the city to thus commemorate the memory of its regained unity.

What the Athenians celebrated exactly is, however, far from obvious. Which event in particular marked in their eyes the reunification of the city and the final end of the civil war? On the twelfth day of the month of Boedromion, when the victors took possession of the city, the Athenian community reacted in two diametrically opposed ways. After eight months of civil war, the army of Thrasybulus entered the town and marched to the Acropolis to make a sacrifice to the goddess Athena.[4] Then, going down to

---

[2] Ancient sources mention between 1,500 and 2,500 victims of the Thirty: Isocrates, *Areopagiticus* (7), 67; Aeschines, *Against Ctesiphon* (3), 235; Pseudo-Aristotle, *Athenian Constitution*, 35.4. The figures vary greatly depending on the sources: See Canfora 2013, pp. 112–21, and *infra*, Conclusion, p. 310–21.
[3] Plutarch, *On the Fame of the Athenians*, 349e–f.
[4] Xenophon, *Hellenica*, 2.4.38–9: 'And they effected a reconciliation on these terms, that the two parties should be at peace with one another and that every man should depart to his home except the

Fig. 0.1 Map of Attica.

members of the Thirty, and of the Eleven, and of the Ten who had ruled in Piraeus. They also decided that if any of the men in the city were afraid, they should settle at Eleusis. When these things had been accomplished, Pausanias disbanded his army and the men from Piraeus went up to the Acropolis under arms and offered sacrifice to Athena.' The combatants would, however, have

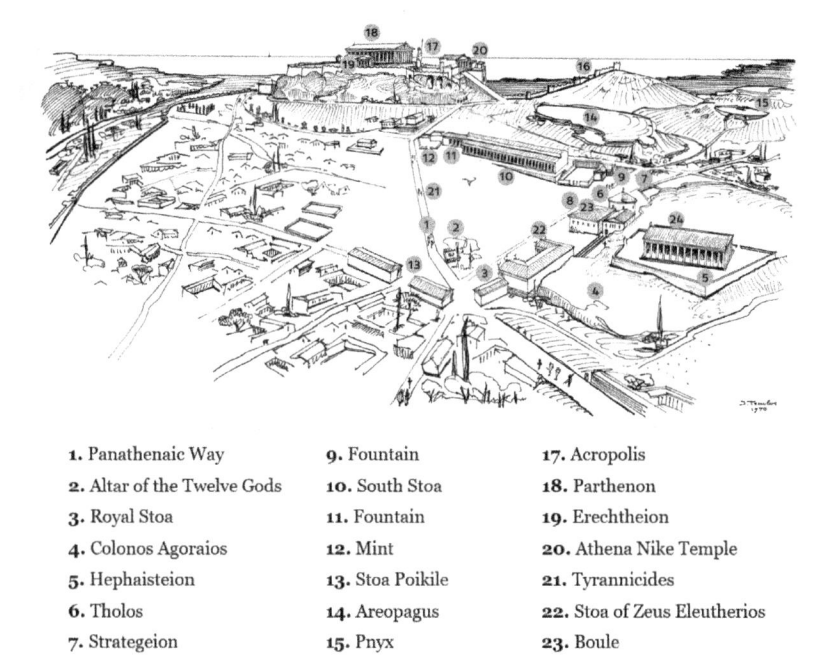

1. Panathenaic Way	9. Fountain	17. Acropolis
2. Altar of the Twelve Gods	10. South Stoa	18. Parthenon
3. Royal Stoa	11. Fountain	19. Erechtheion
4. Colonos Agoraios	12. Mint	20. Athena Nike Temple
5. Hephaisteion	13. Stoa Poikile	21. Tyrannicides
6. Tholos	14. Areopagus	22. Stoa of Zeus Eleutherios
7. Strategeion	15. Pnyx	23. Boule
8. Eponymous heroes	16. Themistocles Wall	24. Hephaistos Temple

Fig. 0.2 The Agora, the Pnyx and the Acropolis (view from northwest).

the Pnyx, the victorious general called together an assembly at which all Athenians undertook to respect the terms of reconciliation, 'to be true to [their] oath' and 'to live under the laws that had previously been in force.'[5]

The city had thus offered up two very different visions: on the one hand, that of a procession giving thanks to Athena; and on the other, that of a political community, gathered together in the main venue for democratic deliberation on the hill of Pnyx.

The Acropolis and the Pnyx: two canonical representations of the city, or, more exactly, two ways to build the ideal type of the Greek city. These two representations function most often in an inverted way. Civic rites are

---

deposited their weapons at the doors of the city before rushing toward the Acropolis: Lysias, *Against Agoratus* (13), 81. This summary of the Athenian civil war is loosely based on Xenophon's testimony in Books I and II of the *Hellenica*. For a more precise chronology of the sequence, see Krentz 1982. On the successive interpretations to which the Athenian defeat in 404 has given rise over the course of history, see the rich special issue of *Ktèma* 42 (2017): 7–205.

[5] Xenophon, *Hellenica*, 2.4.43.

generally considered as a means to build and reinforce the unity of the political community. The procession of 403 could therefore be seen as the definitive symbol of the reunification of the city around a ritual in honor of Athena. It offered the reassuring image of a city united anew, after having been torn asunder by civil war. Conversely, a public assembly is the place where disagreement and, potentially, political division are expressed.

However, on this day of October in 403, these two events functioned the other way around: While the ostensibly inclusive ritual demonstrated the divisions within the community, it was at the Assembly – a locus of often violent political confrontations – that the city regained its unity. It would be wrong, however, to interpret the procession to the Acropolis in the light of the Panathenaia, the great civic rite at which the city's unity took center stage.[6] While it followed the same route, Thrasybulus' procession had a completely different meaning. The scene does not offer any of the Panathenaia's much-admired order, as illustrated in schoolbooks and admired at the British Museum by tourists from all around the world. Beyond a simple reconciliation with the gods, this was the occasion for one camp to claim victory over the other. Indeed, the procession and the sacrifice concerned only the democrats of Piraeus: The men remaining in the city were excluded[7]; furthermore, the participants were undoubtedly armed, as if the threat still loomed large and the democrats were ready to throw themselves on the first tyrants they spotted, just like Harmodius and Aristogeiton, who, one century earlier, had taken advantage of the procession of the Panathenaia to assassinate Hipparchus, the son of the tyrant Peisistratus. Rife with division, the procession exhibited the visible separation between democrats and oligarchs, 'those of Piraeus' and 'those of the town,' participants in the ritual and simple spectators, all breathing in the smoke of the sacrifices without being able to reach the feast.

In contrast to this, it was at the Assembly that the recovered unity of the community became obvious, as the former oligarchs and the exiled democrats stood side by side. All listened to the unifying speech of Thrasybulus, which, in the form that Xenophon gave it, enjoined the victors to keep their word and to respect the vanquished. Far from being a place of dissensus or conflict, the Assembly, on this twelfth day of Boedromion of the year 403, was the place where the two camps sealed their truce.

---

[6] Historians have often interpreted the procession of the Panathenaia as the incarnation of the community in its unity and its articulations, associating the different social groups. See Graf 1996; Kavoulaki 1999.
[7] See the remarks of Shear 2011, p. 288.

The City in Chorus(es)

Of the two conceptions of the city we have just described – the 'city at sacrifice' or 'the city in assembly' (both of which are heirs to ancient sources and have been extensively employed by historians of the Greek world) – neither of them alone says anything about the *true* reality of the city. However, there is another noticeable configuration through which the civic imagination likes to represent the *polis* and the different groups that make it up: that of the chorus. In fact, it is not the metaphor of the procession or of sacrifice that ancient authors used to appraise the union of the community. Rather than the procession moving linearly through space, they preferred to privilege the idea of the chorus, which turns in on itself, organizes a common experience and aims to create harmony among its participants.

To understand this, let us go back a few weeks and to the hill of Mounychia in Piraeus, after the great battle between democrats and oligarchs where the bloodthirsty Critias perished, since this provides the first step toward reconciliation. After the democrats' victory, Cleocritus, the herald of the mysteries of Eleusis – who was on Thrasybulus' side – spoke up. He enjoyed considerable prestige because of the bond his family maintained with one of the most important cults of Athenian civic religion: that of Demeter and Persephone in Eleusis. In his vibrant appeal to the defeated oligarchs, he evoked the notion of the chorus in order to discuss what united Athenian citizens beyond their political differences:

> And Cleocritus, the herald of the initiated, a man with a very fine voice, obtained silence and said: 'Fellow citizens, why do you drive us out of the city? Why do you wish to kill us? For we never did you any harm, but we have shared with you in the most solemn rites and sacrifices and the most splendid festivals, *we danced together in the choruses (sugkhoreutai), followed the same choral formation as children*,[8] and we have braved many dangers with you both by land and by sea in defence of the common safety and freedom of us both. In the name of the gods of our fathers and mothers, in the name of our ties of kinship and marriage and comradeship – for all these many of us share with one another –, cease, out of shame before gods and men, to sin against your fatherland, and do not obey those most accursed Thirty, who for the sake of their private gain have killed in eight months more Athenians, almost, than all the Peloponnesians in ten years of war.'[9]

---

[8] On this translation, see Fisher 2003, p. 203 n. 67.
[9] *Hellenica*, 2.4.20–2, transl. Browson slightly modified.

8   Introduction: Toward a Choral History

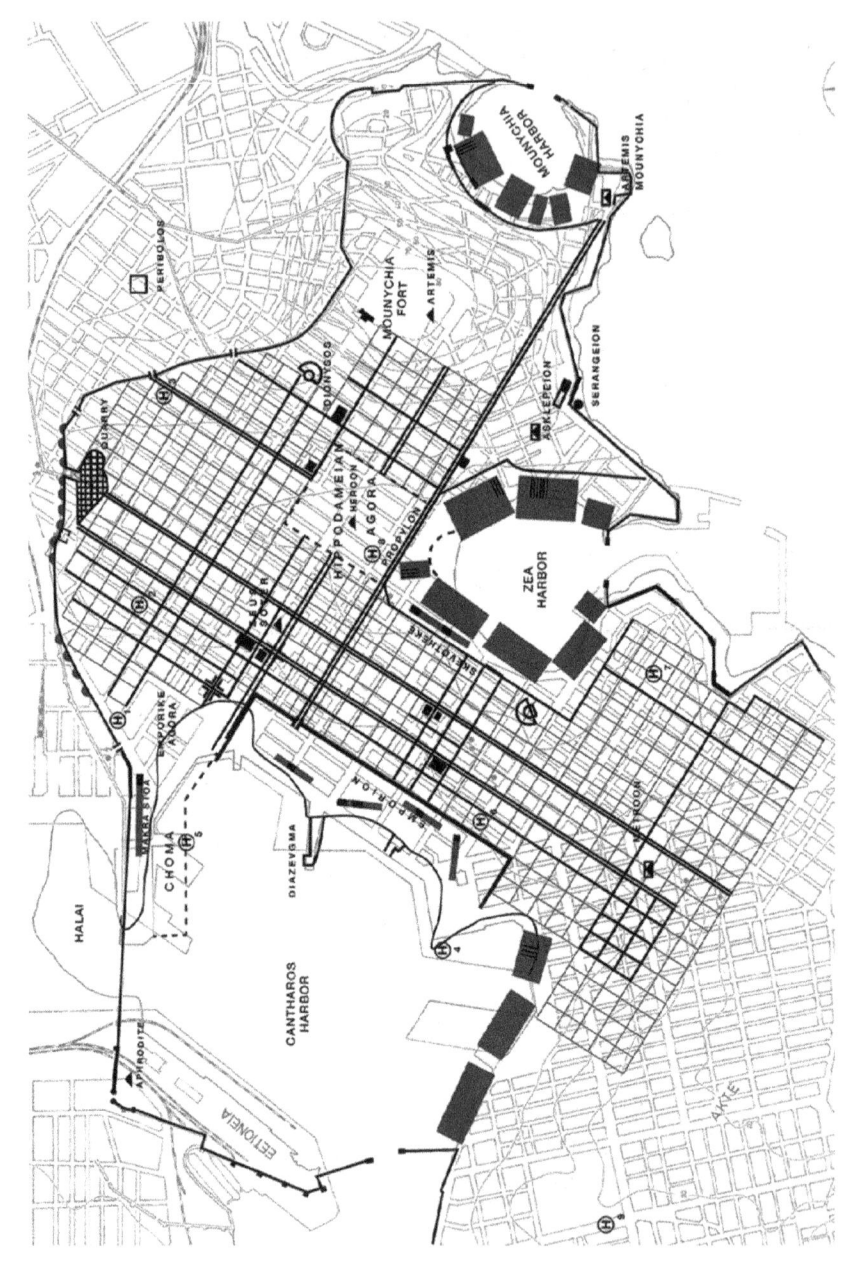

Fig. 0.3   Map of Piraeus.

Festivals, sacrifices, choruses and the army: Cleocritus rapidly listed a group of practices that he felt contributed to making the Athenian community what it was. We have chosen to isolate the chorus from among this range of inclusive activities because the Greeks themselves made special use of the notion of the chorus for thinking about how the city functioned.

The Chorus, an 'Absolute Metaphor'

Let us start with an affirmation: The chorus plays the role of an 'absolute metaphor' in Athenian thought – like other images, such as weaving, slavery or navigation.[10] Chorality evokes the ideal ordering of a collective, be it objects in the domestic sphere, various human groups or the cosmos itself. It is in the form of a chorus that Ischomachus, in Xenophon's *Oeconomicus*, presents the arrangement of the pots in the kitchen of his *oikos* when he affirms: 'There is nothing, in short, that does not gain in beauty when set out in order. For each set looks like a chorus of utensils, and the space between the sets is beautiful to see, when each set is kept clear of it, just as a cyclic chorus (*kuklios choros*) about the altar is a beautiful spectacle in itself, and even the free space looks beautiful and unencumbered.'[11] In the pseudo-Aristotelian treatise *On the Cosmos*, it is the stars and the sky themselves that are assimilated to a chorus in which the divinity is the coryphaeus – that is to say, the entity who regulates its moves:

> Just as in a chorus at the direction of the leader (*coryphaeus*) all the chorus of men, sometimes of women too, join in singing together, creating a single pleasing harmony with their varied mixture of high and low notes, so also in the case of the god who controls the universe: the note is sounded from on high by him who might well be called the chorus-master (*coryphaeus*).[12]

From the domestic arena in Ischomachus' house to the ordering of the stars in the sky, all collective forms can be appraised by means of the choral metaphor.[13] Plato's work offers the most striking illustration of this: In the

---

[10] On the crucial metaphor of weaving (*sumplokē*), see Scheid and Svenbro 1996: As for the chorus, weaving serves to appraise unity as well as the diversity of collectives, political consensus as well as *stasis*. On slavery as a metaphor, see Ismard 2019, pp. 239–41.
[11] Xenophon, *Oeconomicus*, 8.20.
[12] Pseudo-Aristotle, *On the Cosmos*, 399a15. Cf. 392a17–20: '[Ouranos] is full of divine bodies which we call stars; it moves eternally, and revolves in solemn choral dance with all the stars in the same circular orbit unceasingly for all time.' Moreover, in the *Republic*, the chorus represents the procession that accompanies all the improper desires that clutter the psyche devoid of any virtue (560e).
[13] On the analogy between dramatic chorus and hoplitic phalanx, see Calero 2018.

philosopher's dialogues, the chorus is used to represent groups of all kinds, both human and nonhuman, from the entourage of certain sophists or politicians to entire age groups of young men, but also groups of animals, gods and even vices and virtues.[14] The metaphor is all the more structuring as it can describe forms of association that are valued, even enchanting – like shining stars – or, on the contrary, very worrying – like the flatterers who, at the court of Alexander the Great, gathered into a detestable chorus under the leadership of a certain Medeus of Larissa.[15]

What sense can we make of this extensive use of the choral metaphor? Hans Blumenberg has shown that metaphor is an integral part of any philosophical discourse, in which statements and concepts are never fully clarified.[16] Any metaphysics is thus carried by metaphors and representations that cannot be translated back into concepts but 'have never ceased to pervade, tincture and structure them.'[17] The world as a book to be deciphered,[18] truth as light, life as a sea voyage[19] are all absolute metaphors that cross intellectual history, offering horizons of meaning through which thinking can ultimately unfold. These metaphors function to orient and represent the world as a whole, and while they go beyond what can be expressed theoretically, they nevertheless produce knowledge.

In this sense, chorality is indeed an absolute metaphor in Greek thought; that is to say, a means of representing – as part of the order of the world – the arrangement or organization of a collective in the broadest possible terms. If the image is prevalent, it is because it is based on experience and knowledge so common that it does not need to be explained.

At the Heart of Civic Life

It is a well-known fact that choral practice was a deeply rooted reality in the lives of ordinary Athenian citizens – particularly through the widespread

---

[14] *Protagoras*, 315b (the chorus of the disciples of Protagoras); *Euthydemus*, 276b and 279c (the chorus of the admirers of Dionysodoros and Euthydemus); *Theaetetus*, 179d (the chorus of the followers of Heraclitus); *Politics*, 291c (the chorus of the politicians); *Phaedrus*, 250b (the followers of Beauty); *Theaetetus*, 173b–c (the chorus of the wise men); *Laws*, 665e (the chorus of the children, the adult men and the old men); *Timaeus*, 40e (the chorus of the stars); *Phaedrus*, 230e (the chorus of the cicadas); *Phaedrus*, 247a (the chorus of the gods); *Republic*, 490c, 554b and 560e (the chorus of the vices and qualities). See Trédé-Boulmer 2002, pp. 583–4.
[15] Plutarch, *How to Tell a Flatterer from a Friend*, 65c–d: '[Medeus of Larissa] was, if I may call him so, leader and skilled master (*exarchos kai sophistēs koruphaios*) of the chorus of flatterers that danced attendance on Alexander, and were banded together against all good men.' Demosthenes describes a chorus of false witnesses, manipulated by three *chorēgoi*, exercising a shared *chorēgia* (i.e. the financing and the direction of the chorus): *Against Aphobos* 3 (29), 28.
[16] Blumenberg 2010. [17] Blumenberg 2010, p. 7. [18] Blumenberg 2022. [19] Bodei 2004.

performance of the dithyramb, a singular choral formation involving singing and dancing in a circle (the *kuklios choros*). During the fifth century, a thousand citizens (or young men who were about to become citizens) found themselves directly implicated in such performances every year. Such performances – more than comedy or tragedy[20] – formed the civic spectacle par excellence and were characterized by a competition between ten choruses of fifty boys and ten choruses of fifty adult citizens, one from each tribe.[21] These dithyrambic choruses performed not only during the Dionysia but also during the Thargelia in honor of Apollo, the Panathenaia and probably the Prometheia and the Hephaisteia.[22] Furthermore, far from remaining confined to the large civic cults that were held in the urban center (*astu*), choral practice occurred at all levels of civic life. Thus, during the Bendideia of Piraeus, the Tauropolia and in Brauron, choruses in various formations were involved in collective worship, including both boys and girls and men and women at the same time.[23]

Choral activity assumed such importance in the democratic city because it was a part of the *paideia*, or education, of all young Athenian women and men, and it significantly contributed to preparing them for their respective roles within the community. If the ancient authors are to be believed, it was one of the vectors through which the community's core norms were communicated to the whole city. In the *Laws*, Plato suggests that a group of choruses should be created in order to instill the right attitudes in citizens as early as possible, and that these choruses should subsequently be maintained throughout the citizens' lives.[24] According to him, the ideal city would therefore be composed of three choruses, each composed of a different age group: children, those under thirty and men between thirty and sixty years old. The chorus was subsequently presented as the ideal medium for educating citizens and conveying community values, with the city's combined choruses feeding into the 'chorus of choruses' that constituted the city. Plato evokes in particular 'the duty of every man and child – slave and free, male and female –, the duty of the whole city, to charm themselves unceasingly with the chants (*epaidousan*) we have described, constantly changing them and securing variety in every

---

[20] On the tragic chorus, see Calame 2013; Gagné and Govers Hopman (eds.) 2013.
[21] On the social and political implications of that specific organization, see Wilson 2011, p. 24.
[22] See Wilson 2003b, p. 168. Choruses of men sang paeans at the Thargelia (Wilson 2000, p. 314) and choruses of young girls performed on the twenty-eighth day of the month of Hekatombaion during the Panathenaia.
[23] Parker 2005, pp. 182–3.   [24] Plato, *Laws*, 2.664b–667a.

way possible, so as to inspire the singers with an insatiable appetite for the hymns and with pleasure therein.'[25]

The various choruses imagined by Plato, which potentially encompassed all members of the community ('every man and child – slave and free, male and female'), were thus articulated in a skillful composition, the coherency of which lay in dancing and singing together. This shared pleasure exerted an extremely powerful link between members of the community, which Plato conceived as being a true enchantment (*epōidē*). This is a delightful definition of the social magic implied by the choral ritual, which created the community by defining an interior (those who participated in the choruses) and an exterior (those who were excluded from them).[26]

This philosophical fantasy appears radical in that it anticipates including slaves in this enchanted circle. This exaltation of the choral model is not, however, specifically Platonic: There is indeed a *song culture* common to most ancient Greek cities.[27] But perhaps it is necessary to go further. If the chorus is so important in Athens, it is because it represents a properly democratic aesthetic. The hypothesis can be tested in many different ways. By placing its members in a circle or a square, sometimes under the aegis of a coryphaeus – the chorus-leader – the chorus primarily displays visually the principle of equality between citizens. Furthermore, its circular form presupposes that all of its participants can see each other, thus mimicking the transparency that was specific to the democratic regime and made public visibility of the law and of magistrates' supervision an essential aspect of civic life.[28]

As the visual representation of a collective gathered around an empty center, the shape of the circle can offer a model of the type of order that is characteristic of the civic ideal. Jean-Christophe Bailly even believes he can see in circle dances a figuration of the political operation par excellence, in which 'the space of the city comes to conceive itself as a whole, fueled by a center which gives it measure and legality, but which can only do so because it is an inappropriable point, situated between the men.'[29] The chorus thus appears to produce 'a center effect'[30] of a properly political nature. Built around a place that is at the same time not capable of being

---

[25] Plato, *Laws*, 2.665c. On the chorus as 'magical,' see Kurke 2013.
[26] Bourdieu 1982, pp. 58–63. See, for a different perspective, Kurke 2013. [27] Herington 1985.
[28] The chorus exists in a space that is at once empty and central. See Xenophon, *Oeconomicus*, 8.20: 'Just as a cyclic chorus about the altar is a beautiful spectacle in itself, and even the free space looks beautiful and unencumbered (*katharon*).' On the core values of chorality, see the important contribution of Kurke 2013.
[29] Bailly 2005, p. 214. [30] Bailly 2005, p. 231. See in particular Xenophon, *Oeconomicus*, 8.20.

appropriated and under everyone's control,[31] the city could be said to take the ideal form of a *choreia*.

In this respect, the chorus can truly be considered of the same order as 'festivals,' according to the definition Rousseau proposed in his *Letter to M. d'Alembert on the Theatre* (1758). In this work, Rousseau distinguishes festivals from theater, which, by distancing the spectator, provides a moment of separation between the actor and the role they embody, between the audience and the stage, between the spectators themselves and between the spectators and the rest of the social body:

> People think they come together in the theater, and it is there that they are isolated. It is there that they go to forget their friends, neighbors, and relations in order to concern themselves with fables, in order to cry for the misfortunes of the dead, or to laugh at the expense of the living.[32]

For Rousseau, spectacles steal our being, whereas, at a festival, 'the contagion of public friendship' wins over every individual, turning them into the private actors of a collective emotion.[33] In contrast to this, by creating confusion between the stage and the public when playing the role of an emphatic and empathic commentator,[34] the chorus abolishes the distance that is specific to theater and which Rousseau denounces. In this respect, the chorus should be considered one of the key elements of a true democratic aesthetic.[35]

Democratic Chorus, Oligarchic Chorus

To stick to these general remarks is not enough: The organization of choral practice differs appreciably from one city to another, depending on the

---

[31] See Vernant 1983.   [32] Rousseau 1960, pp. 16–17.

[33] Rousseau 1960, p. 126: 'Plant a stake crowned with flowers in the middle of a square; gather the people together there, and you will have a festival. Do better yet; let the spectators become an entertainment to themselves; make them actors themselves; do it so that each sees and loves himself in the others so that all will be better united. I need not have recourse to the games of the ancient Greeks; there are modern ones which are still in existence, and I find them precisely in our city.' Certainly, one could object that the choruses of dithyramb put on stage not all of the people but a fraction of them. However, each individual could imagine being part of it: All citizens were, are or will be *choreutai* and can consequently imagine participating in festivals on the same footing as those who play in the *orchestra*.

[34] Dupont 2007, p. 299.

[35] That is, the aesthetic dimension of politics, which is particularly noticeable in Pericles' famous funeral oration: *philokaloumen te ... kai philosophoumen* (Thucydides, 2.40.1). See Castoriadis 1991, p. 122–3: 'Pericles does not say we love beautiful things (and put them in museums), we love wisdom (and pay professors or buy books). He says we are in and by the love of beauty and wisdom and the activity this love brings forth, we live by and with and through them – but far from extravagance, and far from flabbiness.'

political regime that characterizes them. In Athens, chorality was plural, egalitarian and competitive: the challenge being to prevent the emergence of an overly powerful chorus that could represent, even if only for the duration of a ceremony, the city as a whole. It was quite different in other cities of the Greek world. As Leslie Kurke has shown, Pindar's corpus offers a glimpse of a completely different way of organizing chorality in Thebes during the early fifth century. Through the formation of choruses overseen by important families, the Theban elite sought to embody the city as a whole.[36] In Alcman's Sparta, choral dances came to symbolize the close union between civic and cosmic order, and choruses of young girls were meant to incarnate the whole community.[37] More broadly, despite being divided according to age groups, Spartan choruses expressed a homophony in which the *eukosmia* running through the political community was achieved.

In Athens, however, the city as a whole was never conceived as a single chorus capable of incarnating the city itself, except in the writings of Athenian dissenters such as Plato and Xenophon. In the *Laws*, as we have seen, Plato explicitly defended a noncompetitive conception of choral practice. Delighted with its own singing and dancing, the city found unity in choral practice, in what seems like a form of social magic.[38] The same is true of Xenophon's *Memorabilia*, in which Socrates chooses to celebrate specifically the Athenian chorus sent to work on civic *theōria* (state pilgrimage) for Delos precisely because the city was presented as a single chorus, unlike the multiple choral performances characteristic of the democratic dithyramb.[39] Socrates' two disciples aimed to redefine the choral phenomenon as it existed in Athenian society in their era, and their implicit condemnation of Athenian chorality was part of their wider criticism of the democratic regime.

Athenian practices present another singularity: They strove to dissociate the roles of *chorēgos*, coryphaeus and poet. In Thebes, it seems that the members of the city's most important families were able to hold both the position of *chorēgos* (thus helping to finance the chorus) and the position of

---

[36] Kurke 2007, p. 100. [37] Ferrari 2008; see also Calame 2013b.
[38] While the children's chorus states the doctrine, the young men ask the gods to accept its principles, and the mature men validate the words of the other two choruses as holders of power. See Kowalzig 2013a; Peponi 2013a, 2013b.
[39] Xenophon, *Memorabilia*, 3.3.12. The agonistic character of the choral contests in Delos is debated; the main point for our purpose is that Socrates himself sees in this chorus 'of the whole city' the most beautiful expression of Athenian choral practice. See Rutherford 2004, pp. 89–90.

chorus-leader,[40] while in archaic Sparta, poets most probably also played the role of coryphaeus. This was not the case in Athens, where these three roles were clearly separate.[41] This was a deliberate choice, and one that aimed to avert the charismatic authority that came with the dual power of financing the ceremony and conducting the chorus.

Chorus and Social Hierarchies

Despite mobilizing hundreds of individuals (which made it a vector for spreading civic values not only to citizens but to all members of the community) and creating friendship and unity through the repetition of ritualized performances (a crucial aspect of a true democratic aesthetic), choruses should nonetheless not be considered a factor in cohesion and an ever more perfect union.

Beyond the appeasing discourses of Plato and Xenophon, choral activity obscured a series of tensions and even divisions. Within a given chorus, strong rivalries could divide those within it who apparently danced to the same tune. Who could then be seen as the leader, or coryphaeus? Choruses thus embodied a sphere of competition that illustrates the deep-reaching hierarchies within the group.

In fact, Athenian choruses are far from being loci of perfect equality. First of all, the *chorēgos* plays an eminent role there: He has de facto authority over the various people whom he hires, since he provides directly for their upkeep for several months of the year.[42] It is he who recruits, at his own expense, a professional to train the *choreutai*, and he provides a sufficiently large space (the *chorēgeion*) so that the chorus can comfortably rehearse its complex moves; by the same token, it falls to him to manage the entire troupe and to disburse the expenses related to the performance itself, in particular the costumes. It is also he who, in the event of victory, collects the prize of the dithyrambic contest – a large bronze tripod – which he often dedicates to the gods to ensure his success goes down in history. The *chorēgos* thus wields such power that Xenophon compares his authority to that of the head of an *oikos*, an army or a city.[43] It should not be surprising, therefore, that a real king can be compared to a *chorēgos*, making his followers dance like puppets on strings and, beyond that,

---

[40] Kurke 2007, pp. 100–11.   [41] Wilson 2011, p. 33.
[42] Wilson 2000, p. 124, does not hesitate to speak of a real 'choregic patronage,' recalling that, by this means, rich individuals directly paid a significant percentage of the civic body for several months each year (p. 128).
[43] Xenophon, *Memorabilia*, 3.4.6.

dominating the whole people. It is in this way that Philip of Macedonia allegedly acted, according to the orator Demosthenes, recruiting traitors within several Greek cities who were ready to deliver their fatherland to him.[44] Faced with these choral maneuvers, the *dēmos* thus looked on as it was dispossessed of its own power.

Another character stands out: the coryphaeus; that is to say, the chorus-leader[45] – of whom Aristotle affirms that by becoming autonomous (as a protagonist, the main actor) he gave birth to tragedy.[46] The very form of the dithyramb, such as it was established in the fifth century BC, gives him a privileged place: Strophes (sung by the coryphaeus alone) alternate with antistrophes (sung in unison by the chorus). It is he who intones the song, provides the melody and strikes the rhythm: Everyone follows him.[47] This prominent position is also reflected in the metaphorical use of the term by ancient authors, who see it as a means of symbolizing the ascendancy of an individual over those around him. The metaphor is notably used in a famous passage of the *Theaetetus*, which depicts the philosophers as a chorus, with Socrates specifying that he is only going to 'speak of the chorus-leaders (*coryphae*); for why should anyone talk about the inferior philosophers.'[48] Better still, as we have seen, the divinity itself, in *On the Cosmos*, can be likened to a coryphaeus organizing the world around him.

But the texts provide a glimpse of other forms of more subtle hierarchies proper to choruses. The aulete thus occupies a central place: It is he who organizes the dance and the song of the *choreutai* evolving around him, probably in concentric circles.[49] Within the troupe itself, some *choreutai* even seem to have been more equal than others. The *geranos* (the 'crane dance'), for example, which took place in Delos in honor of Apollo, distinguished within the chorus not only a coryphaeus (called the *geranoulkos*) but also a 'first dancer,' executing solo rather free variations, and a 'second dancer,' in charge of orchestrating the movements of the rest of the troupe.[50] This specific case suggests the existence of micro-hierarchies,

---

[44] Demosthenes, *Third Philippic* (9), 59–60: in Oreos (Euboea), 'many men banded together, with Philip as chorus paymaster (*chorēgos*) and controller.' Cf. Plutarch, *Aemilius Paulus*, 34.1: After his defeat at Pydna, King Perseus marches with 'the chorus of his friends and intimates (*choros philōn kai sunēthōn*)'; Plutarch, *How to Tell a Flatterer from a Friend*, 63a: Kings, 'like the tragedians, want to have a chorus of friends singing the same tune or a sympathetic audience to applaud them.'
[45] Souda, s.v. *koruphaios*; Pollux, 4.106. [46] Aristotle, *Poetics*, 1449a14ff.
[47] Lucian, *On Salaried Posts in Great Houses*, 28; for song, Dion Chrysostom, *Orationes* (56), 4, 1; for melody, Aristotle, *Problems*, 19.22.919a35ff; for rhythm, Pseudo-Aristotle, *On the Cosmos*, 6.399a15. See also Aristotle, *Metaphysics*, 4.11.1018b25–30 and *Politics*, 3.4.1277a.
[48] Plato, *Theaetetus*, 173c-d. [49] See D'Angour 2013, p. 203.
[50] Delavaud-Roux 1994, pp. 78–9.

undoubtedly quite fluid and difficult to locate given the lack of documentation.

The fact remains that these hierarchies between *chorēgoi*, *coryphaeoi*, *auletai* and *choreutai* are clearly less rigidly defined in Athens than elsewhere in the Greek world. Not only is the *chorēgos* not confused with the poet, nor with the coryphaeus[51] – which would increase his influence on the chorus – but *chorēgia* is a *compulsory* duty that rich citizens and metics are obliged to carry out: This limits de facto the gratitude felt by the *choreutai* toward their (more or less) generous financer, as Pseudo-Xenophon deplores.[52] In the same way, the coryphaeus does not crush the *choreutai* with his magnificence but behaves more like a *primus inter pares*. This is especially the case from the end of the fifth century when the music takes ever greater precedence over the words.[53]

The Chorus Put to the Test of Civil War

These internal hierarchies are sufficiently deep-reaching to raise the question of the coherence of the choral group and the rivalries within it. Far from being a purely harmonious place, the chorus is always also a competitive playing field, where each individual strives to better the next coryphaeus and even replace him. These rivalries are rarely manifest, if only because the group must sing and dance in unison to have a chance of winning the competition while pleasing the gods.[54] But some clues suggest that this little world was far from irenic – as in the case of one poisoned young chorus boy, which resulted in his *chorēgos* coming before the Athenian courts (Antiphon, *On the choreutes*). This internal rivalry is also sometimes dramatized. In some tragedies the chorus is divided into two half-choruses carrying opposing voices: The clearest case stages, in the *Eumenides* of Aeschylus, the trial of Orestes and the division of the chorus

---

[51] Perhaps the *chorēgos* could initially – in the time of Aeschylus – also serve as *coryphaeus* in the tragedies, but this was no longer the case at the end of the fifth century. See Wilson 2000, pp. 133–4, and Azoulay 2014, p. 23.
[52] Pseudo-Xenophon, *Constitution of the Athenians*, 1.13: 'In the case of providing support for festivals, for athletics in the gymnasia and for manning triremes, they know that it is the rich pay for the choruses (*chorēgiai*), while are paid to be in the choruses [...]. The common people think that they deserve to take money for singing and running and dancing and sailing in the ships, so that they get more and the rich become poorer.'
[53] Moretti 2001, p. 44.
[54] On the tendency of Athenian sources to value chorus unanimity, see Budelmann 2018.

into two camps unable to decide between the adversaries without the support of a god.⁵⁵

Beyond these internal quarrels, the choral experience translates into intense competition *between* the different choruses within the framework of a competition arbitrated by the community. Each *chorēgos* competes to put together the most beautiful ensemble and to win the prize, even if it means spending a lot of money to achieve it. As Xenophon reminds us in the *Hipparchus*: 'For evidence of this [spirit of emulation] I may refer to the choruses, in which many labors and heavy expenses are the price paid for trifling rewards.'⁵⁶ This competitive spirit sometimes drove participants to try and destabilize their adversaries, such as when Meidias sought by all means (corruption, destruction of material and assault!) to make the *chorēgia* of Demosthenes the least spectacular possible.⁵⁷

Seen from this perspective, the choral model maintained unique connections with *stasis*, and the chorus should be considered within a spectrum of collective activities that run the gamut from war to peace and harmony.⁵⁸ In this respect, the establishment of agonistic choral practices following the clash that opposed Cleisthenes' and Isagoras' respective factions at the end of the sixth century is far from insignificant. As early as 508/7, the reorganization of choruses, in accordance with the Cleisthenic system of ten tribes, can indeed be interpreted as a way of blocking stasis from reoccurring. Through the organization of choral competitions as part of the dithyrambs, a specific form for managing *stasis* was invented, in which the Cleisthenic tribes aimed precisely to break up preexisting cliental ties and factional divisions. By replacing impious *stasis* with healthy competition, the Athenians strove to strike a new internal

---

⁵⁵ This situation of confrontation between two half-choruses is quite common, since it is also found in *Ajax* by the same Sophocles or in *Alcestis* and the *Trojan Women* by Euripides. In *Hippolytus*, the case is a little different since the play introduces two different half-choruses, entering on each side of the orchestra – that of the servants, then that of the women of Troizen. *Contra* Visvardi 2015, p. 242, which does not take into account the seditious potentialities of chorality.
⁵⁶ Xenophon, *Hipparchus*, 1.26.
⁵⁷ Cf. Demosthenes, *Against Meidias* (21), 147: 'And yet what act of insolence did [Alcibiades] commit that equals the crime that this man has been proven to have done? He hit Taureas in the face when he was chorus leader (*chorēgos*). But let that go: he did this to a chorus leader when he too was a chorus leader without even breaking this law (the law was not yet passed).'
⁵⁸ Toward war: cf. Athenaeus, 14.628e: 'Whoever honours the gods best with dances are the best in war'; toward peace: cf. Pausanias, 5.16.6: The quarrel between the sixteen cities of Elis was resolved by organizing *agōnes* for the Heraia, weaving a *peplos* for the goddess and establishing two choruses bearing the memory of the confrontation. See Scheid and Svenbro 1996, pp. 10–21.

civic balance.[59] Choral confrontation, in the agonistic mode, thus made it possible to depict and overcome divisions by sublimating them.[60]

But these tensions inherent in how choruses functioned should not conceal another form of division, which is less visible but no less structural. Like all collective rites, choral activity radically separated those who participated in it – albeit as part of a competition – from those who would never be part of the circle. Athenian society also included a good number of individuals outside of the choruses, who were the objects of a radical form of exclusion. While choruses offer a privileged way into thinking about unity and division within the Athenian community by using its own categories, the rifts within and between the various choruses that exist in the city still need to be taken into account in order to avoid deluding ourselves with an overly positive and harmonious conception of the social world.

A Choral History: Contemporary Theorization

In order to overcome this risk, this book aims to shift our focus from the ancient conception of the chorus to the contemporary theorization of what we will call a *choral history*. We are arguing, in short, that by writing a choral history, we are able to restore the complexity of the Athenian society at the end of the fifth century.

This position has already been taken up by some of the social sciences.[61] When they turned their attention to the organizational frameworks of social life and the relations between the various groups that compose it, the sociologists of the Durkheimian school mobilized the choral metaphor.[62] For Henri Hubert and Marcel Mauss, the memory of the ancient chorus

---

[59] Wilson 2003b, p. 182.
[60] Xenophon, *Memorabilia*, 3.5.16–8: 'When will they reach that standard of obedience to their rulers, seeing that they make contempt of rulers a point of honour? Or when will they attain that harmony, seeing that, instead of working together for the general good, they are more envious and bitter against one another than against the rest of the world, are the most quarrelsome of men in public and private assemblies, most often go to law with one another, and would rather make profit of one another so than by mutual service, and while regarding public affairs as alien to themselves, yet fight over them too, and find their chief enjoyment in having the means to carry on such strife? ... No, no, Pericles, don't think the wickedness of the Athenians so utterly past remedy. Don't you see what good discipline they maintain in their fleets, how well they obey the umpires in athletic contests, how they take orders from the choir-trainers as readily as any?'
[61] For a very general approach, see Azoulay and Ismard 2018; Kowalzig 2013a.
[62] The Durkheimian school's interest in the choral phenomenon was also the result of a dialogue with British social anthropology. In his 1922 ethnographic study of the Andaman Islanders, Alfred Radcliffe-Brown saw dance as a privileged medium for expressing social unity and harmony (Radcliffe-Brown 1922). In 1928, Edward Evan Evans-Pritchard studied the social role of one of

was used metaphorically to examine a founding moment in the 'realization' of the social body along the lines of a primitive scene, with 'the magical act' at its center: 'A circle of impassioned spectators collects around the action being performed. They are brought to a halt, absorbed, hypnotized by the spectacle. They become as much actors as spectators in the magical performance – rather like the chorus in Greek drama. The society as a whole becomes expectant and obsessed by the rite.'[63] In particular, the chorus provided a way of thinking about the connection between individualism and holism:

> The round, the dance, and the rhythm are the work of the crowd, but each individual brings his or her own personal variation to the theme. Within the homogenous horde, gifts of improvisation are widespread, with each individual following the next in the dance and adding a phrase, which is welcomed and repeated by the crowd, thus becoming part of the common heritage.[64]

Marcel Granet was the scholar who extended the choral paradigm the furthest as part of his study of 'seasonal festivals' in ancient China. Indeed, Granet saw the primordial notion of peasant community life in the choral principle.[65] By directing different choruses that embodied the different

---

the most important dancing ceremonies for the Azande: the beer dance (*gbere buda*). For him, the ceremony enacted sexual desire and its condemnation, celebrating the institutions of marriage and family (Evans-Prichard 1928, p. 458). However, neither of these two anthropologists referenced antiquity, and the study of dance was not part of a broader reflection on the choral mode (see the remarks of Rutherford 2013).

[63] Mauss [1902] 2001, p. 162. Mauss continues: 'The rhythmic movement, uniform and continuous, is the immediate expression of a mental state in which consciousness of each individual is overwhelmed by a single idea, a single sentiment, a single hallucinatory idea, a common objective. Each body shares the same passion, each face wears the same mask, each voice utters the same cry. In addition, we have the terrific impression produced by the rhythm of the music and singing. To see all these figures masked with the image of the same desire, to hear all mouths uttering proof of their certainty – everyone is carried away, there is no possibility of resistance to the conviction of the whole group' (p. 163). In an article for the *Année Sociologique* the following year, Mauss (1903, pp. 561–2) again discussed the importance of the choral theme by examining the origin of rhythm: 'Where does [rhythm] come from? From special conditions in which poetry was formed. Indeed, poetry was primitively, regularly, and necessarily sung. Both among primitive peoples and across the various countries in Europe, primitive poetry was essentially something that was spoken in a chorus. "Singing together" and the chorale are what cause rhythm. ... A primitive chorus presupposes ... a group of men who manage to agree in their voices and their gestures, forming one and the same dancing mass. A community animated by rhythmic movements, there you have a condition that is immediate, necessary and sufficient for the rhythmic expression of the feelings of a community .... Thus, a social reality and a determined group of singing and dancing individuals appears behind rhythm.' See Kowalzig 2013a, pp. 180–1.

[64] Mauss 1903, p. 564.

[65] Granet 1959, 1982;. For the singularity of Granet's work within the Durkheimian school and its reception, see Freedman 1975, pp. 624–48; Hirsch 2011. See also the important comments of

elements composing the community during 'sung jousts,' peasant society revealed different aspects of itself. These rites had a primarily religious purpose. During such solemn and important ceremonies, which unfolded in 'holy places,' human order, explains Granet, was anchored to cosmic order. Next came a political purpose – these ceremonies were decisive moments when it came to building seigneurial authority. But Granet further insisted upon a singular aspect involving the portrayal of division and reunion. Through these ceremonies and the distinction between choruses, society as a whole experienced its own divisions at the same time as it resolved them.[66]

However, we have to admit that the reference to ancient chorality vanished after the mid-twentieth century: While the notions of *philia*, *habitus* or *hexis* are part of the current vocabulary of contemporary social sciences, no one today thinks of describing collective action devices by referring to the choruses of classical Athens. Moreover, it is in the field of literary theory or cinema that contemporary reflections on chorality offer precious resources for the historian. If there is no longer any doubt that cinema and literature can inform history as a discipline – not only as a source, but as a specific modality of historical writing[67] – how can we doubt that in return the historian might benefit from a literary or cinematographic narrative form?

Plurality, Polyphony, Dissonance

Since Alfred Döblin's *Berlin Alexanderplatz* and John Dos Passos' *Manhattan Transfer*, the choral novel has provided some of the most beautiful historical reflections within the register of fiction. But the 'choral' mode, far from forming a clearly established genre or having its own aesthetic canon, is embodied in a different narrative logic depending on the way in which the story is 'put together.' One could perhaps attempt to establish a basic taxonomy of the different types of choral films and novels.

Humphreys 1971, pp. 172–96, particularly those on the connections between Louis Gernet and Marcel Granet.

[66] The model of Granet was not entirely ignored by the Hellenists. It is in the background of the study of Louis Gernet in 1928 that is devoted to the peasant festivals of archaic Greece, in which he believed he recognized the expression of 'the social virtue' proper to the world of the cities of the classical time. Gernet 1981, p. 25, writes in particular: 'But in the concrete – in the living organism of festivals – what is the significance of young men acting in unison? Evidently they reinforce the social bond; and their preliminary opposition followed by a rapprochement is symbolic of all the *agōnes* that point to a distant past and yet must have their raison d'être in a rural milieu.'

[67] See most recently de Baecque 2008; Witt 2013.

The first involves to varying degrees the omniscience of the narrator, the great architect of a narrative understood as an organic whole and guided by an explicit principle of composition. Conceived in the manner of a ninety-nine-piece puzzle in which 'it is not the elements that determine the whole, but the whole that determines the elements,'[68] Pérec's *La Vie mode d'emploi* offers the most radical example of this in its description of the lives of the characters living side by side in the Parisian building of 11 rue Simon-Crubellier. The second type does not presuppose any a priori unity between the different characters who are presented in isolation from each other and only run into each other at more or less random junction points. The story then unfolds under a regime of narrative uncertainty and very often finishes with an open ending. Robert Altmann's famous *Short Cuts*, adapted from several short stories by Raymond Carver, is a model of this. In the final type of choral work, the different segments of the action – potentially isolated – can be brought together 'from the outside' by the same, more or less distant event, the effects of which are experienced to varying degrees. Laurent Mauvignier's novel *Autour du monde*, which captures the fate of eleven characters across the globe all affected by the tsunami of March 2011, is an example of this.[69]

This brief typology is obviously rudimentary. Indeed, nothing seems to unite the great monophonic tale that is *In Search of Lost Time* (which is, in its own way, a choral novel) or *The Sound and the Fury*, which is centered on three voices over which a superior truth never prevails. More recently, the literary critic Vincent Message has extended his reflection precisely to the choral genre by attempting to define what he calls the '*le roman pluraliste.*' The kaleidoscopic construction of the story in addition to the multiplication of voices and linguistic registers seem to be at the heart of the pluralist novel, the major representatives of which in contemporary literature would be Thomas Pynchon and Salman Rushdie. Yet, if Message is to be believed, the polyphonic nature of *le roman pluraliste* only hints toward the broader forms of composition of the social, which are given a central place in the narrative. 'Instead of charting the arrival of a subject-in-the-making in a preconstituted Whole, the continuous and difficult movement of organizing a Whole that would like to be more than the sum of its parts is revealed for us to see.'[70] Thus, 'the collective effort of a society that is always in the making' would appear to be the true subject of *le roman pluraliste*. It is easy to imagine how much the historian can gain from these reflections surrounding the choral genre and how it has developed. When

---

[68] Pérec 2010, p. 17.   [69] Mauvignier 2014.   [70] Message 2013, p. 13.

examined through the historian's lens, choral writing leads us to question in an original way the homogeneity of the social arena, the articulation of the various spheres of action plunged in distinct temporal textures and the contemporaneousness of discordant actions.

Dividing Athenian Society Differently

In this respect, the *stasis* of 404–403 offers an exceptional area of study, since the event shows how the various elements of Athenian society were decomposed and recomposed. Indeed, according to Plato – through the mouth of Aspasia – the event resulted in a great blending (*sunmixis*):

> So kindly and so friendly was the way in which the citizens from the Peiraeus and from the city consorted with one another, and also – beyond men's hopes – with the other Greeks; and such moderation did they show in their settlement of the war against the men at Eleusis. And the cause of all these actions was nothing else than that genuine kinship (*suggeneia*) which produces, not in word only but in deed, a firm friendship founded on common descent.[71]

Despite its ironic tone, this vision is well in line with Platonic fantasies of unity – a city first divided in two, then reunited in a single chorus, now singing in unison. However, we would like to take a step back from this grand narrative of reconciliation by showing that the 'great mixture' created by the *stasis* led to the formation of multiple choruses with shifting contours, dismantling and recomposing themselves well beyond the Assembly of the twelfth of Boedromion and the official end of hostilities.

Such a choral approach makes it possible to break away from a set of schematic representations of society and, in particular, to challenge two principles that generally organize its description.

The first usually separates the different spheres of action at work in the city. In this way, political life is considered part of an operational logic distinct from that of economic activity, which is itself independent from religion, and so on. Yet the choral model cuts across these various realms of

---

[71] Plato, *Menexenus*, 243e. Certainly, this presentation of the civil war must be interpreted with care. The speech, as we know, is a pastiche, maliciously placed in the mouth of Aspasia the foreigner: The philosopher lets his irony show in relation to one of the great democratic myths, the autochthony, which, since the middle of the fifth century, had allowed the Athenians to present themselves as brothers; in the same way, he makes fun of the supposed moderation of the winners, insofar as the war against 'those of Eleusis' was far from a minor skirmish. On the Platonic irony of *Menexenus*, see Loraux 1986, pp. 264–8. On the harshness of the repression of the oligarchs of Eleusis in 401/0, see Xenophon, *Hellenica*, 2.4.43, and here, *infra*, Chapter 3, pp. 126–128.

action, making it possible to avoid confining analysis to areas of activity that have already been defined. In this respect, the choral approach makes it possible to observe both politics (which is composed of citizens taking action in places where civic decisions are made) and the political (which is defined as all of the practices that contribute to the expression of a civic identity).[72] It should also be noted that, by its very existence, the chorus in Athens was the product of political institutions (politics) – since, within the dithyrambic framework, it was constituted according to the principle of the Cleisthenic division of the civic body into ten tribes – but that its activity in fact consisted of the ritual celebration of Dionysos (the political).

The second principle seeks to describe this society according to its own classifications of status by distinguishing between metics, citizens and slaves, as if they were distinct and impenetrable groups. Here, each category has attached its own subjective rights that, like property, define the position of every individual in society. A citizen thus 'possesses' the right to do such and such a thing, and this right is sometimes accorded to metics, free women married to full citizens, freedmen or slaves. This kind of description is undeniably efficient, in that it provides a convincing representation that allows us to explain some of the configurations presented in the ancient sources. But it is limited and, in practice, sometimes erroneous. Thinking about Athenian society in choral terms makes it possible to examine in greater depth the various levels of social intensity without considering them to be immediately determined by specific status positions. It should be recalled that the tragic chorus – which was at once the 'voice of the city' and that of other 'marginal' people, women, foreigners and even slaves – shows the city in precisely all its diversity. Let us think of the *Helots* of Eupolis, in which Athenian citizens embody a chorus of Spartan helots, or the *Babylonians* of Aristophanes, with their chorus of tattooed slaves.[73] Similarly, certain choruses were able to welcome and blend citizens and metics, such as the dramatic *choroi* of the Lenaia performed each winter.[74] As for the *chorēgoi*, they could be citizens as well as metics: Holding this office was a question of wealth, not of status, at least in most cases. On another level, numerous female choral rituals in

---

[72] See Azoulay 2014.
[73] According to Storey 2003, p. 176, the play may have concerned helots taking refuge in Athens after the massacre at Cape Taenarum. Cf. Aristophanes, *Babylonians*, fr. 67 K.-A, with the comments of Norwood 1931, p. 286. As for the poet Pherecrates, he put on stage, in the *Didaskalos*, a chorus of slaves whose master taught them domestic service.
[74] See Wilson 2000, pp. 28–31.

classical Athens are known to have existed, from the *arktoi* for Artemis in Brauron to the dancing *parthenoi* for the Erechtheidai, to the Eleusinian cults, which included female dances.[75]

In this perspective, the choral phenomenon cannot be understood in terms of identity and otherness, according to a binary structuralist scheme, but must rather be considered a blurring, displacement or even 'estrangement' of distinctions of gender, origin and status.[76]

Rethinking Collectives through the Chorus' Lens

The choral scheme thus makes it possible to engage in a novel description of Athenian society that seems a priori to be in line with contemporary interpretations based on the notion of networks. This latter approach has given rise to numerous works in ancient history over the last twenty years: The network even seems to have become a fetishized concept capable of defining collective action in its most diverse forms – whether it aims to shed light on the relationships between different characters or groups within a single city or to describe the circulation of information patterns.[77] The contribution of a choral history lies first of all in the fidelity that it claims to a certain 'emic' representation of the social world, since we intend to borrow a descriptive category through which, under the term of *choros*, the Athenians themselves imagined collective action. But this is perhaps not the main tenet of our argument. We suggest that the concept

---

[75] On the *arktoi* for Artemis at Brauron, see Kowalzig 2007, p. 284; on the *parthenoi* dancing for the Erechtheides, see Euripides, *TrGF* 65; on the Eleusinian cults, which included female dances, see Pausanias, 1.38.6. See Budelmann and Power 2015, who highlight the importance of female choral culture in Athens and Attica – often underestimated due to scholars' focus on the Great Dionysia.

[76] On the dithyramb chorus as a way of reconciling openness and inclusiveness on the one hand and social cohesion on the other, see Kowalzig 2013b (for the Archaic period).

[77] We leave aside here all the numerous works that refer to the notion of network to describe relations between cities or between groups of individuals on the Mediterranean scale. See recently, to remain within the Athenian case: Ismard 2010; Karila-Cohen 2018; Ober 2008; Taylor and Vlassopoulos 2015. See also Latour's reservations against the all-out use of the notion (Latour 1999). He insists on the ideas of transformation and translation originally implied. Against the Durkheimian tradition, Bruno Latour and his close relations intended to deconstruct the commonly shared conception that makes 'the' society a 'substance' providing a specific type of causality to all the fields of activity. But Actor–Network Theory was not content to take up the reservations formulated for a long time by ethnomethodology, and it claimed to go beyond the canonical opposition between structure and *agency*. In this sense, it was not so much a question of giving back its place to the actor and to interactions as of highlighting the processes of assembly and composition (going beyond the nature/culture distinction) between heterogeneous elements that would form the heart of the social, conferring on sociology the status of 'science of associations.' On the uses of the notion of network in the framework of Actor–Network Theory, see Latour 2005.

of *choros* allows us to overcome the difficulties generated by the immoderate use of the notion of networks. Indeed, the new rhizomatic landscape of the classical city has too often tended to neglect the breaking points, the discontinuities and the conflicts between the different components of the city in favor of a grand integrating narrative.

In contrast to this, the choral scheme systematically sketches out a closed space in which a circle of participants is distinguished from those who are excluded; at the same time, these choruses, shot through by hierarchies of differing strengths, unceasingly recompose themselves in a dynamic way and, above all, position themselves in relation to each other in a competitive field. Thinking of the Athenian city through the choral prism consists of choosing an observation post at a good distance from both Plato's indivisible *polis* and a radically decentered city of networks.

Our proposal of choral history thus promotes a certain vision of collectives and their mode of composition. What are the salient features?

First of all, the chorus allows us to find a path between individualism and holism. Clearly, chorality does not imply defending the primacy of the individual, much less considering society as a collection of individuals, according to the presupposition of methodological individualism. The chorus offers the spectacle of a collective, created by its monophonic singing,[78] which does not presuppose the independence of each of the participants but immediately considers them collectively. In other words, the chorus represents a more or less stable aggregation of individuals who are never more than (to use the expression of Cornelius Castoriadis) 'moving fragments of the social.'[79] For all that, the *choreutai* do not act as an indistinct, even fusional mass either: Within the group, certain figures stand out – the coryphaeus, the aulete, perhaps the first and second dancers. Above all, the staging tends to distinguish the participants at certain key moments of the performance: In the tragic setting, for example, the *choreutai* seem to enter in three rows of five, or five rows of three, and not as a unified group.[80] According to this perspective, choruses were the supreme embodiment of the 'singular plural' form perfectly illustrated by Attic tragedy, in which chorists often sang the same text, sometimes saying 'I' and sometimes saying 'we.'[81]

---

[78] Aeschylus in the *Libation Bearers* and in the *Eumenides* thus fragments a chorus between several voices: Dupont 2015, p. 38.
[79] Castoriadis 1986, pp. 223–4. [80] Delavaud-Roux 1994, p. 100ff. [81] Nancy 2013.

Rethinking Collectives through the Chorus' Lens

Secondly, a choral perspective highlights the mixture of constraint and adhesion that is present not only at the origin of the collectives but also in their dissolution. While the Athenian choruses were in principle based on voluntary commitment, the *chorēgos* nevertheless held coercive power – for example, that of imposing fines – in the event of recruiting challenges.[82] This balance between obligation and voluntary commitment was also valid for the *chorēgoi* themselves: Obliged to assume these costly charges, the richest Athenians very often voluntarily accepted the call to be able to boast of their generosity during a possible future trial. It is precisely such a combination that presided over the emergence of many choruses in the turmoil of the civil war – be they the successive rallies to Thrasybulus' troops or the constitution of the Three Thousand, who made the choice to remain in the city but at the same time had to obey the orders of the Thirty. It is also what can make them fragile: a lack of sufficient institutionalization.

In fact, this 'choral model' also has the advantage of taking into account forms of grouping that are not necessarily set in stone. Choruses, which were created by repeated performances, had no other existence or duration other than that of the activity of the collective. They subsequently made it possible to approach any social elements as a provisional construction that could indeed find a stable form (e.g. by taking on a legal status that ensured the group's permanency) but without this being a rule. The civil war of 404–403 provides an opportunity to examine the surge in moving choruses that were recomposed numerous times because of the turmoil. The duration was quite similar: In the case of the dithyramb, the experiment lasted a few months, during which the participants met with each other continuously before confronting their rivals and determining a winner. Better still, even though the choruses were destined to dissolve after the competition, they nonetheless produced long-term bonds that could be reactivated periodically within the tribe – the latter serving as a recruitment framework not only for the choruses but also for the army or the Council of Five Hundred. In the same way, if many choruses, active during the few months of the *stasis*, disappeared after the reconciliation, the links that had been forged in them did not vanish all at once.

An analysis in choral terms allows, moreover, the role of emotions in the city to be underlined. For choruses also function – perhaps even

---

[82] See MacDowell 1985, p. 70; Wilson 2000, p. 83, according to whom the power given to the *chorēgos* was all the more exorbitant as it was not subject to accountability.

primarily – as emotional communities, where everyone feels the same joys and sorrows, even if this expression is ritualized.[83] Plato affirms this in his own way by maintaining that choral practice gives rise to joy, a feeling of elation experienced by the participants, not by the spectators.[84] In its tragic dimension, the events of 403 brought to a climax the emotions that build collective identities: The democrat Thrasybulus is well aware of this power when he incites the exiled, just before the battle of Mounychia, to advance 'with the same heart' to the sound of the paean; the oligarch Critias says the same thing when he defines the political regime by the participation of all its members in the same hopes and the same fears, as we will see.

Finally, a choral description of Athenian society avoids analyzing each chorus individually as a social world closed on itself. By multiplying the scales of analysis, it makes it possible to highlight the relations – harmonious or conflictual – between these various choruses. Far from the Platonic dream of a unified choral city, the investigation must give full scope to the phenomenon of competition and complementarity between choruses that are not necessarily placed in the same spheres of action.

To write a choral history of Athens is therefore to specify how the collectives that spread throughout the city functioned. It is to underline the hierarchies and the internal tensions that run through them; it is to estimate their duration and sometimes their institutionalization (or their disappearance); it is also to insist on the role that collective practices and shared emotions play in them; it is finally to scrutinize the relations between the different choruses by paying acute attention to the intervals that separate them and to their exterior aspects. In short, it is to reconstruct a plurality of collectives, without starting from preconstituted and already organized aggregates, and especially without presupposing the existence of a unique whole – 'Athenian society' – clearly hierarchized into distinct groups.

Our approach will consist of starting from an individual, playing the role of coryphaeus, and trying to systematically reconstitute the choruses that surround and encircle them. A crucial question then arises, which is

---

[83] Plato, *Republic*, 5.462c–e, according to whom 'the best governed city (*hē arista politeuomenē polis*)' is the one in which *all* the citizens rejoice and grieve over the same things, as if the whole community behaved as a single individual.

[84] The philosopher plays here on the homophony between choral practice (*choreia*) and joy (*chara*). On the community of emotions created by the chorus, see Plato, *Theaetetus*, 173b and *Phaedrus*, 250b. See Peponi 2013b, pp. 222–3. See also Calame 1977, p. 420ff, on the link between chorus and eroticism.

both an epistemological issue and a writing challenge: How are we to select the individuals who will allow us to observe this choral functioning? Is it not a huge risk that further contributes to the history of great men, as has been written since Antiquity? How can we avoid being prisoners of the documentation that sheds light on certain characters more than others, leaving whole sections of society in the dark? If the historian must necessarily make do with the limits of their documentation, perhaps it is possible to try and mitigate its effects by following two main principles. First of all, we will be attentive to the plurality of the collectives in which each character, even the well-known ones, is involved and which they contribute to structuring. Thus, rather than analyzing the actors of the event by classifying them, following the ancient sources, into two watertight camps – the democrats and the oligarchs – we will try to grasp the dynamics of the heterogeneous groups that temporarily gather around Critias and Thrasybulus, swelling or shrinking according to the circumstances (Chapters 1 and 2). Above all, we will try to bring to light more unexpected figures who serve precisely to thwart this supposed bipartition of political life: Such is the case, in particular, of the numerous 'centrists,' who came from both camps and gathered around Archinus, one of the leaders of 'those of Piraeus,' shortly after the reconciliation (Chapter 3). In the same way, we will highlight all those who do not enter any of these political choruses, by necessity or by choice, of which Socrates is certainly the figurehead (Chapter 4).

But in order to escape from the 'great men trap,' we have also set up a device that ensures an oscillation between two types of chorus-leaders with very different profiles. In an expected way, several chapters of the book are interested in real *coryphaeoi* (i.e. in individuals who, de facto, exert a structuring influence on the groups which surround them, such as Critias, Thrasybulus, Archinus or the priestess of Athena, Lysimache; Chapter 5). However, our investigation also highlights individuals who do not exert any notable influence on those close to them but whose figures benefit from sufficient documentary light to be able to reconstitute the various choruses in which they evolved: The poor worker Eutherus (Chapter 6), the rich heiress Hegeso (Chapter 7), the former slave Gerys (Chapter 8) and the bureaucrat Nicomachus (Chapter 9) are cases in point. As for the orator Lysias, while he appears only at the end of the story, this is because he occupies a special position in the narrative device as the main producer of sources on the civil war (Chapter 10).

This oscillation between structuring figures and small lives is a way of expressing, as a form of unresolved tension, our questioning of the nature of the Athenian community as it appears in the context of *stasis*. It is an attempt to study, from the ground up and without any preestablished hierarchy, not 'Athenian society' – as if such a thing existed – but its mechanisms of composition and recomposition, activated and illuminated by various events.

CHAPTER I

Critias and the Oligarchs

'Critias was indeed the most rapacious, the most violent and the most murderous of all those who were part of the oligarchy.'[1] In the ancient tradition, Critias is a man systematically described in superlatives. The ancient sources readily depict him as an extremist oligarch, a misguided disciple of Socrates, oblivious to the lessons of his former master. This detestable image is admittedly softened in Plato's dialogues, which give a mellower point of view.[2] But the overall picture remains very dark: As a radical counterpart of the 'moderate' Theramenes, Critias embodies the figure of the wolf-man, ready even to spill the blood of his friends to retain his power.

Incomparable Critias? This superlative representation deserves to be deconstructed. Not in order to rehabilitate his tarnished memory but because the man is a convenient bogeyman who acts as the singular representative of what was in reality a collective adventure. Not only does his role as leader of the Thirty remain to be proven, but this exclusive focus also tends to obscure the vast chorus that surrounded him: Far from being a lone wolf, Critias was the spokesman or, rather, the coryphaeus of Athenian oligarchs united by common habits and experiences.

The challenge is therefore to understand the dynamics that led to the emergence of such a group at the end of the Peloponnesian War. Here we are faced with the same burning questions as today: How did men, having fought together, having attended the same chorus in their youth, having danced and sung together as adults – to quote Cleocritus' poignant recitation in the *Hellenica* – come to exclude and even murder their former comrades? In this process of radicalization, what relative weight should be given to the general context (the violence of war), to existential ruptures and, finally, to the force of oligarchic ideology itself?

---

[1] Xenophon, *Memorabilia*, 1.2.12 (our translation).
[2] On the reasons for such an exception, see Danzig 2014.

It is in this broader perspective that the figure of Critias imposes himself, no longer as an evil and all-powerful coryphaeus but as the spokesman of an oligarchic chorus, bonded together by an exclusive definition of the community. Is this a simple choral metaphor? Absolutely not. Speaking of an 'oligarchic chorus' distances us from the idea of an aristocratic 'party' – endowed with a structured ideology and faithful adherents, possibly divided into different schools of thought – in order to conceive of forms of affiliation that are both ephemeral and dynamic, enlisting bodies and mobilizing emotions. A poet and a virtuoso musician, Critias even promoted a true choral policy, striving to convince all the Athenians remaining in the city to align to his radical positions. Breaking with the democratic experiment and its multiple and competing choruses, the oligarch sought to create a single, distinctive and hermetic chorus, of which all the members had to dance in unison and where the slightest deviation was mercilessly punished. Better still, in the tumult of the civil war, Critias had a dream: to establish a permanent state of exception in order to forge a new brand of men entirely devoted to the cause of the oligarchy.

Incomparable Critias?

In the third century AD – more than 600 years after the Athenian civil war – the rhetorician Philostratus reiterated earlier views of Critias: 'for all this I hold him to be the greatest criminal of all who is notorious for crime.'[3] The worst of all: How to better express the evil aura that surrounded Critias?

Let's take a closer look. Even before the civil war broke out, Critias had allegedly already betrayed his country. In the fourth century BC, a litigant compared the patriotism of one of his ancestors to the detestable behavior of the 'kin of Critias' who, in 411 BC, tried to deliver a stronghold in Piraeus to the Lacedaemonians.[4] Even more seriously, he is said to have failed in his faith not only in men but also in the gods: At the end of the second century AD, Sextus Empiricus considered him to be a prominent member of the 'atheist group,' who had blasphemed against divinity in both word and deed.[5] As for his morals, they were supposedly just as

---

[3] *Life of the Sophists*, 1.16.501 = 88 A1 DK.
[4] Pseudo-Demosthenes, *Against Theocrines* (58), 67 (= 88 A6 DK). The participation of Critias in this episode is very unlikely because, in this case, it is difficult to imagine that he could have remained in Athens after the restoration of democracy in 410.
[5] *Adv. Math.* [*Against the Physicists*], 1.54.

corrupt. According to Xenophon, Socrates enjoined him not to harass the handsome Euthydemus: 'As Critias paid no heed whatever to this protest, Socrates, it is said, exclaimed in the presence of Euthydemus and many others, "Critias seems to have the feelings of a pig he can no more keep away from Euthydemus than pigs can help rubbing themselves against stones."'[6] Unable to govern himself, he would therefore have been unable to govern others. Lecherous pigs do not make good shepherds![7] In his *Life of Critias*, Philostratus takes up this pastoral comparison and adds even more sinister overtones: 'he shared in the monstrous design of Sparta to make Attica look like a mere pasture for sheep by emptying it of its human herd.'[8] In contrast to the Homeric shepherd-king who cares about the well-being of his subjects – once studied by Michel Foucault – Critias is depicted as a shepherd determined to decimate his own flock.[9]

Thus an evil figure emerges, oscillating between the impious pig and the wolf-man, devouring even his own flesh and blood. Still, we have to understand the reasons behind such a terrible picture: Like Xenophon, himself involved in the oligarchic revolution of 404, many authors had every interest in blackening Critias' reputation to expunge their own turpitude from people's minds. Above all, this charge aimed, for Socrates' disciples, to dissociate the figure of their master from his cumbersome devotee by stressing their radically incompatible temperaments.[10] Consumed by their desire to right this wrong, the Socratics even tended to credit Critias with an exaggerated influence within the oligarchy, all the better to exalt their master's stubborn resistance to the tyrant's arbitrariness.

The Untraceable Leader

This is particularly true of Xenophon, who, in the *Memorabilia*, makes Critias the leader of the Thirty, presenting him as the legislator of the

---

[6] *Memorabilia*, 1.2.29–30.
[7] *Memorabilia*, 1.2.32: 'It seems strange enough to me that a herdsman who lets his cattle decrease and go to the bad should not admit that he is a poor cowherd; but stranger still that a statesman when he causes the citizens to decrease and go to the bad, should feel no shame nor think himself a poor statesman.'
[8] *Life of Critias*, 1.16.501 = 88 A1 DK.
[9] This disturbing figure is also contrasted to the figure of the shepherd-king put on stage by Plato in the *Republic* (1.345c, 2.375c). Perhaps this elaboration intends to contrast the uncle to the nephew.
[10] Cf. Plato, *Charmides*, 166c, 169c; *Timaeus*, 19a–20a. See Lévy 2001, p. 240.

oligarchy, alongside Charicles.[11] Should we believe him? Probably not. First of all, the selfsame Xenophon does not grant him any particular institutional preeminence in the *Hellenica*, where he appears only as one of the Thirty.[12] Moreover, no other contemporary source ascribes to him a decision-making role. It is true that Critias was a member of the committee of five ephors (named after the famous Spartan magistrates) set up in 404, 'while the democracy was still in existence.'[13] He then represented 'the notables who belonged to the *hetaireiai* and those exiles who had returned after the peace and were eager for oligarchy.'[14] However, this was a position of power that was neither stable (since it was transitory), nor legal (since it took informal groups as its origin), nor hegemonic (since it was collegial). What's more, with the exception of Xenophon and, secondarily, of Lysias, the authors of the fourth century loftily ignore Critias when they evoke the *stasis* of 404: Andocides and Aristotle mention only Charicles at the head of the Thirty, and, in the *Athenian Constitution* of Pseudo-Aristotle, the name of Critias is conspicuous by its absence in the long account devoted to the Athenian civil war.[15]

On balance, it would be just as fair to present Charicles, or even Theramenes, as the real leaders of the oligarchy.[16] Going into more depth, it is probably a mistake to try to isolate a single leader within the oligarchy that took power in Athens: The Thirty were precisely not a tyranny – whatever the ancient authors say – and they should be considered as a dynamic and unstable chorus, in which Charicles, Critias, Theramenes or even Satyrus and Aristoteles played successively or concurrently the leading roles.[17] How then can we explain the process of *reductio ad unum* that finds its final formulation in the later ancient sources? Since the times of Diodorus of Sicily, in the first century BC, the matter seems to have been settled: 'the Thirty called a meeting of the Council. Critias, at their head (*Kritiou de proestōtos autōn*), brought numerous charges against

---

[11] *Memorabilia*, 1.2.31 (nomothete). Cf. Lysias, *Against Eratosthenes* (12), 55. See Németh 2006, p. 23.
[12] Xenophon, *Hellenica*, 2.3.2.   [13] Lysias, *Against Eratosthenes* (12), 43.
[14] Pseudo-Aristotle, *Athenian Constitution*, 34.3.
[15] Andocides, *On the Mysteries* (1), 101; Aristotle, *Politics*, 5.1305b22–7. More significantly, Aristotle in the *Rhetoric* advises recalling Critias' actions when speaking about him, since they are unknown to the general public: *Rhetoric*, 3.16.1416b26. See Gotteland 2018, pp. 179–80.
[16] Son of Hagnon, the founder of Amphipolis, Theramenes controlled a third of the composition of the Thirty: Lysias, *Against Eratosthenes* (12), 76.
[17] Together with Aischines, Aristoteles was the member of the Thirty who asked Lysander to send Lacedaemonian guards (*Hellenica*, 2.3.13); with Critias, he was the only one of the Thirty who Theramenes attacked in his apology (*Hellenica*, 2.3.46). On the role of Satyrus, see Németh 2006, p. 117.

Theramenes.'[18] We must no doubt see there the influence of the Socratic tradition, initially a minor factor but victorious in the long term.[19] Critias, or the misguided disciple, persecuting his former master: This portrayal left little room for what was in reality a collective venture.

The Banality of Evil

Far from being beyond compare, Critias resembles all the laconizing oligarchs – zealous admirers of Sparta – that Aristophanes depicts so often in his plays that they have become a genuine sociological type. Let's try to characterize them briefly, taking Critias as our guide. While there was no real nobility in Athens, some Athenians could boast of a prestigious ancestry – including Critias, the son of Callaischros and a distant descendant of the archon Dropides, a relative and friend of the legislator Solon.[20] These Athenians with their prestigious genealogies were usually rich, even if it is difficult to identify precisely the bases of their wealth. Certain historians have claimed to see, within the Thirty, the broad outlines of a 'mining lobby,' which was exploiting the mines of Laurion and eager to cease all hostilities with the Spartans in order to pick up with their flourishing business.[21] But there is scant evidence of this, and such a theory jars with the contempt in which Critias held craftsmen and, more generally, his disdain for profit[22]: Was he not the one to stigmatize mortals who 'seek shameful profits rather than virtue'?[23] Did he not show his hatred of newly affluent men such as Cleon who, after spending years in debt, supposedly accumulated more than fifty talents during his career?[24]

This criticism of ill-gotten gains does not provide sufficient grounds to see Critias as the figurehead of a hypothetical middle class impoverished by the war, as Németh would have it.[25] There is no doubt that closer inspection of the assets confiscated from the most virulent supporters of the oligarchy after democracy was restored in 403 reveals them to be quite modest. However, the hypothesis is still fragile: While the amounts

---

[18] Diodorus Siculus, 14.4.5 (transl. Loeb slightly modified). Cf. Diodorus Siculus, 14.33.2–3; Philostratus, *Life of the Sophists*, 1.16 (88 A1 DK); Cornelius Nepos, *Thrasybulus*, 2.7: 'Critias, the leader of the tyrants'; Justin, 5.9.15.
[19] See on this subject Gotteland 2018.
[20] On Critias' family, see the prosopographical data collected by Nails 2002, s.v. Critias IV. See also Rosenmeyer 1949.
[21] This is what Rankin 1988 suggests. The hypothesis is taken up by Cox 1998, p. 18, but refuted by Hansen 1991, p. 287, and Brulé and Wilgaux 2018, pp. 150–3.
[22] *Memorabilia*, 1.2.37.   [23] Critias, *Rhadamanthys*, 88 B15 DK.
[24] Aelian, *Various History*, 10.17 (= 88 B45 DK).   [25] Németh 2006, pp. 159–66.

recorded are relatively low, this could just as well reflect a general deflation in Athens, affecting the entire population and not just the oligarchs; above all, these stelai, engraved in 402/1, are highly disfigured and do not allow for an overall view of the fortunes of the condemned.[26]

Whatever their exact level of wealth was, one thing is certain: Critias and his kin did not consider themselves ordinary citizens. On the contrary, Critias expressed the wish, in his elegies, to accede to 'the wealth of the Scopadai, the magnanimity of Cimon, and the victories of the Spartan Arcesilaus.'[27] Such a desire may seem astonishing: Is it not contradictory to celebrate in the same voice the luxury of an opulent Thessalian family – the Scopadai, encountered in exile – and the very Spartan austerity of an Olympic victor? In reality, Critias' remark reflects the choices of a certain number of Athenians who, in order to oppose the democratic ethos, did not hesitate to combine laconism (and its demonstrative austerity) and 'medism' (i.e. the attraction of Persian luxury).[28] In *Wasps*, produced in 422 BC, Aristophanes had already begun to mock these cheap laconizers wearing stark woolen fringes – in imitation of the Spartan Brasidas (v. 473–6) – while appreciating clothes 'woven at great expense by barbarians.'[29]

The Athenian oligarchs readily drew on various external models to differentiate themselves, but they reserved a special place in their imagination for Sparta: At the end of the fifth century BC, laconism had become the common language of the Athenian elites in disarray. This fascination even found, at the end of the Peloponnesian War, an institutional translation under the Thirty.[30] Indeed, Critias seems to have whipped up laconophilia to fever pitch. Considering Sparta 'the most beautiful of regimes,' he praised it in one of his *Constitutions in verse*.[31] In it, he celebrated in particular the Spartans' drinking habits and, furthermore,

---

[26] See Brulé and Wilgaux 2018, p. 152, and Walbank 1982.   [27] Plutarch, *Cimon*, 10.5.

[28] Critias himself allegedly established a link between the luxury of the Thessalians and their fascination for the East. Cf. Athenaeus, 14.663a (= 88 B31 DK): 'The Thessalians are generally agreed to have been the most extravagant Greeks when it came to their clothing and their life-style. This is why they convinced the Persians to invade Greece, because they were eager to adopt their luxurious and expensive habits. Critias in his *Constitution of the Thessalians* describes their extravagance (*poluteleia*).'

[29] *Wasps*, 1145–6. See Ruzé 2007.

[30] The Athenian oligarchs appointed five ephors to ensure the political transition – shamelessly taking the name of the famous Lacedaemonian magistrates: Lysias, *Against Eratosthenes* (12), 43, 46. On this institutional translation, see here, *infra*, pp. 56–7.

[31] *Hellenica*, 2.3.34 (*kallistē politeia*). The *Constitution in verse* (*Politeiai emmetroi*) is evoked by John Philoponos (88 A23 DK). Lévy 2001 underlines, however, that only a *politeia* of the Lacedaemonians in prose is attested.

their sobriety in all things: 'Apart from these matters, the smallest details of their way of life. The best shoes, as well as the robes that are most comfortable, are the Spartan variety.'[32] Laconizing in Athens was as much about promoting a specific institutional model as it was about adopting a certain way of life – a way of drinking wine (soberly), of dressing (simply), of wearing one's hair (long),[33] even of dancing (doing entrechats[34]) or playing music (with the *aulos*, a kind of double oboe).[35]

However, laconism alone was apparently not enough to define the distinctive identity of the Athenian oligarchs: Even Critias willingly drew on other references to feed his political imagination.[36] Beyond a certain number of shared ideas, the Thirty were especially united by experiences that counted at least as much as their ideological motivations.

Generation War

If the case of Critias deserves an in-depth examination, it is above all because his path overlaps with that of many Athenians who, after having initially supported the democratic regime, went on to oppose it with extreme violence. His trajectory therefore makes it possible to analyze the powerful effects of democratic pressure on the civic elites before the experience of exile served to bring out oligarchic tendencies that were all the more disruptive for having been repressed for a long time.

Most of the oligarchs in power in 404 experienced their youth and the beginning of their adult life within a city at war. Indeed, Critias belonged to the generation born in the middle of the fifth century – around 455 in his case – that reached manhood shortly before the Peloponnesian War broke out. This interminable conflict had destabilizing effects in the long term because it accustomed the citizens to an unprecedented degree of violence. Certainly, Greek cities in general and Athens in particular had always marched to the rhythm of war. But in terms of the frequency of

---

[32] Athenaeus, 11.483B = 88 B34 DK.
[33] To 'wear one's hair like a Spartan' (*spartiokhaitēs*), according to the expression of the comic poet Plato, was to arouse the suspicion, even the hatred of the people, as Lysias reminds us, around 390 BC (*For Mantitheus* [16], 18).
[34] According to Eustathius, *Commentary on the Odyssey*, 8.376, p. 1601, 25 (= 88 B36 DK), Critias praised, in his *politeia* of the Lacedaemonians in prose, a form of dance consisting of 'leaping very high and, before touching the ground, making several beats with the feet – a sort of entrechats.'
[35] Athenaeus, 4.184d (= Critias, 88 A15 DK). The fragment is taken from the protreptic of Chamaileon of Heraclea, a peripatetic of the fourth century BC. See Wilson 2003a, p. 195.
[36] See Herrmann 2017, who tends to relativize the Lacedaemonian influence on Critias, showing how much more fascinated he was by an imagined ancient Athens than by the Sparta of his time. See also Powell 2018.

battles, their intensity and, especially, the repeated massacres of prisoners of war and even of civilians, the Peloponnesian War broke with the past.[37] In this respect, it is no exaggeration to speak of a real 'brutalization' of Athenian society – all the more so as the violence built to a crescendo during the conflict, which lasted over twenty-five years. The proof: In 416 BC, the Athenians massacred all the male inhabitants of the island of Melos – who refused to rally to them – and sold the women and the children as slaves. The following year, they enthusiastically launched a great expedition to Sicily, which led, two years later, to a resounding catastrophe and to the annihilation of a quarter of the civic body: 12,000 Athenians died there, including a large number of prisoners living in impossibly cramped conditions deep in the stone quarries of Syracuse. Finally, in 405, after the battle that sealed the fate of the conflict in Aigos Potamos, the 3,000 Athenians who had been taken prisoner were massacred in cold blood on the order of the Spartan Lysander.[38] Knowing they were accustomed to mass extinctions and even torture is crucial to understanding the violence that the Thirty showed in 404.[39]

This brutality was unleashed with such force that, for several decades, the future oligarchs had been forced to show, at least superficially, their attachment to the people's cause. Let us take the case of Charicles, an exact contemporary of Critias, sometimes presented as the true leader of the Thirty: He showed ostensible support for the democratic regime for some time. In 415, he was even chosen to investigate the Herms affair, thereby showing 'a very great devotion to the people.' According to Androcles – himself embroiled in this disreputable affair – Charicles declared that the event was not the work of a few individuals, 'but was aimed at the overthrow of democracy.'[40] Charicles as a defender of the people: This was, for Androcles, a way to highlight his duplicity since, at the time of this speech in 399, the sinister role Charicles had played in the oligarchic revolution in 404 was common knowledge. But, in 415, there was no indication of what was to come. The adhesion of Charicles to democratic values was even sufficiently credible for the Athenian people to elect him *stratēgos* the following year, in 414/3.[41] He was then one of the politicians

---

[37] Payen 2012.   [38] See Lévy 2001, p. 243.
[39] Therefore, we should not be surprised, as was Isocrates, that 'these people ... who claim to be supporters of the Lacedaemonians while having morals contrary to their own ..., [dare] to commit inexplicable crimes against their own fellow citizens' (Isocrates, *Panegyricus* [4], 110). What the orator presents as a contradiction is rather a tragic articulation: The brutality of the conflict favored, without any doubt, the action of the Thirty.
[40] Andocides, *On the Mysteries* (1), 36–7: *epi tēi tou dēmou kataluei*.   [41] Thucydides, 7.20.1, 26.1.

influential enough to be mocked by comic poets, such as Telecleides (c. 440–420 BC), who targeted him over his supposedly dubious origins.[42] However, hardly three years later, the split was confirmed: In 411, Charicles sided with the oligarchs – and, in particular, with Peisandros, previously also devoted to the people – who seized power in Athens while the Athenian fleet was stationed in Samos. After democracy was restored in 410, Charicles went into forced exile.[43]

Critias followed a similar but slightly offset trajectory. In 415, he was one of the 300 or so Athenians who had a hand – guilty or not – in the desecration of the Herms and the profanation of the Eleusinian Mysteries.[44] But after this traumatic episode, Critias showed his attachment to the democratic regime: Not only does he not seem to have taken part in the oligarchic revolt of 411,[45] but he also took the initiative, as soon as democratic order was restored in 410, to bring a posthumous lawsuit against Phrynichus, one of the leaders of the oligarchy.[46]

Is this enough to see Critias as a confirmed democrat? One might question it. His behavior is more of an overblown attempt to prove his attachment to the regime, even though his father, Callaischros, had undoubtedly been one of the influential members of the Four Hundred in 411.[47] Perhaps his initiative was also guided by the desire to gain the upper hand over certain rivals involved in the ongoing struggles between oligarchic factions: Phrynichus was a declared enemy of Alcibiades, of whom Critias was then a staunch supporter, even proposing in 407 a decree granting Alcibiades the right to return to Athens.[48] More positively, it was a question of gaining influence with the people, as Theramenes reminded him during his trial: 'For, said he, you and I also have said and done many things for the sake of winning the favor of the city.'[49] Should one then conclude that oligarchs in general were duplicitous, ready to switch allegiances at the slightest opportunity? This is what the orator Lysias claims a few years later when he recalls 'how often the supporters of

---

[42] Telecleides, F 44 Loeb (Storey 2011) (= Plutarch, *Life of Nicias*, 4.5).
[43] Isocrates, *On the Team of Horses* (16), 42; Andocides, *On the Mysteries* (1), 36.
[44] Andocides, *On the Mysteries* (1), 38, 47.
[45] The testimony of the speech *Against Theocrines*, composed by Pseudo-Demosthenes, is not sufficiently reliable to know the behavior of Critias in 411.
[46] Lycurgus, *Against Leocrates*, 113: 'The people voted on the motion of Critias to put [Phrynichus'] corpse on trial for treason, and if it appeared that a traitor had been buried in their country, to dig up his bones and cast them out of Attica so that not even the bones of a man who had betrayed both his country and his city would lie buried in its territory.'
[47] Lysias, *Against Eratosthenes* (12), 66. See, however, the doubts of Caire 2001, p. 77, according to which he may not have been the father of Critias.
[48] Critias, 88 B5 DK. See Caire 2001, p. 80; Lévy 2001, p. 237.   [49] Xenophon, *Hellenica*, 2.3.15.

each of the two types of constitution [oligarchs and democrats] changed their allegiances,[50] following the example of Phrynichus' and Peisander's changes in allegiance.

Could Athens have been the very first place in history where political actors changed their minds on a dime? Was it the first 'Republic of political weathervanes'? This depoliticized vision calls for some nuance.[51] Far from being purely opportunistic, Critias' path is rather the result of his lucid adherence to a regime that was perhaps despised but also considered too powerful to be publicly challenged. Having always lived in a democracy, the Athenian elite had indeed assimilated the hegemony of the people as an intangible fact of political life. Faced with such a mighty opponent, there were only two possibilities: to serve him (faithfully) or to fight him (to the death).

To prove this point, one need only to read the prose of the Athenian oligarch – known as Pseudo-Xenophon (or the Old Oligarch) – whose work has come down to us in the corpus of Xenophon: the *Constitution of the Athenians*, which specialists agree on dating between 430 and 415 – before the Sicilian expedition weakened the democratic consensus. Relying on a philological argument that is as seductive as it is fragile, the Italian historian Luciano Canfora suggested it might be the work of Critias, composed before his exile.[52] *Si non è vero, è bene trovato*: Whoever wrote it, the treatise expresses quite bluntly the divided *habitus* of oligarchs living under popular pressure. The beginning is famous:

> As to the constitution of the Athenians, I give no praise to their choice of this form of constitution, because this choice entails preferring the interests of bad men (*ponēroi*) to those of good men (*chrēstoi*); this I why I do not praise it. But since this is their decision, I shall demonstrate that they preserve their constitution well, and manage well even the other things which the rest of the Greeks think are a mistake.[53]

Within this unjust but terribly efficient regime, the 'good men' have no choice but to bend to the will of the people, to the point of almost becoming their slaves. For compromise is impossible and the 'middle way' is no more than a pious fiction: Either the elite must accept the undivided domination of the people or it must introduce judicious

---

[50] *Defense Against a Charge of Subverting the Democracy* (25), 9.
[51] Lysias takes in this case the defense of a former member of the oligarchy who has every interest in claiming that the divisions between Athenians were by no means political: 'it is not difficult to recognize, gentlemen of the jury, that differences with each other are not about a constitution but about what is personally beneficial to each individual' (*Defense Against a Charge of Subverting the Democracy* [25], 10).
[52] See Canfora 1994, pp. 404–9.   [53] Pseudo-Xenophon, *Constitution of the Athenians*, 1.1.

measures, although 'as a result of these excellent decisions, the common people would soon plunge into slavery.'[54] Radical democracy or extremist oligarchy: The alternative is all the more clear-cut since democracy is, according to the author of the *Constitution of the Athenians*, incorrigible.[55] This rigid conception makes it possible to understand both why the future oligarchs adhered for so long to the democratic regime (and even defended it vigorously) and, symmetrically, how, once the *demos* had been weakened, they were able to suddenly become its worst enemies: Inherently violent, democracy could not be changed but only overthrown by a superior form of counterviolence. Long in a weak position, the oligarchs thus bowed to pressure – and often served the *demos* with zeal – until they were able to crush their depleted opponent. It was no wonder, then, to discover that most of the Thirty occupied positions of importance within the Athenian democracy, before or after 411 – having been elected as generals or drawn by lot as Council members and treasurers.[56]

If there is anything permanent in the behavior of Critias and his peers, it is ultimately their radical actions, both in serving the people and in opposing them. Several spectacular episodes attest to this: In 415, Peisander and Charicles led a judicial inquiry to uncover the suspects in the profanation of the Eleusinian Mysteries, who were accused of wanting to overthrow democracy; and in 411, Critias proposed to expel the corpse of the oligarch Phrynichus, thus refusing the sacred right to burial to a 'public enemy (*koinos echthros*)'[57] – like the tyrant Creon when he deprived Polynices of a proper funeral in the tragedy of Sophocles. As for the 'moderate' Theramenes, in 406, he persuaded the people to condemn to death the victorious Athenian generals at the Battle of Arginusai, guilty as they were of not having been able to repatriate the remains of the soldiers who died during the campaign. Extremists to a man . . .

The Fracture of Exile

Along this sinuous but coherent path, there are several pivotal moments that had an effect, sometimes immediately, sometimes at a later time. In the case of Critias, the date of 415 breaks with the past. The city was then in turmoil, following the mutilation of the Herms, and the culprits were actively sought. Arrested and imprisoned on the denunciation of a certain Dioclides, dozens of citizens spent an interminable night in prison,

---

[54] *Constitution of the Athenians*, 1.9.   [55] *Constitution of the Athenians*, 3.8–9.
[56] See the prosopographical survey conducted by Brulé and Wilgaux 2018, pp. 148–50.
[57] Lycurgus, *Against Leocrates*, 111.

expecting the same death sentence that had already befallen many of their kinsmen. Andocides delivered a poignant description of the scene:

> We were all imprisoned in the same place. Night came on, and the prison was closed up. One man had his mother there, another his sister, another his wife and children, and there were cries and moans from the men as they wept and carried on about the trouble they were in.[58]

During the night, Dioclides was convicted of lying and, at dawn, the danger was over. But the terror felt on this occasion undoubtedly left a lasting impression on all those who had looked death in the eye: This episode is perhaps one of the unnoticed root causes of the regime of fear that the Thirty put in place a little over ten years later. Fear had simply changed sides.

There is another traumatic experience shared by many oligarchs: exile. The Thirty indeed count among their ranks a number of outcasts, who have returned home with their hearts set on revenge. There are abundant sources to back this up: Onomacles and Charicles had been forced into exile after the failed revolution of 411[59]; likewise for Mnesilochus, Melobius and Aristoteles.[60] As for Critias, he left for Thessaly a few years later, in 407 or 406, perhaps because of his legal disputes with Cleophon, the leader of the democrats.[61] Lysias goes so far as to maintain, in one of his speeches, that 'the Thirty and the Council that held office under them [...] had themselves all been members of the exiled Four Hundred.'[62] This assertion is certainly exaggerated, not only because all of the Thirty were not involved in the revolution of 411, but also because not all of them had experienced exile: The vacillating Theramenes is an example of the latter.[63] It is, however, true of the majority of them, and it was indeed a chorus of former exiles that took power in Athens in 404.

Certainly, the experience of exile was intensely individual, insofar as not all the banished left at the same time, nor did they all take refuge in the

---

[58] Andocides, *On the Mysteries* (1), 48.
[59] Isocrates, *On the Team of Horses* (16), 42, for Charicles; Pseudo-Plutarch, *Lives of the Ten Orators*, 833f, for Onomacles.
[60] See Ostwald 1986, pp. 460–2. If these punishments were harshly felt by those who were victims of them, let us note, however, the relative Athenian moderation in the matter: No measure of expulsion was taken without a preliminary trial, contrary to what happened at the time of the Thirty. See Forsdyke 2005, pp. 181–204, especially pp. 191–6.
[61] Xenophon, *Hellenica*, 2.3.15, 36; *Memorabilia*, 1.2.24; Aristotle, *Rhetoric*, 1.15.1375b32; *Politics*, 1275b26–30. His departure took place before the trial of the Arginusai and probably after the Battle of Notion and the second exile of Alcibiades.
[62] Lysias, *Against Agoratus* (13), 74.
[63] If Mnesilochus, Onomacles, Aristoteles, Melobius and Theramenes were indeed part of the Four Hundred, the participation of Critias and Sophocles is not proven: see Németh 2006, p. 31.

same place. Far from settling randomly, the outcasts relocated to places chosen according to the support and assistance from which they already benefited abroad. Critias thus went to Thessaly because he enjoyed bonds of hospitality (*xenia*) with several powerful families in the area; as for Andocides, he settled in Cyprus because of the commercial contacts that he had made there previously. These networks of mutual aid and solidarity therefore guided the course of the exiles who ended up dispersed throughout the Mediterranean basin.

However, exile was also a collective experience in that it involved a common trauma. If, as Aristotle says, man is by nature a political animal – that is, destined to live in a *polis* – exile is a social death. For these men did not simply leave behind a homeland, but a vibrant community to which they were attached by multiple bonds: The entire existence of every citizen took place within nested circles of sociability, from the family to the city, but also including the deme, the tribe (in which voting took place), the army and the phratries (where citizens had their children recognized during the festival of the Apatouria). Also on the list, in the case of the Athenian elite, was membership of *hetaireiai* – groups of companions who quaffed wine together – and of more informal groups lingering in the Agora to converse, as Plato's dialogues show. It is this rich social fabric, woven by bonds of reciprocal obligations, from which exiles were brutally torn.

On an individual scale, this existential rupture has a truly revolutionary potential. Such an upheaval is sometimes expressed only in thought, as among the first Greek historians. It is because they had all experienced exile that they were able to propose a decentered vision of the past, attentive to each other's views.[64] But exile can also result in a radical change of political attitude. Xenophon shows exactly this in his study of Critias, when he underlines the deleterious effect caused by his distance from Athens[65]: As long as he lived in Athens and regularly visited Socrates, he behaved as a good citizen; as soon as he had to go into exile in Thessaly, he fell under the control of violent men and turned into a real villain.[66] If, for the sake of his argument, Xenophon exaggerates the regulating influence of Socrates, he is still on the mark: Exile accustomed the banished men to other political regimes and, above all, led to a sense of disaffection – in the literal sense of

---

[64] Payen 2010.   [65] *Memorabilia*, 1.2.24.
[66] In the *Lives of the Sophists* (1.16), Philostratus evokes the 'pure arrogance' of the Thessalians. The actions of Critias in Thessaly have been much talked about: he may have been in contact with the Thessalian tyrant Prometheus, whom he apparently helped to take power, even though it meant arming the *penestai* to achieve his ends (cf. Xenophon, *Hellenica*, 2.3.36). See on this subject Németh 2006, p. 37; Lévy 2001, p. 238.

the word – for their community of origin. For want of participation in the daily weaving together of the community, the banished sometimes came to take an outsider's view of their city, as a den of enemies to be eliminated.

It is precisely this process of emotional detachment that explains the violence of the oligarchs during the revolution of 404. Not only did they not want to repeat the failure of 411 – caused, according to them, by too timorous a repression – but they wished to inflict on their adversaries the experience that they themselves had been through. This is why they decided to proceed with the mass expulsion of the people: 'more than half of the Athenians' were driven out of the territory.[67] More broadly, they used an unprecedented level of violence that Xenophon attributes, in the case of Critias, to the experience of exile: 'Critias showed himself eager to put many to death, because, for one thing, he had been banished by the people.'[68]

Even before the civil war broke out, the most lucid Athenians were already conscious of the revolutionary potential of exile – whether they dreaded or hoped for it. At the end of the *Constitution of the Athenians*, Pseudo-Xenophon was thus interested in the Athenians deprived of their citizenship (*atimoi*) and often left in exile, due to their inability to obtain any legal defense:

> Someone might suggest that no one has been unjustly deprived of civic rights (*atimia*) at Athens. I maintain that there are some who have been deprived of civic rights unjustly, but they are few. But it needs more than a few to attack the democracy at Athens, since the situation is that one must not bear in mind people who have been justly deprived of civic rights, but if any have been deprived unjustly.[69]

If it is somewhat tortuous, the Old Oligarch's argument is prophetic: As long as there are only a few disenfranchised men (*atimoi*), democracy is in no danger. But the situation could evolve if their number increases: Forced into exile, such demoted citizens could join forces and bring down the regime responsible for their misfortunes.[70]

---

[67] Diodorus of Sicily, 14.5.7.
[68] *Hellenica*, 2.3.15. See Wolpert 2001, p. 24. This traumatic moment seems thus to have been the matrix of the exactions of the Thirty. Perhaps this is what explains, *a contrario*, the relative moderation of Theramenes in the same circumstances: Having never been banished, he refused to treat his own fellow citizens as enemies.
[69] Pseudo-Xenophon, *Constitution of the Athenians*, 3.12–3 (transl. Osborne 2004).
[70] A few years later, a client of the orator Lysias argued the same point (*Defense Against a Charge of Subverting the Democracy* (25), 11): 'My own opinion is that the people who are likely to have desired an alternative constitution, in the hope that the change would bring some benefit to them, were those who had suffered *atimia* (loss of civic rights) under the democracy after failing to submit their accounts, or had their property confiscated, or suffered some other similar disaster.' It is by virtue of the same reasoning that Aristophanes launched, in January 405, a spirited call to reinstate all of the disenfranchised, in the famous *parabasis* of the *Frogs* (v. 686–705), where the poet

When all is said and done, Critias' path through life seems quite banal: It overlaps with the itinerary of many members of the Athenian elite, initially faithful to the democratic regime, before detaching themselves and then turning violently against it, often following a stay in exile. If he can be considered unique, it is not, ultimately, because he was the leader of the Thirty or 'the most wicked of men,' but rather because he lent his voice to the claims of the Athenian oligarchs and ventriloquized them.

Critias, Champion of Oligarchic Radicality

In his fragmentary work, Critias portrays himself as an oligarch who displays his convictions loud and clear – in words as well as in images, in prose as well as in verse, in form as well as in content. Such is undoubtedly the true originality of his character: his lack of inhibition. During his lively exchange with Theramenes, Critias thus refuses all half-measures and makes no bones about breaking with the democratic regime. Speaking in the name of the Thirty, he addresses the members of the Council in these revealing terms: '[...] you and we have *manifestly* (*phanerōs*) become hateful to the democrats.'[71] Critias is precisely that: a *declared* oligarch.

According to Hermogenes, his eloquence was emphatic and 'often categorical'; according to Aelius, Aristides and he frequently used sentences giving definitive, even peremptory opinions: 'My opinion is that ...' or, 'It seems to me to be right to do ...' As for Philostratus, he qualifies his opinion thus: While Critias had a way with words, he was willingly dogmatic, even sententious.[72] In fact, in the rare fragments that have come down to us, Critias readily uses superlatives, seeking excellence in all things.[73] His opponents took pleasure in turning this distinctive obsession against him: Xenophon described him as someone who 'of everyone in the oligarchy was the most greedy and the most violent!'[74]

This radicalism was even displayed at his tomb. Critias' funeral stele is said to represent the oligarchy in human form setting fire, by means of a torch, to an allegory of democracy. An epitaph in verse was also engraved there:

---

addressed the Athenian people gathered at the theater directly. They did not listen, and disaster struck a few months later: 'those exiles who had returned after the peace were eager for oligarchy' (Pseudo-Aristotle, *Athenian Constitution*, 34.3). The time for compromise was over.

[71] *Hellenica*, 2.3.28.
[72] Hermogenes, *On Types of Styles*, 2.11.10 (= 88 A19 DK); Aelius Aristides, *Art of Rhetoric*, 2.2.7 (= 88 B46 DK); Philostratus, *Lives of the Sophists*, 1.16 (= 88 A1 DK). See Gotteland 2018, p. 180.
[73] Lévy 2001, p. 248; Caire 2018.   [74] *Memorabilia*, 1.2.12.

> This is the tomb of good men who, for a while,
> constrained the excesses (*hubrios*) of the accursed Athenians.[75]

Only a particularly attentive reader can detect a veiled allusion to the deceased, by spotting, in this epitaph, the repetition of a verse by Solon, a distant relative of Critias: In his time, the legislator had himself boasted of having 'constrained the people.'[76] The image, however, gives the epitaph very sinister overtones, far from the Solonian spirit of compromise: The 'compulsion' here is nothing other than the pure and simple destruction of the people, as if democratic *hubris* could only be contained by an even greater violence. Death to democracy, long may it burn![77]

This demonstrative radicality was also expressed in music. A renowned poet, Critias indeed resorted to various musical forms – be they elegies sung at *symposia* or tragedies staged at the theater – to reach the widest possible audience for his ideas: a musical stance intertwined with a certain emotional, even ardent conception of politics.

A Musical Politics

Since the beginning of the sixth century BC, the Greeks attributed powerful political effects to music, for better or for worse.[78] In the *Republic*, Plato worried about the contagious power of music, which 'flows over little by little into characters and ways of life. Then, greatly increased, it steps out into private contracts, and from private contracts, Socrates, it makes its insolent way into the laws and government, until in the end it overthrows everything, public and private.'[79] But in the eyes of the Greeks, music could also have beneficial effects, by purifying a city infected by *stasis*: 'Now that those cities which were governed by the best laws (*eunomōtatais*) took care always of a generous education in music, many testimonies may be produced. But for us it shall suffice to have instanced

---

[75] Schol. Aeschin. I, 39, p. 261 Schultz (= 88 A13 DK). See Bultrighini 1999, pp. 316–34, who argues for the authenticity of the epitaph against those who see it as pure literary fiction. Since the oligarchy lasted five months after the death of Critias, the erection of such a stele is, at least, possible.
[76] See Wilson 2003a, p. 187, on the links between Critias and Solon.
[77] From this point of view, the stele functions as a mirror of the monument of the Tyrannicides that, on the Agora, presented the murder of the tyrant – the oligarchs turning the warlike iconography of democracy against itself.
[78] See Wilson 2003a, pp. 181–2; Wallace 2015, pp. 24–5, 148. The relationship between law and song in the Archaic and Classical periods is the focus of Antoine Chabod's forthcoming book (Chabod forthcoming).
[79] Plato, *Republic*, 424c–e (trans. Cooper modified). Cf. *Laws*, 701a–b.

Terpander, who appeased a sedition among the Lacedaemonians, and Thaletas the Cretan, of whom Pratinas writes that, being sent for by the Lacedaemonians by advice of the oracle, he freed the city from a raging pestilence.'[80] Beyond such shock therapies, music had the power to generate harmony within the community, as demonstrated by Pythocles (or Pythocleides), one of the teachers of Pericles, who 'harmonized (*harmozontos*) the citizens [of Athens] using suitable melodies.'[81]

It was still necessary to choose the right musical forms for each political project. To establish his ideal city, for example, Plato favored Dorian and Phrygian harmonies to the detriment of loose Lydian harmonies, which were associated with corrupt democracies.[82] A few years earlier, his uncle Critias himself had come to a similar conclusion: According to Philostratus, he cultivated a majestic style, diametrically opposed to the artificial solemnity of the dithyramb – a democratic genre par excellence; in the same way, he played the aulos in the Lacedaemonian manner, in order to better distinguish himself from the new democratic style then in vogue on the theatrical stage.[83]

Critias seems to have particularly appreciated the elegiac genre, undoubtedly because, sung at *symposia* for a select audience, this type of poetry was the best vehicle for his oligarchic ideas: Form and content coincided perfectly.[84] Thus it is in elegiac couplets that he celebrated the moderation of the Spartans:

> The Spartan way of life is evenly ordered: to eat and drink moderately (*summetra*) so as to be able to think and work. There is no day set apart to intoxicate the body with immoderate (*ametroisi*) drinking.[85]

How better to say that these 'constitutions *in verse*' (*emmetroi*) were at the same time '*moderate* constitutions' (*summetroi*)?[86] For the oligarch, music and politics were mirror images of each other and had to be *well*

---

[80] Pseudo-Plutarch, *De musica*, 1146b–c. Cf. Aelian, *Various History*, 12.50. See Ellinger 2005. On this question, cf. also Euripides, *Medea*, 190–203, and, more generally, Wallace 2015, pp. 45–7.
[81] Olympiodorus, *On Plato First Alcibiades*, 138, 5–6 (on *Alcibiades I*, 118c). See Griffin 2016, p. 79 (transl.).
[82] Plato, *Republic*, 398e–399c. Cf. Aristotle, *Politics*, 1290a19–23.   [83] Caire 2015.
[84] On Critias as an expert practitioner of a convivial poetry, especially choral poetry, see Iannucci 2002, pp. 111–37.
[85] Athenaeus, 10.432d (= 88 B6 DK, l. 24–7). A few verses earlier, Critias expressed his admiration that the Spartans drank 'just enough to have a happy heart, a friendly tongue and a measured laugh (*metrion*)': 88 B6 DK, l. 14–6. A few other fragments of the *Constitution of the Lacedaemonians* have been preserved (DK 88 B 6–9). See more generally Centanni 1997, ch. 2, and Bultrighini 1999, ch. 5.
[86] Wilson 2003a, p. 197.

balanced in order not to fall into the excesses typical of 'pure democracy' – that is to say, 'without mixture' (*akratos*), as Plutarch characterizes the Athenian regime of the mid-fifth century.[87]

Critias extended his thoughts on the relationship between poetic action and political commitment into an elegy, where he recalled his decisive role in the return of Alcibiades to Athens in 407 BC:

> The decree allowing his return had been ratified earlier (411 BCE), at the motion of Critias the son of Callaeschrus, as Critias himself wrote in his elegiac verses, reminding Alcibiades of the favor as follows:
>
>> 'As for the proposal which restored you,
>> I was the one who delivered it among all the people,
>> and by my motion I accomplished this deed.
>> The seal of my tongue is set on these words [or verses].'[88]

Addressing with familiarity his companion Alcibiades, Critias simultaneously claims the paternity of his verses – performed impromptu at the *symposion* – and of the decree formerly put to the Assembly. To this end, he plays on the ambiguity of the term *sphragis*, which can designate both the seal authenticating official documents and the poetic style of an author. Legislative and poetic works are thus closely associated, probably because Critias sees in them two modes of *nomos* – rules, whether legal or musical.

However, the poem distinguishes and hierarchizes these two registers: Recited with an anonymous crowd as its audience, the speech in prose clearly does not have the same reach as the elegy sung for a group of distinguished companions.[89] More exactly, each is only a means to the other: It is to be able to sing with Alcibiades again that Critias speaks at the Assembly in favor of his friend. From this perspective, the poem is resonant of an ode to friendship – an unbreakable bond between two companions, underpinned by the people.

This minor oligarchic melody can be heard in other works composed by Critias and, in particular, in several choral tragedies that are attributed to him. Such a statement may seem surprising, as tragedy seems intimately associated with the democratic universe, reflecting it like a 'broken mirror,' according to Pierre Vidal-Naquet's formulation.[90] Should we be surprised that a resolute oligarch like Critias could have indulged in such a genre? No, for it would mean forgetting the future oligarch's lasting ostensible

---

[87] Plutarch, *Cimon*, 15.2: This democracy is pure (*akratos*), like wine that would not be diluted with water.
[88] Plutarch, *Life of Alcibiades*, 33 (= 88 B5 DK). [89] Orfanos 2003. [90] Vidal-Naquet 2002.

support for the Athenian regime and, above all, overlooking the role of tragedy in offering a framework flexible enough to allow dissonant voices to be heard.[91] Far from reflecting democratic consensus, Critias' plays seem to have promoted an ardent conception of the community based not on the rule of law, but on the manipulation of emotions.

Deadly Friendships

In his *Constitutions in Verse* as in his tragic plays, Critias indeed shows a certain contempt for the law. This disdain is expressed most clearly in a fragment from his tragedy *Pirithoos*:

> A good character is surer than a law:
> no orator would ever be able to distort it,
> whereas often one of them defiles the law
> with words which cause confusion high and low.[92]

Although it stands alone, this fragment is consistent with the distrust Critias often expressed – in words and in deeds – toward institutions: In 404, he did not hesitate to bend the law to his convenience in order to eliminate his political opponents and, in particular, Theramenes. Rather than relying on a system of legal rules, Critias preferred to rely on trusted men, bound to him by mutual friendship and fear – two powerful emotions, the only ones able to hold the political community together.

It is in the *Pirithoos* that Critias most clearly developed this demanding, even terrifying conception of friendship (*philia*). From this lost drama – whose attribution to Critias is probable, even if certainty is impossible[93] – several fragments have come down to us and allow us to specify the course of the action. After having tried to kidnap the goddess Persephone, the hero Pirithoos is punished by the god Hades and condemned to stay in the Underworld.[94] His companion Theseus decides to stay by his side,

---

[91] See Rhodes 2003. [92] Critias, 88 B22 DK (= Stobaeus, *Anthologia*, 3.37.15).
[93] On these questions of attribution, see the (too skeptical) view of Yvonneau 2018, pp. 19–20.
[94] The play deliberately plays with the image of Pirithoos then in vogue in Athens. For Pirithoos, the king of the Lapiths, was celebrated above all as a heroic defender of marriage, whether on the friezes of the city's temples or on the cups of wine circulating at the *symposion*. The story is famous: Invited to the wedding banquet of Pirithoos, the centaurs – cousins of the groom – got drunk on pure wine and tried to rape his young wife, Hippodamia. This is how the terrible battle between the Lapiths and the centaurs – the centauromachy – began. Theseus was also invited to the party and joined the fight with his friend Pirithoos to defeat the gang of centaur-rapists. By depicting Pirithoos as a sexual abuser of Persephone, Critias reminded us that *all the descendants of Ixion* (the grandfather of Pirithoos and the centaurs) were ungodly rapists – Ixion having attempted to rape Hera, the wife of Zeus.

although he has the option to return to the world of the living. After a series of adventures, Heracles manages, as a good friend, to rescue them both and deliver them together (88 B16 DK). The whole play is thus pervaded with 'the obsessive presence of the code of friendship.'[95]

Found on a papyrus of Oxyrhinchus in Egypt, a long tirade describes the unfailing friendship that binds the two prisoners.[96] Theseus opposes Heracles' offer to free him alone because he cannot abandon Pirithoos to his tragic fate, whatever wrongs his friend may have committed: 'it is shameful to betray a true and faithful friend when he has been seized malevolently' (v. 1–3). Far from blaming him, Heracles then praises his exemplary behavior: 'Theseus, your words become (both yourself) and the city of the Athenians; for you have ever been an ally of those in misfortune' (v. 4–7). The dialogue thus praises a model of uncompromising *philia*, which requires one to support one's friends even in death and beyond, since it is a question of suffering an eternal punishment together. This radical commitment also rings out in an isolated verse, also taken from the *Pirithoos*: 'So isn't not living superior to living in dishonor (*kakōs*)?'[97] How better to sum up the fatal conception of friendship defended in the play as a whole? In a way, it is in death – and only in death – that true friendships are proven and tested. So it is probably no coincidence that the whole play is bathed in a dark, even crepuscular atmosphere, representing a 'circle of the ether, around which the dark night and the innumerable crowd of stars never cease to circle.'[98]

It is an equally demanding form of friendship that links Theseus to Heracles. There again, it implies unequivocal support, whatever the obstacles encountered. When Heracles announces, at first, that he will not be able to come to his aid – because he is preoccupied with his own mission, to capture Cerberus – Theseus nobly answers him: 'But what you desire [...] you have my goodwill, not from impulse (but) freely, in enmity to enemies and good intention (towards friends).'[99] Once granted, friendship cannot be taken back. Better still, it defines a network of cascading solidarities, which affects the entire life of a given companion: Transposing to the individual level the principles of a military alliance between cities, Theseus promises Heracles to have the same friends and the same enemies, no questions asked. Conversely, this absolute solidarity forbids any deviation, however minor.

---

[95] Bultrighini 1999, p. 159. On the *Pirithoos*, see Centanni 1997, pp. 159–70.
[96] *POxy*, vol. 17, n° 2078, not quoted by Diels-Kranz (= *Pirithoos*, fr. 7 Collard and Cropp 2009, to which we owe the translation). See Brisson 2009, pp. 419–20 (n° 38b).
[97] Stobaeus, *Anthologia*, 4.53.23 (= 88 B23 DK).
[98] Critias, 88 B19 DK. See Csapo 2008, p. 273.   [99] *POxy*, vol. 17, n° 2078, l. 12–4.

Deadly Friendships 51

All of these fragments help sketch out the profile of a hero who is certainly exemplary, but also disturbing. Theseus indeed puts friendship above all other considerations – and, in particular, above common good, or even good itself. It does not matter to him that Pirithoos insulted a god and tried to rape a goddess: He will follow him to the Underworld, without the merest hint of reproach. This excessive image broke radically with the soothing representations of the hero then in vogue in Athens. A few years earlier, in 423, Euripides had portrayed Theseus as a good-natured king, voluntarily submitting his decisions to the community and boasting of having established in the city 'an equal right to vote.'[100] Breaking with the democratic imagery associated with the founding hero of Athens, Critias thus made a dissonant voice heard on the theatrical stage: His Theseus promoted an oligarchic conception of friendship, based on exclusive and distinctive choices, in contradiction to the horizontal and democratic vision of friendship – the very same that Aristotle celebrates in the *Eudemian Ethics*.[101] In short, Critias was already outlining the path he would later take: As we shall see, the tyranny of the Thirty was also a tragedy of aristocratic friendship.

Quoted by Plutarch three times, the last line of the *Pirithoos* clarifies the profound importance of *philia* in the eyes of the poet:

> So some persons without deriving any benefit from their friends' good fortunes, perish with them in their misfortunes. This is the experience especially of men of culture and value, as Theseus, for example, shared with Pirithoos his punishment and imprisonment:
>
> 'He [Theseus] is joined [to me?] in the unforged fetters of a sense of honor (*aidous*).'[102]

For Critias, Theseus and Pirithoos are thus linked by immaterial chains – not forged of metal (*achalkeutoisin*), says the Greek text – and yet unbreakable. This extremely powerful link relies on a form of fear: Often translated as 'honor,' *aidos* in fact indicates the fear of dishonor.

---

[100] *Suppliants*, 349–54.
[101] Aristotle's work articulates these two competing conceptions, without trying to reconcile them: on the one hand, a political, more or less egalitarian *philia*, fitting harmoniously into the democratic ideological universe; on the other hand, a 'friendship of character,' contracted between selected and distinguished individuals. Only the latter is the central object of books 8 and 9 of the *Nicomachean Ethics*: It is different in many ways from democratic definitions of *philia*. On the contrary, the *Eudemian Ethics* proposes a much more egalitarian conception of *philia*: cf. *Eudemian Ethics*, 7.1.1234b22, 7.10.1242a9–11. For a discussion of political friendship in the *Eudemian Ethics*, see Schofield 1998 (according to whom the work is not by Aristotle); Pakaluk 1998, p. 425.
[102] *On Having Many Friends*, 96c (= 88 B20 DK). Cf. *On Brotherly Love*, 482a; *On Compliancy*, 533a.

If Theseus decides to stay with his friend in the Underworld, it is ultimately because he fears not doing 'the right thing.' This fatal friendship is therefore based on fear, this other emotion that Critias wishes to instill in the hearts of all men, putting them all on the same sinister wavelength.

A Political Praise of Fear

It was probably in the theater that the Athenian oligarch theorized the political role of terror. At the end of the second century AD, Sextus Empiricus quoted a long passage, explicitly attributed to Critias, in which fear plays an important role.[103] While there is no indication of the exact provenance of the extract, most commentators have recognized it as a fragment of a tragedy or satyr drama, perhaps entitled *Sisyphus*.[104]

In this long tirade in verse, one character delivers a strange account of the origins of the social world. To civilize a still bestial humanity, it is said that wise men invented the first laws, 'so that justice might be sovereign (*tyrannos*).' The actor then gives himself up to a praise of the *nomos*, celebrated for its capacity to 'keep outrage (*hubris*) in slavery (*doulēn*).' However, laws alone are not enough: They can only punish faults that are discovered and committed in broad daylight. Religion may therefore have been invented precisely to make up for the failures of human institutions:

> [...] some shrewdly intelligent and clever man invented for mankind fear of gods, so that there might be something to frighten bad men even if they do or say or think (something) in secret. From that time therefore he introduced belief in gods – that there exists a divine power flourishing with indestructible life {and hearing and seeing with a mind, and both thinking and [attending to?] these things, and bearing a godlike nature} which will hear everything that has been said among men, and will be able to see everything that is being done. 'Further, if you silently plan some evil, this will not escape the gods' notice: for there is intelligent awareness in (them).' In saying these words he introduced the most pleasant of teachings, hiding

---

[103] Sextus Empiricus, *Against the Physicists*, 1.54 (= 88 B 25 DK).
[104] Wilamowitz-Moellendorff 1875, pp. 161, 166. This would make it a satyric drama, concluding a tragic trilogy formed by the *Pirithoos*, the *Rhadamanthys* and the *Tennes*. Many commentators have chosen to attribute this fragment to Euripides and not to Critias, under the pretext that Euripides had also written a satyric drama, entitled *Sisyphus*, probably in 415 (Aelian, *Various History*, 2.8). In reality, Critias and Euripides may both have devoted a play to the same character – as did Aeschylus and Sophocles, who also composed a *Sisyphus*. In any case, there is nothing to dispute the attribution of *this* particular fragment to Critias, insofar as Sextus Empiricus insists heavily on the 'tyrannical' personality of its author. At most, one can question whether it belongs to *Sisyphus*, as Sextus Empiricus does not specify the name of the work of Critias from which he takes this extract.

the truth with words of falsity; [...] Such were the fears (*phobous*) he established all round for mankind, and thanks to these fears this man did a fine job in his story of settling divine power in a fitting place, and quenched lawlessness (*anomia*) with the laws.[105]

Through his actor, Critias shows an incredible audacity here: claiming first of all that the gods were only an invention created by a particularly wise man; then, far from seeking to alleviate the evils of humanity, that this fiction aims to spread terror among men. For these imaginary gods have the power to probe hearts and minds. Invisible from men, they see all and hear all: 'Further, if you silently plan some evil, this will not escape the gods' notice: for there is intelligent awareness in (them).'[106] As Emmanuelle Caire reminds us, 'force can constrain bodies and the law can constrain public behavior, but only religion – and therefore fear – can achieve absolute control, that of the spirits.'[107] Tamed by fear, citizens can be governed more easily.

How original is the scene imagined by Critias? It is certainly not the first time that Fear is placed at the foundation of the social order on stage. In the *Eumenides*, Aeschylus had already evoked its founding role: 'Upon [the Areopagus], the respect (*sebas*) and inborn fear (*phobos*) of the citizens will prevent any wrong being done, alike by day and by night.'[108] However, fear occupied only a marginal place in the Athenian religious landscape, and it is rather from Sparta that Critias, as a good laconizer, seems to have drawn his real inspiration. The Spartans were indeed famous for their 'fear of the gods' (*deisidaimonia*), and they even worshipped fear.[109] Fear, moreover, kept the Spartan community together, by holding a perpetual threat over the citizens' heads. Some magistrates seem to have been primarily responsible for relaying this policy of fear: The sanctuary of Fear was next to the place where the ephors met, and they, according to Xenophon, were precisely in charge of 'frightening the citizens into obedience.'[110]

---

[105] Critias, 88 B25 DK, l. 12–5, 37–40 (transl. Collard and Cropp 2009).
[106] Critias, 88 B 25 DK, l. 21–3. [107] Caire 2018, p. 129. [108] *Eumenides*, 690–1.
[109] Plutarch, *Cleomenes*, 9.1: 'Now, the Lacedaemonians have shrines of Death, Laughter, and those sort of emotional states (*pathēmata*) as well as of Fear. And they pay honors to Fear, not as they do to the powers which they try to avert because they think them baleful, but because they believe that fear is the chief support of their *political regime*.' Cf. *Lysander*, 17.10 (on the fear of the law). Other laconizers have reflected on the singular power of fear. It is fear that, according to Xenophon himself, 'brings down souls the most' (*Cyropedia*, 3.1.25) and 'makes men attentive, obedient and disciplined' (*Memorabilia*, 3.5.5). See Patera 2013, pp. 113, 131; Loraux 1989, pp. 93, 98.
[110] *Constitution of the Lacedaemonians*, 8.3. Cf. *Constitution of the Lacedaemonians*, 7.2, 5. On the sanctuary of Phobos, cf. Plutarch, *Cleomenes*, 9.1. See Mactoux 1993, p. 259; Richer 1998, pp. 220–1.

While it resounds with Spartan tradition, the tirade of *Sisyphus* is, however, an innovation. For the Lacedaemonians never considered fear a complete invention! Relayed by Sextus Empiricus, this extract is, moreover, at the root of the accusations of atheism that have been brought against Critias since antiquity. Might we then compare Critias' verses with the ideas of his nephew, Plato, who praises the 'noble lie'? Perhaps, but with one major difference: Plato never ventured to present the gods as a purely human invention. To lie, for the sake of the greater good, about the origins of the political community is one thing; to claim that the gods themselves are pure fiction is another; moreover, the Platonic lie aimed to develop friendship between citizens, not to unleash fear in the community.[111]

In *Sisyphus*, Critias develops a deeply original theology, even if it means hurting common beliefs.[112] Stranger still, the hero lifts the lid on deception and, so to speak, spills the beans. He reveals religion for what it is: an instrument of domination over men, a means of government in the hands of a sophist-legislator – a revelation all the more shocking as it was undoubtedly placed in the mouth of Sisyphus, a king who, according to the common tradition, had been punished by the gods! This is perhaps the strongest originality of the play: Through the intermediary of his actor, Critias suggests that an intelligent ruler should not hesitate to use law, religion or rhetoric – all human inventions – to establish his power absolutely. In this uncomplicated perspective, religion is only one of the means of government.

At the end of this foray into *Sisyphus*, one last question deserves to be clarified. Is it possible to infer from this simple excerpt Critias' ideas on religion? Is this not falling into the classic interpretative trap of confusing the author and his work, the poet and the characters he gives voice to? The risk is all the greater here since the fragment is totally isolated and we know nothing about how it fit into the play, unlike the *Pirithoos*, whose plot we can reconstruct. If it is indeed an extract from a tragedy, the character was perhaps abused, even punished by the gods, after having pronounced such transgressive words. Isn't it the case of Sisyphus who, according to the almost unanimous tradition, ends up tortured in the Underworld?[113] Tragedies tend to end badly … Moreover, it is far from certain that

---

[111] *Republic*, 3.414b–415e and *Laws*, 2.663e–664b. [112] Caire 2002, p. 42.
[113] On Sisyphus, cf. Homer, *Odyssey*, 11.593–600 (punishment of Sisyphus); Pseudo-Apollodorus, *Bibliotheca*, 1.9.3; 12.6; Pausanias, 2.1.3; 3.11; 9.34.7; Tzetes, *ad Lyc.*, 107, 176, 229, 284, 344; Probus, *ad Verg. Georg.*, I, 137. See, however, Theognis, 703–4, where Sisyphus manages to sway Persephone by 'insidious speeches' and, thus, to leave Hades.

Sextus Empiricus acted neutrally when he selected the passage: He was probably influenced in his choice by what was known about Critias after 404, which could have introduced a 'confirmation bias' reinforcing through a type of feedback loop the already detestable image of Critias.

Should we therefore give up the idea of accessing Critias' true thoughts? At least we can see that his 'atheist' tradition was formed quite early in time.[114] Let us also note that the *Sisyphus* passage strangely echoes the affair of the Thirty, which made fear a principle of government: Poetically stated in the theater, Critias' ideals were brutally put into practice under the oligarchy. It would be a mistake, however, to believe that Critias tried to impose on the Thirty a political line that he had defined beforehand on the tragic stage. The poet simply had the talent to express and to put to music ideas already largely shared by opponents of democracy. A culture of friendship and fear had indeed already bloomed within the *hetaireiai*, and it is these powerful collective emotions that guided the initial development of the oligarchic chorus in 404, before contributing to its ruin.

The Unified Chorus: A Joyful Purification

April 22, 404: The siege of Athens has finally ended. Critias and the other outcasts return to the city, set on revenge. In an initial symbolic gesture, the victors begin to destroy the Walls to the sound of the aulos – the instrument so intimately associated with the Spartan universe. Let us not be mistaken: It is the death of the imperialist democracy of the fifth century that is thus signified. Sheltered behind the Long Walls linking the city to its port, the Athenians dominated the Aegean Sea for over half a century, their fleet punishing recalcitrant allies and importing the food they needed, even when their territory was under invasion.

The enthusiasm generated by victory silenced the divisions and erased the divergent interests between the Athenian exiles and the triumphant Spartans, and, within the oligarchy itself, between radicals and moderates. Created in such joyful circumstances, the chorus of the oligarchs managed,

---

[114] One can no longer assert, as Dihle did, that the tradition of an atheist Critias was only a late construction – on the pretext that the rest of his work does not testify to anything of the sort and that this reputation only appeared in the late testimonies of Sextus Empiricus and Plutarch in the second century AD (Dihle 1977, pp. 28–30). The tradition of an atheist Critias goes back at least to the end of the fourth century or the beginning of the third century BC. The new edition of Philodemus' *On Piety* shows that Epicurus was already criticizing what Critias said about the gods (l. 519–41) according to ideas close to those quoted by Sextus Empiricus (l. 1185–217). See Burkert 1985, p. 467 n. 22, quoting Epicurus, *On Nature*, book 11 (= 27.2.8); Bremmer 2006, p. 16.

for a while, to agree on the punishment of a certain number of scapegoats, before unchained political passions compromised its internal balance.

As always, the good times couldn't last. After a moment of indecision, the Athenians set up a new political regime. Conducted by five ephors designated within the oligarchic *hetaireiai*, the transition ended during the summer of 404 with the election of a commission of thirty members, charged with collecting and restoring the 'ancestral laws' – the *patrioi nomoi* – and, in the meantime, with governing the city.[115] While Xenophon provides the nominative list of the Thirty in a passage using very official language, it is Lysias who makes its principles of composition clear: 'Instructions were given to vote for ten men identified by Theramenes, ten whom the previously established "ephors" should appoint, and ten more from those at the meeting [i.e. the Assembly].'[116] The establishment of the Thirty therefore relied on a skillful balance between various schools of thought with divergent political options. According to the *Athenian Constitution*, the political field was then divided into three distinct groups: 'the people's supporters endeavored to preserve the democracy, but the notables who belonged to the *hetaireiai* and those exiles who had returned after the peace were eager for oligarchy, while those notables who were not members of any *hetaireiai* but who otherwise were inferior in reputation to none of the citizens were aiming at the ancestral constitution.'[117] One should not, however, be misled by this beautiful tripartition: The Thirty did not count any authentic democrats in their midst, but only men whose positions were compatible with the new political relations of force, inside and outside the city. As Xenophon recalls it, the new regime was established 'with the approval of the Lacedaemonians.'[118]

This rather homogeneous recruitment policy explains why the Thirty displayed a united front at first, determined to put an end to several decades of popular hegemony. Brought together through attending the same *symposia*, they even sought to create an ideal community, transposing the principles of Spartan organization to Athens. The Thirty indeed seem to have wanted to break with the Cleisthenic decimal system, with its decentralized structures of power, to privilege a much more hierarchical model, ordered into three concentric circles based on multiples of thirty: It seems that the community counted 3,330 citizens, divided into 3,000

---

[115] On the chronological question, see Salmon 1969, pp. 497–500.
[116] Lysias, *Against Eratosthenes* (12), 76. Cf. Xenophon, *Hellenica*, 2.3.2.
[117] Pseudo-Aristotle, *Athenian Constitution*, 34.3.   [118] *Hellenica*, 2.3.25.

hoplites (100 × 30), 300 horsemen (10 × 30) and 30 leaders (1 × 30). If this hypothesis is correct, one might claim that the Thirty were inspired by a laconizing utopian model, undoubtedly actively promoted by Critias, the 'organic intellectual' of the oligarchy.[119]

Beyond this numerical reorganization, the Thirty wanted to put an end to the Athenian maritime dominance and to anchor the city to the earth. For them, it was a question of going back to a primitive Athens, before the city turned toward the sea and fell into imperial excess – according to the historical reconstruction proposed by Critias himself in Plato's *Timaeus*.[120] This inflexion was reflected, in particular, in the decision to reorient the Pnyx – the place where the citizens' Assembly met – so that the *bema* faced the territory of the city, instead of Piraeus, the port of Athens and symbol of imperialist democracy.[121] When they addressed the people, orators henceforth gazed out upon the territory of a city closed on itself and purged of its foreign elements.

This redefinition of the community was accompanied by a certain violence, initially rather well accepted. Attacking the most radical democrats, the first capital sentences even favored, at first, the unity of the Athenians who had remained in the city. Diodorus of Sicily underlines this momentary state of grace: 'To begin with, [the Thirty] brought to trial the city's most notorious malefactors and condemned them to death; and so far what was going on met with even the most reasonable citizens' approval.'[122] Even the orator Lysias, however little suspected of oligarchic sympathies, agrees: 'you would have regarded the Thirty as honorable men if they had punished only those people.'[123] Better still, these initial measures aroused enthusiasm, according to the *Athenian Constitution*: 'At the outset, therefore, [the Thirty] were engaged [...] in removing the sycophants and the persons who consorted undesirably with the people to curry favor and were evil-doers and scoundrels; *and the city was delighted at these measures*, thinking that they were acting with the best intentions.'[124]

---

[119] The hypothesis was advanced simultaneously by Krentz 1982 and Whitehead 1982–1983. See also Caire 2016, pp. 117–8.

[120] In the *Timaeus* and in the interrupted dialogue of *Critias*, Plato tells the story of the conflict between two cities that disappeared almost 9,000 years ago: the primitive Athens and Atlantis. It is Critias who introduces the story, presenting the victory of the just city of Athens, turned toward the earth, over the Atlantean city, symbolizing *hubris*, excess and thalassocracy. See Pradeau 1997; Vidal-Naquet 2007.

[121] Plutarch, *Life of Themistocles*, 4.   [122] Diodorus of Sicily, 14.4.2 (transl. Green 2010).

[123] *Defense Against a Charge of Subverting the Democracy* (25), 19.

[124] Pseudo-Aristotle, *Athenian Constitution*, 35.3 (our emphasis).

Who were these 'sycophants' and 'evil-doers' whose deaths contributed to temporarily uniting the oligarchic chorus? Lysias evokes by name Cleophon, one of the former leaders of the people, recognized as a 'bad citizen' and quickly executed.[125] Those who refused the new geopolitical order were also attacked, and in particular the *stratēgoi* and the taxiarchs who had opposed the terms of the peace treaty with the Spartans: Arrested even before the Thirty came into being and accused of high treason, they were eventually brought before the Council and condemned to death after a public vote.[126]

These first condemnations aimed, in the literal sense, to *purify* the community, by ridding it of the worst leaders of the 'accursed people of the Athenians' – to paraphrase the funeral epigram of Critias. The Thirty claimed 'that they needed to cleanse (*katharan*) the city of wrongdoers and redirect the remaining citizens towards goodness and justice.'[127] These expeditious punishments were in this respect a cathartic ritual similar to the purifying ceremonies that opened the festival of the Thargelia in honor of the birth of Apollo and Artemis: Charged with all the evils of the city, one or two individuals were chosen as expiatory victims before being, according to ancient sources, either expelled from the city or beaten and stoned so that the regenerated city could get back to normal.[128] The following day, competitions between several cyclical choruses of men and children took place to mark, in the joy of dance and song, the new beginning of the community.

Beyond its ritual resonances, this joyful purification had long been prepared for or, more precisely, prefigured in the theater. For the comedies of the last third of the fifth century had continually staged expulsions, or even the elimination of sycophants,[129] according to a recurrent narrative pattern: A sycophant enters the stage and proudly announces that he is pursuing, on spurious grounds, certain vulnerable individuals; he is then mocked and insulted by the comic hero, before finally being chased away, or even brutally and mercilessly beaten.[130] In the *Demes* of Eupolis, in 412, a sycophant ended up tied up and beaten like a drum, after having opposed

---

[125] Lysias, *Against Nicomachus* (30), 13: *kakon politēn*.
[126] The legality of the decision was, however, undermined because, initially, the Assembly had decreed that the accused would be judged 'by a court of two thousand members' and not by the Council: Lysias, *Against Agoratus* (13), 35–8.
[127] Lysias, *Against Eratosthenes* (12), 5. Cf. Plato, *Letters*, 7.324d.   [128] See Eck 2011, p. 19.
[129] See Christ 1998, p. 52.
[130] Aristophanes, *Birds*, 1468; *Acharnians*, 818–28, 908–58; *Ploutos*, 850–950. See Rosenbloom 2002, pp. 336–7.

Aristides the Just. In Aristophanes' *Lysistrata*, performed in 411, the heroine proposes to unite the citizens after cleaning the dirt – the dung and the burrs – from the shorn fleece that is the city in this metaphor; that is, cleansing the city of the demagogues who would do anything to gain power – even if it meant 'pluck[ing] off their heads one by one.'[131]

It would be a mistake, however, to read these plays in retrospect as genuine calls for the murder of sycophants. First of all, the comic poets were targeting *all* influential political actors, without distinction, and laconizing oligarchs bore the brunt of it as well. Secondly, the violence of comic language was more akin to a ritualized verbal venting than to an articulated political program.[132] In order to switch from verbal insults to real violence, a completely different political situation and the arrival in power of vengeful oligarchs were necessary.

When theatrical fiction found its way into reality, comedy quickly turned to tragedy or, rather, to terror: Instead of purifying passions by representing them on stage – in accordance with Aristotle's famous *katharsis* – the very real executions of 'sycophants and demagogues' aroused terrible fears that quickly became impossible to appease within the community.

For a while, 'those in the town were unanimous.'[133] But the spell was soon broken, for the Thirty quickly attacked not only overt democrats, but also citizens whose only fault was to have adhered to the previous regime. The executions came in quick succession, striking Leon of Salamis, a famous former general, the rich and patriotic Antiphon, and Niceratus the son of Nicias: 'although he was invited to share in the oligarchy by those who were plotting against the democracy, he rejected their request.'[134] Shortly afterwards, it was the turn of 'Strombichides and Calliades and many other excellent citizens (*kaloi kagathoi*)' to be condemned to death by the new oligarchic Council.[135]

Far from targeting only the 'contemptible' (*ponēroi*), the Thirty also focused particularly on rich Athenians: Of the sixteen victims of the oligarchy known by name, eleven were part of the liturgical class.[136]

---

[131] Aristophanes, *Lysistrata*, 574–8. See Scheid and Svenbro 1996, p. 16.
[132] See Saetta Cottone 2005; Stark 2004; Kamen 2020, ch. 2.
[133] Lysias, *Defense Against a Charge of Subverting the Democracy* (25), 21.
[134] Lysias, *On the Property of the Brother of Nicias* (18), 4–5. On these three characters, see Caire 2016, p. 149.
[135] Lysias, *Against Nicomachus* (30), 14.
[136] Németh 2006, p. 152; Canfora 2013, pp. 122–44. According to the latter, the Thirty led a deliberate assault against wealth and intended to establish a new Sparta: The project was to refound the community on virtue and not capital.

Perhaps this relentlessness derived from the fact that these wealthy citizens were regarded as traitors to their class. A few years before, the Old Oligarch had already railed against 'anyone who is not one of the common people, and yet chooses to settle in a city governed by a democracy rather than one governed by an oligarchy.'[137] Still, this extension of violence brought about the first fracture within the oligarchy between the most radical fringe and all those who, like Theramenes, refused this justification. A man should not be executed, he argued, 'because he was honored by the people, provided he was doing no harm to the excellent people (*kaloi kagathoi*).'[138]

Such violence also affected noncitizens and, in particular, wealthy metics who remained in Athens after the defeat.[139] These targeted seizures, of which the family of the orator Lysias was a victim, corresponded to a particularly closed conception of the community. Far from being arbitrary, such persecutions resonated with the new civic organization, which was based on political and spatial segregation. Reduced to three thousand, the citizens were thus registered, then reviewed by the Thirty and, finally, gathered on the Agora; conversely, all 'those who were not on the roll' were distributed 'in various places here and there,' before being disarmed.[140] Dispersed across the entire territory, several thousand Athenians were thus dispossessed of their citizenship and deprived of means of defense both military and judicial.

This drastic redefinition also had strong repercussions within the civic body itself: By setting a strict limit on the number of citizens – 3,000 and not one more – the Thirty also put a strain on the fortunate ones, whose names they could strike off the list with the stroke of a pen: 'for a long time went on postponing the roll of the Three Thousand and keeping to themselves those on whom they had decided, and even on occasions when they thought fit to publish it they made a practice of erasing some of the names enrolled and writing in others instead from among those outside the roll.'[141] To include a citizen was therefore to perfunctorily exclude another. The Thirty probably saw this as a way of maintaining pressure

---

[137] Pseudo-Xenophon, *Constitution of the Athenians*, 2.20.
[138] *Hellenica*, 2.3.15 (transl. Loeb modified).
[139] Xenophon, *Hellenica*, 2.3.21: 'And now, when this had been accomplished, thinking that they were at length free to do whatever they pleased, [the Thirty] put many people to death out of personal enmity, and many also for the sake of securing their property. One measure that they resolved upon, in order to get money to pay their guardsmen, was that each of their number should seize one of the metics residing in the city, and that they should put these men to death and confiscate their property.'
[140] *Hellenica*, 2.3.20.   [141] Pseudo-Aristotle, *Athenian Constitution*, 36.2.

on the closed group of citizens, who had to fight to retain their place and their privileges. This agonistic conception of citizenship was in fact quite coherent with the thought of Critias, according to whom true superiority was established through competition: As Emmanuelle Caire has successfully shown, for the oligarch, 'excellence is never a steady state: it is only conceived in the *agōn*.'[142]

This numerical limit also aimed to prevent the emergence of competing choruses within the oligarchic community. It is, in any case, the justification given for the reform according to Xenophon: 'Accordingly Critias and the rest of the Thirty, who were by this time alarmed and feared above all that the citizens would flock to the support of Theramenes, enrolled a body of three thousand, who were to take part, as they said, in public affairs.'[143] In this matter, the oligarchs seem to have been guided by the fear of seeing 'too large a group gravitating' (*surreō*) around Theramenes – himself a member of the Thirty – since this could have thwarted their radical projects.[144]

Not surprisingly, Theramenes opposed the idea of fixing a precise number of citizens, 'as though this number must somehow be good men and true': He refused to believe that 'they should limit themselves to three thousand, and there could neither be excellent men (*kaloi kagathoi*) outside this body nor rascals within it.'[145] Above all, he thought that such a restriction endangered the maintenance of the new regime: 'Theramenes said that if one did not associate enough people in the public affairs, it would be impossible that the oligarchy maintains itself.'[146] He then became the spokesman of all those who, among the Three Thousand, and even among the Thirty, challenged the exclusive approach defended by Critias and his peers: They soon split into separate factions. *Stasis* insinuated itself within the oligarchy: Even before the first massacres, 'the Three Thousand were in a state of civil strife (*stasiazontas*), [...] the other citizens had been formally expelled from the town, [and] the Thirty were no longer united.'[147] The oligarchic revolution would soon begin to

---

[142] Caire 2018, p. 134 and Caire 2016, pp. 123–4. [143] *Hellenica*, 2.3.18.
[144] Significantly, the Three Thousand were called 'satellites of the oligarchy' (*tria millia satellitum statuunt*): Justin, *Epitome of the Philippic History of Pompeius Trogus*, 5.8.
[145] *Hellenica*, 2.3.19. According to Caire 2018, p. 133, these divergent strategies go hand in hand with distinctive lexical choices: While Theramenes wanted an Athens open to all *kaloi kagathoi* (the 'excellent'), Critias wanted to stick to the *beltistoi* (the 'best'), who were in competition with each other.
[146] See Caire 2016, p. 128.
[147] Lysias, *Defense Against a Charge of Subverting the Democracy* (25), 22.

devour its own children – as was the case at the height of the Terror during the French Revolution.[148]

The Fractured Chorus: Extending the Domain of Fear

Faced with the growing popularity of Theramenes, the Thirty finally decided to bring him to trial for treason. Pretending to respect the law, they assembled the Council, which acted as a judicial court. Critias held the role of principal accuser, and, at the end of a parody of judgment, Theramenes was condemned and executed. Reported in detail by Xenophon, this sequence is marked by a form of intense theatricalization, both in form and in content. Pitting the accuser against the accused, the story has contributed greatly to the legend of an all-powerful Critias, the true leader of the oligarchy. In reality, if he did all the talking during the trial, it was not by virtue of his supposedly exorbitant power, but because he was the most accomplished orator of the Thirty and the only one able to stand up to a rhetorician of Theramenes' caliber.[149] And the fact that the confrontation was so poignant is because the two men had been close – so close.[150]

'Now in the beginning Critias shared the ideas of Theramenes and was his friend (*philos*).'[151] The two men had indeed frequented the same places and, in particular, the same *symposia*, tasting together the pleasures of the wine that Critias sang about so beautifully in his elegiac verses.[152] However, these happy memories were not enough to disarm the growing hostility between the two men. Better still, it is in the name of this earlier friendship that Critias tried to have Theramenes condemned. For, in his eyes, 'treason is a far more dreadful thing than war.'[153] While with an avowed enemy one knows what to expect, a traitor ruins any form of trust and calls into question the very principles of *philia*. He claimed Theramenes had acted precisely in this way: After having been a friend of the Lacedaemonians, he turned against them, becoming their adversary, even their enemy.[154] Without the loyalty of Theseus, who supported Pirithoos in all circumstances, the inconstant Theramenes thus deserved severe punishment. At the end of the trial, Critias had him removed from the list of citizens, depriving him of any legal protection because the Thirty

---

[148] Tackett 2015, pp. 324–34: 'A Revolution Devouring Its Children.'
[149] Cicero, *De Oratore*, 2.93.   [150] On the analysis of the narrative, see Usher 1968.
[151] *Hellenica*, 2.3.15 (our translation).   [152] Critias, 88 B6 DK (= Athenaeus, 10.432d).
[153] *Hellenica*, 2.3.29.   [154] *Hellenica*, 2.3.27–9 (*echthros*). See Caire 2016, p. 308.

'have power of life or death over those outside the roll (*katalogos*).'[155] What better way to show that the traitor is no longer a subject of law, but a man who can be killed with impunity, like the *homo sacer* dear to Giorgio Agamben?

Theramenes obviously did not take the same view. Condemned to death, he delivered a final speech, in which he looked back on the friendship that had tied him to Critias. Mixing pathos with irony, the scene is famous: 'And when, being compelled to die, he had drunk the hemlock, they said that he threw out the last drops, like a man playing kottabos, and exclaimed: "This to the fair Critias."'[156] Far from being anecdotal, as Xenophon pretends to believe, this tirade mobilizes a whole universe of references shared between oligarchs. At one level, this joke is indeed part of the tradition of scathing retorts, specific to the culture of the banquet (*symposion*). More specifically, it refers to the game of *kottabos*, very popular at *symposia*, whose rules are well known: The participants threw the last drops of their cup toward the cup of the friend to whom they wished to show their preference, or even their attraction.[157]

In this context, this last line takes on a very ironic character. Wasn't it a way of mocking Critias, whose taste for drunken banquets and admiration for the sober morals of the Lacedaemonians were well known to everyone?[158] 'This to the fair Critias': The remark was also, at another level, a way to make fun of the codes of the erotic culture specific to *symposia*. For Critias, then about fifty years old, was no longer the handsome young man he had once been, when the two adversaries were still frequenting the *symposion* together. Above all, by addressing the last drop of poison to his former companion, Theramenes was ironically inviting him to join him in death, as Theseus had followed Pirithoos to the Underworld. While the kottabos anticipates in principle love, it announces in this case death – the death that Critias met, a few days later, during the Battle of Mounychia.

Beyond its biting irony, the toast also functioned, on one final level, as a melancholic meditation on how time ravages bodies and dissolves the

---

[155] *Hellenica*, 2.3.51.   [156] *Hellenica*, 2.3.56.   [157] See Pownall 2008a, 2008b.
[158] Critias had indeed sung, in his elegies, the praises of kottabos, 'a remarkable product from the land of Sicily, which we set up as a target for wine-drop arrows from the land of Sicily': Critias, 88 B2 DK (= Athenaeus, 15.666B). Cf. Critias, 88 B6 DK (= Athenaeus, 10.432d), l. 8–10. In the same manner, he had also celebrated Spartan drinking habits, which forbade the slightest toast and made de facto impossible the kottabos game: The cups were never empty, but filled as the meal went on. See also Usher 1979, who views this passage as an illustration of Critias' hypocrisy. In one final change of stance, Theramenes allegedly forced Critias to confront his own contradictions as a laconizing oligarch. For other (not exclusive) interpretations of Theramenes' final remark, see Gray 1989, p. 96, and Dillery 1995, p. 281–2.

bonds of even the strongest friendships. The time of *philia* was now over – and fear had taken its place!

Let's go back, to the moment of the trial itself, to focus this time not on the two main protagonists, but on the audience attending the scene. Everything happens in front of the members of the Council, arranged in a circle and charged with judging the case. As in a real play, the accuser and the accused question the audience in turn: After an initial tirade from Critias, Theramenes replies with conviction and almost wins over the audience. The denouement of the trial is then staged by Xenophon as a theatrical event:

> When with these words [Theramenes] ceased speaking and the Council had shown its good will by applause, Critias, realizing that if he should allow the Council to pass judgment on the case, Theramenes would escape, and thinking that this would be unendurable, went and held a brief consultation with the Thirty, and then went out and ordered the men with the daggers to take their stand at the railing in plain sight of the Council. Then he came in again and said: 'Members of the Council, I deem it the duty of a leader who is what he ought to be, in case he sees that his friends are being deceived, not to permit it. I, therefore, shall follow that course. Besides, these men who have taken their stand here say that if we propose to let a man go who is manifestly injuring the oligarchy, they will not suffer us to do so. Now it is provided in the new laws that while no one of those who are on the roll of the Three Thousand may be put to death without your vote, the Thirty shall have power of life or death over those outside the roll. I, therefore', he said, 'strike off this man Theramenes from the roll, *with the approval of all of us*. That being done', he added, 'we now condemn him to death.'[159]

Through his consummate storytelling, Xenophon brings the scene alive for the reader. However, as Emmanuelle Caire has shown, 'it is above all the staging of a show for the use of the members of the Council, a show in which Critias is both the chorus and the coryphaeus. The appearance of the dagger-bearers is as spectacular as the entrance of the chorus in a dramatic play, even if it remains absolutely silent and even if, paradoxically, the narration ellipses it.'[160] With its two distinguished protagonists, a highly visible chorus and a large audience, all the ingredients of a tragic play, with its adventures and its dramatic denouement, are gathered together.

But it should be noted that it is a very singular play that is acted out here, in complete contradiction with the traditional tragic codes. First of all, Critias combines roles that are normally distinct in the theater: In this

---

[159] *Hellenica*, 2.3.51 (our emphasis). [160] Caire forthcoming.

strange show, he acts at the same time as a protagonist (since he plays the main role), as a coryphaeus (since he speaks in the name of the dagger-bearers), as a *chorēgos* (since he has prepared the entrance of the different performers) and, finally, as a poet (since he has also written the denouement of the plot). Then, throughout the whole sequence, the chorus does not speak, does not dance and does not call out to the spectators, as is the custom in Athens: The armed men remain silent, stationed all around the stage, like threateningly immobile blocks. The spectators themselves remain mute: While they are supposed to decide between the actors by means of a vote – at the end of the trial as in tragic contests – they remain frozen and reactionless, silently acquiescing to the dispossession of their own power. Finally, this disconcerting show does not aim to purge the passions of the audience through a cathartic fictional tale, but on the contrary to unleash fear in citizens' souls, by bringing together reality and its representation.

Indeed, the Council members were seized with terror and abandoned Theramenes to his sad fate. Panic-stricken, the accused took refuge on the altar of Hestia, placing himself under the protection of the gods and the laws. Critias did not care, however, and had him apprehended by his men, in a heavy silence, broken only by Theramenes' protests and calls for help. 'But the councilors kept quiet, seeing that the men at the rail were of the same sort as Satyrus and that the space in front of the Council-house was filled with the guardsmen, and being well aware that the former had come armed with daggers.'[161] The Councilors were thus reduced to the rank of passive citizens, forced to accept the death of one of their own without saying a word.

After this *coup de force*, the oligarchy of the Thirty was transformed into a true phobocracy – a form of government by terror. The Three Thousand were henceforth only a cluster of fearful solo individuals, with no unifying principle other than fear. Critias and the Thirty were not spared either: Like the tyrant who brings in a reign of terror but feels it cruelly in return – according to a cliché in vogue on the tragic scene – the leaders of the oligarchy were tormented by fear. Wasn't it in fact because they '*feared* (*phoboumenoi*)' the charisma of Theramenes that they decided to eliminate him at all costs?[162]

The Frightened Chorus: The Terrorist Climax

At the end of the trial, the Thirty nevertheless felt they had been delivered from their anguish. 'So, then, Theramenes died; but the Thirty, thinking

[161] *Hellenica*, 2.3.55.   [162] *Hellenica*, 2.3.18.

that now they could play the tyrant *without fear*, issued a proclamation forbidding those who were outside the roll to enter the city [...].'[163] But this feeling of safety was illusory, Xenophon immediately specifies: A few weeks later, terror invaded the entire political arena, at the end of a new spectacular trial.

Eleusinians of fighting age – in all, three hundred men, formerly Athenian citizens – were arrested in a single day, at the instigation of Critias and his peers.[164] The very next day, the Thirty summoned to the Odeon the hoplites and the horsemen – that is to say, the whole Three Thousand – to collectively judge the prisoners.[165] Here again, the scene appears to be marked by a powerful theatricality, first of all because of the place chosen for the trial: Next to the theater of Dionysus, wasn't the Odeon in fact a major venue for performances, where the musical competitions of the Panathenaia were held? The unfolding of the trial itself can be seen as reproducing, on a much larger scale, that of Theramenes: Critias again plays every role, at once protagonist, chorus, coryphaeus and poet. But the play quickly turns into a parody, so condensed is the plot and so accelerated the rhythm. If Critias gives voice to the accusation, he no longer has an opponent to counter him. He delivers only a short speech, concentrated into a few sentences, to the Three Thousand:

> 'We, gentlemen', said he, 'are establishing the political regime no less for you than for ourselves. Therefore, even as you will share in honors, so also you must share in the dangers. Therefore you must vote condemnation of the Eleusinians who have been seized, that you may have the same hopes and fears as we.'[166]

Critias confesses here: The trial does not aim to punish criminals – the Eleusinians' only fault being that they are not registered citizens – but to transform the judges themselves into assassins! Alternating 'you' and 'we,' Critias seeks precisely to make the Three Thousand accomplices of a terrible crime, to stop them defecting for fear of reprisal.[167] Beyond this sordid objective, Critias reveals what, according to him, form the real

---

[163] *Hellenica*, 2.4.1: *adeōs* (our emphasis).
[164] *Hellenica*, 2.4.8. Cf. Lysias, *Against Eratosthenes* (12), 52, according to whom 300 citizens (or, rather, former citizens) were condemned to death. To the massacre of the Eleusinians is added – like a sinister double – another mass crime, affecting this time the inhabitants of Salamis. Cf. Diodorus, 14.32.4: The Thirty also 'accused the inhabitants of Eleusis and Salamis of abetting the exiles, and slaughtered them all.'
[165] *Hellenica*, 2.4.9.   [166] Ibid.
[167] Cf. Lysias, *Against Eratosthenes* (12), 93: '[The Thirty] did not want you to share in their profits but forced you to share their bad reputation.' This strategy had perhaps been tried out, on a small scale, a decade earlier in the context of the mutilation of the Herms in 415: This transgressive

founding principles of a political community: Citizenship is less about participation in the Assembly or the Council than about shared hopes and fears. To put it differently, according to the enraged oligarch, a *politeia* worthy of the name is defined emotionally, not institutionally.

For the oligarch, these collective passions must be imposed, not negotiated. In this case, the vote is not only public in order to identify the half-hearted and any possible traitors, but it is carried out under guard. The threat is even clearer than at the time of Theramenes' trial: It is no longer simple dagger-bearers, placed at strategic locations, who impose a reign of terror, but 'the armed Lacedaemonian garrison,' occupying 'half of the Odeon'[168]: the threatening troop transforms the vote into a masquerade and the tragedy into a sinister farce.

In this trial orchestrated by Critias, terror is pervasive and touches every single participant – victims, executioners and accomplices: While the Eleusinians fated to die were seized with terror, the Three Thousand hardly fared any better, fearing as much the ferocity of the Thirty as future reprisals by the democrats who were enraged by this mass crime; and the Thirty themselves also lived in fear since they deemed that 'their government was no longer secure' (*Hellenica*, 2.4.8). Following the initial successes of Thrasybulus and his troop, they had decided to empty Eleusis of its population to contrive a refuge in case they needed one.[169]

We must go further. Pervading the whole civic body, these fears are not the accidental fruit of a political situation out of control, but the product of a deliberate strategy implemented by the laconic oligarchs leading the Thirty. Critias had indeed been interested in the way the Spartans had based their own political freedom on fear and, in particular, on fear of the helots – the enslaved population of Laconia and Messenia who farmed for the *Homoioi*. This is, at least, what is suggested, at several centuries of distance, by the rhetor Libanios in one of his *Discourses*:

> The Lacedaemonians [...] had granted to themselves the freedom to put to death the helots. Critias declares that 'in Lacedaemonia are the most enslaved men (*douloi*) and the most free (*eleutheroi*)'. What does this mean if not what Critias himself says, namely: 'it is because of the distrust which

---

action, carried out as a community, was probably intended to unite the group around a common goal. See on this subject Murray 1990, p. 158.

[168] *Hellenica*, 2.4.10.

[169] The choice of Eleusis is probably not random. Beyond its religious importance, it was a strategic location, situated on the road leading to Sparta. See Hornblower 2011, p. 138. In this respect, Eleusis was to symbolize, in the eyes of the Thirty, the bastion from which they could hope to counterattack with the help of the Lacedaemonians.

he feels towards these helots that the Spartan, at home, removes the strap from his shield.'[170]

The Spartans had apparently even invented the means to prevent helot revolts by removing the strap on their shields (to make them unusable) and by always carrying a spear (to have a constant advantage in the event of hand-to-hand combat). Libanios makes light of such freedoms, the cost of which seems to him inordinate:

> Such was apparently the situation of people living in fear who were prevented from even breathing by those who represented a threat to their hopes. People who are armed with the fear of their slaves while they are eating, sleeping or doing any other activity, how could they, son of Callaischros, enjoy *pure freedom* (kathara eleutheria)?[171]

With all due respect to Libanius, Critias saw in this constant vigilance the very condition of complete political freedom. His reasoning can be expressed in the form of an argumentative chain: To be truly free, a citizen must always remain on the alert; to remain on the alert, he must himself feel fear; to feel fear, he must frighten others; to frighten others, he must enslave them. According to this perverse logic, true freedom is thus inseparable from the enslavement of others, and this is why 'in Lacedaemonia are the most enslaved men (*douloi*) and the most free (*eleutheroi*).' This is also why the whole of society had to live in fear: Terrorized as they were themselves, the helots also terrorized, in turn, the citizens, thus maintaining them in a state of salutary tension.

Transposed to Athens, this vicious reasoning allows us to better understand certain radical decisions taken by the Thirty. In 404, the oligarchs could indeed have reserved access to the magistracies and the Council to a selected elite, without excluding the majority of the people from the civic body and, consequently, from any form of legal protection. If the Thirty decided to enslave the *demos* and to deprive it of the safety offered by the statute of citizen, it was perhaps not only out of a spirit of revenge, but also to create enemies inside the group, determined to restore their old privileges. In the face of such a threat, the oligarchs were forced to form a united front and silence their internal divisions. In this strategy of tension, fear became its own goal – an existential experience designed to prevent any dissension in the oligarchic ranks.[172] This policy was therefore linked to a

---

[170] Libanius, *On Slavery* (25), 63 (= 88 B37 DK, our translation).
[171] Libanius, *On Slavery* (25), 64 (= 88 B37 DK, our translation and emphasis).
[172] See Boucheron and Robin 2015, pp. 64–5.

new form of anthropology: Skillfully maintained, terror was to give birth to a 'new man,' frightened but free – or, rather, free because he was frightened.

Establishing a permanent state of exception to guarantee the freedom of the 'best': Such was perhaps the great dream of Critias and his accomplices. But in wanting to keep the political community perpetually at boiling point, there was a great risk of arousing fatal fury. Rather than creating a virtuous form of vigilance, terror quickly degenerates into paralyzing fear, isolating citizens from each other and plunging them into a dazed stupor.

After the Thirty

Hardly a few days after the Eleusinians' massacre, the Thirty left to reconquer Piraeus, which Thrasybulus and his men had just seized. In spite of their numerical superiority and their heavy armament, the oligarchs suffered a resounding defeat on the slopes of Mounychia, where Critias and Charmides died: Fear had obviously not helped the oligarchs' troops stick together. However, fear was still necessary several months before any true peace negotiations were launched between 'those of the town' and the democratic exiles. Plagued by the fear of reprisal, the Three Thousand entrenched themselves behind the city walls and refused to lay down their arms for a long time. While they did eventually decide to dismiss the Thirty, they replaced them with a ten-man commission that proved to be just as belligerent and intransigent:

> [The Ten], however, having obtained this office did not proceed to do the things for the purpose of which they had been elected, but sent to Sparta to procure help and to borrow funds. But this was resented by those within the constitution, and the Ten, in their *fear of being deposed from office and their desire to terrify the others* (which they succeeded in doing), arrested one of the most leading citizens [of the town], Demaretus, and put him to death, and kept a firm hold upon affairs.[173]

The execution of Demaretus functions here as a duplicate of the condemnation of Theramenes. It has the same objective – to bring the Three Thousand to heel – and resorts to the same means: terror. There again, fear pervades the whole community: The fear felt by the Ten

---

[173] Pseudo-Aristotle, *Athenian Constitution*, 38.1–2 (our emphasis). Even if they were deposed, the Thirty were not immediately victims of a *damnatio memoriae*. On the contrary, Critias benefited from a splendid tomb that celebrated his antidemocratic action in a city still at war with itself. See *supra*, pp. 45–6.

corresponds to the terror that strikes the Three Thousand. However, the narrative has another, less immediately apparent, function: It seeks to impute responsibility for the continuation of the war to the Ten alone, who are accused of having betrayed the mission of appeasement that was entrusted to them.[174] In this version of the story, the Three Thousand are portrayed as frightened citizens, acting against their will and manipulated by the Ten after having been manipulated by the Thirty.

Once democracy was restored a few months later, the former oligarchs adopted this line of defense before the popular courts of justice, at least for those who did not benefit from the amnesty. The anonymous defendant in a Lysianic speech justified staying in the city because he was filled, like so many other citizens, with fear.[175] This argument of the 'terrorized terrorizer' was taken up even within the Thirty. In his speech against Eratosthenes – one of the Thirty, whom Lysias accused of having had his brother, Polemarchus, murdered and of having plundered his family's wealth – the orator anticipated the answers of his adversary in this imaginary dialogue:

SPEAKER: Did you summarily arrest Polemarchus or not?
DEFENDANT: I obeyed the orders of those in power, because *I was afraid.*[176]

Indeed, Eratosthenes had everything to gain by playing the role of the frightened citizen in order to better exonerate himself from any responsibility for the crimes committed by his fellow oligarchs.[177]

Focusing hatred on a few convenient bogeymen – first and foremost, the dazzling Critias – this emotional strategy was accepted by the democrats who had returned from Piraeus, or at least by the most moderate fraction of them. Every effort seems to have been made to help people forget to what extent, until the very last moment, the chorus of the Three Thousand danced in unison: The collective memory targeted, *a posteriori*, a few irredeemable citizens, struck with infamy, in order to better rebuild the unity of the divided city. But it is far from certain that all the democrats of Piraeus accepted this irenic version of the history – and, in particular, those close to Thrasybulus who had shouldered the risk involved in chasing the oligarchs out of Athens and knew what to expect.

---

[174] *Against Eratosthenes* (12), 55. No doubt the Three Thousand were much less frightened than the orator suggests. See Cloché 1915, pp. 125–9.
[175] *On a Charge of Overthrowing the Democracy* (25), 22.
[176] *Against Eratosthenes* (12), 25: *dediōs* (our emphasis).
[177] Cf. *Against Eratosthenes* (12), 50: 'Perhaps he can claim that he was afraid, and to some of you this will seem an adequate defense.'

CHAPTER 2

Thrasybulus and the Democratic Resistance

In distant Pamphylia, one night of the year 389 BC. Exasperated by the looting and the abuses of the Athenian soldiers, some men from the city of Aspendos break into the tent of their general to assassinate him. By a strange twist of fate, it is on the site of one of Athens' most famous victories of the fifth century against the Persian king, near the Eurymedon river, that resurgent Athenian imperialism suffers a cruel humiliation. Did the conspirators of Aspendos know as they awoke that the old general they had just assassinated was none other than the great Thrasybulus, the liberator of 403? One might question this. 'This, then, was the end of Thrasybulus, who was esteemed a most excellent man,'[1] writes Xenophon, seeming to regret the inglorious death of one of the greatest heroes of Athenian history.

There were, however, few Athenians who mourned the death of the general in 389. Diodorus of Sicily indicates only that 'when the Athenians learned of the death of their general Thrasybulus, they sent out Agyrrhius as general.'[2] Fifteen years after the democratic regime was restored, the glorious memory of the liberator had given place to defiance, even rejection, on behalf of the people. The man who had restored democratic institutions in 403 was henceforth suspected of conspiring to their overthrow, whereas many of his friends, described as obscure figures in the pay of a general who left to seek glory and fortune off Ionia, were dragged in front of the courts. Some did not hesitate to compare Thrasybulus to Dionysius, the tyrant of Syracuse, as if he too had only ever aspired to exercise personal power.[3] On the occasion of a lawsuit brought against one of his relatives, Ergocles, an orator even went so far as to affirm that his brutal death in Aspendos was providential, because it saved his memory from the dishonor to which it was promised: 'Thrasybulus did well in ending his life as he did. It was not right for him to live after plotting such deeds, nor to be executed by you (since he was thought to have done you

---

[1] Xenophon, *Hellenica*, 4.8.31.   [2] Diodorus of Sicily, 14.99.5.   [3] Aristophanes, *Ploutos*, 550.

some good in the past), but to be removed from the city in this manner.'[4] Thrasybulus had then become an adversary of the democratic city.

An Illustrious Unknown

When Hellenistic and Roman authors came to write the history of classical Athens, it is, however, the sole memory of the victory of 403 with which they associate the name of Thrasybulus, claiming he personally overthrew the Thirty's tyranny, thereby putting him on an equal footing with the greatest characters of classical Athens, such Miltiades, victor of the Battle of Marathon, or Pericles, the icon of the triumphant democracy of the fifth century.[5] From the beginning of the third century, the 'victory of Thrasybulus (*hē Thrasyboulou nikē*)' is the expression used to name and date the restoration of democratic institutions following the tyranny of the Thirty.[6] Since he 'was not only the first to make war upon them, but in the beginning he was the only one,'[7] as Cornelius Nepos wrote much later, Thrasybulus had become the symbol of all the combatants who had taken part in the restoration of the democracy. This late entry into the glorious crypt shared by the heroes of Athenian history nevertheless conceals the character's lack of biographical depth in the works of ancient authors, as if the man Thrasybulus, son of Lykos and of the deme of Steiria, frozen in the marble of his own statue, was destined to remain no more than a name, confined forever to the memory of the events of 403.[8]

What do we know about Thrasybulus? Very little, for the simple reason that no biographical tradition, whether favorable or hostile to him, has amassed and been transmitted through the centuries. It is with great difficulty that the historian gathers, with the help of some remarks scattered among Athenian writers, the elements that might lend him either allure or personality.[9] Born in the middle of the fifth century, undoubtedly toward 450, the man belongs to the Athenian social elite, and while it appears that his wealth was considerable, since he was designated trierarch twice in less than five years (in 411 and 406), it is quite difficult to

---

[4] Lysias, *Against Ergocles* (28), 8.   [5] See in particular Plutarch, *On the Glory of the Athenians*.
[6] For example, Philochorus (*FGrHist* 328 F 143): '... after the victory of Thrasybulus, Critias dies in Piraeus.'
[7] Cornelius Nepos, *Thrasybulus*, 1.2.
[8] Cornelius Nepos (first century CE) tries to explain this silence (*Thrasybulus*, 8.1): 'I put no one above him in sense of honor, in steadfastness, in greatness of soul and in love of country. For while many have wished, and a few have been able, to free their country from a single tyrant, it was his good fortune to restore his native land from slavery to freedom when it was under the heel of thirty tyrants. But somehow or other, while no one surpassed him in the virtues that I have named, many men have outstripped him in renown.'
[9] See mainly Buck 1998.

ascertain its origin. It should be noted, however, that in the middle of the fourth century his son, also Thrasybulus, was condemned to a fine of ten talents, a considerable sum that implies an exceptional fortune. In addition, his daughter went on to marry the grandson of the great Nicias, confirming with this brilliant matrimonial alliance that the family belonged to the social elite of the civic community.[10] Through scattered allusions present in the works of Xenophon, Aristophanes and Lysias, a few character traits – a psychology in short – take shape. Pride, first of all, the natural preserve of a man who was aware he enjoyed a certain superiority[11]; in the speech *In Defense of Mantitheus*, Lysias thus mocks 'the pretentious man from Steiria who had been reproaching everybody with cowardice'[12] as if, from the heights of his own legendary status, Thrasybulus despised his fellow citizens. Next, recognized oratorical talents, since Thrasybulus regularly spoke at the Assembly with the help of 'the most powerful voice of Athens (*megalophōnotatos Athenaiōn*).'[13] And finally, an undeniable physical courage,[14] which went hand in hand with a certain intellectual coarseness. His adversaries never missed the opportunity to make puns about his name. *Thrasos*, that is to say courage, boldness or temerity, on the one hand, and *Boulē*, meaning council or will, on the other: It didn't take much to turn the combined terms, which might have designated a man of courageous council, into a mockery of his rash and unrefined decisions.[15]

Beyond these few impressionistic touches, the man remains mysterious. This fact is undeniably surprising when you consider his intense participation in political life during one of the most crucial twenty-year period in Athenian history (411–390). When he entered the city in 403 victorious, he already had a reputation among the Athenians for valorous behavior during a particularly dramatic moment of the Peloponnesian War, in the summer 411, on the island of Samos.

Samos, 411: A Political Experiment

The Samos episode opens a decisive sequence of Athenian history that will only close in 403. Let us recall what we know about it. The adversaries of the democratic regime had made the most of the fact that a lot of poor citizens were away with the Athenian fleet stationed in Ionia to overthrow the democratic institutions. The oligarchs indeed intended to replace the

---

[10] Davies 1971, pp. 240–1.
[11] In *Assembly Women*, v. 202–4, Aristophanes shows him in a fury because, in the Assembly, the Athenians had voted a decree without having consulted him.
[12] Lysias, *In Defense of Mantitheus* (16), 15.   [13] Plutarch, *Life of Alcibiades*, 26.6.
[14] Pausanias, 1.29.3.   [15] Aristotle, *Rhetoric*, 1400b, about Conon.

Council of 500 citizens (drawn by lot without distinction of fortune) with a restricted Council of 400 members and to reserve citizenship to the 5,000 richest Athenians. A trierarch – and not a *stratēgos* – Thrasybulus was then part of the Athenian navy present in Samos, the operational base for all Athenian incursions throughout the eastern Aegean. According to the account proposed by Thucydides, it was he and Thrasyllus who, with the announcement that the Four Hundred had seized power in Athens, convinced the Athenian rowers of Samos to take up arms and overthrow the oligarchic regime.[16] The two trierarchs were apparently even the originators of the oath that each of the soldiers present that day had to swear: to 'maintain a democracy (*dēmokratēsesthai*) and live in harmony (*homonoēsein*), to carry out energetically and prevail against the Peloponnesians and, vis-a-vis the Four Hundred, to treat them as enemies without sending them heralds.'[17] By an act of dissidence against the established powers that Thucydides presents as a genuine revolution (*metabolē*),[18] the rowers of Samos then came to proclaim themselves the sole representatives of Athens and, forming an assembly (*ekklēsia*), deposed the *stratēgoi*[19] and elected in their stead Thrasybulus and Thrasyllus.

The scene, as penned by Thucydides, is presented as a heroic Athenian democratic gesture, by which a group of exiles came to refound the political community, and it is not without reason that some have implicitly compared it to the Gaullian experience of Free France.[20] A careful reading of Thucydides' account reveals a singularly complex situation. Two political scenes, Athenian and Samian, collide in the initial episode: The assembly of the Athenian *demos* also aims to prevent the establishment of an oligarchic regime in Samos. Moreover, the oath is sworn not only by the soldiers of Athens, among whom are citizens as well as metics and slaves,[21] but also by some of the Samians. In sum, the Athenian people who refounded the democratic regime in Samos in 411 were made up of free and unfree men, Athenians and Samians. Far from Athens, on the

---

[16] Thucydides, 8.73.4.   [17] Thucydides, 8.75.2.   [18] Thucydides, 8.75.2.
[19] It is impossible to know if only the *stratēgoi* present in Samos were deposed or if this statement referred to all the *stratēgoi* of the year.
[20] Isaac 1946.
[21] The presence of slaves and metics is not in doubt; they are even a constant on Athenian triremes from the 420s onwards: see, in general, Hunt 1998 and Graham 1992, pp. 257–70, and especially *IG* I³ 1032 – on this inscription, see *infra*, Chapter 8, pp. 222–3). Although the status of this long list remains uncertain (obituary? honorary inscription? mobilization list made in a hurry?), it attests to the important presence of slaves on Athenian triremes (on servile onomastics, see Robertson 2008 and the hypotheses of Bakewell 2008). Let us observe, moreover, that in his description of the episode, Thucydides, at 8.74.1, makes the distinction between the trireme Paralos, composed of citizens, and the rest of the troops.

Samos, 411: A Political Experiment

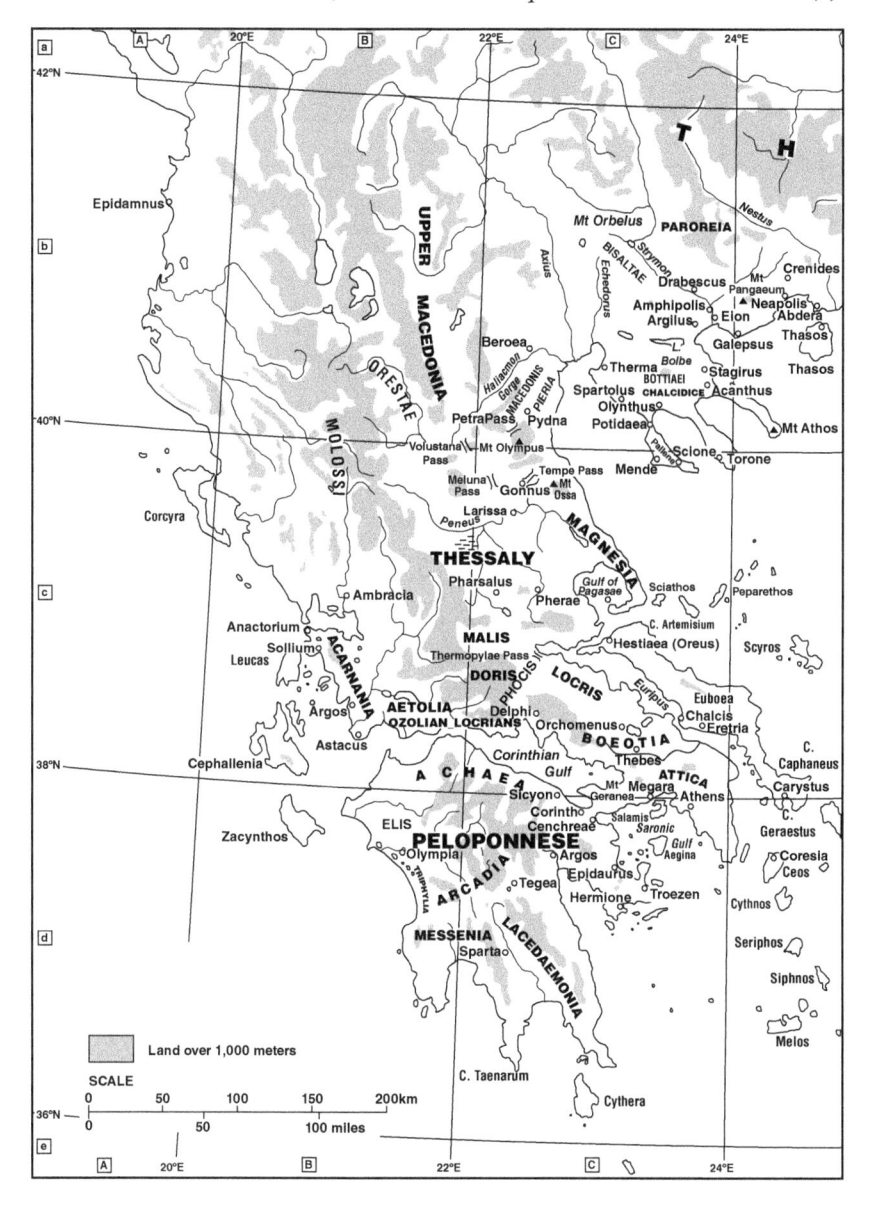

Fig. 2.1 Map of the Aegean world.

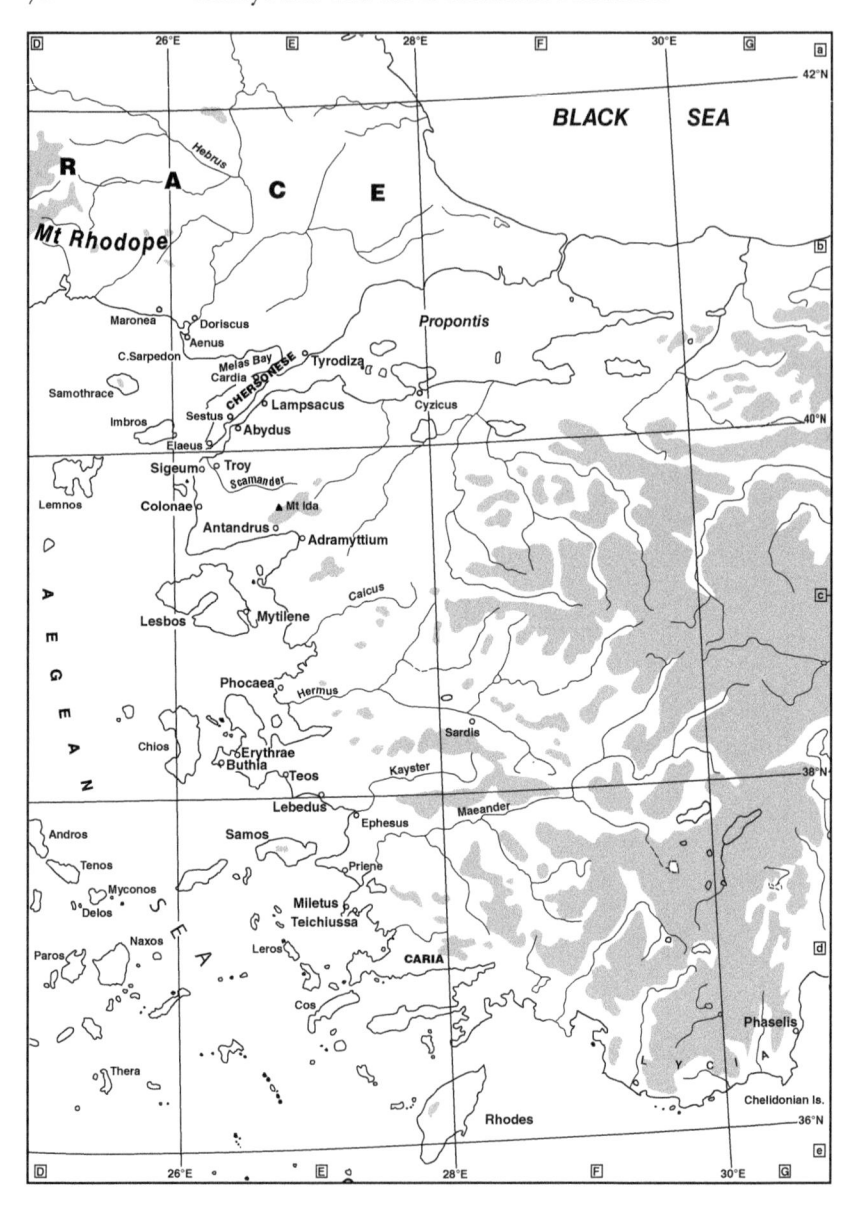

Fig. 2.1 (cont.)

Samos, 411: A Political Experiment

triremes that Plutarch compared to choruses,[22] a political community with new boundaries had been invented. Transcending the restricted framework of citizenry, this even claimed to be the guarantor of the democratic regime.

However, this political experiment was not simply a bright and fleeting moment of Athenian history. It largely accounts for the specificity of Thrasybulan politics over the course of 404–403. It is indeed striking to observe the sustainability of this community that, from 411 to 407, accompanied Thrasybulus while continuing to maintain an ongoing relationship with the Athenian institutions once democracy was restored in 410. It is within this diverse group that Thrasybulus, deprived of his status as *stratēgos* since 410 but enjoying unquestionable authority over his men,[23] carried out the siege of Eresos and took part in the appropriation of Cyzicus, and these same men were still at his side when the fleet reached Thrace in 409 and took part in the captures of Thasos and Abdera in 407.[24] Everything suggests that this political experience, lived through exile, greatly contributed to widening the distance that separated Thrasybulus from the other members of the Athenian elite – and when the litigant of Lysias' *Against Ergocles* denounces Thrasybulus in 390 as a man whose interests are now 'separate from those of the town,'[25] he obviously points out a constant in his life since the Samian episode. The experience of exile unites Critias and Thrasybulus, beyond their political antagonism, and this probably also explains their dissonant behavior compared to the ordinary practices of the elite and the singularity of their positioning in the Athenian political field.

It is tempting to interpret the action of the trierarch of 411 in the light of that of the liberator of 403. Thrasybulus initially appears to be a man of his oath, refounding on two occasions the democratic regime by means of a successful speech: In 411, he was the originator of the oath by which everyone committed themselves to overthrowing the regime of the oligarchs, whereas in 403 he exhorted the Athenians, once the city was reconquered, not 'to violate any one of the pledges to which [democrats and oligarchs] have sworn' in order to live together again.[26] The echoes between the two episodes attest, in any case, to the constancy of Thrasybulus in his political commitment to the service of Athenian

---

[22] Plutarch, *On Having Many Friends*, 94b–c. [23] See Potts 2008, p. 192.
[24] See in particular Potts 2008 and Karamoutsou-Teza 1988.
[25] Lysias, *Against Ergocles* (28), 6. On the background of the speech, see Bearzot 2014.
[26] Xenophon, *Hellenica*, 2.4.42.

democracy and imperialism. The rupture with the oligarchic city in 411 was a solitary act that Thrasybulus went on to reproduce in the final months of the confrontation against the Thirty. While he and his men had a firm grip over the fort of Phyle, the Thirty indeed urged him 'to break up the group of exiles, and instead to join them, the Thirty, in the running of the city, as the elected replacement for Theramenes. He would, they added, have the authority to bring back into the country any ten exiles he chose.'[27] Thrasybulus remained unmoved, answering 'that he preferred his current exile to power with the Thirty and, further, that he would not stop fighting until every citizen was repatriated, and the people got back their ancestral constitution.'[28] Attachment to the democratic regime risked exile, as if loyalty to Athens was above all to its democratic institutions. The constancy of Thrasybulus contrasts singularly with the underwhelming path taken by the majority of Athenian politicians of the last decade of the fifth century, especially Theramenes and Alcibiades – that is, one of successive volte-faces.

Fortunes and Misfortunes of a *Condottiere*

But if the memory of Thrasybulus since Hellenistic times was restricted to his role in liberating Athens in 403, this was due to his repeated failures on the Athenian political scene. Whether it concerned the first oligarchic revolution of 411, that following the restoration of the democracy in 403 or that during the Corinthian War, which started in 395, Thrasybulus had no idea how to convert his military glory into political victory, meaning that his destiny followed the trajectory of all great men quick to save the fatherland in dark times but unsuited to the prosaicness of peace. The same misadventure repeats itself throughout the life of our hero, one in which he gets eclipsed by politicians he himself helped bring to the forefront of political life: Alcibiades, first of all, in whose service he placed himself until the defeat of Notion (407). Indeed, Cornelius Nepos comments that 'in the Peloponnesian war he often won victories without the aid of Alcibiades, the latter never without his help; but Alcibiades by some innate gift gained the credit for everything.'[29] Next, Theramenes, who was a trierarch like Thrasybulus at the time of the Battle of Arginusai (406) but who upheld the charge against the *stratēgoi* alone and therefore amassed all the profit from this dark political maneuver.[30] Finally,

---

[27] Diodorus of Sicily, 14.32.5.   [28] Diodorus of Sicily, 14.32.6.
[29] Cornelius Nepos, *Thrasybulus*, 1.3.   [30] Xenophon, *Hellenica*, 1.7.8, 31.

Archinus, who, in the aftermath of the restoration of democracy in 403, managed to marginalize the victorious general by reconnecting with the Three Thousand.

It would be naive, however, to compare Thrasybulus to a man like Cato, who offers a model for republican virtue fallen victim to the machinations that make up the ordinary course of political life. Because, if the commitment of Thrasybulus to the democratic regime is incontestable, another, less flattering representation is no less appropriate: that of a *condottiere*, more at ease on the battlefield than in the Assembly and resistant to the necessarily egalitarian order of democratic life. This is also the reason for the city's disenchantment at the end of the Corinthian War. Sent out by the Athenians at the head of forty triremes, Thrasybulus indeed put into place a highly personal form of diplomacy and military policy: Not only did he free himself from the control of the Assembly and the Council by forging ties of *philia* with certain cities – and even with the Thracian king Seuthes, whose daughter he perhaps thought of marrying[31] – but he also imposed heavy taxes on some allies. Many Athenians disapproved of the violence of the general who, during the expedition, did not hesitate to overthrow the political regime of cities such as Byzantium, where he established institutions of a democratic type,[32] or, still worse, to allow his men to plunder his allies' communities.[33] Undoubtedly some of these measures were inevitable given that the city was reluctant to finance its own military expeditions, tacitly leaving it up to its *stratēgoi* to fund them by all and any means that they judged appropriate.[34] Nevertheless, some of the Athenians saw in the general's behavior the specter of tyranny, as if Thrasybulus had privatized imperial policy and the benefits that the Athenian *demos* could draw from it: This is why he was recalled to Athens to justify his conduct as *stratēgos*, his death saving him *in extremis* from facing this test.[35] One can also imagine how those close to Thrasybulus must have benefited from this policy of plunder and brutal exploitation. Ergocles, who was denounced as the courtier of the 'tyrant' Thrasybulus by an orator of the beginning of the century, is a good example of this.[36]

---

[31] Lysias, *Against Ergocles* (28), 5.   [32] Xenophon, *Hellenica*, 4.8.25–30.
[33] Xenophon, *Hellenica*, 4.8.30.   [34] See the remarks of Low 2011.
[35] Lysias, *Against Ergocles* (28), 5.
[36] One hears here a distant echo of the destiny of the Spartan regent Pausanias, crowned in success following the second Persian War but whose aura was tarnished by his outrageous behavior toward other Greek cities, particularly Byzantium, which was a geographic and symbolic junction point between Greece and Asia (see Thucydides, 1.130). In the background, there is always the threat of

In sum, Thrasybulus' political career is located at the crossroads of two conceptions of politics in Athens, and it is perhaps an anachronistic standpoint which gives the best perspective of this. Thrasybulus seems indeed to believe that he is the worthy successor of Pericles, adopting his austere ethics, competing with his oratorical talents and, especially, putting the alliance of democracy and the imperial project at the heart of his policies. But his political position after 403 also prefigures that of Timotheus or Chabrias, the great generals of the fourth century, admired and feared in equal measure by the Athenian people who preferred to see them defending their interests far from the city than to support them on a day-to-day basis in Athens. It is, moreover, what Pausanias seems to suggest, in his way, when he indicates that the tomb of Thrasybulus was next to those of Pericles and Chabrias, as if the political destiny of Thrasybulus symbolically bridged the gap between these two figures of Athenian political and military life.[37] True, the political failure of Thrasybulus in the aftermath of 403 announces, in a fashion, the separation between the military and oratorical sources of power that characterizes political life in the fourth century. Whereas a Cimon, a Pericles or a Nicias, in the fifth century, founded their political legitimacy in part on the basis of their military victories, a Demosthenes or a Lycurgus in the fourth century would hardly venture out into the battlefield; likewise, great generals like Timotheus or Chabrias would deliberately avoid the political arena.

But if the name of Thrasybulus has come to designate the entire group of victorious combatants from 403, to which chorus does it refer? Let us return to the crucial moment when our hero is preparing for the reconquest of Athens. The ancient sources agree that the victory of Thrasybulus' army revolves around three key moments: the capture of the fort of Phyle during the winter of 404, the military victory against the Thirty in Piraeus at the end of spring 403 and the entrance of the democratic army into Athens and their ascent of the Acropolis a few months later.[38] Focusing on the changing composition of the men with Thrasybulus through the way the army absorbed various fractions of the political community reveals how the democratic city gradually found its new center of gravity. But to capture each progressive coalescence of Thrasybulus' chorus before it

---

Persian behavior and customs (sense of distinction and superiority toward his soldiers, lavish lifestyle, etc.) that the warlord would be likely to import into the world of the Greek cities.

[37] Pausanias, 1.29.3.
[38] On the problematic chronology of the civil war, see *infra*, Conclusion, pp. 309–15.

eventually evolved into a reunified civic community in 403 also implies questioning the very existence of a Thrasybulan policy and, consequently, how it may have evolved as events unfolded. This is because the same applies to Thrasybulus' army as to those of Garibaldi or Mao Zedong: The group of men who took the fortress of Phyle during the winter of 404 was quite different from those who wound their way to the top of the Acropolis a few months later. While the group mutated, just as the chorus continued to grow, contradictions could not fail to appear, and the Thrasybulan project likewise evolved.

The Hundred Heroes of Phyle

It is undoubtedly when his exile and the confiscation of his property were announced at the end of the year 404 that Thrasybulus left Athens to take refuge with Thebes.[39] 'And further, when I saw that many in the city were becoming hostile to this domination and that many were becoming exiles, it did not seem to me best to banish either Thrasybulus or Anytus or Alcibiades; for I knew that by such measures the opposition would be made strong, if once the crowd should acquire capable leaders and if those who wished to be leaders should find a multitude of supporters,'[40] declared Theramenes at the time of his own trial. With seventy men by his side,[41] some of whom had perhaps been with him since the Samos episode, Thrasybulus was welcomed to Thebes while the city was under the influence of Ismenias, who had undertaken to disengage it from its traditional alliance with Sparta. Thrasybulus would never forget the protection that Thebes granted to him, erecting in the Herakleion of the Boeotian city two gigantic statues of Athena and Heracles, works of the Athenian sculptor Alcamenes.[42] Placed side by side, the two divinities recalled the precarious alliance between the two cities and the crucial support that Thebes, defying its own history, had given to the restoration of the Athenian democracy. The dedication that may have accompanied this monumental offering remains unknown, but one might suppose that, with this gesture, the victorious general also wished to celebrate the memory of the first soldiers, 'those of Thebes,' whose combat, initially led while they were few and far between, was not to be confused with that of the larger army that later went on to strike the blow that proved fatal to the Thirty. The

---

[39] Isocrates, *Against Callimachus* (18), 23; Diodorus of Sicily, 14.32.1.
[40] Xenophon, *Hellenica*, 2.3.42.
[41] Pseudo-Aristotle, *Athenian Constitution*, 37.1, and Xenophon *Hellenica*, 2.4.2, similarly mention seventy men, whereas Pausanias, 1.29.3, speaks of sixty.
[42] Pausanias, 9.11.6.

monument was therefore the depositary of the Thrasybulan memory of the event, irreducible to civic memory. This Boeotian connection persisted over time, since, in 395, Thrasybulus would be sent as ambassador to the Athenians to forge an alliance with Thebes against the Spartans.[43]

From Thebes, Thrasybulus and his men entered into the north of Attica and managed to seize the fortress of Phyle, which constituted one of the outposts ensuring the military defense of the Athenian territory. The capture of Phyle and the resistance that followed constitute the founding acts of the Thrasybulan legend, of which Xenophon and, after him, Diodorus wrote a detailed account. Once it was announced that the fortress had been captured, the Thirty immediately sent out a group of young combatants, but a miraculous event spared the besieged: Snow – yes, snow! – began to fall as winter came around in Attica,[44] an unexpected phenomenon in which Thrasybulus saw a sign from the gods,[45] which obliged the Thirty's army to retreat and to set up camp several kilometers to the southwest of Phyle. A few weeks later, Thrasybulus and his men attacked the oligarchs' camp by night on the plain of Acharnai. In the weeks that separated the capture of Phyle from the 'Acharnian surprise,'[46] the chorus of Thrasybulus had swollen by several hundred men, since, according to Xenophon and Diodorus, there were between 700 and 1,200 men on the democratic side who took part in the night raid.[47] The mission was a resounding success, since 120 hoplites and three of the Thirty's horsemen were slaughtered during the assault. Thrasybulus did not fail, moreover, to erect a memorial on the site of the confrontation, raising this simple raid to the status of a founding battle, which ushered in the military reconquest of Athens.

In the account they forged of these events, once democracy was restored the Athenians clearly distinguished between the initial group of men who had heroically resisted the siege of Phyle and those who took part in the raid against the Thirty's camp in Acharnai. Aeschines is indeed quick to point out that the day after democracy was restored, the Council, at the instigation of Archinus, carried out an investigation to establish the identity of those who had been besieged in Phyle.[48] On the stele that recorded

---

[43] Xenophon, *Hellenica*, 3.5.16. [44] Xenophon, *Hellenica*, 2.4.2–14.
[45] Xenophon, *Hellenica*, 2.4.12. [46] The expression is from Cloché 1915, p. 24.
[47] Xenophon, *Hellenica*, 2.4.5–10, mentions 700, but they were apparently 1,000 a few weeks later at the time of their departure for Piraeus. Diodorus of Sicily, on the other hand, estimates the figure at 1,200.
[48] Aeschines mentions quite explicitly 100 individuals (or a few more), since the expenditure of 1,000 drachmas must correspond to fewer than 10 drachmas per individual (Aeschines, *Against Ctesiphon* [3], 187).

their names, set up in the Metrôon in the center of the Agora, they even had the following epigram engraved: 'These men for their virtue were honored with crowns by the ancient people of Athens, because once when men with unjust ordinances (*adikois thesmois*) ruled the city, they were first to check them and lead the way, accepting mortal danger.'[49] By decree, the Athenians decided, moreover, to finance a sacrifice and a number of offerings in their honor – rites, the timing and regularity of which we know nothing – as well as to crown each one of them. This admittedly minor honor brought them considerable prestige. The very existence of an investigation carried out by the Boule indicates the importance that the city attached to defining this community of early fighters precisely.[50]

The decree mentioned by Aeschines is also recorded on a long fragmentary inscription found in the Agora and published for the first time in 1933 by Benjamin Meritt.[51] It consists of a dedication made by about sixty individuals, whose names are engraved and divided into two columns according to the Athenian tribes to which they belonged, and it was probably placed under the epigram quoted by Aeschines. Only the names of citizens seem to have been engraved, as if metics and slaves had been excluded from the commemorative group.[52] Their presence at the battle is, however, confirmed by Aeschines: When he mentions the 'first men' who

---

[49] Aeschines, *Against Ctesiphon* (3), 190.
[50] The community of Phyle, honored by this decree, resembles *mutatis mutandis* the order of the *Compagnons de la Libération* created by General de Gaulle on November 16, 1940, and which was always conceived as a closed order.
[51] Merritt 1933, no. 3. See, following the first publication of Raubitschek 1941, Taylor 2002 (= *SEG* 52.86), and especially Malouchou 2014 (= *SEG* 62.50) and Malouchou 2015. Malouchou relies on the rereading of a now illegible inscription made in the nineteenth century by Panayiotis Eustratiadis (died 1884), whose papers are in the archives of the Archaeological Society of Athens, and which she associates with our inscription. She has recognized in this the expression employed by Aeschines (*kindunos sōmasin*), but the given fragment precedes the formal mention of a decree. The addition of this fragment changes the materiality of the monument as a whole, which is wider and deeper than Raubitschek and Taylor conceived it (in particular because fragments a and b are no longer joined). Malouchou thus hypothesizes that it is the base of a statue, perhaps of the Athenian *demos*, which would have been placed near the Metrôon. On the other hand, it should be acknowledged that only sixty-five to seventy names are engraved upon it.
[52] Raubitschek 1941 and Taylor 2002 considered that the list, on which only citizens' names are legible, must also have included noncitizens whose presence is in Phyle is proven. It remains to be seen, first of all, if the list of noncitizens really starts at l. 69: It depends on whether one restores *Eleutherathēn* or *Engraphoi*. But whatever restoration is adopted, we would still need to ascertain where the forty missing individuals are mentioned and who the noncitizens, whose presence is implied by the quotation of Aeschines, are likely to be. The interpretation of Malouchou 2015 solves the difficulty, insofar as she shows that the inscription is not the decree itself but a dedication, the text of which recalls the decree that Aeschines mentions (in a way rather similar to the prytanic inscriptions of the end of the fifth and the fourth centuries). The commemorative group seems, therefore, to have been restricted to the citizens among the combatants of Phyle, given that the inscription could not hold more than seventy names.

contributed to saving democracy, he makes no distinction between the citizens and noncitizens among them. An honorific community had therefore sprung up around the memory of Phyle, including both free men and noncitizens, even if only the former commemorated the privilege that had been granted to them in 401. It must therefore be admitted that the men honored by Archinus' decree are not exactly those who erected the monument from which the fragments of our inscription derive, since noncitizens, whether they were free or not, have been excluded. In short, statutory hierarchies do not unfold in a homogeneous and continuous fashion in the social arena.

How can we identify the one hundred heroes of Phyle? It seems like a difficult task since the stele delivers the complete name of only two individuals. The first can be identified as a certain Theocles, son of Leucios, of the deme of Sounion (l. 33). While he is unknown, his son, who was an important mineowner in Laurion,[53] went on to be known in the mid-fourth century for offering no less than an agora to his own deme,[54] attesting to the wealth of the family. To him, we can probably add two men in Athens destined to greatness: Firstly, Archinus of Koile, whose name can be made out on the stele, and of whom Demosthenes affirms that he 'captured Phyle,' by adding that, 'next to the gods, he was the person most responsible for the return of the democracy.'[55] The presence of Archinus in Phyle is moreover confirmed by an author of the third century BC, Cratippus, who classifies him among the seventy 'of Phyle' who rose against the oligarchy.[56] Second, Anytus, known for having taken part in the accusation against Socrates in 399, was also present in Phyle.[57] A well-to-do man, he was the son of Anthemion, who commemorated a statue on the Acropolis on the occasion of his passage from the class of the thetes to that of the horsemen (*hippeis*), indicating a recently acquired fortune. Owner of a tannery in the city – just like Cleophon and Hyperbolus – he belonged to the category disparagingly designated by ancient authors as that of the demagogues.[58] Elected *stratēgos* in 409, he allegedly abused his position. Plutarch and Aristotle even attribute to him

---

[53] *Agora* 19, P 29, l. 5–6, P 26, l. 72–3. Moreover, its property is mentioned in the *poletai* records of 367/6: *Agora* 19, P 5, l. 46, l. 80 and P 13, l. 5–6.
[54] *IG* II² 1180 (with Stanton 1996).
[55] Demosthenes, *Against Timocrates* (24), 135. See *infra*, Chapter 3.
[56] Plutarch, *On the Glory of the Athenians*, 1.345d.
[57] Lysias, *Against Agoratus* (13), 78, affirms that he was one of the *stratēgoi* of Phyle. One can imagine that this function had been entrusted to him precisely because he was part of the first group present in the fortress itself. Cf. Xenophon, *Hellenica*, 2.3.42.
[58] Xenophon, *Apology of Socrates*, 29–31, presents him as the very model of the new politician.

an unflattering invention: that of having been the first to corrupt an entire Athenian jury during the trial following the rending of accounts (*euthynai*) of his generalship (*stratēgeia*).[59] However, it would be wrong to reduce him to the stereotype of the vengeful demagogue. In 403, Anytus opted for a policy of appeasement: He refused to bring to trial those who had seized his property during the civil war.[60] The *Athenian Constitution* is not mistaken when it presents him as a man attached to the *patrios politeia*, close to the moderate oligarch Theramenes in 404.[61]

To these three names, it is undoubtedly necessary to add that of Aisimus. If nothing explicitly indicates that he was present at Phyle, it is he who led the procession to the Acropolis when it entered Athens in September or October 403, and such an eminent role would not have been entrusted to a man who was not an early freedom fighter.[62] Whatever the case may be, he went on to play a political role during the first few decades of the fourth century as the ambassador of the city at the time of the King's Peace in 386,[63] and he took an active part in the reconstitution of Athenian power when he was designated ambassador to Chios in 384[64] and to Methymna in 378/7.[65]

Apart from these four characters, it is difficult to define precisely the community of the men of Phyle. Among the orators of the fourth century, many individuals are praised for having 'brought back' the people 'from Phyle' (*apo Phulēs*). Among them, it is very difficult to distinguish those who were besieged in the fortress from those who fought only in Acharnai. This is the case for Thrasybulus of Collytos,[66] for Atrometus (Aeschines' father)[67] and for Ergocles.[68] An episode related by Lysias testifies, moreover, to the conflicts that arose between the men of Phyle and those whose arrival, after the siege of the fortress began, came across as opportunistic rallying. It involved a certain Agoratus, accused in 402 by the litigant of a speech by Lysias of having caused the death of his cousin, Dionysodorus,

---

[59] Plutarch, *Life of Coriolanus*, 14, and Pseudo-Aristotle, *Athenian Constitution*, 27.5; Isocrates, *Against Callimachus* (18), 23. The latter allegation is probably false, as shown by Lenfant 2016. This accusation of corruption would have been based only on the mockery of comic poets, taken a posteriori at face value. See in general, about Anytus, Davies 1971, n° 1324, and Nails 2002, pp. 37–8 (with previous bibliography).
[60] See *infra*, Chapter 3, pp. 119–21.
[61] Pseudo-Aristotle, *Athenian Constitution*, 34.3. On this conservative political orientation of Anytus, see *infra*, Chapter 3.
[62] Lysias, *Against Agoratus* (13), 81. [63] Aristophanes, *Assemblywomen*, 208.
[64] *IG* II² 34, l. 36. [65] *IG* II² 42, l. 19.
[66] Demosthenes, *Against Timocrates* (24), 134, and Aeschines, *Against Ctesiphon* (3), 138.
[67] Aeschines, *On the Embassy* (2), 147. On the character, see *infra*, Chapter 3, p. 116.
[68] Lysias, *Against Ergocles* (28), 12.

during the Thirty's reign. The orator denounces his adversary's successive acts of treason after having perhaps taken part in the plot that led to the murder of Phrynichus, one of the principal figures of the Four Hundred, in 411.[69] It seems that he served the Thirty during the initial months of the oligarchy, denouncing the members of a plot formed by former generals and trierarchs, who aimed to restore democracy. Then, changing camp once again, it is said that he went to Phyle, whence some of the citizens he had just denounced had fled. Apparently, as soon as they saw him, these combatants arrested him and, just as they were about to execute him,[70] Anytus, designated *stratēgos* by the army, stayed their hand. In spite of this providential protection, Agoratus had to live carefully separate from the remainder of the troops: 'no human being spoke to him – it was as if he were polluted,'[71] affirms the litigant. Even if this biased account cannot be proven, it testifies at least to the tensions that had been unravelling the army of Thrasybulus since the first weeks of its existence.

In the course of his diatribe, the speaker returns several times to the allegedly servile origins of Agoratus, whom he describes as 'a slave son of slaves.'[72] The status of Agoratus is more uncertain than the speaker suggests: Perhaps he was in fact not a slave but a freedman or a foreigner who had recently become a citizen. But no matter; the presence of Agoratus in Acharnai reminds us of a crucial fact: While the most easily identifiable men on the expedition belonged to the citizen elite, they obviously did not make up the largest part of it. On the contrary, there is every reason to believe Thrasybulus' army had been a heterogeneous group from the start. Admittedly, the first fighters of Phyle were not predominantly noncitizens; but the troop was composed of many poor citizens, non-property-owning peasants or minor craftsmen from the town of Athens who wanted to defend the democratic regime.

The Enlarged Chorus of Piraeus

After the victory at Acharnai, Thrasybulus and his men moved toward the Piraeus, which they reached in fewer than five days.[73] Their military confrontations occurred in two distinct phases. The exiles managed first of all to seize the hill of Mounychia, which overhangs the port of Piraeus. This was a highly strategic spot because it forced the Thirty's army, even

---

[69] Lysias, *Against Agoratus* (13), 72.
[70] Lysias, *Against Agoratus* (13), 78.
[71] Lysias, *Against Agoratus* (13), 79.
[72] Lysias, *Against Agoratus* (13), 18 and 64.
[73] Xenophon, *Hellenica*, 2.4.13.

though clearly in the majority, to attack from the plain of Piraeus, rendering all missiles ineffective. At the end of a 'long and violent' fight,[74] during which Critias was killed, the Thirty failed to recapture the hill. This decisive victory apparently convinced a great mass of Athenians, who had been biding their time, to join the camp of the democrats in Piraeus.[75]

After the fight, Thrasybulus' army changed in nature for the second time by incorporating at its heart not only those who were former members of the Three Thousand but also the heterogeneous population of Piraeus itself. Many citizens had been forced by the Thirty to leave the city because they did not participate in the regime of the Three Thousand.[76] These forced exiles were then joined by the many opportunists at whom Lysias took aim when he decried those who 'changed sides ... when they saw that those from Phyle were succeeding in their efforts,'[77] or more precisely still, those 'men like this, who shared in the activities of those at Piraeus but shared in the attitudes of those from the town.'[78] With this, Lysias was targeting the mysterious Phormisius, Theramenes' former ally, who tried to bring in a new constitution once the city had been reconquered.[79] According to Lysias, adding these last-minute recruits to Thrasybulus' army constituted a true turning point. It might be said that some oligarchs, by returning at little personal cost to the city, subverted the democratic dimension of Thrasybulus' gesture, cutting short his time as a hero. A parallel, once again, comes to mind if one thinks of the installation of General de Gaulle's 'government' in Algiers in June 1943. When a whole section of the administrative and economic elite, who had previously supported the Vichy regime, rallied to the new power, for many combatants this meant the end of the 'Resistance as Revolution.'[80] Similarly, some of Thrasybulus' soldiers may have had the impression that the new recruits from Piraeus distorted the very heart and soul of the expedition.

To define the contours of Piraeus' chorus, it is necessary to question the place that noncitizens – metics or slaves – occupy within it. Thrasybulus' task was indeed pulled in two contradictory directions. The need to gather

---

[74] Diodorus of Sicily, 14.33.4. [75] Pseudo-Aristotle, *Athenian Constitution*, 38.3.
[76] See also Diodorus of Sicily, 14.32.4: 'The Thirty, perceiving that those citizens in Athens who had no part in the regime of the Three Thousand were elated by the possibility of overthrowing the current government, relocated them to Piraeus and maintained their control of the city by means of armed mercenaries.'
[77] Lysias, *Against Philon* (31), 9.
[78] Lysias, *Against the Subversion of the Ancestral Constitution* (34), 2.
[79] Dionysius of Halicarnassus, *Lysias*, 32. See *infra*, Chapter 3, p. 121.
[80] See Bourdet 1975, pp. 248–9.

together the whole of the civic community clashed with the growing number of noncitizens among the fighters. For just as the former members of the Three Thousand rallied to their cause, the army received an enormous influx of partisans, among whom poor citizens rubbed shoulders with slaves and metics. According to Xenophon, Piraeus' democratic soldiers were 'numerous and of all conditions.'[81] Their contribution made all the difference: Behind the scant rows of hoplites, vastly outnumbered by the Thirty's men, they formed the contingents armed with slingshots and javelins who routed the oligarchic army and drove them out of Mounychia.[82]

The participation of these noncitizens in Thrasybulus' army is proven by a decree of the year 401/0 with which the Athenians, at the instigation of Thrasybulus himself, granted honors to the foreigners and the slaves who had taken part in battle on the democratic side. The text is fragmentary, and all attempts at restoration have been the subject of debate. Since Michael Osborne's systematic survey of Athenian citizenship decrees, however, a consensus has gradually emerged among epigraphists of classical Athens to render the first nine lines of the inscription as follows[83]:

> Lysiades was secretary; Xenaenetus was archon [401/0].
>
> Resolved by the council and the people. Hippothontis was the prytany; Lysiades was secretary; Demophilus was chairman. Thrasybulus proposed:
>
> So that worthy gratitude may be obtained by the foreigners who joined in returning from Phyle or who joined with those who had returned in coming back to Piraeus: concerning these, be it decreed by the Athenians that there shall be citizenship for them and their descendants; and distribute them

---

[81] Xenophon, *Hellenica*, 2.4.25.   [82] Xenophon, *Hellenica*, 2.4.12.
[83] Osborne 1981–1983, D6. The text restored by Osborne was notably taken up and accepted by Lambert 1993 and Rhodes and Osborne 2003, n° 4. Gauthier 1986, pp. 119–33, while rightly pointing out a difficulty as to what should be understood by the mention in l. 9 of the *enguēsis*, does not fundamentally question the restoration of Osborne. The only truly alternative reading is that proposed by Krentz 1980 and 1986, who argued that *ateleia* would have been granted only to the men of Mounychia and Piraeus. If the restoration by Osborne of *isoteleian* in l. 9 is correct, it is essentially because it corresponds to the promise that Thrasybulus appears to have made to his foreign combatants before the Battle of Mounychia (Xenophon, *Hellenica*, 2.4.25). In a more general way, the distinction made between the fighters of Phyle and those of Piraeus fits the account of the events proposed by book 2 of the *Hellenica*. The difficulty lies in the fact that it is impossible to restore the decree, which is the product of exceptional circumstances, in the light of the form of citizenship-granting decrees in the fourth century. Osborne's restorations draw their strength from two prosopographical comparisons: Two fourth-century epitaphs record homonyms honored as *isotelēs* (Gerys, mentioned in column III, l. 13, and in *IG* II² 7863, as well as Dexandrides, mentioned in column VI, l. 49, and in *IG* II² 7864). Insofar as only twenty-five funerary inscriptions of men with *isoteleia* are known, the comparison established by Osborne seems convincing.

immediately into the tribes tenfold; and the officials shall use the same laws concerning them as concerning the other Athenians.

Those who came later, joined in fighting the battle at Mounychia and made the Piraeus safe, who remained with the People in Piraeus when the reconciliation took place, and were doing what they were instructed: for these there shall be *isoteleia* if they live in Athens, and the right to contract a legal marriage, like the Athenians.[84]

Following the decree, three lists of names were engraved according to Athenian tribe: It is estimated that the first, which listed the men returned from Phyle, included between 70 and 90 names[85]; the second, which brought together those who had fought at the Battle of Mounychia,[86] included around 290 individuals; while the third, approximately 580 names strong, tallied those who had been present at Piraeus[87] and had joined the army of Thrasybulus the day after the decisive battle. These lists show just how much Thrasybulus' army had grown since the capture of Phyle, but that is not the crux of the matter. First and foremost, they demonstrate the important role played by noncitizens, of all trades, in the combat. Study of the names suggests, moreover, that there were not only many foreigners resident in Athens but also large numbers of slaves.[88]

The decree does not resemble any other decrees granting citizenship. And for good reason: The Athenians did not decide to grant citizenship to a clearly delimited community, like the Samians or the Plataeans, who had shown their loyalty to Athens, or to a benefactor of the city, as would become common in the fourth century. They intended to reward two categories of clearly distinguished individuals, to whom specific rights and honors were granted, but who were obliged to join the system of Cleisthenic tribes in return. Thus, the foreigners who had rallied to Thrasybulus' army in Phyle during the winter of 404/3, whether they joined it before the siege or on the way from Phyle to Piraeus, were granted citizenship and had to integrate into one of the ten Cleisthenic tribes rather

---

[84] Rhodes and Osborne 2003, n° 4, l. 1–9 (with Gauthier 1986 for l. 9).
[85] [*hoide sunkatēlthon apo Phulēs*], at the top of the first column, face A.
[86] [*hoide sunemachēsan de tēn machēn tēn Monichiasin*], logically at the top of the second column, face A.
[87] *hoide [p]arem[enon tôi] em Peraiei*, face B, col. II, l. 56–7.
[88] Pseudo-Aristotle, *Athenian Constitution*, 40.2: 'Archinus seems to have acted politically in a good way [*politeusasthai kalōs*], and also later when he attacked for illegality the decree of Thrasybulus admitting to citizenship all those who had come back together from Piraeus, some of whom were clearly slaves' (transl. Loeb modified). Slave onomastics are often difficult to discern, but certain names, such as Cnips, Egersis or Abdes, are quite transparent. See the remarks of Rhodes and Osborne 2003, p. 27.

than a deme or a phratry. To these men the 'same laws as [those] concerning the other Athenians' applied. To those who had rallied to the cause 'later' (*husteron*), whether they had fought only at Mounychia or they had been on the democrats' side during the reconciliation in Piraeus, only the tax privilege of *isoteleia* and the right to *enguēsis* were granted.[89] Under this last term, it is necessary to understand 'the right to ally with a member of this community (that of the Athenians) and to have legitimate children of it.' Thus, these noncitizen *isoteleis*, henceforth an integral part of the Cleisthenic tribes, could marry their daughters to Athenians in order to beget legitimate grandchildren with full citizenship, just as they could take Athenian women for their wives and 'produce within wedlock legitimate Athenian children of their own.'[90] This should be recognized as an exceptional privilege that set this honorific community apart from all the other metics present in Athens. While the law of Pericles, guaranteeing citizenship only to the sons and daughters of citizens, had just been officially reinstated in 403, and just as the Athenians were about to prohibit marriages between Athenians and noncitizens,[91] the combatants were given an opportunity to incorporate their descendants into the civic community.

It is probable that Thrasybulus' decree was supplemented by another measure. In his funeral oration, Lysias refers to a decision undoubtedly dating back to the year 401/0 that concerned the foreigners who had died during the campaign at Piraeus:

> These men are respected by all mankind, because of the dangers they faced at Piraeus. But we should remember also to praise the foreigners buried here, who assisted the democracy and fought for our safety. They regarded bravery as their fatherland and made a noble end to their lives. In return, the city gave them official burial and mourning, and allowed them for all time to have the same honors as citizens.[92]

The speaker explicitly evokes the situation of the foreigners who had fought in the army of Piraeus. They benefit from the same honors as citizens since their deeds have been commemorated at the public cemetery (*dēmosion sēma*). The speaker insists on the significance of this privilege: It is indeed a considerable honor, unprecedented in the fifth century,

---

[89] It is not surprising that these *isoteleis* were included in the framework of the *phylai*. All the texts insist on the fact that the *isoteleis* participate in civic life as citizens to the exclusion of the domain of the *archē*: see Roubineau 2007, p. 193.
[90] Vérilhac and Vial 1998, p. 237.   [91] [Demosthenes], *Against Neaira* (59), 52.
[92] Lysias, *Funeral Oration* (2), 66.

which we should consider to be the indirect consequence of the *isoteleis*' integration into the Athenian tribal system.

To the Slaves: The Promise of Thrasybulus

The decision of 401/0 concluded a sequence during which the status of Thrasybulus' combatants had been the subject of bitter debate among the Athenians once democracy was restored. The experience of battle had deeply subverted the theoretical isomorphism between the community of fighters and the civic community since the Samian episode of 411. Which attitude would be adopted with regard to all the noncitizens who had shown their attachment to democratic mores? By contrast, many citizens had remained passive or, worse still, had supported the Thirty. In 403, Thrasybulus had proposed granting citizenship to all the combatants of Piraeus regardless of their legal status. The *Athenian Constitution* specifies that Thrasybulus wanted to grant citizenship to 'all those who had come back together from Piraeus, some of whom were clearly slaves,'[93] but he had failed following an 'indictment for illegality' (*graphē paranomōn*) initiated by Archinus. According to Plutarch's *Lives of the Ten Orators*, the assembly even voted to grant citizenship to Lysias (who was not part of the fighting group but helped the resistance financially), before Archinus also attacked the proposal made by Thrasybulus.[94]

Let us take stock of the revolutionary character of the proposal. Like a new Cleisthenes, Thrasybulus envisaged no less than to redefine the contours of the civic body by massively incorporating slaves and foreigners. The decree of 401 suggests that this concerned approximately 1,000 men. Such a figure is far from being negligible when correlated to the Athenian demographic situation of the end of the fifth century. Decimated by the plague of 429 and the accumulation of military defeats since the dramatic expedition to Sicily in 415, the civic community counted few more than 20,000 men in 403, so Thrasybulus' project consisted in renewing (at least) 5% of all citizens.

An echo of this astonishing initiative can be found in the remarks Xenophon places in the mouth of Theramenes, a figure of political

---

[93] Pseudo-Aristotle, *Athenian Constitution*, 40.2.
[94] The *graphē paranomōn* of Archinus is further confirmed by Aeschines, *Against Ctesiphon* (3), 195 and *P. Oxy.* XV, 1800, fr. 6–7. According to Xenophon (*Hellenica*, 2.4.25), Thrasybulus promised *isoteleia* to the foreigners who had taken part in the Battle of Mounychia. See *infra*, Chapter 3, p. 122 and Chapter 10, pp. 257–8.

moderation par excellence, during his own trial. They were certainly aimed, as if by anticipation, at Thrasybulus' proposal.

> But I, Critias, am forever at war with the men who do not think there could be a beautiful democracy (*kallistē by kalē dēmokratia*) until the slaves and those who would sell the city for lack of a drachma should share in the public affairs, and on the other hand I am forever an enemy to those who do not think that a good oligarchy could be established until they should bring the city to the point of being ruled absolutely by a few.[95]

No doubt Xenophon places in the mouth of Theramenes the arguments that were those of Archinus against the proposal of Thrasybulus.[96] Theramenes' remarks are in any case disturbing: They suggest that a radical democratic design existed, implying 'the lifting of all exclusions' and that democracy contained the potential to radically extend the privilege of citizenship. *Dēmokratia* would thus cease to designate the complete rights of a community all the more egalitarian for having its power rest on the domination of the others (women, metics or slaves) and would instead be the name of a promise: that of the abolition of all these relationships of domination. Granting citizenship to slaves, as Thrasybulus defended it, would therefore be no more than a simple consequence of the founding gesture of the democratic regime (i.e. the extension of political rights beyond the narrow circles of the social elite). In other words, the dissociation of political rights and wealth capability, at the very foundation of the Cleisthenic reform, revealed the true nature of the democratic regime, monstrous according to its detractors in that it could imply the eventual political participation of slaves.[97]

Perhaps it is adventurous to want to see in this a specifically Thrasybulan conception of democracy. The proposal of the victorious general aimed, after all, only to reward the partisans of the democratic regime, and not to open citizenship to slaves for good; and one might rightly object that this measure is presented from the standpoint of its adversaries, who accuse it of destroying the very foundations of civic order. True ... But at least it is clear that already in Thrasybulus' speech to these men before the Battle of Mounychia he defended a broadened conception of the civic community. Let us listen to the *chorodidaskalos* as he faces his own chorus:

---

[95] Xenophon, *Hellenica*, 2.3.48 (transl. Loeb modified). On this decisive tirade, see also *infra*, Chapter 3, p. 114.
[96] Loraux 2000, pp. 130–1.   [97] Loraux 2000, p. 131.

And now, comrades, we must so act that each man shall feel in his breast that he is chiefly responsible for the victory. For victory, God willing, will now give back to us fatherland and homes, freedom and honor, children, to such as have them, and wives.[98]

Thrasybulus exhorts each of the combatants individually to defend the fatherland (*patris*), the family (*oikos*), freedom (*eleutheria*) and honor (*timē*) – or, to put it differently, to safeguard the democratic city as if it were his own *oikos*. Through this complex invocation, Thrasybulus boldly exalts 'the claim of a collective identity linked, because it is rooted in it, to a territory, as the Athenian freedom had been to Attica since Solon,'[99] and in this, it comes across as a premature funeral oration that, as penned by Xenophon, recalls that of Pericles. But the situation is paradoxical, to say the least: While qualifying them as citizens, Thrasybulus addresses de facto Athenians, foreigners and slaves, and his speech also aims to mask the heterogeneous character of his troops by, in word if not in deed, integrating all combatants regardless of their statutory differences into the civic community.

The City and Its Borders: Back to Order

But Thrasybulus' project was doomed to failure. The decree of 401/0, while delivering an exceptional testimony to the composition of the democratic army, demonstrates this, since it did not grant citizenship to all the noncitizens present at Piraeus but only to the combatants of Phyle. The idea of an inclusive civic community conflicted with that of Archinus, which, remaining faithful to Theramenes' views, refused to grant citizenship to those who had not been born Athenian. Archinus prevailed, and Thrasybulus' proposal was rejected by the Athenians. By refusing to incorporate into the civic body the 1,000 noncitizen combatants of Thrasybulus' army and, at the same time, reinstating Pericles' law on citizenship, Athens affirmed how inflexible its borders were.

Debate only took place among the Athenians after the democratic institutions were restored in the summer of 403. However, Thrasybulus' chorus, once it returned to the city, no longer resembled the Piraeus troupe, since it had absorbed every member of the Three Thousand who had remained in the city and supported the Thirty. Back within city limits, the civic community recovered its traditional form, and the legal distinctions within the civic body, temporarily neutralized within the

---

[98] Xenophon, *Hellenica*, 2.4.17.   [99] Sébillotte 2006.

heterogeneous army of Thrasybulus, came back to full strength. The refoundation of the democratic regime thus ushered in two new forms of exclusion: that, numerically derisory, of some of the Thirty and the Ten, who were banished from the ranks of the community with their crimes deemed unforgivable; and that of all the metics and the slaves whose the integration into the civic body was refused, even though they had fought for the restoration.

During their speeches, the orators of the fourth century did not fail to address the judges of the courts by referring to the moment when the aforementioned men had 'returned from Piraeus,'[100] as if the city as a whole, and in its abstract form, had been constantly by the side of Thrasybulus' men. This rhetorical platitude should not mislead us. While the men of Piraeus came to qualify by metonymy the whole Athenian *demos*, this identification took the form of a double denial: On the one hand, it made it possible to leave untold the integration of those who had supported the Thirty until the end while remaining in the city; on the other, it erased from memory the city's crucial debate on the place of metics and slaves in the new civic order.

* * *

From the siege of Phyle, during the winter of 404, until the ascent of the Acropolis in the fall of the following year, several fighting communities had succeeded one another under Thrasybulus' direction, reconstituting little by little, as if in ripples, the whole of the Athenian community. The city's mantle – to refer to the Platonic image again – was, however, far from being unified and homogeneous at the end of the civil war. Torn and patched back together, its seams were visible, and the political life of the initial years of the fourth century made them periodically reappear.

The memory of these events reflected these struggles: In the aftermath of the civil war, various accounts coexisted and contradicted each other, before being replaced, during the fourth century, by a univocal civic account. There is every reason to believe that Thrasybulus tried, in the aftermath of the democratic restoration in 404–403, to put the memory of his epic journey on public display. Lysias evoked shortly after his death the arrogance of the general who had continued to reproach the Athenians for their behavior during the *stasis*. And we have seen that the *stratēgos* tried at all costs to have his acts commemorated directly where they happened by

---

[100] For example: Isocrates, *Against Callimachus* (18), 2 and 17.

setting up a trophy on the battlefield or, in the case of the two statues, in Thebes. However, just as he did not succeed in imposing himself durably in public life after 403, Thrasybulus lost the battle of history and memory by failing to impose his own account of the events in Athens – and this is most certainly what ultimately explains why he got left out of ancient sources. In fact, there is every reason to believe that another chorus – associated with the name of Archinus – won, and entirely rewrote the account of the events of 403 to its own benefit.

CHAPTER 3

Archinus or the Victory of the 'Moderates'

On their return to the city in September or October 403, the victorious democrats showed great restraint. Both sides swore solemnly to 'not recall past evils' (*mē mnēsikakein*), or, more precisely, to 'not hold a grudge,'[1] an injunction that is often considered to be one of the first amnesties in history.[2] Amnesty, not amnesia: In a famous book, Nicole Loraux showed that this oath corresponded to a paradoxical form of memory – a denied memory or, to put it another way, a memorable forgetfulness.[3] To ward off the hideous specter of civil war (*stasis*), the democrats made the choice to forget and, in a way, to remember that they had to forget this traumatic moment.[4] Loraux sees this as an eminently political decision, pointing to the very wording of the *Athenian Constitution*: 'the Athenians appear both in private and public to have behaved toward the past disasters in the most completely honorable and *political manner* (*politikotata*) of any people in history.'[5] For the historian, politics is identified both with the conflict and with its necessary repression. The Athenian amnesty of 403 offers a striking summary of this inasmuch as it promoted the active repression

---

[1] On the translation of *mē mnēsikakein*, see the remarks by Agamben 2015, p. 16: 'In the formation of compound verbs of this type in Greek, the second term is, in general, active. *Mnēsikakein* means less "to have bad memories" than "to do harm with memory, to make bad use of memories".'. There are, however, exceptions to this rule, especially for compound nouns with a verb as the first term (verb-first compounds); see Tribulato 2014, pp. 344–7. To respect the polysemy of the verb, we follow here the translation proposed by Cohen 2001, pp. 335 and 339: '*mē mnēsikakein* signifies "not to hold a grudge," that is, in a society of vengeance like Athens, "not to seek revenge".'
[2] After the one concluded at Megara in 424 (Thucydides, 4.74). The Athenian amnesty was intended to prohibit the prosecution in the courts of all crimes committed during the period of the Thirty, if not before. However, according to Carawan 2013, the amnesty was limited to a group of written provisions (*sunthēkai*) that the oath merely reinforced. See the decisive analyses by Joyce 2014 and 2015.
[3] Loraux 2002. The subtitle chosen by the author (*On Memory and Forgetting in Ancient Athens*) expresses this tension well.
[4] On the need to reiterate the memory of forgetting by various means, including epigraphic ones, see Shear 2011, pp. 214–7.
[5] Pseudo-Aristotle, *Athenian Constitution*, 40.2 (translation Loeb slightly changed).

of the civil war and, at the same time, displayed its trace, as an amputated limb attracts all eyes.

This chapter takes as a starting point one of the great figures of the Athenian civil war: Archinus, a resistance fighter against the Thirty from the outset and the main architect of the reconciliation in 403. By a strange turn of events, Archinus endeavored to recast Athenian law and to mark the permanence of the community beyond the vicissitudes of the civil war. Archinus, a tireless promoter of a reunified city, managed to gather two groups around his project, which each presented symmetrical evolutions: on the one hand, all the democrats who, having fought against the Thirty, did not want to open the civic body to new entrants, even deserving ones; and on the other hand, all 'those from the town' who were ready to cooperate with the restored democracy, such as Rhinon, a fascinating political 'weather vane' who appears, in many respects, to have been Archinus' alter ego in the oligarch camp. After violently opposing each other during the civil war, these men agreed to merge into a single chorus, dancing in step within a seemingly pacified city.

However, this irenic vision must be put into perspective in view of the violent upheavals experienced during the reconciliation process. Far from being a foregone conclusion, reconciliation actually went hand in hand with the maintenance of a strong political conflict, as illustrated by an astonishing profusion of trials between 403 and 399, attested to both by numerous law court speeches and by extraordinary epigraphic sources (i.e. curses [*katadesmoi*] engraved on lead tablets and buried in the ground). These clashes clearly worked to the advantage of the 'moderates' on both sides, who succeeded, at the time, in winning before the Assembly and in the courts and, subsequently, in imposing their version of history in the city.

Indeed, this victory had a historiographic translation. Already perceptible in some of Lysias' speeches, the 'winner's version' was definitively formalized in the *Athenian Constitution* by Pseudo-Aristotle shortly after 335 BC. Discovered fortuitously on a papyrus in Egypt and first published in 1891, this famous treatise opens with a history of different constitutional (r)evolutions (*metabolai*) from the origins of the city until 403.[6] The detailed account of the Athenian reconciliation is given a significant place (chapters 39–41); it depicts democrats who did not seek revenge in any way and oligarchs who welcomed them with open arms. This favorable representation can be counterbalanced by other contemporary sources,

[6] Rhodes 1981, pp. 2–5.

including the testimony of Xenophon – himself a civil war actor on the oligarchic side[7] – as well as by fragments of comedies performed in the aftermath of democratic restoration.

It is therefore time to return to the hypothesis formulated by Loraux: Undoubtedly, it was not 'the city' that repressed the conflict but certain groups, clearly identified within it, who had an interest in promoting this active forgetfulness, even if this meant imposing it on others with a certain violence.

Archinus' Reconciled Athens

Archinus occupies a special place in the Athenian memory of the civil war. In the middle of the fourth century, he was considered not only as 'one of the men who brought back the people' to the city but was even raised to the level of Thrasybulus.[8] Archinus even sometimes overshadowed the latter, whose memory had been tarnished in the 390s.[9] Not content to make Archinus one of those 'who occupied Phyle,' the orator Demosthenes added, with some exaggeration, that he was 'after the gods, [the one] we have chiefly to thank for the restoration of popular government'[10]: In this account, the name of Thrasybulus is not even mentioned. In this regard, the agreement between Aeschines and Demosthenes is all the more notable since the two orators never failed to contradict each other wherever the opportunity presented itself.[11] The portrait of Archinus was just as laudatory in philosophical circles; the *Athenian Constitution* praises him after the return of the democrats to the city: 'Archinus seems to have acted politically in a good way (*politeusasthai kalōs*).'[12]

Like so many other figures of antiquity, however, Archinus remains only an evanescent silhouette. When they deign to take an interest in him, the ancient authors rush through his case in a few lines to draw a portrait that is certainly flattering but devoid of any depth. Demosthenes illustrates this tendency to the point of caricature: '[Archinus] achieved success on many occasions both as statesman and as commander.'[13] Beyond the

---

[7] On Xenophon's biography and his role in the civil war, see for instance Azoulay 2018, pp. 2–4 (with bibliography).
[8] Aeschines, *Against Ctesiphon* (3), 187 and 195.   [9] See Bearzot 2014.
[10] Demosthenes, *Against Timocrates* (24), 135.
[11] Plutarch, *On the Glory of the Athenians*, 345d, 350b. Relaying the words of Cratippus of Pergamon, Plutarch distinguishes Archinus among the seventy men 'of Phyle' who stood up against the oligarchy.
[12] Pseudo-Aristotle, *Athenian Constitution*, 40.2 (translation ours).
[13] Demosthenes, *Against Timocrates* (24), 135.

conventional praise, commentators struggled to highlight the slightest salient feature. Should we be surprised by this? Is this not a drama common to all 'middle men,' too insipid to polarize strong emotions – be they positive or negative – and, therefore, incapable of giving rise to a proper biographical tradition?

Nevertheless, if we take the trouble to cross-reference all the available sources, the different pieces of the puzzle assemble to form the image of a character who was much less bland than expected: As an advocate of a closed conception of the civic community and ready to resort to violence to impose his views, Archinus deserves, in some respects, to be compared to the 'authoritarian centrists' who took power in Thermidorian France after the fall of Robespierre. Unnatural political alliances, violence against 'extremists' and the active promotion of forgetfulness: These are all traits that resonate with Archinus' project.[14]

Archinus before 404

Even before the civil war broke out, Archinus had already made a name for himself in the city, albeit in spite of himself: He was one of those politicians who were made fun of in the theater – those whom the ancient sources call the *komodoumenoi* ('those who are mocked'). Several comic poets had violently attacked him for having proposed to reduce their wages while he was in charge of the public treasury (*dēmosion*). In 405, he was targeted in this passage of *The Frogs* by Aristophanes:

> Let him be mute and stand aside from our sacred dances [...] he who bites off the pay of the poets for being ridiculed in the ancestral rites of Dionysus.[15]

Through the voice of the *coryphaeus* (the leader of the chorus), Archinus was expelled from the circle of initiates accompanying Dionysus to the Underworld, which represented the entire Athenian community in miniature. Thus the politician was symbolically expelled from the community in the same way as the corrupt magistrates and all those who '[do] not eliminate hateful factionalism, and [are] disagreeable to the citizens, but

---

[14] Serna 2005.
[15] Aristophanes, *Frogs*, v. 354–71. The same attack had been carried out by at least two other poets: Plato the Comic and Sannyrion. Cf. Sannyrion, fr. 9 K.-A. (= Scholia to Aristophanes, *Frogs*, 367): 'This [is directed] against Archinus, and perhaps also at Agyrrhius. Plato mentions them in his *Costumes* [*Skeuai*] and Sannyrion in his *Danae*. They were in charge of the public finances and reduced the pay for the comic poets because they had been made fun of.'

kindle and fan civil strife, in [their] thirst for private advantage.' And the head of the chorus concludes: 'All these I warn, and twice I warn, and thrice I warn again, stand aside from our mystical dances.'[16]

Should we, then, see Archinus as one of those radical democrats whom Aristophanes stigmatized and wished, as in the *Lysistrata*, to purge the city?[17] Some doubt still remains. Although the *Athenian Constitution* first presents him as one of the 'leaders of the people' (*prostatēs tou dēmou*), it subsequently depicts him as a moderate man, attached to the ancestral constitution: after the defeat at Aigos Potamos in 405 BCE, 'the popular faction endeavored to preserve the democracy, but the notables who belonged to the *hetaireiai* (comradeships) and those exiles who had returned after the peace were eager for oligarchy, while those notables who were not members of any *hetaireia* but who otherwise were inferior in reputation to none of the citizens were aiming at the ancestral constitution; members of this party were Archinus, Anytus, Cleitophon and Phormisius, while its chief leader was Theramenes.'[18] The Aristotelian treaty therefore presents Archinus, even before the beginning of the civil war in 404, as the promoter of a balanced regime, equidistant from the 'extremists' on both sides: in a word, in the very middle.

Surely this reconstruction is highly suspect. On the one hand, it aims to rehabilitate the controversial figure of Theramenes by surrounding him with other characters with less scandalous reputations, such as Archinus[19]; on the other hand, it implies the existence of a 'third party' in Athens at the end of the fifth century – which contemporary sources are far from confirming.[20] However, this chapter argues that the narrative of the *Athenian Constitution* must be considered to be at least partially valid. Although there was never a 'moderate party' with a defined political line and a stable composition, it is nevertheless possible, in the aftermath of the civil war, to identify the temporary coalition of ancient oligarchs and former democrats around a shared conception of the community. Archinus is one of the leading figures, as evidenced by his journey after reconciliation.

An Active Promoter of Continuity

Although he accompanied Thrasybulus to Phyle and held his own in the military resistance to the Thirty, it was only after the return of the

---

[16] Aristophanes, *Frogs*, v. 354–71.   [17] Aristophanes, *Lysistrata*, v. 551–97.
[18] Pseudo-Aristotle, *Athenian Constitution* 34.3.   [19] See on this subject Bearzot 1979.
[20] Bearzot 2007, pp. 52, 97.

democrats to the city that Archinus began to play a major role in the city. He certainly took part in the interim government that was set up, composed of twenty men and appointed to watch over the community until a new code of laws was established.[21] In these troubled times, Archinus appears to have pursued a single goal: affirming the continuity of the city beyond the divisions induced by the civil war. Institutional continuity first of all, since the magistrates appointed under the oligarchy were allowed to render accounts under democracy, as if nothing had happened; financial continuity secondly, insofar as the money borrowed by the oligarchs to wage the battle against the democrats of Piraeus was eventually repaid by all the Athenians; religious continuity finally, since it was decided to make the sanctuary of Eleusis common to both sides, even though the Eleusinians had been massacred by the Thirty, with the complicity of 'those from the town.'[22]

According to the author of the *Athenian Constitution*, Archinus was the main architect of this voluntarist policy. Perhaps he was even the herald of such a strategy. The term must be understood literally here: It is indeed possible that Archinus was chosen in 403 to pronounce the funeral oration in honor of the Athenians who had died over the course of the past year.[23] In the *Menexenus* – a Platonic dialogue supposed to take place between 403 and 399 BC[24] – Socrates says that Archinus (or Dio) was expected to give this speech on the following day,[25] and a late tradition presents him as the author of a funeral oration, like Thucydides and Lysias.[26] The idea that Archinus was appointed in 403 for this honorary task – which consisted of celebrating the glory of Athens through the praise of the dead – is an alluring hypothesis, though impossible to prove. This would have been the perfect occasion to celebrate the reunification of the city, weeping over the dead fallen on both sides – in the manner of Cleocritus, in the vibrant speech he gave to the people of the city in Xenophon's *Hellenica*, after the Battle of Mounychia: 'Yet for all that, be well assured that for some of

---

[21] Andocides, *On the Mysteries* (1), 81. On the *patrios politeia* in 404, see Caire 2016, pp. 265–75.
[22] On these three forms of continuity, see Pseudo-Aristotle, *Athenian Constitution*, respectively 39.4; 39.6 and 40.3; 39.2.
[23] See Bertoli 2003.
[24] The dialogue evokes civil war and reconciliation (243), but the Platonic irony is such that Plato's Socrates evokes the history of Athens until 387, more than ten years after the death of the historical Socrates.
[25] Plato, *Menexenus*, 234b.
[26] Photius, *Bibliotheca*, 8.487b32–40: 'One might accuse him of theft, for having appropriated in his *Panegyricus* ('Festival Speech') many things said by Archinus, Thucydides and Lysias in their funeral speeches (*tous epitaphious logous*)' (transl. Waterfield, in Roisman and Worthington (eds.) 2015, p. 291). See, however, the doubts expressed by Loraux 1986, pp. 8, 345, n. 53.

those now slain by our hands not only you, but we also, have wept bitterly.'[27] Rather than regard the oligarchic government as a foreign body in the history of Athens – the way that the Gaullists kept insisting that the Vichy regime 'wasn't France' – Archinus seems to have drawn a link between before and after 403.

State of Exception or Transitional Justice?

This solution, however, was not achieved easily. On the contrary, to be successful, it required the exercise of a certain violence. The tradition thus attributes several exceptional measures to Archinus, which aimed at preserving the community from returning to *stasis*.[28] Perhaps the most striking was the summary execution of one of the democrats who had returned from Piraeus and had dared to 'hold a grudge' (*mnēsikakein*) – in violation of the amnesty oath. Although this execution was carried out with the approval of the Council, it was nevertheless an extraordinary, if not illegal, decision. This speedy execution deserves to be compared with the extrajudicial convictions carried out under the Thirty and subsequently under the Ten, also with the approval of the Council.[29] Moreover, the author of the *Athenian Constitution* makes no mystery of the fact that this execution was intended to bring the recalcitrant democrats to heel by means of terror: 'never since he was put to death has anybody broken the amnesty.'[30]

This voluntarist policy was also reflected in the choice made for the settlement of the civil war debts. Whereas the conventions formally stipulated that the repayment of the sums borrowed by the two sides would be made separately,[31] the Athenians decided that payment would be made without taking previous political divisions into account. The democrats therefore repaid – in part – the money borrowed by the

---

[27] Xenophon, *Hellenica*, 2.4.22.   [28] Pseudo-Aristotle, *Athenian Constitution*, 40.2.
[29] Under the Thirty, these extrajudicial executions, carried out with the agreement of the Council, were numerous. In addition to Theramenes (Xenophon, *Hellenica*, 2.3.51), the Eleusinians were also among the victims (*Hellenica*, 2.4.8–10). However, the most striking parallel took place after the dismissal of the Thirty and the installation of the Ten at the head of the oligarchy: 'having obtained this office [the Ten] did not proceed to do the things for the purpose of which they had been elected, but sent to Sparta to procure help and to borrow funds. But this was resented by those within the constitution, and the Ten, *in their fear of being deposed from office and their desire to terrify the others* (which they succeeded in doing), arrested one of the most leading citizens, Demaretus, and put him to death, and kept a firm hold upon affairs' (Pseudo-Aristotle, *Athenian Constitution*, 38, 1–2; our emphasis).
[30] Pseudo-Aristotle, *Athenian Constitution*, 40.2.
[31] Pseudo-Aristotle, *Athenian Constitution*, 39.6, 40.3.

oligarchs to wage war against them. Regardless of who initiated it, this exemption was certainly surprising, even shocking.[32] It was tantamount to contravening a written commitment that was no less binding, on the face of it, than that of the oath of amnesty, sworn orally by all citizens.[33] Yet no one dared to attack this clear violation of the reconciliation agreement, which passed into posterity as the very symbol of Athenian political wisdom.[34]

These violations of legality also found a judicial translation at the initiative of Archinus, who proposed a law forbidding the Athenians to 'hold a grudge' under penalty, for the accused, of being placed in an unfavorable legal position – the individual in question could make an 'exception' (*paragraphē*) that considered him as a plaintiff and allowed him to speak first in court.[35] Furthermore, in the event of an acquittal, the accuser was forced to pay a large fine (*epobelia*), equivalent to one-sixth of the amount in dispute.[36]

Summary executions, violation of written conventions, reversal of the normal course of judicial proceedings: To suture the wound opened by the civil war, Archinus and his entourage therefore seem to have promoted a state of exception, marked by the temporary suspension of the legal order.[37] It is as if it had been temporarily necessary to maintain the extraordinary situation characteristic of the civil war. Should we then see in this sequence the evidence of the underground continuity between the state of exception and the ordinary legal order? This temptation is all the stronger since certain measures taken in 403 – such as the *paragraphē* – were subsequently incorporated into the common law of Athenian trials: The exceptions were therefore normalized. In this perspective, Pseudo-Aristotle's eulogy of Archinus may well take on a less conventional resonance: 'Archinus seems *to have acted politically in a good way* [*politeusasthai*

---

[32] Although the author of the Aristotelian treatise does not explicitly attribute this exemption to Archinus, he nevertheless cites the latter, in the preceding lines, as the architect of this policy of appeasement.

[33] On this failure to implement the Reconciliation Agreement, see Loening 1987, pp. 85–8, according to whom this decision occurred before 399 and constituted a 'breach' of the Reconciliation Agreement.

[34] Demosthenes, *Against Leptines* (20), 11–2 sees it as a measure of civic agreement.

[35] Athenians considered it a great advantage to speak first in court: Demosthenes, *On the Crown* (18) 7. See Calhoun 1918; Loening 1987, pp. 29, 57–8.

[36] Isocrates, *Against Callimachus* (18), 2–3. On the date of the reform (shortly after 403/2, and not later, as it has sometimes been claimed), see Whitehead 2002, pp. 83–6; Carawan 2011, pp. 254–95.

[37] To this can be added the authoritarian shortening of the time limits for the registration of oligarchs wishing to leave the city: Pseudo-Aristotle, *Athenian Constitution*, 40.1 and *infra*.

kalōs].'³⁸ Politics could be understood here not as forgetting the conflict, as Loraux argues, but as the sovereign act of discriminating against the friend of the enemy in a crisis situation – in the wake of Carl Schmitt's reflections.³⁹ Might not all of these exceptional decisions have been a way to redefine Athenian politics based on a new distinction between friends and enemies – between those who accepted the terms of reconciliation and those who rejected them?

Although this Schmitt-inspired analysis is attractive at first glance, it does not stand up to scrutiny. Firstly, these extraordinary decisions had an extremely limited field of application – in contrast to those taken by the Thirty, who made the suspension of legality the ordinary practice of their government.⁴⁰ Secondly, with the exception of the *paragraphē*, these emergency measures had no institutional posterity in Athens after 403. On the contrary, they seem to have led to legal adjustments designed to prevent the recurrence of such excesses. The summary execution of the Piraeus democrat – in the strange continuity of the Thirty – could therefore explain the introduction after 403 of a new clause in the oath taken by the *bouleutai* (Councilors), which specified: 'Under the terms of that oath you swear to exile no one, to imprison no one, to put no one to death, without trial.'⁴¹ Far from becoming the norm, the exception therefore apparently contributed to better delineating the boundaries of legality and to giving new legal guarantees to citizens in the fourth century. Finally, these measures were aimed less at differentiating the friend from the enemy than at ensuring that this deadly distinction was definitively neutralized: Every effort was made to ensure that the Athenians would no longer consider each other with radical hostility.

---

³⁸ Pseudo-Aristotle, *Athenian Constitution*, 40.2 (our emphasis).
³⁹ The Nazi jurist elaborated two successive definitions of sovereignty, which only imperfectly overlap. In the early 1920s, he linked sovereignty to the establishment of the state of exception (Schmitt 1985, p. 5): 'Sovereign is he who decides on the exceptional case.' In *The Concept of the Political*, published ten years later (1932), Schmitt gave a specific content to the decision taken in exceptional circumstances: Sovereign is he who has the capacity to decide the identity of friends and enemies in the event of conflict (Schmitt 1996). For a more in-depth discussion of the (problematic) adaptation of the Schmittian conception of politics to Greek history, see Azoulay 2014, pp. 479–83.
⁴⁰ On the suspension of the characteristic legality of the Thirty – who repeatedly postponed the drafting of a formal *politeia* – see Caire 2016, p. 318.
⁴¹ Andocides, *Against Alcibiades*, (4), 3. This addition is, if not certain, at least probable. Of the ten known clauses of the Bouleutic Oath, at least two were added in 403/2: see Lysias, *Against Philon* (31), 2, and Andocides, *On the Mysteries* (1), 91, with the comments of Sommerstein and Bayliss 2013, pp. 40–3.

In fact, Archinus' actions had probably less to do with a *state of exception* than with *transitional justice*. The notion, which emerged in the 1990s following the fall of communist regimes in Eastern Europe and the end of the apartheid system in South Africa, covers the study of all judicial mechanisms, institutions, policies and memorials that enable a community to emerge from civil war. The whole challenge is to reconcile, on the one hand, the desire to punish the executioners and repair the harm suffered by the victims and, on the other hand, the need to prevent any return to violence and, if possible, stabilize a democratic government.[42] In this regard, the emergency measures taken at the initiative of Archinus signal less the maintenance of a state of exception than the establishment of a transitional regime, as Jon Elster argued in a book that gave the notion of 'transitional justice' its philosophical credentials.[43]

Does this mean that we must radically reject the Schmittian angle to shed light on Archinus' actions in 403? Perhaps not. The jurist and philosopher Giorgio Agamben has argued that the exceptional situation never identifies itself with the reign of pure lawlessness, but constitutes the decisive moment from which new norms can be set.[44] Although he temporarily suspended the legal order, Archinus was the one to propose an in-depth reform of it.

The Reformer of the Athenian Legal Order

With others, Archinus worked to prioritize and homogenize the institutional functioning of the city. Firstly hierarchization: It was in 403 that the Athenians established a clear distinction between laws, of general scope, and decrees, with a more circumstantial aim, resulting in the creation of a relatively stable and coherent legal corpus.[45] In this new configuration, writing took on an increased importance, to the point of

---

[42] On the notion itself, see Teitel 2000, which evokes the Athenian case in passing (pp. 52, 58); more generally, Andrieu 2012.

[43] Elster 2004, pp. 3–23. Although he refers to Nicole Loraux's work (p. 15), Elster relies primarily on Ostwald 1986, pp. 488–500, and Hansen 1991. In a striking loop effect, some specialists of Greek antiquity have in turn reconsidered the Athenian reconciliation in this new legal light in order to highlight its singularity: see Lanni 2010 and Cohen 2001. David Cohen, a Professor of Law at Stanford and specialist in Greek antiquity, was personally involved in the transitional justice processes in Cambodia and East Timor: The Athenian reference therefore not only nourished his historical reflection, but also his concrete legal practice.

[44] Agamben 2005, and, earlier, Schmitt 1985. We will not discuss here the eminently problematic assertion by Giorgio Agamben – inspired by a decontextualized quotation from Walter Benjamin – that the state of exception has now become the rule. On these shifts, see Paugam 2004.

[45] On the procedure for creating laws (*nomothesia*) after 403, see Canevaro 2013b.

becoming the guarantor of the civic order[46]: a law of 402 thus stipulates that judges should in no case use an unwritten law, since the sovereignty of *demos* was henceforth limited by the authority of *nomos*. Secondly, homogenization: 403 also marked the end of the slow process – begun a decade earlier – that saw the reorganization of the civic archives, the collation and revision of the laws of Draco and Solon (henceforth displayed in the Agora in plain sight) and the establishment of the list of Athenian archons – a set of measures aimed at streamlining the processing of official documents and also reflecting the establishment of a new relationship to the past.[47]

This harmonization even extended to the manner of written law, since Archinus was behind the initiative of a profound reform of the alphabet.[48] The measure deserves attention: Even as the reconciled Athenians were celebrating the constitution of their ancestors (*patrios politeia*), they decided to turn their backs on their linguistic heritage by adopting the Ionian alphabet to transcribe their official documents. How can this apparent contradiction be explained? It undoubtedly reflected the desire to break with the practices of the imperial democracy of the fifth century, which had shamelessly imposed its manner of writing on the Ionians, subjected by decrees written in the Attic language and installed at the heart of the cities of the Delian League.[49] By adopting the writing of their former allies, the Athenians took note of the end of their imperial power while paving the way for the affirmation (or even the reaffirmation) of their cultural hegemony.[50] From an internal point of view, it was also a way to standardize the writing of laws and decrees, putting an end to the anarchic cohabitation between different written forms: From now on, the reunified city would speak with one voice and make it known by means of the same writing.

Beyond these institutional aspects, the main objective of Archinus' policy seems to have been the preservation of the traditional contours of the civic community, even if this had to be enacted by force. On the one hand, he attacked as illegal the decree proposed by Thrasybulus – his former ally – that granted citizenship to the metics, and even to the slaves,

---

[46] Herrenschmidt 1996, p. 174.
[47] Pebarthe 2005 proposes the date of 410 (but, in fact, the inscription could just as easily have been engraved in 403).
[48] Theopompus of Chios, *FGrHist* 115 F 155; Duris of Samos, *FGrHist* 76 F 66 J.
[49] We think first of Clearchus' decree, whatever its date (around 425 or 414 BC?), fragments of which have been found in various parts of the Athenian empire and which imposed on allied cities the use of the 'Athenian coins, weights and measures' (*IG* I³ 1453).
[50] D'Angour 1999, p. 128; Ferrandini Troisi 2003.

who were on the side of the democrats in 404[51]; on the other hand, showing a surprising authoritarianism, he manipulated the terms of the amnesty in order to prevent the oligarchs from deserting the city out of fear of possible reprisals:

> Those were the terms of the reconciliation. The men who had fought on the side of the Thirty were afraid, and many intended to emigrate but postponed their registration until the last possible deadline. But Archinus, seeing how many they were and wanting to keep them back, moved back the deadline for registration, so that many were compelled to remain, unwillingly, until their confidence returned.[52]

Archinus therefore seems to have behaved opportunistically, sometimes pretending to defend legality (against Thrasybulus), sometimes trampling on it (against 'those from the town'). But these reversals were in fact a reflection of the same authoritarian policy, aimed at preserving the integrity of the civic body by all means and maintaining the political balances in place[53]: the integration of new citizens – close to Thrasybulus – and the concomitant exile of many 'people of the City' would have inevitably changed the equilibrium of power in favor of the most radical democrats, in the same way that Ephialtes, in 462, had taken advantage of the momentary absence of the 'moderate' Cimon and of 4,000 hoplites – rich enough to pay for their heavy combat equipment – to reorient the *politeia* in a sense that was more favorable to the people.[54]

To carry out this conservative policy – in the literal sense of the word – Archinus was able to rely on two groups who appeared to be antagonistic, but who were ready to make common cause to defend the supposed 'ancestral constitution': on the one hand, many 'people of the City' who had a vested interest in making a pact with the victors to make people forget about their collaboration with the Thirty; on the other, all those among the resistance fighters of Piraeus, who were not eager to extend the community to include foreigners, even deserving ones. The events in Athens in 403 call to mind certain theater plays where the chorus, initially divided in two, ends up merging in joy.

---

[51] Pseudo-Aristotle, *Athenian Constitution*, 40.2.

[52] Pseudo-Aristotle, *Athenian Constitution*, 40.1. On this manipulation and its probable timing, see Shear 2011, p. 209. This is a flagrant violation of the reconciliation agreement (*contra* Loening 1987, pp. 68–9).

[53] On this articulation, see Wolpert 2001, pp. 42–3. Nevertheless, we have difficulty in viewing this conservative policy as a 'victory of the democratic faction,' as the author does (p. 48): This would be to ignore the dissensions among former 'heroes' of Piraeus themselves.

[54] Aristophanes, *Lysistrata*, v. 1137–44; Pseudo-Aristotle, *Athenian Constitution*, 25.1–2.

The Half-Chorus of the Oligarchs Rallied to Democracy

The Honorable Rhinon and His Virtuous Colleagues

Among the Three Thousand who remained in Athens under the oligarchy, the ancient tradition distinguishes an eminent figure: a certain Rhinon, from Paiania. Somewhat paradoxically, this individual came to embody the reunified Athens in civic memory. Three centuries after the events, Heraclides Lembus wrote in a treatise on the *Athenian Constitution*:

> After [the Thirty] were overthrown, Thrasybulus and Rhinon, a good and honorable man, governed.[55]

It is not too surprising that Archinus should disappear from the picture here: In a certain way, Rhinon was his alter ego in the camp of oligarchs, and the two men appear, up to a certain point, to be interchangeable.

Let us pause for a moment on his winding journey. Until the defeat of Athens in 404, Rhinon seems to have acted as a citizen committed to maintaining democracy. Coming from an honorable family, he was involved in the management of the Athenian empire in the early 410s[56] and probably did not take the side of the oligarchs in 411: At least, he was not exiled in the years that followed. Although he remained in the city in 404, he did not appear to have exercised any responsibility under the government of the Thirty. According to the *Athenian Constitution*, it was only after the Battle of Mounychia and the dismissal of the Thirty that he became one of the principal leaders of 'those from the town,' actively involved in the process of reconciliation:

> [They] deposed the first board of Ten and appointed another Ten, those who seemed to be *the best men* (*tous beltistous*): under these Ten, and with their enthusiastic support, the reconciliation took place and the people returned to Athens. Chief among them were Rhinon of Paeania and Phayllus of Acherdous: before Pausanias' arrival they sent messages to the men at the Piraeus, and after he had come they joined *eagerly* (*sunespoudasan*) in working for the return. [...] Rhinon and his supporters were praised for *their good will towards the people* (*eunoian eis ton demon*): having accepted responsibility under the oligarchy they submitted to examination under the democracy, and no complaint was made against them either by those who

---

[55] Dilts (ed.) 1971, pp. 16–7 (Pseudo-Aristotle, *Athenian Constitution*, § 6 = Aristotle, fr. 372 Rose).
[56] His father might have been Charicles of Paiania, whose name is engraved on a casualty list of the last quarter of the fifth century: Raubitschek 1943, p. 45 (inscription no. 8, fr. K, l. 2). On his office of *paredros* of the *Hellenotamiai*, see Davies 1971, pp. 67–8, n° 2254.

had remained in the city or by those who had returned from the Piraeus; indeed, on account of this Rhinon was immediately elected general.[57]

Rhinon's trajectory is a perfect illustration of the leniency shown by the victorious democrats when they returned to the city: The magistrates elected under the oligarchy were able to render their accounts without hindrance. This indulgence is all the more surprising since the Ten – as well as the Thirty – had been specifically excluded from the amnesty because of their direct involvement in the horrors of the civil war.[58] In this case, Rhinon and his colleagues benefited from an exemption, echoed in the *Athenian Constitution*:

> Otherwise no one was to hold a grudge against anyone except the Thirty, the Ten, the Eleven and the governors of the Piraeus, and not even of these if they successfully rendered their accounts.[59]

Moreover, the Ten were honored by the city, no doubt after they had rendered their accounts. Indeed, they received public praise and perhaps even a crown as thanks for their devotion (*eunoia*): Voted by the Assembly, such honors reflect the astonishing popularity of these former oligarchs who had recently rallied to restored democracy. But the most surprising was yet to come: Rhinon was immediately elected general by the Assembly, the highest office to which Athenians could aspire. Passing without transition from a college of ten magistrates (the Ten) to another (the generals), Rhinon is probably the most striking embodiment of the civic continuity that Archinus promoted at the time.[60]

Although Rhinon's career was certainly remarkable, his case is by no means isolated, and he appears, in some respects, to be the leader of a much larger chorus. Besides these direct colleagues, recipients like him of public praise, many Athenians who had remained in the city were thus distinguished in Athens in 403. A speech written by Lysias makes it

---

[57] Pseudo-Aristotle, *Athenian Constitution*, 38.3–4 (our emphasis).
[58] There is no evidence to suggest that two colleges of the Ten should be distinguished – one excluded from the amnesty and the other benefiting from it. On this Aristotelian invention, see *infra* and Rhodes 1981, pp. 459–60.
[59] Pseudo-Aristotle, *Athenian Constitution*, 39.6. Some have claimed that this clause only concerned the oligarchs who were refugees in Eleusis: This seems unlikely, since the *Athenian Constitution* mentions the possibility of leaving for Eleusis *after rendering accounts*. See Carawan 2002, p. 9.
[60] Rhinon continued to hold important positions in the years that followed, as he was appointed treasurer (*tamias*) of Athena in 402/1, a position that bore witness to his wealth while giving him some control over the city's finances: *IG* II² 1370 + 1371, l. 10: Rhin[-]. It should be noted, however, that this does not appear to have been an elective magistracy, but a function drawn by lot from among the richest Athenians (the *pentakosiomedimnoi*, according to the tax classification attributed to Solon: Pseudo-Aristotle, *Athenian Constitution*, 47.1).

possible to measure the phenomenon. A certain Euandros, a former member of the Three Thousand, had been appointed *archon basileus* by lot, some time after the restoration of democracy (probably between 401 and 399). During his *dokimasia* – intended to verify that the chosen individual was worthy to occupy his office – he was attacked by an anonymous citizen who asked Lysias to compose the speech delivered before the Council of the Five Hundred. Not only does the accuser note that the institution is full of former members of the oligarchy – whom Euandros could hope to win over – but he points out that many of them had been given high office after the reconciliation: '[*the people of the city*] received no less *honor* (*tetimēke*) from the city than those who marched on Phyle and got possession of the Piraeus.'[61] He also refuses to take offense – probably not to alienate part of the jurors – because, according to him, the people are capable of separating the wheat from the chaff: It was only the 'oligarchs in spite of themselves' to whom the *demos* conferred 'the highest honors (*megistai timai*), appointing them to cavalry commands, generalships and embassies in their service.'[62]

Although this assertion must be taken with caution, since its foremost aim is to disqualify Euandros, there is no reason to reject it outright, since Lysias had nothing to gain by lying about it. Rhinon's trajectory is therefore only a particularly striking illustration of a more general phenomenon: the rapid reintegration of repentant oligarchs into the institutions of restored democracy.[63] A final case allows us to measure the phenomenon and, perhaps, to better understand its motivations.

Cephisophon, from Oligarchy to Democracy

In the *Hellenica*, Xenophon mentions two members of the Three Thousand who were sent to Sparta, without a real mandate, to negotiate peace with 'those of Piraeus': Cephisophon and Meletus.[64] The latter, not to be confused with Socrates' accuser,[65] showed a great capacity for adaptation in Athens after 403, going so far as to give lessons of patriotism

---

[61] Lysias, *On the Scrutiny of Euandros* (26), 17 (our emphasis).
[62] Lysias, *On the Scrutiny of Evandros* (26), 20.
[63] Rhodes 2000, p. 135, cites the case of Chariades, member of the *epistatai* of the Erechtheion in 409/8, and part of the board of the *Hellenotamiai* in 406/5, who remained in Athens under the Thirty, and who nevertheless served as treasurer of Athena in 404/3.
[64] Xenophon, *Hellenica*, 2.4.36.
[65] On the possible confusions between several individuals called Meletus, see Nails 2002, pp. 199–202.

to Andocides. This is nothing, however, compared to the skill shown by Cephisophon, who performed an astonishing political reconversion in the space of a few weeks.

In all probability, this individual must indeed be identified with Cephisophon of Paiania,[66] who was part of the first Council of Five Hundred of the restored democracy in 403/2. He therefore passed the scrutiny (*dokimasia*) required to enter the institution without incident.[67] And Cephisophon did not stop there. Like Rhinon, elected general by the assembly, he was appointed secretary to the prytany (*grammateus kata prutaneian*) and therefore became, for a month, the guarantor of the proper functioning of the Council. The secretary 'is responsible for documents, is keeper of the decrees that are passed and supervises the transcription of all other documents, and who attends the sittings of the Council'; he was therefore initially chosen from among 'the most distinguished and trustworthy' citizens.[68] To hold this office, Cephisophon may have been elected by a show of hands by all the Councilors, and not drawn by lot[69]; this would be proof that he enjoyed a certain aura, despite the functions he had occupied under the oligarchy – or perhaps because of them.

This prestigious magistracy, in turn, guaranteed its holder a high degree of visibility in the city: 'this officer's name is inscribed on the monumental slabs above records of alliances and appointments to consulships and grants of citizenship.'[70] Indeed, the name of Cephisophon is engraved, in large, visible letters, on one of the most famous Attic stelai, currently preserved in the Acropolis Museum (Fig. 3.1).[71]

Recording three decrees concerning Athens and its ally Samos, this inscription has an exceptional character. Dated to 405/4, a first decree (lines 5–40) rewards the Samians for their loyalty after the defeat of Aigos Potamos (at the very end of the Peloponnesian War), granting them Athenian citizenship and full autonomy. The second decree (lines 41–55), passed two years later after the fall of the oligarchy, reaffirms the

---

[66] On Cephisophon (Cephisophon I Paianieus), see Kirchner 1901, n° 8401 = 8400? = 8415? = 8416? ; Davies 1971, n° 148. On this probable identification, see Németh 2006, p. 123.
[67] Pseudo-Aristotle, *Athenian Constitution*, 55.2.
[68] Pseudo-Aristotle, *Athenian Constitution*, 54.3.
[69] According to the *Athenian Constitution*, drafted shortly after 335, the office of secretary to the prytany (*grammateus kata prutaneian*) was formerly (*proteron*) subject to an election (54.3). This was still very probably the case in 403: Besides Cephisophon, we know the name of another secretary designated in the same year. But the latter was actually an important politician, Agyrrhius of Collytus (see later). It seems statistically unlikely that, in the same year, two citizens playing leading roles in the city were drawn by lot to perform this function. See Rhodes 1972, pp. 134–6, and Stroud 1998, p. 18. On the role of the secretary to the prytany, see Osborne 2012.
[70] Pseudo-Aristotle, *Athenian Constitution*, 54.3.   [71] M.Acr. 1333. *IG* I³ 127 = *IG* II² 1.

Fig. 3.1   Stele displaying three decrees in honor of the Samians voted in 405/403 BC.

privileges that had been granted previously, while a final decree (lines 56–75) honors a Samian citizen, named Poses, for services rendered. The stele is capped with a magnificent relief: The patron deities of the two cities, Athena and Hera, shake hands, according to the codified ritual of *dexiōsis*, to manifest the solidity of their alliance.

How can we understand this unusual artifact that combines decisions taken at different dates on the same stele? In 405, the first decree was engraved and displayed on the Acropolis of Athens – as stated in the inscription (lines 38–40) – before being destroyed probably by the Thirty in 404: They must have seen it as a reflection of undue privileges, granted to a doubtful ally by a hated regime. In 403/2, the Assembly reiterated the honors accorded to the Samians in two stages: While in the last decree Cephisophon played the role of secretary, it was Agyrrhius of Collytus who carried out this function for the second decree, which was voted on a little earlier in the year. Was this just a meaningless shift? Perhaps. It is, however, tempting to see it as a way for Athenians to display the reconciliation in progress, in capital letters. For this Agyrrhius was far from being unknown in Athens.[72] Before the civil war, the comic poets had booed him, along with Archinus, for reducing their pay.[73] And like the latter, he had undoubtedly taken the path of exile at the time of the tyranny of the Thirty: Half a century later, Demosthenes presented him as 'a fine man and a democrat who had many times demonstrated his loyalty to you the people.'[74]

Let us summarize the story so far. In 403, Cephisophon, a former influential member of the Three Thousand, and Agyrrhius, a democrat close to Archinus, were successively elected as secretary to the Council, a particularly honorific office. It was as if the Athenians had been careful to give an equal place to the 'moderates' from the two camps in the institutions of the city as well as on the marble of the stelai. To take this one step further: The two men were involved in the decrees voted in honor of the Samians, whose function was, in a way, to restore the continuity broken by the tyranny of the Thirty. The sculpted image is eloquent in this regard: The handshake exchanged between the goddesses symbolizes the unwavering friendship between Athens and Samos, as if the city still had an empire (and allies) and had not been violently torn apart between

---

[72] Stroud 1998, pp. 18–9.
[73] See *supra*. On Agyrrhius, see the in-depth discussion in Sartori 1983, pp. 60–6.
[74] Demosthenes, *Against Timocrates* (24), 134. If Agyrrhius had remained in the city, it is likely that Andocides, his opponent, would not have failed to stigmatize him as one of the Three Thousand in the speech *On the Mysteries* (133–6).

the first decree, voted in 405, and the next two, dating from 403.⁷⁵ But on what political basis could the alliance between the 'moderates' of the two camps be concluded?

The Half-Chorus of the 'Moderate' Democrats

Many democrats doubtless shared Theramenes' position as he expressed it just before being sentenced to death by the Thirty:

> But I, Critias, am forever at war with the men who do not think there could be a beautiful democracy until the slaves and those who would sell the city for lack of a drachma should share in the public affairs, and on the other hand I am forever an enemy to those who do not think that a good oligarchy could be established until they should bring the city to the point of being ruled absolutely by a few.⁷⁶

The New Definition of 'Moderation' in Athens in 403

Certainly, Theramenes cannot be taken at his word here. No known democrat had ever advocated for a total openness of the civic community: The 'beautiful democracy (*kalē dēmokratia*),' which even integrated slaves, was only a fiction, intended to justify Theramenes' conservative position on citizenship. Moreover, political moderation did not always go hand in hand with such a restrictive conception of citizenship. In the previous century, on the contrary, it was the partisans of a more radical democracy – starting with Pericles – who decided to tighten the criteria of access to the community to better regulate the redistribution of wealth and benefits of all kinds linked to the growing imperialism of the city.⁷⁷ Symmetrically, some very undemocratic Athenians defended a more open approach to citizenship, willingly stigmatizing the city's retreat into its autochthonous nucleus.⁷⁸

However, it is not illegitimate to speak *situationally* of 'moderation' and 'moderate democrats' in Athens in 403. Indeed, moderation is never an absolute, but always a slogan claimed by certain groups in a given situation. At the turn of the century, the very definition of political

---

⁷⁵ Blanshard 2007. On the difficulty of articulating the different registers, see Elsner 2015.
⁷⁶ Xenophon, *Hellenica*, 2.3.48 (transl. Loeb slightly modified). ⁷⁷ See Azoulay 2014, pp. 82–3.
⁷⁸ Irwin 2015, p. 77. First developed in the rather elitist milieu of *metroxenoi* – the sons of foreign mothers, marginalized in 451 by Pericles' citizenship law – these criticisms were later taken up in oligarchic philosophical circles and, in particular, by Plato, who mocked the native claims of the Athenians in the parody funeral oration in the *Menexenus*.

The Half-Chorus of the 'Moderate' Democrats

moderation was reconfigured around a single criterion: the maintenance of the limits of the civic body. This was because this question had taken on a central character. Barely ten years before, the Sicilian expedition had caused terrible bloodshed among the civic body: At least 10,000 citizens had lost their lives in a few months in this catastrophic adventure, at the same time as the Athenians were just beginning to recover from the ravages of the 'plague' of 430–426.[79] To replenish the depleted ranks of their army, the Athenians had resolved to free hundreds of slaves who had fought alongside them on the triremes, no doubt during the Battle of Arginusai in 406: According to the historian Hellanicus, they were even granted citizenship, subject to certain restrictions.[80] Shortly before, the Euboeans also obtained intermarriage rights (*epigamia*) with the Athenians, whereas the Samians, as we have seen, were collectively granted citizenship following the Battle of Aigos Potamos.[81] When Isocrates, a few decades later, criticized the laxity with which the Athenians granted citizenship rights at the end of the fifth century,[82] his remarks are certainly exaggerated, but they probably reflect a feeling shared by the ranks of many Athenians, concerned about this (relative) openness of the civic body. It is in this tense context that Theramenes' tirade must be interpreted, which sought precisely to impose a new definition of 'radicality' and 'political moderation,' indexed to the greater or lesser openness of the Athenian civic body. By his resolute opposition to the enlargement proposed by Thrasybulus, Archinus revealed himself to be a genuine Theramenian.[83]

The 'Moderate' Democrats: A Group Portrait

If Archinus managed to convince the Athenians to reconsider these decisions to enlarge the civic body – by proposing, in 401/0, to grant more modest honors to only the first set of resistance fighters in Phyle[84] – it was

---

[79] On the mortality caused by the epidemic, see Thucydides, 2.47, 2.52.4, 3.87.3. Numerical estimates have been proposed by Hansen 1988, pp. 14–6 (15,000 adult citizens died between 430 and 426, plus at least 10,000 other citizens who were killed in Sicily between 413 and 411).
[80] Hellanicus of Lesbos, *FGrHist* 323A F 25; Aristophanes, *Frogs*, 190–1, 693–4; Diodorus of Sicily, 8.97.1.
[81] Lysias, *Against the Subversion of the Ancestral Constitution of Athens* (34), 3 (for the Euboeans); *IG* I³ 127 (for the Samians). It was also at this time that the desperate Athenians passed a decree authorizing the return of those who had been banished: Andocides, *On the Mysteries* (1), 73. On the *epigamia* of the Euboeans, see Oranges 2013 (who dates the measure to shortly before 412, when the Euboeans defected from the Delian League).
[82] Isocrates, *On the Peace* (8), 88.   [83] See *supra*, Chapter 2, pp. 91–3.
[84] Rhodes and Osborne 2003, n° 4, pp. 20–6; Aeschines, *Against Ctesiphon* (3), 187–90.

because he was able to count on the support of former resistance fighters from Piraeus, who shared the same reservations. Such was the case of the father of the orator Aeschines, Atrometus, who had returned to the city with the democrats of Piraeus. Atrometus made no secret of his preferences when he evoked this troubled period with his son: Although he admired Thrasybulus, he praised the indictment for illegality that Archinus had brought against him without reservation, precisely with regard to the decree granting citizenship to foreigners who had fought against the oligarchy.[85]

Aristophon of Azenia had similar convictions: Honored in 403 for his resistance against the Thirty and rewarded by an exemption from taxes (*ateleia*), he quickly asserted himself as one of the most active orators in Athens in the first half of the fourth century.[86] There can be little doubt about his democratic convictions, since he was personally involved in having the Athenians repay a man who had lent five talents to 'the democrats in the Piraeus.'[87] However, this did not prevent him from having probably been the initiator of the decree that, in 403, updated the law of 451, reserving access to citizenship to children of two Athenian parents.[88] Whereas, thanks to the upheavals brought about by the Peloponnese War, bastards (*nothoi*) had been able to discreetly integrate into the civic body – since the so-called 'Pericles' law was no longer being systematically enforced[89] – this possibility was therefore closed to them again. That's not all: According to Demosthenes, the same Aristophon also proposed to reactivate a Solonian law that imposed specific taxes on foreigners working on the Agora (*xenika*).[90] Likely voted on in the same year,[91] this decision was clearly part of a coherent policy aimed at reaffirming the boundaries of the civic body and the privileges associated with citizenship.

---

[85] Aeschines, *Against Ctesiphon* (3), 191, 195.
[86] Demosthenes, *Against Leptines* (20), 148 (on the *ateleia* accorded to him). Aristophon spoke again at the Assembly in 346, during the debates on the Peace of Philocrates (Theopompus of Chios, FGrHist 115 F 166).
[87] Demosthenes, *Against Leptines* (20), 149.
[88] Demosthenes, *Against Eubulides* (57), 30; Isaeus, *On the Estate of Ciron* (8), 43. See Vérilhac and Vial 1998, pp. 56–9. Whereas Athenaeus (13.577b) credits Aristophon with proposing the decree, there is another tradition, relayed by Eumelos the Peripatetic (scholia to Aeschines 1.39), according to which a certain Nikomenes, unknown elsewhere, was at the origin of it.
[89] Diogenes Laertius, 2.26: '[...] when the Athenians, because of a shortage of men, wished to increase their population, they decreed that a man could marry one Athenian woman and have children by another; and that Socrates accordingly did so.' Others have interpreted this as the institution of a kind of legal bigamy: see Roussel 1926, p. 106.
[90] Demosthenes, *Against Eubulides* (57), 31–4.   [91] See Hansen 1983, p. 188.

The Half-Chorus of the 'Moderate' Democrats

It is in this same perspective that we must interpret the actions of a certain Theozotides, who, at the end of the fifth century, was the proposer of a decree for the sole benefit of the orphans of 'Athenians who died violent deaths during the oligarchy in aid of democracy'[92]: The children of the metics or bastards killed during the struggle were explicitly excluded from the scope of the measure.[93] The case is complex, because the measure must, in all likelihood, have referred to the oligarchic revolution of 411, and not to the tyranny of the Thirty.[94] Nevertheless, it remains possible – if not probable – that Theozotides repeated the same proposal after the restoration of democracy in 403.[95] In fact, a speech by Lysias accuses him of having proposed that only the legitimate sons of the citizens who perished under the oligarchy should benefit from the support of the city, thus manifesting his hatred for 'bastards' (*nothoi*) and 'adoptive sons' (*poiētoi*).[96] This plea was probably pronounced after 404, for two reasons. On the one hand, Lysias evokes the fallen 'on the battlefield' (*in tōi polemōi*) – a formula that would not make much sense in relation to the oligarchic revolution of 411 and its targeted assassinations; on the other hand, he probably would not have been able to compose such a speech before 404 if it is true that it was not until after the fall of the Thirty that he became a logographer – an activity consisting of writing speeches made by others in exchange for wages.[97]

We must make no mistake about it: The discriminatory decrees proposed by Theozotides in 410/9 and reiterated, probably, in 403 did not only reflect the legitimate concern not to overburden the accounts of a financially beleaguered city. The addition of a few dozen deserving foreign

---

[92] *SEG* 28.46, ll. 4–6.   [93] Woodhead 1997, n° 106A.
[94] Matthaiou 2011, according to whom the inscription was engraved around 410/9. His argument is based, in particular, on the mention in the inscription of the *Hellenotamiai* (l. 18) – magistrates linked to the management of the Athenian empire and who disappeared, in all likelihood, with the defeat of Athens in 404. Added to this is the fact that the estimated number of deaths in the decree (between thirty-five and forty-five, according to Matthaiou), well below the number of victims attributed to the Thirty (1,500), would correspond better to what is known about the oligarchic revolution of 411 (Thucydides, 8.70).
[95] The hypothesis of two successive decrees proposed by Theozotides, one in 410/9 (attested by the epigraphy) and the other in 403 (contested before the courts with the support of Lysias), is formulated by Matthaiou 2011, pp. 77–8, *contra* Blok 2015, pp. 95–6, who suggests that Lysias' speech was delivered in 410/9. However, the main argument put forward (the mention of *diobelia*) is not entirely convincing, especially since it does not take into account the probable chronology of Lysias' logographic activity.
[96] Lysias, *Against Theozotides*, fr. 6 Gernet (= fr. 128–50 Carey).
[97] Lysias claims to have never composed speeches before the fall of the Thirty: *Against Eratosthenes* (12) 3. However, this is a rhetorical cliché, of which it is difficult to assess the veracity. On logography as a shameful activity, see Pseudo-Aristotle, *Rhetoric to Alexander*, 1444a16 sq.

children would hardly have endangered the public treasury in view of the modest amount that was planned to be allocated to each beneficiary (one obol per day per orphan). Probably coming from the ranks of the democrats of Piraeus – since he took the initiative of a measure benefiting them specifically[98] – Theozotides appears, like Archinus, as the promoter of a restricted conception of belonging to the city.[99]

Close to Archinus and, like him, a renowned resistance fighter, Agyrrhius does not stand out in this group picture, even if, at first sight, it would be easy to classify him on the side of the radicals, favorable to the increase of popular hegemony. It was he, in fact, who, shortly after 403, took the initiative of defraying the citizens who attended the Assembly sessions forty times a year.[100] The measure was generally interpreted, following an early reading of the plays of Aristophanes and the *Athenian Constitution*, as a way of combating absenteeism in the *ekklēsia*, in a particularly depressed demographic context. Above all, it was seen as an eminently democratic measure, inasmuch as it encouraged the poorest Athenians to take part in these crucial moments of civic life.

In reality, this interpretation, far from being satisfactory, does not do justice to the various reasons – both technical and symbolic – that presided over the introduction of Assembly pay (*misthos*) by Agyrrhius. Technically, first of all, the measure was foremost aimed at encouraging citizens to be punctual, since only the first six thousand who arrived received the *misthos*.[101] At the outset, it was probably a question of being able to reach the quorum necessary for the secret ballot votes as quickly as possible, which were sometimes held even before the Assembly session itself began. This procedure was required to ratify decisions affecting the legal status of certain individuals – and thus the legal contours of the community – either for the better (granting of citizenship) or for the worse (*atimia*; i.e. civic disenfranchisement).[102]

Beyond this technical goal – quickly achieving the quorum and not unduly delaying the Assemblies – the *misthos* also had a political aim. However, despite appearances, the objective does not seem to have been to

---

[98] Although he should probably be identified with the father of two disciples of Socrates (Plato, *Apology of Socrates*, 33d), Theozotides was not one of the fierce opponents of the philosopher, since Plato invokes the names of his children to prove that Socrates did not corrupt youth. In another context, Theozotides was also the author of an amendment to an honorary decree for the benefit of a family whose interests he supported (*SEG* 14.36, revising *IG* II² 5).

[99] Vérilhac and Vial 1998, p. 59.

[100] Hansen 1991, p. 150. It is difficult to specify the exact date of its establishment: In 392, Aristophanes reported that its amount had already been raised twice, to reach three obols (*Assemblywomen*, v. 182–8, 289–93).

[101] Gauthier 1993, p. 232 dates the measure to the years 403–400.   [102] Gauthier 1990, pp. 78–9.

The Half-Chorus of the 'Moderate' Democrats 119

encourage the participation of impoverished and vengeful citizens in the *ekklēsia*. In fact, this allowance was not allocated on a means-tested basis, but only on the basis of the order in which the participants arrived. This criterion therefore benefited urban dwellers and small-scale farmers who lived close to the urban center – a population in which wealthy citizens were overrepresented.

This incentive may have had another objective, ideological this time: When it was created, the *misthos* might have served as a tangible marker of the separation between citizens, who were eligible to receive it, and all the other categories of the population, who were not. Indeed, the amount of compensation was so low at the outset – one obol per session and per citizen – that it was foremost symbolic. The measure amounted to less than seven silver talents (40,000 drachmas) in a full year, and moreover, according to Aristophanes, it did not prevent delays in the Assembly in any way:

> Let's be sure to jostle the assemblymen from town, who before now never used to attend, when their pay was only one obol, but would sit gossiping in the garland shops. Now they fight hard for seats.[103]

When it was introduced shortly after 403, the measure was therefore akin to a privilege intended to symbolically reaffirm the distinction between citizens and *isoteles* (i.e. the metics who were exempted from the poll tax paid by foreign residents), whereas in practice these two categories of the Athenian population lived in an almost identical way.

By proposing to establish the *misthos* of the Assembly, Agyrrhius therefore fit perfectly into the conservative ideological line defended by Archinus. The aim was to ensure that decisions requiring a quorum could be voted on more quickly – decisions that were particularly sensitive in the aftermath of the civil war inasmuch as they affected the expansion or, on the contrary, the contraction of the civic community.[104]

In this chorus of democrats opposed to the widening of citizenship, we must add two last characters, Anytus and Phormisius, presented as close to

---

[103] Aristophanes, *Assemblywomen*, 300–3. The objective of ensuring punctuality at the meetings of the Assembly does not seem to have been met, at least in the early stages.

[104] In this context, should we be surprised to find the name of Agyrrhius (as a secretary) on the decree reiterating the granting of Athenian citizenship to the Samians in 403? Here again, this is only a paradox at first glance. This decision was foremost an honorary measure, since most Samians were not integrated into a phratry or a tribe – a *sine qua non* condition for being able to implement the citizenship granted to them. References in the decree to the Samian constitution and autonomy indicate that the measure was not intended to be implemented in a significant way. However, it was also not purely symbolic: The people voted on an amendment in 405/4 ($IG\,I^3$ 127 = $IG\,II^2$ 1, l. 32–40) that allowed the Samians present in Athens to really benefit from their Athenian citizenship by distributing them, if they so wished, within the tribes of the city.

Theramenes in the *Athenian Constitution*.¹⁰⁵ At first glance, the figure of Anytus does not seem to correspond to the cliché of the 'moderate' citizen: His trajectory is more reminiscent of that of Cleon, the belligerent demagogue of the Peloponnesian War, ready to do anything to humiliate the oligarchs. Like Cleon, he was the son of a rich tanner, named Anthemion, who went from the status of *thetes* (the poorest property class in the Solonian classification) to that of *hippeus* (cavalryman), according to Plato¹⁰⁶; like Cleon, he was mocked by the comic poets, who reduced him to the rank of a simple 'shoemaker'¹⁰⁷; like Cleon, he was sent as a general in 409 to prevent the loss of Pylos – the military base of the Athenians in Messenia that Cleon had taken from the Lacedaemonians in 425.¹⁰⁸ Unable to accomplish this mission, Anytus was taken to court and owed his salvation to his wealth, which could have been used to corrupt the jury.¹⁰⁹ His involvement as an accuser in Socrates' trial in 399 adds the finishing touch to this dark picture of a democratic social climber, vindictive, corrupt and corrupting.

However, this is only a selective reading of the ancient sources, which must be put in perspective, as Philippe Lafargue recently has done with regard to Cleon.¹¹⁰ In Xenophon's account, Anytus appears in a much better light: Theramenes regrets loud and clear that the Thirty banished him from Athens, because it risked strengthening the camp of the exiles by giving them a capable leader.¹¹¹ Appointed as a general in Phyle, he behaved with great moderation, sparing Agoratus, a new supporter suspected of having played an unclear role at the beginning of the oligarchy¹¹²; above all, in a speech composed in 402, Isocrates depicted Anytus as the very model of the virtuous citizen, respecting the terms of the amnesty to the letter, even though he was robbed of a large part of his possessions under the Thirty and was perfectly aware of the persons responsible for his misfortune.¹¹³ Anytus seems to have acted in 403 and subsequent years in the wake of Archinus, as a moderate democrat, and not as a militant demagogue.¹¹⁴ Without it being possible to administer proof,

---

¹⁰⁵ Pseudo-Aristotle, *Athenian Constitution*, 34.3.   ¹⁰⁶ Plato, *Meno*, 90a.
¹⁰⁷ Archippus, *The Fishes*, 30 K.-A.; Theopompus, *Soldierettes (Stratiōtides)*, 57 K.-A.
¹⁰⁸ Pseudo-Aristotle, *Athenian Constitution*, 27.5.
¹⁰⁹ Pseudo-Aristotle, *Athenian Constitution*, 27.5. This last allegation is probably false, as Lenfant 2016 has shown. This accusation of corruption is based solely on mockery by comic poets, taken *a posteriori* at face value.
¹¹⁰ Lafargue 2013.   ¹¹¹ Xenophon, *Hellenica*, 2.3.42.   ¹¹² Lysias, *Against Agoratus* (13), 78.
¹¹³ Isocrates, *Against Callimachus* (18), 23–4. On the character, see Nails 2002, pp. 37–8 (with bibliography).
¹¹⁴ In a passage describing the Athenian political situation in 395, the *Hellenica Oxyrhynchia* makes Anytus one of the leaders of the 'moderate men and property owners' (*hoi epieikeis kai tas ousias*

this former close friend of Theramenes probably shared an equally closed conception of citizenship.

Phormisius has a somewhat different profile in this regard. At the end of the Peloponnesian War, nothing yet distinguished him from Archinus and Anytus: Like them, he went into exile under the Thirty and, according to Lysias, then became one of those who returned with the people to the city.[115] But once democracy was restored, he became the promoter of a policy that, in many ways, brought him closer to his former enemies, the oligarchs: He presented a project reserving citizenship only to the owners of land (*gen*) in Attica. If the measure had been adopted by the Assembly, it would have effectively excluded 5,000 citizens from taking part in the *politeia*.[116] This was a way of pushing the logic of closing the civic body one step further than his comrades, by excluding not only foreigners, but also the poorest Athenians from active citizenship. However, he was not followed in this direction, and the Assembly rejected the proposal.

The case of Phormisius provides a glimpse into the existence of tensions within the 'moderate' group, whose members were, in fact, united by fragile ties, and not by a coherent political agenda. From this point of view, to speak of an 'Archinian party' is an abuse of language: It was more like an ephemeral chorus, based on a momentary convergence of interests and animated by centrifugal forces.[117] Nevertheless, these internal quarrels had nothing in common, in terms of intensity, with the violent confrontations that pitted the 'moderates' against all those who refused to enter the fold: The struggles were so harsh that they can even be considered as being a continuation of *stasis* by other means.

An Illusory Reconciliation

The reconciliation of 403 was certainly not a quiet family reunion gathering erstwhile enemies in a peaceful atmosphere. Although the 'moderates' from the two sides managed to impose their choices on the Assembly by joining forces, it was no easy feat. The political field remained divided into several poles: On the one hand, there were those close to Thrasybulus, in favor of a more open conception of citizenship; at the

---

echontes), opposed to the more radical democrats (*hoi polloi kai demotikoi*). See Strauss 1987, pp. 90–1, 94–6; Goukowsky and Feyel 2019, pp. 237–9.
[115] Lysias, *Against the Subversion of the Ancestral Constitution of Athens* (34), 2.
[116] Dionysius of Halicarnassus, *Lysias*, 32.
[117] On the remarkable fluidity of Athenian political life in classical times, see the founding remarks of Sealey 1955, pp. 80–1, and, more recently, Luraghi 2014.

center was Archinus' group, bringing together the defenders of the *status quo ante*; and at the other extreme were the partisans of an oligarchic intensification, supported by a 'defector' of Piraeus, Phormisius.

A Profusion of Trials

These strong tensions were expressed in particular through the numerous indictments for illegality (*graphai paranomōn*) brought between 403 and 399. Thrasybulus was the most famous victim: Archinus sued him before the courts, as we have seen, in order to quash the decree granting citizenship to foreigners who had been engaged in the resistance. In the opposite camp, Theozotides was probably brought to trial in 403 – rather than in 410/9 – for having proposed the decree concerning Athenian orphans: Composed by the orator Lysias, the accusation speech reflects the animosity between the two camps.[118] As for Phormisius, his proposal provoked the offended response of an anonymous democrat before the Assembly: In charge of drafting its contents, Lysias accused Phormisius of sharing the sentiments of the Three Thousand and of proposing decrees with an oligarchic tendency.[119] Finally, although there is no formal proof of it, Aristophon of Azenia may also have been prosecuted for his two decree proposals, one of which was to impose a tax on foreigners trading in the Agora and the other to reactivate Pericles' citizenship law: According to the orator Aeschines, he boasted of having faced seventy-five indictments for illegality during his career, without ever having being sentenced![120]

Moreover, these political trials are only a small sample of the many legal actions (trials linked to *dokimasia* and accountability) brought in the three years following reconciliation.[121] Scores were far from being settled, despite the proclamation of amnesty: While some democrats of Piraeus tried to obtain the condemnation of certain oligarchs, even if it meant circumventing their oath of 'not holding a grudge,' 'those from the town' demanded, on the contrary, the application of the most severe penalties against those who dared to transgress this sacred commitment. Thus, no less than seven cases are known in which accusers and accused used their

---

[118] As explained earlier, we prefer to continue to date Lysias' speech to the year 403/2, and not to 410/9, even though the (first?) decree of Theozotides was probably proposed in 410/9.
[119] Lysias, *Against the Subversion of the Ancestral Constitution* (34), 1–2.
[120] Aeschines, *Against Ctesiphon* (1), 194. Although the figure is probably exaggerated, it is nonetheless indicative of certain activism. See Whitehead 1986.
[121] On the violence of the 403–399 sequence, which is sometimes underestimated, see Wolpert 2001, pp. 48–71, and especially Loening 1987, pp. 151–4, appendix 1 (with the list of the twenty-three known trials related to the reconciliation agreement).

imagination to restrict or broaden the scope of the amnesty.[122] The trial of Socrates also emerged from this contentious context: Although he was prosecuted for impiety and the corruption of youth, the real motives of the prosecution lay elsewhere. In the middle of the fourth century, the orator Aeschines calmly explained that the philosopher had been sentenced for having notoriously trained (*pepaideukōs*) Critias, 'one of the Thirty who put down the democracy.'[123]

A Latent State of Stasis

It would be a mistake to see this profusion of trials as a peaceful way to put an end to the civil war. Since Loraux's studies, no one has been unaware of the connections between justice (*dikē*) and discord (*stasis*): In Greece, trials always had a potentially seditious scope.[124] In fact, political antagonisms sometimes went beyond the court – and the public exchange of reasoned arguments – and took a very disturbing turn. To subdue their enemies, some litigants did not hesitate to resort to curse tablets (*katadesmoi*), composed of thin strips of lead, often rectangular in shape, rolled or folded, and which could be pierced with nails.[125] Before they were buried in the ground, these strips were carefully engraved with the names of their opponents, possibly accompanied by references to the parts of the body that were to be 'bound' (tongues, limbs, genitals). In some quite exceptional cases, they were associated with figurines representing the person or persons targeted by the ritual.

Such an artifact was discovered during the excavations of Kerameikos Cemetery in Athens in the 1960s. In the vicinity of the tomb of two young boys who died around 430,[126] archaeologists discovered three rectangular boxes containing lead figures, with their arms tied behind their backs and prominent genitals (Figs. 3.2 and 3.3). Given the existence of contextual elements, commentators agree that this finding is a set of 'judicial curses' dating from the very end of the fifth century.[127]

---

[122] Lysias, *Against Andocides* (6); *Against Agoratus* (13); *Defense Against a Charge of Subverting the Democracy* (25); Andocides, *On the Mysteries* (1); Isocrates, *Against Callimachus* (18). To this must be added two other speeches by Lysias, well after 403, but where the reference to the Thirty remains decisive: *On the Scrutiny of Euandros* (26), and *In Defense of Mantitheus* (16). See Shear 2011, pp. 217–24.
[123] Aeschines, *Against Timarchus* (1) 173. See Ismard 2013, pp. 115–27.
[124] Loraux 2006, pp. 229–44.   [125] See Carastro 2009.   [126] *SEG* 13.46–7.
[127] Another lead tablet found in the immediate vicinity is therefore explicitly linked to the world of the law courts: Jordan 2000, n° 12 (*kai hoi alloi antidikoi*); Faraone 1991, p. 190. On the wider cultural context of judicial curses in classical times, see Faraone 1989.

124   Archinus or the Victory of the 'Moderates'

Fig. 3.2 Curse box (photograph and inscription), Kerameikos Cemetery, late fifth century BC.

Fig. 3.3 Cursed figurine (photograph and inscription), Kerameikos Cemetery, late fifth century BC.

On the lead lid of one of these boxes are engraved the names of Theozotides, Cephisophon, Diophanes and Diodoros – names that are also inscribed on the body of the doll that was nestled there.[128]

[128] Costabile 2000, pp. 99–108 and figs. 35–47.

The name of Theozotides is sufficiently rare that it can be related with reasonable certainty to the proposer of the (second?) decree on orphans, the target of Lysias' speech.[129] Cephisophon,[130] for his part, was undoubtedly the oligarch who had become secretary of the Council in the context of the restored democracy. Given that they both belonged to the chorus of the 'moderates,' it is not surprising to find them associated during a trial because it was customary, in the Athenian judicial system, for the accused or the principal accuser – in this case, probably Theozotides, whose name is engraved first – to be assisted by several collaborators (*syndikoi* or *synēgoroi*).

It is therefore necessary to imagine that these two eminent figures of Archinus' chorus were taken to task by an opponent – perhaps close to Thrasybulus – in a struggle in which any means, even extrajudicial ones, were admissible. Not only does this archaeological discovery validate the hypothesis of active collusion between former oligarchs and 'moderate' democrats after 403, it also reflects the violence of the reactions that this collaboration provoked on behalf of part of the population: The ritual artifact aimed to destroy the ability of the four individuals to act, by soliciting the magical help of the two boys who died prematurely (*aōroi*) and who were buried in the nearby tomb. Beyond the case at hand, this could also be seen as an allegory of the persistent effects of the *stasis* in Athens in 403: Like these lead figurines, still active although buried in the ground, the civil war was repressed, but ready to reappear at any moment. Ultimately, the restored democracy experienced its 'years of lead,' both literally and figuratively.

The Imposition of the Agreement

Far from being accomplished in one day by the magic of the oath of amnesty alone, reconciliation was therefore actively imposed by all those who ensured that no one would 'hold a grudge.' And they did not hesitate to use violence to enforce their conception of moderation: We have already shown how Archinus short-circuited the normal legal path to execute a former resistance fighter who did not accept the terms of the amnesty in a very specific form of state of exception. As for the oligarchs, they were careful to ensure that the political compromise of which they were the

---

[129] Lysias, *Against Theozotides*, fr. 6 Gernet (= fr. 128–50 Carey).
[130] His name is also found on another unpublished tablet from Kerameikos Cemetery: Inv. no. JB 45. See Costabile 2000, pp. 101, 108.

great beneficiaries was respected, demanding the utmost severity for those who dared to defy it.[131] In the case of Isocrates' *Against Callimachus*, the anonymous accuser, a former member of the Three Thousand, condemned the victims of the Thirty who had the audacity to claim reparations: 'Indeed, *you ought to hate (chrē misein)* such people and regard them as bad citizens, those who have experienced the same misfortunes as most have but think it right to exact different punishments from the others.'[132] The orator even goes so far as to demand a toughening of the laws protecting the amnesty: Callimachus and his ilk must perish, otherwise the *stasis* could well make its return.[133]

We must not think, however, that the 'moderates' only went after recalcitrant democrats. The staunch oligarchs were also brutally brought to heel, even though they benefited from a guaranteed refuge in Eleusis under the terms of the agreement passed in 403. Under the influence of vague rumors, the Athenians launched a massive expedition against this oligarchic stronghold in 401/0. Blood flowed: Not only did the democrats besiege the place, they also did not hesitate to physically eliminate the generals who had come from Eleusis to conduct peace talks, even though the leaders of the oligarchs should, in principle, have benefited from the inviolability guaranteed to ambassadors.[134] Although the confrontation ended with the reiteration of the amnesty oath, the brutality of the sequence reminds us of the extent to which the reconciliation was by no means self-evident.

A few weeks later came a final significant episode. The Spartans had sent one of their own, Thibron, to Asia, and he asked the Athenians for the support of three hundred cavalry: 'And the Athenians sent some of those who had served as cavalrymen in the time of the Thirty, thinking it would be a gain to the democracy if they should live in foreign lands and perish there.'[135] While Xenophon probably intended to criticize the versatility, even the disloyalty of the Athenian *demos* – breaking the oath of 'not

---

[131] Cloché 1915, pp. 365.
[132] Isocrates, *Against Callimachus* (18), 38 (transl. Mirhady and Too 2000, our emphasis).
[133] Isocrates, *Against Callimachus* (18), 47.
[134] On the siege of Eleusis, see Lysias, *Defense against a Charge of Subverting the Democracy* (25), 9; on the elimination of the generals, see Xenophon, *Hellenica*, 2.4.43. In Xenophon's work, this treacherous assassination cannot fail to echo the murder of the Greek generals that took place on exactly the same date (in September 401), at the end of the Battle of Cunaxa. Trapped in Tissaphernes' tent, the generals were similarly executed in one fell swoop (Xenophon, *Anabasis*, 2.5.31–2.6.1). Athenian democrats and imperial Achaemenid elites therefore shared the same treacherous behavior in the author's eyes.
[135] Xenophon, *Hellenica*, 3.1.4.

holding a grudge,' if not *de jure*, at least *de facto*[136] – the passage reveals all the suppressed violence that continued to plague Athenian society several years after the end of the civil war. From this point of view, the great political trials held in 399 – against Socrates and Andocides – contributed to this persistent conflict, despite repeated proclamations of forgetfulness.

When it comes to reporting these final throes, the author of the *Athenian Constitution* nevertheless provides a very strange summary, which is ultimately biased as a result of being condensed: '[The Athenians] also made a reconciliation with those that had settled at Eleusis two years after the migration, in the archonship of Xenaenetus [401/0].'[137] Nothing is therefore said of the bloody assault against the oligarchs, nor of the treacherous assassination of their generals. Was this a simple omission by an author summarizing the history of Athens in broad strokes? Rather, it seems to us to be the effect of a deliberate strategy. For the 'moderates' did not only strive to enforce amnesty through violence, but also to rewrite the entire history of the civil war, by camouflaging the divisions that had separated the two sides.

History Rewritten: The Winner's Version

Isocrates proclaims that 'since we gave each other pledges and joined together in unity, we have run our city nobly and for the common good, *as if no misfortune had happened to us.*'[138] To act as if nothing had happened: How better to express the will to promote an irenic history, aiming to erase the very traces of the conflict? It was undoubtedly a question of reconstructing the 'one and undivided [city], as it is described in the official praises of Athens.'[139] It should also be noted that this version of history was especially promoted by the 'moderates,' whose vision is expressed by the *Athenian Constitution*.

The Historiographic Victory of the 'Moderates':
The Athenian Constitution

Indeed, this text gives a biased representation of the civil war and its aftermath, which gives (excessive) pride of place to the 'moderates' on both sides – in short, to Archinus' chorus. It is not an exaggeration to see

---

[136] Krentz 1989, pp. 191–2; Dillery 1995, p. 24.
[137] Pseudo-Aristotle, *Athenian Constitution*, 40.4.
[138] Isocrates, *Against Callimachus* (18), 46 (our emphasis). [139] Loraux 2006, p. 153.

this as genuine historiographic revisionism that comparison with other sources allows us to put into perspective. This rewriting process extended both upstream and downstream of the reconciliation.

Upstream, the Aristotelian treatise ignores the participation of the Three Thousand in the abuses of the 'tyrants' and, in particular, in the summary execution of the Eleusinians, related by Xenophon.[140] Without the latter's account, it would be almost impossible to grasp the degree of involvement of the Three Thousand in the terror orchestrated by the Thirty: Because he wrote his work in exile, this former member of the oligarchy had no interest in clearing the names of the ex-collaborators of the regime, of which he had incidentally been a member.

In the account of these troubled times, Theramenes enjoys very singular preferential treatment. According to the *Athenian Constitution*, he is not even presented as being part of the Thirty, contrary to what the rest of the unanimous tradition affirms; even better, the author of the treatise endeavors to situate the worst crimes of the oligarchy after the death of Theramenes, as if the latter had been able to moderate the 'tyrants' in his lifetime.[141] What was the reason for such a twisting of reality? Probably the fact that the man was the missing link between the 'moderates' on both sides: Theramenes was nicknamed the 'Buskin,' after a platform shoe that could be worn on the right foot as well as on the left.[142] As for the promoters of this historiographic rehabilitation, a passage from Lysias allows us to glimpse their silhouettes in Athens in 403: 'I see [Theramenes' friends] referring their defense (*apologias*) to him, and we have *his associates attempting to compete for honors* (*tous t' ekeinōi sunontas timasthai peirōmenous*) as though he had been responsible for many benefits, and not of grievous injuries.'[143] Clearly, his former associates – Archinus, Phormisius and Anytus in particular – had a vested interest in rehabilitating the memory of their former accomplice in order to present themselves in a good light.[144] That Lysias could denounce the maneuver shows, however, that this defense and illustration of Theramenes remained a matter of controversy: Other versions of history circulated in the city, much less favorable to one of the most famous political 'weather vanes' of antiquity.

---

[140] Xenophon, *Hellenica*, 2.4.8–20.
[141] Pseudo-Aristotle, *Athenian Constitution* 36.1–2, 37.2. See Rhodes 1981, p. 422.
[142] Xenophon, *Hellenica*, 2.3.47.
[143] Lysias, *Against Eratosthenes* (12), 64 (our translation and emphasis).
[144] *Contra* Hurni 2010, pp. 346 sq., whose argument is biased by the desire to rehabilitate the figure of Theramenes.

The 'moderates' from both camps also took care to edit the account of the reconciliation as such, to make it a beautiful story of shared desires, which the *Athenian Constitution* recounts indulgently: According to the text, just after the Battle of Mounychia, the Three Thousand immediately wished to conclude a peace treaty with the exiled democrats.[145] They allegedly deposed the Thirty and elected a college of ten magistrates in their place who, unfortunately, betrayed their trust by appealing to the Spartans in order to crush the resistance of the democrats. Once again, Xenophon's account undermines this version, which is too consensual to be honest[146]: According to the historian (present in the city at the time of the events), it was indeed the Three Thousand – not the Ten – who decided to send ambassadors to Lacedaemon and to call on Lysander to take advantage of the democrats in exile.[147] If, a few weeks later, the Three Thousand resolved to make offers of reconciliation to 'those of the Piraeus,' it was only because the Spartan king Pausanias, jealous of Lysander's popularity, had 'set about dividing the men in the city.'[148] Moreover, the litigator of Isocrates' *Against Callimachus* makes no mystery of the mutual hatred between the two sides until the last moments of the conflict: 'before concluding it we were at war, one group holding the city, the other having captured Piraeus; *we hated each other more than the enemies that were left us by our ancestors.*'[149]

Downstream, these reconfigurations of historical reality also affected the narrative of the months following the restoration of democracy. As we have seen, the author of the *Athenian Constitution* ignores the violent upheavals generated by the reconciliation after 403, effectively overlooking the multiple trials that took place at this time and the violent assault launched against the last oligarchs who were refugees in Eleusis. At most, to congratulate Archinus, he mentions the summary execution of the democrat who dared to transgress the oath of amnesty. The concealment of the conflict is, once again, striking.

---

[145] Pseudo-Aristotle, *Athenian Constitution*, 38.1–2. Twenty years after the events, in 382, Lysias took up this enchanted vision, pretending that 'those from the town' had always wanted to reconcile with their democratic opponents. Thus, in *On the Scrutiny of Euandros* (26), 19, the litigant exclaims: 'As to the further point which some find unaccountable – how it was that their large numbers were worsted by the little band of the Piraeus – this can only be attributed to the prudent policy of those citizens; for they chose to concert a government with the restored exiles rather than an enslavement to the Lacedaemonians with the Thirty.'
[146] Xenophon, *Hellenica*, 2.4.28–9. See the detailed argument made already by Cloché 1915, pp. 120–32.
[147] Xenophon, *Hellenica*, 2.4.28–9.   [148] Xenophon, *Hellenica*, 2.4.35.
[149] Isocrates, *Against Callimachus* (18), 45 (our emphasis).

Thus is the whole history of the civil war – from its first clashes to its final consequences – reread and corrected from the perspective of the 'moderates' in the Aristotelian treatise. This historiographic revisionism is particularly striking in the case of Rhinon, who, as Archinus' alter ego in the Three Thousand camp, is transformed into a true icon of reconciliation, in defiance of historical reality.

Rhinon, a Virtuous Citizen or a Skillful Weather Vane?

According to the *Athenian Constitution*, Rhinon only had real influence in the very last days of the oligarchy. To play the leading role, he had to wait not only for the fall of the Thirty, but also for the dismissal of a first college of ten magistrates (decarchy), who were reluctant to negotiate with the democratic camp. It was only as part of a second decarchy, elected some time later, that he was finally able to influence the course of events and put an end to the conflict.[150]

We must be clear: This reconstruction is a pious fiction intended to make us forget Rhinon's active engagement in the service of the oligarchy.[151] Indeed, there is nothing to suggest the existence of two successive decarchies – the first recalcitrant to all negotiations, the second much more conciliatory toward democrats. Neither Xenophon nor Lysias utter a word about it, and the amnesty oath makes no mention of it.[152] In addition, a speech by Isocrates explicitly contradicts this version of the story. In *Against Callimachus*, the litigant refers to Rhinon as one of the Ten.[153] The action takes place just after Mounychia and the deposition of the Thirty – that is to say, precisely at the time when the first decarchy was supposed to be cracking down on the democrats, according to the *Athenian Constitution*. In fact, there was no question of peace talks: Isocrates' speech, on the contrary, evokes the violent fighting that, some time later, pitted the people of the city against the exiles.[154] The second decarchy is therefore very likely only an *ad hoc* fiction created by the 'moderates' after 403 to absolve Rhinon and his colleagues. In all likelihood there was only one College of the Ten, whose political positions evolved under the pressure of events. Resolutely hostile at the outset to any compromise (even if it meant terrorizing the opponents of their political

---

[150] Pseudo-Aristotle, *Athenian Constitution*, 38.1–4.
[151] Rhodes 1981, pp. 459–60; Piovan 2011, p. 62.
[152] Xenophon, *Hellenica*, 2.4.29; Lysias, *Against Eratosthenes* (12), 54–9.
[153] Isocrates, *Against Callimachus* (18), 6, 8.   [154] Isocrates, *Against Callimachus* (18), 49.

line[155]), the Ten gradually adopted a more accommodating attitude toward the democrats, as the military setbacks piled up and the Spartans' support for them weakened.

Moreover, Isocrates' same speech sheds a very murky light on Rhinon. The case can be summed up in a few words. Shortly after the Ten had taken up office, Patrocles, the *archon basileus*, walked with his friend (Isocrates' client) and met Callimachus, who was carrying a large sum of money. Patrocles then decided to seize the loot on the pretext that Callimachus got it from a certain Amphilochus, who was 'a member of the party of the Piraeus.'[156] At this very moment, Rhinon, as a member of the Ten, intervened in the dispute and decided to take the two opponents before his colleagues, who referred the matter to the Council: The money was finally confiscated for the benefit of the public treasury. Although Rhinon did not decide the case himself, he did not oppose a seizure that was nevertheless based on factious criteria. He was therefore, at least passively, endorsing the plunder of the exiled democrats in accordance with a tradition initiated by the Thirty and shamelessly taken up by the Ten.[157]

How can we understand, in this context, that Rhinon was able to get away with things so lightly after the fall of the oligarchy? Let us say that, as a good political 'weather vane,' he probably felt the wind turning and decided to get involved, before the others, in a process of reconciliation that, in reality, was largely dictated from the outside, according to the divisions between Spartan leaders. Above all, by rallying to Archinus' position early on, he was able to benefit from the precious support of the moderate democrats on their return from Piraeus.

It was this political alliance, much more than their moral virtue, that enabled Rhinon and his accomplices to render their accounts unhindered under the restored democracy. In this respect, the former magistrates of the oligarchy enjoyed preferential treatment. Under the terms of the agreement signed by both parties, it was stipulated that the Ten would render their accounts before 'those possessed of a property qualification in the city (*tous d'en tōi astei en tois ta timēmata parechomenois*).'[158] The conduct of

---

[155] Indeed, Rhinon was certainly a member of the Ten when they, 'in their fear of being deposed from office and their desire to terrify the others (which they succeeded in doing), arrested one of the most leading citizens, Demaretus, and put him to death' (Pseudo-Aristotle, *Athenian Constitution*, 38.2). As Cloché 1915, pp. 118–9, 181–2, points out, it is unlikely that Rhinon opposed this drastic and apparently illegal measure.
[156] Isocrates, *Against Callimachus* (18), 5.   [157] Cloché 1915, p. 119.
[158] Pseudo-Aristotle, *Athenian Constitution*, 39.6 (our translation).

Rhinon and his accomplices was therefore examined by an *ad hoc* commission, composed of Piraeus democrats and former members of the Three Thousand, to the exclusion of the poorest and potentially most vindictive Athenians.[159] Ultimately, the whole system seems to have been designed so that these political weather vanes would not be unduly compromised.

This exemption, however, does not explain how Rhinon managed to get being elected general thrown into the bargain. But should we really be surprised? At the end of the civil war, arithmetic worked in favor of the 'moderates.' Indeed, the Three Thousand attended the Assembly sessions en masse, both because they feared that the victorious democrats would want to take revenge on them and because their material ease allowed them to do so. Conversely, many *thetes* could not afford the luxury of losing a day's work to go to the *ekklēsia*, in an economic context degraded by decades of conflicts; the amount of the *misthos* was not enough to attract them in significant numbers. By combining the votes of the former oligarchs (the Three Thousand) and a fraction of the democrats who had returned from Piraeus, the 'moderates' could reasonably hope to win the majority of the votes – moreover, the Pnyx could only accommodate 6,000–8,000 citizens at most. It was certainly due to these political power relationships that Rhinon was able to be elected general and Archinus was able to win his trial for illegality against Thrasybulus.

Nevertheless, not all Athenians were fooled by his political sincerity. Before being canonized by the Aristotelian tradition – a reflection of Athenian history such as a moderate like Androtion could write[160] – it appears that Rhinon was the object of sharp criticism in the city. His name was therefore given to two works whose content was doubtless derogatory toward him: The first, with a restricted circulation, emanated from Socratic circles; the second, with a wider diffusion, was composed by a comic poet for all Athenians gathered at the theater.

Aeschines of Sphettos, a close friend of Socrates,[161] wrote a dialogue called *Rhinon*, of which unfortunately only the title has reached us.[162] In all likelihood, the work was the staging of an encounter between

---

[159] For an in-depth discussion, see Cloché 1915, pp. 268–72. Elster 2004, p. 14, sees this as an example of 'loser justice' intended to protect the defeated from the civil war.

[160] Bearzot 2010. The author shows, from an analysis of a number of fragments by Androtion that are rarely taken into account, that Androtion had a 'moderate' political orientation and that his work most likely exerted a great influence on the *Athenian Constitution*. (See *FGrHist* 324 F 10, on the decarchy replacing the Thirty.)

[161] He attended his trial (Plato, *Apology of Socrates*, 33e). See Goulet-Cazé 1989.

[162] Diogenes Laertius, 2.61.

Rhinon and Socrates. In the absence of tangible information, we can hazard two contradictory hypotheses as to its content. Either the dialogue emphasized the convergences between two men from the 'middle,' who had remained in the city during the civil war and had acted as best they could under the circumstances; or, on the contrary, the work accentuated their differences, highlighting the winding path of one and the ideological coherence of the other. While Rhinon had adapted to two diametrically opposed political regimes, moving from one chorus to the other with admirable flexibility, Socrates had turned his back on both oligarchs and democrats, refusing to bow to orders that he considered to be illegal regardless of where they came from. The idea that Aeschines of Sphettos staged such a contrast would not be surprising in view of what we know of his other dialogues, in which the interlocutors of Socrates seldom came out on top – such as Alcibiades or Miltiades, son of Stesagoras, who were ridiculed by the philosopher.[163]

Although it remains difficult to know in what light Rhinon was portrayed by Aeschines of Sphettos, there can be no doubt in the case of Archippus, who attacked Rhinon in the theater in an eponymous play.[164] Probably performed shortly after 403 – since he was not previously well-known enough to justify a poet devoting an entire work to him – the play belongs to a well-known genre, the 'demagogue's comedy,' made famous by Aristophanes and particularly popular in the last years of the Peloponnesian War.[165] The authors liked to stigmatize leading political figures, systematically painting a caricature of the 'hero,' who was accused of every possible flaw.

According to the rules of the genre, the tone of the play must have been scathing: Although it is difficult to discern the types of attack that were deployed, we can assume that Rhinon's versatility and his Theramenes-like capacity to adapt were probably grist to the poet's mill. A passage by Athenaeus allows us to glimpse one of the characteristic elements privileged by Archippus:

---

[163] See, for example, Rossetti and Lausdei 1981, pp. 154–65.
[164] Archippus had already won the Dionysian competition between 415 and 412. Sixty-one fragments and six titles of his work have reached us. In addition to *Rhinon*, he composed an *Amphitryon*, a *Ploutos*, as well as a play entitled the *Fishes* (*Ichthyes*), which depicts a fish city, modeled on the Aristophanic city from the *Birds*.
[165] Lind 1990, pp. 239–41; Sommerstein 2002b. In keeping with Aristophanes' *Knights*, Plato the Comic composed three pieces (*Hyperbolus*, *Peisandros* and *Cleophon*), each attacking a supposed 'demagogue.' To this must be added the *Teisamenos*, a play by Theopompus aimed at a 'moderate,' like Rhinon, and which was probably also performed in 403 or shortly thereafter.

I find also, in the comic poets, mention made of a kind of garland called *kulistos* [crown braided in a circle], and I find that Archippus mentions it in his *Rhinon*, in these lines – 'He went away unhurt [*athōios*] to his own house, having laid aside his cloak, but having on his *ekkulistos* garland.'[166]

Without any context, the quotation remains difficult to interpret, but it is tempting to see in it a reference to the rendering of accounts from which Rhinon managed to emerge unscathed: The term *athōios* is almost always used in a judicial context to describe crimes that remained unpunished.[167] To take the argument one step further, the *Athenian Constitution* evokes the public praise received by Rhinon and his colleagues, and Lysias even claims that some citizens from the city involved in the reconciliation process received 'the highest honors' (*megistai timai*).[168] Is it therefore conceivable that Rhinon obtained a crown in addition to the praise since the two awards often went hand in hand in Athens?[169] In this hypothesis, Archippus is attacking the honors granted to Rhinon, honors that were all the more undue in his eyes because they were equivalent to, or even greater than, those granted to the most courageous resistance fighters, according to the terms of Archinus' decree – an olive wreath and a few drachmas.[170]

Although this reconstruction remains uncertain in the absence of other fragments to corroborate it, one unmistakable fact remains: In the years following the reconciliation, Rhinon was booed in front of all Athenians by a recognized poet, a discordant voice in the apparent concert of praise surrounding the character.[171] In a way, Archippus' play reflects both the victory of the 'moderates' and the tensions it provoked: Even though Rhinon was honored and elected general thanks to the support of Athenians from both sides, he was nevertheless a controversial figure in a community that was still plagued by the specter of civil war.

At the end of this journey, it may be appropriate to return to the hypothesis previously advanced by Loraux in *The Divided City*. *Mē*

---

[166] Archippus, *Rhinon*, fr. 41 K.-A. (= fr. 274 Miccolis = Athenaeus, 15.678E) (our translation). On this play, see Miccolis 2017, pp. 251–63 (with no political contextualization).

[167] Demosthenes, *On the Crown* (18), 125; Demosthenes, *On the False Embassy* (19), 258, 284; Lycurgus, *Against Leocrates*, 79, 144.

[168] Pseudo-Aristotle, *Athenian Constitution*, 38.4; Lysias, *On the Scrutiny of Euandros* (26), 20. The orator's remarks are certainly exaggerated, to the extent that the *megistai timai* consisted in granting *sitēsis* to the prytaneis and proedria (a place of honor in competitions) – distinctions that were not attested in these circumstances.

[169] Demosthenes, *On the Crown* (18), 118.   [170] Aeschines, *Against Ctesiphon* (3), 187.

[171] Although the caricature of politicians was very commonplace in Athens and often targeted influential and popular men such as Pericles and Cleon, the memory of the recent civil war gave a special resonance to the attacks on Rhinon. On the differentiated scope of comic insults according to the political context, see Azoulay 2014, pp. 150–1.

mnēsikakein, 'do not hold a grudge': The amnesty oath promoted an active forgetting of the civil war, using the method of the paradoxical injunction. According to her, this unprecedented decision was all the more significant since the victorious democrats thereby gave themselves the latitude to take revenge. Is this not proof that, in the manner of a Freudian subject, the city suppressed the *stasis*, that terrible specter lodged in the unconscious of the community always ready to reappear?[172]

As attractive as it may be, this hypothesis must be revised. First of all, the amnesty was not a decision that was taken willingly by both parties. The negotiations took place while the Spartan troops were camped in Attica and had just inflicted their first military setback on the Piraeus-based democrats.[173] In a context where the Spartans were leading the dance, did the exiles really have the possibility of following another policy when they returned to the city?[174] It was under Lacedaemonian pressure that Phormisius, a former fighter from Piraeus, proposed that the full extent of civic rights be reserved for private landowners: According to his anonymous opponent, it was a question of yielding to the 'Lacedaemonians['] demand[s].'[175]

Secondly, the amnesty seems less to reflect the community's anxiety about the *stasis* than to mark the victory of one side over all the others. The anthropology of politics, proposed by Loraux, must be accompanied here by a refined sociology: In 403, it was not *the* unanimous city that wanted to suddenly forget the evils of the civil war, but the temporary chorus of former oligarchs and democrats that forced people to respect the amnesty, then camouflaged the violent clashes that this decision subsequently provoked.[176] These 'moderates' succeeded in imposing an image of

---

[172] This hypothesis was recently taken up and developed by Shear 2011, pp. 286–312, according to whom the Athenians officially reinterpreted the regime of the Thirty as a moment of external war (*polemos*), and not of civil war (*stasis*). See Grangé 2015, pp. 64–9. However, as Simonton 2012 noted in his review of Shear's book, the absence of the word *stasis* in the inscriptions of the time does not in any way prove that the idea of civil war had been banished from Athenian memory. In these same decrees, the use of the term 'oligarchy' implies the idea of division and discord, without trying to mask this unpleasant reality.

[173] Xenophon, *Hellenica*, 2.4.35–8.

[174] On this subject, see Wolpert 2001, pp. 27–8. On the crucial role of Sparta in the reconciliation process, see Ostwald 1986, pp. 488–500.

[175] Lysias, *Against the Subversion of the Ancestral Constitution of Athens* (34), 6. See Todd 2000, pp. 337–8, according to whom the pressure was all the more intense because Pausanias was the subject of a trial in Lacedaemon for having accepted a reconciliation agreement that was too favorable to the Athenians of Piraeus.

[176] In another context, see Mellet and Foa 2016.

consensus within the city, so that this ultimately came to be conceived as the only possible, if not the only conceivable, representation.

It is in this militant context that it is necessary to interpret the intensive references to the figure of Solon after 403.[177] No doubt the idea was to snatch the great legislator from the appropriation attempted by Critias – he who boasted of being his direct descendant.[178] The stakes, however, were much greater than that. By transforming Solon into the patron saint of restored democracy, the 'moderates' legitimized their own political position in the middle of the road. It is therefore not surprising that it is precisely the *Athenian Constitution* that relays Solon's famous poem: 'But I stood in the middle ground between them/Like a boundary-stone (*horos*).'[179]

Here, at the end of the journey, we come to another thesis dear to Loraux: The choice of the 'middle ground' (*mēson*) must be restored to its anthropological vigor and intensity, far from the 'gray mediocrity of "nothing in excess".'[180] The 'moderates' were no angels, and on the contrary displayed an extraordinary radical bitterness to impose their vision and bring the uncooperative parties into line. Moderation was therefore the product of an active, even violent policy, and it is in the context of a struggle that we must consider the establishment of a 'middle ground,' equidistant from vindictive democrats and radical oligarchs.

This brutal victory of the 'moderates' opens up a final interrogation, of a historiographic nature this time. Does not all this analysis offer an opportunity to revisit the debate on the nature of Athenian democracy in the fourth century? Controversy still rages on this subject: Was the Athens of Demosthenes more moderate than that of Pericles, or is this separation only an illusion?[181] By the place it gives to the 'moderates' in the process of reconciliation, the present study seems to argue, at first sight, for the first of these alternatives: After the trauma of the civil war, the city entered a new phase of its political history, guided by the holy alliance of Athenians from both sides.

---

[177] Pseudo-Aristotle, *Athenian Constitution*, 39.2; Andocides, *On the Mysteries* (1) 83. See Psilakis 2014.

[178] Critias, son of Callaischros, was a descendant of the archon Dropides, a relative and friend of the legislator Solon: Plato, *Critias*, 113a–b; *Timaeus*, 20e. On the Critias family, see the prosopographic data collected by Nails 2002, s.v. Critias IV, as well as Rosenmeyer 1949; on the links between Critias and Solon, see Wilson 2003a, p. 187.

[179] Pseudo-Aristotle, *Athenian Constitution*, 12.5. See Loraux 2005, p. 146 ('*Solon au milieu de la lice*').

[180] Loraux 2005, p. 147.

[181] For the first of these alternatives, see Ostwald 1986 and Hansen 1991, pp. 300–4, who speaks of 'if not a "moderate," then a "modified" democracy.' For the second, see Harris 2016.

However, this would be too hasty a conclusion. On the one hand, it is difficult to discern a clear break between the political strategy of someone like Archinus and the democratic practices of the previous century. From the time of Pericles, orators had sought to impose the image of a unified people, capable of deciding in one direction and with one voice – even if this meant going back, just as unanimously, on the decision that had been taken beforehand.[182] On the other hand, the 'moderation' of Archinus and his supporters only applied to one, very localized question: that of the widening of the civic body. There is no evidence that, beyond this point of agreement, they all shared the same political positions – especially about the degree of sovereignty that the people should exercise once the contours of the community had been redefined. These divergent interests explain why this chorus of 'moderates' was probably only ephemeral: Its imprint on Athenian political life is hardly noticeable after the early 390s.

Ultimately, if the reconciliation of 403 did represent a break, it was not because it marked the advent of a more moderate democracy, but because it tipped the city into a new regime of historicity. It was in this forcibly reconciled Athens that a more consensual way of writing the history of the community was born,[183] at the risk of silencing dissonant voices.

---

[182] This is one of the main contributions of the article by Canevaro 2019.
[183] On this standardized rewriting of the Athenian past in the fourth century – in sharp contrast to the lively debates of the fifth century – see Azoulay 2017, pp. 93–114; for a different perspective, see Rhodes 2011.

CHAPTER 4

Socrates and the Voices of Neutrality

'Anyone who, when the *polis* was in a state of civil strife (*stasis*), failed to take up arms with either side should be deprived of his civic rights (*atimos*) and have no part in the *polis*.'[1] Attributed to the legislator Solon, it seems that this law established an imperative for all Athenian citizens: to take sides in case of *stasis*, under penalty of being excluded from the community. According to Nicole Loraux, this ancient legislation is clear proof that political neutrality did not exist in ancient Greece. Because neutrality has nothing to do with moderation: Archinus or Rhinon, Theramenes or Anytus, the 'moderate' Athenians were, as we have seen, actively involved with one camp or the other during the civil war, and it was only later that the enemies of yesterday finally decided to join forces. In trying times, each had chosen his side without taking refuge in the comfort of abstention.[2]

The contours of an all-embracing political universe were therefore taking shape, where participation was not only an ideal, but a civic obligation. Pericles had already pointed this out in 431, in his funeral oration for the soldiers who had died during the first campaign of the Peloponnesian War: 'We are unique in the way we regard anyone who takes no part in public affairs (*ta politika*): we do not call that a quiet individual, we call it a useless one (*achreion*).'[3] Whatever his professional occupations or personal inclinations, an Athenian citizen would have had a duty to get involved in the life of the community. In Athens, it seems there was a categorical imperative to show commitment, which all the citizens were forced to respect, on pain of suffering the reprobation of, or even exclusion from, the community.

This picture is, however, puzzling. How can we explain the discrepancy that Solon's law was never invoked in the judicial speeches of the early fourth century to incriminate those who had not taken sides in the civil

---

[1] Pseudo-Aristotle, *Athenian Constitution*, 8.5.   [2] Loraux 2006, pp. 102–4.
[3] Thucydides, 2.40.2.

war?[4] There were many such people, as we shall see. Moreover, the orator Lysias explicitly specifies that such legislation was not in force in Athens. Anticipating the defense of his opponent – an Athenian banished by the Thirty, but who did not join the democrats – the speaker writes thus: 'I understand he claims that if not being present during that crisis had been a crime, *there would be a law dealing with it explicitly*, as there is for other offenses.'[5] But this is not the case, the speaker concedes. How better to show that Solon's law was not in force?

Perhaps this paradox is not one at all: At the end of a precise philological study, a Dutch scholar recently proposed a quite different translation of the Solonian law: 'whoever, when the polis is in a state of *stasis*, does not ground his arms (*mē thētai ta hopla*) without allegiance to either party, shall be *atimos* and have no share in the city.'[6] It therefore seems that the legislator did not in any way propose to punish neutrality in the event of civil war, but instead recommended citizens should put their weapons down to remain in a position of vigilant neutrality. As for Pericles' speech, its normative value should probably not be overestimated. Delivered in honor of the soldiers who had died for their country, the funeral oration aimed to remobilize the mourners and to convince them to imitate the sacrifice of the deceased at a critical moment for the community. In this context, it is not surprising to see Pericles celebrating an imaginary Athens, composed only of committed citizens: His speech was more prescriptive than descriptive.

If one listens carefully, it is possible to discern discordant voices. The judicial speeches give voice to many citizens who remained outside the conflict, out of necessity or by choice. Out of necessity: The *stasis*, being a form of war, required certain physical or financial capacities, which some did not have – for example, 'the oldest of the citizens, who had remained in their demes with little but the bare necessities, people who supported your democracy but were unable to assist it because of their age'[7]; likewise, minors were not yet able to take part, as regrets an anonymous litigant in the 380s: 'I am thirty-two years old, and this is now the twentieth year since you returned from exile, so clearly I was thirteen when my father was killed by the Thirty. At that age I did not know what an oligarchy was, and I could not have assisted him when he was wronged.'[8]

---

[4] Ruschenbuch 1966, pp. 82–3 (who thinks it inauthentic). See Forsdyke 2005, pp. 98–9.
[5] Lysias, *Against Philon* (31), 27 (our emphasis). See Bers 1975.   [6] Van't Wout 2010.
[7] Lysias, *Against Philon* (31), 18.
[8] Lysias, *Against Theomnestus I* (10), 4 (384/3 BC). At the end of his speech (§31), the litigant specifies that he sought to avenge his father's murder as soon as he could, in this case at his majority (probably as early as 398).

But neutrality could also be the result of an informed choice: The sources mention many Athenians who settled abroad during the troubles to quietly go about their business, or remained in the city, secluded in their *oikos*, without joining either camp. To take an interest in these 'nonaligned' individuals is to give their place in history back to the many protagonists who resisted the all-encompassing logic of the *stasis* and the contradictory injunctions that it gave rise to: Choose your side, comrade! But not everything is political in the same way and with the same intensity, either today or in the past: Even in the midst of turmoil, politics does not invest all spheres of existence and all the different layers of society in equal measure. Let us take the case of the small Sicilian city of Nakone, wrenched apart by *stasis* at the beginning of the third century BC and often invoked to demonstrate the centrality of civil war in ancient Greece.[9] With the aim of reconciling the community, each camp was asked to establish a list of thirty enemy citizens; then groups of five 'chosen brothers' (*adelphoi airetoi*) were drawn by lot, associating each time two former enemies and three other citizens taken from the remainder of the civic body. If the ingenuity of this scheme has been widely discussed, little attention has been paid to a fairly major fact: These groups counted only a minority of the former rebels. This evidently shows that the *stasis* had not involved all the citizens of Nakone to the same degree and that many of them were not immediately identifiable as activists of one camp or the other.

The fact remains that the numerous individuals who stayed 'outside any chorus' and refused to play their expected political roles are often difficult to pinpoint objectively in the ancient documentation. This is probably because political neutrality is always the result of a rhetorical construction, either for the prosecution or for the defense: It generally appears to be an argument used by litigants sometimes to defend their own behavior and sometimes to tarnish the reputation of their opponent. Indeed, orators readily stigmatized the Athenians expelled by the Thirty who, instead of rallying to the democrats in Piraeus, had preferred the comfort of exile; symmetrically, many Athenians who remained in the city tried to demonstrate that they had not participated in any way in the exactions of the oligarchy. Socrates represents in this respect a case that is both common and exceptional: common, in that he was far from being the only one not

---

[9] *SEG* 30.1119. On the Nakone inscription, see Dubois 1989, n° 206 and Van Effenterre and Van Effenterre 1988, pp. 687–700 (with translation). See e.g. Loraux 2006, pp. 197, 215–28; Gray 2015, pp. 37–41 (translation, commentary and modeling).

to take sides during the civil war; exceptional, in that he declared this neutrality loud and clear, even if it meant arousing suspicion on both sides.

A final question remains: Did all these 'neutral individuals' form a chorus in their own right? What links can be established between people who have remained outside the field of political confrontation – strangers to the 'bond of division,' to paraphrase Nicole Loraux? To put it another way: Is it possible to 'make community' out of abstention, even if it is an active choice?

Negative Neutrality: In Exile

If the Peloponnesian War had obliged many Athenians to leave their residences temporarily to take refuge in the city or in the Piraeus (Thucydides 2.17.1–3), the *stasis* in 404 led to population movements of a completely different scale. The Thirty indeed forced many citizens into exile, in particular the most committed democrats. This exodus was accentuated when the list of the Three Thousand was published: Many Athenians left the city thereafter because they were henceforth deprived of the legal protection attached to citizenship.[10] If these upheavals mechanically swelled the ranks of Thrasybulus' army, all the exiles were, however, far from joining the fighters in Phyle and the Piraeus, or did so only much later, during the very last weeks of the conflict.[11]

Illness as an Excuse

In front of the juries of the popular courts, these former exiles tried to make people forget their prudence of that time – which could pass for cowardice – as shown by a speech pronounced by a disabled Athenian and composed by Lysias, shortly after the end of the civil war. Threatened with being deprived of the allowance that helped him to survive, the litigant makes a point of recalling his conduct under the Thirty. Never was he associated, in any way, with their acts of *hubris*, he claims: 'But I went into exile at Chalcis with the people, and although I could have shared in the *politeia* with them, I preferred *to share in the danger* with all of you.'[12] The soaring rhetoric is beautiful: The *adunatos* claims to be a full member of the Athenian resistance. However, his statement is enough to make one smile. First of all, the Athenian oligarchs had probably never envisaged

---

[10] Diodorus of Sicily, 14.32.4.   [11] Lysias, *Against Philon* (31), 9.
[12] Lysias, *On the Refusal of a Pension* (24), 25 (transl. Todd slightly modified, our emphasis).

making this destitute invalid an active member of their *politeia*!¹³ In all probability, he had no choice but to remain in the city and was forced to go into exile once the civic body was redefined by the Thirty; then, as he partially admits himself, he was never an active resistance fighter: Not only did he not rally to the partisans of Thrasybulus in Phyle (who mostly came from Thebes) since he chose to settle in Euboea, far from the combat zone, but he also did not join 'those of Piraeus,' a few weeks later, otherwise he would surely have bragged about it in front of the jury. His 'share in the danger' was therefore limited to undergoing exile and settling as a metic in a city bordering Athens. He was not the only one to make this choice: 'But I went into exile at Chalcis *with the people*,' he says. This is where the truth comes out and reveals, in passing, how many exiles made this prudent choice, while waiting to see how the military situation was going to evolve.

At the other end of the social spectrum, one case allows us to show the full extent of this chorus of individuals banished by the Thirty and yet not involved in the resistance. Shortly after the restoration of democracy, between 402 and 398, a member of the outgoing Council attacked one of the new councilors drawn by lot – a certain Philon – on the occasion of the examination prior to his entry into office (*dokimasia*). The accuser entrusted Lysias with the task of composing the speech that, beyond the case in point, stigmatized all the citizens who had bided their time: 'My contention is that it is not right for anybody else to offer advice in our affairs, other than those who in addition to being citizens are also enthusiastic (*epithumountas*) about their citizenship.'¹⁴ To deliberate properly, it is not enough to be a citizen in name; it is also necessary to manifest the *desire* (*epithumia*) to participate in the affairs of the community. How better to express that citizenship is not only a matter of rights and status, but also of attachment, even of passion?

Far from respecting this ideal of commitment, Philo apparently acted as a simple 'citizen by birth,' preoccupied only by his personal comfort. To demonstrate this point, the accuser gives an account of his behavior during the civil war. 'This man, together with the majority of the citizens, was banished by herald from the town by the Thirty. For a time, he lived in the countryside (*en agrôi*)' – that is, in Attica, where he owned land. At this point, nothing can be blamed on him yet. But everything changes a few weeks later:

---

¹³ See Wolpert 2001, p. 104.   ¹⁴ Lysias, *Against Philon* (31), 5.

> When those from Phyle returned from exile to Piraeus, not only those from the countryside but also those from abroad rallied together, some of them to the town and others to Piraeus, each bringing help to the fatherland to the extent that he was able, this man did the opposite of all the other citizens.[15]

Like the invalid defended by Lysias, Philo thus spent most of the civil war outside Athens, taking up residence as a metic. Like him too, he seems to have used his infirmity as a pretext to justify his attitude. But his accuser rejects in advance the argument of disability by underlining that, even though physically diminished, he possessed a 'sufficient property'[16] to support the democrats financially, 'as many other citizens did, because they were unable to undertake this duty in person.'[17] Worse still, it seems that Philo remained comfortably sheltered until everything was over: He was not even one of the resistance fighters of the eleventh hour, who changed sides 'when they saw that those of Phyle succeed in their efforts.'[18] The conclusion is therefore without appeal: 'So it is not fitting that he should be treated as a friend of those who were in the town, because he did not deign to join them when they were in danger, or as a friend of those who captured Piraeus, because he was not willing to return with them from exile, even though he himself had also been made an exile.'[19]

A Nonaligned Party?

Beyond its explicit target, this speech indirectly reveals what a mass phenomenon neutrality was in Athens. For, in listening carefully to the accuser, we learn that many Athenians waited a long time before taking sides. For what is Philo reproached? To have not chosen a side *after* the capture of Piraeus by Thrasybulus. More than half of the civil war had already gone by at this precise moment: While the Thirty had taken power in September 404 (at the latest) and democracy was restored a little more than one year later, in September or October 403, the capture of Piraeus occurred probably only in April or May.[20] That is to say, for more than half of the conflict involvement in the democratic resistance was much

---

[15] Lysias, *Against Philon* (31), 8–9. [16] Lysias, *Against Philon* (31), 14.
[17] Lysias, *Against Philon* (31), 14. Lysias knows here what he is talking about: Forced into exile to escape the Thirty, he spent (a part of) what was left of his fortune to support financially 'those of Phyle,' even though he was not himself a citizen (cf. *Against Hippotherses*, fr. 170 Carey). See *infra*, Chapter 10, p. 267.
[18] Lysias, *Against Philon* (31), 9. [19] Lysias, *Against Philon* (31), 13.
[20] On these decisive chronological questions, see *infra*, Conclusion, pp. 309–15.

more the exception than the rule, even among the Athenians banished by the Thirty.[21]

Furthermore, the speech suggests that even once Piraeus was in the hands of the democrats, many exiles refused to join Thrasybulus and his men, not believing they would win. The orator alludes to this by making Philo the leader of a true 'nonaligned party':

> If any group of citizens remain who shared in the same activities as this man, and if ever they take control of the city – though I pray this may never happen – let him claim with them that he has a right to be a Council-member.[22]

The logic of the sentence is tortuous. What are in fact the 'activities of Philo' mentioned by the speaker? Precisely that he didn't act in these troubled times! The speaker thus imagines, around his opponent, a chorus of citizens actively engaged in disengagement. This remark, which aims to turn Philo into a zealot for inaction and to unite a party of abstention around him, should probably not be taken too literally. But beyond the rhetorical exaggeration, the speech does suggest the existence of a mass of nonaligned citizens who, at least imaginatively, could be considered as a group in their own right within the restored democracy.

This 'third party' was nevertheless very heterogeneous, since it associated individuals with varied profiles – rich and poor, young and old, former exiles as well as recent outcasts. There were also Athenians with even more atypical trajectories, defying the beautiful bipartition between 'those of the city' and 'those of the Piraeus': Some Athenians belonged to one camp before rallying to the other during the conflict. In fact, the civil war cannot be seen as one block, where political choices were fixed forever. The case of Callimachus, attacked by a client of the orator Isocrates, is in this respect symptomatic. The accused is undoubtedly part of the Athenian elite: He is a member of the Three Thousand and remained in town for most of the civil war. It was only at the beginning of the summer of 403 that he finally decided to leave Athens following a conflict of interest with another member of the oligarchy. According to Isocrates, Callimachus acted as a good opportunist: Initially, he was a passionate participant in the regime of the Thirty, before joining 'those of the Piraeus' just as victory seemed to be within their grasp. As a proof of his duplicity, he apparently left Thrasybulus' troops with haste: When the Spartans went to the aid of 'those of the city,' momentarily reversing the balance of power during the summer of 403, 'again he escaped from there and lived in

---

[21] See Krentz 1982, p. 152 (table); Stern 2003.   [22] Lysias, *Against Philon* (31), 14.

Boeotia. Therefore, he ought to be inscribed among the deserters rather than named among the exiles.'[23]

Isocrates certainly shows immense bad faith in his description.[24] If we stick to the factual elements given by Isocrates' client and free them from the cloak of rhetoric that surrounds them, Callimachus seems actually to have been a citizen with little political inclination. He is the perfect embodiment of all those individuals who, during the civil war, tried to survive in troubled times, navigating as best they could between the two camps.

Ultimately, Callimachus' itinerary reminds us how far the Three Thousand were from unanimously supporting the Thirty. Apart from a small but active minority – the Thirty, the Ten and the Eleven, as well as the Councilors and the cavalry, often unwillingly involved in the repression of the opponents – the majority of the Athenians who had remained in the city looked on at the crimes they committed as simple spectators. This is at least what they tried to pretend in the aftermath of the civil war. When they were dragged before the popular courts, they readily emphasized their inaction – for example, consider Diognetus, who, according to his nephew, 'under the oligarchy, did not exercise any magistracy.'[25] Stigmatized among the exiles, neutrality was on the contrary a cardinal virtue for 'those of the city.'[26]

Positive Neutrality: In the City

Let us return for a moment to the speech against Callimachus. Contrary to his adversary who left late, Isocrates' client remained in town during the whole civil war. Worse still, his connections with several magistrates of the

---

[23] Isocrates, *Against Callimachus* (18), 49.
[24] The whole speech must be read as a preventive attack by Isocrates' client, intended to make people forget his own involvement in the oligarchic regime. See in this respect Wolpert 2001, p. 105. There is no indication that Callimachus actively participated in the oligarchic regime, except that the speaker asserts this without proof in order to better discredit him in front of the jurors: He obviously did not hold any official position under the Thirty – otherwise his opponent would not have failed to point it out; he even seems to have cultivated good relations with some exiles of Piraeus, since one of them trusted him enough to leave with him a large sum of money before going into exile (*Against Callimachus* [18], 5). It is rather his opponent – Isocrates' client, himself a member of the Three Thousand – who seems to have benefited from powerful support within the oligarchy: Doesn't he admit to having been a friend of the *archon basileus* Patrocles, appointed under the Thirty? Is he not also supported by Rhinon – one of the members of the decarchy that succeeded the Thirty, already discussed in the preceding chapter – who comes to testify in his favor at the trial?
[25] Lysias, *On the Property of the Brother of Nicias* (18), 9–10. Probably exiled in 411, this brother of Nicias had come back to Athens under the Thirty; instead of seeking revenge against the democrats, it seems he used his influence with the king of Sparta, Pausanias – with whom he had a bond of hospitality (§10) – to warn him against the bloody drift of the Athenian oligarchy.
[26] Wolpert 2001. The men of the city therefore distinguished themselves from the Thirty and their supporters by recounting not what they did but what they did not do.

oligarchy were sufficiently notorious for he himself to mention them in his speech. In this context, it was all the more important for him to show that he had in no way taken part in the sinister actions of the Thirty: 'I shall be shown to have caused no one monetary loss, nor have I put anyone in physical danger, nor have I erased anyone from the list of those having citizenship, nor have I inscribed anyone on the list with Lysander.'[27] While the Thirty encouraged 'those of the city' to do evil, he never did anything of this kind, he proclaims. How then could anyone imagine him misbehaving during the ultimate phase of the *stasis*, 'when the Thirty had been thrown out, when Piraeus had been taken, when the people (*dēmos*) were in power and there were discussions about a reconciliation'?[28] While it is not very convincing, his demonstration quite clearly reveals the expected behavior of the citizens who remained in the city during the oligarchy: They could not be reproached as long as they had not *actively participated* (*metechein*) in the oligarchy – by criminal acts or by the exercise of important functions.

Declarations of Tranquility

Still, it is necessary to specify what was at stake: The majority of the Three Thousand risked absolutely nothing in legal terms, since they were protected by the amnesty set up in 403 and the commitment 'not to hold grudges' (only the Thirty, the Ten and the Eleven had been excluded from the agreement, as we have seen).[29] On the other hand, 'those of the city' could be barred from access to the magistracies in the restored democracy if they were convicted of having been magistrates under the oligarchy or of having served as cavalrymen – the armed wing of the Thirty.[30]

Such is precisely the accusation brought against a certain Mantitheus, about ten years after 403, when he took his preliminary examination to enter the Council. Composed by Lysias, his defense aimed to prove that he 'did not serve in the cavalry, and was not even present in Athens, under the Thirty, nor did [he] have a share in the constitution that existed at that time.'[31] His line of defense rested in this case on a temporal argument: Having settled with his family by the Black Sea during the last phase of the Peloponnesian War, Mantitheus claimed to have returned to Athens only

---

[27] Isocrates, *Against Callimachus* (18), 16.   [28] Isocrates, *Against Callimachus* (18), 17.
[29] This is not quite true, since they could be reintegrated into the community, provided they explained themselves: Pseudo-Aristotle, *Athenian Constitution*, 39.6.
[30] Lysias, *On the Scrutiny of Euandros* (26), 9–10.
[31] Lysias, *In Defense of Mantitheus* (16), 3: *oude metechon tēs tote politeias*.

at the very end of the Thirty's reign. 'We were not in Athens either when the walls were being destroyed or when the constitution was being changed. We came back only five days before the men from Phyle returned from exile to Piraeus' – that is to say, in April/May 403.[32] This choice of date owes nothing to chance: The accused had every interest in maintaining that he had returned to the city as late as possible, so as not to be associated with the crimes of the Thirty (deposed only one week after his return); but he also had to claim to have arrived *before* Thrasybulus had taken Piraeus. For otherwise how could he justify not rallying to the resistance fighters, even though he had reached Piraeus? One thing is clear: Neutrality was not only a matter of space – between the city and its port – but also of time – neither too early, nor too late.[33]

Lysias had already praised the neutrality of the Three Thousand in an earlier speech, composed for an anonymous citizen on the occasion of the scrutiny (*dokimasia*) to serve on the Council. Undoubtedly delivered shortly after 400,[34] his speech was given at a time when democratic power was solidifying (i.e. shortly after the liquidation of the last oligarchic bastion in Eleusis and at the very moment Socrates was brought to justice). Accused of having conspired against democracy, the defendant starts by relativizing the cleavage between democracy and oligarchy.[35] He is, nevertheless, keen to differentiate his own behavior under both regimes. During the time of the democracy, he asserts that he always behaved as an active and loyal citizen: He provided several trierarchies (costly warships), fought at sea on four occasions and even paid numerous contributions for amounts higher than what was required of him. He stepped up personally and paid from his own pocket for the survival of the regime. During the oligarchy, on the contrary, he became a citizen, who, if not passive, was at least 'quiet' (*apragmōn*): He did not exercise any magistracy and was not a member of the Council appointed at the time: 'But if I was unwilling to hold office when I could have done so, it is right that I should now be

---

[32] Lysias, *In Defense of Mantitheus* (16), 3–4.
[33] Obviously, the argument of Mantitheus is fragile, even reversible. One could accuse him of having returned to Athens at the precise moment when the oligarchs needed reinforcements to crush the democratic resistance in the process of constitution. This is why Mantitheus resorts to an argument of plausibility to reinforce his demonstration: 'It was hardly likely that after arriving at such a critical time, we should have wanted to share in other people's dangers (*epithumein metechein tōn allotriōn kindunōn*)' (*In Defense of Mantitheus* [16], 5). The accused thus presents himself as a disengaged man, raising his nonparticipation to the rank of a political ideal.
[34] Lysias, *Defense Against a Charge of Subverting the Democracy* (25). See Piovan 2011, pp. 181–230 and, in particular, pp. 191–4: the speech is not fictitious and was undoubtedly delivered, despite the doubts of Dover 1968, pp. 188–9.
[35] Lysias, *Defense Against a Charge of Subverting the Democracy* (25), 8, 12. See Lateiner 1981b.

honored by you.'³⁶ As we might expect, he also claims not to have committed any crime during this troubled period.³⁷

But the praise of his own inaction goes even further: 'For it is clear that during the oligarchy, nobody suffered summary arrest (*apagoge*) at my hands, none of my enemies was punished, *and I did not do any good to a single friend*.³⁸ After having recalled that he did not harm anyone during the oligarchy – according to an argument often used³⁹ – the accused even argues that he did not help any of his relatives either! How can we explain this paradoxical apology for not helping friends in need? To cut short suspicion, the defendant wanted to present himself as an inactive individual in public as well as in private, for good as well as for bad. Radical passivity is indeed the argument he puts forward to demand the jury's indulgence:

> You should regard as enemies not those who did not go into exile but those who sent you there; *not those who wished to preserve their own property* but those who stole the property of others; not those who remained in the town *for the sake of their own safety* but *those who took a part in public affairs* because they wanted to destroy other people.⁴⁰

This drastic cut-off between participation (in public affairs) and withdrawal (into the private sphere) certainly arouses suspicion: How could the litigant have avoided any reversal of fortune without being involved in any way in the oligarchy?⁴¹ But the truth matters little in this instance. Beyond his personal case, the speech of this anonymous man gives us access to what was the line of defense probably adopted by all 'those of the city' after 403: It is for having been 'quiet' under the oligarchy that they could argue for their right to go back to being active citizens in the restored democracy.⁴²

---

³⁶ Lysias, *Defense Against a Charge of Subverting the Democracy* (25), 14.
³⁷ Lysias, *Defense Against a Charge of Subverting the Democracy* (25), 16: 'It is also clear that I did not place anybody on the catalogue of the Athenians, or obtain an arbitration verdict at anybody's expense, or become rich because of your misfortunes.'
³⁸ Lysias, *Defense Against a Charge of Subverting the Democracy* (25), 15 (our emphasis).
³⁹ Cf. Isocrates, *Against Callimachus* (18), 16; Lysias, *In Defense of Mantitheus* (16), 8.
⁴⁰ *Defense Against a Charge of Subverting the Democracy* (25), 18 (our emphasis). See Cloché 1915, pp. 86–7.
⁴¹ Wolpert 2001, p. 112.
⁴² This opposition appears in the choice of the terms employed by the orator (*Defense Against a Charge of Subverting the Democracy* [25], 17 [our emphasis]): 'But in fact I have consistently followed this principle: during oligarchy *not to covet* (*mē epithumein*) other people's property, and during democracy to spend my own property *eagerly* (*prothumōs*) on yourselves.' Another speech by Lysias (*Defense in the Matter of the Olive Stump* (7), delivered in 397/6) takes the defense of a citizen with a rather similar profile. The accused is a rich and influential man (§21), owner of several fields (§24) and 'living far from business (*hēsuchian agonti*)' (§1). A member of the Three Thousand in 404, he took advantage of the civil war to acquire land, probably at a low price, before

Autarky as a Political Fiction

One final piece of testimony makes it possible to better define the profile of these individuals who remained in the city but claimed to have sought only the 'safeguarding of their own interests.' It has the advantage of coming from someone directly involved in the conflict, Xenophon, who was actively engaged as a cavalryman in the oligarchic camp.[43] In the *Memorabilia* – a work devoted to defending the memory of Socrates – he stages a dialogue dating from 404–403, during which his master gives advice to an Athenian from the city, a certain Aristarchus, who is worried about not being able to feed his whole household in these difficult times.

In many ways, Socrates' interlocutor appears less as a real character than as the incarnation of a social type. First of all, Aristarchus is not known by any other source, and thus has no biographical depth other than that Xenophon gives him[44]; secondly, his name seems to have been chosen on purpose to point out to the reader that he was a distinguished Athenian: *Aristarchos* means 'the power (*archè*) of the best (*aristoi*)'. The rest of the dialogue does not contradict this etymology: In a few sentences, Xenophon portrays him as a rich landowner with a lot of capital to his name and a member of the Three Thousand.

At the time of the dialogue, however, Aristarchus is in dire straits:

> 'Ah yes, Socrates, I am in great distress (*aporia*). Since the *stasis* began, there has been an exodus to the Piraeus, and a crowd of my women-folk, being left behind, are come to me – sisters, nieces and cousins – so that we are fourteen people of free condition (*eleutherous*) in the house without counting the slaves.'[45]

Aristarchus therefore accommodated in his house many relatives abandoned by their guardians, who had left to join the army of Thrasybulus in exile. This is a way to remind us that the *stasis* tore Athenian families apart and that brothers, cousins, uncles and nephews did not all support the same side; it also highlights the fact that the civil war was not only the business of adult men, but also affected in turn the women and the children placed under their protection. Likewise, it suggests, in implicit contrast with the 'people of free condition,' the presence of many slaves

---

immediately leasing it (§9): Here again, personal interest seems to have taken precedence over any political consideration. See *infra*, Chapter 6, pp. 188–91.

[43] Canfora 2001, pp. 28–9 (Xenophon may even have been one of the two hipparchs commanding the Athenian horsemen).

[44] *LGPN* 2, s.v. Aristarchos n° 3; see also Nails 2002, pp. 46–7.

[45] Xenophon, *Memorabilia*, 2.7.2 (translation Loeb modified).

within the household, who were equally affected by the consequences of the conflict. Finally, it indicates that Aristarchus personally did not suffer the consequences of his role in the government of the Thirty: If he was able to remain in the city, it is because he was part of the Three Thousand, as was his interlocutor Socrates.

Nothing is, however, said about Aristarchus' possible oligarchic leanings. On the contrary, Xenophon presents him as a man entirely absorbed by the management of his household, without any apparent political commitment. This is because of his dire situation: Cut off from his lands because of the occupation of Piraeus by the democrats, he cannot rent the various houses that he possesses in city – the plural reflecting his fortune – for lack of interested tenants. Even borrowing has become impossible as trust between citizens is gone. He fears that he will not be able to feed his family. In this tense atmosphere, there is a risk the *oikos* may quickly fall apart.

To keep this sinister fate at bay, Socrates recommends Aristarchus puts his relatives to work producing clothes to ensure the survival of the *oikos*. The philosopher invites his interlocutor to go beyond the prejudices of the Athenian elite, which sees in these productive tasks only a slave's occupation: According to the philosopher, such work would set in motion a virtuous circle, producing benefit upon benefit[46]: 'but if you exert your authority and make them work, you will love them, when you find that they are profitable to you, and they will be fond of you, when they feel that you are pleased with them. Both you and they will like to recall past kindnesses and will strengthen the feeling of gratitude (*charin*) that these engender.'[47] No sooner said than done: Aristarchus manages to get the necessary funds to buy wool, and the women of the household set to work. Very quickly, cheerfulness comes to drive out the gloom.

In this festive *oikos*, all the positions are, however, not equal. While the women of the house work willingly, Aristarchus does not get his own hands dirty. To justify this inaction, Socrates encourages his friend to remind his female relatives of the fable of the dog protecting the flock: 'Do not I keep you from being stolen by thieves, and carried off by wolves,'[48] says the dog to the sheep. Like an attentive shepherd, Aristarchus thus ensures the protection of the group from external dangers. This is precisely where the fiction of a politically inactive owner, withdrawn into his household and living in isolation, brutally bursts apart. No *oikos* is an

---

[46] See Azoulay 2018, pp. 173–6, 214. [47] Xenophon, *Memorabilia*, 2.7.9.
[48] Xenophon, *Memorabilia*, 2.7.14.

island: To protect his family, Aristarchus cannot stay at home, but must necessarily get involved in the life of the city: politically, to protect his relatives from outside intrusions; financially, to be able to borrow the seed capital for his new enterprise; economically, to find commercial outlets for his produce; socially, since he has to go and ask for the help of Socrates to elaborate this safeguard plan.

But for Aristarchus, as for the majority of the Athenians who remained in the city, it was important to maintain the fiction of their political disengagement: They claimed *a posteriori* not to have taken any part in the oligarchy, having lived in seclusion in their own houses and looked after their own interests alone. This is not a paradox in the least, considering that the Thirty's project was to reserve to the Three Thousand the right to participate actively in the city. It was as if the only citizens who had the right to be active were in actual fact passive and voluntarily gave up their exclusive privilege.[49]

There is, however, a member of the Three Thousand whose behavior challenges this strange inversion of normality: Socrates, Aristarchus' interlocutor, who promoted radical neutrality and militant noncommitment.

Radical Neutrality: Elusive Socrates

Let's postpone Socrates' entry into the fray for a few more moments, or, more precisely, let's observe his career as reflected by another Athenian, who was brought before the courts at the same time as him: the orator Andocides. Between their respective judicial paths, there are indeed powerful parallels which allow, *in fine*, to show Socrates' singularity with all the more clarity.

False Twins: Socrates and Andocides

First of all, let us note the synchronism of the two trials: While the philosopher was tried in the spring of 399,[50] Andocides went to court six months before or six months later (in the fall of 400 or in the fall of 399). In both cases, the indictment had a religious background: Socrates was accused of introducing new gods into the city, and Andocides was attacked for having taken part in the Eleusinian Mysteries while a previous decree expressly forbade him to do so because of his participation, fifteen years earlier, in the desecration of that ceremony. Furthermore, Socrates

---

[49] Mossé 1979.   [50] Diogenes Laertius, 2.44.

and Andocides were both prosecuted by the same man, Meletus.[51] The two defendants had one final point in common: Neither of them had taken sides in the civil war – a fact for which they were bitterly criticized.

However, the two cases are not a perfect match. First of all, the two defendants did not share the same network of friends: While Andocides counted Anytus among his supporters, the latter was, on the contrary, among Socrates' accusers. Next, the two men followed two opposite defense strategies: While the philosopher provoked the jury with challenging statements, Andocides tried by all means to convince his listeners to decide in his favor. Above all, their neutrality during the civil war had not taken the same form at all. Whereas Socrates had remained in the city and refused to obey the injunctions of the Thirty, Andocides had kept himself entirely apart from the conflict: Exiled in 415 following the mutilation of the Herms, he had remained abroad until democracy was reestablished in 403, without ever rallying either to the oligarchs in the city or to the democrats in Piraeus. This is, indeed, what he is reproached for in a speech attributed to the orator Lysias.[52] According to his adversary, the reconciliation agreement indeed applied only to 'those of the city' and to 'those of the Piraeus,' and not to those who were already in exile at the time of the *stasis*:

> On this point I shall argue that Andocides has nothing to do with the agreements: certainly not, by Zeus, the ones you arranged with the Spartans, nor the ones that those from Piraeus swore towards those in the town (*astu*). [...] We were not fighting for his sake, and did not become reconciled only when we could extend a share in the agreement to him as well. The agreement and the oaths took place not for the sake of one man, but for the sake of us – those from the town and those from Piraeus. It would be strange if, when we were in a difficult situation, we had taken an interest in Andocides (who was not in Athens) and how his offenses could be wiped out.[53]

To benefit from amnesty, he should have chosen one side or the other, or at least he should have suffered the misfortunes caused by the civil war.

---

[51] See Todd 2007, pp. 408–9. This is why Andocides and Socrates both allude, in their respective pleas, to the killing of a virtuous citizen, Leon of Salamis, under the Thirty (Andocides, *On the Mysteries* [1], 94; Plato, *Apology of Socrates*, 32c-d): This was probably to embarrass Meletus, their common accuser, who had been involved in this summary execution. See here, *infra*, pp. 160–1.

[52] On these questions of attribution, see Todd 2007, pp. 408–9, according to whom the speech could have been composed by Meletus himself.

[53] Lysias, *Against Andocides* (6), 38–9. It is on this polemical passage that Carawan 2013 argues that the amnesty was not general in scope, but only a set of written provisions (*sunthēkai*) with a limited scope. This interpretation, however, does not stand up to scrutiny: see Joyce 2014, 2015.

Since he did not meet any of these conditions, Andocides was placed in a legal limbo that eventually would lead to his death, at least according to his accuser. Since no convention protected him, he could even be killed with impunity: 'You should realize that by punishing Andocides and getting rid of him, you are purifying the city and freeing it from pollution, driving away the scapegoat (*pharmakos*), and getting rid of something accursed – because this man falls into that category.'[54]

It is in the light of these heavy charges that the defense of Andocides makes sense. Not only does the defendant want to point out his active commitment to the service of the city since his return in 403, but he also seeks to justify his absence during the civil war. His argument then takes an original turn: Andocides asks his audience to imagine the fate he would have suffered if he had been present in town at that time. In an exercise of counterfactual history, Andocides stages, in the form of a dialogue, the judicial questioning to which Charicles, one of the most fanatical of the Thirty, would have inevitably subjected him:

> 'Tell me, Andocides,' he'd ask, 'did you go to Deceleia and fortify it against your country?' 'No, I didn't.' 'Well, did you plunder the countryside, and rob your fellow-citizens by land or sea?' 'No.' 'Didn't you even fight against Athens at sea, or help to demolish the walls, or help to subvert the democracy, or force your way back to Athens?' 'No, I haven't done any of those things.' 'None at all? Then do you expect to get away without being put to death, as a lot of other people have been?' Do you think I'd have got any other treatment than that, because of my loyalty to you, gentlemen, if [the Thirty]'d caught me? [. . . T]hey would have put me to death like other people because I committed no offense against Athens.[55]

Through fictionalized conversation, Andocides is therefore presented as a potential victim of the oligarchy, put to death at the end of an expeditious trial: Only his providential absence from Athens allowed him to escape a programmed execution. How could he, then, be reproached for having remained in exile?

Obviously, this thought experiment did not explain, in particular, why Andocides had not joined the democrats in Piraeus to assist them in their fight.[56] But whatever the weaknesses of the argumentation, it testifies to a fine effort, on the part of the defendant, to justify his absence: In short, he claims his neutrality was imposed, not chosen. This is the most striking

---

[54] Lysias, *Against Andocides* (6), 53. See Eck 2011.   [55] Andocides, *On the Mysteries* (1), 101–2.
[56] See Wolpert 2001, p. 106.

difference with the trial of Socrates, during which the philosopher actively declared his noninvolvement in the civil war.

Socrates the Extravagant

Approaching Socrates' case is always to step out upon shaky ground insofar as the philosopher has left no written record behind him: While he never stops speaking in the Platonic dialogues or the comedies of Aristophanes, it is never actually he who speaks, but always others give him voice for apologetic or critical purposes – think of the *Apologies of Socrates* written by Xenophon and Plato, or, symmetrically, the *Accusation of Socrates* (*Katēgoria Sokratous*) composed by Polycrates.[57] Thenceforth, we risk getting trapped in these distorting mirror images that all share the same goal: to build up the Socratic exception, for better or for worse. If this polemical construction hinders analysis, it may be possible to control these biases by comparing Socrates' trajectory with that of other Athenians who, like Andocides, claimed they remained neutral during the civil war. It is indeed in the light of this vast 'neutral' chorus that Socrates' path appears both banal and exceptional; banal, in that, like so many others, the philosopher chose to stay in town and proclaimed *a posteriori* that he had not participated in the crimes of the oligarchy; exceptional, in that the philosopher also refused to get involved in the functioning of democracy, declaring he would remain radically neutral whatever the regime.

To understand the originality of the Socratic position in this matter, we should probably start by exploring the very particular relationship the philosopher had with the city of Athens. If Andocides embodies the figure of the exile, wandering from place to place without any real attachment – at least until his return in 403 – Socrates appears on the contrary as the man of a single city. Rooted in the soil of Athens from his birth to his death, the philosopher stubbornly refuses to leave his homeland, proving to be the most Athenian of all Athenians:

> You would not have dwelt here *more consistently of all the Athenians* if the city had not been exceedingly pleasing to you. You have never left the city, even to see a festival, nor for any other reason except military service; you

---

[57] On the exact content and purpose of this work, see the opposing positions of Chroust 1957 and Livingstone 2001, p. 39. Apologetic speeches were particularly numerous: According to Diogenes Laertius (2.121–5), Antisthenes, Aeschines, Phaedo, Euclides and many others composed such dialogues. The trial of Socrates was a founding event, giving birth to an authentic literary genre: the 'Socratic discourse' (*logos sokratikos*), explicitly recognized as such by Aristotle: *Poetics*, 1.1447a28–b13; *Rhetoric*, 3.16.1417a18–21; fr. 72 Rose.

have never gone to stay in any other city, as people do; you have had no desire to know another city or other laws.[58]

Before, during and after the civil war, Socrates always remained in the city, without ever seeking shelter abroad, regardless of the circumstances. Even after his death sentence, he refused to flee to Megara, Boeotia or Thessaly, as his friends urged him to do[59]: This was a puzzling choice, since most condemned men, when able to choose, preferred exile to death.

While he was viscerally attached to Athens, for better or for worse, Socrates behaved like a stranger within the city:

> And you, my remarkable friend, appear to be *totally out of place* (*atopotatos*). [...] Really, just as you say, you seem a foreigner who needs a guide, not to be one of the locals. Not only do you never travel abroad – as far as I can tell, you never even set foot beyond the city walls.[60]

With this lapidary sentence, Phaedrus captures the essence of the Socratic paradox. On the one hand, the philosopher embodies the Athenian *par excellence*: He is, even before the outbreak of the civil war, 'one of the city,' in the literal sense of the expression, since he spends all his time inside the walls, rain or shine, be it the Thirty who are reigning as despots or the demagogues who lead the dance. On the other hand, Socrates acts as a stranger in his own country, as if he were not a full member of it. For we must take Phaedrus at his word: Socrates is a man 'out of place' (*atopos*) – that is, elusive, confusing and extravagant.[61] This is because the philosopher never followed the expected paths: He liked nothing more than to confound his interlocutors with his provocative thoughts, his repeated feints and his contradictory doctrines, often causing perplexity, even stupefaction.[62]

Elusive and unlocatable, Socrates evades understanding on all levels. Socially, he is hard to place: If the philosopher seems poor at first sight, walking barefoot and wearing a modest outfit,[63] is he really? Isn't he rich enough to fight as a hoplite, owner of his weapons?[64] Doesn't he consider

---

[58] Plato, *Crito*, 52b (transl. Cooper 1997; our emphasis). Cf. *Meno*, 80b; *Phaedrus*, 230c–d. In this, Socrates is the counterpart of Aristippus of Cyrene, one of his interlocutors, who refuses to 'lock himself into any citizenship' (Xenophon, *Memorabilia*, 2.1.13).
[59] Plato, *Crito*, 44c; *Phaedo*, 99a.
[60] Plato, *Phaedrus*, 230c–d (transl. Cooper 1997; our emphasis).
[61] On this translation of *atopia*, see Pontier 2006, p. 185.
[62] Plato, *Meno*, 80a. Cf. *Symposium*, 215a, 221c–d; *Phaedrus*, 229c, 230c; *Theaetetus*, 149a. See Dorion 2013, pp. 416, 422–4, on the doctrinal lability of the philosopher (cf. e.g. Plato, *Alcibiades*, 106a).
[63] Plato, *Apology of Socrates*, 23b–c, 31c, 36d.
[64] Plato, *Laches*, 181b; *Apology of Socrates*, 28e; *Symposium*, 220c–221c.

himself a good household manager who knows how to save money, leaving him with a surplus?[65] And above all, isn't the philosopher reputed to have left a certain fortune to his children?[66]

The political position of Socrates is even more confusing: While his disciples readily present him as a 'man of the people' (*dēmotikos*), open to all and counting among his closest friends apparent democrats – such as Chaerephon of Sphettos[67] – his opponents stigmatize him as the educator of bloodthirsty oligarchs and as a tireless fighter against democratic irrationality. If he arouses such contrasting assessments, it is precisely because his behavior thwarts the expected divisions and, in particular, questions the traditional oppositions between commitment and tranquility, activism and neutrality.

Throughout his life, Socrates chose to stay away from active political life because his divine sign – his famous 'daimon' – dissuaded him from doing so: 'This is what prevents me from *getting involved in politics* (*ta politika prattein*) and I think it was quite right to prevent me. Be sure, men of Athens, that if I had long ago attempted *to take part in politics* (*prattein ta politika pragmata*), I should have died long ago.'[68] However, this choice does not correspond to a radical withdrawal into the private sphere, in spite of what some of his opponents may claim[69]: Far from neglecting his duties as a citizen, Socrates always scrupulously obeyed the magistrates and the laws,[70] regularly made sacrifices on the public altars of the city,[71] and he fought with courage in the ranks of the Athenian phalanx.[72] Better still, he participated in the Council of Five Hundred at the end of the Peloponnesian War,[73] which implies that he voluntarily presented himself

---

[65] See Toole 1975; Pébarthe 2014a, pp. 227–31.
[66] Cf. Plutarch, *Aristides*, 1.9 = Demetrius of Phalerum, fr. 102 (Fortenbaugh and Schütrumpf 2000). Socrates is said to have bequeathed to his children, in addition to his house, no less than seventy mines – more than one talent – invested to earn interest by Crito. See Ismard 2013, p. 182.
[67] Xenophon, *Memorabilia*, 1.2.48. Exiled by the Thirty, Chaerephon of Sphettos joined the democrats of Piraeus (Plato, *Apology of Socrates*, 21a). See Rankin 1987.
[68] Plato, *Apology of Socrates*, 31d–32a (transl. Cooper modified; our emphases). See Dorion 2013, p. 173.
[69] In the *Clouds*, Aristophanes presents him as the leader of a sect cut off from the world, according to a clearly Pythagorean model: He cultivates secrecy (v. 140: His word is revealed only to his disciples) to the point that Aristophanes draws a parallel with mystery cults (v. 143). His disciples are presented as initiates (v. 258–9) who gather their teachings in a buried place (v. 198–9), compared to the cave of Trophonios (v. 506–9). However, this is a polemical representation, and the Socratics tend to represent Socrates in public and not in secret.
[70] Xenophon, *Memorabilia*, 4.4.1–4.   [71] *Memorabilia*, 1.1.2.
[72] Plato, *Laches*, 181b, *Apology of Socrates*, 28e, *Symposium*, 220c–221c.   [73] *Hellenica*, 1.7.15.

for the drawing of lots that takes place prior to the exercise of such a function.

Moreover, his (relative) disengagement from 'public affairs' (*pragmata*) is the counterpart of a kind of overcommitment to the informal public space. Although he never spoke at the Assembly, Socrates roamed the city in all directions to question anyone who seemed knowledgeable, be they a citizen or a foreigner.[74] Querying passersby in the streets, in the gymnasium or in the stoas, he favored a form of 'sensitive conception' of the public sphere, breaking with the institutional one.[75] To this end, he spent time in particular public places, such as the stalls of craftsmen located in the immediate surroundings of the Agora. It is therefore, according to a tradition relayed by Diogenes Laertius, in a shoemaker's store located just outside the great Athenian public square that he usually conversed.[76] It is also 'in a saddler's workshop near the Agora' that Socrates talked with the young and ambitious Euthydemus, after realizing that the latter 'did not enter the Agora owing to his youth.'[77] This is undoubtedly one of the most striking characteristics of Socratic action, and also one of the reasons for the hostility aroused by the philosopher, as witnessed in Aristophanes' *Clouds:* Unlike the sophists working in the shadows of private houses,[78] Socrates was eminently *visible*. Traveling through the city and its public spaces – squares, streets and porticoes – he pestered his fellow citizens with questions in the manner of a gadfly,[79] even if it meant hurting common beliefs.

We can therefore better understand what characterizes Socrates' specific mode of engagement in the Athenian city. While the philosopher did not habitually spend time in *institutionalized public places*, such as the law courts or the Pnyx where the Assemblies took place, he did frequent *informal public space*, in the sense meant by Jürgen Habermas – that is, a space for discussions and polemics that passed through unofficial channels and involved citizens and noncitizens, young and old, men and women.[80] Clearly, Socrates saw this as a way to continue to practice politics by other means, through influencing the behavior of his contemporaries and,

---

[74] Plato, *Apology of Socrates*, 23b.   [75] Macé 2009.
[76] Diogenes Laertius, 2.122. See *infra*, Conclusion, p. 300.   [77] *Memorabilia*, 4.2.1.
[78] The opening of the *Protagoras* (314c–315b) is paradigmatic in this respect: Housed in the lodging of the rich Callias, the sophist of Ceos is surrounded by a crowd of citizens and strangers who have come to hear him. Cf. *Gorgias*, 447b–c.
[79] Plato, *Apology of Socrates*, 30e.
[80] Habermas 1989. For a reflection on the adaptation of this concept to Greek history, see Azoulay 2011. On the distinction between public and civic, see Ismard 2012. For a parallel reflection, see Vlassopoulos 2007.

especially, the youngest among them. His opponents were not fooled by this strategy: The Thirty specifically forbade him to speak to young people under thirty,[81] while the radical democrats took him to court for having corrupted the Athenian youth.

Socrates' political neutrality did not aim to assure him a radical form of tranquility (*apragmosunē*), but to give him the time he needed to intervene *differently* in the public space.[82] Besides, he himself was proud of his influence on the political life of the city, in spite of his disdain for institutionalized politics: 'I believe that I'm one of the few Athenians – so as not to say I'm the only one, but the only one among our contemporaries – to take up true political craft and *practice true politics* (*prattein ta politika*).'[83] Of what precisely does the Socratic political art consist? This was a matter of debate among the philosopher's disciples. According to Plato, the philosopher's mode of intervention is characterized by the relentless questioning of the beliefs and prejudices of his contemporaries – by the practice of refutation (*elenchos*) – in the hope of making men better and more just.[84] Xenophon prefers to portray his master's political teaching as more substantial: If Socrates is the only one who really practices politics, it is because he possesses the royal art (*basilikē technē*) – that is, the art of governing men. The philosopher is all the more efficient in this matter since he transmits his knowledge to the largest possible number of apprentices:

> On yet another occasion Antiphon asked him: 'How can you suppose that you make politicians of others, when you yourself avoid politics even if you understand them?' 'How now, Antiphon?' he retorted, 'should I play a more important part in politics by engaging in them alone or by taking pains to turn out as many competent politicians as possible?'[85]

His disengagement from active political life was therefore not meant to renounce any form of influence on the community, but rather to help him act with much greater effectiveness, through all those he had trained.[86]

---

[81] *Memorabilia*, 1.2.35; 4.4.3.
[82] To be a quiet citizen (*apragmōn*) – literally, 'far from business' – did not imply refusing all political participation, but only staying away from forms of excessive involvement in public affairs (speaking in the Assembly, suing others in court, running for office and, in another register, trading aggressively on the Agora). See Demont 2009.
[83] Plato, *Gorgias*, 521d (our emphasis). [84] Plato, *Gorgias*, 517b. Dorion 2013, p. 187.
[85] Xenophon, *Memorabilia*, 1.6.15. Dorion 2013, p. 188.
[86] Cf. *Memorabilia*, 1.2.17; 3.1.7; 4.2, 4.3.1. Only exceptionally does Xenophon deny the political dimension of Socrates' teaching: cf. *Memorabilia*, 1.2.48, and the commentary by Dorion 2013, p. 182 n. 28. In *Memorabilia*, Xenophon wants to offer a concrete example of this art of political mediation in which Socrates excels. He thus reports how the philosopher exhorts the young

Radical Neutrality: Elusive Socrates

If Socrates' puzzling attitude could arouse annoyance, even anger – bringing to mind Aristophanes' snarl against the philosopher in the *Clouds*, at the beginning of the 410s – his disengagement from active political life usually protected him from the most ferocious attacks. However, the situation changed at the end of the Peloponnesian War in a context of exceptional tension: This is when the philosopher clashed head-on with the politicians of his time – be they oligarchs or democrats – in the very name of the conception of active neutrality that he defended.

Socrates the Dissenter

In the Socratic writings, the philosopher comes to embody the figure of the dissident – a man who, at mortal peril, has the courage to oppose democratic excesses as well as oligarchic drifts. In Plato's *Apology*, Socrates evokes two particularly tragic moments that justify, according to him, his choice 'not to get involved politically'[87]: first, his refusal to vote, as a member of the Council, on the condemnation of the generals after the Battle of Arginusai in 406; second, his opposition to the Thirty's order to go and arrest a certain Leon of Salamis in 404/3.

Let's start with the famous Arginusai affair. In 406, the Athenians won an important naval battle against the Spartans not far from the Arginusai islands, off the western coast of present-day Turkey. But their victory left a bitter taste: Because of an unexpected storm, the Athenian generals could not collect the dead or wounded sailors at the end of the combat and thus save the survivors and ensure the dead were given the appropriate funeral

---

Charmides to go up to the Assembly's *bēma*, because of his 'shyness' and because he fears 'ridicule' (3.7.7). According to the philosopher, Charmides should not blush at the idea of speaking in front of the Athenian people, composed of artisans and merchants all more ignorant than the others. Instead of being paralyzed by anxiety, Charmides should not 'neglect the public affairs, if [he has] the power to improve them' (3.7.9). What better way to demonstrate Socrates' political usefulness? However, the interpretation of the passage remains ambiguous because of the identity of Charmides. Born around 440, Charmides is none other than Plato's maternal uncle and Critias' cousin: Accused of having been part of the group that parodied the Eleusinian Mysteries, Charmides is one of the ten magistrates appointed by the Thirty to govern Piraeus (see Nails 2002, pp. 90–4). Is it not therefore paradoxical to present Socrates as the one who allegedly convinced one of the future oligarchs of 404 to enter politics? Should we see it as a blunder on Xenophon's part? It is unlikely. It was probably rather to defend the memory of Charmides: By describing him as a close friend of Socrates, shy and without political ambition, Xenophon was probably trying to distinguish him from his rascal cousin, the enraged Critias, who died at his side during the Battle of Mounychia.

[87] Plato, *Apology of Socrates*, 32a: *mē dēmosieuein*. Xenophon establishes the same connection in the *Memorabilia*, 4.4.2–3, by evoking each of these two episodes in turn.

rites.⁸⁸ As the opportunist he was, Theramenes then excited the anger of the Athenians against the generals, who were accused of high treason before the Assembly.⁸⁹ As a member of the *prytaneis* – that is, the executive committee of the Council of Five Hundred⁹⁰ – Socrates decided to speak out (in vain) against the collective judgment of the generals, which in his eyes symbolized the transgression of all established legal norms.

Plato links this episode to another sequence that took place two years later, during the reign of the Thirty:

> When the oligarchy was established, the Thirty summoned me to the Tholos, along with four others, and ordered us to bring Leon from Salamis, that he might be executed. They gave many such orders to many people, *in order to implicate as many citizens as possible in their crimes* [...]. When we left the Tholos, the other four went to Salamis and brought in Leon, but I went home.⁹¹

Mentioned by Plato as well as by Xenophon,⁹² the episode was primarily intended to exonerate Socrates from any collusion with the Thirty, just as his detractors were accusing him of having collaborated with the oligarchy. But this evocation was probably also meant to hinder one of his accusers, Meletus, who, according to Andocides, was precisely one of the four men who had obeyed the orders of the Thirty and agreed to arrest Leon:

> Again, Meletus here arrested Leon in the time of the Thirty as you all know, and Leon was executed without trial. [...] So the reason why Leon's sons aren't allowed to prosecute Meletus for murder is that the laws have to be applied from the Archonship of Eucleides [403 BC]; for not even the man himself denies that he made the arrest.⁹³

---

⁸⁸ Diodorus of Sicily, 13.100-2 and, especially, Xenophon, *Hellenica*, 1.7.4–11. Pritchett 1985, pp. 204–6, has pointed out that the Athenian generals were accused of abandoning men still alive on sinking ships and not drowned men who had fallen into the sea: Everyone knew that, once in the water, corpses sink immediately and only come to the surface after several days – the time it takes for the decomposition process to proceed sufficiently.

⁸⁹ The *stratēgoi* were subjected to an *eisangelia* procedure before the Assembly after having been deposed – probably after a first vote by a show of hands (*apocheirotonia*): see Hansen 1975, pp. 23, 84–6.

⁹⁰ Depending on the source, Socrates was then member of the *prytaneis* (*Hellenica*, 1.7.14–5) or epistates of the *prytaneis* (*Memorabilia*, 1.1.18, 4.4.2). See Hatzfeld 1940; Dorion 2000, p. 66.

⁹¹ Plato, *Apology of Socrates*, 32c–d (transl. Cooper 1997 modified; our emphasis).

⁹² Cf. Xenophon, *Memorabilia*, 4.4.3 (where the victim is not named); Plato, *Letter VII*, 324d–325a. Xenophon also mentions the execution of Leo of Salamis in the *Hellenica* (2.3.39), but without mentioning the role of Socrates. This silence can be explained by the fact that the episode is mentioned by Theramenes, who had no interest in recalling the philosopher's opposition on this occasion.

⁹³ Andocides, *On the Mysteries* (1), 94. Xenophon also suggests this connection in *Memorabilia* (4.4.3), by mentioning Meletus just after having evoked the arrest of Leon of Salamis. It remains

Linked by Plato as well as by Xenophon, these two transgressive episodes are perhaps even more closely related than they seem. It is indeed possible that Leon of Salamis – the man executed by the Thirty – had previously been part of the board of generals prosecuted in 406 and who fortuitously escaped condemnation.[94]

If this hypothesis is right, the comparison between the two episodes becomes all the more striking: In a certain way, it appears the Thirty completed the persecution initiated by the Popular Assembly! This was a clever way to dismiss radical democracy and bloody tyranny in the name of their common excesses. It was also a way to put Socrates above the fray, by presenting him as a stubborn opponent to any denial of justice, whatever its origin. In the case of Arginusai, Xenophon insists several times on the illegality of the procedure of judging the *stratēgoi* collectively.[95] In the same way, he states that Socrates refused to obey the 'orders' of the Thirty because he considered them 'contrary to the laws' – that is, to the laws as the philosopher himself understood them: 'And when the Thirty gave him an order that was illegal (*para tous nomous*), he refused to obey. [. . .] And when they commanded him and certain other citizens to arrest a man [i.e. Leon of Salamis] on a capital charge, he alone refused, because the command laid on him was illegal (*para tous nomous*).'[96]

Reflected in this way, Socrates' disciples ultimately contributed to transforming the philosopher into a promoter of a new form of neutrality, strictly identified with legality. It is precisely such a depoliticized conception of legality that prevails in the *Crito*, where the laws of the city appear unrelated to the fleeting decision of the judges who condemned the philosopher.[97] Far from being eccentric, this representation resonates with the legislative evolutions of the end of the fifth century. A procedure for

---

to be seen whether it is indeed the same man or a homonym: If the question is ultimately undecidable, at least we can notice that Xenophon chooses here to mention only Meletus, and not his two other coaccusers. See Nails 2002, p. 199–200.

[94] An Athenian named Leon was indeed elected *stratēgos* shortly before Arginusai (Xenophon, *Hellenica*, 1.5.16). How did he escape the trial that led to the death sentence of his colleagues? Let us follow here the hypothesis formulated by McCoy 1975 and preceded by Breitenbach 1873, *ad loc*: In 406, the *stratēgos* Leon was one of the commanders of the Athenian fleet trapped by the Spartans in the port of Mytilene on the island of Lesbos (*Hellenica*, 1.6.16). He was perhaps then among those who, trying to break the blockade, were captured by the Lacedaemonians (*Hellenica*, 1.6.21). Held prisoner, he was unable to fight at the Battle of Arginusai, which apparently allowed him to escape the trial that followed. Leon finally returned to his homeland only at the end of the hostilities, in 404. In fact, Leon is not quoted in Xenophon's account of the battle (*Hellenica*, 1.6.31), whereas all the other *stratēgoi* are named. He also does not appear in the list of the *stratēgoi* given by Diodorus of Sicily (13.71.1). See also Nails 2002, pp. 185–6.

[95] *Hellenica*, 1.7.12; 14; 16–34; *Memorabilia*, 1.1.18; 4.4.2.

[96] *Memorabilia*, 4.4.3. See Gray 2004, p. 150–1.   [97] Ismard 2013, p. 80.

revising the Athenian laws had indeed been initiated as early as 410 and led, after many vicissitudes, to the republication of all the laws in 400/399. Laws (*nomoi*) were henceforth clearly distinguished from simple decrees (*psēphismata*): No decree could come to contradict an existing law, while the introduction of new laws (*nomothesia*) was made more complex and solemn. The sovereignty of the laws became then the watchword of the democracy of the fourth century.[98] In defending a conception of legality independent of the political regime in place, Socrates was part of an ongoing historical process.

Obviously, this representation of Socrates as above the fray is largely the invention of the philosopher's disciples, who were anxious to respond to all those who made of Socrates a sophist and a 'friend of tyranny' (*tyrannikos*), transmitting to his audience the contempt of laws and democracy.[99] But perhaps we should go one step further: Far from being a purely defensive argument, this claim of neutrality also contributed *positively* to the extraordinary aura of the philosopher. For Socrates, in spite of his unattractive physique, seduced his listeners, as suggested by the vocabulary used to describe his engagement with his disciples: *Sunousia* evokes sexual union as much as socializing and living together.[100]

However, his power of attraction resided precisely in the neutrality that he displayed at all levels, including the erotic. Better still, his open disdain of *aphrodisia* made him all the more attractive to those whom he inspired by his words and his conduct: Displaying a sovereign indifference can indeed intensify the charisma of an individual, in the manner of the monk who owes his prestige to his rejection of the worldly desires and the pleasures of the flesh.[101] Political neutrality and erotic indifference thus contributed to reinforce Socrates' seduction of his listeners. From this point of view, it is probably not an exaggeration to speak of a real chorus gravitating around the philosopher, of which he was the munificent *chorēgos*. These links were so intense that they aroused jealousy among

---

[98] Ostwald 1986, pp. 497–524. On the *nomothesia* procedure itself, see Canevaro 2013b.

[99] Gathering some elements of Polycrates' accusation, the *Apology* of Libanios makes it possible to specify the nature of the reproaches addressed to Socrates: Libanius, *Apology of Socrates*, 38 ('Men of Athens, Socrates is training the youth against the laws – the regime is endangered. The sophist is fashioning against us individuals who are bold, tyrannical, insufferable, and who despise equality') and 53 ('Socrates is a hater of the Demos and he is urging his associates to deride the democracy'). See on this subject Humbert 1930, pp. 14–6 and Calder III et al. 2003 (for the translation).

[100] Cf. e.g. *Memorabilia*, 1.1.4; 1.2.8; 3.8.1; 4.8.10; 4.6.1, and the comments of Wolff 1997, pp. 42–3, 45.

[101] See in particular Arthur-Katz 1989 and Brown 1990. Iogna-Prat 1998, pp. 364–6 ('*Refouler le sexe, contrôler l'échange*'), shows how, by renouncing sex, the monks managed to control the Eucharistic sacrifice and, consequently, spiritual power.

the parents of his disciples, who believed themselves supplanted by the philosopher in the hearts of their children. According to Xenophon, this was one of the main reasons why he was prosecuted in the Athenian courts.[102]

Here is what separated Socrates from the other neutral individuals of the city: While neutrality aimed to bring the former oligarchs closer to the city, Socrates' neutrality contributed to separating him from it, by intensifying feelings of love and hate toward him.

The Divided City and Its Backstage

Let's leave the tiny Socratic world and return to the mass of citizens who, during the civil war, had taken refuge in neutrality without making it a policy position. Clearly, this nonaligned chorus was numerous, even if its contours remain a matter of debate. This indetermination is inherent in the polemical nature of the sources that mention the phenomenon: Speaking of neutrality was never neutral, but always an argument for the prosecution or the defense, invoked in legal speeches without it ever being possible to establish with certainty the reality of the commitment (or disengagement) of the various parties.

It does not matter, however, whether Mantitheus or Aristarchus were *really* neutral during the civil war. Whether true or false, their speeches suggest the existence of a political field that cannot be reduced to the sole confrontation between oligarchs and democrats. In this respect, politics cannot be identified with the opposition between friends and enemies – to use the disturbing definition proposed by Carl Schmitt. It must also take into account the situations of uncertainty and the avoidance strategies adopted by many protagonists during the conflict. Even in the turmoil of the civil war, there was therefore room for what Nicole Loraux calls the 'antipolitical.' According to her, indeed, it is possible to discern, at the heart of Athenian tragedies, voices – particularly those of the bereaved women – that contravene the established codes: '[...] any behavior that diverts, rejects, or threatens, consciously or not, the obligations and prohibitions constituting the ideology of the city-state (which in turn creates and maintains civic ideology) is antipolitical.'[103] Is it not therefore

---

[102] Xenophon, *Apology of Socrates*, 20. See Azoulay 2018, pp. 214–6. In Plato too, Socrates plays the role of father: In the Platonic *Apology*, Socrates reminds the Athenians, like a father to his children, that by killing him, they will first harm themselves (*Apology of Socrates*, 31b). Cf. *Phaedo*, 116a and the comments of Derrida 1981, p. 146–7.
[103] Loraux 2002, p. 26.

tempting to extend Nicole Loraux's proposal to another civic genre: that of judicial oratory?[104] In fact the form of communication in court is quite similar to that of the theater: two speakers, surrounded by witnesses and *synēgoroi*, adding their voices to that of the litigant, seeking to move a large audience in charge of choosing the best performance.[105]

Should we take another step forward and suggest the existence of a chorus made up of 'out-of-chorus' participants, or even of a self-aware 'party of no parties' whose members shared common goals? This is doubtful, given the divergent trajectories we have studied. However, the question is perhaps more relevant if we look at the situation after the civil war. Didn't political and judicial conflict give coherence *a posteriori* to experiences that were initially extremely different? In this perspective, conflict and neutrality, far from being incompatible, may have maintained a dialectical relationship: While neutrality had initially been a default choice, it became, due to the hostility it aroused, a political line to defend. Certainly, such a chorus cannot be assimilated to a real political party as the links between its members were ephemeral. But these precarious connections seem emblematic of the more general functioning of political oppositions in Athens, also marked by their changing, even reversible character.

More prosaically, the lives of all these individuals suggest at least the existence of a political backstage that reminds us that other (not directly partisan) preoccupations continued to organize the lives of the inhabitants of Attica, even in the midst of turmoil: Beyond the effervescence of the civil war, it was necessary to continue to live. This is what the story of Aristarchus in the *Memorabilia* allows us to perceive, portraying the daily life of a family in the city, cloistered within its own household and seeking simply to survive in a world turned upside down. Of course, this closure to the outside world is only partial and, as we have seen, Xenophon's text reveals the compromises that the master of the household had to make with the oligarchy in order to protect his family and his property. But if

---

[104] There remains a major difference linked to the judicial genre. Contrary to the theater, this form of antipolitics can never be asserted frontally – in the manner of Antigone – but can be discerned *between the lines*, in the apologetic strategies of the accused as well as in the attacks made by the accusers.

[105] Hall 2006, pp. 353–92. The device used to deliver judicial speeches put the litigants into performance situations close to those of theatrical actors: They spoke from a platform (*bēma*) in the middle of a space toward which the judges' benches were turned. Moreover, the speakers reappropriated certain linguistic devices used in comedy (puns, neologisms, irony, use of incongruity). See Harding 1994, pp. 196–221.

total neutrality is a chimera in times of civil war, the case of Aristarchus allows us to gain access to other experiences of the *stasis* – those of the free women and, undoubtedly, of the children affected by the conflict, while we can also guess at the activities of many slaves in the service of Aristarchus. It is all these lives, illustrated by the abundant documentation produced in the wake of the *stasis*, that we must now bring to light.

CHAPTER 5

Lysimache
The Priestess of Athena and Her Doubles

Freeze frame: It's Boedromion 12, 403. With his troops, Thrasybulus is marching up the Acropolis to make a sacrifice to Athena. At first sight, we can only distinguish men: On one side stand the people of the town, frightened spectators of this intimidating procession; on the other, the victorious democrats – citizens, foreigners, slaves and freedmen – who are already preparing to forgive. As the Athenian civil war comes to an end, women appear absent, as if erased from the picture.

Their presence can be sensed in the background, not only among the anonymous crowd who has come to watch, but also on the Acropolis itself. In a majestic role, the priestess of Athena Polias was necessarily present at Thrasybulus' side, since she was to help him accomplish his sacrifice in the honor of the goddess: 'For if a sacrifice could legally be organized, even carried out, by people not exercising priestly functions, it could not normally be done without the priest or the priestess, especially when consecrating victims or reciting prayers.'[1]

In all likelihood, the priestess of Athena played a central role in this ritual sequence, embodying the very specific participation of Athenian women in the resolution of the conflict. Her name – Lysimache – is known to us thanks to an extraordinary piece of evidence: After her death a few decades later, the priestess was commemorated with a bronze statue erected on the Acropolis, the work of a famous sculptor. But how did he manage to flesh out this fleeting and evanescent figure? Erased from history as written by men, she was nevertheless a central figure of the community; it is only necessary to take the trouble to read the ancient sources between the lines, being as attentive to what they express as to what they conceal.

---

[1] Georgoudi 1993, pp. 190–1. See also Pirenne-Delforge 2005, pp. 61–2: 'Textbooks repeat over and over that Greek sacrifice, like Roman sacrifice, does not require an intermediary between the worshipper and his god. However, in a sanctuary served by a priest, or a priestess, it is imperative to ensure her assistance.'

By means of some inscriptions and, especially, thanks to a play by Aristophanes performed in 411, it is possible to give back to Lysimache her full human dimension and to restore her singular mode of action within the city that went against the clichéd view of Athenian women as passive and legally in the minority. Better still, if we listen carefully, we can give voice to all those who surrounded her – not only the women directly involved in the cult of Athena, but more widely all Athenian women, including the foreigners to whom the priestess served as a mouthpiece in these 'dark times.'

The Guardian of an Immutable Ritual?

In 403, the figure of Lysimache was familiar to all the members of the community who sometimes ran into her on the Acropolis, busy with her priestly tasks. A member of the prestigious *genos* of the Eteoboutadai and a direct descendant of one of the legendary royal families of Athens, she had been appointed, probably in the 420s, as priestess of Athena Polias serving at the temple of Athena located on the Acropolis, and, as such, she was tasked with presiding over all sacrifices in honor of the goddess. Even after her death, she continued to occupy this sacred space and to attract the attention of passersby, in the form of a statue erected in around 360. Archeologists have unearthed the circular base of this statue, and the skillfully restored inscription celebrates her long years spent working in the service of Athena[2]:

> [This old woman? Lysimache?] was by her descent (daughter) of Dracontides;
> she completed [eighty-eight] years;
> ... sixty-four years she [served] Athena
> and lived to see four [generations] of children.
> *Uninscribed space*
> [Lysimache] mother of – of Phlya.[3]
> *Uninscribed space*
> [Demetrius] made it.[3]

In this short epigram time is both omnipresent and suspended: While the inscription is full of temporal markers – the age of Lysimache, the time she served as a priestess, the generations she saw pass – it is all the better for freezing the priestess out of time in the eternal practice of ritual. Cast in

---

[2] Cf. Pliny the Elder, *Natural History*, 34.76: 'Demetrius [is the author] of a Lysimache who was sixty-four years priestess of Minerva.'
[3] *IG* II² 3453 (transl. S. Lambert, https://www.atticinscriptions.com/inscription/IGII2/3453).

Fig. 5.1 Base of Lysimache statue, priestess of Athena Polias (*IG* II² 3453), transl. S. Lambert (www.atticinscriptions.com/inscription/IGII2/3453).
Photo: E. Feiler, Deutsches Archäologisches Institut, Athens (neg. D-DAI-ATH-Akropolis 2296).

bronze, the priestess is presented as the guarantor that the community will always go on as before. No place is given here to the impact of history: It is as if the 'four generations of children' that Lysimache saw had followed one another smoothly and had not been bled dry by the wars and revolutions of the end of the fifth century; as if, too, the very definition of the community – and, consequently, the identity of the children who took part in it – had not been profoundly disrupted in the course of the terrible years during which she exercised her priestly office.

Tasked with performing ritual acts according to an immutable calendar, Lysimache thus seems to be placed outside of History, anchored in the repetition of biological and religious cycles – in short, the very symbol of the 'cold city' of rituals, as opposed to the 'hot city' of events.[4] Historiography tends to represent her as the simple incarnation of a line of interchangeable priestesses: 'Lysimache can act as a worthy

---

[4] On this established opposition, see Loraux 2006, pp. 54–6.

representative of these successive priestesses whose activity – as enforced by cult traditionalism – does not seem to have undergone any significant changes over the centuries.'⁵ A priestess for life, a wife and the mother of a family, she is only one link in an uninterrupted chain that goes back to the dawn of time – that of the quarrel between Athena and Poseidon, fighting for the privilege of patronizing the territory of future communities.

It is, however, possible to animate somewhat this portrait of an ageless woman by inscribing it in its own time. Let us consider the statue of Lysimache from another angle, by looking into the reasons that caused the Athenians to erect it on the Acropolis – an unprecedented act that had no equivalent in Athens for a long time to come.⁶ If the priestess was honored in this way, it is precisely because she officiated at a time of major upheaval for the community.

On a ritual level, she was attached, if not to a new cult, at least to a new place of worship, the Erechtheion, completed in 406, barely two years before the start of the civil war.⁷ This religious change coincided with a thorough reworking of one of the founding Athenian myths, autochthony. The history of the first Athenian, born of the earth, is common knowledge: Seized by a violent desire for Athena, the lame Hephaestus attempted, unsuccessfully, to rape her. His semen did spatter the goddess's thigh, however, and she grabbed a twist of wool (*eru*) to wipe her leg, and then dropped it on the Attic ground (*chthon*). From that fertilized earth, Erechtheus emerged and was taken in and raised by Athena, becoming the ancestor of all Athenians.⁸

To this well-known myth – alluded to as early as the *Iliad* – the Athenians added extra material during the fifth century. In the *Erechtheus*, performed in the theater of Dionysus in 423 or 422, just before construction of the Erechtheion began,⁹ the poet Euripides chose to concentrate not on the birth, but on the death of the native hero. The play portrays an Attica torn apart by internal conflicts: The Athenians are fighting for their survival against the people of Eleusis who have received the providential assistance of Eumolpos, a Thracian and a son of Poseidon. The oracle of Delphi announces that Athens can be saved on one

---

⁵ Georgoudi 1993, p. 171. ⁶ Keesling 2012.
⁷ It is perhaps for this reason that she was honored with a statue on the Acropolis by the Athenian *demos*, if one follows the attractive hypothesis of Keesling 2012, p. 495.
⁸ See Gantz 1993, pp. 235–6.
⁹ Some commentators prefer to date the play to around 416 because of its characteristic metrical style: They question the testimony of Plutarch (*Nicias*, 9.7) that is generally used to date the play to just before the Peace of Nicias in 421. See Cropp and Fick 1985, pp. 78–80.

condition only: Erechtheus must sacrifice one of his daughters, a demand to which he and his wife Praxithea accede. Among the daughters of Erechtheus, those who are not married then make the oath to die together in solidarity with their condemned sister. Thanks to this courageous sacrifice, the Athenians prevail over the Eleusinians, while Erechtheus kills Eumolpos in single combat. Upset by the outcome of the fight, Poseidon strikes his son's murderer with his trident, driving him into the ground, the very earth from which he came. Balance having thus been restored, the play ends with reconciliation between gods and men: Athena orders the Athenians to found a new cult to Poseidon and his victim Erechtheus. At the same time, the goddess grants to Praxithea the right to make bloody sacrifices on her altar: 'To you, Praxithea, who have restored this city's foundations, I grant the right to make burnt sacrifices for the city on my altars, and to be called my priestess.'[10]

Marking a major inflection of the myth of autochthony, this play grants a crucial role to women and especially to Erechtheus' wife. Far from the misogyny that is sometimes attributed to him, Euripides thus entrusts Praxithea with the task of celebrating the autochthonous origins of Athens in a passage marked by outspoken xenophobia.[11] More broadly, Praxithea appears to be endowed with a real capacity for action. It is indeed she who takes the initiative, in agreement with her husband, to sacrifice one of her daughters.[12] There is not the slightest passivity in this woman, who goes on to proclaim: 'I love my children, but I love my homeland more.'[13]

As Claude Calame writes, 'not only does autochthony end up being also a women's affair (even if men occupy the central stage), but motherhood, far from being denied, is put at the service of the city.'[14] If Athenian

---

[10] *Erechtheus*, fr. 370 l. 94–6 Loeb = fr. 22, l. 94–6 Jouan-Van Looy.
[11] Euripides, *Erechtheus*, fr. 360 Loeb = fr. 14, l. 5–13 Jouan-Van Looy: 'My reasons are many, and the first of them is that I could get no other city better than this. In the first place, we are not an immigrant people from elsewhere but born in our own land, while other cities are founded as it were through board-game moves, different ones imported from different places. But someone who settles in one city from another is like a bad peg fixed in a piece of wood: he's a citizen in name, but not in reality.'
[12] Euripides, *Erechtheus*, fr. 360 Loeb = fr. 14, l. 1–4 Jouan-Van Looy: 'People find it more pleasing when someone gives favors generously – but to act yet take one's time is considered ill-bred. I for my part shall offer my daughter to be killed.'
[13] Euripides, *Erechtheus*, fr. 360a Loeb = fr. 15 Jouan-Van Looy.
[14] See Calame 2015, p. 229, which highlights the importance of the voluntary suicide of the royal couple's other two daughters, a sacrifice given as an example to all Athenians: 'It is indeed the blood of women that ensures the continuity of the city: it is necessary that native daughters are sacrificed and that their blood returns, in part, to the original soil, to ensure the continuity of the city and the reconciliation between Athens and Poseidon, the good functioning of generations. Women are necessary for the city's sustainability, not only in terms of begetting children, but in ritual terms.'

The Priestess on Stage 171

women generally benefited from this rewriting of the story, the play especially honored one of them, Praxithea, and, in turn, Lysimache, her direct descendant. For the Athenians could not fail to make the link between the very first priestess of Athena and the woman who then held this position on the Acropolis as they watched the play being performed in the sanctuary-theater of Dionysus, with an unobstructed view of the Acropolis where Lysimache fulfilled her office.[15]

At the end of fifth century, the priestess of Athena was therefore celebrated under the gaze of all the Athenians on the tragic stage. But it is on the comic stage that Lysimache was really brought to the fore, in a play by Aristophanes performed in 411, barely a few weeks before the momentary abolition of democracy: In *Lysistrata*, the priestess was presented as a key player in the political life of the city and a depositary of the hopes and fears of the whole community.

The Priestess on Stage

The plot of the play is famous. Determined to put an end to the interminable Peloponnesian War, Greek women agree among themselves to seize power. To this end, Lysistrata, a cunning and energetic Athenian woman, convinces her sisters to withhold sexual privileges from their husbands and to launch a surprise attack on the Acropolis, where the city's treasury – the sinews of war – was stored. The plan succeeds without a hitch, and the women manage to stop the hostilities between Greeks while restoring the true values of civic marriage, the sole guarantor of the city's continuity.

Lysistrata ('she who breaks up armies') has long been recognized as a clear transposition of Lysimache ('she who breaks up battles').[16] With this slight shift, Aristophanes alerted the audience to the meaning of a name that, as is often the case in Greek literature, is also a program of action – in this case, to stop the war. Lysistrata/Lysimache is portrayed as a positive figure throughout the play, unlike the other (feminine and masculine) characters, who are constantly ridiculed.

Above all, like the Athenian political leaders, Lysistrata behaves with authority and constantly takes decisions for the common good. Hailed as 'the bravest of all' (*andreiotatē*) – a very masculine quality, as the etymology suggests – it is she who summons the women to deliberate, in the manner of the *prytaneis*[17]; it is also she who directs the rituals in which

---

[15] Calame 2011.　[16] This identification goes back to Lewis 1955.
[17] Aristophanes, *Lysistrata*, 14, 22, 93.

those who participated in the conspiracy are involved, presiding over the oath taken by the women as well as over the parodic sacrifice that accompanies it (v. 201–4); again, it is she who suggests capturing the Acropolis and doing so on the occasion of a sacrifice, precisely the kind of ritual that the real Lysimache performed (v. 176–9).

Once the Acropolis is taken, she asserts her authority. She becomes the treasurer of Athena, occupying de facto a role that corresponds to one of the most prestigious magistracies in the city (v. 489–98). The stakes are decisively high, insofar as the men will continue the war as long 'as their warships have feet and [as] they have that bottomless fund of money in Athena's temple.'[18] At the end of the play, Aristophanes even lends her the stature of a real legislator: Athenians and Spartans agree to consider her as the only one who can establish concord and put an end to the *stasis* between Greeks, in the manner of a female Solon (v. 1103–4): 'Why don't we ask Lysistrata to join us? She's the only person who can bring about a true reconciliation.' And the Coryphaeus adds: 'Hail, bravest of all women! To your charms all Greeks surrender! Now be awesome, gentle, noble, common, proud, experienced, tender: the two great warring states now share joint determination.'[19]

A priestess, treasurer, councilor and even legislator: Lysistrata/Lysimache receives a majestic portrayal in Aristophanes' play. It would obviously be absurd to take the poet at his word, by falling for what Pierre Vidal-Naquet called a 'sociological illusion': Comedies do not reflect the reality they claim to describe, and Aristophanes' play represents above all the way in which men fantasize about the place of women in the city. Should we then see in *Lysistrata* only a pure fantasy, giving as much power to women as they were deprived of in reality?

To confine the play to the sole register of carnivalesque inversion would, however, be to fall for the opposite illusion. For Lysistrata/Lysimache is not just another individual that Aristophanes could manipulate at will: Inspired by one of the most prominent figures in the community, his heroine has singularities that guided how the poet could imagine his theatrical plot. Thus, it is not by chance that Lysistrata acts in a way that echoes the experience of her double, Lysimache, and, in particular, manifests her intimate knowledge of the Acropolis and the rituals that take place there: Aristophanes' heroine takes action just as the real priestess of Athena did. The same is true when the poet depicts his heroine with exceptional agency: Aristophanes only overstates the point, rather than inventing it

---

[18] Aristophanes, *Lysistrata*, 173–4.
[19] Aristophanes, *Lysistrata*, 1110–1 (transl. Sommerstein 2002a).

from scratch. In fact, we know from various sources how much the priestess of Athena was *really* capable of: Since she was free to do as she pleased and received payment for her duties, she could work together with other magistrates, such as the treasurers of Athena, in order to make dedications.[20] Better still, she could manifest her piety in her own name. Recording the list of offerings dedicated in the Parthenon between 398/7 and 385/4, an inventory includes the following entry: 'A silver phiale that Lysimache, mother of Telemachos, dedicated, and on which is the *gorgoneion*, weight 3+ drachmas.'[21] In all likelihood, the inscription reflects the wording chosen by the priestess herself for the dedication of the object and, therefore, her capacity for action.[22] And that is not all: The priestess of Athena enjoyed prerogatives that, most of the time, were the privilege of male citizens, or even of magistrates alone. Thus she had the power to bring a lawsuit against someone, since the Athenian orator Lycurgus wrote a speech *On the Priestess*. This probably spoke of the priestess of Athena Polias, to whom Lycurgus was related as a member of the *genos* of the Eteoboutadai. More strikingly, she had the right to put her mark on certain official documents, in a society where the anonymity of women was the rule and where the proclamation of their name was often made only after their death on their funerary steles: Just like a priest, the priestess could 'affix her seal on the records,' which no doubt detailed monies given to the goddess and included inventories of offerings.[23]

Moving freely around the Acropolis, handling money, consecrating offerings in her name, introducing lawsuits, affixing her seal – the priestess of Athena thus seems to have had significant agency. The city recognized the exceptional character of the responsibility that was entrusted to her by forcing the priestess to account for her management of the sanctuary, just like any male magistrate in charge of public goods.[24] She even had the power to influence the policies of the community in moments of need: Just before the Battle of Salamis in September 480, it was the priestess of Athena Polias who had tipped the balance in favor of the interpretation of the oracle of Delphi proposed by Themistocles.[25]

---

[20] Georgoudi 1993, pp. 208–9.   [21] *IG* II² 1388, side B, l. 55–7.   [22] Keesling 2012, p. 493.
[23] Lycurgus, *On the Priestess*, fr. 6, 4: *sussēmainesthai ta grammata*. The fact that this speech refers to the priestess of Athena Polias can be deduced from two elements: the use of the singular (On *the* priestess) in the preserved title of the speech and the reference to the *grammata*, which cannot concern any other cult.
[24] Aeschines, *Against Ctesiphon* (3), 17–8.
[25] Herodotus, 8.41: The priestess had then 'made known' that the honey cake, offered every month to the great living snake 'in the sanctuary,' had not been touched by the sacred animal, identified by some as Erichthonios. It is this – as much as Themistocles' speech to the Assembly – that had

Like her illustrious predecessor from the Persian Wars, Lysimache had a real capacity for action. In a way, the very existence of Aristophanes' play reflects the influence the Athenians attributed to her: Lysimache was one of those people prominent enough to become the subject of an entire play, like the *komodoumenoi*, those politicians who were mocked on stage and whose luminous counterpart she embodies.

In the end, what best testifies to the extraordinary aura of Lysimache is the famous statue of her erected on the Acropolis after her death. While some see in this an offering made by a member of her own family (her son?),[26] the statue may well have been voted for at the initiative of the Athenian people. Admittedly, the inscription does not include the words 'the *demos* dedicated . . .' common in later honorific decrees, but this formula was not yet established in the 360s.[27] Apparently, Lysimache received the greatest honor that the city could grant, at a time when only a few great generals had been distinguished in this way in the Agora of Athens. It was undoubtedly a question of showing public gratitude toward the priestess who was the first to have served in the new temple of the Erechtheion and, perhaps, also of thanking her for the exceptional services that she had rendered during the 'dark times' of the war.

Female Chorality: The Servants of Athena

Another question then presents itself: Is Lysimache/Lysistrata only an exception, all the more striking because the play veils the reality of male domination over the remaining Athenian women? Certainly, the priestess of Athena was an extraordinary woman, if only due to her distinctive status. Temptation is therefore great to see her only as a hapax and to revert to the vision of passive women totally dominated by their guardians, whether this meant their father, husband or son.

Such a gloomy picture deserves, however, some nuance. Let's take Aristophanes as a guide: While she is certainly exceptional in terms of her intelligence and her charisma, Lysistrata/Lysimache is far from being alone in the play. Presented as a model to be followed, she arouses forms of projective identification on the part of other women who strive to imitate her to varying degrees of success. She appears at the head of a chorus, in the literal sense of the term, being likely to act in concert with others and

---

encouraged the Athenians to leave their city en masse, by convincing them that the goddess had abandoned the Acropolis.
[26] Bielman 2002, pp. 22–5.   [27] Keesling 2012, pp. 494–5.

Female Chorality: The Servants of Athena

even to bring the city, as run by men, to heel. If this is a pious fiction – for Athenian women never imposed their views on men in this way – the way their choral nature is portrayed invites us to take seriously the forms of solidarity and even sisterhood that were woven between women in a ritual framework.

What is the precise composition of the group evolving around the heroine? Let us start from the words spoken by the chorus of *Lysistrata* who, in the play, sketch out a collective self-portrait, in a strange oscillation between "I" and "we":

> We shall give good advice to the City:
> For my nurture, I owe her no less.
> I became, at the age of just seven,
> An Acropolis child priestess (*arrhēphoroi*);
> Then, after I'd served as a Grinder,
> To Brauron, aged ten, I went down
> As a Bear in the rites of the Foundress,
> And discarded my saffron-dyed gown;
> And finally I was selected
> The ritual basket to bear (*kanēphoroi*),
> With a string of dried figs for a necklace.[28]

Arrhēphoroi, 'bearess,' *kanēphoroi*: These successive statuses all refer to prestigious Athenian rituals, accessible only to young girls from good families.[29] It is therefore a group of handpicked women who sang and danced in a chorus around Lysistrata. And, there again, this comic fiction was inspired by very real ritual practices: We know that the priestess of Athena Polias supervised a certain number of young girls, hired to serve the goddess. When they made the *peplos* – the garment given as an offering to Athena every four years at the time of the great Panathenaia – the priestess presided over the inauguration of the weaving and had under her supervision all those who worked together, for a period of several months, to manufacture the garment: the two *Arrhēphoroi*, maybe the Ergastinai (young girls) and all married women.[30] Between all these women collaborating in the same ritual task a particularly strong bond was established, symbolized precisely by their weaving, which is the usual metaphor for union in ancient Greece.[31]

---

[28] Aristophanes, *Lysistrata*, 638–47.   [29] Brulé 1987.
[30] Brulé 1987, p. 99. The Ergastinai may be a later creation (from the second century BC?). See Mikalson 1998, pp. 255–6; Connelly 2007, p. 39.
[31] Scheid and Svenbro 1996, pp. 9–34.

Thus it is necessary to restore around the historical Lysimache a whole chorus composed of those who, year after year, had occupied these prestigious functions and worked under her direction. But the group also included a core of other women who, like Lysimache, served the goddess throughout their lives and not just for a short period of time: There were in particular the other priestesses of Athena and also the personnel attached to these various priestly functions. We are fortunate to know the name of one of the main contemporary priestesses of Lysimache: Myrrhine, the first priestess of Athena Nike.

Myrrhine, Athena's Other Priestess

Between 440 and 420, the Athenians launched a new construction program on a bastion at the entrance of the Acropolis in order to create a temple and an altar for Athena Nike (the Victorious). An Athenian decree mentions the project and specifies the ritual put in place:

> [...]ikos proposed: to select (or: establish) as a priestess for Athena Nike whoever will be [allotted] from all Athenian women and to provide the sanctuary with doors in whatever way Callicrates will specify; [...] the priestess is to receive fifty drachmai [per year] and to receive the backlegs and hides of the *dēmosios* sacrifices; and that a temple be built in whatever way Callicrates may specify and a stone (marble) altar.[32]

The Athenians therefore decided to create a new priesthood attached to an already very old cult that went back at least as far as the first half of the sixth century BC. Its mode of appointment was a full-blown innovation: The priestess was not chosen from a family with prestigious ancestry, but drawn by lot from all the Athenian women. Such a measure was revolutionary: It potentially granted to any (female) citizen a major religious role. This was the first 'democratic' priesthood attested in Athens, open to all and not reserved to the members of a *genos*, such as the Eteoboutadai, from whom the priestess of Athena Polias was chosen. In a society where politics and religion were closely intertwined, radical democracy thus extended its egalitarian logic to the realm of cult practices, supposedly reticent to innovations.[33]

---

[32] *IG* I³ 35, ll. 3–8, 9–12 (transl. Blok 2014, p. 121). Perhaps this decision was taken following a previous decree that instituted public sacrifices (*dēmotelēs*) for the goddess, to be performed after military victories: The priestess apparently took charge as soon as everything was agreed, without waiting for the temple to be completed. See on this subject Blok 2014.

[33] See Parker 1996, pp. 125–7; Lambert 2010, pp. 153–6.

In addition to her singular mode of designation, it is the magnitude of the remuneration granted to the new priestess that attracts attention. She received a fixed sum, similar to a real annual salary, to which were added a share in the spoils of sacrifice, the resale of which could generate significant profits. These sums went far beyond what was generally granted to other priests and priestesses – often a handful of obols, at best a few drachmas – for the performance of specific sacrifices. The new priestess was thus given a real allowance, like the magistrates who, since the middle of the fifth century, were paid for the time they spent serving the community.

A well-preserved funerary stele bears the name of this first priestess, who died shortly after the completion of the temple of Athena Nike in the years 420–410:

> Far-shining memorial (*mnēma*) of Callimachus' daughter
> who was the first to watch over the temple of Nike.
> Her name accompanied her glory, as by divine
> good fortune she was rightly called Myrrhine.
> She was the first to watch over the statue [or seat] (*hedos*) of Athena Nike,
> (chosen) from all the Athenians by a fortunate lot, Myrrhine.[34]

In a poetic form, the inscription echoes the name of the deceased, whose sound in Greek brings to mind the myrtle often used in ritual occasions, and celebrates the care she took in fulfilling her office; the epigram makes a point of returning twice to the way Myrrhine was chosen by lot as the very first priestess of Athena Nike.[35]

To this beautifully made stele, it is tempting to associate a superb marble funerary lekythos, more than 1.30 m high, unearthed in 1873 three kilometers from the Acropolis. It shows a woman led by Hermes into the other world, passing in front of three figures, probably her husband and her children. Her name, Myrrhine, is engraved in large letters above her head, distinguishing her at first glance as the main character of the scene.

Is this the same Myrrhine as the one mentioned on the stele? Wearing an intricately draped garment, a bracelet on her right arm and a diadem on her head, she has a distinguished appearance, but this is not enough to identify her as the first priestess of Athena Nike. The estimated date of the lekythos – the end of the fifth century – nevertheless encourages such a comparison. In this case, one could imagine that the vase flanked the funerary stele, in accordance with a practice very common at the time.[36]

---

[34] *IG* I³ 1330 (transl. Connelly 2007, p. 227). See Brown Ferrario 2014, pp. 162–5.
[35] On the drawing of lots as a choice left to the gods, see Plato, *Laws*, 559b–c.
[36] Clairmont 1979, pp. 103–10. See, however, the doubts of Connelly 2007, pp. 228–9.

Fig. 5.2 Funerary lekythos of Myrrhine (420–410 BC).

What interactions might this Myrrhine have had with the priestess of Athena Polias, Lysimache? The two women must certainly have been in contact, since they both exercised their roles as priestesses on the Acropolis, where the temples to which they were attached were located. Were they in competition or did they collaborate for the greater glory of the goddess? If it is difficult to give a definitive answer to this question, certain indications suggest that the two priestesses did not enjoy the same recognition within the community. On the monumental level, first of all, the difference is obvious: In spite of the beauty of the lekythos and the quality of the epigram, Myrrhine's funerary commemoration cannot compare – in terms of cost and prestige – with the bronze statue of Lysimache erected on the Acropolis.[37] But there is more: In a thinly veiled form, Aristophanes' *Lysistrata* establishes a clear hierarchy between the two women.

For the priestess of Athena Polias is not the only one alluded to in the play: Lysistrata is indeed assisted by a certain Myrrhine, whom the Athenians could not fail to identify with the priestess of Athena Nike who had taken office a few years prior. Not only did the poet not even bother to find a pseudonym for her, but he placed in Lysistrata's mouth a mischievous evocation of the drawing of lots, describing the moment when the female conspirators – including the famous Myrrhine – had to take the oath to abstain from any sexual intercourse with their husbands.[38] And these allusions continue in the play: While the women take over the Acropolis, Myrrhine quickly manages to get her hands on a bed, a mat, a pillow and a blanket (v. 916–36), as if she had intimate knowledge of the place, just like her alter ego, the priestess of Athena Nike.

If, in the play, Myrrhine behaves as a faithful ally to Lysistrata, she is, however, portrayed in a much less favorable light than her colleague: At the beginning, she arrives late for her appointment, attracting the wrath of the heroine (v. 70–1); we then see her reluctant to stop sleeping with her husband (v. 130), and, sometime later, she is very close to breaking her oath of abstinence, consumed as she is by *erōs* (v. 916–36). Aristophanes thus depicts her as a mercurial woman, submissive to her desires – a good representative of the average Athenian woman, from among whom she is drawn by lot. Aristophanes therefore amuses himself, *mezza voce*, by opposing the virtuous Lysistrata/Lysimache, born within a venerable *genos* and fully mistress of her actions, to Myrrhine, the democratic priestess drawn by lot, unable to keep her word without being forced. Even if one must be careful not to take too seriously these masquerades, intended first

---

[37] Holtzmann 2003, p. 224. [38] Aristophanes, *Lysistrata*, 207–8. See Connelly 2007, p. 63.

and foremost to make people laugh, the poet undoubtedly relays here a feeling shared by most Athenians: In their eyes, Lysimache remained at the head of the 'servants of Athena' of whom she was symbolically the master.

If the priestess of Athena Nike did not enjoy the same prestige as her colleague, she was nevertheless equally responsible for guaranteeing harmonious bonds between the divinity and the community. This is why it was perhaps necessary to restore her presence on the Acropolis when Thrasybulus and his troop marched there. Should we imagine that these men came to a halt in front of the temple of Athena Nike, the very first religious building they had set eyes upon after several months spent unable to take part in the great civic rituals? The symbolism of the building (victory) and the mode of designation of its priestess (through the drawing of lots) must have had a particular resonance for the democrats who had just come back from Piraeus. Without hard evidence, we must remain in the register of hypothesis. On the other hand, there is another woman who must have been present when Thrasybulus sacrificed to Athena and whose image should be added to the great fresco of the Athenian reconciliation: the faithful assistant of the priestess of Athena Polias.

Syeris, the Subordinate Double of Lysimache

On the base of a statue found on the Acropolis is inscribed, in large letters, the name of a woman who was honored in the following way:

> Sye[ris] [. .]gou S[- - -], servant (*diakonos*) of Lysimache.
> This image of my form (*tupou*), the one in the sanctuary, shows me clearly;
> my deeds and spirit now live on, clear to all. A reverend fate led me
> into the most beautiful temple of holy Pallas, where I performed
> this labor not without glory for the goddess [...]
> Nicomachus made [this statue].[39]

During his stay in Athens, several centuries later, Pausanias saw the statue of Syeris still standing near the temple of Athena and described it as that of an old woman.[40] Until recently, it was thought that the effigy had only been erected in the third century BC and that the Syeris it depicted was therefore not the servant of 'our' Lysimache, but a homonymous priestess, active a century later.[41] However, Catherine Keesling has recently shown convincingly that the monument actually dates from the 350s. Her argument is based both on the atypical dimensions of the pillar

---

[39] *IG* II² 3464 (transl. Keesling 2012, p. 469). [40] Pausanias 1.27.4.
[41] See in particular Georgoudi 1993, p. 205; Denis 2009, p. 367.

that housed the statue – shaped like many other examples from the middle of the fourth century – and on the name of the sculptor, Nicomachus, who should be identified as the painter of the same name mentioned by Pliny the Elder and active between 370 and 320.[42]

Therefore, the inscription in honor of Syeris can only refer to the assistant of the Lysimache who officiated on the Acropolis for sixty-four years. What was the exact role of this servant (*diakonos*) who depended directly on the priestess of Athena Polias? In charge of the maintenance of the sanctuary, she must have had a variety of tasks, some very prosaic (like keeping the temple clean) and others more significant: Her missions probably included keeping alive the eternal flame that remained lit, day and night, in the Erechtheion.[43] Undoubtedly she was also directly involved in the preparation and the management of all festivals in honor of the goddess, just like the 'assistants (*diakonoumenai*)' who, in Olympia, organized all the great festivals for Hera.[44] Far from being a vague subordinate, her role as 'servant' implies that she worked closely with the priestess, whom she had to assist and sometimes replace. Their two statues located on the Acropolis certainly provide the best testimony to this constant cooperation, as if, even in death, the two women were continuing to take care of the sanctuary together.

What more do we know about Syeris? The inscription is incomplete and does not tell us the name of either her father or her husband, or her exact origin. Here again we must resort to conjecture and, first of all, note the foreign consonance of her name, of which there are many examples in Egypt. It is possible that the inscription mentioned her ethnicity – that is, her place of origin outside Athens. According to Keesling, Syeris' family could therefore have come from Saïs, a city on the Nile delta.[45] This would not be surprising since some Egyptians settled in Athens as early as the classical period.[46]

---

[42] Pliny the Elder, *Natural History*, 35.108–10. Keesling 2012, p. 489. The name at the top of the pillar was engraved at a later date, presumably because the original name was inscribed on a now-lost capital; it would seem the reengraving dates from the second century BC, a time when intense energy was being put into commemoration of the Acropolis' priestesses.

[43] Plutarch, *Numa*, 9.11.   [44] Pausanias, 5.16.2–3.

[45] See Keesling 2012, p. 496–7 and n. 96. Some have argued, however, that Syeris may in fact have belonged to the prestigious *genos* of the *Eteoboutadai*, and could therefore be a relative of Lysimache, since the orator Lycurgus, who served as priest of Poseidon Erechtheus, was nicknamed 'the Egyptian' in Attic comedy (see Blok and Lambert 2009, p. 111, n. 2). The argument is, however, weak: There is a huge difference between a nickname *assigned* by an ill-intentioned poet and a name *chosen* by the family itself.

[46] The Egyptian presence in Attica is proven by the mention of a sanctuary of Isis founded by a community of Egyptians in the decree of the merchants of Kition in 333/2 (*IG* II² 337, l. 42–5). The mention of an Isigenes, a citizen born in about 400 (*IG* II² 1927, l. 150), allows us to think

That Lysimache's 'servant' was probably a foreigner (or a recent citizen) was not an obstacle to her integration into the Athenian community: not during her lifetime, through her association with the most prestigious cult of the city, nor after her death, through the statue set up for her on the Acropolis. This was an exceptional honor, because the erection of a statue in such a strategic place could not be done without the agreement of the people who either must have let the family do as they wished or initiated the project themselves. Whatever the case may be, such an act must be seen as a mark of exceptional recognition of the role Syeris played, under the direction of the priestess of Athena Polias, in particularly trying times when it was important to cultivate the best possible relations with the goddess.

Gravitating around Lysimache, the chorus of Athena's handmaidens was essentially characterized by strong polarities: on the one hand, between the priestesses of Athena themselves – Myrrhine, an average Athenian chosen by lot, in contrast to Lysimache, the 'über-autochthonous' descendant of Erechtheus; and on the other hand, between these different priestesses and all the women working under their direction – sometimes occasionally, such as the *arrhēphoroi* and other *kanephoroi*, and sometimes permanently, like the *diakonos* Syeris. Cohabiting the same places, living together on a daily basis and sometimes working together, these women formed a community united by strong ritual ties, transcending the barriers of status, or even ethnicity, for the greater glory of Athena. The presence of a foreigner in this group allows us to imagine that the chorus extended beyond the civic circle and was potentially open to all those who wished to enter it. Here again, it is Aristophanes' *Lysistrata* that gives flesh to this enlarged collective, dominated by the prominent figure of the priestess of Athena Polias.

'All of the Lysimachai!'

While Lysimache exercised her power over the 'servants of Athena,' her influence went well beyond this restricted circle. For all Athenians crossed paths with her at certain cardinal moments of their existence: The priestess of Athena received a donation upon the birth and the death of each citizen, and this had been the case since Hippias, son of Peisistratus: 'Moreover, whenever a citizen died, the priestess of the temple of Athena on the Acropolis was to receive one quart measure of barley, one of wheat, and a

---

that there were Egyptians in Attica from at least the fifth century. In addition, one famous – albeit 'mythical' – example is known of a place of worship founded by an old Egyptian slave: the sanctuary of Dodona (Herodotus, 2.56).

silver obol. And when a child was born, the father paid the same dues.'[47] Furthermore, she was in close contact with each woman who married: It is she who welcomed the bride and her parents to the Acropolis when they came to make a sacrifice to the goddess before the wedding; she also left her sanctuary and traveled across the city to visit young brides, if the Suda is to be believed: 'The priestess in Athens, carrying the sacred *aigis*, used to visit the [houses of] newly-married women (*tas neogamous*).'[48]

Birth, marriage and death: The priestess of Athena therefore intervened in all transitional moments – the famous 'rites of passage' dear to anthropologists – which gave her a visibility of which few men, even influential ones, could boast. In this perspective, the epigram engraved on the base of the statue of Lysimache must be understood in a completely literal way: 'She *saw* (*epeide*) four generations of children.' In a city that, by its size, guaranteed a certain anonymity to its members, the priestess was one of the rare few to have really *seen* all the Athenians and to have been seen by each of them.

In 403, Lysimache had probably already been exercising her office for more than twenty years, and, as such, she must already have welcomed many a bride and shared in their expectations, their excitement or their fears; in the minds of the Athenians, she must have been associated with their joys and their sorrows, having comforted them at deaths and having rejoiced with them at weddings and births. The effect could only have been cumulative: Over the years, Lysimache's fame must have grown until the priestess became a familiar figure, a rock to which the Athenians could cling in a city characterized by endless change (*metabolai*).

The priestess of Athena could therefore boast of knowing *visually* all the Athenian women, whatever their social or geographical origins. Furthermore, Aristophanes offers a striking theatrical representation of this when he shows Lysistrata/Lysimache surrounded by women from all across Attica: The group of conspirators includes not only Athenian women from the city, but also women from the coast, the island of Salamis and the north and south of Attica.[49] This intimate bond between Athenian women can also be found in the account of the city's origins. The priestess embodied, as we have seen, autochthony in its highest degree, since she was symbolically descended 'from Boutes and beyond, from Erechtheus,

---

[47] Pseudo-Aristotle, *Economics*, 2.2.4. See Georgoudi 1993, p. 205. Holtzmann 2003, p. 220, wonders whether this measure survived after the fall of the tyrant.
[48] Suda, s.v. *Aigis, alphaiota*, 60.3 Adler.
[49] Aristophanes, *Lysistrata*, 58–9 (Salamis); 62 (north of Attica, Acharnai); 67–8 (deme of Anagyros, in the south).

son of Gaia and Hephaestus.'⁵⁰ However, since the middle of the fifth century, Athenian women could also be proud of being 'born of the earth,' just like men. The law on citizenship, created through the initiative of Pericles in 451, required two Athenian parents to be recognized as a citizen: The purity of Athenian blood was henceforth considered to be passed down from both men and women.⁵¹ But this shared belief also transformed Athenian women into sisters sharing a common ancestor who was born on the Acropolis, where Lysimache, the most autochthonous of them all, officiated.

This imaginary kinship did not prevent the maintenance of a certain hierarchy between old and new autochthons. Aristophanes amuses himself in the play by distinguishing his main heroine from all those who surround her. While the women are frightened by the sight on the Acropolis of 'the guardian snake' (v. 759) – the figure of Erichthonius and a symbol of autochthony⁵² – Lysistrata remains unmoved. Here, again, the poet is playing on the knowledge his public shares of Lysimache, whose identity is discernable under the mask of Lysistrata: It was in fact the priestess of Athena Polias who was responsible for feeding the sacred animal. She could not be afraid of such an encounter.

Aristophanes' play is an invitation to widen the chorus gravitating around the priestess still further. By no means in favor of Athens closing in on itself, Lysistrata wove links beyond the civic framework, integrating in her conspiracy Spartan, Boeotian and Corinthian women. It was together – no matter their origins – that they decided (v. 39–41) to put an end to what Lysistrata considered a war between 'relatives' bound by a common cult (v. 1128–32). And to achieve this goal, all Greek women had to join forces under the sign of *erōs*. It was indeed the birth of a community of desire that Lysistrata/Lysimache called for (v. 551–4):

> So long as Aphrodite of Cyprus
> and her sweet son Eros breathe hot desire over our bosoms and our
> thighs, and so long as they cause our menfolk to suffer from
> long, hard, truncheon-shaped tumescences – then I believe that
> before long we will be known throughout Greece as the
> *Lysimachai* ['those who break up battles'].

Here is Lysistrata's plan stated in its most radical formulation: to create an immense chorus regulated only by the law of desire, even if this meant

---

⁵⁰ [Plutarch], *Life of Lycurgus*, 843e. Cf. Lycurgus, fr. VI.11 Conomis.   ⁵¹ Blok 2009.
⁵² The snake is also the symbol of the male sex: All these women decide to go on a 'sex strike,' thus interrupting momentarily the lineage of the Erechtheidai by generating no more natives.

transgressing affiliations and inherited statuses. To achieve her ends, the heroine intended to mobilize the power of *erōs*, capable of both untying – 'undoing conflicts' (*lysimachai*) – and recomposing an enlarged community on new foundations. But there is more: With the support of Aphrodite, Greek women were all invited to metamorphose into *Lysimachai* – that is, to merge with Lysimache in a form of mimetic contagion. How better to express the central importance of the priestess of Athena Polias in this evolving community?

Obviously, Aristophanes ventures into the register of utopia here. The women in question never stormed the Acropolis, and the Athenians did not stop the Peloponnesian War until their consummate defeat in 404: The law of desire never got the upper hand over the urge to kill. The bonds uniting Lysimache to her sisters were probably too fitful and weak to translate into active solidarity and to generate forms of action: In a certain way, the chorus gathered around the priestess was as evanescent as it was encompassing.

So was this the end of the story and a return to the male norm? Not quite. The potential chorus gathered around Lysimache deserves to be taken into consideration by anyone who wishes to write, in full, the history of the Athenian reconciliation of 403, even if it means dreaming a little.

Lysimache's Dream: The Unacknowledged Community

From one utopia to another: Let us extend for a few moments Aristophanes' reverie by taking, in our turn, a detour. For dreams are by no means the historian's enemy, as long as they are taken for what they are and nourished by a critical reading of the ancient sources. Let us therefore return for a moment to the Acropolis, on Boedromion 12, 403, just as Thrasybulus and his men arrive at the temple of Athena. Here they are welcomed by Lysimache the priestess: How lonely she seems in front of this compact mass of men swollen with the pride of victory! But let's adjust our gaze a little: Here comes Syeris, her 'servant' who has come to assist her, and, a little farther in the background, there are the other priestesses of the Acropolis and their assistants. Let us listen: Through the priestess, it is a whole chorus of women who now give voice to a prayer for peace and reconciliation. Without saying a word, Lysimache speaks for all Athenian mothers, wives and daughters, exhausted by decades of war and discord.

This already gives a more balanced view of the meeting. And let's look again: Here we go, the sacrifice has begun. The beasts are being slaughtered on the altar, the blood is flowing freely, the animals are being carved up, and, suddenly, the gods are there. Behind the priestess, it is the shadow of Athena that appears, prolonging the mute prayer of the women of the city: 'It is necessary to forget all evils! Is there not, in my temple, an altar to Forgetfulness, intended to seal the reconciliation with Poseidon who had disputed me the territory of Attica?' It is thus an entire chorus, of women and deities together, that now demands peace from Thrasybulus. Is this all a daydream? Undoubtedly, but a Greek like Plutarch would not have found it so fanciful: By letting his resentment of Athena last, 'Poseidon was every way more *political* (*politikōteros*) than Thrasybulus, since not being like him a winner, but the loser [...].'[53]

Let us gaze again upon the scene at the Acropolis. What do we see there? Men, of course, waiting to receive their share of the sacrificial animals, sliced into pieces of the same size. From a distance, they all look alike, probably because 'so far as clothing and general appearance are concerned, the common people here are no better than the slaves and metics,' as the anonymous author of the *Constitution of the Athenians*, identified by some as the oligarch Critias,[54] put it. But little by little, several groups distinguish themselves: Here, one can see men crowding around Thrasybulus and eating pieces of viscera grilled on the altar – liver, heart, kidneys – which are also shares in honor. Might they not be the early fighters of Phyle, who chose to resist when all seemed lost? And, a little further on, who are these men with marked bodies? Perhaps they're slaves about to be freed for having joined 'those of Piraeus'? And those, clustered around the statue of Athena Parthenos, aren't they speaking with a slight Ionian accent? Might they be former metics rallied to the cause of the democrats? They definitely all make up a very heterogeneous troupe ... But, at this moment, who cares? However different their origins may be, all these men had shared the same experience and fought side by side, without distinction.

Lysimache attends the scene. She stands there, near the altar, after having accomplished her service, exchanging a few words in a low voice with her assistant, Syeris: They are pleased that the ceremony has proceeded without a hitch, in spite of the palpable tension that reigns in the town. Between the native priestess and her Egyptian assistant, there is total mutual understanding. And suddenly, the men and the women present exchange glances and, in a striking mirror image, recognize themselves for what they are: citizens and foreigners communing together under the

---

[53] Plutarch, *Symposiacs* (*Quaestiones Conviviales*), 9.6.741b (our emphasis).
[54] Pseudo-Xenophon, *Constitution of the Athenians*, 1.10. Canfora 1989, pp. 17–8. On this hypothetical identification, see *supra*, Chapter 1, p. 40.

benevolent gaze of Athena. Hermes suspends his flight and, for a moment, status barriers seem to be abolished.

This imaginary scene is based on the very real social and ethnic mix that characterizes both the army of Thrasybulus and the entourage of Lysimache. Above all, this dream is not so far from the utopia represented on stage by Aristophanes, less than a decade before, at the theater of Dionysus. There also, for as long as the play lasted, the spectators had been able to indulge in the dream of a radically 'other' community: Spinning a long textile metaphor, Lysistrata envisages gathering into a single basket the best strands of fiber – not only the citizens, but also the metics, the debtors of the treasury (deprived of their citizenship) and, abroad, the friends of Athens and the *klērouchoi* – before 'putting them all together in one great ball of wool – and from that you can weave the People a nice warm cloak to wear.'[55] And, whatever one might claim, this project was not as utopian as it seems. In 405, as they were about to be defeated by the Spartans, the Athenians granted citizenship to the rare allies who remained faithful to them – in particular, the Samians – while they reinstated the majority of the Athenians who had been deprived of their citizenship (*atimoi*).[56]

Let us risk a last glance toward the Acropolis. On the altar, the embers are glowing and the sacrifice is being consumed. Silence falls and, suddenly, it's all over: Leaving the sanctuary of Athena, the leader of the democrats moves toward the Assembly to address citizens, males and Athenians alone: *Exit* the foreigners, the metics and the women.

> On this exceptional day, no-one had to give an order to disperse. They separated by the same countless necessities that had brought them together. They separated instantaneously, without leaving anyone behind, without those nostalgic after effects that were formed and in which the very event, which the combat groups purported to preserve, is altered. People do not act like that. They are there, then they are no longer there. They ignore the structure that could stabilize them.[57]

The whole thing had only been a dream: The emergence of an ephemeral chorus, sketching out an alternative community, dissolved at the very moment it came into being.

---

[55] Aristophanes, *Lysistrata*, 585–6.
[56] Andocides, *On the Mysteries* (1), 73. See *supra*, Chapter 3, pp. 111–4.
[57] Blanchot 1988, pp. 32–3.

CHAPTER 6

Eutherus and the Precarious Workers

Somewhere in the Attic countryside, far from the political turbulence agitating the city, a banal real estate transaction took place in 403: A rich Athenian citizen, whose name is unknown, convinced a certain Anticles to sell him a small piece of land. On the edge of the field, surrounded by a fence, stood an olive tree, carefully bypassed by the local road. About ten years later, this very same man was accused before the venerable Areopagus Council of having uprooted the tree. At first sight, the situation seems incongruous to say the least: More than a decade after it happened, in a city rife with political conflicts of all kinds and which aspired to play a leading role in the Greek world again, how should we interpret the fact that the fate of a modest olive tree gave rise to such a solemn lawsuit?

It is well known that olive cultivation was central to both religious and political Athenian identity. When the Athenians had to decide between Poseidon and Athena for their guardian, it was by giving them an olive tree that the goddess won the contest. As a result, she became the protective divinity of the new community, to which she offered her name. Placed in front of the Erechtheion, the stump of the olive tree donated by the goddess had even started growing branches again the day after the army of Xerxes set fire to the Acropolis in 480, symbolizing the invulnerability and the permanence of the city.[1] At the heart of the classical period, the festival of Panathenaia showed how important cultivating olives was in Athenian life. Its celebration coincided first of all with the arrival on the market, under the city's control, of the oil produced in Attica, which had been the main Athenian export since the beginning of the sixth century.[2] More importantly, winners of competitions were honored with large amphorae of oil from the sacred olive trees scattered around Athenian

[1] Herodotus, 8.55.   [2] Papazarkadas 2011, p. 273.

territory, which were the property of Athena.[3] It is precisely one of these sacred olive trees that our man was accused of having uprooted, constituting a crime inflicted on the goddess herself and making him liable for capital punishment.[4]

A Scene of Rural Life: The Olive Tree of Discord

We owe the knowledge of this astonishing judicial case to the existence of a short speech attributed to Lysias. Its anecdotal character paradoxically suggests to historians that they have their hands on a document of exceptional significance, allowing them to observe the slow pace of a rural society supposedly insensitive to the hectic course of political and military history as described in the narratives of writers like Thucydides and Xenophon. In fact, better than any other source, the speech sensitively brings to life elements of the rural landscape of classical Athens. Visible from all sides, the field bought by our man was not surrounded by dry stone walls[5]: Should we deduce from this that open fields dominated the Athenian rural landscape? The account of the litigant invites us to imagine the existence of scattered settlements, without knowing if this configuration is representative of the Attic countryside. Let us also observe that while our man belongs to the city's elite, his properties are composed of several plots dispersed across the whole civic territory, which undoubtedly constitutes a characteristic feature of the Athenian agrarian structure.[6] Finally, the speech reveals some of the features of rural sociability: In particular, it shows the social control exercised by the neighborhood over a small community of classical Athens.[7]

And yet, historians would be wrong to claim that reading this speech allows them to understand the *longue durée* and to dissipate the 'delusive smoke'[8] of political events. While they may believe it allows them to observe the structural features of rural Athenian society – how to size up the distribution of landed property and identify the way in which peasant work was organized – these elements escape them or, more exactly, let themselves be grasped only in a very singular configuration. Beyond the

---

[3] A Solonian law forbade the export of all products outside Attica except olive oil: Plutarch, *Life of Solon*, 24.1.
[4] [Aristotle], *Athenian Constitution*, 60.2: Whoever uprooted or cut down a sacred olive tree was judged by the Council of the Areopagus and, in case of conviction, punished by death.
[5] Lysias, *Defense in the Matter of the Olive Stump* (7), 18, 26, 29.   [6] See Bresson 2015, p. 143ff.
[7] Lysias, *Defense in the Matter of the Olive Stump* (7), 18, 26, 29. See Schmitz 2004.
[8] Braudel 1980, p. 27.

illusory stability of agricultural life in a small Attic deme, the situation depicted by the litigant is indeed inseparable from the political events of the end of the fifth century.

The land in question has an exceptional history, since it had been confiscated by the city from property belonging to Peisander, one of the leaders of the Four Hundred, after democracy was restored in 411/10. It was then offered as an honorary gift to Apollodorus of Megara, celebrated as one of the glorious assassins of Phrynichus, another representative of the regime of the Four Hundred.[9] Apollodorus, undoubtedly threatened by the return of the oligarchs in 404, had sold it to a certain Anticles, from whom our man bought it in 403.[10] One cannot therefore deny that the accusation made by Nicomachus may have had a political dimension, taking aim at a man who, having easily acquired property in Attica in the middle of a civil war, seemed to support at least implicitly the regime of the Thirty.[11] Moreover, far from attesting to the permanence of an immobile ritual life, disconnected from political agitation, the specific attention brought to the question of olive production is explained by the new scale that the city intended to confer to the festival of Panathenaia in the aftermath of the restoration of democracy.[12]

Disturbed by this political event, the underlying structures of Athenian rural life that Lysias' speech sheds light on only appear through a lens that is by nature distorting, in their own way falling under the 'exceptional normal' (or 'exceptional typical') category theorized by Edouardo Grendi.[13] One of the main contributions of the speech lies nevertheless in the portrait it paints of the world of agricultural work at the turn of the

---

[9] Lysias, *Defense in the Matter of the Olive Stump* (7), 4. Lycurgus, *Against Leocrates* (1), 112. Apollodorus is, moreover, mentioned in a decree dating from 410/9, in an amendment proposed by a certain Eudikus that notes the honors that had already been given to him: *IG* I³ 102, ll. 40–1.

[10] Lysias, *Defense in the Matter of the Olive Stump* (7), 4–5, 9.

[11] The litigant does not fail to indicate, obviously, that he had been neutral during the events of 403, in a formula that has all the makings of a denial: 'Was it easier for me, members of the Council, to act illegally during the democracy or under the Thirty? I say this not as one who was powerful then or is under suspicion now, but because it was much easier then than it is now for anybody who wanted to commit crimes' (§27).

[12] The trial is, moreover, contemporary with a reform that affected the collection of olives, making olive trees henceforth the leasable property of the city, a change to which Pseudo-Aristotle, *Athenian Constitution*, 60.2 testifies (see Papazarkadas 2011, pp. 265–70).

[13] Edouardo Grendi saw in this the ideal configuration for micro-historians (Grendi 1977). An exceptional case would thus be paradoxically richer in general elements than 'representative' examples approached as a series. 'The exception is richer than the norm because the norm is systematically implied in it,' considers Ginzburg 2003, p. 122, suggesting that an exceptional configuration offers the opportunity to observe the norm in unstable or uncertain moments particularly rich in meaning.

fifth and fourth centuries by highlighting two different categories of workers, farmers and slaves. The litigant belongs to the liturgical class of the richest Athenians.[14] While he claimed he now intended to work his field himself, he had initially chosen to rent it out to four successive farmers from 403 to 396. After a certain Callistratus worked the field the first two years (403–401), Demetrius then Alcias, a freedman of Antisthenes, took turns (400–399), before Proteas worked the field for the first three years of the fourth century, from 399 to 396.[15] Such a high turnover, which is exceptional with regard to our knowledge of most ancient leases,[16] is difficult to explain: Should it be attributed to the particular situation of Athens at the end of the Peloponnesian War, characterized by an underexploitation of the land with regard to the number of available men?[17] Should it lead us, on the contrary, to reevaluate the importance of the land rental market in classical Athens, which was much more active than we are used to thinking?[18] It is impossible to settle the matter. But the speech suggests above all the importance of servile labor on farms. According to the litigant, slaves were the only labor force working regularly in the field; only they could have cut the trunk of the olive tree in question. And this is the reason why he pretends to want them to testify, under torture, before the court.[19]

Elusive Men: Free Employees

On reading the speech in question, however, historians may come to doubt its veracity, for it seems that this description of farming ignores,

---

[14] Lysias, *Defense in the Matter of the Olive Stump* (7), 31: 'I have fulfilled all the duties laid upon me, more eagerly than was required by the city. As trierarch, as contributor to war taxes (*eisphorai*), as *chorēgos*, and in all the other liturgies, I have been as generous as any other citizen.'

[15] Lysias, *Defense in the Matter of the Olive Stump* (7), 9–10. The presence of the freedman Alcias is obviously intriguing: Does he farm the land on behalf of his former master, Antisthenes? Did he become a farmer only after the death of Antisthenes? See the different hypotheses suggested by Todd 2007, pp. 521–2.

[16] Pernin 2014. [17] Akrigg 2007.

[18] Most of what we know about land rental in classical Athens is due to the leasing of public or sacred lands. The profitability, for private individuals, of their landed properties is undoubtedly one of the specificities of the *oikonomia attikē* of the end of the fifth century. The case of Ischomachus' father, presented by Xenophon, is representative of this (see in particular Xenophon, *Oeconomicus*, 20.22).

[19] Lysias, *Defense in the Matter of the Olive Stump* (7), 16–17, 19. On the more general debate concerning the importance of servile agricultural labor, see mainly Jameson 1977–1978; de Ste Croix 1981, pp. 505–6; Wood 1983; Amouretti 1986, pp. 208–14; Ameling 1998. In this respect, it is necessary to be able to determine to which status category most of the individuals mentioned in the famous decree of Thrasybulus of 401 (*IG* II² 10) under the term *geōrgoi* belong. These men did not possess land. Should one consider them former slaves or metics? Let us note that Xenophon's *Oeconomicus* (3.10) explicitly mentions the practice of buying young slaves to make them *geōrgoi*.

or conceals, an essential component of agricultural labor. Like an alchemist, they need to divine a vital ingredient, without which the social history of classical Athens would remain incomprehensible: free men, whether metics or citizens, who had no property rights and who worked on the farms of other citizens for varying lengths of time.

A passage in Xenophon's *Memorabilia* features just such a man, called Eutherus, in the aftermath of the restoration of democracy in 403. As he meets his 'old comrade' Socrates, Eutherus describes his sad situation:

> I came home when the war ended, Socrates, and am now living here', he replied. 'Since we have lost our foreign property, and my father left me nothing in Attica, I am forced to settle down here now and work for my living with my hands. I think it's better than begging, especially as I have no security to offer for a loan.

Pitying him, Socrates advises him to do paid work for a rich landowner who needs workers on his estate:

> Then it would be better to take up some kind of work at once that will be sufficient for you when you get old, and to go to somebody who is better off and wants an assistant, and get a return for your services by acting as his bailiff, helping to get in his crops and looking after his property.[20]

Reluctant, Eutherus claims that he 'shouldn't like to make [him]self a slave,' and that he has 'no inclination to expose [him]self to any man's censure,' but the philosopher ends up convincing him by pointing out that 'it is by no means easy to find a post in which one is not liable to censure.'[21]

Of course, the character of Eutherus is likely to be a pure invention of Socratic literature. His name is significant, depending on whether one literally recognizes in him the *good prey* (*eu-theros*; i.e. the good game in the hunt of the *philoi* described by Xenophon) or the *good hunter* (*eu-theros*). His fate was nevertheless similar to that of many Athenians after the Peloponnesian War. While his father did not have any land, he had been allotted a plot in the territories of the Athenian empire, undoubtedly cultivated by the local workforce. Once the Delian League had collapsed, however, Eutherus, now deprived of any property, had no other solution other than to temporarily accept work on a farm.[22]

---

[20] Xenophon, *Memorabilia*, 2.8.3.   [21] Xenophon, *Memorabilia*, 2.8.4–5.
[22] See Gauthier 1976b, p. 167: 'We have here, one would say, a good example of a poor *klērouchos*, a *thēs* in Athens, happy to have been able to settle elsewhere (provided with a plot taken from the territory of an allied city), forced to abandon everything after the decisive reverses of 405 and to return to poverty at his return to Athens.'

To what collective does Eutherus lend his name? Or more precisely: To what extent is this character the spokesman of a chorus, that of free men who are not property-owners and who work temporarily on the lands of Athenian citizens? Measuring the influence of this category of workers is not an easy task. The difficulty lies first of all in the disdain shown by ancient literature, which sees this group as a negligible part of the composition of any *polis* worthy of the name. When he undertakes to list the different professions in his ideal city, Plato places those 'who sell the use of their strength for a *misthos*' last, after craftsmen and merchants.[23] Because of their lack of intellectual qualities, they are the least prestigious – and least necessary – part of the community. These free men who 'voluntarily place themselves at the service of others'[24] cannot claim to have acquired any political knowledge. In fact, the way Xenophon's Socrates presents Eutherus' work reveals his contempt for any form of paid work, viewed as it is through the prism of servitude, even when it is temporary.[25] Socrates suggests to Eutherus that he should turn to a large landowner to 'act as his bailiff, helping to get in his crops and looking after his property.' He therefore places two very different activities on the same level: the harvesting of the fruits and the stewardship of the farm, because they are both tasks accomplished for others and are therefore devalued. Eutherus, on the other hand, only agrees to consider working for another free man on an occasional basis, considering long-term work as a form of slavery.

This episode is indicative of a dominant feature of Greek political thought in the fourth century, which assessed work as a servile relationship between master and slave. 'Slavery (in one form or another) is on the horizon of every relationship of service,'[26] meaning that work performed by free men appears to be fundamentally servile. Thus, in *Politics*, Aristotle comes to describe the work done for others by free men as 'servitude' (*douleia*), apparently distinguished from legal slavery only because of its limitation in time.[27]

More broadly, the very notion of wage labor in the sense in which it has been understood since the nineteenth century has hardly any equivalent in

---

[23] Plato, *Republic*, 2.371e: 'There are other servants, I think, whose minds alone wouldn't qualify them for membership in our society but whose bodies are strong enough for labor. These sell the use of their strength for a price called a wage and here are themselves called wage-earners (*hoi dè pōlountes tēn tēs ischuos chreian, tēn timēn tautēn misthon kalountes, keklēntai, hōs egōmai, misthōtoi*) [...]. So wage-earners are the complement (*plērōma*) of our city' (transl. Cooper and Hutchinson 1997).
[24] See in particular Plato, *Politics*, 290a. [25] Garlan 2007. [26] Garlan 2007, p. 254.
[27] Aristotle, *Politics*, 1277b.

classical Greece. Labor was never envisaged as an abstract category that could be isolated from the person who performed it, quantified numerically and exchanged for wages.[28] On the building sites of the city as well as in the craftsmen's workshops, pay calculations usually took into account the result of the activity and not the amount of time worked.[29] The term *misthos* itself does not refer to a form of remuneration indexed to work time and retains 'the meaning of a [somewhat] casual and honorific remuneration.'[30] Eutherus is a *misthōtos*, and if we wish to translate this term as 'salaried' or 'waged,' it is in the sense in which the French of the *ancien régime* used it to designate the '*gens de peine*' (day laborers) who are distinguished from the '*gens de métier*' (carpenters, physicists or lawmen). Uncertainty and social vulnerability characterized wage conditions at that time, a far cry from the role that salaries play in European societies of the twentieth century that include a certain number of guarantees and protective measures attached to the exercise of a job.[31]

The devaluation of free work done for others in the political thought of the classical period tells us nothing, however, of its importance in the economic life of cities. To measure it historians are unfortunately reduced to hypothetical reconstructions, which are based on singularly fragile documentary evidence. The decree proposed by Phormisius, the day after democracy was restored in 403, wanted to reserve full citizenship to the owners of land. The Athenians were opposed to such a restriction. According to Dionysius of Halicarnassus, applying this decree would have deprived 5,000 Athenians of their citizenship. Thus, in the Athens of the end of the fifth century, the model of the citizen-owner apparently remained in the majority, leading us to believe that citizens who were *misthōtoi* may have been few and far between.[32] The figure invoked by Dionysius of Halicarnassus nevertheless arouses a certain skepticism, especially as nobody really knows from which data his calculation proceeded.[33] To this doubtful figure, derived from a late source, it is necessary to oppose

---

[28] See Vernant 1983, pp. 275–92.   [29] See Feyel 2006, pp. 402–3.   [30] Will 1975.
[31] See Castel 2002.
[32] In this sense, see Burford 1993, pp. 187–9, who considers that free *thetes* were marginal in agriculture. Her evaluation does not say anything about the distribution of land ownership. It is also quite possible that citizens who owned very modest amounts of land were forced to rent out their skills as laborers to earn a living.
[33] Dionysius of Halicarnassus, *The Ancient Orators [Lysias]*, 32. See the remarks of Todd 1990, p. 164. Even assuming that Dionysius of Halicarnassus has picked up a figure quoted by Lysias in his speech against the proposal of Phormisius, is it a figure put forward by Phormisius (and on what basis) or an assessment made by Lysias himself? In both cases, it is difficult to understand on what such a calculation could be based.

a determining fact in the social and political history of classical Athens. The disconnection of land ownership from citizenship had been a characteristic of the democratic regime since the end of the sixth century; the history of the democratization of Athens coincided with the rise in power of citizens with no property, together with the 'craftsmen' of the city, in the development of democratic institutions and the assertion of an imperialist policy. Several specific features of fifth-century Athenian politics find their explanation here. If the Periclean strategy at the beginning of the Peloponnesian War, which recommended everyone abandon the territory and withdraw behind the city's walls, was a lasting success among the people, one would be wrong to impute this to the oratory talents of the general. It is rather that the majority of the Athenian *demos* were not impacted when Spartan troops periodically ravaged the countryside.[34] Although the connection is inaccurate, it is significant that a lexicographer like Pollux considers all *thetes* to have been *misthōtoi*: 'The words *pelates* and *thetes* designate the free who serve as slaves for money, because of their poverty.'[35]

Certainly, most ancient authors present recourse to paid work as the product of exceptional circumstances, resulting from the misfortunes that can suddenly strike a family.[36] But Isocrates' complaints should not deceive us: There is every indication that free men working in the service of other free men were in fact very numerous. Eutherus is by no means an exception, and in the course of Athenian speeches or comic plays we encounter other individuals of free status who 'live by the work of their hands' in the Athenian countryside. In Menander's *Dyskolos*, a character weeps over the fate of a peasant forced to harvest the crops alone, having no slaves and no *misthōtos* to help him.[37] The Boor in Theophrastus' *Characters* is a man who, throwing caution to the wind, reports everything he has heard in the Assembly to the *misthōtoi* who work in his fields,[38] while the litigant of *Against Euboulides* evokes the case of Athenian women obliged to become 'nannies, housekeepers and grape-pickers' because of a reversal of fortune.[39] The link that unites an employer to his *misthōtoi* even serves as a model to assess relationships based on reciprocal and temporary interests, and which for this very reason prove to be fragile. While in Aristophanes' *Wasps*, Athenian judges are compared to olive-pickers ready

---

[34] Azoulay 2014, pp. 38–9.   [35] Pollux, 3.82.
[36] Isocrates, *Plataicus* (14), 48; Isaeus, *On the Estate of Dicaeogenes* (5), 39; Demosthenes, *Against Euboulides* (57), 45.
[37] Menander, *Dyscolos*, 327–32.   [38] Theophrastus, *Characters*, 4.2.
[39] Demosthenes, *Against Euboulides* (57), 45.

to serve anyone for a *misthos*,⁴⁰ Demosthenes portrays Aeschines as the employee of Philip, whom he compares to 'harvesters or those who do something for pay.'⁴¹

Reading all of these texts, one realizes how much the valorization of the peasant-owner working on his own land is above all an ideological stereotype in ancient literature. The *autourgos* of Aristophanes or Menander is a comic archetype that masks the reality of the agricultural world, which largely ran on the work of slaves and the temporary work of free men and women.⁴² There is little knowledge of salaried employees working long term in craft workshops,⁴³ but the evidence for *misthōtoi* exercising their activity in town is not negligible. For example, in the bank of the famous Pasion, *misthōtoi* of free status practiced their trade alongside slaves.⁴⁴ The father of Hagnon, general from 431–429, was, according to the chorus of Cratinos' *Ploutoi*, 'formerly a hardworking stevedore, a wage earner (*misthōtos*) of Pithias.' ⁴⁵ According to an ancient tradition, the philosopher Cleanthes 'was renowned for his industry, being indeed driven by extreme poverty to work for a living (*misthophorein*).'⁴⁶ In Aristophanes' *Frogs*, Xanthias suggests to Dionysus that he hire (*misthōsai*) a dead man to carry furniture to Hades, and Dionysus comes to negotiate with one of the resurrected dead men for the amount of his wages.⁴⁷

The Intermittent Chorus

The contours of a specific category of workers therefore take shape little by little around the figure of Eutherus. It gathers together both citizens without property, forced to work temporarily in the workshops or the fields of Attica, and foreigners resident in Attica. Indeed, the *misthōtoi* made up a considerable share of the metic population. At the time of the battle of Mounychia, two men, Astyages and Eucolion, fought under Thrasybulus' orders the army of the oligarchs alongside Gerys. In the decree of 401 that honors them with the privileges of *isoteleia* (fiscal

---

⁴⁰ Aristophanes, *Wasps*, 712.
⁴¹ Demosthenes, *On the Crown* (18), 51; see also Xenophon, *Hiero*, 6.10, on the bond between the tyrant and his guards.
⁴² See lately McHugh 2019.
⁴³ Recently, Rihll 2008, p. 131, and Acton 2015, p. 272. Like Finley before them, they deduced that the phenomenon never existed, which is probably excessive.
⁴⁴ Pseudo-Demosthenes, *Against Timotheus* (49), 51–2; see more generally Mossé 1976 and Zimmermann 1974.
⁴⁵ Cratinos, *Ploutoi*, fr. 73 K.-A.; see Bakola 2010, pp. 208–20, 313–9.
⁴⁶ Diogenes Laertius, 7.168.   ⁴⁷ Aristophanes, *Frogs*, 164–78.

equality with citizens) and *engguēsis* (the right to marry a member of the community of the Athenians and have legitimate offspring), these two men are qualified as *misthō(toi)*. Contrary to the other honored individuals, whose names are accompanied by the mention of their profession, be they peasants, bakers or porters, Astyages and Eucolion are designated by the mention of this 'wage relationship' alone. Eucolion and Astyages, like Eutherus, were workers of free status who sold their skills as laborers according to market needs.

The particular features of this category of workers deserve to be placed in the context of the Athenian economy, within which coexisted complex forms of forced labor that did not fall under the category of slavery. These 'free wage earners' are quite different from the debt slaves who placed themselves at the service of a creditor until they had repaid them.[48] They should also be distinguished from *pelatai*, bound to their employer by a relationship of personal dependence akin to a form of clientelism, and which probably implied legal protection on the behalf of the patron.[49] Likewise, they were not to be counted among the freedmen who were so present in all sectors of Athenian economic life, and whose work was very often one of the obligations they owed to their former master. All these men enjoyed an intermediate status between full freedom and slavery, and their activity was determined by a legally enshrined bond of personal dependence, which guaranteed the stability of the workforce. It was quite different for free men like Astyages, Eucolion or Eutherus, who were hired for temporary farmwork: Their right to break off this engagement at any time was an essential component of their freedom. Clearly, these men of different statuses were able to share the same work space: Many poor citizens worked alongside slaves or freedmen in the countryside of Attica as well as in the urban workshops of the city. The status of free men nevertheless played a determining role in the form their work could take, limiting the employer's ability to impose physical and legal constraints, while depriving these individuals of certain forms of protection offered by the relationship of dependency.

Identifying a category of workers is one thing. But when a type of work comes to define a shared identity, that is another matter. The invisibility of free-status 'wage earners' in Athenian political thought in the classical period is in itself intriguing. Was there a chorus of *misthōtoi* active in the year 404/3? Certainly, Eutherus, Eucolion and Astyages belonged to a

---

[48] Zurbach 2014, p. 277.   [49] Zurbach 2014, p. 279.

singular group in the city, distinguished from both the owners of workshops or agricultural lands, be they citizens or metics, and from all the workers exercising their activity as part of a personal relationship of dependency. They were vulnerable, living hand to mouth, always adjusting to circumstance.[50] At first glance, one concept seems an apt characterization of these men's condition: *precariousness*. The term has been used over the last thirty years to describe, beyond the overly general term of poverty, the new neoliberal ordering of labor relations. 'To the realm of the poor can correspond a collective and individual identity, a universe of stigmas, of symbols [. . .]. To the realm of the precarious, which is mobile and discontinuous, seems to correspond the paradox of an identity built on "the provisional",' wrote Claudine Offredi, in one of the first attempts at a systematic definition of the 'phenomenon of precarity.'[51] The weakening of social ties and the loss of professional identity in a context of great occupational instability are constitutive of the contemporary 'precariat.' It is tempting to draw a parallel with the condition of *misthōtos*, characterized in civic epigraphy by the absence of a professional identity. The category of free employees is based, in short, on a negative identification, collectively qualifying all those who do not have any particular *technē*.[52]

It goes without saying, however, that both individual and collective forms of subjectivation differ radically in modern wage societies and in the ancient city. The absence of a professional identity is not the stigma of a hypothetical disaffiliation but experienced as relegation from the community. Eutherus, as described by Xenophon, defines his position in Athenian society primarily in terms of his status as a free man. Athenian society of the classical period therefore remained a status-based society in two ways: Firstly, in the sense that the logic of status, and not of the market, determined the different ways production was organized – even when they worked side by side, free and dependent individuals did not perform ostensibly identical tasks in the same way, as we have seen; and secondly, insofar as all forms of individual and collective identification remained essentially defined by legal status.

---

[50] Castel 2002. For the specific case of classical Athens, see Taylor 2017.   [51] Offredi 1998, p. 28.
[52] Is it to be imagined that, unlike the other individuals whose professional specialty is specified, Eucolion had no precise professional specialization? Mentioning a profession undoubtedly implies a long-term commitment to a farm, or to an occupation that is part of an interdependent relationship – for example, like that of Pancleon, whose alleged master could affirm that his *technē* was that of a fuller.

The Impossible Union of Wage Workers

But the *misthōtoi* of free status are perhaps not the only men of classical Athens whose work was subject to a 'wage,' at least if one understands by this term the payment of money in return for completing a specific task. It is appropriate here to note a category of workers whose importance has been largely underestimated by historians: that of slaves who were rented out by their masters to a third party. Compared to a Eutherus, who was a citizen, or a Eucolion, who was a metic, these rented slaves were at the opposite end of the city's status spectrum, but from the point of view of the mechanisms of the Athenian economy, they were, on the contrary, singularly close to them and belonged to the same labor market, however embryonic that may have been.

At the end of the fifth century, Pseudo-Xenophon depicts slave hiring as a common feature of Athenian social life, and it is very tempting to attribute the rise of this practice to the modernity of the Attic economy.[53] Athenian oratory of the fourth century reveals numerous cases of rented slaves exercising their activity in a wide variety of sectors.[54] When we are allowed a glimpse of the composition of a rich Athenian family's estate, these rented slaves often constitute an important part of it.[55] We can therefore guess that they formed a supplementary workforce, essential to the activity of many craftsmen's workshops as well as to large agricultural holdings. Thus, at the beginning of the fourth century, a certain Therippides had placed three of his slaves in the workshop of Demosthenes' father. In the middle of the fourth century, a man named Arethousius regularly received rent for the slaves he had temporarily entrusted to landowners to carry out agricultural work. Entire sectors of Athenian economic activity, such as the mining industry or prostitution, were dependent on the hiring of slaves. In the middle of the fourth century, over 5,000 slaves worked, it seems, in Laurion. The renting of slaves was largely regulated by the city, which levied a tax on the income

---

[53] Pseudo-Xenophon, *Constitution of the Athenians*, 1.18. On the *oikonomia attikē*, see the remarks of Descat 1995, pp. 967–71.
[54] Agriculture: Demosthenes, *Against Nicostratus* (53), 20, 21. Craftsmen's workshops: Demosthenes, *Against Aphobus* I (27), 18–20, and *Against Aphobus* II (28), 12; Theophrastus, *Characters*, 30.15; Lysias, *Against Pancleon* (23), 7, describing the situation of a supposed slave whose master apparently placed him in a fuller's workshop (*gnapheion*). Mining: Andocides, *On the Mysteries* (1), 38; Xenophon, *Poroi*, 4.14–7; Xenophon, *Memorabilia*, 2.5.2; Demosthenes, *Against Pantaenetus* (37), 4, 26; Hyperides, *For Lycophron*, fr. 4. See Ismard 2019, pp. 80–95.
[55] See Aeschines, *Against Timarchus* (1), 97; Isaeus, *On the Estate of Ciron* (8), 35.

paid to the owner,[56] and a law dating back to the Solonian period had carefully delimited the respective responsibilities of those who hired out their slaves and those who rented them.[57] Slaves were paid according to how long they worked, not what they actually did; this system is, without a doubt, the most similar thing to modern wage employment within the ancient economy.[58]

Now, insofar as they were present in the various sectors of the Athenian economy, these slaves could compete with the *misthōtoi*. Certainly, it may be risky to look for traces of 'a real labor market, which would be organized with clear rules and whose evolution would be autonomous' in the classical city.[59] The work of most of the productive forces in the city (i.e. slaves working under the direct management of their masters) was not subject to competition on the part of an organized market. But this observation, which in fact applies as much to eighteenth-century France as to fifth-century Athens,[60] should not lead us to overlook the existence of specific configurations within which free workers and slaves were de facto placed in competition. Since it offered a labor force that was always available, capable of working over long periods of time without any remuneration other than the cost of physical upkeep, the institution of slavery relegated the salaried work of free men to a necessarily intermittent and always marginal occupation. In this sense, slavery hindered the development of a stable and durable wage-earning system within the free population. Based on the internal arrangements of the servile relationship, the renting of slaves nevertheless led to limited but very real competition between the *misthōtoi* of free status and the *misthophoroi* (slaves who provided their masters with a regular income). From an external point of view, which was that of the workshop-owners or farmers, this generated a chorus of enslaved *misthophoroi* and free *misthōtoi*, among whom it was possible to recruit workers.

But the competition between these two categories could obviously not give rise to any form of common subjectivation or solidarity: *Misthōtoi* and *misthophoroi* lived in two different worlds. In classical times, the renting of

---

[56] This is how we should interpret Xenophon's mention of such a tax dating back to the fifth century, *Poroi*, 4.25.
[57] See the interpretation of Hyperides, *Against Athenogenes* (3), 22, by Phillips 2009, pp. 89–122.
[58] See the reflections on Roman law of Thomas 1999.
[59] Feyel 2006, p. 431. See also Descat 1987, p. 252, who writes: 'Athens indeed represents what could be called a partially market economy where the market conquers a part of the economic circuits, but not all, and where there is no real labor market.'
[60] See Guerreau 2001.

slaves and the recruitment of free men for seasonal activities was organized in two very different places. In the Anakeion, located near the Theseion on the northern slope of the Acropolis, anybody could come to hire slaves for a limited period of time.[61] To the west of the Agora, in the deme of Colonus, there was a specific place that the Athenians called the *misthōterion*[62]: Here, free men could come to sell their skills as laborers for one day or one month.

Dividing the workforce that fed into the same labor market between two specific locations is in itself significant. While from the point of view of those who hired them, these two groups of workers were one and the same, with price variations likely correlating to each of the two markets, it was essential to keep them separate. No form of collective identity could result.

Friendship as a Mask for Subjection

Around the name Eutherus, historians are therefore condemned to a highly paradoxical operation, which consists of identifying a large and yet invisible category in the sources of the classical period. The end of the dialogue reported in Xenophon's *Memorabilia* sheds light on the value of this invisibilized work. Socrates concludes the conversation with his old friend Eutherus by recommending he finds 'benevolent men' to work with. 'In this way, I think, you are most likely to escape censure, find relief from your difficulties, live in ease and security, and obtain an ample competence for old age,'[63] he adds. If the whole of book II of the *Memorabilia* is devoted to a reflection on the nature of friendship (*philia*), the dialogue with Eutherus is part of a succession of four reported conversations in which Socrates gives advice to his friends who are experiencing financial hardship. In the first two dialogues, Socrates defends the value of an individual life based on work. The philosopher's purpose is indeed to highlight the value of the work of free men and women, considering that it is, by nature, different from that of slaves and can allow

---

[61] Bekker 1814, I, 267, p. 212. See also [Demosthenes], *Against Stephanus I* (45), 80. On the sanctuary of the Anakeion, see Luce 1998, p. 12. The fact that the twin figures (the Dioskouroi) worshipped here welcomed slaves shared between two masters is food for thought.

[62] See all the lexicographical sources collected by Fuks 1951. See also Taylor 2017, p. 179. There is also evidence of such places outside Athens: See the decree of Paros in the second century, which regulated conflicts between employers and *misthōtoi*; *IG* XII 5, 129, l. 16–20; in Magnesia of the Meander, at the time of Hadrian, there was a place south of the Agora for masons' employees: *I Magnesia*, 239a.

[63] Xenophon, *Memorabilia*, 2.8.6.

the fulfilment of individual virtue. While Eutherus provides us with the case of a citizen impoverished by the end of the Athenian empire, the character of Aristarchus embodies the rich Athenian who can no longer enjoy the income from his properties because of the *stasis* tearing the city apart. His sisters, cousins and nieces have even taken refuge in his house, and Aristarchus does not see how he can feed them.[64] In both cases, Socrates suggests turning to work: Just as he advises the poor Eutherus to work for a wealthy Athenian, he recommends the rich Aristarchus puts the fourteen free women who have moved into his house to work, as spinning wool will allow him to make the profit necessary for the survival of his *oikos*. In these two instances, Socrates truly vindicates the idea of work, which is unusual, to say the least, among classical authors.

However, we must remember that Eutherus cannot commit himself permanently to a job in the service of another without seeing it as a form of slavery. For Eutherus, the challenge is to make his work for others last, ensuring him a form of protection in the long run without affecting his status as a free man. Now, if Socrates defends the idea that working for others may be necessary in order to achieve a self-sufficient life, a relationship based on work can only legitimately be considered an extra-economic bond – a relationship of dependency, in short – that takes a clientelist form. In the *Memorabilia*, the dialogue with Eutherus is only the first in a series of three chapters in which Socrates comes to defend a utilitarian conception of *philia*, based on the complementarity and reciprocity of interests.[65] In this respect, Eutherus has Crito, a rich childhood friend of Socrates, who is prey to the Athenian sycophants, as his polar opposite. The philosopher advises the latter to establish patronage relationships with poor Athenian citizens. To keep the 'wolves' away from his fortune, he is encouraged to feed the 'dogs'; in other words, to establish stable bonds of *philia* with those we might call his 'clients' and maintain them in exchange for protection against the sycophants' attacks. The reciprocal exchange of benefits is at the heart of a client-like relationship 'adorned in the flattering attire of *philia*.'[66]

According to the same utilitarian conception of *philia*, Socrates convinces Eutherus to place himself under the patronage of a powerful citizen, engaging in a long-term unequal relationship based on the exchange of goods or services. Thus, it is only in the form of friendship that the work a free individual does for others can find its ideal social form: that of a

---

[64] Xenophon, *Memorabilia*, 2.7.2. See *supra*, Chapter 4, pp. 149–51.
[65] See Dorion 2013, pp. 195–218.
[66] Azoulay 2018, pp. 174–80 (citation p. 176). See also Taylor 2017, p. 134.

durable, asymmetrical but consensual social link, whose logic exceeds that of the exchange of goods. The register of *philia* can therefore enchant and veil what stay usually hidden: the dependency inherent in work carried out for others, which is always in danger of being interpreted as a form of slavery.

* * *

To what extent is the political commitment of the Athenians in 403 explained by their economic condition, regardless of whether they were owners of land and workshops or simply workers in a precarious situation? The character of Eutherus invites us to consider the role played by forms of collective identification based neither on adherence to a political camp – that of the democrats, neutrals, oligarchs or moderates – nor on membership of a statutory group, but on 'work status.'[67] In fact, Thrasybulus' army, in Samos in 411, as in Piraeus in 403, included *misthōtoi* citizens and metics, as well as former slaves, and one might be tempted to recognize in them the coalescence of free and nonfree individuals forming a chorus of precarious workers. At the same time, one cannot underestimate the elitist dimension of the policy conducted by the so-called moderates, such as Archinus, who, when democracy was restored, took care to destroy any possible alliance between workers brought together by the shared experience of battle.

As pertinent as it may be in explaining the events of 403, such an interpretation, which seemingly anchors political confrontations in the forms of social conflict rife in Athenian society (beyond the divide between free men and slaves), is nevertheless difficult to uphold in the light of the ancient sources, which tend to render invisible the world of free workers. In Xenophon's *Memorabilia*, the bond of dependence between Eutherus and his future patron relegates the chorus of the precarious *misthōtoi* of classical Athens to an off-stage position, which is so difficult to reconstitute and yet so very real. The Socratic discourse is indeed an ideological enterprise, in that it aims to conceal the conflict that sometimes divided the community of free men. Viewed through the lens of *philia*, the enhanced vertical bonds between rich owners and precarious workers tend to obfuscate the forms of subjectivation that perhaps brought together free workers and some of the slaves or freedmen, despite their different statuses.

---

[67] On the notion of work status, see Tran 2013.

CHAPTER 7

Hegeso or the Family Torn Asunder

To be of Irish or Italian stock, to piece together a family tree or to list the different branches of a given family: In our everyday vocabulary, origin, filiation and matrimony are often expressed through vegetal metaphors, as if we were unknowingly thinking of family and kinship as organic elements.[1] In fact, it is by no means certain that the family is a historical object like any other. Structural anthropology has taught us that the rules that organize exchanges within families can only be understood through structures and codes that are unaffected by historical events, since 'kinship phenomena are of the same type as linguistic phenomena.'[2] Claiming there had been an epistemological break with the historical discipline, Claude Lévi-Strauss thus assigned a mission to the anthropology of kinship to 'provide a logical framework for historical developments, which, while perhaps unpredictable, are never arbitrary.'[3] For their part, it is most often from the angle of studying 'private life' that historians have assessed this difficult subject, conceived of as a 'zone of immunity to which we may fall back or retreat, a place where we may set aside arms and armor needed in the public place, relax, take our ease, and lie about unshielded by the ostentatious carapace worn for protection in the outside world.'[4]

Is kinship a 'logical framework' indifferent to history? Is the family a 'zone of immunity' offered for withdrawal? The idea would have seemed strange to the ancient Greeks. In its very form, the city did not differentiate between ontology and kinship. In their view, the city had not been built in opposition to the family, but within its folds, by working around its tensions and dissonances. The ancient authors constantly meditated on the links that connected family feuds to civil war, as if any conflict in lineage could devastate a given community at any moment. Aristotle even tells the story, in the manner of a founding myth, of a dispute between two

---

[1] Klapisch-Zuber 2000; see Bretin-Chabrol 2012.   [2] Lévi-Strauss 1963, p. 34.
[3] Lévi-Strauss 1963, p. 23.   [4] Duby 1992, p. viii.

204

brothers from the small town of Histiaia. Initially spreading to close relatives, their dispute over their paternal inheritance eventually affected the whole town, which apparently split into two irreconcilable factions.[5] The way the Athenian tragic authors imagined the destiny of the rival cities of Argos and Thebes is barely any different. In both Oedipus' and Agamemnon's families, the same chain of events constantly reproduces itself: An entire family is torn apart and leads the community inevitably to its own end.[6] Athenian tragedies of the fifth century therefore offered a countermodel to the city of equals, which was also a city of brothers.

Family breakdowns reciprocally offer the most striking representation of the tragic consequences to which the *stasis* can lead. 'Sons were killed by their fathers, and suppliants dragged from the altar or slain upon it.'[7] It is in these terms that Thucydides describes the civil war that struck Corcyra during the Peloponnesian War. It seems that political conflict even came to corrupt all family bonds, since 'even kinship became a weaker tie than faction.'[8] Also, to refound the community at the end of a civil war very often implied not only restoring public institutions, but also recreating bonds of fraternity between citizens in the manner of a fictional family. In Nakone in Sicily at the beginning of the third century, the reconciled city thus undertook, under the observant eye of neighboring Segesta, to mix the partisans of its two opposing factions and, to that end, associate each one of its members with a group composed of five 'elected brothers,' drawn from each of the city's two conflicting halves. This civic decision even intended to establish new bonds between citizens at the expense of the traditional structures of kinship, since natural relatives (*anchisteis*) could no longer live together within the same group.[9] Civic kinship therefore supplanted the bonds that organized real kinship while adopting their essence and vocabulary.

The Domestic Chorus: The Oikos *of Ischomachus*

Encompassed by the double dimension of union and disunion, the family and the city, far from being opposed, are related. In the literature of the classical period, the choral metaphor is a beneficial resource for assessing the link between these two realities; it is in the shape of a well-ordered

---

[5] Aristotle, *Politics*, 1303b31–7.
[6] On the different dimensions of intrafamily conflict, see Damet 2012.   [7] Thucydides, 3.81.5.
[8] Thucydides, 3.82.6.   [9] See *supra*, Chapter 4, p. 140. See Loraux 2006, pp. 222–3; Asheri 1989.

chorus that Ischomachus, addressing his wife in Xenophon's *Oeconomicus*, appraises the community of work and life that is the *oikos*:

> My dear, there is nothing so convenient or so good for human beings as order. Thus, a chorus is a combination of human beings: but when the members of it do as they choose, it becomes mere confusion, and there is no pleasure in watching it; but when they act and chant in an orderly fashion, then those same men at once seem worth seeing and worth hearing.[10]

The interior space of the house, in its ideal form, even borrows the form of the cyclical chorus of the dithyramb: 'For each set looks like a chorus of utensils, and the space between the sets is beautiful to see, when each set is kept clear of it, just as a cyclic chorus about the altar is a beautiful spectacle in itself, and even the free space at the center looks beautiful and pure.'[11] The chorus therefore constitutes an ideal architectural model for organizing the various components of the *oikos*.

But let us not be mistaken: The choral household that Ischomachus celebrates is far from being an egalitarian community. On the contrary, it consists of two half-choruses, placed under the authority of two chorus-leaders: the virtuous wife, qualified as a 'Queen Bee,' and the father of the family, whose respective spheres are clearly delimited.[12] Ischomachus' statement establishes a spatial and functional partition between masculine and feminine, public and private[13]: 'And since both the indoor and the outdoor tasks demand labor and attention, the divinity from the first adapted the woman's nature, I think, to the indoor and man's to the outdoor tasks and cares.'[14] If Ischomachus' wife's prominent position at home is acknowledged, she remains nevertheless subordinate to her husband, as suggested by the fact that she is never named, making of her a generic representative of the 'female race' (*genos gunaikon*). Above all, any coryphaeus worth his salt must demonstrate the ability to make people respect the internal hierarchies that distinguish stewards, servants and slaves. The model proposed by Ischomachus is therefore indeed a 'theoretical construction aiming at putting the city in order.'[15] The choral paradigm provides a standard of authority as relevant for managing an *oikos* as for leading a city, which is why the knowledge of the domestic coryphaeus is fully political.

---

[10] Xenophon, *Oeconomicus*, 8.3.   [11] Xenophon, *Oeconomicus*, 8.20 (transl. Loeb modified).
[12] Xenophon, *Oeconomicus*, 3.15; 7.11–3; 7.17.   [13] Azoulay 2007b.
[14] Xenophon, *Oeconomicus*, 7.22.   [15] Schmitt Pantel 2009, p. 18.

A Disputed Heritage

A speech by Isaeus allows us to observe in detail a family chorus caught up in the turmoil of the Athenian civil war. It is at its heart that the heroine of this chapter, Hegeso, lived for most of her life. But before we can discuss her experiences as a wife and the mother of a citizen, as detailed on a funerary inscription, we need to look at the family dispute that mobilized the Athenian courts in 399.

Its rather confused origins date back to the year 411.[16] A rich Athenian by the name of Dicaeogenes died during the Battle of Cnidus. With neither a son nor a brother as heir, he had legally adopted one of his cousins. At first sight, this was very banal: The procedure of adoption, by which an old man made a young adult member of his extended family his successor and his heir – that is, the equivalent in law of a legitimate biological son (*gnēsios*) – was fairly common in classical Athens. The adopter thus secured the transmission of his assets to his kin and, above all, ensured that the funeral rites in his memory would be regularly performed.[17]

But let us look more closely at this agreement. Childless, Dicaeogenes (II) had chosen as his successor the biological son of his rich uncle by marriage, Proxenus of Aphidna, who took his name after the adoption (therefore becoming Dicaeogenes III). However, Dicaeogenes (II) had four sisters, meaning that many of his nephews, in the absence of a natural heir, could have claimed a share of his considerable fortune, which totaled almost ten talents.[18] According to Isaeus' speech, the will envisaged that only one third of the inheritance would go to the adopted son, the remainder being shared between the other nephews of Dicaeogenes (II). This agreement seems to have been respected during the first part of the decade 410–400. But in 403, Dicaeogenes (III) reneged on the agreement by taking Dicaeogenes (II)'s entire inheritance for himself, which led to him being sued by one of the nephews of Dicaeogenes (II), Menexenus, in 402. The lawsuit, which consisted of an *epidikasia* (a motion to contest the inheritance),[19] found in favor of Dicaeogenes (III), who was authorized to seize his adoptive father's house, demolish it and turn it into a garden adjacent to his own residence. Thus, the judgment was a clear victory for

---

[16] On the exact chronology of all the proceedings, see Cobetto Ghiggia 2002, pp. 34–40.
[17] See this point as particularly highlighted by Rubinstein 1993.
[18] Davies 1971, n. 3773, pp. 145–7. See also Humphreys 2018, pp. 203–7.
[19] Isaeus, *On the Estate of Dicaeogenes* (5), 6.

the adoptive son, who was also the deceased's cousin by his mother, to the detriment of the descendants of his sisters. Now, for our litigant, this legal action was intimately linked to the situation of *stasis* that the city was going through:

> During all this period, though the courts sat, no one of them thought of claiming that there was any injustice in what had been done, until, when the city suffered misfortune and strife arose, Dicaeogenes (III) here, acting at the instigation of Melas the Egyptian, whose advice he followed in everything, claimed from us the whole estate, alleging that he had been adopted as sole heir by our uncle.[20]

'When the city suffered misfortune and strife arose': The expression deserves to be more clearly defined. The situation indeed demonstrates that Dicaeogenes (III) took advantage of the restoration of the democracy to appropriate his adoptive father's estate in its entirety. If the crime had been committed during the civil war, it would be hard to find a reason for the litigant to avoid mentioning the fact that his adversary had rallied to the regime of the Thirty.

But how could a dispute over an obscure matter of inheritance be resolved in the aftermath of the civil war? A man of few words, our litigant contented himself with imputing his adversary's victory to the false testimonies to which he claimed he resorted, as well as to the intervention of a foreigner:

> However, on coming into court, though we had by far the better case, we were cheated of our rights, not by the judges but by Melas the Egyptian and his friends, who thought that the misfortunes of the city gave them liberty to possess themselves of other people's property and to bear false witness in support of one another, and by their acting in this manner the judges were misled.[21]

One cannot, however, take at face value what Isaeus' client affirms, and bringing up false testimonies under the influence of a foreigner seems to have been no more than a delaying tactic.

In fact, the matter was difficult to settle in legal terms. Although they undoubtedly appeared in the same document, the trial unfolded as if in 411 Dicaeogenes (II) had carried out two distinct legal actions, of which the two family branches, represented by the brothers-in-law of the deceased and Proxenus himself, were witnesses: By means of the first, the adoption, he had instituted a successor, designated as his son, and had

---

[20] Isaeus, *On the Estate of Dicaeogenes* (5), 7   [21] Isaeus, *On the Estate of Dicaeogenes* (5), 8.

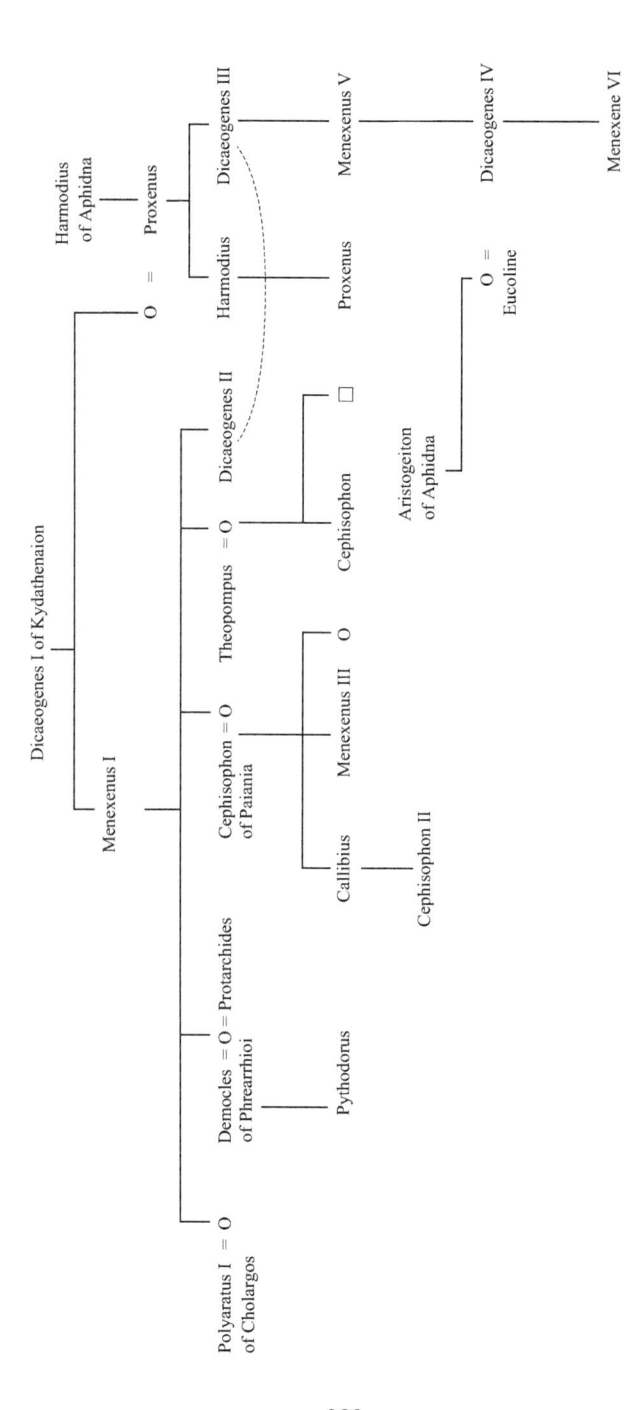

Fig. 7.1 *Stemma* of the family of Dicaeogenes of Kydathenaion.

entrusted to him the transmission of the rights of his *oikos*; by means of the second, his testament, he had limited the range of the inheritance by specifying that his adopted son would only inherit one third of his property.[22] Thus, his successor was not the full heir enjoying absolute rights over the *oikos* and its possessions. Such a case constituted a major and exceptional restriction with regard to the law of Solon on wills, which made the adopted son the universal heir.[23] Dicaeogenes (III) had, moreover, undoubtedly referred to this law in 399 to plead his case, considering that his status as adopted son made him the universal and incontestable heir, even to the detriment of the rightful claimants in the collateral line. It must be admitted that, by finding in favor of Dicaeogenes (III), the Athenian judges had defended a restrictive interpretation of the law of Solon, according to which one could not dissociate the transmission of the property from the recognition of filiation in a testamentary adoption.[24]

A Political Trial?

Such an interpretation has its charms, but it might lend to the Athenian court a legal rigor that it did not possess; furthermore, this alone is not enough to explain Dicaeogenes (III)'s victory. In fact, the denouement of the trial of 402 certainly had a political subtext, present in every aspect of the confrontation affecting the entire family of Dicaeogenes (II), which the litigant preferred not to mention. Several of the main characters were waiting in the wings of our family drama. Dicaeogenes (III)'s biological father was Proxenus of Aphidna. One of the Hellenotamiai in 410/9,[25] he had held an important position in Athens at the end of the fifth century.

---

[22] It is uncertain whether this may be considered testamentary adoption, strictly speaking, as Cobetto Ghiggia 1999, pp. 192–205, suggests. He does, however, point out (pp. 195–6) the initially contradictory nature of this form of adoption as compared to adoption as set out by Solon's law.

[23] See also Gernet 1920.

[24] This is notably the reading of Humphreys 2018, vol. 1, pp. 203–5, and, to a lesser extent, of Cobetto Ghiggia 1999, pp. 195–6. See also Cobetto Ghiggia 2002, pp. 18–33. It is perhaps only in the Hellenistic period that it became common to make individuals heirs by will without adopting them (see Rubinstein 1993, pp. 81–3, which reviews the historiography of the question and challenges the idea that adoption is the only way to transmit property by will). One might also consider that Dicaeogenes (II) benefited here from the law of amnesty that, according to some, implied that all judgments, but also contracts, conventions, etc., were rendered void. From this point of view, the will, which predates 403, would have been made null and void by the oath of amnesty. See Joyce 2008, which answers the thesis of Carawan 2002. The affair took a new turn ten years later when Leochares, convicted of false testimony, initiated a *diamarturia*, swearing that Dicaeogenes (III) was indeed the only heir. On adoption, see also the general remarks of Leduc 2011.

[25] *IG* I³ 375, l. 17, 28, 31, 37–8; Isaeus, *On the Estate of Dicaeogenes* (5), 6, 15.

A Political Trial? 211

More importantly, he was an eminent member of the *genos* of the Gephyreans and a direct descendant of Harmodius, one of the two famous Tyrannicides who were said to have freed Athens from the yoke of the Peisistratids in 514. Furthermore, the memory of the Tyrannicides had taken on a new flavor in the aftermath of the restoration of democracy: The ritual activities that took place around their two bronze statues are attested for the first time, and a hymn was included in the great festival of the Panathenaia in which the two 'liberators' were commemorated and honored 'on a par with the gods and heroes.'[26] It is, moreover, possible that these songs simultaneously celebrated the Tyrannicides and the resistance fighters of Phyle led by Thrasybulus.[27] How could we then imagine that during the trial of 402 the memory of this illustrious family did not play to the advantage of Proxenus' natural son? A few years later, the natural brother of Dicaeogenes (III), Harmodius, attacked the honorific decree granting a statue to Iphicrates. This was a rare distinction that would have put the victorious general on the same footing as his own ancestors. On this occasion, the accuser outlined the *eugeneia* of his prestigious lineage and the constancy of his commitment to serve the democracy.[28] The temptation is great, therefore, to see in the family of Proxenus a hotbed of democrats in a position of power in the city in 402.

Our litigant, Menexenus (II), was the nephew of Cephisophon, the brother-in-law of Dicaeogenes (II), whose sister he had married. A close friend of Rhinon, Cephisophon, as we have seen, was an important political character in the civil war, since he was the ambassador of the oligarchy in Sparta in the summer of 403.[29] The man was clearly on the side of the Three Thousand, and his position in the city, once democracy was restored, remained fragile and disputed. Above all, he was the son of Polyaratus of Cholargos, who had been secretary to the Council during the decisive year of 405/4 and perhaps played an important role in negotiating the Athenian surrender. Finally, one should perhaps recognize in the litigant's own brother-in-law a certain Eryximachus, mentioned in a fragmentary speech by Lysias, in which he was accused of having remained in the city during the oligarchy.[30] Therefore, the trial of 402 seems to lend

---

[26] Demosthenes, *On the Embassy* (19), 280, with the hypotheses of Azoulay 2017, pp. 75–7.
[27] Azoulay 2017, pp. 75–7.
[28] See Azoulay 2017, pp. 112–3. One of the sons of Harmodius, Proxenus of Aphidna (II), went on to be *stratēgos* himself on three occasions in the middle of the fourth century (*PAA* 789835).
[29] On Cephisophon, see *supra*, Chapter 3, pp. 111–3.
[30] Lysias, fr. 106 Carey: *huper Eruximachou meinantos en astei* (Carey 2007); see Davies 1971, n. 11907. On this speech, see *infra*, Chapter 10, pp. 287, 293.

itself to a political reading, the decision of the judges sanctifying the victory of a man, Dicaeogenes (III), whose biological family had proven their unfailing commitment to the democrats, and the defeat of a family who lined up on the side of the Three Thousand.

The City of the Dead: The Blended Family

As attractive as it may be, such a reading is also fragile. Considering Athenian political life as a confrontation between lineages with clearly defined positions tends to identify family solidarities and ideological positions too hastily. There is much to be gained from examining the Dicaeogenes affair in a different light. It should be noted that the result of the lawsuit recognized the defeat of the collateral kin of the deceased in favor of his direct, adopted descendant. The legal relationship of rights and duties, the *anchisteia*, codified according to the right of succession, acknowledged the primacy of the adopted son over all the collateral relatives. Taken from this point of view, the Athenian judges' decision can be seen in light of the shifts that characterize Athenian civic discourse at the turn of the fifth and the fourth centuries. Termed by some a 'politics of the *oikos*' promoted by the city, the *oikos* provided an ideological pattern for thinking about the ideal form of the community and, by extension, about the city itself.[31]

In 403 the restoration of democracy was accompanied by the reactivation of the law of Pericles, enacted for the first time in 451, but whose application had been suspended de facto during the years of war.[32] By establishing that only the children of citizen fathers and mothers would be citizens, the law granted an unprecedented place to the Athenian wife in the transmission of status. Uterine siblings, and, more broadly, what we would call the nuclear family, took on a new importance, to the detriment of the looser forms of solidarity based on membership of a shared male lineage.

The evolution of funerary practices is undoubtedly the best vantage point for viewing the new symbolic role given to the *oikos*, which now became the locus for familial belonging. It was indeed at the end of the fifth century that the use of the family *peribolos* (funerary enclosure), which first appeared in Attica in the 430s, became widespread.[33] Beyond their morphological diversity, hundreds of stelai erected along the main streets of the Kerameikos Cemetery came to portray an idealized representation of the *oikos* through the use of a limited repertoire of gestures and postures.

---

[31] See Marchiandi 2011a. [32] See *supra*, Chapter 2, p. 90. [33] Marchiandi 2011a, pp. 35–50.

By celebrating the memory of one or several individuals of the same lineage, these decorative reliefs exalted an ideal vision of harmony and concord as well as the filiation that allowed a single family chorus to unite several generations of the living and the dead. As Geneviève Hoffmann writes, 'to compensate for the sorrow of death, the funerary monument expresses a hope: that the inter-generational solidarity in time is reinforced by an alliance expressed in a precise place and eternalized in stone.'[34] What was new at the end of the fifth century was the 'publicization' of the *oikos*, now displaying itself in the public space, trying to draw the attention of passersby.[35] An idealized version of the family was projected and offered itself up to the public eye in the form of a funerary *oikos* within which all its members live together beyond death. Moreover, Daniela Marchiandi has shown that the arrangement of funerary markers within a family enclosure very often reproduced the internal hierarchies of the family structure, with the founding couple in the middle and the couples formed by their sons arranged around them.[36] Immediate family is presented as a harmonious, almost immutable rampart against the outside world and its divisions. Might we go so far as to assert that the development of this type of funerary art was also intended to offer a response to the conflicts of the city at the end of the fifth century?

Hegeso, the Seated Woman

Let us get a closer look at the city of the dead by taking one of the streets that led from the Sacred Gate across the Kerameikos Cemetery. By chance, the modern traveler can easily see an impressive funerary enclosure, arranged on a terrace like a small sanctuary.[37]

Several funerary monuments are still visible. To the right stands a large aedicula surmounted by a sculpted block (1.49 m high, 0.92 m wide) on which one can still make out slight traces of paint.[38] Framed by two columns, supporting a pediment, according to the canonical model of the *naiskos*, a domestic scene is represented. Seated on a comfortable armchair, a woman in a long, neatly draped *chiton* is shown; her left foot, wearing a beautiful sandal, rests on a small stool. A veil is slipping down her shoulder and there are jewels adorning her hair. Less formally dressed, but also wearing a long *chiton*, the young maid facing her is handing her a jewel box (*pyxis*), from which she has just removed a necklace that she is

---

[34] Hoffmann 1993, p. 175.   [35] Clairmont 2001, p. 18.   [36] Marchiandi 2011b, p. 148.
[37] Breder 2013, on the connection between the family *peribolos* and the sanctuary.
[38] Archaeological Museum of Athens 3624.

holding in her right hand.³⁹ The beauty of the stele has impressed archaeologists and historians so much that some recognize in it the style of the great sculptor Callimachus, to whom are attributed the sculptures in the frieze of the Athena Nike temple. The cost of the stele and the luxury of the goods represented (the chair and the jewels) testify to the fact that the deceased belonged to the Athenian elite: This is the enclosure of a powerful Athenian family. In the same way, there is no doubt that this woman was a wife, since she is represented in a stereotyped form corresponding to her role in the world of the living. Her seated position unambiguously indicates her status as a married woman according to the iconographic convention used for both mortals and immortals.⁴⁰

On the pediment of the *naiskos*, one can easily read a name:

> Hegeso (daughter) of Proxenus.

This woman is not unknown to us: The daughter of Proxenus of Aphidna, she is none other than the biological sister of Dicaeogenes (III). A woman alone, whose portrait is on display in a public space, without any male presence: It's a rare enough occurrence that we may be tempted to think this stele is an exceptional document testifying to a particular form of recognition not of womankind, but of an individualized woman. However, this would be wrong. For the very name of Hegeso can only be established through interaction with the other funerary monuments nearby, and this tends to erase the singularity of her presence by confining her to the role of the model wife.

The family *peribolos* can be read as an *orchestra*, in the center of which a chorus-leader speaks, offering the true meaning to the memorial of Hegeso. In the same funerary enclosure stood two other stelai. On the first one, 3 m high and crowned by a beautiful palmette, five names are engraved, in the following order:

> Sosicles, (son) of Euthydemos of the deme of Eitea
> Coroibos, (son) of Cleidemides of the deme of Melite
> Cleidemides, (son) of Coroibos of the deme of Melite
> Coroibos (son) of Cleidemides of the deme of Melite
> Euthydemos, (son) of Sodicles of the deme of Eitea.⁴¹

---

[39] Clairmont 1993, pp. 95–8. The necklace must have been painted on the stele and not carved.
[40] See in particular Lissarrague 2000, pp. 163–70.
[41] *IG* II² 6008. For Weber 2001, whereas the memorial of Hegeso may date back to the years 420–410, the erection date of the stele of Coroibos seems to be prior to 429 (an assumption picked up by Hildebrandt 2006, pp. 105–6). The presence of the two rosettes between the first and the following names assures us that, in any case, they were engraved during two different periods.

Fig. 7.2 The stele of Hegeso. National Archaeological Museum of Athens.

Fig. 7.3 The enclosure of Coroibos of Melite (Kerameikos, Athens).

On the second one, which had the shape of a loutrophoros vase, was engraved the following epigram:

Lady Sophrosune, daughter of great-minded Aidos,
one who has given much honor (*pleista se timēsas*) to you and to Arete, good in war,
Cleidemos of Melite, son of Cleidemides, lies here,
once the source of his father's pride, now of his mother's pain.[42]

This epigram celebrates the memory of an Athenian who died at war. If it recalls the hoplite values that the deceased showed in combat (his *sophrosunē* and *aretē*), it does not, however, say a word about the battle during which he died. We will never know where and when Kleidemos gave the shining proof of his courage. The celebration of his glorious death in combat and the exaltation of his excellence as a warrior make it possible to silence the memory of the civil war.

One name is particularly striking in this long engraved list: that of Coroibos of Melite. Perhaps we should recognize here the famous architect

---

[42] *IG* II² 6859 (= Clairmont 1970, n° 79), transl. González González 2019. On the different and always fragile dating hypotheses, see Breder 2013, p. 184.

Fig. 7.4 Funerary stele of Coroibos of Melite (Kerameikos, Athens) (= *IG* II² 6008).

of Pericles, designer of the Telesterion in the Eleusinian sanctuary, who died at the beginning of the Peloponnesian War.[43] It is, however, very difficult to establish the links that unite all of these men. According to the custom that the same names are repeated every two generations within the same family, one can guess that the first stele was engraved with names belonging to two distinct male lines: on the one hand, that of Coroibos of the deme of Melite, which included at least his son Cleidemides and his grandson Coroibos (to which it is necessary to add Cleidemos, son of Cleidemides, celebrated on the adjacent monument)[44]; and on the other hand, that of Sosicles of the deme of Eitea, whose son, Euthydemos, was honored in the same enclosure.[45] The link between these two male lines, whose history is rooted in two different demes of Attica, is impossible to establish. It seems difficult to imagine that, like a cuckoo that has come to roost in the nest of another bird, members of the family of Eitea wished to list their deceased with the men of Melite if they had no family ties. Family alliances can be guessed at in the background but do not mention those who mainly brought them about: the mothers and wives. Just as it celebrates the union of two *oikoi*, this monument makes no mention of the women who made it possible.

How then can we interpret this face-to-face encounter between a woman, designated by her name and patronymic alone, and the whole of the male lineage extending over five generations? First, let us observe that Hegeso was not buried with her father, since the tomb of Proxenus of Aphidna was far from the Kerameikos Cemetery.[46] It is therefore in her husband's family *peribolos* that she found her final resting place. To determine the name of her husband and guardian (*kurios*) among those engraved on the stele is, however, difficult; no conclusions can be drawn, although the son of the great architect, Cleidemides, seems the best candidate.[47]

---

[43] Plutarch, *Pericles*, 13.7; *IG* I³ 32, l. 26 (= K. Clinton, *I. Eleusis*, n° 30, l. 25 – now lowered to 432/1).
[44] According to Clairmont 1970, p. 154, Cleidemos, son of Cleidemides, was Hegeso's brother-in-law. He may also be the brother of Coroibos (II).
[45] Let us, moreover, note that the inscription *IG* II² 6001, which mentions Euthydemos, son of Sosicles of Eitea, was found near the *peribolos*.
[46] *IG* II² 5765.
[47] The reconstruction proposed by Weber 2001 poses a chronological problem. Coroibos apparently died at the beginning of the 420s. If Dicaeogenes (II) was born in the 420s, as, it seems, did Harmodius (the other son of Proxenus), there is no reason to date the birth of Hegeso, their sister, to any earlier than the initial years of the 420s. That she was the wife of Coroibos then seems hardly credible; she could, on the other hand, have married his son, Cleidemides. Marchiandi 2011a, pp. 304–5, adopts a hypercritical approach by suggesting that she could even have been the wife of Cleidemides' son, Coroibos (II), treasurer of Athena, in 370/69 (*IG* II² 1424a, l. 4). It is, however, difficult to date the erection of the *naiskos* of Hegeso to the fourth century for stylistic reasons.

But the absence of any explicit link between Hegeso and her *kurios* is in itself significant. It is as if it was less important to recall the memory of them as a couple than to celebrate the alliance that had been concluded between the two *oikoi* of Proxenus and Koroibos and sealed by the transfer of Hegeso from one house to the other. We should bear in mind that marriage in classical Athens took place in two acts: the *enggue* and the *ekdosis*. Whereas the *ekdosis* consisted in the transfer of the authority of the bride's father to her future husband, most often in the presence of the other family members, the *enggue*, which was an essential preliminary, took the form of an oral agreement by which the father and the future husband agreed on the amount of the dowry. The prominence given to the jewels on the stele should be understood in this sense; their presence indirectly recalled the dowry of Hegeso, on which the two parties had agreed and whose transfer sealed the alliance.[48]

The scenic arrangement also celebrated, according to well-known iconographic stereotypes, the functional partition between male and female within the *oikos*. It is at first sight a representation of the two half-choruses – male and female – that constitute the *oikos* according to the ideological construction formulated by Ischomachus. The symmetry was, however, far from perfect: While all of the men are mentioned by their name, Hegeso, placed by their side, seems to occupy a different position. Certainly, her memory is individualized, but she is not commemorated as a member of any community of women within the *oikos*. The reason is simple: The very figure of Hegeso assures a metonymic function.[49] Just as the nameless woman of Ischomachus in Xenophon's *Oeconomicus* serves as the archetypal model wife, Hegeso plays the role of representative – or coryphaeus – of several generations of wives of the *oikos*, whose memory was presumably also honored in the enclosure; she is, in this sense, an impersonal figure embodying the feminine protagonist indispensable to the reproduction of the *oikos* from generation to generation.[50]

This partition also makes it possible to symbolically oppose interiority and immutability to exteriority and movement. The deceased wife is represented in a domestic scene; the long-backed chair on which she is sitting is an interior item, and the jewels symbolize better than anything else the *kosmos* proper to the female world. Ordering the space around her,

---

[48] Leader 1997, p. 692.
[49] Schmaltz 2002 (especially on the relationship between name and image).
[50] On the other hand, Xenophon explicitly attacked the wives 'who sit about like fine ladies, expose themselves to comparison with painted and fraudulent hussies' (*Oeconomicus*, 10.13).

Hegeso is enthroned here in the manner of Hestia, the divinity of the hearth and a pledge to fixity, immutability, permanence,[51] to whom Zeus, in return for staying unmarried, offered a central place in the *oikos*.[52]

* * *

The family chorality celebrated by Ischomachus leads us, then, to two children of one of the most illustrious families of fifth-century Athens: that of Proxenus of Aphidna. Hegeso and Dicaeogenes (III) were in their way caught in symmetrical forms of logic, which led them both to leave the paternal *oikos*: Whereas Dicaeogenes (III) inherited his cousin's *oikos*, whose name he took following his adoption, his biological sister left the paternal *oikos* to join that of her husband in Melite. The paths they took are good examples of the games of alliance and the circulation of wealth organized through adoption and marriage within the Athenian social elite.

The destiny of the two children of Proxenus of Aphidna reveals two contradictory faces of the same family group caught up in the events of 403. Union and disunion: The two opposing factions must be considered together. Far from constituting a zone of withdrawal and intimacy, families were rife with political conflicts. The memorial of Hegeso nevertheless exhibits the harmony of the family sphere in the form of two half-choruses singing in tune: the regulated game of exchanges from which marriage proceeds, as well as the regulated gender divisions within it. Celebrating the fixity and the permanence of family lineage, this portrayal masks, or staves off, political turbulence by presenting the *oikos* as existing in an unchanging temporal space: that of its cyclic reproduction from one generation to the next.

Finally, the history of the family reveals the impact of war on the life of Athenian families from the fifth century. It was during the Battle of Cnidus in 411 that Dicaeogenes (II) died, shortly after having adopted the biological son of Proxenus of Aphidna, just as Cleidemos, the son of Cleidemides, then a young man, fell in a foreign war during the early decades of the fourth century. The epigram engraved in his honor is remarkably discreet about the nature of the battles in which he perished: We will never know the date or the place where Cleidemos made his ultimate sacrifice. The exaltation of his glorious death on the battlefield makes it possible to hush up the memory of the civil war.

---

[51] Vernant 1983, p. 161: 'To Hestia belongs the world of the interior, the enclosed, the stable, the retreat of the human group within itself; to Hermes, the outside world, opportunity, movement, interchange with others.' See in particular the reflections of Hoffmann 1993, p. 161–2.

[52] *Homeric Hymn to Aphrodite*, 30: *mesō oikō*.

CHAPTER 8

Gerys and the World of the Merchant Agora

This scene has no Thucydides to narrate it, and very few ancient historians count it among the great political confrontations of fifth-century Athens. Aristotle and Xenophon only mention it in the course of more extensive developments, almost reluctantly, as if a nagging discomfort persisted by simply recalling it. Let us summarize it, once again: Following his victory, Thrasybulus proposed a decree granting citizenship to 'all those who had come back together from Piraeus, some of whom were clearly slaves.'[1] Acting as a 'good citizen,' as Aristotle writes, Archinus sued him for 'indictment for illegality' (*graphē paranomōn*) and won the case.

The laconism of ancient sources has not prevented some modern scholars from making this a major episode in the history of Athenian slavery, to the point of designating Thrasybulus as one of the precursors of modern abolitionism. The man who had given freedom back to the Athenian citizens had also been the defender of the freedom of *all men*. Thrasybulus thus became the name under whose aegis the humanist heritage of classical Athens and the abolitionist movement could meet, even proving, for some, that there was a hidden link, a common source, for democratic principles and the abolition of the slave order.

To this desire, or this fantasy, one must issue a firm denial. Thrasybulus' proposal aimed only to grant citizenship to the slaves who had joined his fight and not to emancipate all enslaved people. Above all, there is no evidence that in democratic Athens chattel slaves were treated better than elsewhere because of the existence of democratic institutions. On the contrary, Athens seems to offer the first example in history of a genuine slave society; indeed, the experience of political freedom to which we attach the name of democracy is inseparable from it.[2]

Let us listen again to the way Theramenes harangues his judges as his execution is imminent: 'But I, Critias, am forever at war with the men who

[1] Pseudo-Aristotle, *Athenian Constitution*, 40.2.   [2] Ismard 2019.

do not think there could be a beautiful democracy until the slaves and those who would sell the city for lack of a drachma should share in the public affairs.'[3] The sentence is surprising, and if it echoes the violence of the political controversy rife in the city of the final two decades of the fifth century, it seems at first sight to deny the intimate link between the democratic regime and the exploitation of slaves. Did such a discourse providing for those 'without shares' ever exist in classical Athens? Or is it a pure rhetorical exaggeration, with Theramenes imputing to his ancient adversaries an unthinkable transgression? The dilemma is difficult to solve. Theramenes' statement at least invites us to grasp in the same hand two propositions that are ostensibly contradictory, but whose combination condenses the peculiarities of the Athenian experience: On the one hand, slavery was an indispensable condition for the emergence of a direct democracy; on the other hand, the term *dēmokratia* contained in itself the principle of equality that potentially, at least, could lead to the granting of political rights to slaves, however unlikely that may have been in practice.

Slave Names

Theramenes' statement comes at a singular moment in the history of the Athenian institution of slavery, which was severely tested during the final decades of the Peloponnesian War. Many slaves had made the most of the repeated invasions of Attica by the Spartan troops to take flight, contributing to the disorganization of Athenian production. So, in 413, more than 20,000 slaves had fled following the Spartan occupation of the fortress of Deceleia.[4] Faced with adversity, the Athenians had also had to integrate contingents of slaves into their army, de facto dissociating the privilege of carrying a weapon and fighting for the city from the status of citizen.

It is during these same years that slavery acquires an exceptional visibility on the documentary level. Several epigraphic documents tell us the names of hundreds of Athenian slaves, briefly freeing them from the anonymity in which literary sources traditionally kept them. The stelai of the Hermokopidai (also known as the Attic stelai), engraved in 411, take stock of the goods seized by the city from the men convicted for having mutilated the Herms. Among these goods were forty-five slaves whose names the inscriptions provide. If some of these names are very conventional (such as Pistos, the 'faithful man'), the majority indicate their ethnic

---

[3] Xenophon, *Hellenica*, 2.3.48.
[4] Thucydides, 7.13.2, 7.27.5, on the escape of slaves hired in Sicily.

origin (for example, the name Thraitta, 'Thracian woman,' is used to indicate a female Thracian slave).[5] The accounts of the building of the Erechtheion temple on the Acropolis, compiled in 407/6, moreover provide the names of several dozen slaves alongside their masters, who worked for the city in the company of free men, citizens or metics. Finally, a long inscription from the last decade of the fifth century lists the men hired to work on eight Athenian triremes during one of the last battles of the Peloponnesian War. Under the category of 'servants' (*therapontes*), the names of 146 slaves are listed, representing between a quarter and a half of the whole naval crew.[6]

What use can the historian make of these lists? The matter is more complex than it seems. If the scholarly poetics of history indeed imply that 'we must name subjects [and] attribute to them states, affections, events,'[7] they certainly meet a limit here, due to the onomastic regime specific to all slave societies. Let us remember that the name of a slave does not follow the same rules as those of a free man.[8] Nothing is more eloquent in this respect than the acts by which a master manumitted one of his slaves, consecrating or selling his body (*sôma*) to a divinity. Thus, in the sanctuary of Apollo at Delphi, in the second century BC, according to a well-documented formulary model, 'Ateisidas son of Orthaios sold to Pythian Apollo three female bodies, whose names are Antigona, of Jewish origin, and her daughters Theodora and Dorothea, at the price of seven silver mines, and he has the whole price.'[9] By dissociating the body, gender and the name, the formula emphasizes the social death that characterized slave status. The name given to a 'body' that is also a commodity is no more than a pure artifact and not the repository of any civil or legal identity. Masters were free to change any slave's name without affecting their identity: 'When we give names to our domestic slaves, the new ones are as correct as the old,' Hermogenes asserts in Plato's *Cratylus*.[10] In short, the servile regime removed all names from their own truth – that is to say, from being registered in the order of filiation.

Because it does not cover any positive identity, servile onomastics alone reveals the difficulties encountered in analyzing the institution of slavery through the ordinary methods of social history. In fact, if historians have sometimes considered slaves as a collective subject, to be appraised as a

---

[5] *IG* I³ 421.   [6] *IG* I³ 1032; see *supra*, Chapter 2, p. 74.   [7] Rancière 1994, p. 2.
[8] See, for example, in very different contexts, the reflections of Cousseau 2013; Hébrard 2003; Williamson 2017.
[9] *CID* V 379.   [10] Plato, *Cratylus*, 384d.

class or an order, and if they have questioned the civic imagination of Greek slavery, they have hardly ever ventured to tell the story of an Athenian slave. Let's try to do so, however, by following the exceptional adventures of one of the soldiers in Thrasybulus' army ...

An Exemplary Greengrocer

The decree voted by the Athenians in 401 lists the name of several hundred combatants by distinguishing between two categories of individuals. The men present by Thrasybulus' side in Phyle are granted the statute of citizen, probably without being integrated into the demes and the phratries. On the other hand, for those who joined the combat later, the Athenians granted only *isoteleia* (tax equality) and *engguēsis* (the right to marry a member of the Athenian community and produce legitimate offspring). These men, around 850 in all,[11] were registered as members of the Athenian tribes, within which they enjoyed the privilege of being able to fight for the city. On the thirteenth line of the third column of this long inscription, one can easily decipher the name of a certain Gerys. Let us try to unroll a series of hypotheses to identify who he was.

On the onomastic level, it is initially tempting to consider that before 403 Gerys was a slave. Certainly, when we encounter him in 401, he has just acquired the status of a privileged metic (*isotelēs*), but there is every indication that he had been one of the slaves fighting at Thrasybulus' side. This name can indeed be found nine times in the Athenian documentation of the last decade of the fifth century and the beginning of the fourth century[12]; and, in eight cases out of nine, it refers to a slave: The name obviously carries a servile stigma. As Kostas Vlassopoulos noted, it is therefore necessary to admit that Gerys kept his slave name when he became an *isotelēs* in 401. This is completely exceptional: In doing so, he undoubtedly aimed to commemorate his democratic engagement in 403.

Derived from *gēruō* ('to make a voice heard, to celebrate'), the name Gerys is nevertheless paradoxical for a slave, symbolically designating as the holder of a 'voice' one who, legally speaking, was deprived of precisely this.

---

[11] Rhodes and Osborne 2003, n° 4, l. 1–9. See *supra*, Chapter 2, pp. 88–90.
[12] See Osborne 1981–1983. *IG* I³ 475, l. 69, 254, 290 (in 409/8); *IG* I³ 476, l. 82, 231, 313; *IG* I³ 1032, 116; 261; 265; 325; 404; 459. The ninth attestation undoubtedly concerns a freedman *chōris oikountēs* (i.e. freed from all obligations toward his former master and registered in his place of residence in the fourth century): *SEG* 19, 173. A miller named Gerys (*mulōthros*) of uncertain status can also be identified (*IG* II² 10995, fourth century BC). See Vlassopoulos 2015, pp. 125–6, and, more generally, Canevaro and Lewis 2014.

This is perhaps the result of the Hellenization of a name of Thracian origin: Based on the Thracian root *Ger-*, the Greeks may have come up with a name of Greek appearance, but whose foreign origin remained perfectly audible.[13] This attractive hypothesis would therefore make Gerys one of the many Athenian slaves originating from Thrace, a region that became, with Scythia and Anatolia, the main source for slaves in the Greek world of the classical era.

Exceptionally, the decree mentions the profession of each of the individuals that the Athenians chose to honor. Beside the name Gerys was engraved the word *lachanopō(lēs)*, greengrocer. Our man therefore sold figs, cabbages or turnips on the Athenian markets, and we like to imagine him going every morning to the Agora and setting up in his allotted place, where the fruit and vegetables were sold. In the center of one of the circles (*kukloi*) in which sales took place, we envision him, under the watchful eye of the *agoranomoi*, haranguing the passersby. His activity undoubtedly forced him to make frequent round trips into the Attic countryside to fetch supplies, but also to sell his products in the local markets spread across the demes of Attica. If Gerys was indeed a greengrocer slave even before he became an *isotelēs* in 403, one must suppose that his activity granted him a certain independence from his master, so he may in fact represent a specific category of slaves well known in Athens: 'Settled slaves,' placed by their masters at the head of a store or a workshop, in exchange for which they paid them a regular income, while enjoying a certain autonomy in running the business.[14] Once he became a metic, Gerys had to pay a special tax, created in 403, which targeted foreign merchants in the Agora.[15]

Thrasybulus' decree therefore illuminates fleetingly, in the manner of a snapshot, the situation of the former slave Gerys in 401, just as he acquired the status of metic. Two further inscriptions allow us to reconstruct the activities of our character both before and after this crucial date.

If Dying Is a Beautiful Thing …

Perhaps Gerys was involved in the final battles of the Peloponnesian War. The name Gerys indeed appears five times in the list of the fighting slaves present on the eight Athenian triremes during this period.[16] The man who

---

[13] See Middleton 1982, p. 300.   [14] Ismard 2019, pp. 96–105.
[15] Demosthenes, *Against Euboulides* (57), 34; also Bekker 1814, I, 267.
[16] *IG* I³ 1032, l. 116, 261, 265, 404, 459. On this inscription, see *supra*, Chapter 2, p. 74. On the identification of the battle in question, see the cautious conclusions of Funke 1983, pp. 164–9, who dates the list more generally to the years 408–400. There is no indication that slaves were only called

fought on the hill of Mounychia by Thrasybulus' side in 403 was perhaps experienced in military matters.

But our knowledge of Gerys comes above all from a splendid epitaph that was engraved in the fourth century on a stele and placed within a family funeral enclosure. On it, Gerys, his wife, Nico, and his son, Theophilos, recall their status of *isotelēs*: We can therefore be sure this is the same Gerys to whom this privilege had been granted because of his participation in the battle at Mounychia.[17] The epitaph gives voice to two speakers, Gerys and Nico:

Gerys, *isotelēs*. Nico. Wife of Gerys. Theophilos, *isotelēs*.
If dying is a beautiful thing, [then] Fortune has assigned this to me too.
I, who was not prizeless (*agerastos*) by the gods while I was looking at the light (of life),
I offered myself without reproach to all men (*pasin anthrōpoisi*)
The earth received me as an honorable man for the gods who live below[18]
I was by nature the wife of this man, matching in all respects old age and meditation because of my piety.[19]

Dating from between 340 and 317, the inscription was engraved after the death of Theophilos. As a son, he recalled the privilege of *isoteleia* once granted to his father, perhaps indirectly celebrating the glorious deed that gave rise to it. The mark of honor (*geras*) formerly granted to Gerys is undoubtedly the *isoteleia* that had been conferred to him by the city in 401. Since his son Theophilos designates himself as an *isotelēs* metic, we must imagine that Gerys did not benefit from the privilege of *egguēsis*, by virtue of which he could have married an Athenian and given birth to a citizen. His wife, Nico, is probably therefore not be Athenian, and perhaps their union took place prior to the events of 403.[20]

Philologists agree that the first lines of the epitaph are a paraphrase of an epigram attributed to Simonides: 'If the greatest part of virtue is to die nobly, then Fortune granted it to us above all others; for we strove

---

on for the battle of Arginusae mentioned by Xenophon (*Hellenica*, 1.6.24), nor moreover that slaves were confined to the role of auxiliaries. If Arginusae represents an exceptional configuration, it is because citizenship was granted to slaves who fought there (Aristophanes, *The Frogs*, 693–4). Thucydides (7.13.2) even seems to imply that the latter played an important role during the Sicilian expedition. See Graham 1992.

[17] The link, established by Osborne 1981–1983, has rarely been questioned.
[18] Gallavotti 1979, pp. 152–3, surprisingly sees in it an allusion to the Demeteric religion.
[19] *IG* II² 7863 (= Peek 1689 = Hansen 1989, vol. 2, n° 595). Transl. Tsagalis 2008, p. 70.
[20] The union formed by Gerys and Nico deserves to be compared with the over twenty-year-long marriage that united Pasion, the former slave banker turned citizen, with Archippe, a free woman who was undoubtedly a metic, before her husband willed her to Phormion, also a freed slave. "(Ismard 2018)", and in the bibiography = P. Ismard, "Phormion l'Athénien", Dike, 21, 2018, p. 183–200.

If Dying Is a Beautiful Thing . . . 227

to crown Greece with freedom and lie here in possession of unaging praise.'[21] This epigram, which seems to have been engraved on the tomb of the Athenians who died at Plataea (479) or at Chaeronea (338),[22] celebrates the military action of the Athenians in the service of their fatherland and of the freedom of the Greeks. The civic ideology is implicitly used by Theophilos for the benefit of his own lineage, as if his father's participation in the liberation of Athens in 403 echoed the combat of Athenian citizens in the most heroic moments of their history. The epitaph therefore seems to correlate the military glory of Gerys with that of the heroes of Athenian history who had given their lives for the fatherland.[23] Moreover, by mentioning the three names of Gerys, Nico and Theophilos, it celebrates the exemplary integration of the family of a former slave who became not only a metic but an *isotelēs*. If one accepts that Gerys, once freed, kept his slave name, it must simultaneously be noted that he gave his son, Theophilos, a very common Athenian name.

But assimilating Gerys to the heroes of Athenian history also deserves to be examined in relation to the complex rhetorical strategy implied by epigrammatic writing itself, which is based on the convergence of several identities. Jesper Svenbro emphasized the unusual position of the epigrammatic genre between orality and writing, by which the reader of an epitaph becomes the 'the vocal instrument of the writing that cannot do without it.'[24] Written in the first person, an epitaph is intended to be read publicly. 'For the text to achieve complete fulfilment, the reader must lend his voice to the writing'[25]: The reader is therefore invited to project themselves onto the figure of the deceased, for whom they become the spokesperson. The epitaph conjures up an open stage upon which different identities converge by exalting service to the city. The glorious combat of Gerys is placed under the aegis of the Athenians who died in heroic circumstances at Plataea or Chaeronea, and the audience of the inscription becomes the instrument of his fame and his memory by embodying him, even if only for as long as they are reading the inscription.

Now, this singular device truly comes into it own when you read aloud the text of the epitaph. Gerys boasts of having given himself entirely *to all men* (*pasin anthrōpoisi*), by which he means all human beings in the broadest possible sense, whether they are men or women, citizens, metics or slaves. The epitaph claims to offer an ethical lesson to passersby of all

---

[21] *Palatine Anthology*, 7.253 (= fr. VII Campbell 1991).
[22] See the discussion in Kowerski 2005, pp. 193–4, and Tsagalis 2008, pp. 70–4.
[23] See the remarks of Tsagalis 2008, p. 73.   [24] Svenbro 1993, p. 47.
[25] Svenbro 1993, pp. 45–6.

social statuses: that of a pious and good man, whose life was devoted to serving the Athenian city. In a funerary context, it shows how status distinctions have been suspended in favor of the exaltation of Athenian patriotic rhetoric.

With what thread should we weave our hero into Athenian social life? Reconstructing a social context in which slaves may have participated is obviously perilous, considering the act of fundamental desocialization that is at the origin of slavery and seems to forbid slaves from any participation in the shared world of free men. Aristotle thus establishes that a master and his slave cannot share the bond of friendship (*philia*) necessary for the existence of any community:

> It is like the relation between a craftsman and his tool, or between the soul and the body [or between master and slave]. All these instruments it is true are benefited by the persons who use them, but there can be no friendship, nor justice, towards inanimate things; indeed not even towards a horse or an ox, nor yet towards a slave as slave. For master and slave have nothing in common: a slave is a living tool, just as a tool is an inanimate slave.[26]

Aristotle's statement is revealing of an ideology of slavery that envisages the relationship of a master to his slave in its instrumental dimension. If it is based on violence, the bond of mutual, dissymmetrical, involuntary dependence that unites a master and his slave is obviously much more complex and often includes an emotional dimension. More broadly, no slave society can survive without the development of spaces within which free and enslaved people come to mingle, and classical Athens is no exception. As a slave and then as an *isotelēs*, Gerys was obviously involved in all sorts of relationships with Athenians, both free and unfree. Several choruses can be inferred at the various sites where this former slave was active.

Men and Women of the Agora

The Agora is the first of these. As the speeches of the fourth century show, the vast space of the Agora and the set of stalls that occupied it were regular gathering places for all forms of groups in Athens. The residents of the deme of Deceleia, in the north of Attica, used to gather around a barber's stall, while the Plataeans, recently integrated into the civic community,

---

[26] Aristotle, *Nicomachean Ethics*, 1161a–b.

used to meet once a month at the fresh cheese market.[27] In this vast open space, at the center of the urban arena, men and women of very different statuses rubbed shoulders, the logic of commercial exchange neutralizing the status distinctions that structured political life. One document among others reveals the heterogeneous and variegated character of the Athenian Agora. A curse tablet from the fourth century, written by a merchant, dooms a multitude of individuals to misfortune:

> Side A: I bind Callias the innkeeper in the neighborhood, and his wife Thraitta and the inn of the bald man, and the inn of Athemion nearby ... and Philon the innkeeper. Of all these men, I bind spirit, work, hands, feet, their inns. I bind Sosimenes his brother and Carpos his servant, the fabric seller, and Glycanthis whom they call Malthake and Agathon the innkeeper, who is the slave of Sosimenes. Of all these I bind spirit, work, life, hands, feet. I bind Cittos the neighbor, the maker of wooden frames [ropes?] and Cittos' craft and work, and spirit and mind and the tongue of Cittos. I bind Mania the innkeeper, the woman near the spring, and the inn of Aristandros of Eleusis and their work and mind. Spirit, hands, tongue, feet, mind. All of them I bind in the ... grave in the presence of Hermes the Binder.
> Side B: (I bind) The slaves of Aristandros.[28]

It is likely that some sort of commercial rivalry is at the origin of these threats, but that is not the main point. The tablet offers above all a striking insight into the Athenian commercial sphere, in which individuals of very different statuses crossed paths. Only one individual is mentioned with a demotic, which attests to his citizenship (Aristandros of Eleusis); beyond this, determining the legal status of these people proves difficult. While some of them have names that were widespread among Athenian citizens, such as Callias or Philon, others by contrast have typical slave names, such as Carpos or Thraitta. The writer of the tablet did not bother to qualify all his opponents with their legal status: Within the world of the *agoraioi* – the craftsmen and merchants of the Agora – legal distinctions had only marginal importance compared to the professional activity of each of its members. There is even an example of a man with a typically servile name, Sosimenes, who owns or at least has in his possession slaves, which confuses things still further. This curse also shows the extent to which women played a role in the economic activity of the Agora. Finally, it appears that slaves are at the head of real stalls and, under the more or less

---

[27] See Lysias, *Against Pancleon* (23).
[28] *IG* III Appendix: *Defixionum Tabellae*, 87. See Eidinow 2007, p. 371.

rigorous control of their master, seem to enjoy a certain autonomy. Carpos, the slave of Sosimenes, therefore manages a stall, whereas Cittos, with his name of servile origin, seems to have been a manufacturer of ropes. Our greengrocer Gerys, a slave then a metic, blends into this landscape perfectly, and one can imagine how he came to find his place within the chorus of the *agoraioi*.

It would be wrong, however, to reduce the Agora to its commercial dimension and to imagine, consequently, the world of the *agoraioi* as cut off from a political life reserved for citizens only. The Agora was both a market and a politicized space within which political information circulated during particularly bitter debates. In this sense, it constituted well and truly one 'of the complementary, even parallel, places of political participation,'[29] where noncitizens found their rightful place. In Aristophanes' *Wasps*, Bdelycleon gives voice to a colleague of Gerys, who is also a greengrocer, suggesting that the political fate of the city could rest on plots hashed out at the vegetable stall:

> And if he asks for a free onion to spice his sardines a bit, the vegetable lady gives him the fish eye and says, 'Say, are you asking for an onion because you want to be tyrant? Or maybe you think Athens grows spices as her tribute to you?'[30]

It does not matter here the reasons for which buying a leek came to constitute a sign of rallying to the oligarchic camp or an aspiration to tyranny; the important thing is to note that the behavior of each person in the marketplace of the Agora could be observed, analyzed and discussed in political terms and that, in this passage, a woman played the role of political analyst. It may be in this same Agora that Gerys forged the democratic convictions that led to him joining the army of Thrasybulus.

The Thracian Chorus of Mounychia

There is proof of Gerys' presence at another site in 403: the Piraeus. Now, Piraeus, and more precisely the hill of Mounychia at its heart, constituted a place of utmost importance for the Thracian population residing in Attica.

---

[29] Mansouri 2010, p. 148, and, already, Vlassopoulos 2007, pp. 44–5.
[30] Aristophanes, *Wasps*, 488–99: 'How you see tyranny and conspirators everywhere, as soon as anyone voices a criticism large or small! I hadn't even heard of the word being used for at least fifty years, but nowadays it's cheaper than sardines. Look how it's bandied about in the marketplace. If someone buys perch but doesn't want sprats, the sprat seller next door pipes right up and says, "This guy buys fish like a would-be tyrant."'

This community can be observed during the annual festival in honor of the goddess Bendis, the *Bendideia*, of which Plato offers a vibrant description in the first lines of the *Republic*.[31] The entry of this Thracian divinity into Athens can be traced back to the early years of the Peloponnesian War. Each year, two distinct processions – that of the Thracians and that of the citizens – wound their way up to the sanctuary at the top of the hill of Mounychia. The festival, which ended with the organization of a race with horses and torches (*lampadēdromia*) followed by a great nocturnal celebration (*pannuchis*), was of a considerable scale and involved the sacrifice of several dozen animals.[32]

The organization of the festival was the responsibility of the city, represented by the priestess of the divinity and its magistrates (the *hieropoioi*), and of a religious association made up of Thracian men and women (the *orgeōnes*). This association was undoubtedly also responsible for building the sanctuary of the goddess on the hill of Mounychia.[33] The *orgeōnes* and the magistrates of the city organized cult practices for both the Athenian citizens and for all the Thracians of Attica. However, the sanctuary of Mounychia formed the center of a Bendidean cult network whose branches extended across the entire southern coast of Attica: On the island of Salamis, as in Laurion, the goddess was honored by various Thracian communities, some of whom were mainly composed of slaves.[34] However, this Bendidean network was closely associated with another cult network linked to Artemis, to which it offered a sort of counterpart. Whereas in Mounychia, the Bendideion adjoined a sanctuary of Artemis, in Kamatero, on the island of Salamis, the two sanctuaries faced each other. The celebration of Bendis seems to have played on a complex set of echoes between Thracian and Athenian identities, as demonstrated by the procession of Piraeus being divided into two separate lines, one including citizens and the other Thracians, and by the duality of the sanctuaries of Artemis and Bendis in Piraeus and Salamis. In this, these festivities helped integrate all of the Thracians residing in Attica, whether they were free men or slaves.

---

[31] Plato, *Republic*, 327a–328a. The action is difficult to place in time but is necessarily later than the end of the 430s and the introduction of the cult to Attica. See *infra*, Chapter 10, p. 255.

[32] In 334/3, the *hieropoioi* were able to add 457 drachmas to the civic treasury thanks to the sale of the skins of the animals sacrificed at the *Bendideia*, which undoubtedly implies a very large sacrifice.

[33] Ismard 2010, pp. 261–70; see also Guicharrousse 2023.

[34] See Ismard 2010, pp. 270–4. SEG 2.9 and 10: the Salaminian group. On the basis of onomastics, the group appears to have been made up primarily of slaves.

Pausanias documents the existence of a similar configuration when he reports the introduction of the cult of Heracles to Erythrae in Asia Minor. The celebration of Heracles was here entrusted to the members of a Thracian community, composed of free men and women as well as slaves. The story of the cult began when the Erythraeans failed to transfer the statue of the god from Tyre in Phoenicia. A blind man from Erythrae, named Phormion, had a vision in a dream in which all the Erythraean women cut off their braids to make a cable and managed to bring the statue back to the city. However, according to Pausanias, the Erythraean women refused to submit to the dream. In contrast, he notes that 'the Thracian women, both the slaves and the free who lived there, offered themselves to be shorn. And so the men of Erythrae towed the raft ashore. Accordingly no women except Thracian women are allowed within the sanctuary of Heracles, and the hair rope is still kept by the locals.'[35] Pausanias thus describes a Thracian community in charge of a civic cult in Erythrae that brings together free and slave women. The Thracian *orgeōnes* of Bendis must have likewise blurred the legal distinction between free men and slaves.

Furthermore, there are a few hints that suggest the presence of many Thracians within the army of Thrasybulus in the Piraeus. If the Thracian identity of Gerys cannot be definitively proven, one of his brothers in arms was named Bendiphanes, a name directly related to the Bendis goddess herself.[36] Better still, among the twenty or so names that we can read on Thrasybulus' decree, several of them – Blepon, Egersis, Epictas, Dexios – hint at a Thracian origin.[37] It is therefore tempting to reconstruct a Thracian chorus around Thrasybulus, of which Gerys may have been a member.

Another argument also supports this assumption. According to Xenophon's account, Thrasybulus' army was composed essentially of lightly armed soldiers. A few scant rows of hoplites supported by a heterogeneous troop of men of all classes armed with lances and light shields: These are the men who routed the oligarchs in 403.[38] However,

---

[35] Pausanias, 7.5.8.   [36] See on this point Masson 1988 = *OGS* II, pp. 605–11.
[37] Middleton 1982. The personal connections between Thrasybulus and the Thracian kingdoms, which appeared particularly during the decade 390 (Xenophon, *Hellenica*, 4.8.26 and Diodorus, 14.94.2), are moreover suggestive of this.
[38] Xenophon, *Hellenica*, 2.4.25: '[The men of Piraeus], who were now numerous and included all sorts of people, were engaged in making shields, some of wood, others of wicker-work, and in painting them. And having given pledges that whoever fought with them should be accorded equality in taxation (*isoteleia*) with citizens even if they were foreigners, they marched forth before ten days had passed, a large body of hoplites with numerous light troops.'

Thracians were unanimously known in the Greek world to provide the best *peltastai* (soldiers with light weapons), and the Athenians had already called on them during the first decade of the Peloponnesian War. The Battle of Mounychia was perhaps the theater of a war 'in the Thracian style,' carried out by a composite army, reinforced by men of all classes. Moreover, Thrasybulus deliberately chose to fight the army of the Thirty from a strategic position: the hill of Mounychia. This choice of site, protected by the goddess Bendis, is far from innocent once the presence of a strong Thracian contingent is acknowledged. It is, in fact, beside the sanctuaries of Bendis and Artemis that Thrasybulus and his men found refuge, and it is thanks to the assistance of the two goddesses – and of the Thracian chorus of Gerys – that, in spite of being outnumbered, they still managed to crush the army of the Thirty.

* * *

The figure of Gerys, a slave who became an *isotelēs*, *agoraios* and member of the Thracian community of Piraeus, is exceptional. If his case is revealing of the multiple affiliations that cross Athenian society, his upward trajectory undoubtedly tells us very little of the ordinary destiny of the slaves of classical Athens. It even serves to create a mirage. Indeed, he makes it look as if the slave population only ever spoke up to offer us an image reassuring to our democratic sensibilities: that of individuals able to free themselves from their servile condition and to obtain privileged positions within Athenian society. Gerys cannot stand for all slaves, nor for all Athenian metics, as the figure of Lysias, antinomic to this in almost in every way, will show. Ultimately, it is within a Thracian chorus, made up of free men and slaves, that our character should be placed.

But how can we represent this Thracian community that brought together men and women of different statuses? Athenian society by no means consisted of a mosaic of ethnically homogeneous communities closed on themselves, since it was dominated by a core of autochthonous Athenians. Indeed, Gerys' epitaph allows us a glimpse into the complex logic of identification, through which the family of this former slave mimics patriotic civic rhetoric, but for their own benefit. Meanwhile, the *orgeōnes* of Bendis maintained close relations with civic authorities in the name of the entire Thracian population, and the Bendidean cult network unfolded like a mirror image of the Artemisian cult network of civic origin. We can only understand this Thracian community through its relations with the whole civic community around the cult of Bendis. Gerys is the coryphaeus of a Thracian chorus that, far from constituting a community closed in on itself, is in constant contact with the other components of the city, and conceives of itself as part of the community of Athenians.

Once our representation of Athenian society acknowledges the standing owed to the Thracians of Piraeus, our overall perspective on the events of the year 403 is reversed. It is from the topographic and symbolic periphery of Athens – and thanks to some of its Thracian metics and slaves – that democracy was restored; it is in Mounychia – where the Thracians of Attica met in honor of Bendis – that the men of Thrasybulus took shelter and carried off their greatest victory. We usually imagine that the great Thrasybulus accommodated within his army the various components of Athenian society gradually. On this day, however, it was perhaps the Thracians of Attica who welcomed the brilliant Athenian soldier and his men and then led them on to victory and the restoration of democracy.

CHAPTER 9

Nicomachus and the Servants of the City

At the Lenaia of January 404, the spectators gathered together in the sanctuary of Dionysus witnessed a rare, if not unprecedented, event in the history of Athenian theater: Less than a year after its first performance, a play was put back on stage while its author was still alive.[1] The situation of the city at the time was desperate. The Spartan fleet, which now controlled the Aegean Sea, had begun a siege, and the conditions for Athenian surrender were the subject of bitter negotiations. Even twenty-five centuries later, we can still hear the fright of the Athenians if we read the words people sang that day in the theater of Dionysus. Who will save Athens? Such is the worried question that the chorus of Aristophanes' *Frogs* asks.

Spectators then witness a strange descent into the Underworld of the god Dionysus and his slave Xanthias, tasked with bringing back to life the

---

[1] In his treatise *Peri tōn Dionusiakōn agōnōn* (= *Poetae Comici Graeci*, Kassel-Austin, 3.2), the student of Aristotle Dicaearchus says that Aristophanes' play was put on stage again after its first performance at the Lenaia of 405: 'The play [*The Frogs*] was produced in the archonship of Callias [406/5], who came after Antigenes, through Philonides at the Lenaia. He [Aristophanes] was first, Phrynichus second with *Muses*, and Plato third with *Cleophon*. The play was so admired because of the *parabasis* which it contains, that it was performed again, as Dicaearchus says.' It is therefore the contents of the chorus's *parabasis* that seem to have justified such an honor, made still greater by the granting to Aristophanes of a crown of foliage taken from the sacred olive trees (*Life of Aristophanes*). Historians cannot, however, agree on the date of this second performance. Salviat 1989; Dover 1993, pp. 73–5; Sommerstein 1993, pp. 461–76, or, more recently, Canfora 2017, pp. 294–305, 340–2, have provided two definitive arguments in favor of the Lenaia of 404 (or even the Dionysia of 404, as suggested by Dover) and not the Dionysia of 405: Aristophanes' charge against Adeimantos can only be understood in the aftermath of the defeat of Aigos Potamos (in the fall of 405) for which he is partly held responsible; moreover, precise references to Cleophon's trial, which was held in December 405 or January 404, appear in the preamble of the *parabasis* of the chorus. One might add that the portrait of Theramenes in the play can only be understood in relation to his ambiguous role in 404 (see the remarks of Allan 2012). The difficulty in fixing a date lies in the support that Aristophanes seems to give, through the voice of the chorus of initiates, to Patrocleides' decree, which is dated to the end of 405. Some have considered that since the play defends the contents of the decree, it would not make much sense for it to be put on stage again after it had been voted on. But one can also observe – as we shall see – that the words of Aristophanes' chorus radicalize the very meaning of Patrocleides' decree, so that it is possible to recognize in it an overstatement of the point subsequent to its vote.

late Euripides, who had died less than two years previously. After having received the advice of Heracles, the god and his slave cross the Acheron, accompanied by a croaking chorus of fabulous beasts, half-swan and half-frog. Once they have passed this first test, they meet a second chorus of initiates, devotees of the god Iacchos, who lead them to the residence of Pluto. Finally reaching the land of the dead, a strange poetic contest is organized, opposing Aeschylus and Euripides, who fight for the right to reign over tragedy in the underworld. In the words of Aristophanes, the *agōn* between Aeschylus and Euripides embodies the confrontation between two radically different conceptions of the city. The latter is moreover presented, in the mouth of Ajax, as a 'full-blown *stasis*,' and it is obviously tempting to recognize in this strange expression a premonition of the civil war that is on its way.[2] While Aeschylus embodies the city of an ancient, venerable time, in which governed 'well-born, well-behaved, just, fine, and outstanding men (*kalous te kagathous*), men brought up in wrestling schools, choruses, and the arts (*en palaistrais kai chorois kai mousikē*),'[3] the poetics of Euripides are associated with the deadly reign of democratic passions. The blurring of status distinctions is the rule, as is the leveling of discourse, since women and slaves speak in the same way as free men. In fact, Euripides defends the democratic dimension of his art, boasting that in his tragedies '[he]'d have the wife speak, and the slave just as much.'[4] The 'maker of words (*pseudologos*)'[5] also asserts the clarity of his expression and his recourse to logical reasoning, as if tragic language could be deployed in the continuity of the democratic deliberative speech. His poetry had in short 'the same defects as democracy [. . .]: as everyone could speak, the slave as well as the king, the king disguised as a slave as well as the debauched queen, no tradition was valued and there was no authority, except that of speech.'[6]

Aristophanes' adherence to the oligarchic camp is hardly in doubt when we read the play. It is easy to divine from Aeschylus' triumph over

---

[2] Aristophanes, *Frogs*, 760 (*stasis pollē panu*). It is for this reason that the battle Aeschylus fights against Euripides (v. 902–4) can be implicitly compared to a centauromachy: see Schneider 1999.
[3] Aristophanes, *Frogs*, 727–9.
[4] Aristophanes, *Frogs*, 949. Aristophanes' scholiast (v. 949) comments on this line in the following way: 'for this too he mocks Euripides, for attributing inappropriate speeches indiscriminately to his characters.'
[5] Aristophanes, *Frogs*, 1521.
[6] Judet de La Combe 2012, p. XLIII. See in particular Aristophanes, *Frogs*, 952–67. As Judet de La Combe 2012, p. XLII, also writes: 'with Euripides, a linguistic community can be established, and tragedy, which will deal with obvious and not mysterious or authoritarian realities, will thus enter into a real practice of democratic exchange.'

Euripides, but that's not the main point: Aristophanes' inclinations mainly come through when he evokes the Athenian political conflicts of the years 405–404. The chorus of the initiates speaks for him in the *parabasis* when it demands that power should be entrusted to the honest men (*chrēstoi*; i.e. the social elite), and that the exiles of 411 be recalled and restored to their political rights: 'I say that those who slipped up at that time should be permitted to dispose of their liability and put right their earlier mistakes. Next I say that no one in the city should be disenfranchised (*atimon*).'[7] The chorus's words explicitly supported the decree of Patrocleides, which restored the rights of the citizens exiled following the oligarchic coup of 411,[8] and it is for this advice that the poet was crowned by the city.[9] Aristophanes even wanted to extend the scope of the decree: While the measure primarily concerned public debtors, Aristophanes wished to extend it to all Athenians exiled for political reasons, among whom were many former oligarchs. These were precisely the men who would later return to Athens after the surrender of the city and become the core of the new oligarchic regime.

Aeschylus in the Underworld: Chorus and Anti-Chorus

The *Frogs* occupies a singular place in the history of Athenian theater due to its representation of two seemingly opposite choruses. The first was composed of strange frogs–swans chirruping cacophonously from perhaps underneath the stage.[10] From here, the croaking of the frogs and the harmonious song of the swans were mixed together. In the tradition of animal choruses of ancient comedies, this grotesque ensemble accompanied Dionysus with its 'magnificent and admirable' song as he rowed behind Charon to cross the infernal marshes of the Acheron. Inversely, just as Odysseus had to resist the seductive song of the sirens, Dionysus had to struggle against these terrible sounds in order to move forward.[11] Here, Aristophanes was mocking the new authors of dithyramb, whose sophistication and mannerisms produced only dreadful cacophonies. In contrast to this, the second chorus, accompanied by flutes and sacred songs, and marked by Eleusinian solemnity, provided an idealized version of the Athenian community.[12]

---

[7] Aristophanes, *Frogs*, 690–2.   [8] Andocides, *On the Mysteries* (1), 77.
[9] See MacDowell 1995, p. 298.
[10] According to the suggestion of the scholiast of the *Frogs*. From the first dialogue between Dionysus and Heracles, to the duality between master and slave (Dionysus/Xanthias) and the confrontation between Aeschylus and Euripides, the *Frogs* is full of doubles, mirror images and inversions.
[11] See Corbel-Morana 2012, pp. 222–48.   [12] See also on this point Belis 1991.

It is especially striking to observe that the salvation of the city is identified with choral practice at the end of the play. 'So our city could survive and continue her choral festivals (*in hē polis sōtheisa all chorous agēi*)'[13]: This is the mission that Dionysus finally assigns to the best of the poets. The formula must be understood in two ways: Aeschylus must save the city so that choral activity may go on, as if the permanence of Athens was guaranteed by the ritual repetition of choral practice. He also had to lead choruses himself (*chōrous agēi*), as if theatrical rites had the power, at least for as long as a play lasted and thanks to the power of musical choruses, to heal the city. No sooner said than done: At the end of the comedy, Aeschylus becomes the head of a chorus embodying a reconciled and pacified city. In it are gathered mortals and gods, women and men, free citizens and slaves singing and dancing in unison in a beautiful final *parodos*.[14]

But this poetic community is also a vigilante chorus, full of violence. The beautiful city is guided back together by its best poet, but only after announcing several death sentences. When he releases Dionysus and Aeschylus from the Underworld, Pluto entrusts to Aeschylus the task of sending several malefactors back to him:

> Fare you well then, Aeschylus. Save our city with your fine counsels, and educate the thoughtless people; there are many of them. And take this and give it to Cleophon; and this to the Commissioners of Revenue (*toisi poristais*), together with Myrmex and Nicomachus; and this to Archenomus; and tell them hurry on down here to me, without delay; and if they don't come quickly, by Apollo I'll tattoo them, clap them in leg irons, and dispatch them below ground right quick, along with Leucolophus' son, Adeimantus![15]

Aeschylus therefore had to provide several individuals with the instrument of their own death, since otherwise Pluto would brand them like runaway slaves before sending them underground. Like a 'tragic Erinys,'[16] the poet had to lead several Athenians to the Underworld, whose names were offered up to the wrath of the assembly of spectators. Who were this anti-chorus of men destined to be sent to the Underworld?

It included prominent politicians, such as Adeimantus and Cleophon. A close friend of Alcibiades, Adeimantus had taken part in the profanation of the Mysteries and the mutilation of the Herms. His

---

[13] Aristophanes, *Frogs*, 1418.
[14] On Xanthias' role as part of the chorus, see Griffith 2013, pp. 209–11. Aeschylus 'is going back home again, a boon to his fellow citizens, a boon as well to his family and friends' (v. 1487–9), therefore to a community that is not limited to the circle of citizens.
[15] Aristophanes, *Frogs*, 1500–14.   [16] Judet de La Combe 2012, p. XIV.

goods confiscated,[17] he had been condemned to exile, before returning to Athens in 407. A *stratēgos* during the year 405/4, he was accused of having 'delivered the fleet' to the Spartans during the defeat at Aigos Potamos.[18] The dishonor that struck him undoubtedly explains in large part Aristophanes' violent accusation. Cleophon, by contrast, was a well-known politician, who was depicted by ancient authors as the archetype of the demagogue. At the first performance of *The Frogs*, Aristophanes was in competition with Plato (the comic poet), whose play expressly targeted Cleophon.[19] A dominant figure in Athenian political life since 416, the 'lyre maker' had made intransigence toward the Spartans his trademark. In 405, he was clearly a staunch supporter of continuing the war against the Spartans, and he opposed the destruction of the Long Walls. Well before Pluto demanded that he join him in the Underworld, Cleophon was the subject of accusation earlier in *The Frogs*. In the opening of his famous *parabasis*, the chorus of Initiates alluded to the Thracian origins of his mother, who, like an exotic swallow, was sitting on a barbarian branch:

> Embark, Muse, on the sacred dance (*Mousa chorōn hierōn*),
> and come to inspire joy in my song,
> beholding the great multitude of people,
> where thousands of wits are in session
> more high-reaching than Cleophon,
> on whose bilingual lips
> some Thracian swallow (*Thrēkia chelidōn*)
> roars terribly,
> perched on an alien petal,
> and bellows the nightingale's weepy
> song, that he's done for,
> even if the jury's hung.[20]

Here, the chorus was alluding directly to the trial of Cleophon by hoping – in contradiction to Athenian customs – that the demagogue would be convicted even in the event of a tied vote. This passage is, however, incomprehensible if it is read in relation to the trial brought by Satyrus and the 'partisans of the oligarchy'[21] against Cleophon in January 404, to which the second performance of the *Frogs* is contemporary. In this

---

[17] His name appears on the stele of the Hermokopidai: *IG* I³ 426, l. 10, 43, 106, 141, 185, 190.
[18] Xenophon, *Hellenica*, 2.1.32. At the beginning of 405, he opposed the decree that proposed to mutilate the Peloponnesian sailors by cutting off their hands. The scholiast of the *Frogs* (v. 1513) adds: 'Perhaps he was the one who is said to have been fraudulently registered as a citizen: for the expression "to brand them" is peculiar to him: he was a foreigner.'
[19] See Pirrotta 2009, pp. 143–5.   [20] Aristophanes, *Frogs*, 675–85.
[21] Lysias, *Against Agoratus* (13), 12; Lysias, *Against Nicomachus* (30), 11.

period already dominated by *stasis*,[22] Aristophanes took a vigorous stand in favor of the death sentence for the demagogue; it seems, therefore, that the poet contributed, at least poetically, to the installation of the Thirty ...

Nicomachus, Scribe and Administrator

Behind these well-known figures of Athenian political history, three men denounced by Pluto seem to form a coherent group: Myrmex, Archenomus and Nicomachus. We know almost nothing about the first two of them, and this quasi-anonymity perhaps demonstrates their subordinate position in the service of the civic administration. It is possible that the first was a member of the *poristai*, a college of magistrates in charge of civic finances, or that he was one of their assistants.[23] The name of the second is in itself noteworthy. It consists of two parts: *archē* (command) and *nomos* (law); the man seems to merge with his professional role, ensuring the laws of the city were respected. But it is actually the third character, Nicomachus, who allows us to identify the nature of this chorus destined for Aeschylus' vengeance. Known because of the indictment for treason (*eisangelia*) brought against him in the summer of 399, for which Lysias wrote the prosecution speech,[24] he belongs to the circle of the city's administrators and servants.

After the first restoration of democracy in 410, the Athenians had decided to completely revise the city's laws. They even instituted a board of 'writers' (*anagrapheis*) of the laws, tasked with working closely with the *nomothetai*, and Nicomachus was one of its members.[25] The work of the commission lasted longer than expected, from 410 to 404, then from 403 to 399, after a brief interruption under the regime of the Thirty. For almost eleven years, Nicomachus was one of the board's principal

---

[22] Xenophon, *Hellenica*, 1.7.35: 'in the civil war during which Cleophon found death (*husteron de staseōs tinos genomenēs, en hē Kleophōn apethanen*).'

[23] We favor the second option. The scholiast of Aristophanes (v. 1506) writes: 'Myrmex is not exactly one of ther *poristai* [...] neither Nicomachus. He [Nicomachus] was either the actor of tragedies, either the citizen about whom we have spoken.' It is possible that Myrmex was the father of Euphanes, known to us from an epitaph dated to the early decades of the fourth century (*SEG* 13, 201), or he may be seen as one of the citizens hired to work on a trireme at the very end of the fifth century (*IG* I^3 1032, l. 187). Our knowledge of the *poristai* is very scarce, but there is evidence of this office in 419 (Antiphon, *On the Choreutes* [6], 49), as well as in the fourth century (Demosthenes, *First Philippic* [4], 33). It is not known how the possible link between Archenomus and his homonym (*IG* II^2 1145, l. 2; fourth century) can be understood.

[24] Lysias, *Against Nicomachus* (30).

[25] On the whole process, initiated by Teisamenus' decree (Andocides, *On the Mysteries* [1], 83), see Volonaki 2001.

members, and therefore his contribution to rebuilding Athenian legislation after the civil war was considerable. There is, moreover, every indication that during the oligarchic year of 404–403 Nicomachus had sided with the democrats. Certainly, Lysias' speech suggests that he played some kind of role in the trial against Cleophon at the beginning of 404 by producing rare laws that apparently facilitated the demagogue's conviction.[26] But he also indicates that Nicomachus had been banished (or had fled) under the Thirty[27]; he even suggests that his opponent blamed the Athenians for their behavior during the *stasis*. Believing that 'he should be allowed to rake up grudges (*mnēsikakein*) unjustly against others,' he was accused of having defied the duty of forgetting established by the city.[28] One might also conclude that if Nicomachus was reelected to the commission once democracy was restored, it must be because his democratic engagement was not in doubt.

But how can we explain the violence of the attack against Nicomachus? Lysias' client denounces, in particular, the role that he supposedly played in establishing a new cult calendar after the *stasis*. He blames him for introducing new cults to the detriment of traditional rites. Historians agree that the remnants of this new calendar can be recognized in a vast inscription placed inside the Stoa Basileios in the Agora of Athens. The calendar is engraved on two sides of the same stone, before and after the year 403, and there is every indication that it was already in use before Nicomachus' trial.[29] Its structure is particularly complex. In the manner of an inventory, it lists a series of sacrifices following a logic that appears erratic, grouping each according to whether they were the responsibility of the 'chiefs of the tribe' (*phulobasilikoi*), took place every month, had no fixed day, or even came from a previous inscription or other written material.[30]

Lysias' speech fortunately makes it possible to grasp the way in which Nicomachus undertook his work. Following the instructions of the board in charge of revising the laws, he drew up the new calendar by gathering together two distinct types of sacrifices: on the one hand, those that, already engraved on the plaques deposited in the Stoa Basileios, could be

---

[26] Lysias, *Against Nicomachus* (30), 10–1.
[27] Lysias, *Against Nicomachus* (30), 15: 'I would not have mentioned this, if I had not heard that he would try to save himself in defiance of justice by portraying himself as a democrat and that he would use his exile as an indication of his goodwill towards the People (*kai tēs eunoias tēs eis to plēthos tekmēriōi chrēsomenon hoti ephugen*).'
[28] Lysias, *Against Nicomachus* (30), 9.
[29] See Lambert 2002 (= *SEG* 52.48). Side A is in Attic script, side B in Ionian. On this change of writing, see *supra*, Chapter 3, pp. 106–7.
[30] See side A, fr. 3, l. 77: *ek tōn st[ēlōn]* or *ek tōn s[uggraphōn]*.

traced back to an archaic calendar; and on the other hand, those that had a more recent origin and were inscribed 'on the stelai.'[31] In the course of this operation, it seems that Nicomachus deleted old sacrifices and replaced them with new cults. This is at least what Lysias' client would have us believe, although it obviously exaggerates the role of his adversary whose name does not appear on the stele.[32] The full religious dimension of the confrontation remains obscure, however. Is the litigant an advocate of religious conservatism, furious at witnessing more recent cults become official? Or is he, in fact, disturbed by the writing down of these rites, since it might endanger ritual knowledge based on the oral tradition?[33] Is it, on the other hand, the excessive cost of certain cults that seemed unreasonable? It is illusory to pretend to be able to answer these questions, and this in any case is not the crux of the matter.

Politics and Its Borders

The main reason for the hatred directed at Nicomachus, and which Aristophanes manifested as early as 405, was not that he drafted this calendar. More generally, it was due to the anomalous position that he had acquired in the city, allowing him to undermine representations of political authority as the Athenians understood them.[34] By compiling and reorganizing the corpus of Solonian laws, this simple secretary apparently appropriated for himself the power of a legislator and a *nomothetes* like Solon: This is the scandal that our litigant unceasingly denounces. The power acquired de facto by the *anagrapheus* called into question one of the constitutive features of civic order: that which required civic administration to be subordinated to the magistrates' authority. It obscured the necessary distinction between the order of politics and that of 'service,' or administration.

In the *Statesman*, Plato shows the importance of this hierarchical distinction at the heart of Greek thought. When apprentice philosophers undertake to define the authentic royal function (the *archē basilikē*), they

---

[31] Lysias, *Against Nicomachus* (30), 17: *ek tōn kurbeōn kai tōn stēlōn kata tas suggraphas*.
[32] This was the interpretation of Dow 1960, 1961, which made Nicomachus a fervent democrat. Dow suggested that Nicomachus had introduced new cult rites open to most people into the calendar by suppressing old traditional cults of an aristocratic nature.
[33] This is suggested in particular by Heinrichs 2003, pp. 56–7.
[34] Lysias, *Against Nicomachus* (30), 28, makes Nicomachus a *hupogrammateus* (*kai heterous anthrōpous hupogrammateas*). Hansen 2019 argues that Nicomachus was probably in the service of other magistrates. One might also see this as a generalization on the part of the litigant, reducing Nicomachus' role to the tasks of any *hupogrammateus*.

come to circumscribe, by means of successive dichotomies, what political competence consists of. This is distinguished, they explain, from all the other 'auxiliary arts': Even though they are essential, the production of goods or ritual practices could never be part of the political art. Among these auxiliary arts, one in particular creates a problem for the young philosophers: that acquired by 'all those who become accomplished at writing by having repeatedly given their services in this respect, and certain others who are omnicompetent (*pandenioi*) at working through many different tasks relating to public offices.'[35] Because of their administrative expertise, these individuals could stake a claim to the title of holders of royal competence. The Stranger even states that politics is based on 'the class of slaves and all those people who are subordinate to others,' who 'dispute with the king about the woven fabric itself.'[36] Slaves and servants as masters of authentic political competence? The hypothesis is absurd, and Socrates the Younger refutes it bluntly: Since they are 'subordinates, and not themselves rulers in cities,'[37] these false rivals of the politician cannot participate in any way in royal functions, and the Stranger is forced to recognize that it would be absurd to look for anyone with such skills 'in a servant class.'[38] The Platonic dialogue therefore reveals the potential confusion between two types of skill at work in the governing of the city, while seeking to ward it off by reminding the reader of the necessary exclusion from the field of politics of those with administrative knowledge.

However, Nicomachus transgressed this division, carrying out, in the manner of a magistrate, tasks that, in an ordered world, should have been entrusted to a slave. This is the reason why his allegedly servile origins are constantly recalled by the litigant, as if this son of a public slave had only become a citizen by some kind of infraction. Nicomachus, in short, personified a form of usurpation, by which the effective power in the city fell to its servants and its magistrates, to the detriment of the civic community as a whole.

This charge appears already in the comedy of Aristophanes, if one listens to the reproaches that the chorus of the initiates addressed to Euripides:

> And what evils can't be laid at his door? Didn't he show women procuring, and having babies in temples, and sleeping with their brothers, and claiming that 'life is not life?' As a result, our community's filled with under-secretaries (*hupogrammateōn*) and clownish monkeys (*bōmolochōn*

---

[35] Plato, *Statesman*, 290b.   [36] Plato, *Statesman*, 289c.   [37] Plato, *Statesman*, 290b.
[38] Plato, *Statesman*, 290b–c.

dēmopithēkōn) of politicians forever lying to the people, and from lack of physical fitness there's nobody left who can run with a torch.[39]

Hupogrammateus – that is to say, the undersecretary in the service of a magistrate: This is the scandalous term that in itself says so much about the sad destiny of the democratic Euripidean city.[40] Left in the hands of its servants and administrators, civic hierarchies are reversed. And if Euripides embodied this vicarious threat better than any other, it is not only because he had portrayed it in his tragedy about Palamedes, as Dionysus reminds him,[41] but also because an insistent rumor, relayed by Aristophanes, was circulating about him, saying that his own slave Cephisophon was the real author of his plays. 'By Palamedes, that's good; you're a genius! Did you think that up yourself, or was it Cephisophon?' asks Dionysus.[42] The scholiast delivers the end of the story by affirming that 'Cephisophon the slave composed with Euripides his plays, and especially the lyric parts; one makes fun of him also because he frequented the wife of Euripides.'[43] Of democratic inspiration, Euripides' poetry was as erudite as it is inauthentic, to the extent that a slave might be considered its true author.

But let us return to Nicomachus. His office as an *anagrapheus* was not an ordinary magistracy. The litigant is scandalized that no inspection was organized after Nicomachus had succeeded in abusively extending its duration, suggesting that he escaped the 'universal accountability' of the classical Athens magistracies.[44] He is especially indignant that, contrary to the principle of noniteration governing most magistracies, it led the same individual to occupy the same office for a long time, freed de facto from

---

[39] Aristophanes, *Frogs*, 1078–88.
[40] Aristophanes' scholiast (on v. 1084) glosses Aeschylus' statement by saying that the city 'has become full of people who wanted to be secretaries and not go on military expeditions; he attacks the secretaries for their intrigues.'
[41] Aristophanes, *Frogs*, 1451. According to Jouan and Van Looy (eds.) 2000, pp. 490–2, the Euripidean version of the Palamedes legend was the following: Agamemnon, Odysseus and Diomedes seized a slave and forced him to write a letter in Phrygian characters, signed with the name of Priam and addressed to Palamedes. After having killed the slave, they corrupted one of Palamedes' slaves and had him place under the bed of his master the letter and the Phrygian gold, proving his treason. Palamedes' tent was then searched, the gold and the letter were discovered and he was sentenced to be stoned to death. Thus, the inventor of writing was apparently the victim of his own invention; the written proof, intended to constitute the surest means to decide a legal case according to Palamedes, turns out here to be a forgery that condemns him to death. In this etiological account, therefore, the slaves play a determining role in Palamedes' misfortunes, writing the letter of denunciation or hiding it to prove his treason. It is through a slave that writing comes to betray its inventor (see Ismard 2019, pp. 158–60).
[42] Aristophanes, *Frogs*, 1451–2. Euripides replies: 'All by myself, but Cephisophon thought up the vinegar bottles.'
[43] Scholiast of Aristophanes, *Frogs*, 944a.
[44] Fröhlich 2004, p. 333. See in particular Lysias, *Against Nicomachus* (30), 2–3, 29.

the control of the people: 'Worst of all, even though a man cannot legally serve twice as clerk under the same official, you have allowed the same man to remain for an extended period in full control of matters of the greatest importance.'[45] Now, the position acquired by Nicomachus is explained largely by his expertise in the field of the law and in writing. It was also his Achilles' heel, isolating him from a political field that refused to believe specialized skills entitled someone to govern.[46] A citizen, but the son of a public slave, not strictly speaking at the head of a magistracy, Nicomachus was the only visible representative of the working people without which the democratic city could not function, but whose existence it preferred not to mention.

A Chorus of Bureaucrats

By the side of the coryphaeus Nicomachus, there was in fact a vast chorus of city servants, who worked behind the scenes with the magistrates, and without whom city administration would have been impossible. So it was with the *paredroi*, chosen by the archons when they took office. Like magistrates, they were scrutinized by *dokimasia* and had to render accounts at the end of the year. They could even be honored by decree. Their appointment did not, however, rely on an election or the drawing of lots from the community as a whole, but from the discretionary choices of the archons. As a result, the *paredroi* were men who often had family or friendly ties with the archons.[47] At the same time, many citizens acted as secretaries (*grammateis*) or undersecretaries (*suggrammateis* or *hupogrammateis*) to the magistrates, although it is not always possible to determine whether their office was considered a magistracy in itself.[48] Their number

---

[45] Lysias, *Against Nicomachus* (30), 29.   [46] Todd 1996, p. 115. See also Ismard 2017.
[47] On the *paredroi*: Pseudo-Aristotle, *Athenian Constitution*, 56.1: 'The Archon, the King and the polemarch also take two assessors (*paredroi*) each, chosen by themselves, and the qualifications of these are checked in the Jury-court before they hold office, and they are called to account when they retire from office.' On the link between the archon and his *paredros*, see Demosthenes, *Against Meidias* (21), 178–9 (father and son), [Demosthenes], *Against Neaira* (59), 72, where the *archon basileus* marries the presumed daughter of his *paredros* (and 79–84). Cf. *IG* II² 2811 (the *paredros* is the archon's brother). It should also be noted that the *paredros* could also be honored with the archons (Clinton 2008, n° 100, end of the fourth century; *IG* II² 668, l. 17–22, from 281/0 BC) or form dedicatory communities with them (probably *IG* II² 2811).
[48] They should probably be distinguished from the secretaries of the Council and the People, the secretaries to the prytany or the secretaries in charge of the laws (*epi nomou*), who were *bouleutai*, and whose office constituted indeed an *archē*. On these different secretaries of the Council, see Rhodes 1972; Sickinger 1999; Pébarthe 2006. In Delos, in the middle of the second century, the *grammateus* who assisted the *agoranomos* was decided by lot (*ID* 1833, l. 6).

and the scope of their work are difficult to determine, as the function of undersecretary (*hupogrammateus*) seems to be presented in Athenian judicial speeches as an insult, the term only serving to qualify, in a pejorative way, the office of *grammateus*. There is every indication, however, that it was an ordinary position, generally devolved to citizens, and did not constitute in any way a magistracy.

Demosthenes' diatribe against Aeschines, in the speech *On the Embassy*, is enlightening in this regard. Intending to detail the past political career of his opponent, he twice attacks his role as undersecretary and servant of the Council.[49] Next, he attacks Aeschines and his brother Aphobetus by claiming that they 'took bribes while working as petty clerks in all the civic offices (*hupogrammateuontes d'autoi kai hupēretountes hapasais tais archais*) until, finally, elected by you citizens to the rank of secretary (*grammateis*), they were maintained for two years in the Tholos.'[50] Demosthenes' statement indicates that there were undersecretaries (*hupogrammateis*) for most of the magistracies.[51] But it also suggests that Aeschines accomplished two different tasks within the Council for two years in a row, working first as a simple undersecretary, then, once chosen as Council member himself, as a secretary to the Boule and the people.[52] In this regard, Aeschines' trajectory can be compared with that of Anticles, the undersecretary of the *epistatai* of the Parthenon for seven years and then a secretary (*grammateus*) for the following four years between 443 and 432.[53] The case of Aeschines highlights an interesting configuration, according to which the principle of noniteration of office could be subverted de facto by the presence of the same citizen for two consecutive years: spending the first year as secretary to a magistrate and the second year as a magistrate himself. This pattern is confirmed by several inscriptions honoring *prytaneis*.[54] It is possible to hypothesize that the skills acquired by an individual as undersecretary could be mobilized once he became a magistrate, and might even explain his appointment, despite the principle of drawing lots.

---

[49] Demosthenes, *On the Embassy* (19), 70, 249; in § 237, he mentions only his activity as *hupogrammateus*.
[50] Demosthenes, *On the Embassy* (19), 249.
[51] Hansen 2019, p. 345, lists all the attestations of *grammateis* or *hupogrammateis* attached to magistracies.
[52] It may be that the distinction between *hupogrammateus* and *hupēretes* refers to this succession of the two tasks (see MacDowell 2000, p. 238).
[53] *IG* I³ 436–51, l. 115, 171, 240, 287, 312, 344, 366, 370, 411.
[54] For example, Euthymachos, son of Ergochares of Kerameis, was undersecretary in 193/2 (*Agora* 15.168, l. 39), then secretary of the Council and the People in 190–189 (*Agora* 15.170, l. 11).

Next to all these free men who assisted the magistrates, there were many public slaves, collectively owned by the Athenian people, and if the office of undersecretary was so easily mocked, it is precisely because it was dangerously similar to the offices held by these slaves. These public slaves (*dēmosioi*), who allegedly included Nicomachus' father himself, were placed in the service of the Council or the law courts, counting votes, making sure that sessions ran smoothly or filing and copying the civic archives, but they also regularly assisted the magistrates in their tasks, sometimes outside Athens. Insofar as their work was very similar to that of citizens who were *hupogrammateis*, they were part of the same chorus: that of the city's bureaucrats. Like the latter, they received pay but were exempted from rendering accounts and could fill the same position for several years in a row, and the relative technicality of their tasks allows us to imagine that, very often, they may have helped new magistrates in the performance of their tasks. The Athenians sometimes even honored these public slaves, implying that they understood their influential role in the operation of the civic institutions.[55] But one thing is certain: Their slave status was used to justify the tasks they were given. By entrusting slaves with indispensable duties that were carefully kept out of the field of politics, the Athenians aimed to conceal the bureaucratic work inherent in the democratic regime: These tasks were projected onto a figure of radical otherness – that of the slave. In other words, relying on slaves made it possible to mask the inevitable gap between state and society, the necessary administration of public life and the democratic ideal.[56]

Public slavery therefore gives substance to the Platonic distinction between authority (*archē*) and service (*hupēresia*), since slaves were required to perform administrative jobs that were not magistracies. It is difficult, however, to determine the bonds that these slaves could maintain with citizens who also held administrative positions. Was there a unitary chorus of bureaucrats, whose common identity, or dignity, based on professional pride and knowledge of administrative workings, transcended statutory distinctions?[57] Or should we imagine two half-choruses within it,

---

[55] See Ismard 2017. In addition to their role in the service of the Council and the Courts, public slaves assisted the *stratēgoi*, their treasurers, the archons, the *astunomoi*, the treasurers of the goddess, the *epimeletai* of the arsenals, the *epistatai* of Eleusis and the Eleven, but one may assume that the list was in fact much more extensive (see the recent synthetic survey of Hansen 2019, p. 339).

[56] See Ismard 2017.

[57] See the particularly suggestive case of the salaried officials (*apparitores*) who attended the Roman magistrates and priests of the Roman Republic, manifesting the dignity and the power attached to their functions. David 2019, pp. 140–7, has clearly shown that while they shared a collective

according to whether city services were accomplished by slaves or free men?

Beyond Freedom and Slavery

Answering such a question is an intrepid undertaking, since the ancient sources say so little about all the minor employees who ensured institutions ran smoothly. This enterprise requires us in any case to look far downstream from the events of 403 and to focus on the honors (*timai*) granted to slaves and citizens who performed administrative tasks in the service of the city. The dedicatory inscriptions and the honorific decrees of the *prytaneis* of the Council of the fourth and third centuries offer, in this respect, the best documentation. The members of the Council, including secretaries and undersecretaries, but also the public slaves working for the institution, are indeed honored on three occasions. The latter are first mentioned in the fragment of a prytany inscription of 343/2.[58] The slave of the Council, Metrodorus, is named just after the secretary (*grammateus*) to the Council and the People, Blepyrus of the deme of Paiania.[59] But in another inscription from the same year, a dedicatory inscription of the *prytaneis* of the Aigeis tribe, the secretary is again mentioned but not the public slave, whose name is consciously omitted. In the eyes of the *prytaneis*, the *dēmosios* had never been the recipient of the honors that had been granted to them.

However, the situation was different in 303/2, just one century after the Athenian civil war. Eight public slaves of the Council (*hupēretai tēs boulēs*)[60] were this time mentioned following a list of *prytaneis* of the Pandionis tribe. It would, however, be a mistake to believe that the *dēmosioi* were henceforth part of the honorific community that constituted the *bouleutai*, and among whom the secretary to the Council and the People, Procleides of the deme of Xypete, was distinguished.[61] The slaves of the Council are grouped together as a collective, but their names were added *a posteriori*, as if they did not clearly belong within the honored community.[62] Moreover, the purpose of this list of names, which brings together the Council members and its administrative support, is unknown.

---

identity, there was a clear hierarchy of prestige and dignity between *ingenui* (free men born free) and freedmen *apparitores*.

[58] *Agora* 15.37, l. 4.   [59] *Agora* 15.36, col. II, l. 35.   [60] *Agora* 15.62, col. V, l. 10–8.
[61] *Agora* 15.62, fr. col. IV–V, 350.
[62] They were engraved by different hands: see Traill 1968, p. 4.

Although their names were engraved, the Council's slaves were not part of the honorific community.

Finally, in a list of members of the Council, drawn up in 281/0, public slaves are mentioned, but in a substantially different form. The name of each of them is engraved after the list of *prytaneis*, as if their activity was associated with the exercise of a specific prytany.[63] It is not known why the slaves of the Council are mentioned in 303/2 in the form of a collective made up of (at least) eight individuals, whereas twenty years later their presence is individualized and associated with a prytany. Let us simply observe that, once again, their names must have been engraved *a posteriori* and were therefore presented as an addition to the list of the *prytaneis*.

The prytany inscriptions therefore reveal a paradoxical situation. The inclusion of public slaves in these lists is remarkable. Individualized in the form of a personal name, they are given prominence with regard to the operation of the institution. However, there is no evidence that they were granted any honors. They never appear in the dedicatory inscriptions of the *prytaneis* of the classical period, and if, from the third century onwards, their names are visible, it is always in lists that have no honorific function. Above all, the engraving of their names always seems to be a matter of supplement or exception. The slaves of the Council are certainly recognized as members of the community, indispensable to the administration of public affairs, but they cannot receive the same honors as the citizens who were secretaries or undersecretaries. Among the Council's servants, the statutory distinction between free men and slaves remained an essential dividing line.

* * *

Around Nicomachus, the alleged son of a public slave, who became the collector and transcriber of the city's laws, a group of men in the service of Athenian institutions takes shape. Radically distinct from that of the magistrates, their activity was well and truly outside the political field, as described in Plato's *Statesman*. It brought together slaves and free men, whether they played the role of *paredroi* to the archons or of undersecretaries to certain magistrates. Reading the prytany inscriptions suggests that, within it, the distinction between free men and slaves prevented the

---

[63] *Agora* 15.72, col. I, l. 5, col. II, l. 67, 211, col. III, l. 83, 266. This inscription does not concern all the prytanies, but according to J. S. Traill, who edited the text, while three of them do not mention the name of any public slaves, a blank space was left so that they could be added later: Traill 1969, p. 463.

formation of a collective identity based on a specific skill and professional dignity. The chorus of bureaucrats that surrounds Nicomachus, in short, is only a mirage.

Trapped by the city's self-representation, such a reading would, however, be erroneous. It undoubtedly underestimates the existence of an administrative culture of which these men, whether they were free *or* slaves, could be the guardians, and about which our sources are admittedly tenuous. Above all, it ignores the opportunities public slaves were given to accede, if not during their lifetime, then possibly via the intermediary of descent, to the society of free men. Nicomachus, after all, was perhaps the son of a *dēmosios*, and, if this was the case, it allows us to suggest, on the one hand, that service to the city could lead some of these slaves to see their descendants acquire citizenship and, on the other hand, that citizenship could be acquired through the transmission of professional skills from father to son, which were put to service for the common good. Therefore, it is perhaps through the transmission, over several generations, of a skill used in the service of Athens that the chorus of the bureaucrats of the city came into being, which transcended the distinction between free men and slaves.

CHAPTER 10

Lysias, a Multifaceted Man

Lysias, the son of Cephalus, was an Athenian logographer, a wealthy metic and a staunch democrat: In the *Dictionary of Received Ideas* about Greek antiquity, the entry devoted to Lysias would probably read along these lines. If there was ever a man identified with a status, a social class, a professional function and a political identity, it is indeed the orator Lysias, whose family, originally from Syracuse, benefits from an exceptional documentary focus. Along with Socrates, he is certainly the most famous figure in our gallery of characters, celebrated throughout antiquity as one of the principal Attic orators. Lysias was admired by grammarians and rhetoricians already in antiquity, and his career path can be reconstructed both through his own works – in particular, the morsels of oblique autobiography that he slips into *Against Eratosthenes* – and through the various *Lives* that were devoted to him in Roman times.[1]

Let us recall, one by one, the popular beliefs about him.[2] That Lysias was a metic – and even a model or ideal metic – emerges from his own speeches. Doesn't he in fact say so himself to contrast the exemplary conduct of his family with that of the Thirty and their supporters? 'They clearly did not believe that we as metics should behave in the same way that they behaved as citizens [that is, unjustly].'[3] His enemies also viewed him in this way, since it was *as metics* that he and his brother Polemarchus were arrested by the Thirty. As Xenophon indicates, 'One measure that [the Thirty] resolved upon, in order to get money to pay their guardsmen, was that each of their number should seize one of the foreigners residing in

---

[1] Two *Lives* have come down to us in their entirety: The first was written by Dionysius of Halicarnassus, in the first century BC, the second by Pseudo-Plutarch, probably in the third century AD. On the dating and composition of the *Lives of the Ten Orators* by Pseudo-Plutarch, see Roisman and Worthington (eds.) 2015, pp. 11–4. On the relationship between Dionysius' *Life of Lysias* and that of Pseudo-Plutarch, see Martin 2014, pp. 323–4.
[2] In French historiography, see for example Baslez 2008, pp. 130–1.
[3] Lysias, *Against Eratosthenes* (12), 20.

the city, and that they should put these men to death and confiscate their property.'[4] Lysias therefore seems to embody this status of foreign resident, and this defines him for better or for worse.

If Xenophon suggests greed was the only reason for these arbitrary arrests, Lysias maintains that he was also persecuted for political reasons: 'It was at a meeting of the Thirty that Theognis and Peison raised the subject of the metics, claiming that some were hostile to the new regime (*politeia*). This would provide an excellent pretext for appearing to punish them while in reality making money, because the city was completely impoverished, and the regime needed cash.'[5] When faced with the jurors, Lysias unceasingly brought to the fore his attachment to the democratic regime and his opposition to the oligarchy. The implication is clear: It was not only because he and his brother were rich metics that they were targeted by the Thirty, but because they belonged to a family that, for several decades, had shown a particular devotion to democracy. This political fidelity had terrible consequences: Polemarchus was executed, and while Lysias managed to escape death at the last moment, the Thirty apparently left him not 'the least bit of [his] fortune.'[6]

By its brutality, it seems this sequence of events led Lysias, who was utterly ruined, to reorient his career and become a logographer (a 'speech-writer'), composing speeches for hundreds of clients due to go to court. In fact, it is as a judicial orator that Lysias went down in history and how he was eventually canonized as an eminent example of the ten Attic orators: In the Western imagination, Lysias is emblematic of those rhetoricians who were capable of adjusting their style to their clients in order to make them sound all the more convincing to their listeners.

One initial observation is essential. All these clichés were developed during the civil war, the intensity of which produced a powerful stylizing effect on the lives of those who lived through it. It was the *stasis* that led Lysias to define himself as a democratic metic; not unlike the Sartrean Jew, whose identity is constructed in response to the attacks he endures, it was the civil war that forced the wealthy craftsman to become an orator after the family workshop was ruined. However, this exceptional moment tends to obscure the twists and turns of Lysias' life, which cannot be summed up

---

[4] Xenophon, *Hellenica*, 2.3.21. Cf. Lysias, *Against Eratosthenes* (12), 6–8. According to Xenophon, Theramenes refused to engage in such exactions against the metics, and this refusal triggered the campaign of denigration against him and led to his trial, and then to his execution: Xenophon, *Hellenica*, 2.3.22–3. Lysias could hardly speak about it, insofar as he was accusing a close relation of Theramenes, Eratosthenes, who had agreed to carry out the arbitrary arrests prescribed by the Thirty.
[5] Lysias, *Against Eratosthenes* (12), 6.   [6] Lysias, *Against Eratosthenes* (12), 20.

in such a simple outline. Considering all the available evidence and his path through life as a whole, a completely different image of the man emerges. Outside of the brief context of the civil war, Lysias was never depicted as a metic and never defined himself as such; nothing, moreover, indicates that he particularly suffered from this status or that he sought to be a naturalized Athenian at any price after the failure of his bid for citizenship in 403. Likewise, considering his life as a whole, his attachment to the democratic regime is not as clear to see as his vibrant proclamations in *Against Eratosthenes* suggest: The company he kept and the choice of his clients plead for a much more nuanced approach. Finally, his conversion to logography also deserves to be put into perspective: Was he not already considered a brilliant 'sophist,' albeit not a logographer, before the beginning of the civil war? He certainly continued to be considered as such after the reconciliation.

Beyond the din of *stasis*, which forced everyone to choose their camp and froze individuals in clear-cut positions, Lysias' life reveals that Athenian society was much more fluid than it appears in terms of status, partisanship or profession. On deeper examination, the life of Lysias seems marked by a form of uncertainty due not only to gaps in the source material, but also to the irreducible complexity of Athenian community life. Around this ill-defined man gravitate shifting choruses whose principles of composition and recomposition can be defined by taking advantage of the exceptional light shone on them by the shock of the civil war.

An Uncertain Date of Birth

Lysias was a prolific author and, with the exception of Demosthenes, his work is the best preserved of all the Attic orators. In addition to the thirty-five complete speeches that have come down to us, there are nearly 500 fragments documented through indirect or papyrological tradition, as well as 145 titles of works and about fifteen summaries of speeches. However, this is only a fraction of a much larger body of work lost to us: Only 15 percent of the Lysianic corpus considered authentic has been preserved today.[7] Worse still, this sampling is not based on the historical value of the speeches, but on rhetorical and legal considerations.[8]

---

[7] Pseudo-Plutarch, *Lives of the Ten Orators [Lysias]*, 836a: Caecilius of Calacte and Dionysius of Halicarnassus recognized the authenticity of 233 Lysianic speeches out of 425.
[8] Going back to the Hellenistic period, the corpus was roughly organized according to the type of lawsuit concerned (trials for assault and battery, acts of impiety, property cases and confiscations, *dokimasiai*, etc.) and not according to their historical significance: Todd 2007, pp. 21–2. The corpus

What is known about the life of the orator is like his writings: incomplete and uncertain. While there is some remarkable documentary evidence about him, many ambiguities remain, and the *Lives* of Dionysius of Halicarnassus and of Pseudo-Plutarch swarm with partial, even contradictory information.[9] It is therefore difficult, even impossible, to establish so much as the year of birth of the orator[10]: Was Lysias born in 459/8 or fifteen years later, around 445/4? Far from being anecdotal, this chronological question affects our whole interpretation of his path through life. To put it differently: In 404/3, was Lysias still a dashing forty-year-old ready to embark on a second career or was he an almost sixty-year-old forced to become a logographer just as he entered old age?

The earlier dating is often favored because Dionysius of Halicarnassus, followed by Pseudo-Plutarch, places the birth of the orator 'under the archonship of Philocles' – that is to say, in 459/8.[11] However, it is probable that the two biographers are working by inference here: It is because they believe that Lysias was fifteen years old when he left for Thurii in southern Italy and that the foundation of this colony goes back to 443 that, by extrapolation, they have placed his birth at such an early date.[12] Now, this hypothesis implies that Lysias developed most of his oratorical activity between fifty-six and eighty years old, between 403 and 379. Even more disturbing is a testimony preserved in Demosthenes' corpus that makes this dating unlikely: The litigator of *Against Neaira* explains how 'Lysias the sophist' fell in love with a *hetaira* named Metaneira, when he was already married and his mother still lived in their house.[13] However, in view of the indications given in the speech, this torrid episode cannot have taken place any earlier than the decade of the 380s. If Lysias had been born in 459, he would have been between seventy and eighty years old, while his mother would have been over ninety:

---

probably goes back to the cataloging done in Alexandria by Callimachus, as shown by Carey 2007, pp. vii–viii. The surviving work is, however, only a fragment of the complete corpus in its final iteration, which is similar to the one attested by the *hypotheseis* of *P. Oxy.* 2537.

[9] The biography of Dionysius of Halicarnassus tries to reconstruct Lysias' life story from partial information, drawn partly from the works of Lysias himself and from which the author infers the essential dates of his life: Todd 2007, p. 7.

[10] His death is, on the other hand, easier to place in time: Dionysius of Halicarnassus simply hesitates between 379/8 and 378/7 BC. This fits well with the last datable speech of the orator, *On the Scrutiny of Evandros* (26), delivered in 382.

[11] Pseudo-Plutarch, *Lives of the Ten Orators [Lysias]*, 835c.

[12] Dover 1968, p. 42, according to whom Dionysius of Halicarnassus found the information about Lysias leaving at fifteen years old in a judicial speech, perhaps in *Against Hippotherses* (of which we have some fragments). See also Chiron 2015, p. xxviii.

[13] Pseudo-Demosthenes, *Against Neaira* (59), 21–3.

An Uncertain Date of Birth 255

We would then have to imagine an orator with a Berlusconian profile, blessed with a mother who had an iron constitution.[14]

Dating Lysias' birth so early poses one final difficulty. It is hard to reconcile with the (certainly fictitious) setting of Plato's *Republic*, which, as we know, takes place in the house of Lysias' father, Cephalus.[15] Mentioned in the speech, Lysias does not take part in the discussion, unlike his elder brother, Polemarchus, who actively participates in the dialogue. This is probably because the future orator is too young to speak, like Plato's brothers who, equally silent, keep him company. But these men were not born before the 440s; Glaucon, for example, was born c. 445. How could Lysias be fifteen years older than the comrades with whom Plato imagines him in the *Republic*?

It is all these difficulties that led Kenneth Dover to place the birth of Lysias around 445/4, about fifteen years later. According to the British scholar, the biographical reconstructions of the ancient authors are based only on one single reliable piece of information, probably given by the speaker himself in *Against Hippotherses*: Lysias was fifteen years old at the time of his departure to Thurii.[16] However, nothing proves that he emigrated to the colony as soon as it was founded in 444/3, as Dionysius of Halicarnassus and, after him, Pseudo-Plutarch assume. He could just as well have settled there only after the beginning of the Peloponnesian War. That is, this dating offers the advantage of being compatible with the (fictitious) context of the *Republic*.[17] The later dating is all the more attractive as it fits better with the testimony of *Against Neaira* about the love affair between the orator and Metaneira: He would have been only about fifty years old at the time of the episode.

However, this assumption is itself problematic in that it comes to contradict the calculations of Dionysius of Halicarnassus, according to which Lysias spent over thirty years in Thurii.[18] Certainly, the argument is

---

[14] See Kapparis 1999, pp. 211–3; Hamel 2003, pp. 16–26.

[15] See Dover 1968, p. 42; Todd 2007. It has been confirmed that the Bendis cult was introduced at the latest in 429. The dialogue could therefore have taken place at any time between the late 430s and 404. None of these dates agree with the chronology established by Dionysius of Halicarnassus and Pseudo-Plutarch, according to whom Polemarchus and Lysias left for Thurii in 444/3, after the death of Cephalus: Pseudo-Plutarch, *Lives of the Ten Orators*, 835d; Dionysius of Halicarnassus, *The Ancient Orators [Lysias]*, 2.1.2. See Nails 2002, pp. 324–5.

[16] On the speech *Against Hippotherses*, which has reached us in a fragmentary state, see here *infra*, pp. 276–7.

[17] The Platonic dialogue can indeed hardly have taken place before the introduction of the Bendideia festival in Athens, at the very beginning of the war, since this opens the dialogue. See Planeaux 2001, who dates the dialogue back to June 429.

[18] Pseudo-Plutarch, *Lives of the Ten Orators [Lysias]*, II, 1. See Edwards 1999, who, for this reason, follows the traditional chronology.

not critical, insofar as the ancient biographer could very well have deduced this duration by calculating the interval between the foundation of Thurii (443/2) and the return of Lysias to Athens (412/1). But it is another of Plato's dialogues that makes this chronological adjustment particularly fragile. In Plato's *Phaedrus*, Socrates talks with the young Phaedrus, who speaks with admiration of Lysias and presents him as an already accomplished sophist, which suggests he is a man of a certain age.[19] But Phaedrus was born around 444, or even a little earlier.[20] The dating proposed by Dover would imply that Lysias was the same age as his admirer and still a very young man. Is this enough to reject definitively Dover's hypothesis? Perhaps not, insofar as this Platonic dialogue seems in any case impossible to locate at any given moment in history.[21] Should we be surprised by this chronological imbroglio? Not at all. As usual, Plato likes to blur times and places to make his speech all the more universal for being unlocatable.[22]

If we had to settle this undecidable issue, we would tend to prefer the traditional chronology, precisely because of Plato's *Phaedrus*. For it may not be the fictitious date of the dialogue that matters, but rather the particulars of the discussion that is staged within it: A very young man, Phaedrus, conversing with Socrates about an accomplished sophist, Lysias. Might Platonic irony go so far as to represent the young Phaedrus as being impressed by a fellow student of the same age? This seems doubtful.

Whatever the solution, these chronological uncertainties have serious consequences for the way in which Lysias' status, political affinities and professional activities are viewed.

---

[19] Phaedrus is explicitly qualified as a young man (*neanias*): Plato, *Phaedrus*, 257c.
[20] Nails 2002, p. 432.
[21] Let us proceed by elimination: Firstly, the dialogue cannot have taken place between 415 and 404, since Phaedrus was then in exile following the profanation of the Eleusinian Mysteries in which he was implicated; secondly, it cannot have taken place after 403, since Lysias' brother Polemarchus is supposed to still be alive at the time of the dialogue (*Phaedrus*, 257b). Should we therefore conclude that the exchange could have taken place in 404, *after* Phaedrus' return to Athens and *before* Polemarchus' death at the hands of the Thirty? This is also difficult to imagine, both because the dialogue mentions Sophocles and Euripides as if they were still alive (the two tragedians died one after the other in 406) and because, in 404, Phaedrus had not been a young man for quite some time! Should the dialogue then be situated at the very beginning of the Peloponnesian War, before Lysias left for Thurii? This hypothesis is also problematic: How could Lysias already be such a famous sophist when he had only just reached adulthood? Should we then go back to the traditional dating? This would unfortunately solve nothing because the orator would not have been able to converse with Phaedrus. In this hypothesis, Lysias would have left for Thurii as early as 443, while his interlocutor had only just been born! Having returned to Athens in 412, it would have been just as impossible for him to meet Phaedrus, who had left in exile three years earlier.
[22] See Nails 1998, who refuses to try to date the dialogue precisely.

A Model Metic?

In 403, for a few hours, a few days, even for a few weeks, Lysias believed that he would become Athenian. According to Pseudo-Plutarch, Thrasybulus proposed that citizenship be granted to him because of his loyal services, and the Assembly voted to ratify this.[23] Did he have time to benefit from his new rights by integrating into a phratry? It is unlikely, since Archinus was undoubtedly quick to attack the decree of naturalization for illegality, thereby blocking the procedure, and he succeeded in having the decision overturned in the courts.[24] According to the testimony of Pseudo-Plutarch, 'Lysias spent the rest of his life as an *isotelēs*'[25] – that is, as a privileged metic exempt from the *metoikion* tax, an honor he may have already enjoyed before the outbreak of the civil war.[26]

By concentrating on this single dramatic moment, it is quick work to write the history of Lysias – and, beyond that, of Athenian society – in terms of clearly defined legal statuses. From this perspective, Lysias can be seen as the model of every individual who, in spite of all their merits, remained separated from full citizens by an unbridgeable chasm. Lysias' life story encourages us to look at this legal status-based conception of Athenian social history in a whole new light. Was the acquisition of a new status indeed a vital prize for Lysias and his peers? Was he obsessed by the prospect of becoming an Athenian citizen? Accentuated by the magnifying effect of the civil war, this legal vision is, if not false, at least only partially true.

In fact, Lysias was not the man of a single status. While he was indeed a metic in his early youth, he arrived in Thurii when he was fifteen years old and, upon reaching his majority, became a citizen with full rights for fifteen or maybe even thirty years if one defers to the traditional chronology. Whether Lysias died at eighty (according to the early-dating hypothesis) or at sixty-five (according to the late-dating hypothesis), he still lived as a citizen for half of his adult life. Pseudo-Plutarch even confirms it: 'And once he had bought himself a house there and been granted an allotment, he was citizen of Thurii thirty-three years, up to and

---

[23] Pseudo-Plutarch, *Lives of the Ten Orators [Lysias]*, 835f–836f.
[24] See *supra*, Chapter 3, pp. 91–3.
[25] Pseudo-Plutarch, *Lives of the Ten Orators [Lysias]*, 836a. Beyond this procedural aspect, it seems that only the metics who were part of the contingent of Phyle (or who joined Thrasybulus in Piraeus) were granted citizenship: *IG* II² 10. Exiled to Megara during the civil war, Lysias could not count himself among these lucky few.
[26] Todd 2007, p. 15.

including the archonship of Cleocritus in Athens (413/2).'[27] It is only once he returned to Athens that Lysias again became a metic, perhaps enjoying some privileges like *enktēsis* (the right of a foreigner to own land and a house).[28] And the story was far from over: After a few months of exile in Megara in 404/3, he briefly became a citizen again before becoming (or becoming again) an *isotelēs*, a legal status in its own right, putting him on an equal fiscal footing with citizens.[29] This quick summary therefore allows us to consider Lysias as much as a citizen as a metic. From this perspective, the aborted naturalization of 403 no longer stands out as an exceptional moment, but seems rather to be an (aborted) return to the civic norm: In 403, Lysias had lived much longer as a citizen than as a metic!

The case of Lysias suggests, then, that metic status should not be given undue importance in the ordinary circumstances of everyday life. It was, above all, during the civil war that Lysias was considered from this legal perspective, first by his enemies, the Thirty, who sought to rob him, then by his friends, such as Thrasybulus, who wanted to reward him. For the rest of his life, Lysias hardly seems to have been preoccupied by the matter: His status is mostly ignored and, in a way, neutralized. In the *Republic*, for instance, Plato never mentions that Cephalus and his family are foreign residents. Better yet, Lysias, his father and his brothers ostensibly share the same lifestyle as the Athenian elite, treated as 'friends and familiars (*philous te kai oikeious*)': They all share in the revels of the city.[30] They eat and drink at the same banquets, attend the same festivals and parade in the same processions, such as the one organized in the honor of the Bendis goddess at the beginning of the *Republic*.[31] Moreover, at the (fictitious) time of the dialogue, Lysias is not yet of age: Considering him a metic

---

[27] Pseudo-Plutarch, *Lives of the Ten Orators [Lysias]*, 835d (transl. Roisman and Worthington (eds.) 2015, *ad loc.*).

[28] Lysias, *Against Eratosthenes* (12), 18: The funeral procession of his brother Polemarchus could not leave 'from one of the three houses which belonged to us (*triōn hèmin oikiōn ousōn*).' These houses could, however, have been rented: see Todd 2007, p. 15 n. 58, and, already, Reinach 1919, pp. 444–5.

[29] In a definition transmitted by Harpocration, Lysias himself defines *isoteleia* as 'an honor (*timē*) attributed to metics who are worthy (*axiois*), exempting them from the *metoikion*; the *isoteleis* were also exempted from the other things weighing on the metics': Lysias, *Pros Sōstraton hubreōs*, quoted by Harpocration, s.v. *Isotelēs kai isoteleia*.

[30] Plato, *Republic*, 328d. See Cohen 2000, pp. 19–21.

[31] Plato, *Republic*, 327d: 'Just then Polemarchus caught up with us. Adeimantus, Glaucon's brother, was with him and so were Niceratus, the son of Nicias, and some others, all of whom were apparently on their way from the procession [in honor of Bendis].' A few lines further on, the selfsame Polemarchus asks Socrates and Glaucon to stay with them so that they can attend together the torchlight race that is to take place that evening in honor of the goddess: 'After dinner, we'll go

makes all the less sense as he shares the relative marginality of all the young inhabitants of Athens – whatever the status of their parents – symbolized by their shared silence during the dialogue.

This neutralization of legal status is also striking in the *Phaedrus*. Lysias has grown up this time: He is presented as an accomplished orator, already well known to Athenian politicians. Yet, no allusion is ever made to his status as a foreigner. The real foreigner of the dialogue is Socrates, a foreigner in his own city.[32] The dialogue presents him only as 'Lysias, son of Cephalus,' 'the best of our contemporary writers' in Athens.[33]

Plato is not the only one to make such an omission. In *Against Neaira*, Apollodorus refers, without any further precision, to 'Lysias the sophist' (§21): His social identity is based on his stylistic virtuosity, not on his condition as a foreigner.[34] Beyond these questions of naming, Apollodorus' speech reveals how, in the private sphere, nothing differentiated Lysias from a full citizen: He observed the same matrimonial practices as the Athenians, having married his own niece, according to a very common practice in the city.[35] In the same way, he protected his *oikos* from the presence of *hetairai*, as the members of the Athenian elite did in general, whatever their status: In Athens, prostitutes were not admitted into the house of a free person if there was any risk of them being in contact with a legitimate wife or a woman protected by a guardian.[36] This is why Lysias installed Metaneira in the house of one of his 'intimate friends' (*philon ... kai epitēdeion*) who was not yet married, a citizen named 'Philostratus, son of Dionysius, of the deme of Colonos.'[37] The relevant boundary here is not between citizens and noncitizens, but between married and unmarried men.

---

out to look at the all-night festival (*pannuchis*). We'll be joined there by many of the young men, and we'll talk' (*Republic*, 328a). See Whitehead 1977, pp. 18–9. This does not mean, however, that their metic status is irrelevant to the interpretation of the dialogue. According to Kasimis 2018, pp. 51–83, the *Republic* may even be a 'metic space': If the metics are not identified as such, the choice of the house of Cephalus as the setting for the dialogue was not philosophically neutral. Plato apparently played on the very close proximity, in the dialogue, between citizens and metics to highlight the dangerous proximity between the two statuses in a democratic context (p. 61). Although subtle, the argument is hardly convincing in view of the way Plato willingly blurs the status boundaries in his political utopias.

[32] Plato, *Phaedrus*, 230c–d. See *supra*, Chapter 4, p. 155.   [33] Plato, *Phaedrus*, 228a.
[34] In the testimony quoted in §23, Lysias is presented, in what is a text with legal value, as 'Lysias, son of Cephalus.' Only the absence of the deme indirectly reveals the foreign origin of the speaker.
[35] Pseudo-Demosthenes, *Against Neaira* (59), 22. On the identity of his wife, see *infra*, p. 275.
[36] Müller 2018, pp. 243–70: 'The house of the metic functions exactly like that of a citizen and the speaker makes no difference between the two.'
[37] Pseudo-Demosthenes, *Against Neaira* (59), 23.

On many occasions, the life of Lysias was not very different from those of the citizens and even of the richest of them, whose leisure practices he shared. It is by no means certain that Lysias wanted to become a citizen at all costs, and even less so that he aimed to enlarge the civic body to include deserving metics, as has sometimes been argued from a one-sided reading of *Against Philon*.[38] On the contrary, some speeches in the orator's corpus show a strong hostility toward those who seek to change their status when they do not deserve to.[39] Furthermore, he probably had nothing but contempt for most of the poor metics, a sizeable proportion of whom were freed former slaves, such as Gerys.[40]

In sum, Lysias should not be considered a metic seeking to acquire citizenship by any means, but rather as an individual endowed with significant agency whose life and activities remained unhindered by his legal condition. Can it be said, then, that his status was of little consequence? That would certainly be an exaggeration. For his condition as a foreigner, even a privileged one, came flooding back in certain contexts and at certain times: on the battlefield, when he had to fight in a separate contingent; at certain feasts, when he could not share the same meats as the

---

[38] In this speech, the accuser argues that only those 'who in addition to being citizens are also enthusiastic (*epithumountas*) about their citizenship' should participate in civic affairs (*Against Philon* [31], 5). Is this sufficient proof of the will to redefine citizenship on the basis not of heredity, but of the adherence to democratic values? Could this be an oblique way of pleading for the naturalization of foreign benefactors who manifested the *desire* to be citizens? The hypothesis, put forward by Bakewell 1999, is risky. In this case, the litigant does not seek to deprive Philo of his citizenship, but only to prevent him from accessing the Council: This is not a far-reaching proposal that aims to reconfigure the contours of the civic community, but a strategic argument intended to hinder the access of a former member of the Three Thousand to the main deliberative institution of the Athenian democracy. At most, one could say that Lysias – echoing his own experience – does not wish deserving metics to be unduly prosecuted in Athenian courts, like a certain Callias who had rendered 'many good deeds' (*pola agatha*) to the city: Lysias, *For Callias* (5), 2–3. Cf. Lysias, *Against Philon* (31), 29. Symmetrically, he does not hesitate to compose speeches against other metics: cf. Lysias, *Against the Corn-Dealers* (22), with the remarks of Whitehead 1977, pp. 44, 54.

[39] *Against Pancleon* targets an individual accused of having usurped citizenship by claiming to be of Plataean origin and to have been enrolled in the deme of Deceleia, which the client of Lysias fiercely contests. There are two other cases: *Against Agoratos* (which targets a recent citizen or a privileged metic, perhaps freed, who had fought for democracy in 411 and 404) and *Against Nicomachus* (whose accused is indeed a citizen, but perhaps the son of a public slave: see *supra*, Chapter 9). Lysias was also involved in actions brought by a former master against his freedman accused of shirking his obligations: cf. Lysias, *For Dexios*, fr. XIX Gernet (= fr. 75–7 Carey); *Against Andocides, Failure to Have a Patron* (fr. 15–6 Carey). One must also add another speech, *Against Calliphanes, for Usurpation of Citizenship* (fr. 193 Carey), which probably aimed to prosecute an illegitimately born man (*nothos*) accused of having tried to integrate the civic body.

[40] See *supra*, Chapter 8, pp. 224–34. On the suspicion of some metics toward slaves and freedmen, cf. Lysias, *For Callias* (5), 5. See more generally Akrigg 2015, pp. 164–5.

citizens[41]; at court, where he had to go through the intermediary of his *prostatēs* (patron) in order to file a claim.[42] The fact remains that outside of these special events – be they festive or conflictual – Lysias did not live and probably did not see himself as a metic, even a model one, but rather as an active member of the Athenian community.

An Equivocal Democrat

Just as it is difficult to reduce Lysias to his status, it is equally complex to associate him with a single political stance. There is, however, a rich tradition that tends to portray him as a staunch democrat: The orator himself claims, at the beginning of *Against Eratosthenes*, to have led an exemplary life under the democracy.[43] This attachment to the Athenian political regime may even hark back to the previous generation, since his father boasted that he came to Athens at the invitation of the great Pericles.[44] This is why Lysias has long been considered a 'radical' democrat – in the words of Wilamowitz-Moellendorff[45] – or a 'democratic intellectual,' or even the 'official logographer of the democracy.'[46] In fact, he wrote a vibrant eulogy of the Athenian political system in the funeral oration preserved in his corpus and composed between 395 and 386.

---

[41] In the case of the Hephaisteia, see, for example, *IG* I³ 82. While metics did take part in the ceremony, they played a minor role: They received only a share of raw meat and therefore did not have access to the sacrificial banquets reserved for citizens only. Cf. also *IG* I³ 244, side C, l. 7–9 (475–450): The decree of the deme of Skambonidai accorded metics the same rights as demesmen in terms of worship, which suggests that in general this equality was not a given. See Parker 2005, p. 66; Humphreys 2004, pp. 145–6; Wijma 2014, p. 104. The latter, however, shows that metics were integrated into the Athenian ritual community, in their own role and in specific ways, such that it would be wrong to interpret this in terms of honor or humiliation (pp. 51–6). For a nuanced approach, see Guicharrousse 2023.

[42] On the judicial role of the *prostatēs*, see Gauthier 1972, p. 133. On the 'dishonors' (*atimiai*) attached to the condition of a metic, see Xenophon, *Poroi*, 2.2, who, in 355, suggested relieving metics of such obligations in order to attract more foreigners to the city and therefore contribute to its prosperity. Gauthier has decisively argued that these *atimiai* were to be understood metaphorically as 'affronts' and referred to dishonorable *practices*: They have nothing to do with the modification of the metic *status* per se (Gauthier 1976a, pp. 57–9).

[43] Bearzot 2007, pp. 9, 140, who forces (voluntarily) the translation of *ôikoumen dēmokratoumenoi* (*Against Eratosthenes* [12], 4) into 'we were living as democrats' (and not 'we were living under a democratic regime') in order to emphasize Lysias' desire to be at one with the Athenian political experience.

[44] Lysias, *Against Eratosthenes* (12), 4. But making Pericles the patron (*prostatēs*) of Cephalus would be a step too far, as in Schindel 1967, p. 44.

[45] Wilamowitz-Moellendorff 1893, p. 361.

[46] See respectively Mansouri 2011, pp. 39, 99, 112; Desrousseaux and Egger 1890, p. xviii. See also Baslez 2008, p. 131 ('a democrat, faithful to the city in good and bad days').

However, for more than a century historians have insisted on the difficulty of identifying the orator's political convictions. Wilamowitz-Moellendorff was one of the first to remind us that Lysias had defended many 'enemies of his political camp,'[47] while Paul Cloché underlined the fact that he had supported people of all parties, including both aristocrats and democrats.[48] Such observations have sometimes led to a very dark image of the orator, portrayed as an opportunistic logographer, willing to sell his talents to the highest bidder. This characterization culminated in Friedrich Ferckel's thesis, published in Germany in 1937, which likens Lysias to 'a Jewish element alien to the people and the state (*volks- und staatsfremde Jüdische Element*)': Like the Jews, Ferckel suggests that Lysias did not have the slightest consideration for the form of the political regime (*Staatsform*) in which he lived, pursuing only his own personal interest.[49] Ferckel even went so far as to hope that Lysias' works would be banned from the curricula of German schools![50]

This vile attack was based on the exegesis of a passage of speech 25 (*Defense Against a Charge of Subverting the Democracy*), in which the anonymous client of Lysias formulates this relativistic profession of faith: 'In the first place, it is important to remember that no human being is by nature either oligarchic or democratic: instead, he wants that regime (*politeia*) to be established which would most benefit himself.'[51] In addition to the fact that such a proclamation is not particularly original and is expressed differently in other contemporary writings,[52] we must be careful not to carelessly assign this opinion to Lysias, given that it was intended to clear the name of a citizen who had remained in the city during the civil war. Rather than being satisfied with a single, biased testimony, it is better to take a second look at the orator's political career over the long term and highlight all the uncertainties that surround it.

Let us begin by interrogating the figure of his father, whose memory Lysias invokes in *Against Eratosthenes*. Do we have to see Cephalus

---

[47] Wilamowitz-Moellendorff 1924, pp. 106–7.   [48] Cloché 1915, p. XI.
[49] Ferckel 1937, pp. 158–9: Lysias apparently only took into account 'which system brings the most advantages (*welches System gerade den grössten Nutzen bringt*).' These racist attacks explain, through the reaction to them, the enchanted vision defended by Romilly 1980, p. 137: 'Lysias was a democrat; and the experience of 404 did nothing but reinforce his feelings [...]. Undoubtedly he sometimes wrote speeches for aristocrats [...], but he defends their innocence: Lysias did not disown himself by pleading for them.'
[50] Ferckel 1937, p. 163. If it were not so nauseating, the attack would almost be comical because the author forgets that Lysias, originally from Syracuse, was a good Dorian, a people that the Nazis took for the ancestors of the Aryans.
[51] Lysias, *Defense Against a Charge of Subverting the Democracy* (25), 8.
[52] Cf. e.g. Pseudo-Xenophon, *Constitution of the Athenians*, 1.4.

choosing to settle in Athens as an act of democratic faith? Here again, chronology matters. In all probability, Lysias' father left Syracuse after 466, when the Sicilian city had already freed itself from its tyrants and adopted a democratic regime.[53] If this was the case, Cephalus' emigration takes on an ambivalent meaning: If he came to Athens, it was not to live in a democracy, since his home city was just as democratic.

These chronological questions are also important in determining how deeply Lysias himself was committed to the democrats. The moment when, after the death of their father,[54] Lysias and Polemarchus left Athens to establish themselves in Thurii is a particular subject of debate. Did the two brothers leave Athens in 443, as members of a grandiose colonization project initiated by Pericles, or did they abandon a city at war, ravaged by the plague and the Lacedaemonians, shortly after 430? Everything depends, once again, on Lysias' date of birth.[55] At least one thing is certain: The orator does not say a word about his departure to Thurii in *Against Eratosthenes* because this episode was difficult to portray in a positive light.[56] Even his return to Athens in 412/1 is open to discussion. According to Dionysius of Halicarnassus, it may have been the consequence of the Athenians getting routed out of Sicily[57]: It was a forced departure toward a destination imposed by the circumstances. Worse still, Lysias could not claim that his return had been motivated by the desire to live in a democracy: Until 406, Syracuse was a city every

---

[53] It is indeed difficult to imagine they might have arrived earlier in Athens, insofar as Pericles, who instigated the move, was, before 466, a young man with no influence. Moreover, if Cephalus had been driven out by the tyrants of Syracuse, his son would no doubt have boasted of it in *Against Eratosthenes*. The difficulty in justifying such a departure politically was probably the origin of the tradition according to which Cephalus 'was banished from Syracuse during Gelon's tyranny [in 485 BC]' (Pseudo-Plutarch, *Lives of the Ten Orators [Lysias]*, 835c). Highly unlikely from a chronological point of view, this version shows the desire, on the part of ancient authors, to maintain the 'antityrannical' reputation of the orator's family. See Dover 1968, pp. 39–41.

[54] In any case Cephalus died in Athens, not in Thurii: Pseudo-Plutarch, *Lives of the Ten Orators [Lysias]*, 835d. *Contra* Kasimis 2018, p. 65 (who speaks of 'Cephalus' role in the founding of the Athenian colony at Thurii').

[55] Among those who follow the second option, see Dover 1968, pp. 41–2; Gauthier 1972, p. 114 (who proposes to date the departure 'around 425' without, however, justifying this); Goulet 2012, pp. 1186–8; Roisman and Worthington 2015, pp. 124–5. Let us recall here the reasoning of Kenneth Dover: In his biography, Dionysus of Halicarnassus (2.1.2) maintains that the orator left for southern Italy at the age of fifteen; the ancient biographer apparently drew this information from one of the orator's speeches – perhaps *Against Hippotherses* – in which it seems he sought to justify leaving Athens shortly after 430 at the beginning of the Peloponnesian War, giving his young age as an excuse. In fact, the accusation was serious: Departing after 430 made Lysias and his brother cowards, even traitors, fleeing their adopted city in the middle of a war. Let us recall that the Athenians even voted a law during the fourth century that forbade a metic to leave the territory in case of conflict (Hyperides, *Against Athenogenes* [3], 29, 33).

[56] See Baslez 2003, p. 100.   [57] Dionysius of Halicarnassus, *The Ancient Orators [Lysias]*, 2.1.3.

bit as democratic as Athens! Furthermore, Lysias disembarked in Piraeus just as the oligarchs had taken power in the city. According to Pseudo-Plutarch, 'he arrived in Athens and began to live there in the year of the archonship of Callias (the Callias who succeeded Cleocritus), at the time of the regime of the Four Hundred in Athens.'[58]

From this perspective, it is less surprising that Plato chose to depict the close links between Lysias and other citizens known for their oligarchic sympathies. If the *Republic* portrays Lysias in the company of many Athenians later involved in the revolutions of the end of the fifth century, it is especially the *Phaedrus* that attracts attention in this respect. Plato portrays Phaedrus as an admirer of Lysias, whereas everyone knew at the time of the dialogue's composition in the 380s that he had been forced into exile for having profaned the Eleusinian Mysteries in 415.[59] If it is difficult to take Plato's word for it, it is at least worth noting that Lysias himself mentions Phaedrus in a favorable light in a speech delivered around 388: One of his clients assures us that Phaedrus, when he married his cousin after his return from exile, was 'a man who had become poor not because of any wickedness.'[60]

This exercise of methodical doubt can even be extended to the period of the civil war. Can we really be so sure that Lysias acted as a committed democrat at that time? *Against Eratosthenes*, followed by the whole ancient biographical tradition, certainly presents him as a strong supporter of Thrasybulus and of those who resisted the oligarchy, and we do not wish to deny that here. On the other hand, one can wonder if this was truly a voluntary choice. As when he left Thurii, torn apart by *stasis*, in 403 Lysias was *forced* to go into exile to save his life; moreover, it is by no means certain that in arresting him and his brother the oligarchs wanted to attack democrats: It was primarily their fortune they were interested in, as Lysias himself admits to those who came to arrest him: 'I have done nothing wrong but am being killed for my wealth.'[61] Let us, moreover, note that, until their arrest, the two brothers had remained in the city and had not sought to rally the embryonic resistance to the Thirty.[62]

---

[58] Pseudo-Plutarch, *Lives of the Ten Attic Orators [Lysias]*, 835e.
[59] *IG* I³ 426 (414 BC). Phaedrus' property was confiscated and the city auctioned off a house and a piece of land he owned. See Dorandi 2012, p. 286.
[60] Lysias, *On the Property of Aristophanes* (19), 15.   [61] Lysias, *Against Eratosthenes* (12), 14.
[62] The collective arrest of metics is difficult to date precisely. Did it occur relatively early in the reign of the Thirty? It is difficult to say. Xenophon certainly mentions it rather quickly in his account of the civil war, but he also suggests that these acts of violence generated disapproval of Theramenes and soon led to his trial and execution, an episode that took place only a few weeks before the Battle of Mounychia and the end of the Thirty.

This political uncertainty does not stop with the end of the *stasis*. After 403, it is also difficult to identify a well-defined political line in the speeches of the orator. More precisely, if there is one, it is not the 'radical' line of Thrasybulus, as we will see by studying the choruses that gravitate around Lysias. Let us simply say here that he had among his clients many neutral citizens or moderate oligarchs, and, more disturbingly still, that he did not hesitate to attack, in the late 390s, his own 'side' – or, at least, the 'side' with which he is often associated. While the speech *In Defense of Mantitheus* (16), delivered around 392–390, takes an early dig at Thrasybulus, the attack became more ferocious in the speech *Against Ergocles* (28), dated 389 or 388. In it, the former leader of the resistance to the Thirty is blamed for the excesses of his campaign in Asia in 390, during which he had just died.[63]

At the end of this rereading, it would be easy to draw a disturbing portrait of Lysias and his family, far from the democratic vulgate: Here is a man born into a family of rich Syracusans, who left their fatherland just as it declared itself as a democracy; a man who left Athens perhaps in about 429, while his adopted city was fighting against enemy troops and disease; a man who returned in 412/1 and settled in a city that was in the hands of the Four Hundred; a man who mixed with well-known oligarchs, be they Plato's family or the impious Phaedrus; a man who remained in the city in 404 until he was arrested by the Thirty, without trying to rally to the early resistance fighters; a man, ultimately, who chose to defend the former members of the Three Thousand and ended up trampling on the memory of his 'patron,' Thrasybulus ...

However, this account is not only tendentious – there are still a great many uncertainties about Lysias' life – but also trapped in a partisan vision of Athenian politics. In Athens, political affiliations were not fixed once and for all and did not take as their basis stabilized ideological programs. Lysias' trajectory is in fact emblematic of a world where the two sides are not as clear-cut as the civil war suggests. This principle of uncertainty characteristic of Athenian politics was strengthened still further in the case of Lysias by his activity as a logographer. Because he wrote for others in return for payment, he found himself defending political positions that he did not necessarily endorse personally.

The Paradoxes of Logography

Lysias the logographer? Here, again, doubt must be cast over this statement, as it seems impossible to reduce him to this sole function. For the

---

[63] Bearzot 2014. See *supra*, Chapter 2, pp. 73 and 79.

facts are stubborn: If Lysias was indeed born in 459 and only became a logographer after the reconciliation in 403, he only began his new career at the age of fifty-six. Even if he had been born fifteen years later, he would have been over forty already at the time of his career change. It is therefore difficult to identify Lysias with this activity alone: His rhetorical career lasted fewer than twenty-five years, while he was a rich landowner and/or a wealthy owner of a workshop for at least as long (if he was born around 444), if not much longer (if he was born in 459).[64]

However, these chronological considerations cannot exhaust the subject, not only because the year 403 probably does not constitute a clear cut-off point in Lysias' career, but especially because it is illusory to define the identity of a member of the social elite by means of the 'profession' they exercised, according to a very anachronistic standard. Let us begin by questioning the radical break that the civil war would have represented in Lysias' 'professional' career. The idea that he converted to logography is in fact based on a single testimony, that of Lysias himself in *Against Eratosthenes*: 'For myself, gentlemen of the jury, I have never taken part in public affairs, *either on my own or on anybody else's account*, but because of what has happened.'[65] But should we take him at his word here? It is all the more doubtful since this claim is a rhetorical platitude.[66] It was in every litigant's interest to assert their inexperience in legal matters so as not to be seen as a sycophant or an expert in quibbling.

If many historians have nevertheless agreed to take Lysias' statement seriously, it is because they rely on an implicit reasoning: It seems that Lysias was forced to become a logographer to compensate for the plundering of his goods by the Thirty, like Isocrates, the son of a craftsman was impoverished by the Peloponnesian War.[67] However, here again the

---

[64] However, nothing is known about his activities in Thurii. Did he work as a craftsman in southern Italy? He could just as well have made a living from farming, since in Thurii 'he had bought himself a house there and been granted an allotment' (*Lives of the Ten Orators*, 835d). Dionysius of Halicarnassus, *The Ancient Orators [Lysias]*, 2.1.2, specifies only that he 'continued to reside there as a citizen in considerable prosperity (*en euporiai pollēi*).'
[65] Lysias, *Against Eratosthenes* (12), 3 (our emphasis). [66] Demont 2009, pp. 96, 259–60.
[67] Todd 2007, p. 13: 'It is certainly possible that financial need will have driven him to exploit professionally an existing amateur talent.' See also Carey 2007, p. v, n.1. The parallel between Isocrates and Lysias goes back to Plato (*Phaedrus*, 239e). Like Cephalus, Isocrates' father was a wealthy workshop-owner who made musical instruments (*auloi*); like Lysias, Isocrates received an expensive education and, like him, lost his fortune during the Peloponnesian War (*Antidosis* [15], 161). Like Lysias, he also had to (momentarily) become a logographer after 404 in order to reestablish his material situation: In the speech *On the Exchange*, his opponent blames him for having occupied his time in 'writing judicial pleas (*dikographia*)' (§2). However, contrary to Lysias, this activity was only transitory (for about fifteen years?): While logography was often the destiny for metics, it was usually only a phase for citizens. See Azoulay 2010, pp. 36–9.

parallel is misleading for the reason that Lysias was probably far from being totally ruined in 404. If he maintains, in *Against Erastosthenes*, that the oligarchs had not left him 'the least bit of his fortune' (§20), he still had enough resources left to support the democrats after his flight from Piraeus: 'Once the men of Phyle had resolved to recover Athens, there was no one who proved more supportive than Lysias. He supplied them with 2,000 drachmas and 200 shields; he was dispatched, along with Herman [?], to hire 300 mercenaries; and he persuaded Thrasydaeus of Elis, a guest-friend of his, to donate two talents.'[68] Moreover, he seems to have been able, on his return to the city, to make an (unsuccessful) offer to buy back some of his property.[69] This shows that his fortune probably consisted partly in loans and mobile capital, which was easily transportable from one end of the Mediterranean to the other, from Athens to Thurii, then from Thurii to Athens.

Better still, several testimonies tend to indicate that Lysias was already working as a rhetorician even before the civil war. According to Dionysius of Halicarnassus – who does not mention the episode of the Thirty at all in his biography – Lysias started his rhetorical career as early as 412/1, on his return from Thurii: 'Returning to Athens in the archonship of Callias, when his age was presumably forty-seven, he lived and worked for the remainder of his life in Athens. He wrote many speeches for the law courts, and for debates in the Council and the Assembly, each well-adapted to its medium.'[70]

From this perspective we would be well advised to imagine a long overlap between his work as a businessman and his career as an orator. This would provide the advantage of making the large number of speeches that Lysias managed to compose during his career more understandable. If he had only started his activity in 403, he would have had to produce an average of nearly ten speeches per year to arrive at the 233 'authentic' speeches that the ancient tradition recognizes![71] However, it is necessary to

---

[68] Pseudo-Plutarch, *Lives of the Ten Orators [Lysias]*, 835f (transl. Roisman and Worthington (eds.) 2015). On Herman (or Hermon), see *infra*, p. 281. Cf. Justin, 5.9.9, who speaks of 500 mercenaries. For an evocation of these services to the resistant fighters, cf. Lysias, *Against Hippotherses*, fr. 1 Gernet (= fr. 170 Carey), l. 165–70.

[69] This is what emerges from a reading of *Against Hippotherses*, fr. 1 Gernet (= fr. 7a Todd = fr. 164 Carey), §1, l. 13–7 and fr. 1 Gernet §4 (fr. 7c Todd = fr. 167 Carey), l. 79–86, in spite of the partial contradiction between these two passages.

[70] Dionysius of Halicarnassus, *The Ancient Orators [Lysias]*, 2.1.4.

[71] On this question, see Todd 2007, p. 8 n. 28. The idea of a gradual transition would better fit with the way he is presented in Plato's *Phaedrus*: He is portrayed as a flamboyant sophist – like his compatriot, Gorgias – even before the beginning of the civil war. Taking this into account also makes it easier to explain why *Against Eratosthenes* displays such rhetorical talent: Far from being an early speech, it was the work of a man already well versed in all the oratorical codes.

take into account all the consequences of this hypothesis, which might also cause certain speeches to be attributed to him in cases where Lysianic authorship is usually denied for chronological reasons.[72]

This shift in viewpoint also means Lysias is no longer confined to the sole practice of logography. It is true that the orator's corpus is essentially composed of speeches delivered before Athenian courts. Cicero even assures us that Lysias specialized in legal matters after having realized that he could not compete with Theodoros of Byzantium (an important sophist at the end of the fifth century) in theoretical speculations.[73] However, this legend is highly suspect, not only because it may well be a rather free adaptation of Plato's *Phaedrus*,[74] but especially because ancient biographers present Lysias as a *polygrapher*, excelling in all types of rhetoric.[75] His corpus includes a *Funeral Oration* and an *Olympic Oration*, of which Dionysius quotes a large excerpt,[76] as well as a speech *On Love* (*Erotikos*), even if the latter is probably only a Platonic pastiche.

Posterity is the best judge of such rhetorical versatility: In the speech *Against Neaira*, delivered in the 330s, Lysias is indeed defined as a 'sophist,'[77] without it being necessary to specify his patronymic or his city of origin. This was certainly an ambivalent term, often taken in the wrong way, including by Lysias himself.[78] However, the term is far from always

---

[72] The speech *For Polystratus* (20) was therefore rejected from Lysias' corpus because it was composed before 404 (Dover 1968, p. 56, is one of the few to leave open the question of its authenticity). In the same way, Lysias could also have composed the speech *For Nicias*, around 412, as the ancient tradition indicates. As for *Against Theozotides* (of which only a few fragments are extant), if it is generally attributed to Lysias, it is not impossible that it was delivered in 410, and not in 403. See Matthaiou 2011 and *supra*, Chapter 3, pp. 117–8.

[73] Cicero, *Brutus*, 12.48, perhaps drawing on Aristotle. On the sophist Theodoros of Byzantium, see Kennedy 1959, p. 178; Rambourg 2015, pp. 39–54.

[74] In Plato's *Phaedrus* (257c), the young Phaedrus claims that Lysias might stop writing after hearing Socrates' speech, which was so superior to his own.

[75] Dionysius of Halicarnassus, *The Ancient Orators [Lysias]*, 2.1.5: In addition to speeches for the courts, the Council and the assemblies, Lysias 'wrote also panegyric and amatory discourses, and discourses in the epistolary style. With these he eclipsed the fame of his predecessors and of contemporary orators, and left few of his successors with the opportunity of improving upon his performance in any of these media, indeed, not even in the most trivial.' Cf. ibid. 2.16.2; 2.3.7.

[76] Lysias, *Olympic Oration* (33). On the context of this speech, cf. Diodorus, 14.109.3.

[77] That this is indeed Lysias is confirmed by the mention of his father, Cephalus, a few lines further on. See Dover 1968, pp. 34–8.

[78] Lysias, *Olympic Oration* (33), 3: '[...] I have not come here to talk about trivialities or to fight about names. In my view these are the tasks of those sophists who are wholly useless (*sophistōn lian achrēstōn*), and who are desperate for a livelihood, whereas the task of an honorable man and of a worthy citizen (*andros de agathou kai politou*) is to give advice about great matters [...].' Cf. Aeschines, *Against Timarchus* (1), 125, 173, 175 (about Socrates); *Against Ctesiphon* (3), 202.

being pejorative[79] and, at the very least, tends to prove that Lysias was never considered a pure logographer. Should we, then, trading one social identity for another, consider him a 'sophist'? That would not be doing justice to his successive and, sometimes simultaneous, social activities: Lysias certainly partook of various rhetorical practices at the *same time* during his career, including when he was still the owner of a flourishing shield workshop. Plato provides the best evidence of this when he amuses himself by depicting Lysias as both a sophist (i.e. belonging to that category of men who are not 'ashamed to write speeches') and a 'logographer.'[80] If the term does not have its usual meaning of 'writer of judicial speeches' here, the allusion is nevertheless transparent: The philosopher is playing on the interferences between the fictitious context of the dialogue – situated before the civil war of 404 – and the real context of composition, in the 370s, when Lysias was well known for his logographical activity.

Beyond its polemical dimension, Platonic irony, as it often did, gets right to the heart of things. Lysias is characterized precisely by his versatility and the fact it was impossible to confine him to a single sphere of activity[81]: Depending on the place and the time, he could be understood – and could define himself – as a businessman, a sophist or a logographer.

Let's narrow the focus, finally, to his activity as a logographer. In this particular register, uncertainty is exacerbated, because it is difficult to know who is speaking in a speech composed by Lysias. With the exception of *Against Eratosthenes*, he never speaks himself, but always gives voice to others. One could say – to paraphrase Flaubert – that, in his works, the logographer is 'present everywhere and visible nowhere.' Present everywhere, since he acts as a ventriloquist, placing his own words in the mouths of his clients; visible nowhere, insofar as Lysias must always adjust his words to the interests of his clients and, above all, erase his name from the work he has created.

---

[79] This is the case, for example, in Xenophon, who often associates sophists with *sophoi* and even uses the term to talk about philosophers (cf. *Memorabilia*, 4.2.1; 4.2.8; *Poroi*, 5.4; *Cyropaedia*, 6.1.41). See Classen 1984. In the fourth century, the term 'sophist' could have at least three different meanings according to the context: firstly, a neutral sense to indicate a scholar or a specialist in all the fields; next, a pejorative sense, which denigrated nitpicking intellectuals; and finally, a platonic sense, stigmatizing those who refused the science of being.

[80] Plato, *Phaedrus*, 257c-d.

[81] Moreover, we should not excessively broaden the distance between the sophist, the logographer and the owner of a workshop: All of them make products and respond to the demands of customers who orient, through their use of such products (*chrēsis*), the production process (*poiēsis*). See Vernant 1983, pp. 296–8.

This tension between anonymity and authorship has a paradoxical effect over time. While in court, the client appropriates the speech of the logographer and erases all trace of its true author who, incidentally, has no interest in being recognized as such.[82] However, in the long term, it is very often the client who sinks into anonymity: The speech then becomes the work of Lysias alone, to the extent that, in the great majority of cases, the identity of the client remains unknown.[83] Initially erased, the name of Lysias is even transformed over time into a powerful magnet likely to attract to it other 'inauthentic' speeches that come to swell an ever more imposing corpus.

These contradictions characteristic of logography are explored in the *Phaedrus*, a decidedly crucial, if one-sided, testimony. This is because, in the dialogue, Lysias is not only qualified as a 'logographer,' but acts as such: He composes a written speech, of which the young Phaedrus obtains a copy in order to deliver it before a new audience – just as a client buys a speech to deliver it later in court. Of course, the analogy is only partial, since, in the Platonic dialogue, Lysias' speech is not composed for a fee and is dedicated to love, not to a lawsuit. Besides, in the end, it is not pronounced from memory but read aloud by the young Phaedrus: 'Do you think that a mere dilettante like me could recite from memory in a manner worthy of him a speech that Lysias, the best of those who write (*graphein*) nowadays, took such time and trouble to compose?'[84] However, as we have seen, the verb *graphein* leads the reader to connect this to the later career of Lysias,[85] especially since the whole dialogue functions as the

---

[82] Dover 1968, p. 156: 'The consultant, for his part, might find it preferable, on many occasions, not to incur such opprobrium as could be attached to the *logographos*, but rather to become known by word of mouth as a man whom it was profitable to consult; he stood to gain more by exaggerated rumour than by a label on a written text.'

[83] This is the case for twenty-five of the thirty-five speeches preserved in the corpus: *Against Simon* (3); *On a Wound by Premeditation* (4); *For Callias* (5); *Against Andocides* (6); *Defense in the Matter of the Olive Stump* (7); *Accusation of Calumny* (8); *Against Theomnestus I & II* (11–2); *Against Agoratus* (13); *Against Alcibiades I & II* (14–5); *On the Property of Eraton* (17); *On the Property of Aristophanes* (19); *Defense against a Charge of Taking Bribes* (21); *Against the Corn-Dealers* (22); *Against Pancleon* (23); *On the Refusal of a Pension* (24); *Defense Against a Charge of Subverting the Democracy* (25); *On the Scrutiny of Evandros* (26); *Against Epicrates and His Fellow-Envoys* (27); *Against Ergocles* (28); *Against Philocrates* (29); *Against Nicomachus* (30); *Against Philon* (31); *Against the Subversion of the Ancestral Constitution* (34).

[84] Plato, *Phaedrus*, 228a. Cf. *Phaedrus*, 230e: Phaedrus carries Lysias' manuscript off under his coat and finally decides to *read* it aloud to Socrates, whereas in court litigants always had to declaim the text from memory. Cf. Alcidamas, *On the Sophists* (17), 11, 18, 21, 34; Patillon 2009.

[85] It should be remembered that analogy does not mean identity, or even term-to-term comparison; rather, to build an analogy is to *establish a system of similarities and differences* between two objects, which are then linked together, without being assimilated to each other. See in particular Lahire 2005, p. 66.

parody of a trial: Phaedrus ends up delivering Lysias' speech to Socrates, who plays the role of a juror; after listening to him, the philosopher turns into an accuser, elaborating a counter-speech to tear his opponent's argument to pieces. Finally, the verdict comes in: Having become a juror in turn, Phaedrus recognizes Socrates' clear superiority over Lysias.[86] End of story!

But the dialogue plays with logography in an even more subtle way. Plato has fun portraying Lysias as a character who is both omnipresent and radically absent according to the principle of logography. On the one hand, his name is constantly quoted, and the speaker insinuates himself into the dialogue through his manuscript with which he is one, like Christ in the host: As Socrates ironically points out, 'Lysias himself is present' through his text.[87] On the other hand, he is only a ghost and, lacking any physical presence, is unable to defend his own text against Socrates' criticism. Here, again, the parallel with logography is obvious: The author is always at the mercy of a client who may deliver a poor oral performance, disfiguring the speech. How better to illustrate the main thesis of *Phaedrus*, according to which the written text always needs the assistance of its 'father' – of the one who conceived it – at the risk of seeing its meaning distorted?[88] Because it implies genetically (so to speak) a need to dissociate the work and its creator, logography exposes the risk inherent in any written production.

However, the Platonic critique is based on a questionable conception that tends to establish a rigid division between the author, Lysias, and the performer, Phaedrus, deprived of any autonomy. But this is the exact opposite of the way logography worked, as Kenneth Dover once showed. Most of the speeches cannot be assigned to a single, clearly identified author: In them, Lysias always mixed his own voice with those of his clients, even if it is difficult to discern their respective contributions.[89] It was in the litigants' interest to be personally involved in writing their speeches, not only because they risked a great deal – both as the accused, of course, but also as the accusers if they suffered too bitter a failure – but also

---

[86] The dialogue represents the principle of logography at one final level. In the end, it is Plato who gives Socrates and Phaedrus voice, and they in turn give voice to Lysias. From this point of view, Plato is the ultimate logographer and the real arbitrator between sophistry, logography and philosophy.
[87] Plato, *Phaedrus*, 228e. One can obviously doubt the authenticity of this manuscript attributed to Lysias.
[88] Cf. Plato, *Phaedrus*, 275d–e. See on this subject Derrida 1981.
[89] Dover 1968, pp. 148–74, who speaks of 'composite authorship.'

because they themselves had to speak in front of the jurors. Moreover, most of them were far from being devoid of any rhetorical capacity. Often rich and well educated, Lysias' clients were able to contribute to their own defense.[90]

This principle of coproduction applied to all stages of the logographic process: Downstream, the client had to deliver his own account of the case, find possible witnesses for the prosecution or the defense and participate in the development of a judicial strategy with Lysias, who acted as a legal advisor, like Antiphon in Thucydides' work.[91] Preparing the speech also implied close collaboration, insofar as Lysias had to adjust his style to the rhetoric skills of the litigant and to his 'idiolect,' his singular way of speaking. As for the speech actually delivered in court, the client needed to make his mark on it, if only to make it sound natural. Finally, the logographer perhaps needed to have the client's agreement to 'publish' the speech – even if it meant touching it up – by means of written copies put on sale in selected 'bookshops.'[92]

Obviously, not all clients got involved to the same extent in the logographic process, whether by necessity or by choice, and some ancient testimonies mention utilitarian relationships, reduced to the strict minimum, between Lysias and his buyers.[93] Even if these interactions are limited, they are nonetheless sufficient to modify the terms in which questions of authenticity are generally raised. Thus, it is undoubtedly futile to try to identify a work by Lysias on the sole basis of stylistic considerations: This would mean retrojecting an anachronistic conception of the author – specific to the Hellenistic and Roman periods, and to the 'invention of literature'[94] – but above all forgetting that Lysias did not act as a solitary demiurge, and that he worked to make himself literally (and literarily) indistinguishable.[95] From this perspective, it is important not to mechanically assign to him the words he puts in the mouths of others

---

[90] The speech *On the Refusal of a Pension*, made by a relatively poor man, is more the exception than the rule: see *infra*, pp. 288–9.
[91] Thucydides, 8.68.1; cf. Aristophanes, *Clouds*, 462-475. See Dover 1968, p. 149.
[92] Publication involved forms of *ex post* rewriting, as shown by the arguments of Aeschines and Demosthenes which respond to each other: certain arguments, raised by the opponent, are not found in the published speeches, suggesting *ex post* alterations. See MacDowell 2009, p. 382.
[93] Plutarch, *Concerning Talkativeness*, 5, 504c. The excerpt does not imply, however, that the client played no role in the composition of the speech delivered to him by Lysias. See Usher 1976, p. 34.
[94] Dupont 1994.
[95] This does not mean, however, that one cannot recognize Lysias' own style in the speeches, since he gave them their finished form and his stylistic patterns are incorporated almost unconsciously in the text. See Usher and Najock 1982.

and that do not necessarily correspond to his own convictions.[96] By nature, the logographer had to act like a chameleon and adopt as his professional ethic the principle of not aligning his speeches with his own thoughts.

His logographic activity therefore brings to a head the uncertainties that characterize Lysias' entire life, be they his fluctuating legal status, his unclear political opinions or his varied professional occupations. To this multifaceted and ambiguous man corresponded multiple and moving choruses of which he was sometimes the coryphaeus, sometimes a simple participant: an enlarged chorus of family and friends; a chorus of the Athenian 'gilded youth,' caught up in the excitement of banquets and processions; a chorus of the colonists in Thurii, which mixed Athenians and foreigners in a shared political project; a chorus of exiles and the banished, forced to leave the city to save themselves during the civil war; and, finally, a chorus of SUPPRIMER Athenian litigants, of which he was the invisible coryphaeus and with whom he wove bonds that were not purely mercenary.

A Family Epic

Everything begins with the family circle. In the ancient sources Lysias is often portrayed as a family member rather than as an autonomous and independent individual. In the *Republic*, Plato represents him as a mute figure, overshadowed by his father, Cephalus, and his brother, Polemarchus, in whose house the dialogue takes place.[97] After the death of his father comes the time of his departure to Thurii, either in 444/3 or closer to 429. There, again, the adventure remains collective: According to Pseudo-Plutarch, 'Lysias went there with his eldest brother Polemarchus,' while Dionysius of Halicarnassus specifies: 'At the age of fifteen he sailed

---

[96] In this, logography does not correspond to the writer/reader model, according to which, 'at the moment of reading, the reading voice does not belong to the reader', but to the writer. See Svenbro 1993, pp. 44–63 (quote p. 46).

[97] Nails 2002, p. 84: The text of the *Republic* (328b) does not, however, imply that they all lived together. If some have thought that the conversation took place in Cephalus' house (Todd 2000, p. 4), the text explicitly speaks of Polemarchus' house (Polemarchus may even have taken his elderly father under his roof). Indeed, an elderly father could very well cede control of his *oikos* to his son, even before his death. Polemarchus' position as preferential heir is metaphorically suggested in the *Republic* (331d–e). When Cephalus slips away to attend to a sacrifice, his eldest son, Polemarchus, calls out to him: 'So, Polemarchus said, am I then to be your heir in everything? You certainly are, Cephalus said, laughing, and off he went to the sacrifice. Then tell us, heir to the argument, [Socrates] said …' Polemarchus is both the heir of the conversation and of the family fortune mentioned previously – at least until his younger brothers come of age.

away to Thurii *with his two brothers* to join in the foundation of a colony there, a Panhellenic venture promoted by the Athenians in the twelfth year before the Peloponnesian War.'[98] The departure therefore does not result in us being able to see Lysias' individual trajectory, but rather one in solidarity with that of his brothers. At the time, of course, it was likely that both he and Euthydemus, still minors, were under the supervision of their eldest brother, Polemarchus. As for their return to Athens in 412, it does not put an end to this fraternal solidarity: There, still, Lysias and Polemarchus act in concert and both settle in the Piraeus.[99]

In a revealing way, the Thirty jointly attack the two brothers, the better to plunder them. Moreover, Lysias and Polemarchus seem to have owned and managed in common the flourishing shield factory that made them extremely prosperous metics, perhaps even the most prosperous of the whole community.[100] When, in *Against Eratosthenes*, the orator gives his poignant account of their simultaneous arrest, the 'we' is omnipresent: '*We* owned plenty of cloaks, but when *we* asked, they would not give us a single one for the burial. [...] The Thirty had seven hundred shields *of ours*. They had a huge amount of silver and gold, bronze and ornaments, [...] and also one hundred and twenty slaves [...]. *We* received not the smallest degree of pity from them; instead, because of *our* money, they behaved towards *us* just as others would have done if angered by very serious offenses.'[101] The two brothers even seem to have considered their dwelling

---

[98] Pseudo-Plutarch, *Lives of the Ten Orators [Lysias]*, 835d, and Dionysius of Halicarnassus, *The Ancient Orators [Lysias]*, 2.1.2 (our emphasis).

[99] With his usual irony, Plato set up this family constellation in the *Phaedrus*. If the dialogue confirms the importance of Lysias as a sophist, it also reserves a prominent place to his elder brother, Polemarchus. After having torn to pieces his speech on love, Socrates encourages Phaedrus to try to convert Lysias to philosophy and, therefore, to imitate Polemarchus (*Phaedrus*, 257b). The 'sophist' Lysias is thus diminished to the status of an immature young man unable to follow in the footsteps of an elder brother made untouchable by the tragic death he met under the Thirty.

[100] Lysias, *Against Hippotherses*, fr. 1 Gernet (= fr. 7 Todd and fr. 170 Carey), l. 152–5, who defines Lysias as 'the richest of the metics.' See Todd 2007, pp. 12–3. His fortune amounted to thirty-six or even seventy talents according to the restoration adopted from another fragment of the same speech (fr. 165 Carey, l. 28–31). The text can be rendered either as *ebd[omēko]nta talantōn* (seventy talents) or as *ex [kai triako]nta talantōn* (thirty-six talents), which would divide Lysias' wealth by two. On the other hand, it is not known whether this was the amount of his personal fortune or the amount he shared with his brother.

[101] Lysias, *Against Eratosthenes* (12), 18–20 (our emphasis). It is necessary here to dismiss a hypothesis that is still commonly accepted. The shield workshop was probably not founded by their father, Cephalus, as pointed out by Karabélias 2005, p. 338 n. 25 and p. 339. In Plato's *Republic* (330a–b), when Cephalus speaks of the inheritance he wishes to pass on to his children, he speaks only of his 'goods' (*ousia*), without specifying their nature, whereas, in *Against Eratosthenes*, the shield factory is never presented as a paternal inheritance. Such a legacy would, moreover, suppose a very strange continuity: One would have to imagine an Athenian workshop managed from Thurii for fifteen, even thirty years, since the two brothers left for southern Italy at the latest in 425, after the

A Family Epic   275

places as one unit: Lysias evokes 'the three houses' (§18) that he and his brother occupied without feeling the need to distinguish them.[102]

Lysias' family chorus did not, however, function only along the patrilineal and male line. The women around Lysias also played a major role in the transmission of his patrimony and, more widely, in the integration of the family within the Athenian community. Let us return briefly to the already much-noted passage of Apollodorus' *Against Neaira*: 'When the women arrived, Lysias did not take them to his own house, since he was embarrassed to do so in front of *his wife, Brachyllus' daughter, who was also his niece, and his elderly mother*, who lived there too.'[103] If there is no reason to be surprised that Lysias brought his old mother under his roof out of affection or, at least, out of obligation,[104] marrying his own niece was also quite a common practice. It was even an advantageous marriage that aimed to avoid splitting any inheritance between the collateral branches of the same family.[105] However, Lysias' marriage starts to look less banal as soon as one wonders about the probable identity of his wife, who is not named according to the customs of Athenian judicial rhetoric[106]: She was probably the daughter of his sister, who was in turn married to a certain Brachyllus.[107] An anecdotal detail? Not quite. This Brachyllus – who became both the brother-in-law and the father-in-law of Lysias – could in fact be a well-known Athenian citizen from the deme of

---

death of their father. The shield factory may therefore have been set up by the two brothers on their return to Athens, in 412, thanks to the fortune accumulated during their stay in Thurii. On the wealth amassed by the citizens of Thurii, cf. Diodorus of Sicily, 12.11.3. One could certainly argue that in Greece, as elsewhere, specialized crafts were very often transmitted from father to son. However, there is no mistake about it: Lysias and Cephalus did not have any particular skills as craftsmen, contrary to painters, sculptors or even poets. At most the two brothers supervised the smooth running of the factory, perhaps divided into several production units and placed under the effective control of a workshop manager (Karabélias 2005, p. 342). They were therefore not craftsmen in the technical sense of the term, but workshop owner-managers.

[102] It might be tempting to think of them as the houses of the three brothers who, like the little pigs in the fairy tale, faced attack by the wolves (i.e. the Thirty). However, Euthydemus is not mentioned in *Against Eratosthenes*: Should we then imagine a third house in which we might find Lysias' sister, married to a certain Brachyllus?

[103] Pseudo-Demosthenes, *Against Neaira* (59), 22: *adelphidēn* (niece; our emphasis).

[104] Nails 2002, p. 84, put forward the hypothesis that she may have been the second wife of Cephalus, which would make it possible she was not necessarily a centenarian in the 390s.

[105] See Damet and Moreau 2018, pp. 139–43, 154–5.

[106] Schaps 1977; Schmitt Pantel 1994–1995. Women are, with rare exceptions, identified through their relationships with male relatives.

[107] Contrary to what Pseudo-Plutarch claims, wrongly, in *Lives of the Ten Attic Orators [Lysias]*, 835d. See on this subject Dover 1968, pp. 39–40.

Erchia.[108] If this is the case, Lysias' family would thus have been allied by a double marriage to an important Athenian *oikos*.[109]

As a relative by marriage, Brachyllus was part of the many 'familiars' (*oikeioi*) who gravitated around the house of Lysias.[110] Still, one should not imagine these as a homogeneous chorus, made up only of free men and women, whether they were metics or citizens. This second circle also included, at the other end of the social and legal spectra, many slaves. While these dependents, essential to the production and reproduction of the *oikos*, hardly appear in the ancient sources, the shock of the civil war made it possible to perceive their outline fleetingly – for example, in the speech *Against Hippotherses*, delivered shortly after the reconciliation. Published in fragmentary form in 1919,[111] the text is difficult to reconstruct, but certain elements seem certain. After the amnesty of 403, a certain Hippotherses, unknown in other respects, brought a lawsuit against Lysias, whom he accused of having tried to recover all or part of the goods the Thirty had confiscated from him.[112] If the details of this affair remain obscure, the speech attests to the exceptional wealth of Lysias before 404 and, implicitly, his relative financial prosperity after the reconciliation.[113] More importantly, it gives voice to a slave who provides the speech's

---

[108] Lambert 2000, p. 494 n. 3. A citizen named Brachyllus, son of Bathyllus of Erchia, happens to be the man behind the *Agora* decree 15.34, l. 10 (dated 343/2) and may have been related to a certain [B]athyllus [son of Brachyllus], mentioned on a funerary stele (*SEG* 21.1013). The name Brachyllus is very rare: The testimony of the *Against Neaira* is the only other known example of it. All these men, starting with the brother-in-law of Lysias, may therefore belong to the same family of Athenian citizens.

[109] Until the fourth century, there was no legal prohibition against marriage between a citizen and a foreigner: This prohibition was formalized and enforced only later. Cf. Pseudo-Demosthenes, *Against Neaira* (59), 16–8; Canevaro 2013a, pp. 187–90.

[110] On the *oikeiotēs*, see Will 1995, pp. 301–3. As Will puts it, the *oikeioi* are 'the familiars of the *oikos* (to be distinguished from the real "family"), people who, for various reasons (customary, institutional), are in a more or less close and constant relationship with the *oikos*.' See more generally Gherchanoc 2012.

[111] *P. Oxy.* 1606 (Grenfell and Hunt (eds.) 1919). The speech contains 236 lines that are partially mutilated and divided into several noncontinuous blocks, often difficult to read: fr. 1 Gernet (= fr. 7 Todd and fr. 164–73 Carey).

[112] See Todd 2000, p. 368. The speech cites a hitherto unknown clause in the amnesty, which seems to distinguish between property sold by the Thirty (and nonrecoverable) and that still in the hands of the public Treasury (and which could be returned to its original owner). But another distinction may be at work: The speech (fr. 172 Carey) seems to oppose visible (*phanera ousia*) and invisible (*aphanēs ousia*) property. While visible property could have been recovered by its former owner (through buying it back), the latter could not be returned, even in exchange for payment.

[113] Cf. Lysias, *Against Hippotherses*, fr. 1 Gernet (= fr. 164 Carey), l. 13–7: 'Now that he is back, however, he cannot recover it, not even by paying the price to those who purchased it.' That this reimbursement can be envisaged implies that Lysias retained some financial means, as he had already proved his capacity to help (with arms and money) the democratic resistance materially *after* the confiscations carried out by the Thirty: fr. 1 Gernet (= fr. 170 Carey), l. 165–7.

subtitle: *Against Hippotherses, on the female servant* (*huper therapainēs*). In the absence of any precise indications in the text, it is possible to make two hypotheses: Either the servant girl was the very object of the dispute – the property over which (*huper*) Lysias and his adversary were fighting – or Lysias was being sued for the actions that this slave had undertaken in his service, perhaps in an attempt to recover some of his property, the speech therefore being made 'in favor (*huper*) of a servant girl' targeted by the lawsuit at the same time as her owner, Lysias.[114]

Both hypotheses raise some difficulties. On the one hand, it is difficult to understand why anyone would sue over the possession of a single slave, especially since the preserved fragments suggest that the financial stakes of the lawsuit were considerable; on the other hand, some scholars find it difficult to conceive that a servant could have acted as a commercial agent on behalf of her master.[115] However, this may be an anachronistic projection, since it is known that some slaves could enter into contracts instead of their owners, even if the latter remained *ultimately* legally responsible for their actions.[116]

In any case, this anonymous servant is certainly just one representative (on the documentary level) of a chorus of familiars, where individuals of various statuses were living together: metics, of course, but also citizens, such as Brachyllus, and slaves.[117] Gravitating around the *oikos* of Lysias, all contributed, voluntarily or not, to preserving, restoring or increasing the family patrimony.

A Very Small and Rich World

Let us pause for a few moments and examine the speech *Against Hippotherses*, by focusing on its performance context. Obviously, the speech was not delivered by Lysias himself, but by an anonymous citizen, tasked with defending him, because the speaker is mentioned in the third

---

[114] The lawsuit was obviously aimed at Lysias, and this is clearly indicated at the end of the text (fr. 1 Gernet = fr. 171 Carey, l. 219–22: 'Lysias deserves to receive gratitude from the People, given that he has been a great benefactor. So I beg you, gentlemen of the jury, to acquit *him*' [our emphasis]). See Cloché 1921.
[115] Todd 2000, p. 367 n. 6.
[116] *Against Athenogenes* by Hyperides attests to this possibility. See Ismard 2019, pp. 109–12, on the slave's capacity for commercial action, which does not, however, affect the master's unlimited responsibility.
[117] It is very likely that, among the 120 slaves mentioned by Lysias himself in *Against Eratosthenes*, some worked in the three houses of the family and not in the shield factory. See Karabélias 2005, p. 339.

person in the fragments transmitted on papyrus. Is this because metics were not allowed to speak in court and had to use a third party to defend themselves? This is highly unlikely. On the contrary, everything indicates that they could sue in the courts, as attested by the speech *Against Eratosthenes* delivered by Lysias himself.[118] As Philippe Gauthier has demonstrated, it is only for the application – and not for the trial itself – that a metic had to resort to a *prostatēs*.[119] Why then did Lysias not deliver the speech himself? We don't know, but it is possible to put forward an argument from silence. Lysias could very well have spoken in court without leaving a written trace, and this speech – his *Against Hippotherses* – was composed for a friend who came to support him as a *sunēgoros* ('cospeaker').[120]

This anonymous citizen testifies to the dense relational network on which Lysias could rely. He was certainly one of the numerous friends in Lysias' social circle before, during and after the civil war. As we have already seen, from his childhood on, Lysias frequented the Athenian gilded youth. Portrayed on stage in Plato's *Republic*, this proximity is confirmed by Pseudo-Plutarch: 'He was educated along with the sons of the most distinguished Athenian families.'[121] When he reached middle age, but still before the civil war, Lysias seems to have cultivated close links with powerful citizens. The opening of the *Phaedrus* shows him as the guest of Epicrates, a politician and a democrat.[122] The house, Plato specifies, belongs to another citizen, Morychos, known for his dietary extravagances and, therefore, for his oligarchic leanings.[123] The glutton Morychos, the democrat Epicrates, the controversial Phaedrus: In this dialogue, Plato was probably right in linking Lysias to a single social milieu with varied political orientations.

---

[118] It is unnecessary to assume that Lysias was a citizen when he delivered his speech against Eratosthenes (*contra* Edwards and Usher 1985, p. 235). As we have seen, lawsuits against proposals contrary to the laws (*graphai paranomōn*) had a suspensive effect on the decisions concerned. Therefore, there is no reason to suppose that *Against Eratosthenes* was never delivered in court and consisted only of a pamphlet intended to show what Lysias *could have said* if he had had the right to do so: Todd 2000, pp. 114–5.

[119] Gauthier 1972, p. 133.

[120] This friend should not necessarily be identified with Lysias' guarantor (*prostatēs*): see Gauthier 1972, p. 127 n. 67.

[121] Pseudo-Plutarch, *Lives of the Ten Orators [Lysias]*, 835c: *hoi epiphanestatoi athenaioi*.

[122] Plato, *Phaedrus*, 227b. On Epicrates, cf. scholia to the *Assemblywomen*, 71, with commentary by Ryan 2012, p. 81.

[123] Plato, *Phaedrus*, 227b. On the reputation of Morychos, cf. Aristophanes, *Wasps*, 506; *Acharnians*, 887; *Peace*, 1008–9. See Ryan 2012, pp. 82, 96. Plato implicitly – and ironically – connects the 'word feast' to which Lysias invites Phaedrus (*Phaedrus*, 227b) with the rich banquets he was to share with his extravagant friends: Yunis 2011, pp. 86–7; Davidson 1998.

A Very Small and Rich World 279

In fact, this friendly chorus was far from being a harmonious little world where all danced as one: As is often the case, proximity went hand in hand with rivalry.[124] The relations between Socrates and Lysias are perhaps the best illustrations of this. On the one hand, Lysias seems to have been quite close to Socrates, since several scholiasts attribute to him a speech *For Socrates, against Polycrates*, in response to a pamphlet written against the philosopher in 394.[125] On the other hand, the 'sophist' never managed to fully integrate the Socratic circle, as demonstrated both by the *Phaedrus'* acrimonious tone toward him and a speech attributed to Lysias against Aeschines the Socratic.[126] To this should also be added a probably apocryphal but revealing tradition. According to Diogenes Laertius, Lysias offered his services to Socrates during his trial in 399:

> The philosopher then, after Lysias had written a defense for him, read it through and said: 'A fine speech, Lysias; it is not, however, suitable to me (*ou mēn harmottōn g'emoi*).' For it was plainly more forensic than philosophical. Lysias said, 'If it is a fine speech, how can it fail to suit you?' 'Well', he replied, 'would not fine raiment and fine shoes be just as unsuitable to me (*anarmosta*).'[127]

Despite his willingness, then, Lysias could not *accord* (*harmottein*) himself with Socrates. Even though they were in the same intellectual chorus, in the eyes of most Athenians, who barely distinguished between philosophers and sophists,[128] their relations were nonetheless *dissonant*.[129]

With the trial of Socrates, however, we sidestep the episode of the civil war, which sheds a harsh light on Lysias' network of friends, since it was severely strained at this time. Everything took place in the Piraeus: Lysias and Polemarchus both lived there and had established multiple links, as revealed in *Against Eratosthenes*. After having escaped from the Thirty, Lysias states: 'I went to the house of Archeneus the shipowner and sent him to the town (*eis astu*) to find out about my brother.'[130] Probably a

---

[124] In a restricted community, only a limited number of positions can coexist at the same time. This 'law of small numbers' brought about fierce competition between intellectuals: see Collins 1998, pp. 81–2, 91.
[125] Lysias, fr. 272a–b and fr. 273 Carey.   [126] Lysias, fr. 1–4 Carey (= Athenaeus, 13.611d).
[127] Diogenes Laertius, 2.40–1 (= fr. 271f Carey).
[128] On the role of the trial of Socrates in the emergence of an intellectual arena that was both autonomous and competitive, see Azoulay 2007a, pp. 182–3.
[129] This dissonance was not linked to Lysias' condition as a foreigner, but to his activity as a logographer. Let us recall that his brother Polemarchus, also a metic, was praised in the Platonic tradition: cf. Plato, *Phaedrus*, 257b; Plutarch, *On the Eating of Flesh*, 2.4.998b.
[130] Lysias, *Against Eratosthenes* (12), 16. This passage does not imply that his brother lived in the city. On the contrary, he probably also lived in Piraeus, since Peison goes to Polemarchus' house from Lysias' (§12): the two locations are obviously not far from each other.

citizen,[131] the aforementioned Archeneus is obviously one of the family's relatives, since he is ready to take calculated risks to do a favor for a man pursued by the authorities. Perhaps he was both a friend and a business partner of Lysias. As a *naukleros*, he could have chartered the ships intended to export the productions of the family workshop. Was he also the one who helped Lysias to settle in Megara in favorable financial conditions? We don't know, but *Against Hippotherses* suggests that somebody aided Lysias with his escape: He obviously managed to take with him some of his possessions – perhaps in the form of maritime loans or cash – without which he would not have been able to assist, as he did, 'those of Piraeus.'[132]

Far from being an isolated supporter, the shipowner Archeneus is the most prominent figure of a chorus that included not only citizens and metics, but also foreign visitors. An excerpt from *Against Eratosthenes* gives a fleeting glimpse of them at the time of Lysias' arrest: 'They found me entertaining guests at dinner, drove them out, and handed me over to Peison.'[133] While denouncing a flagrant violation of the laws of hospitality, the passage draws attention to the presence of *xenoi* – both guests and foreigners – in Lysias' house. The cosmopolitan company of a man who had lived for fifteen or even thirty years outside Athens is hardly surprising, and it must be noted that these relations of hospitality (*xenia*) functioned in a reciprocal way. Once in exile, Lysias could count on a number of faithful hosts to welcome and support him – first of all in Megara, where he settled a few months as a metic and found a patron (*prostatēs*) to vouch for him; then in the Peloponnese, where he managed to persuade Thrasydaeus of Elis – the leader of the city's democrats – to provide financial and military aid to the resistance fighters of the Piraeus.[134] Perhaps his role as intermediary was in this case facilitated by his long stay

---

[131] PA 2362. On his probable citizenship, see Reed 2003, p. 120, n° 36.

[132] Lysias, *Against Hippotherses*, fr. 1 Gernet (= fr. 170 Carey), l. 163–7. Cf. Pseudo-Plutarch, *Lives of the Ten Orators [Lysias]*, 835f: 'He supplied them with 2,000 drachmas and 200 shields.' About his silence in *Against Eratosthenes* on his deeds in Megara, see Baslez 2003, p. 100: '[T]he dispersion of his business and interests could have seemed to contradict his attachment to Athens.' In this respect, Lysias had clearly been more careful than Amphilochus, a citizen who had left to join the resistance fighters in Piraeus and had entrusted a significant sum of money to Callimachus, a citizen who had remained in the city. The latter ended up being confiscated by the *archon basileus*, a decision thereafter confirmed by the Council: Isocrates, *Against Callimachus* (18), 5. See *supra*, Chapter 4, p. 131.

[133] Lysias, *Against Eratosthenes* (12), 8. This tradition of hospitality goes back several decades: As early as the *Republic* (328b), Polemarchus and Cephalus are portrayed as guests, since, when Socrates arrives at their house, Thrasymachus of Chalcedon is already staying with them.

[134] Pseudo-Plutarch, *Lives of the Ten Orators [Lysias]*, 835f. On Thrasydaeus of Elis, cf. Lysias, *Against Hippotherses*, fr. 1 Gernet (= fr. 170 Carey), ll. 165–70. Thrasydaeus was the leader of the democrats of Elis: Xenophon, *Hellenica*, 3.2.27–30. Justin, 5.9.9, speaks of 500 mercenaries.

A Very Small and Rich World

in Thurii, where he rubbed shoulders with numerous Eleans, engaged in this Panhellenic foundation.[135]

During his mission in the Peloponnese, Lysias was accompanied by a certain Herman, to whom he must have been close.[136] For a very long time, a number of scholars have suggested correcting the name of this man – totally unknown otherwise – to Hermas, or even to Hermon.[137] The latter proposal would have the advantage of linking Lysias to an Athenian citizen well known for his commitment against the oligarchy, since a certain Hermon had participated in the conspiracy against the 'tyrant' Phrynichus in 411.[138] Let us take the suggestion seriously for a moment. If this was the case, it would mean Lysias acted in concert with an authentic resistance fighter. However, this Hermon was by no means a rabid democrat: A close contact of Theramenes, he had even served as a magistrate under the Four Hundred – he was in charge of the ephebes in Mounychia.[139] He therefore seems to have been, in fact, a 'moderate' Athenian, tired of the oligarchic excesses of 411. And if Hermon was forced to take exile in 404, it was undoubtedly because the Thirty counted among their ranks several friends of Phrynichus, who were unwilling to forgive his complicity in the attack.[140] In this context, it seems all the more coherent to associate Lysias with this man who belonged to the same privileged social circle and who was also personally targeted by the oligarchs.

But it would be a mistake to tell an irenic story, full of nothing but solidarity and assistance. The friendly chorus of Lysias was also pushed to breaking point by the civil war. In 404, underlying disagreements burst into the open, and certain close relations turned brutally against him. Lysias touches on this without dwelling too much on the subject, probably because he does not want to draw attention to his elite friends. After having been arrested by the Thirty's envoys, Lysias was led to the residence of a citizen named Damnippus, to be momentarily locked up there. Now, the two men knew each other well, and the prisoner hoped to convince his

---

[135] See Roisman and Worthington (eds.) 2015, p. 128, according to whom this connection with Thrasydaeus may have been facilitated by the presence of Eleans at Thurii (Diodorus of Sicily, 12.11.3).

[136] Pseudo-Plutarch, *Lives of the Ten Orators [Lysias]*, 835f.

[137] This suggestion goes back to Westermann 1833, p. 38, based on the spelling given by Photius, *Library, Codices*, 262 [Lysias], 489b. For Herman, see Roisman and Worthington (eds.) 2015, p. 128.

[138] See Fowler 1969, p. 364 n. 2.

[139] Thucydides, 8.92.2–5 (*peripoloi*); Plutarch, *Alcibiades*, 25.10.

[140] His presence in the Piraeus in 411 could also explain how he was in contact with Lysias, who, in all probability, had just settled there with his brother after having been forced to leave Thurii.

jailer to set him free: 'So I called Damnippus and said, "You are a close friend (*epitedeios*) of mine, and I am in your house".'¹⁴¹ After having heard his supplication, Damnippus promised to help him, before changing his mind and warning the oligarchs.¹⁴² Clear-sightedly, Lysias did not, however, wait too long for his help and escaped: 'as it happened, I was familiar with the house and knew it had two doors; [so] I decided to try and save myself.'¹⁴³ This is clear proof that he had been quite intimate with his jailer in the past.

Beyond this specific case, the episode reflects the way in which the civil war transformed former close friendships of Lysias, if not into radical enemies, at least into 'nonfriends' (since friendship is defined, in Greece as elsewhere, by a duty of mutual assistance).¹⁴⁴ Conversely, Lysias seems to have established new bonds with Athenians – like Hermon? – placed in the same uncertain situation. Should this lead us to believe that the traumatic experience of the *stasis* led to a total reconfiguration of the speaker's social circles?

Shared Suffering: A Chorus of Exiles?

At first sight, this idea is attractive. As the Greeks themselves had already theorized, it is not only joys that unite men, but also sorrows, through the feeling of solidarity that *stasis* arouses between comrades in misfortune.¹⁴⁵ And Lysias certainly had more than his fair share of misfortune in life. For we should bear in mind an often-overlooked fact: The orator suffered through the torments of civil war and exile not once, but twice: first in Thurii, then in Athens. Although he makes no mention of it in *Against Eratosthenes*, his long stay in southern Italy was probably a foundational experience. It is in Thurii that Lysias became an adult and a citizen, a community in which he lived for fifteen or even thirty years, and where he seems to have forged close links with 'best men.'¹⁴⁶ The ancient tradition

---

¹⁴¹ Lysias, *Against Eratosthenes* (12), 14. On the meaning of *epiteideios*, see Eernstman 1932, according to whom the term refers to friends, but can include more casual relationships (cf. Xenophon, *Hellenica*, 1.4.12, 18–9).

¹⁴² Here, again, Lysias wishes to underline the impiety of which he was then victim. Being in Damnippus' house, he should have enjoyed the protection accorded to guests (*xenoi*), especially since he asked him for assistance in terms that evoke the ritual of supplication (*hiketeia*). See Edwards and Usher 1985, p. 239.

¹⁴³ Lysias, *Against Eratosthenes* (12), 15.   ¹⁴⁴ See Blundell 1989, and *supra*, Chapter 1, pp. 49–51.

¹⁴⁵ See Macé 2014, pp. 681–2: Evil, the common scourge, is offered to each person in as many shares as needed, according to a principle of omnidistribution.

¹⁴⁶ According to the expression of Diodorus of Sicily, 12.11.3–4.

mentions several famous participants in the expedition, such as the architect Hippodamus of Miletus, the historian Herodotus of Halicarnassus, the sophist Protagoras of Abdera and the Athenian soothsayer Lampon, one of the founders (*oikistai*) of the colony.[147] The enterprise was so successful that it is sometimes described in the ancient tradition as a utopia come to life, combining a geometric urban grid, equally distributed land and democratic laws.[148]

Thirty years later, the dream turned into a nightmare. After the Athenians were routed in Sicily, old antagonisms revived in the city of Thurii: 'After that disaster there was a civil strife (*stasiasantos*), and he [Lysias] was exiled along with three hundred others on the charge of pro-Athenian sympathies (*attikismon*).'[149] The orator and his brother therefore returned to Athens not only as a family, but in a group: Expelled as one, many 'Atticizers' probably sought refuge in Athens. Nothing, however, indicates that there was a significant Thurian community in the democratic city: The experiment had undoubtedly been too short to create a strong collective identity between colonists. The Athenians did not grant any special status to these refugees from southern Italy, unlike the 212 Plateans who, after the destruction of their city in 428, had been collectively granted Athenian citizenship.[150]

In 404 Lysias had to undergo the trauma of the civil war and banishment a second time. This was also a collective experience. While he went alone to Megara to save his life, he shared in the fate of a great number of Athenians who had been exiled and separated from their relatives because of the Thirty. He himself, in *Against Hippotherses*, proclaims he was a full member of this suffering community:

> For while you were prosperous, Lysias was the richest of the metics, and when the disaster took place, he remained here: *he did not avoid even the smallest part of your misfortunes.*[151]

---

[147] On Protagoras, cf. Heraclides Pontus, *On the Laws*, fr. 150 Wehrli (= Diogenes Laertius, 9.8.50).
[148] On the urban grid (often attributed to the presence of Hippodamus), cf. Diodorus, 12.10.7; on its democratic regime and the equal distribution of lots, Diodorus of Sicily, 12.11.2–3. See García Quintela 2002, p. 139, who describes 'a quadrangular and ideally expansive layout in space (in agreement with the open character of the citizenship of Thurii which accepts all the Greeks), which is opposed to the circular layout, with a limited number of citizens, defined by Plato in the *Laws*.'
[149] Dionysius of Halicarnassus, *The Ancient Orators [Lysias]*, 2.1.3. Cf. Diodorus of Sicily, 12.11.1.
[150] On the citizenship granted to the Plateans, cf. e.g. Thucydides, 3.55.3, 3.63.2; Pseudo-Demosthenes, *Against Neaira* (59), 104; Lysias, *Against Pancleon* (23). See Canevaro 2010.
[151] Lysias, *Against Hippotherses*, fr. 1 Gernet (= fr. 170 Carey), l. 150–66: [oude g]ar' elachiston me[ros tōn hume]terōn dustu[chiōn apela]usen (our emphasis).

Here, the speaker mobilizes the memory of the hardships shared during the civil war to build a collective of victims, associating citizens and metics indiscriminately. He uses the same rhetorical technique in the peroration of *Against Eratosthenes*, when he tries to revive the memory of past sufferings in order to obtain the conviction of his opponent, Eratosthenes:

> In return for this, display your anger as you did when you were in exile. Remember also the other evils *you* suffered at their hands. They executed people after forcibly seizing them, some from the Agora and others from shrines; they dragged others away from children, fathers, and wives, compelling them to be their own killers [. . .].[152]

Lysias immediately specifies the composition of this emotional community. It includes all 'those who escaped death found danger in many places, who wandered to many cities and were banished from all of them.' These suffering people broke down into two groups: on the one hand, those who had remained 'in a hostile fatherland' (i.e. 'those of Piraeus') and, on the other hand, those who had left 'in foreign territory' (i.e. those who, like the speaker, had settled temporarily in another city to escape persecution).[153] The final words of the speech return to these shared misfortunes that united the dead with the living. It is, indeed, as the dead look on that the jurors are called to vote: 'You have heard, you have seen, *you have suffered*, and you have them in your grasp. Give your verdict!'[154]

It remains to be seen how strong the bonds created by this shared suffering were. If it was intensely felt at the time, the solidarity between victims obviously vanished quickly, since once they had returned to the city, some of the democrats of Piraeus opposed naturalizing the foreigners who had fought by their side, either directly or indirectly.[155] In the case of Lysias, these moving appeals obviously had limited effectiveness: In all likelihood, the orator did not recover the property confiscated from him by the Thirty, while his opponent, Eratosthenes, may well have been acquitted by the popular court.[156] This is probably because exile had not been a real collective experience, creating lasting solidarity, unlike the enduring ties that bound, for example, the rowers of the fleet of Samos between 411 and 407.[157] But Lysias himself does not seem to have felt part of this resistance community: As a logographer, he only very rarely gave his support to those who had suffered together with him.

---

[152] Lysias, *Against Eratosthenes* (12), 96 (our emphasis). Cf. §91. See Baslez 2003, p. 101.
[153] Lysias, *Against Eratosthenes* (12), 97.   [154] Lysias, *Against Eratosthenes* (12), 99 (our emphasis).
[155] See *supra*, Chapter 2, p. 91.   [156] Bizos and Gernet 1924, p. 159.
[157] On the links forged at this time, see *supra*, Chapter 2, pp. 73–8.

The Discreet Charm of the Oligarchy

This is to enter into a very complex question: Is it possible to reconstruct a coherent chorus of clients revolving around the orator? The idea may seem strange, even paradoxical. Isn't logography based on purely contractual bonds between the producer and his clients? Lysias seems to have produced ten speeches per year: Could he really have been picky about the identity of his clients?[158]

This approach cannot get to the bottom of the question, not least because a chorus could also include the existence of fee-paying relationships within it: The coryphaeus maintained, or even paid, the *choreutai* it recruited to its service, even if their ties were not limited to their monetary aspect.[159] Logography has similar features in that it is not a craft like the others: In principle, it supposes that intimate links are forged with the client over a long period of time, from their introductory talks to the verdict of the trial, or even the publication of the speech. And the exchange is not a one-way street: As we have seen, while Lysias lent his voice and his talent to his client, he had to adapt to his attitudes and, above all, to momentarily espouse his friendships and hatreds, so as to compose a *well-tuned* speech.[160] These bonds of identification were all the more powerful because the logographer was obliged to write the speech in the first person and because the stakes were much higher than in the context of an ordinary craftsman's activity: While the client risked his property, even his life, the stakes for the logographer were his reputation and, therefore, his economic survival.

These specific features suggest that a logographer's choice of clients did not depend on the law of supply and demand alone, and even less on any supposed (and anachronistic) obligation to act as a 'court-appointed lawyer.'[161] Is it therefore possible to identify, if not selection criteria, at least some consistency in the cases selected by Lysias? A thorough investigation into this subject deserves to be carried out, in spite of the

---

[158] In this respect, it could even be said that Lysias did not really become a craftsman until *after* 403: Whereas he had previously managed a shield factory without getting his hands dirty, he became a real *poiētēs* – a maker of things – when he had to write speeches with his own hands to meet the demands of his clients.

[159] Pseudo-Xenophon, *Constitution of the Athenians*, 1.13. See Wilson 2000, pp. 124–8.

[160] This dissonance is precisely what Socrates reproaches Lysias for, according to the (apocryphal?) tradition reported by Diogenes Laertius (2.40). See *supra*, p. 279.

[161] Logographers were under no obligation to accept a client due to 'professional ethics' in the manner of a contemporary lawyer, contrary to the claims of Kennedy 1963, p. 139. See Dover 1968, p. 149 n. 2.

uncertainties linked to the partial conservation of the corpus. We will take into account here the seventeen speeches referring directly or indirectly to the civil war written between 403 and the 380s in order to try and think this through.[162]

Let us begin by dismissing two false leads often followed by scholars. The first one consists in attributing to Lysias a leaning toward the 'radical' democrats, because of the support that Thrasybulus had given him for his (aborted) naturalization attempt in 403. In reality, there is nothing to support this assumption: If he perhaps supported Thrasybulus at the time of the reconciliation – although we have no proof of this – he was by no means his right-hand man in the long term; less than fifteen years after 403, he even took on as clients two men who were challenging the great man of Phyle.[163] As for the second error of perspective, it consists of overestimating the hatred that Lysias felt for the oligarchs in general, based on the sole reading of *Against Eratosthenes*. In reality, Lysias only prosecuted the citizens he considered directly responsible for his family misfortunes: Eratosthenes, his brother's 'murderer,' and Hippotherses, who, it seems, had appropriated their fortune for his own benefit. Now these initial misunderstandings have been cleared up, let us review the available evidence, focusing on Lysias' clients on the one hand and on their opponents on the other.

In the sample of works preserved to this day, Lysias' clients are, for the most part, Athenians who remained in town during the civil war: No less than eight of them can be identified as such. In *Against Andocides* (speech 6), the litigant is none other than Meletus, one of Socrates' accusers and, above all, one of the Three Thousand involved in the arrest of Leon of Salamis[164]; in a more discreet way, the anonymous client of the *Defense in the Matter of the Olive Stomp* (speech 7) is obviously one of 'those of the city,' since he admits having bought a plot of land under the Thirty and

---

[162] Here is the list: *Against Andocides* (6), *Defense in the Matter of the Olive Stump* (7), *Against Eratosthenes* (12), *Against Agoratus* (13), *In Defense of Mantitheus* (16), *On the Property of the Brother of Nicias* (18), *Defense Against a Charge of Taking Bribes* (21), *Defense Against a Charge of Subverting the Democracy* (25), *On the Scrutiny of Evandros* (26), *Against Ergocles* (28), *Against Nicomachus* (30), *Against Philon* (31) and *Against the Subversion of the Ancestral Constitution* (34). Added to this are fragmentary speeches or others known by their title alone: *Against Hippotherses*, fr. 1 Gernet (= fr. 7 Todd = fr. 164–73 Carey); *Against Theozotides*, fr. 6 Gernet (= fr. 10 Todd = fr. 128–50 Carey); *For Eryximachus who Remained in the City*, fr. 9 Todd (= fr. 106–7 Carey); *Against Archinus*, fr. 52a–c Carey.

[163] *In Defense of Mantitheus* (16), a speech given in around 392–390; *Against Ergocles* (28), dating from 389 or 388. Lysias is also credited with *Against Thrasybulus* (*Kata Thrasybulou*), *for Treason* (fr. 156–63 Carey). See *supra*, Chapter 2, p. 71.

[164] Todd 2007, pp. 408–9. See *supra*, Chapter 4, pp. 159–61.

appears to have taken advantage of the setbacks of the previous owner (associated with the democrats) to buy at a low price.[165] Mantitheus, another client of Lysias (speech 16), is also a member of the Three Thousand, since he has to defend himself from his supposed connections with the Thirty and claims to have been absent from Athens for a long time during the civil war. In addition, there are three speeches whose litigants present similar profiles and a similar line of defense: Whether it is the anonymous citizen accused of corruption (speech 21), the man accused of activities against democracy (speech 25) or a certain Eryximachus (fragment 9c Todd), all of them recognize that they remained in the city, but fiercely deny having actively participated in the oligarchic regime.[166]

This clear preference of Lysias for 'those of the city' persisted with time. Delivered twenty years after the reconciliation, *On the Scrutiny of Evandros* (speech 26) is a good example. In 382/1, a certain Leodamas was dismissed from the Council after his initial examination (*dokimasia*) because of his past involvement in the regime of the Thirty; one of his friends then commissioned a speech by Lysias to attack his replacement, a certain Evandros, and, through him, Thrasybulus of Collytos, an influential general among the democrats (who should not be confused with his great homonym, Thrasybulus of Steiria). The accusations seem to have been made on both sides. While the litigant blamed Evandros for having supported the Thirty,[167] his ally Leodamas seems to have done even worse: According to Aristotle, he had been banished in 411 after the first oligarchic revolution and his name had even been engraved on a stele of infamy; during the reign of the Thirty, it seems he opportunely got rid of this compromising record.[168] As for the litigant himself, given his insinuations against 'those of Piraeus,' we can guess that he remained in the city during all of the civil war.[169]

Two other speeches deserve also to be considered from this perspective. In *Against Nicomachus* (speech 30), composed in 399, Lysias has as a client

---

[165] See *supra*, Chapter 6, pp. 188–91.
[166] *Defense Against a Charge of Taking Bribes* (21), 14; *Defense Against a Charge of Subverting the Democracy* (25), 14; *For Eryximachus Who Remained in the City*, fr. 9c Todd = fr. 107 Carey. This last speech was perhaps also given at a *dokimasia*. Should the client be identified as Eryximachus, son of Acumenos, the physician who is among the guests at Plato's *Symposium*? While the name is not very common, his identity is not certain: The litigant claims to have participated (as a *stratēgos*?) in the Battle of Aigos Potamos in 405, whereas his Platonic namesake was exiled from Athens after the Herms affair in 415.
[167] Lysias, *On the Scrutiny of Evandros* (26), 2–3, 5, 17. [168] Aristotle, *Rhetoric*, 2.23.1400a32–6.
[169] Lysias, *On the Scrutiny of Evandros* (26), 17: 'the city has honored these men [the ancient Three Thousand] no less than it has honored those who returned to Phyle and captured Piraeus.'

a man who may have been a member of the Four Hundred, despite his denials,[170] and who, in 404, probably remained in the city: If he had been able to do so, he would not have failed to mention his banishment by the Thirty or his participation in the democratic resistance like his opponent, Nicomachus, who did go into exile.[171] The same argument can be applied to *Against Ergocles* (speech 28), which dates from 389 or 388. Lysias' client refuses what we might call the 'excuse of Phyle (or Piraeus)': He should not be punished for his present crimes because, fifteen years before, his adversary fought against the Thirty.[172] Here, again, the accuser would undoubtedly have put forward his own democratic service record, if he had been able to do it, to better counter the argument of Ergocles.

In short, of the fifteen clients of Lysias who were involved in the civil war (if we exclude *Against Eratosthenes* and *Against Hippotherses*), nine or ten obviously belonged to the Three Thousand.[173] And the orator not only put his talent at the service of former oligarchs forced to defend themselves against vengeful democrats,[174] but also assisted them in *attacking* their political enemies.[175]

That leaves five clients – one-third of the sample – who do not fall into this category. Does this mean they are committed democrats? The reality is much more nuanced. Let us start with the famous speech *On the Refusal of a Pension* (24), which occupies a special place in Lysias' corpus. This colorful speech was composed for the benefit of – in his own portrayal – a pitiable and disabled citizen who was in danger of being deprived of his

---

[170] Lysias, *Against Nicomachus* (30), 7–8.   [171] See *supra*, Chapter 9, pp. 241–2.
[172] Lysias, *Against Ergocles* (28), 12–3. Cf. *Defense Against a Charge of Subverting the Democracy* (25), 33: 'They believe that because of the dangers at Piraeus, they can now do whatever they wish.' Lysias' speeches sometimes give the impression of a strange 'double standard': While the 'Piraeus excuse' is often rejected (my opponent was with the 'good' resistance fighters, but that doesn't mean anything ... positive), the excuse of neutrality (I was with the 'bad' oligarchs, but that doesn't mean anything ... negative) is frequently invoked.
[173] Certainly: *Against Andocides* (6), *Defense in the Matter of the Olive Stump* (7), *In Defense of Mantitheus* (16), *Defense Against a Charge of Taking Bribes* (21), *Defense Against a Charge of Subverting the Democracy* (25) and *For Eryximachus Who Remained in Town*. More hypothetically: *On the Scrutiny of Evandros* (26), *Against Ergocles* (28) and *Against Nicomachus* (30). We can perhaps add to this final list the accuser of *Against Philon* (31): While the accuser says nothing about his own behavior during the *stasis*, his silence makes it likely he was on the side of 'those of the city.' Otherwise, would he not have invoked his past deeds on the side of the democrats, the better to denounce his opponent accused of having 'gone into hiding abroad'? On this bias of oligarchic selection in Lysias, see the early sources in Kennedy 1963, p. 139; Lateiner 1971; Todd 2007, p. 17.
[174] *Contra* Lateiner 1981b.
[175] This is the case in the speeches *Against Nicomachus* (30), *On the Scrutiny of Evandros* (26) and *Against Ergocles* (28).

living allowance. Whether it is a real case or a covert sophist exercise,[176] the *adunatos* cannot be qualified as a democratic freedom fighter: On the one hand, he may not be as poor as he claims, since it is in his interest to hide his possible assets in order to obtain his pension; on the other hand, he never rallied to the men of Phyle or Piraeus, but fled to be a metic abroad, without contributing in any way to the fight against the Thirty.[177]

Delivered between 397 and 395, *On the Property of the Brother of Nicias* (speech 18) is also difficult to interpret. Lysias' client in this case is one of the nephews of the famous Nicias, who was killed during the expedition of Sicily. To avoid having his goods confiscated, the young man recalls his family's democratic service record. However, in spite of his proclamations, his relatives could not all be regarded as staunch democrats. His uncle Nicias was certainly a great Athenian general, but also a resolute opponent of the most radical democrats.[178] As for his father, Eucrates, his execution by the oligarchs at the very beginning of the civil war did not make him a hero in the eyes of the democrats: His sons were dragged before the courts because Eucrates had been accused – and convicted – for having acted in a criminal way while he was a *stratēgos* at the end of the Peloponnesian War.[179] Worse still, having become an orphan, Lysias' client was taken in, at the time of the Thirty, by another of his uncles, Diognetus, who was very close to the oligarchs. Exiled by the democracy, this former member of the Four Hundred had returned to Athens in 404 and, far from trying to join the resistance in Piraeus (§10), had remained in the city.[180]

Beyond these two very difficult cases, three clients could have belonged to the camp of Piraeus. The anonymous litigants of *Against a Proposal Tending to Destroy the Regime of the Ancestors* (speech 32), *Against Theozotides* (which has come down to us in fragmentary form) and *Against Archinus* (of which we only know the title) might be seen in this light.[181] But it should be noted that, in the latter two cases, this

---

[176] Usher 1999, pp. 106–10; see the reservations of Chiron 2015, pp. 143–6.
[177] Lysias, *On the Refusal of a Pension* (24), 25. See *supra*, Chapter 4, pp. 141–2.
[178] The author of the *Athenian Constitution* (28.3) even claims he was the chief of the notables (*tōn epiphanōn*), opposing him to the demagogue Cleon and suggesting he was close to the oligarch Theramenes.
[179] Gernet 1926, p. 28.
[180] Lysias, *On the Property of the Brother of Nicias* (18), 10–2. Using a tried and tested line of defense, the litigant claimed that his uncle had not taken an active part in the regime of the Thirty and, better still, that he drew on the privileged relations that he maintained with the Spartans to help with the reconciliation – although nothing forces us to believe him.
[181] Lysias, *Against Archinus*, fr. 52a–c Carey. This last speech may have been delivered during the lawsuit for a proposal contrary to the laws (*graphē paranomōn*) initiated by Archinus in order to oppose the decree granting naturalization to Lysias.

identification is only a pure inference, not based on any concrete proof.[182] More importantly, these three speeches targeted Piraeus veterans, and not oligarchs who remained in the city.[183] Lysias therefore seems to have participated more willingly in the internal struggles between former fighters of the Piraeus than in the prosecution of former members of the Three Thousand.

Through their complexity, these last three cases indicate that we must take into account not only the identities of the clients, but also those of their enemies in order to reconstruct the other side of the story, as it were. Out of fifteen identifiable opponents, five are formerly of the Piraeus, or even of Phyle. In addition to the three speeches opposing former 'men of Piraeus' to one another,[184] we must add *Against Agoratus* (13), which attacks a citizen or a metic who had rallied to the army of Thrasybulus,[185] as well as *Against Ergocles* (28), in which, twenty years after the civil war, the litigant attacked a former member of the Phyle army by reproaching him for hiding his crimes behind this flattering front.

There are also four opponents whose political position is not explicit, but who seem to have been, if not resistance fighters, at least fervent democrats: The *adunatos*' (24) accuser is likely to have been close to 'those of Piraeus,' otherwise Lysias would have had good reason to blame him for having been a member of the Three Thousand. As for the three speeches composed for the benefit of citizens who remained in town (*Defense Against a Charge of Taking Bribes* [21], *Defense Against a Charge of Subverting the Democracy* [25] and *For Eryximachus Who Remained in Town*), it would be logical to conclude they were written in response to accusations emanating from the democratic camp. Finally, the opponents

---

[182] Only the speech *Against the Subversion of the Ancestral Constitution* (34) seems to support this: 'It would be terrible, men of Athens, if while we were in exile we fought the Spartans in order to return from exile, but after returning we will go into exile in order not to fight' (§11). We should, however, note that the speaker remains very vague on this subject, and his *pedigree* shows him as actually quite close to 'those of the city': He boasts that he is of good lineage and very rich (§3).

[183] See *supra*, Chapter 3, pp. 146–8.

[184] *Against the Subversion of the Ancestral Constitution* (34), *Against Theozotides* and *Against Archinus*, to which one could moreover add *Against Thrasybulus, for Treason* (fr. 156–63 Carey), of which only the title is known today.

[185] The speech dates back to the spring of 399: see Todd 2000, p. 137. The case of Agoratus should be compared to that of Meletus, the accuser of the speech *Against Andocides* (6). While one was forced by the Thirty to denounce his accomplices – thus condemning them to death (Agoratos) – the other obeyed the oligarchs who asked him to arrest Leon of Salamis, who was then executed Meletus. But their destiny then diverges: Whereas the former joined the resistance in Piraeus Agoratus, the latter stayed in the city until the end Meletus. However, Lysias took on the latter as a client and participated in the accusation against the former. Here, again, the orator's preference for 'those of the city' is confirmed.

of Lysias' clients also included some individuals who, without having taken part directly in the resistance, had suffered from the regime of the Thirty: *Against Nicomachus* (30) and *Against Philon* (31) fall into this category, since these speeches attack individuals who had been banished under the oligarchy.[186]

Therefore, out of the fifteen opponents of Lysias' clients, we count five former Piraeus fighters and four who had probably been banished by the Thirty, to which we have to add two individuals who are difficult to pinpoint: the equivocal Andocides and the anonymous accuser of the speech *Defense in the Matter of the Olive Stump* (7). Only two speeches composed by Lysias against former members of the Three Thousand remain; and, again, these are borderline cases, since they are confrontations between citizens who remained in the city: The speech *On the Property of the Brother of Nicias* (18) pits a former member of the oligarchy, Poliochus, against Nicias' nephew, who also remained in the city in the company of his uncle and guardian; as for the speech *On the Scrutiny of Evandros* (26), it not only pits former oligarchs against each other, but ends up praising 'those of the city' rather than the 'those of Piraeus':

> And rightly so: in the case of the latter [those of Piraeus], the *demos* knows what sort of men they are only under a democracy, and has not experienced what sort of people they would be under an oligarchy. For the former group [those of the city], the *demos* has had a sufficient indication under both constitutions, such that it is reasonable to trust them.[187]

At the end of this quick prosopographical survey, some consistencies deserve to be highlighted. Lysias did not, as far as we know, ever compose a speech for a man of the Piraeus fighting against a man from the city: His few 'resistance' clients were involved in conflicts between themselves and other democrats, not former oligarchs. Symmetrically, Lysias never went after former members of the Three Thousand unless their opponent was also in the same camp: In this respect, the speeches *Against Hippotherses* and *Against Eratosthenes* are more the exception than the rule. More generally, his clients were, for the most part, former members of the Three Thousand who denied their active involvement in the regime of

---

[186] Lysias, *Against Nicomachus* (30), 15–6. The litigant accuses his opponent of using his legal knowledge to have helped have the democrat Cleophon convicted at the very beginning of the oligarchy (§11). The accusation is, however, hardly credible, if only because Lysias' client, who had stayed in the city, had certainly been among those who had rejoiced at the condemnation of this 'bad citizen' (Pseudo-Aristotle, *Athenian Constitution*, 35.3; Lysias, *Against Nicomachus* (30), 13). See *supra*, Chapter 1, p. 57.
[187] Lysias, *On the Scrutiny of Evandros* (26), 17.

the Thirty, while their opponents were most often former resistance fighters from Piraeus or men banished by the Thirty.

This general panorama increases the likelihood that Lysias composed the speech *For Polystratus* (20) insofar as this (chronologically possible) attribution is in line with the same logic: There is nothing to prevent the orator from taking as a client a former member of the Four Hundred who claimed to have acted as best he could under the circumstances.[188] Similarly, it now seems easier to believe that Lysias offered his help to Socrates during his trial in 399: The philosopher was – like many of his clients – a prominent member of the Three Thousand, who claimed to have been in no way involved in the crimes of the Thirty.[189]

We still need to explain these preferential choices, which are far from random. Is it out of simple opportunism that Lysias chose such customers? In fact, 'those of the city' were at the same time those most in need of defense in the (barely) reconciled Athens of 403, and also those who had the economic resources to pay for the orator's services. However, this pragmatic explanation overlooks the personal reasons that might have motivated the speaker's choices. Might not Lysias also have been guided by a certain animosity toward the fighters from Piraeus who, in some cases (the chorus of Archinus), had joined forces to deprive him of his citizenship and, in others (the chorus of Thrasybulus), had not provided him with sufficient support at this time? It is nevertheless necessary to take into account another factor: Lysias mainly took on as customers men to whom he was sociologically close, and he had done so since his youth.

If this observation seems reductive, it is nonetheless crucial: For his entire career, Lysias was at the service of a coherent group, to which he himself belonged – the socioeconomic elite of the city. With the exception of the (self-proclaimed) *adunatos* and, perhaps, Eratosthenes' murderer, Euphiletus,[190] Lysias wrote only for wealthy men, who were usually obliged to pay for liturgies, those costly public services to which only wealthy citizens and metics were subject. In the fourth century, this

---

[188] Lysias, *For Polystratus* (20), 13. In 411, the accused had been one of the hundred commissioners elected, ten per tribe, to draw up the citizen list, and he claims he did everything in his power to integrate as many Athenians as possible into it, raising the limit to 9,000 instead of 5,000.

[189] Scholia to the *Apology of Socrates*, 18b; cf. Diogenes Laertius, 2.40, and, here, *supra*, Chapter 4, pp. 154–9.

[190] Lysias, *On the Refusal of a Pension* (24), even if he had every interest in underestimating his level of wealth. In the speech *On the Murder of Eratosthenes* (1), Euphiletus may not be very rich – if it is true that he has only one or two slaves. Nevertheless, his house has two floors, and his wife is not obliged to work or to go out to the market. Might Lysias have accepted the case because his client had murdered a relative of the 'tyrant' Eratosthenes? As a friend, Lysias perhaps cut him a deal! See Todd 2007, pp. 58–60, recognizing that this is 'wild speculation.'

privileged group numbered barely a thousand individuals out of several tens of thousands of taxpayers.

Many of Lysias' clients thus boasted of their multiple contributions to the common good,[191] and even claimed loud and clear to draw political and legal benefits from this. 'But the reason I spent more than was required by the city was to improve my reputation among you *and to be able to defend myself better if I were to encounter any misfortune*,' assures one[192]; 'the expenditure is the reason I am justly being rescued by yourselves,' claims another.[193] As for Lysias himself, he recalls how generous his family had been to the Athenian people in the past: 'we had sponsored all our choral performances and contributed to many war taxes (*eisphorai*).'[194] This shows the orator as *chorēgos* in the true sense of the term. This is far from surprising: Rich metics had to carry out such tasks as much as Athenians did (although the trierarchy was only for citizens).

It is still necessary to take the stock of what a *chorēgia* implied in terms of prestige and, more broadly, of relations with society. First of all, it was a practice that functioned in part beyond the established distinctions of status: At the Lenaia and the rural Dionysia, metics could not only participate in the procession in honor of the god, but also could act as a *chorēgos* during the drama competitions that took place thereafter.[195] A metic could therefore find himself in an eminent position that involved directing and maintaining a group of *choreutai* that could include full citizens for several months; in the same way, they could gain victory over other *chorēgoi* who were Athenians. Of course, certain differences

---

[191] *Against Simon* (3), 20, 47: The litigant has 'assumed so many liturgies'; *On a Wound by Premeditation* (4), 5; *For Callias* (5), 3: This rich metic had 'rendered many services to the city,' probably in the form of liturgies (see Todd 2007, p. 395); *Defense in the Matter of the Olive Stump* (7), 24, 31; *On the Property of the Brother of Nicias* (18), 21: All three of Eucrates' sons were trierarchs; *On the Property of Aristophanes* (19), 12, 57–9: The client came from a family of trierarchs and *chorēgoi*, and he himself had exercised 'all the *chorēgiai* he should and has been trierarch seven times'; *Defense Against a Charge of Taking Bribes* (21): The litigant had been trierarch in the time of Aigos Potamos (see Kapellos 2014, pp. 14–6); *Defense Against a Charge of Subverting the Democracy* (25), 12: Lysias' client had been a trierarch five times and provided all the other liturgies; *For Eryximachus Who Remained in the City*: The client is one of the trierarchs who escaped death at Aigos Potamos (see Kapellos 2009, p. 270, n. 73).
[192] Lysias, *Defense Against a Charge of Subverting the Democracy* (25), 13 (our emphasis).
[193] Lysias, *Defense Against a Charge of Taking Bribes* (21), 17. Lysias' client obviously came from a family involved in the oligarchy of the Four Hundred. He clearly embarked on a massive spending spree to make amends: see Todd 2000, p. 229.
[194] Lysias, *Against Eratosthenes* (12), 20.
[195] Cohen 2000, pp. 73–5 and Wijma 2014, pp. 66–75 (the metics as *choreutai* in the Lenaia) and pp. 167–8 (list of the known *chorēgoi* in the demes).

remained, since metics could not be *chorēgoi* at the time of the city Dionysia,¹⁹⁶ but their partial integration is no less significant for all that.

Full participation implied the establishment of specific links between groups of liturgists, metics and citizens alike. On the one hand, the *chorēgoi* were in competition with one another, and the contest could sometimes degenerate into a feud, according to a deleterious process revealed by some of the judicial speeches.¹⁹⁷ On the other hand, liturgists were distinguished as a collective in the social space, whatever their status, especially during any procession preceding the contest: They could not fail to recognize themselves as a coherent group – the 'liturgical class'¹⁹⁸ – who shared the same interests and were bound to frequent each other's company, and even join together (e.g. through reciprocal marriages with the women in their families).

In the case of Lysias, the social links between *chorēgoi* appeared after the civil war and not before. Let's go back one last time to *Against Neaira*: According to Apollodorus, Lysias installed his concubine Metaneira, not in his own *oikos*, but 'at the home of Philostratus of the deme Colonos, a friend of his, still a young man.'¹⁹⁹ However, Philostratus was not an average citizen, but in fact came from a very small, fortunate world: A well-known orator, he was a victorious *chorēgos* in the Dionysia and, in 342, a trierarch alongside his father.²⁰⁰ The episode is a good demonstration of the almost carnal proximity between Lysias and a young citizen – who took in his adulterous lover – and is presented as an 'intimate friend (*philon kai epitedeion*).'²⁰¹ *Epitedeios*: It is the same term that qualified Damnippus, the powerful Athenian who chose not to help Lysias when he was arrested by the Thirty.²⁰² Thanks to the civil war, Lysias had perhaps changed some of his friends, but not his social class.

The Civil War or the Great Simplification

At the end of this survey, Lysias stands out as resolutely different in the gallery of characters that we have considered. His trajectory connects

---

¹⁹⁶ Wilson 2000, pp. 29–31, 80; Wijma 2014, pp. 83–5. At the city of Dionysia, metics participated only in the procession, but could nevertheless perform as poets, actors or musicians.
¹⁹⁷ Cf. Demosthenes, *Against Meidias* (21), 147. See *supra*, Introduction, pp. 17–8.
¹⁹⁸ Davies 1971, pp. xvii–xxxi; Davies 1981, pp. 15–37. On this 'liturgical class,' which accumulated not only a social and economic but also a cultural and religious capital, see Degand 2011.
¹⁹⁹ Pseudo-Demosthenes, *Against Neaira* (59), 22.
²⁰⁰ Kapparis 1999, pp. 213–4 and the earlier source Davies 1971, p. 552 n° 14734.
²⁰¹ Pseudo-Demosthenes, *Against Neaira* (59), 23.
²⁰² If Damnippus is otherwise unknown, there is no doubt that he belongs to the Athenian elite. Lysias indeed asks him to use his power (*dunamis*) with the Thirty (*Against Eratosthenes* [12], 14). This confirms that he belonged to the small wealthy milieu that was in contact with both Lysias and the oligarchs. See Hauck 2018, pp. 161–2.

several figures of the choral city that we have tried to bring to light. For better or for worse, Lysias was connected to Thrasybulus, whom he perhaps supported before turning away from him; to Archinus, who was his adversary at the time of the reconciliation; to Nicomachus, whom he pursued with his hatred as a *parvenu* bureaucrat; to Socrates, with whom he maintained strong but dissonant ties; to the 'neutral' citizens who remained in the city and of whom he was an unfailing supporter; to the rich Athenian families, torn apart by the civil war and to whom he often lent his legal assistance; and to Gerys, with whom he shared the status of *isotelēs*, while living in a completely different social world.

Because he benefits from a privileged documentary status – due to the multiple sources produced by him and about him – Lysias also allows us to emerge from of an *aporia* characteristic of writing the history of the civil war. At the beginning of the investigation, we wagered that, through its destructive ability, the *stasis* was the ideal opportunity to appraise how Athenian society functioned and how its various parts hung together. This event, which disturbed the normal order of things, had the capacity to unveil and make visible what would normally remain unseen. It nonetheless tends to obscure as much as illuminate our view, functioning like a 'device,' or '*dispositif*' according to Gilles Deleuze's definition: 'Each device (*dispositif*) has its way of structuring light, the way in which it falls, blurs and disperses, distributing the visible and the invisible, giving birth to objects which are dependent on it for their existence, and causing them to disappear.'[203] In this case, the civil war tends to oversimplify Lysias' life story by reducing him to the role of a democratic metic, forced by circumstances to become a logographer. This distortion is further amplified by the extraordinary prestige of one speech, *Against Eratosthenes*.[204] Canonized by modern tradition – but ignored by Dionysius of Halicarnassus[205] – the speech seems to deliver the definitive truth about Lysias' identity, while it in fact actually hardens and freezes it in time.

It is therefore appropriate to dial down the blinding glare of the civil war and, through a longitudinal approach, restore to Lysias his multifaceted

---

[203] Deleuze 2006, p. 339.
[204] Chiron 2015, p. 55, speaks rightly of the 'most serious' and 'most intense of all the speeches that Lysias left us'; Bizos and Gernet 1924, p. 155, describe the speech as 'the most important of all our collection.'
[205] In his *Life of Lysias*, Dionysius of Halicarnassus cites only four speeches: *On the Statue of Iphicrates* and *On the Defense of Iphicrates* (2.12.2–6), *Olympic Oration* (2. 29.1–2.30.9) and *Against the Subversion of the Ancestral Constitution* (34) (2.32.1–33). The manuscript tradition of *Against Eratosthenes* is, however, rich and old: see Avezzù 1991, p. 54 (especially in Cicero).

nature. Obviously, this perspective also entails danger: to end up with an anachronistic description of Athenian society as overly fluid; in short, an Athens reread through the prism of our time – that of intermittent careers, the decline of political parties and the emancipation from legal constraints. In fact, following Lysias does not lead to the conclusion that legal status or political choices counted for nothing in Athens at the end of the fifth century, but rather to grasp the moments and places where these distinctions played a decisive role or, on the contrary, were neutralized. These variations explain precisely why metics – as a fetishized category – could be considered, in historiography, sometimes as quasi-citizens, sometimes as anti-citizens, depending on whether the emphasis was on their participation in cult, the army, the city's finances or their exclusion from political institutions and land ownership.[206] This is, it seems to us, a false alternative – doubly false, in fact. First of all, it neglects the evidence that individuals with the same status but radically different origins and existential experiences coexisted: A whole world separated the freedmen, still carrying the stigma of slavery, from the foreigners who had come from all over the Greek world to seek wealth in Athens. In addition, it forgets that all metics, even those with privileges, like Lysias, could, according to the time and place, be included or excluded from society.

Likewise, reinstating all the uncertainties about Lysias' life also fails to bring about any underestimation of the strength of class distinctions. His multiple choruses are the proof of this: From the beginning until the end of his life, Lysias was part of the who's who of the Athenian community, in circles where citizens and wealthy metics rubbed shoulders and mostly stayed on good terms.[207] Certainly, the civil war put the coherence of this small world severely to the test: The discords sometimes tore through the social fabric at this moment of truth. However, while Lysias was sometimes betrayed by those close to him, he was never a traitor to his class. His networks of friends, allies and clients were reconfigured on the same distinctive basis after the civil war. As is often the case, everything had to change for everything to remain the same.

---

[206] The former position was defended, as early as the end of the nineteenth century, by Wilamowitz-Moellendorf 1887, pp. 219, 246 (for the expression of 'quasi-bürger'); the latter opinion is eloquently formulated by Whitehead 1977, p. 70 (the metic as 'anti-citizen').

[207] Aristophanes, *Acharnians*, 502–3: 'for I count the resident foreigners as the bran of our populace.' The metics are to the citizens what bran is to flour – that is to say, two inseparable elements, though hierarchically distributed, both necessary to make bread. See earlier reference by Clerc 1893, p. 233.

Conclusion
The City in Chorus

Ha, ha! keep time: how sour sweet music is,
When time is broke and no proportion kept!
So is it in the music of men's lives.
And here have I the daintiness of ear
To cheque time broke in a disorder'd string;
But for the concord of my state and time
Had not an ear to hear my true time broke.
I wasted time, and now doth time waste me;
For now hath time made me his numbering clock

Shakespeare, *Richard II*, Act V, Scene 5

Throughout his intellectual career, Pierre Bourdieu has constantly returned to a text from ancient literature: Plato's *Theaetetus*.[1] One passage in particular attracted the attention of the sociologist. As he looks down upon the Athenian Agora, before an audience made up of his companions, Socrates celebrates the philosophical detachment from the democratic city and comes to distinguish two groups. To the men engaged in the ordinary functioning of democratic life, who act in a hurry because 'running water doesn't wait,' are opposed those who have time to talk things over at leisure. The latter are like strangers in the city, to the point that they are entirely ignorant of its topography: 'To begin with, then, the philosopher grows up without knowing the way to the Agora, or the whereabouts of the law courts or the council chambers or any other place of public assembly.'[2]

Pierre Bourdieu sees this digression as the locus of an original theorization of the 'scholastic disposition' and of the illusion that accompanies it like its shadow. For him, philosophy proceeds from twofold ignorance: 'the (active or passive) ignorance not only of what happens in the world of

---

[1] The reference to the *Theaetetus* appears first in Bourdieu 1972. It is also present in his lectures at the Collège de France (see Bourdieu 2016, 2017) and is particularly well developed in Bourdieu 2000.
[2] Plato, *Theaetetus*, 173c–d.

practice [...] and, more precisely, in the order of the *polis* and politics [...],' but also 'the ignorance, more or less triumphant, of that ignorance and of the economic and social conditions that make it possible.'[3] Bourdieusian sociology, in fact, aims to dissipate this illusion, forcing us to risk the following hypothesis: Presenting the choice of philosophy as a breaking point, the Platonic text offered an inverted mirror through which Bourdieu could appraise his own conversion to sociology.

The Philosophical Fantasy

But let's go back to classical Athens and the passage from *Theaetetus*. Plato presents the community of philosophers and the different groups that walk around the Agora as rival choruses. The choral metaphor is used here to describe philosophical companionship, under the authority of a master who plays the role of coryphaeus. 'Would you like us to have a review of the members of our chorus?' Socrates asks Theodorus.[4] Plato dramatizes the gap that separates this chorus of disinterested intellectuals from political factions, regardless of whether these lean toward democracy or oligarchy. Evolving in a closed circuit and prescribing its own laws, the chorus of philosophers claims to have escaped any form of involvement in the city: 'the scrambling of political cliques for office, meetings, dinners, parties with flute-girls – such doings never enter their head even in a dream.'[5]

Plato's dramaturgy deserves, however, a closer look.[6] For it is not by chance that Socrates' companions were on the outskirts of the Agora that day. Their teacher had just been summoned by the *archon basileus* following the accusation that Meletus had made against him.[7] The reference to the trial of 399 gives Socrates' words a strange resonance. The account he provides of the opposition between the two choruses is filled with the foreboding of their confrontation and of his own death. His conviction also contributed to the withdrawal of the philosophers' chorus

---

[3] Bourdieu 2000, p. 15. For an ancient historian's view of the Bourdieusian reading of the *Theaetetus*, see Pébarthe 2014b.
[4] Plato, *Theaetetus*, 173b. Such a metaphor appears several times in Plato, whether it refers to the chorus of Protagoras' disciples (*Protagoras*, 315b), to the chorus of Dionysodoros' and Euthydemus' admirers (*Euthydemus*, 276b, 279c) or to Heraclitus' followers (*Theaetetus*, 179d). We find this same idea in Plutarch in relation to the rivalry between Zeno and Theophrastus (Plutarch, *On Progress in Virtue*, 78d).
[5] Plato, *Theaetetus*, 173d.
[6] On the importance of digression in the analysis of the Athenian intellectual field in the fourth century, see Azoulay 2007a.
[7] Plato, *Theaetetus*, 142c.

into itself, since it convinced his disciples to stop participating actively in the political life of the city.

This process of secession comes fully to light in Plato's *Letter VII*.[8] In this strange autobiographical text, Socrates' disciple tells the story of his own conversion to philosophical life, concretized by the foundation of the Academy in 387/6. He claims that a double disappointment convinced him to leave the political arena: the violence and the injustice of the Thirty on the one hand and the disorder, impiety and injustice of the restored democracy on the other. This beautiful symmetry, however, is misleading, since it puts the radical oligarchy and the restored democracy on an equal footing. The *Letter* implies it was only natural for Plato to fall in with the oligarchs, because of his family ties: 'Some of these men happened to be familiars (*oikeioi*) and acquaintances of mine, and they invited me to join them at once in what seemed to be a proper undertaking.'[9] It seemed so obvious he must have been close to the Thirty that he had to convince his audience, sixty years after the civil war, that he had dissociated himself from the crimes committed by his relatives.[10] Reading between the lines, however, we can see how extraordinarily attractive Critias and his allies were to the young man, convinced, as he confessed at the time, that when they seized power, it would mark a new golden age for the city.[11]

But Plato does not stop there and, to explain his abandonment of any political ambition, invokes his inability to bring together friends and partisans after democracy was restored. The order of the *hetaireiai* had been overturned, and the relations of *philia*, essential for participating in political life, were corrupted[12]: The city, in short, was *out of tune*. Rife with

---

[8] This letter was obviously intended for public reading in accordance with the epistolary model of which the two texts entitled *Letter to Philip* by Isocrates and Speusippus are the best examples in the fourth century. The existence of *Letter VII* within the corpus of texts attributed to Plato is documented as early as the third century BC, but the question of its authenticity has been widely discussed. Approaches to the question include examination of its historical authenticity (i.e. the relationship between the Platonic account and what has been documented elsewhere), its linguistic authenticity (stylometry indicating, in particular, a lexical similarity with the *Laws*) or its philosophical authenticity (to what extent the philosophical digression of the *Letter*, which begins in 342e, agrees with or contradicts the doctrine of other Platonic dialogues). As Brisson 1987 has shown, following on from many other scholars, there is no reason to consider it apocryphal: *Letter VII* can rightly be considered as an autobiographical text written by Plato himself, probably toward the end of his life.
[9] Plato, *Letter VII*, 324d.
[10] Plato, *Letter VII*, 325a. Describing the episode during which Socrates refused to obey the Thirty and arrest Leon of Salamis, he states that he was 'indignant and dissociated himself from the crimes that were then committed.'
[11] Plato, *Letter VII*, 324d.
[12] Plato, *Letter VII*, 325e: The young man, distraught, even says he is in the grip of vertigo (*iliggia*).

new harmonies, it had become cacophonous, to the extent that Plato decided to travel far from Athens to found another chorus, which would be monophonic and dance in unison. To break with democratic chorality, with its radical plurality, and found a chorus far from the city: Such was the Platonic project.

Democratic Polyphony

Faced with the civil war of 403 and then with the death of their master, not all of Socrates' followers made the same choice as Plato, who took refuge for a few years in Megara before returning to Athens to live, as if in exile, within the walls of the Academy. Far from breaking with the democratic city, on the contrary some continued to walk its main streets and participate in its political life. Tradition has preserved the name of one of them, Simon, who owned a shoemaker's workshop on the outskirts of the Athenian Agora. It even claims that he was the first to have published a Socratic dialogue ...

Let us imagine for a moment the cobbler-philosopher sitting at the threshold of his store, and let us suppose that, over the course of the year 403, he encountered most of the protagonists of our book. From his workshop, he might have observed the procession of the 12th of Boedromion that Lysimache was to welcome at the top of the Acropolis, just as he might have seen Archinus and Thrasybulus battling to convince the people to grant or refuse citizenship to the metics and the slaves who had taken part in the restoration of the democracy. He could have been intrigued by Nicomachus when he examined the documents necessary to reorganize Solon's laws in the archives of Metrōon, a stone's throw away from his store; he might even have had several conversations with Gerys, who came to sell his vegetables in the Agora, not far from the law courts where the speeches of Lysias were delivered and where the inheritance of Hegeso was disputed. Around each of these characters, he could have seen groups being formed, institutionalized and sometimes dissolved. Each one of these choruses greatly varied in terms of composition and the logic driving its acts, whether they were a political gathering, a religious community, a philosophical brotherhood, an extended *oikos* or a group of workers.

We have suggested that the notion of choruses offers a metaphor through which these diverse collectives can be understood. Granted, this metaphor is not a typical concept that historians ordinarily use to describe community life, such as the association or the network, which seem at first sight to offer a more stable descriptive framework. We nevertheless argue that the choral reference makes it possible to obtain fine-grained knowledge of the modulations of the Athenian city in 403, since it is anchored in Greek thought and social practices. Indeed, viewed through the lens of chorality, the Athenian community landscape appears in a new light, defined by plurality and contingency. Legal status is no longer a fixed barrier assigning place to individuals once and for all: Divergent temporalities constantly overlap and weave together the polyrhythmic fabric of the city.

The question that guides the whole of our investigation is ultimately about the choral essence of the city. Is it possible to see the Athenian *polis*, and all the groups of which it is composed, as a choral song? Illustrating the scope of the Athenian social space does not consist only in describing its polyphony, but also in listening to the harmonics, be they consonant or dissonant, which cut across it. The idea that musical harmony can provide the organizing principle of the civic community seems incongruous to us. It was, however, familiar to the Greeks. In the city of Camarina in Sicily, civic subdivisions were represented as the strings of a lyre, the first and the last of them (*hupatē* and *nētē*) giving their name to two phratries. The lyre thus served as a 'geometrical and arithmetic model to appraise the city,' and relations between the various communities were envisaged as musical intervals (*diastēmata*).[13] Elsewhere, as in Tenos, the term *tonos* (the musical tone) could indicate a civic subdivision, with the city then taking the shape of an arpeggio.

In the same way, a whole field of meaning associates music and song with conflict resolution, as if they had the power to put an end to the *stasis* by instilling harmony inside a community torn apart. The *eunomia* that Solon celebrates in his poems is precisely this civic harmony that foreshadows, in the manner of a promise, the beauty of its own song.[14] It is, moreover, striking to observe that the identification of civic discord with musical dissonance reappears on the stage of the Athenian theater at the very end of the fifth century, a few months before the democratic regime was overthrown. In the *Frogs*, performed during the Lenaia of 404, Aristophanes denounced not only the cacophonous harmonies but also the rhythmic complexity that characterized the new dithyramb. With its excessive polyphony, losing its way in overly sophisticated modulations, its

---

[13] See in particular Helly 1997.
[14] On sung laws in the Greek world, see Piccirilli 1981; Ruzé 2001; Ellinger 2005.

choral song was, in the poet's view, no more than an emblem of the chaos (*dusnomia*), toward which the new poets risked leading the city.[15]

If, following on from the ancient authors, we identify the city with a more or less dissonant chorus, it is ultimately the consistency of what we call *Athenian society* that becomes unclear. Because, after all, does Athenian society even exist? Formulated in these somewhat abrupt terms, this question is not so absurd if we bear in mind that the very term 'society' has no equivalent in Greek. The word *koinon* (or *koinōnia*) designates all forms of gathering from the *oikos* to the *polis* without ever encompassing all the inhabitants of a city beyond its citizens. However, the notion of society, since the Middle Ages, has implicitly supposed a unitary approach to community, which is often described in the manner of an organism, within which each individual and group has its place. With the exception of *Laws*, in which Plato envisages the city as a hierarchical organism associating citizens, women, children and slaves, such an organicist conception of the city is absent from ancient Greek thought. The latter only acknowledged the existence of a *polis* once a community of citizens or rights-holders had been strictly delimited, and this never came to include all of its inhabitants.

To undertake a choral reading of the Athenian city, it might be more appropriate to walk in the footsteps of Plato's most famous student, Aristotle, and, more precisely, book III of *Politics*. The move may seem paradoxical, as Aristotle considered the city to be a whole, in which, according to his teleological perspective, each of the different fields of action in human life serves as a function for its end. But this ignores the fact that within it, like an insistent refrain, the choral metaphor eventually sketches out an alternative social ontology.

Aristotle, or the Choral City

When Aristotle sets out to define the *polis*, it is initially described as a composition or mixture of parts.[16] 'Like any other whole that is made up of many parts, the city is to be classed as a composite thing,'[17] and chorality provides exactly the model required to illustrate this principle of composition (*sunthesis*). The identification of the city with a chorus

[15] On the criticism of the new dithyramb in Aristophanes' *Frogs*, see *supra*, Chapter 9, p. 235–8.
[16] On the specific stakes of the 'definition machine' that is book III, see Pellegrin 2017, p. 191.
[17] Aristotle, *Politics*, 3.1.1274b38–40 (transl. Saunders and Sinclair 1992). There is therefore no ideal constitution, but an ideal constitution in each of the given situations that are those of a particular city.

naturally encourages us to consider the permanence of the city beyond its changes of political regime:

> For the city is a kind of association – an association of citizens in a constitution; so when the constitution changes and becomes different in kind, the city also would seem necessarily not to be the same. *We may use the analogy of a chorus, which may at one time perform in a tragedy and at another in a comedy, so that we say it is different – yet often enough it is composed of the same persons. And the same principle is applicable to other associations and combinations, which are different if the combination in question differs in kind. For example, we say the same musical notes are fitted together differently, to produce either the Dorian or the Phrygian mode.* If this is right, it is clear that the main criterion of the continued identity of a state ought to be its constitution. This leaves it quite open either to change or not to change the name of a city, both when the population is the same and when it is different.[18]

The city is here presented as a community of constitution shared between citizens (*koinōnia politōn politeias*): Aristotle establishes the principle of identifying a community with the political regime it has chosen. It is only out of linguistic habit that we persist in using the same name – 'Athens' – for the democratic *polis* of 450 and the oligarchic city of 404–403: The natural substratum of the political community (i.e. its territory and the successive generations of its inhabitants) is not enough in itself to ensure the continuity of a political community. It is its political regime and its customs and not any abstract identity – nor indeed the permanence of its legal identity – that define a city. That is, Aristotle explicitly mobilizes the choral model to appraise the impossible permanence of the city beyond its changes of constitution: The same group of *choreutai* never constitutes an identical chorus, since the tonality and the harmony of its song are different every time.

Under the aegis of the chorus, Aristotle also undertakes to expose the principle of composition that defines the *polis*. Consisting of the same parts, two wholes may differ according to their own *arrangement*, and the choral model illustrates this principle of composition from one community to another. Like a chorus, the city presents itself as a composition (*sunthesis*), and it is the arrangement of its parts alone that gives it its identity. Populated by the same citizens, two cities can differ according to the harmonies generated by the way their members are placed in subgroups.

---

[18] Aristotle, *Politics*, 3.3.1276b1–13 (our emphasis).

A few paragraphs later, Aristotle continues his choral reading about how individual excellence can be disseminated throughout the whole civic body:

> Again, a city is made up of unlike parts [*ex anomoiōn*]. As an animate creature consists of body and soul, and soul consists of reasoning and desiring, and a household consists of husband and wife, and property consists of master and slave, so also a state is made up of these and many other sorts of people besides, all different. *The virtue of all the citizens cannot, therefore, be one, any more than in a troupe of choreutai the goodness of the chorus-leader and that of the followers are one.*[19]

Here, Aristotle contrasts two types of political excellence (*aretē*) according to whether they derive from the reproduction of identical qualities in each of the citizens or whether they are born from the combination of distinct capacities. Because, for the philosopher, since the city is 'made up of dissimilarities (*ex anomoiōn*),' common excellence must be attained through the dissimilarity of the expertise of each of its parts.[20] Dissimilarity is therefore a prerequisite for political excellence, and it is the chorus that offers the best model for this, through the contrasting voices of the coryphaeus and all those who surround him.

Even more surprisingly, Aristotle also uses the choral model to ascertain the benefits of unequal relations in the city for the common good (*to koinē sumpheron*):

> Indeed this whole question concerns all constitutions, not merely the divergent ones, which resort to such methods for their own advantage, but also right forms of constitution, which aim at the common good. This same point may be observed also in the other skills and fields of knowledge. A painter would not allow his representation to have one foot disproportionately large, however magnificent the foot might be. A shipbuilder would not let the stern, or any other part of the ship, be out of proportion. A chorus-master will not allow among the members a performer whose voice is finer and more powerful than the whole chorus. On this showing there is no reason at all why monarchs should not remain on good terms with their states, provided that in taking this action their own rule is beneficial to those cities. Therefore the theory behind ostracism has some measure of political justice, in cases of admitted disproportion.[21]

---

[19] *Politics*, 3.4.1277a5–12 (transl. Saunders and Sinclair 1992, modified; our emphasis). See Romeyer-Dherbey 2005, pp. 192–3.

[20] See in particular Cassin 1995, p. 243: 'the Aristotelian definition of the city and the constitution does not have for model the unicity of an organism but the composition of a mixture.'

[21] Aristotle, *Politics*, 3.13.21.1284b3–17.

The choral metaphor makes it possible to describe (relative, albeit necessary) inequality within the civic community. Aristotle uses it to appraise the common utility of hierarchical relationships as soon as a collective limits the horizon. A chorus could never accommodate a relationship so unequal that it fails give rise to any measure (such as that which links a free man to a slave, or a tyrant to his fellow citizens). Chorality makes inequality proportional and not incommensurable, even when it favors a monarch over a city.

Book III of *Politics* therefore offers an ideal representation of what the *polis* is in the light of the choral model. It could be formulated as follows: A city is a moveable arrangement of heterogeneous elements, and a good city is one that knows how to utilize dissimilarity for the common good, which supposes the recognition of unequal, though proportionate, relationships. It is not such a big step from this to considering that, seen as a chorus, Aristotle's city converges with the 'new ontologies' of the social world defended by contemporary philosophy and social sciences when they invite us to think in terms of coordination rather than subordination, of interlinking relationships rather than substance or of the fractal rather than the unitary.[22] We could then say that the city is an assemblage, in the sense that it always presents itself as the interweaving of multiple choruses. Its

---

[22] See, for example, Tsing 2015, p. 22, who attempts to understand 'how the varied species in a species assemblage influence each other,' and how 'divergent, layered, and conjoined projects [...] make up worlds'; DeLanda 2006, who proposed a definition of the notion of assemblage based on four elements: Every human entity is made up of heterogeneous elements, with each of these elements having its own dynamics. The whole composed by the assemblage of these elements evolves and transforms according to the interactions that take place between its elements. An element can be extracted from one assemblage and introduced into another, where it will enter into new interactions. See also Viveiros de Castro 2014, p. 105, who speaks of a contemporary 'eido-aesthetics' that sets knowledge the task of 'multiplying the agents and agencies populating our world' and no longer unifying 'diversity through representation.' Such a paradigm, which places in its center the notion of agency, is essentially inspired by the work of Gilles Deleuze, who defined the notion in this way: 'What is an assemblage? It is a multiplicity which is made up of many heterogeneous terms and which establishes liaisons, relations between them, across ages, sexes and reigns – different natures. Thus, the assemblage's only unity is that of co-functioning: it is a symbiosis, a "sympathy." It is never filiations which are important, but alliances, alloys; these are not successions, lines of descent, but contagions, epidemics, the wind. Magicians are well aware of this. An animal is defined less by its genus, its species, its organs, and it functions, than by the assemblages into which it enters' (Deleuze and Parnet 1977, p. 69). The Deleuzian agency, reflected in the English language in the term *assemblage*, although sometimes misunderstood, radicalizes in a way what Foucault defined as a '*dispositif*' (device, machinery or apparatus). In its contemporary theoretical use, it intends to describe the social world not as based on structures with fixed and established properties, but as fluid agglomerations of heterogeneous and contingent processes, by acknowledging the importance of nonhuman agentivity. It is also a question of insisting on the autonomy of the compounds in play in the process, by considering that the properties of an assemblage emerge from the interaction between its parts; if these interactions cease, it is the whole that disappears.

unity, far from being presupposed, takes the form of a task or a question constantly brought to the fore as the sum of its gatherings is either cemented or broken down. Seen as a chorus, the city can no longer be considered a community if we persist in using the term to recognize a unitary and organicist conception of the social world.[23]

But are we fully faithful to the Aristotelian perspective when we apprehend the *polis* from the angle of association and plurality? This seems to be confirmed by another passage from book III, in which the philosopher considers, distantly echoing the thoughts of Protagoras, how the necessary political skills in the city are put together from the point of view of a communal potluck:

> For it is possible that the many, no one of whom taken singly is a sound man, may yet, taken all together, be better than the few, not individually but collectively, in the same way that a feast to which all contribute is better than one supplied at one man's expense. For even where there are many people, each has some share of virtue and practical wisdom; and when they are brought together, just as in the mass they become as it were one man with many pairs of feet and hands and many senses, so also do they become one in regard to character and intelligence. *That is why the many are better judges of works of music and poetry: some judge some parts, some others, but their collective pronouncement is a verdict upon all the parts.*[24]

This democratic epistemology is both pluralist and associationist, since a gathering of men 'without political value' is better than the monody of an elite, even a very learned one. Undoubtedly nothing would be possible without each citizen's individual skills, but the alchemy in which politics consists relies on common deliberations that transform the aggregation of individual expertise, always incomplete, into useful knowledge for the community. It is indeed plurality that makes the best judgments possible, and, to present a model for this collective form of intelligence, Aristotle gives the striking example of the common deliberations of the judges during the choral contests of the Dionysia.

But let's not go too far, nor too fast, because Aristotle's choral city is not identical to democratic chorality. In fact, if Aristotle thinks of the city as a chorus, he never conceives of it as a potentially dissonant association of choruses, since his conception of plurality relies on organic unity. While the choral model allows us to appraise the city's internal plurality, Aristotle

---

[23] In other words, the *choros* would highlight the gap between the idea of the *koinon* and the order of the community-*communitas*.
[24] Aristotle, *Politics*, 3.1281a42-b9 (our emphasis). See the thoughts of Ober 2013 and Ismard 2017, pp. 93–5.

does not consider the city to be a combination of heterogeneous choruses. In this, it does not allow us to entirely think through the form of democratic plurality that is initially accomplished through the activities of the citizens.

Let us recall the words that Thucydides gives to Pericles, in his famous funeral oration:

> In summary I declare that our city as a whole is an education to Greece; and in each individual among us I see combined the personal self-sufficiency to enjoy the widest range of experience and *the ability to adapt* (*eutrapelos*) with consummate grace and ease.[25]

The Athenian citizen that Pericles celebrates here is a multifaceted and even versatile (*eutrapelos*) man, able to change identity according to the contexts that require him to show different characteristics. This is, moreover, how he attains autarky: Like a city that ensures every element of production, deliberation and consumption without depending on the outside world, the Athenian citizen can also play any role, whether he speaks at institutions, works in the Agora or takes part in community festivals.

But how can we conceive of *stasis* in a city viewed through the lens of plurality? Does conflict still have a place in a rhizomatic and decentered city? By tearing people apart, doesn't the *stasis* oblige us to put *the* community back center stage, if only because that is where competing conceptions of what the city should be clash with one another? Shouldn't the experience of *stasis* make these different choruses exist as one community, not in spite of division, but because of it? For, as Nicole Loraux has reminded us, civil war creates a powerful bond between opponents and, as if in a chemical reaction, helps melt them into a single whole.

Back to the Event

Let us consider this hypothesis for a moment. In the heat of the moment, it seems that this process of coalescence was expressed in three complementary ways. First, the *stasis* reduced human plurality to a Manichean confrontation between friends and enemies or to the logic of the One and the Two.[26] Secondly, by forcing every man to choose his camp and prohibiting neutrality, the dynamics of the conflict would have introduced

---

[25] Thucydides, 2.41.1 (transl. Hammond and Rhodes 2009; our emphasis).
[26] Loraux 1994, p. 285.

a specific emotional regime. United in fear, hatred or hope, the different choruses of the city harmonized according to a phenomenon we could describe as an 'emotional form of communal relationship (*Vergemeinschaftung*).'[27] Finally, through the common affects that it generated, the civil war ushered all individuals into a unified time – that of the state of exception, where the usual norms were suspended, even subverted, and where words could even change their meaning.

Confrontation between friends and enemies, emotional communalization, a state of exception: Through this triptych an ideal type of *stasis* takes shape, which seems to have been fully realized in the Athenian civil war. Let us briefly recall a certain number of facts, fully developed during the preceding chapters, starting with the state of exception, which has become such a central element in political studies in the Western world.[28]

As we have seen, the Thirty dismantled democratic legality. Appointed to write a new constitution, they postponed its publication to establish a legal void which was favorable to arbitrary decisions. The publication of the nominal list of the three thousand Athenian citizens did not change a thing: 'and even on occasions when they thought fit to publish it they made a practice of erasing some of the names enrolled and writing in others instead from among those outside the roll.'[29] To include one citizen was therefore to mechanically drive out another, which amounted to institutionalizing *anomia*. Once they had returned to the city, the democrats made no mistake in dismissing all the political and legal decisions made during this whole period. They decided to erase from the Athenian archon's list the name of the magistrate designated under the Thirty – who gave his name to the year and appeared at the top of all official documents – and replace it with the term *anarchia* (absence of power).

In this case, the state of exception went hand in hand with the drastic redefinition of friend and enemy. From the point of view of the Thirty, all those who were not registered on the civic list mechanically became enemies, killable at will. It was enough to cross a name off the register to deprive someone of all legal protection.[30] What better way to show that the excluded were no longer subjects of law, but radical enemies who could be slaughtered with impunity? This was certainly done to make summary executions possible, even legitimate, be they individual or collective: The

---

[27] Weber 1978, p. 243.
[28] Significantly, in the last twenty years, with the new reading of Carl Schmitt by Giorgio Agamben (Agamben 2005). For a recent overview of the issue, see Goupy 2016.
[29] Pseudo-Aristotle, *Athenian Constitution*, 36.2.   [30] Xenophon, *Hellenica*, 2.3.51.

metics targeted by the Thirty come to mind, and the three hundred Eleusinians massacred all together after a mock trial.

The civil war also gave rise to intense shared emotions. In the city, it initially generated joy and expectation: The Thirty had a certain number of 'sycophants and bad people (*ponēroi*)' executed and 'the city was delighted at these measures.'[31] But soon, people's joy gave way to anguish and even terror: All the Athenians of the city came to share in the same hopes and the same fears, in accordance with the desires of the Thirty, who wished to make them accomplices of their crimes. Symmetrically, all the outcasts experienced the suffering of being uprooted and henceforth living a precarious existence. At the end of this process of polarization, the entire Athenian population found itself affected. In the manner of a pandemic, the civil war struck each man and woman in the comfort of their own homes, as described in an earlier song by the poet-legislator Solon:

> So the public evil comes into the home of everyone,
> and courtyard-gates no longer wish to keep it out;
> it leaps right over the high wall, and surely finds anyone
> even if he flees and runs to a corner of his room.[32]

This apocalyptic vision deserves, however, to be questioned. The civil war waxed and waned, with moments of intense conflict and more peaceful times. However powerful it may have been, the 'bond of division' never managed to reduce entirely the choral plurality of the Athenian city. To begin this process of theoretical and rhetorical de-escalation, we must take as our base chronological considerations and a very often forgotten fact: The *stasis* cannot be considered as a whole as the French Revolution once was. To put it another way, the civil war cannot be assimilated with the government of the Thirty, which was itself divided into several phases of unequal intensity.

Of Stasis *as Arrythmia*

We chose not to discuss thoroughly the chronological framework in this book. Our choice – for it is one – does not in any way mean that we reject an event-based history that means only to scratch the surface. It is rather

---

[31] Pseudo-Aristotle, *Athenian Constitution*, 35.3. Cf. Lysias, *Defense Against a Charge of Subverting the Democracy* (25), 21: 'Whenever you heard that those in the town were *unanimous*, you had little hope of returning from exile' (our emphasis).

[32] Solon, fr. 3 Gentili-Prato (= 4 West), v. 27–30 (quoted by Demosthenes, *On Embassy* [19], 255). See Loraux 1994, pp. 288–9.

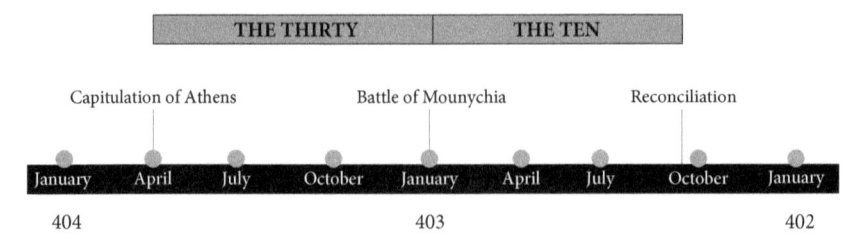

Fig. 11.1 Chronology of the Athenian civil war according to Canfora.

because we do not wish to consider chronology as a definite framework, acting as a backdrop for events, but as a historical and historiographical *problem* in its own right: Establishing how the *stasis* unfolded amounts in itself to proposing an interpretation whether the historian is aware of it or not.

Let us recall in this respect some stubborn facts. Of the Athenian civil war, only the start and end points seem certain. It began with the capitulation of Athens in April 404 and ceased with the reconciliation agreed at the end of September or at the beginning of October 403. However, within this one-and-a-half-year interval, the Thirty's experiment lasted only eight months at most, according to the democrat Cleocritus.[33] Beyond such rare fixed dates, everything is subject to debate, first and foremost the most appropriate timing of those eight bloody months. According to Luciano Canfora, this macabre sequence began as soon as Athens capitulated in the spring of 404 and ended in December 404 or January 403: Following the argument of the Italian scholar, it seems the Thirty were therefore removed from power over nine months before the reconciliation, which amounts to attributing an equivalent or even greater time in power to the Ten (Fig. 11.1).[34]

Providing little evidence to support it, this proposal remains historiographically isolated. This is because most specialists agree that the 'reign' of the Thirty occurred between September 404 and May/June 403 for two reasons. First of all, the *Athenian Constitution* maintains, in a passage written in an official style, that the Thirty were established under the

---

[33] Xenophon, *Hellenica*, 2.4.21: 'do not obey those most accursed Thirty, who for the sake of their private gain have killed *in eight months* more Athenians, almost, than all the Peloponnesians in ten years of war' (our emphasis).

[34] Canfora 1994, pp. 239, 372, 400. The author uses the same framework in his other books, without ever justifying his choices except through short asides in his footnotes. See Canfora 2013, pp. 113–4 n. 184–5, according to whom the eight months mentioned by Cleocritus occur immediately after the surrender (in April).

archonship of Pythodoros (i.e. after June or July 404).[35] Secondly, Xenophon indicates that the Battle of Mounychia did not take place in winter, but at the end of the spring of 403: The Athenian historian specifies that, in the days that followed the confrontation, the democratic resistance fighters were able to collect fruit (*opōra*) fallen on the ground as provisions.[36] Unless the manuscripts are to be corrected, this implies that the episode took place at the end of May or the beginning of June 403.

Taking this as a general framework allows us to roughly situate the various events of the civil war.[37] As the first act of the democratic reconquest, the capture of Phyle could have taken place between December 404 and February 403, because of the abundant snowfalls mentioned by Xenophon on this subject.[38] The following phase – sometimes called the 'Acharnai surprise' – could have taken place in April or May, shortly before the capture of Piraeus by the army of Thrasybulus.[39] Finally, sounding the death knell of the Thirty, the decisive battle in Mounychia must have been fought in May or June 403 for the reasons presented previously (Fig. 11.2).[40]

Whatever the chronological solutions adopted, one thing seems certain, even if it is rarely mentioned. The reign of the Thirty covered only half of the duration of the civil war, whereas the reign of the Ten, often considered a simple epiphenomenon before the reconciliation, lasted at least three to four months. Would it not therefore be an erroneous view to align the Athenian *stasis* only with the duration of the Thirty's reign? Certainly. But we should still note that this one-sided perspective derives largely from the ancient sources. If it is difficult to establish the relative chronology of

---

[35] See Munn 2000, pp. 340–4 (appendix D, 'the capitulation of Athens and the installation of the Thirty'). Canfora 2013, pp. 37–8, does not argue for any particular dates, although he does agree that the eight months mentioned by Cleocritus start in April. See also Stem 2003, according to whom the Thirty did not come to power before September 404: Appointed in April, an initial commission was apparently replaced by the 'true' Thirty when Lysander returned to Athens at the end of the summer.

[36] Xenophon, *Hellenica*, 2.4.25.

[37] See Krentz 1982, pp. 131–52. The foundations for this theory were laid by Hignett 1952, pp. 378–89, and Rhodes 1981, pp. 436–7, 462–3. The reconstruction proposed by Krentz is supported, apart from a few minor details, by Loening 1987, pp. 21–2, and Wolpert 2001, pp. 15–24.

[38] Xenophon, *Hellenica*, 2.4.14. Cf. Pseudo-Aristotle, *Athenian Constitution*, 37.1. On the date Phyle was captured, see Rhodes 1981, pp. 449–50, and Krentz 1982, pp. 70, 126, 151. While the latter places the episode in January 404, Hignett 1952, p. 387, argues that a date in February, or even early March, is just as likely, since the mention of snow is the only clue at our disposal.

[39] Krentz 1982, p. 152.

[40] On the date of this battle, see the early texts Cloché 1915, pp. 27–30, Rhodes 1981, pp. 461–2, and Krentz 1982, pp. 91–2, 151–2. Canfora 2013 is the only scholar who places the battle in December 404 or January 403.

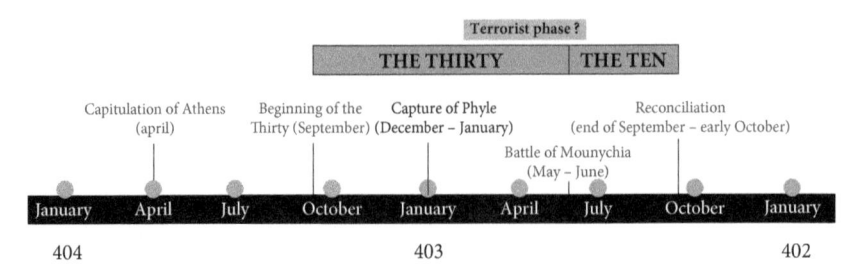

Fig. 11.2 Chronology of the Athenian civil war according to Krentz

the civil war, it is not because of the gaps in our documentation, but because it was in most Athenians' interests to maintain confusion over the matter. While some sought to prolong the period of the *stasis* to better stigmatize their adversaries (such as Nicomachus, accused of oligarchic crimes in anticipation for acts committed before Athens even surrendered),[41] others wished to reduce it in order to minimize their own collaboration with the disgraced regime (such as Mantitheus, who claimed to have come back to Athens 'only five days before the men from Phyle returned from exile to Piraeus').[42] As for the exiles or resistance fighters, most of them had nothing to gain by specifying the exact date they left the city, having sometimes done so extremely late.[43] From this point of view, the amnesty acted like amnesia: A whole part of the civil war was deliberately forgotten by the Athenians and, following in their footsteps, by some parts of historiography.[44]

Far from being anecdotal, these chronological considerations make it impossible to interpret the civil war solely through the lens of its most brutal features, as if, during those eighteen long months, political intensities had not varied at all. But the same criticism deserves to be applied to the paroxysmal phase of the civil war – or, to put it another way, to its core of terror. For the reign of the Thirty itself cannot be considered from beginning to end as a pure moment of *anomia*, marked solely by violence and arbitrariness.

---

[41] Lysias, *Against Nicomachus* (30), 10–1. See here, *infra*, p. 317.
[42] Lysias, *In Defense of Mantitheus* (16), 3–4. See Wolpert 2002, pp. 105–6.
[43] In opposition to 'those of Phyle' engaged from the winter against the oligarchy, 'those of Piraeus' sometimes rallied very late – in April or May – to the army of Thrasybulus: Lysias, *Against Philon* (31), 8–9.
[44] It is striking in this respect that Nicole Loraux 2006 does not give any consideration to chronology in order to be able to put together an ideal type of the *stasis* reduced to its paroxysmal phase.

Again, chronology is crucial. During the eight months that the Thirty spent at the helm of the city, violence was not meted out evenly. In all likelihood, the dynamics of terror were unleashed after the capture of Phyle – that is to say, at the earliest in December 404, or even January or February 403.[45] It was only after the democrats' initial successes that Theramenes was condemned to death and that the Thirty, freed from this internal opponent, multiplied their exactions against the population.[46] The true pivotal moment perhaps came even later. According to Xenophon, it was the surprise of Acharnai (in March or April 403?) that brought about the massacre of 300 Eleusinians – the worst crime of the entire civil war – when, 'deeming their government no longer secure,' the Thirty 'formed a plan to appropriate Eleusis, so as to have a place of refuge if it should prove necessary.'[47] Whatever the case may be, this murderous upsurge certainly came quite late in the day.[48] This periodization is all the more attractive as it chimes with an allusion by Isocrates in *Panegyricus*, composed in 380, and mentioning the Laconizers who 'put to death without trial more men in the space of three months than Athens tried during the whole period of her supremacy.'[49] These three months could indeed correspond to the final phase of the Thirty's government.

To examine this in greater depth, the oligarchic terror must be put into perspective, as Luciano Canfora has clearly shown. Certainly, the Thirty carried out numerous executions without trial; however, it is also true that after the reconciliation the Athenians tended to exaggerate the extent of their crimes in order to establish a true 'black book of the civil war.'[50] A repugnant 'arithmetic of the victims' intended to cause fright and anger was then developed: While the majority of the ancient authors speak about 1,500 deaths,[51] certain orators go so far as to mention 2,500 summary executions.[52]

---

[45] Wolpert 2002, p. 26.
[46] Pseudo-Aristotle, *Athenian Constitution*, 37.1. There is, however, no obligation to believe the author who, in this passage, tries to exonerate Theramenes of any responsibility in the civil war.
[47] Xenophon, *Hellenica*, 2.4.8.
[48] Hignett 1952, pp. 378–89, and, in particular, pp. 384–9 (appendix 14, 'The Order of Events during the Reign of the Thirty').
[49] Isocrates, *Panegyricus* (4), 113.   [50] Canfora 2013, p. 112.
[51] Isocrates, *Against Lochites* (20), 11; *Areopagiticus* (7), 67; Aeschines, *On the Unfaithful Embassy* (2), 77; Pseudo-Aristotle, *Athenian Constitution*, 35.4 (deriving from Androtion's *Atthis*?).
[52] Cf. Lysias, fr. 307 Carey (= scholia to Aeschines, *Against Timarchus*, 39), with the commentary of Canfora 2013, pp. 117–8. On the other hand, the latter is mistaken when he suggests that Lysias, in *Against Eratosthenes*, mentioned a much lower number of victims (which, he believes, better matched reality). In reality, the speaker does not seek, in the passage concerned, to take stock of all the deaths caused by the Thirty, but only of a single massacre. Cf. Lysias, *Against Eratosthenes*

While Canfora's argument aims to feed into a debatable analogy between the regime of the Thirty and Stalin's USSR,[53] it nonetheless highlights the uncertainty surrounding the number of victims of the oligarchy. Rather than trying – in vain – to arrive at an objective total, it is necessary to understand the reasons that explain these strong variations. To this end, we should probably take Cleocritus at his word in the *Hellenica*: The oligarchs had unleashed, not a *stasis*, but a real *polemos* – a term designating war against an external enemy.[54] Far from being innocent, this lexical choice suggests that the democrats tended to merge together the summary executions ordered by the Thirty and the victims who fell during the battles between the oligarchs and the democrats in the same macabre accounts, and even to aggregate to them the losses caused by the sporadic clashes between the Spartans and the army of Thrasybulus.[55] In the same way, it is very probable that, to inflate the number of victims, the Athenians imputed to the Thirty *all* deaths during the civil war, from surrender to reconciliation, without seeking to discriminate between its various phases.

Let us be clear: There is no question here of exonerating the Thirty from their weighty responsibilities, but instead of showing that in 403 it was in the interests of every party to exaggerate their crimes and depict them as bloodthirsty monsters – or, more exactly, cruel 'tyrants' – according to the qualification chosen by the Athenians after the reconciliation.[56] This *damnatio memoriae* helped impose a totalitarian reading of events, whereas the exactions of the Thirty, in reality, far from affected all the inhabitants of Attica to the same degree and according to the same rhythms. In terms of time, first of all, the outburst of terror was brief, as we have seen. Until the capture of Phyle (in December or January 403), many excluded from

---

(12), 52: '[Eratosthenes] marched out with his colleagues to Salamis and Eleusis, dragged off three hundred citizens to prison, and condemned them all to death by a collective vote.'

[53] For the Italian scholar, this comparison was merited due to the two powers' common desire to homogenize the civic body and, also, to the way both resorted to confiscating riches in order to fight against wealth. Canfora 2013, pp. 122–43.

[54] Cf. Xenophon *Hellenica*, 2.4.22: 'And when we might live in peace as fellow citizens, these men bring upon us war with one another, a war (*polemon*) most utterly shameful and intolerable, utterly unholy and hated by both gods and men.'

[55] Canfora 2013, p. 121.

[56] The term 'Thirty Tyrants' was coined just after the reconciliation: Lysias used it as early as in *Against Eratosthenes* (12), 35. It then appeared in Xenophon, in the mouth of Critias (*Hellenica*, 2.3.16): 'But if merely because we are thirty and not one, you imagine that it is any the less necessary for us to keep a close watch over this government, just as one would if it were an absolute monarchy, you are foolish.' Cf. Xenophon, *Hellenica*, 2.4.1; Aristotle, *Rhetoric*, 2.24.1401a34–6; Diodorus of Sicily, 14.2.1, 4. See Mitchell 2006, pp. 178–87.

the list of the Three Thousand remained in the city without being any worse off.[57] In the same way, the Eleusinians lived quietly in their deme, preserving their goods and their freedom, until they were brutally arrested and executed after the 'surprise of Acharnai' (in March or April 403?).[58] In terms of space, then, whole sections of the Athenian population were hardly affected by the conflict, even in its phase of terror. Let us think in this context of all those who remained in the countryside to take care of their fields, going to the city only on rare occasions, like the anonymous litigant of the *Defense in the Matter of the Olive Stump* composed by Lysias.[59] As for the numerous slaves (almost half of the population of Attica), the civil war only marginally disrupted their existence: With the exception of the few who rallied to Thrasybulus' army, most continued to serve their owners, or, if they changed, only switched one slave master for another.

Extension of the Domain of Civil War?

By questioning its central truth – the reign of the Thirty – the very definition of *stasis* is shaken to the core. Should we reduce the civil war to these few weeks of outbursts of terror? Doesn't this simply embrace the version of all those who had an interest in blaming the Thirty in order to make people forget their own turpitude (on the side of 'those of the city') or who were committed to facilitating the reconciliation (on the side of 'those of Piraeus')? For one could also sketch out an alternative history of the *stasis* that, instead of reducing its perimeter, would considerably enlarge it. Couldn't the civil war in fact have begun well before the Thirty took power, in the aftermath of the terrible defeat of Aigos Potamos in 405? Mightn't it have continued long after the reconciliation, until the oligarchic stronghold of Eleusis was taken over, in 401/0, or even until the trial of Socrates in the spring of 399? Can we not discern, upstream as well as downstream, the distinctive symptoms of the *stasis* – the creation of emotional communities, the distinction between friends and enemies, the state of exception?

Let us experiment by going back to a few months before the surrender of Athens. It was in the fall of 405 that the last great battle of the Peloponnesian War took place. Lysander managed to surprise the

---

[57] This is what Diodorus of Sicily, 14.32.4, and Justin, 5.9, suggest. See Cloché 1915, p. 2.
[58] Some Athenians even remained in the city until the final hours of the Thirty without choosing sides, such as Callimachus, who only deserted the city after the Battle of Mounychia: Isocrates, *Against Callimachus* (18), 48.
[59] See *supra*, Chapter 4, pp. 148–9.

Athenian fleet at Aigos Potamos in Thracian Chersonese: It was annihilated, while 3,000 citizens were captured, then summarily executed.[60] Having witnessed this first hand, Xenophon reported on the great fear this stirred up throughout the city. The Athenians were scared that their former 'allies,' so long tyrannized within the Delian League, would decide to take revenge over the exactions they had suffered. Mixing sorrow and guilt, the people's lamentations spread across the whole city like wildfire.[61] The announcement of the disaster gave birth to an emotional community, as explored in the theater over the previous decades. Men executed en masse, women taken captive: Everyone was aware, having seen it many times on stage, of the terrible fate promised to a defeated city.[62]

This regime of high emotional intensity lasted until Athens capitulated, while, in parallel, new definitions of friend and enemy came into force in the city, as did the beginnings of a true state of exception. To understand this, let us return for a moment to Aristophanes' *Frogs*: On the one hand, the poet pleads in the *parabasis* for the rehabilitation of all those who had been compromised during the regime of the Four Hundred (v. 686–705); on the other hand, he vilifies a number of internal enemies, dead or alive.[63] Nothing new under the Athenian sun? Hadn't Aristophanes used personal attacks since the start of his career twenty years earlier just like his comic rivals, who were every bit as vindictive as him? In reality, it's all a matter of context: While comedies usually provided an opportunity for cathartic venting without any political consequence,[64] the situation was very different in early 404. The Athenians were in disarray after the decisive defeat of Aigos Potamos, and comedy was an active part – and not a passive reflection – of the political game in which expeditious condemnations and sudden amnesties were cooked up. At the time of the performance, the trial of Cleophon had been ongoing for a few weeks (since December 405),[65] while Patrokleides was undoubtedly already thinking about the decree – voted in a little later – that was to authorize the exiled oligarchs to return to their fatherland.

This redefinition of friend and foe – through a double game of integration and exclusion – was carried out in part by temporarily suspending the

---

[60] Xenophon, *Hellenica*, 2.2.27–32.
[61] Xenophon, *Hellenica*, 2.2.3. Cf. Olivetti 2011, pp. 74–100, especially p. 86.
[62] Macé 2019, p. 37.
[63] Phrynichus (v. 689); Adeimantos (v. 1513); Nicomachus (v. 1506); Cleophon (v. 684–5). On the suspicions weighing on Adeimantos, cf. Xenophon, *Hellenica*, 2.1.32. See *supra*, Chapter 9, pp. 238–9.
[64] Azoulay 2009, pp. 303–4.
[65] Canfora 2017, pp. 306–13: 'The conspiracy against Cleophon (December 405).'

law. To understand this, we must leave the stage of the theater and enter the courts to meet up one last time with one of our characters, Nicomachus. A few years after the reconciliation, Lysias recalled his deleterious role after Aigos Potamos. He accused him of having contributed to Cleophon's arrest by the Council at the instigation of Satyrus and, consequently, of having been 'blatantly part of the oligarchic plot (*sunestasiasen*).'[66] Occurring even before the surrender of Athens, this episode allowed his accuser to transform Nicomachus into a partisan by recalling the Thirty, of which Satyrus was one of the most virulent members.[67] Above all, it aims to show that the state of exception and the *stasis* were already established in the city. From this point of view, the – extraordinary, even illegal – role of the Council in Cleophon's condemnation can be linked to the regime of the Thirty, during which this institution was the instrument of all arbitrary convictions.

Of course, nothing here obliges us to believe Lysias' client, who is developing an ad hoc argument to blacken the reputation of his opponent knowing that Nicomachus could not be accused of having collaborated directly with the Thirty, who had even forced him into exile. But the testimony of Lysias is not entirely without parallel: Xenophon also tends to place the beginning of the civil war at this precise moment (i.e. before Athens surrendered), mentioning clearly 'the civil war (*staseōs*), in the course of which Cleophon was put to death.'[68]

In the same way that it is possible to trace the beginning of the *stasis* upstream, one could extend its course downstream from the reconciliation. For the official end of the civil war, on the 12th of Boedromion 403, did not make the conflict magically disappear. Certainly, all the Athenians then agreed 'not to hold a grudge,' whatever side they had been on. But it is doubtful that they forgot everything in the blink of an eye. With all due respect to Plato, 'the citizens from the Piraeus and from the city' could not be said to have 'consorted with one another so kindly and so friendly': The large Athenian family does not seem to have instantaneously reunited in concord or, to use a musical term, in harmony.[69]

Political life even continued to function according to the dialectic of friend and foe. For Athens' sacred union was achieved at the expense of a few individuals, in particular of the Thirty, the Ten and the Eleven, who

---

[66] Lysias, *Against Nicomachus* (30), 10–1.   [67] Xenophon, *Hellenica*, 2.3.52–6.
[68] Xenophon, *Hellenica*, 1.7.35.
[69] Plato, *Menexenus*, 243e. Maybe Plato is being ironic here, which would not be surprising in a funeral oration supposedly composed by a foreign woman, Aspasia. See Loraux 1986, pp. 267–70.

were judged to be responsible for the people's shared misfortunes and were nominally excluded from the amnesty: The oath established a clear line of demarcation between citizens who could be rehabilitated and those who could not. Conflict therefore remained on the horizon in a ritual that expressed both the strongest union (that between co-jurors) and the most intense division (through the targeting of unforgivable enemies). Even within the reconciled community, political antagonisms were far from being extinguished. Not only in the years that followed were many citizens who had remained in the city hauled off to trial for having collaborated with the Thirty, but also the former resistance fighters quickly divided into partisans of a relatively open democracy (Thrasybulus and his close relations) and supporters of a more closed community (Archinus and his followers).[70]

Even more disturbingly, reconciliation seems to have been achieved by maintaining a sort of state of exception. Tradition indeed attributes to Archinus several extraordinary measures to prevent any return of the *stasis*. The one that struck people the most was, as we have seen, the summary condemnation of one of the democrats who had returned from Piraeus and dared to 'hold a grudge' (*mnēsikakein*), in contravention of the oath of amnesty.[71] In many ways, this summary execution echoes the expeditious sentences carried out under the oligarchy in agreement with the Council.[72] In addition, there were several decisions that contravened written commitments or reversed the normal course of legal proceedings. As for the oligarchs who took refuge in Eleusis, they were also subjected to violence in 401/0 at the end of a siege and after the assassination of the generals whom they had sent to negotiate with the democrats.[73] Everything points to the fact that the Athenians had maintained certain exceptional practices to better ensure the return to civil peace. Should we see in this the proof of a subterranean continuity between a state of exception and the ordinary legal order?[74] The temptation is all the stronger since certain measures taken in the emergency of 403 (such as the *paragraphē*) were subsequently

---

[70] See *supra*, Chapter 3, pp. 114–27.
[71] Pseudo-Aristotle, *Athenian Constitution*, 40.2. See *supra*, Chapter 3, p. 102, 134–7.
[72] Before the surrender, the trial of Cleophon (Lysias, *Against Agoratus* [30], 10–4); under the Thirty, the conviction of Theramenes (Xenophon, *Hellenica*, 2.3.51) and of the Eleusinians (*Hellenica*, 2.4.8–10); under the Ten, the expeditious trial of Demaratus (Pseudo-Aristotle, *Athenian Constitution*, 38.1–2)
[73] Lysias, *Defense Against a Charge of Subverting the Democracy* (25), 9; Xenophon, *Hellenica*, 2.4.43. See *supra*, Chapter 3, p. 126.
[74] It is possible to recognize in this the thesis of Agamben 2005.

integrated into the ordinary legal practice of the Athenians: The exception eventually became the norm.

From barely three months to more than five years: Depending on the definition one chooses, the chronological depth of the *stasis* therefore varies. Extending the perimeter of the *stasis* in such a way is not without its problems, however. First of all, it sets in motion a revisionist dynamic that is difficult to end. Why see the *stasis* beginning only after the defeat of Aigos Potamos? Why not go back to the trial of Arginusai in 406? Or even to the preceding oligarchic revolution in 411 and to the confrontation between the oligarchs who remained in the city and the fleet of Samos? And why stop there? Hadn't the seeds of what was to come already been sown in 415 at the time of the mutilation of the Herms and the parody of the Mysteries of Eleusis? An endless regression therefore seems to be set in motion, making the Athenian *stasis* truly interminable. Above all, this chronological extension is based on partial analogies, false continuities and problematic equivalences.

For it must be stated loud and clear: Athenian democracy, even in its dysfunctional form before the surrender of the city, even when it was transitional after the reconciliation, never functioned on the same basis as the oligarchic regime of the Thirty or of the Ten, who waged a deliberate war against the majority of the city's former citizens. Certainly, after Aigos Potamos in the fall of 405, the city entered into an emotional maelstrom; certainly, judicial manipulations occurred, leading to the execution of Cleophon and others. However, until the establishment of the Thirty, democratic institutions continued to function, and the citizens did not fear being disenfranchised or losing the protection attached to their status. While fear permeated the community, and there were plenty of low points, there was not yet a campaign of terror orchestrated by a minority against the majority. Between condemnable excesses under democracy and the institutionalization of *anomia* under oligarchy there is an extremely wide gap.

It is equally problematic to extend the civil war downstream. For however violent they may be, confrontations in court cannot be interpreted as maintaining a form of radical hostility. In spite of the similarities noted by Nicole Loraux,[75] the judicial *agōn* is not equivalent to *stasis*, but rather is a means of taming it. As for the oath of amnesty, it would be a

---

[75] Loraux 2006, pp. 229–44 ('Of Justice as Division'). In her view, typical Athenian trials were intimately associated with dissension (*stasis*), to the extent that one could not exist without the other.

mistake to interpret this in terms of a confrontation between friends and enemies. Admittedly, the oath excluded a certain number of oligarchs; however, some additional clauses undid this exception, since even the Thirty, the Ten and the Eleven were able to reintegrate the community after having rendered their accounts, according to a procedure that, moreover, outrageously favored them.[76] In reconciled Athens, radical enemies, who could be killed at will, no longer belonged.

Should we then invoke the way in which the state of exception resurfaced just as the reconciliation was taking place? Again, this is an attractive but misleading parallel. If there were indeed some extraordinary decisions, such as the summary execution of the democrat accused of having broken the oath of amnesty or the violent depletion of the oligarchic stronghold of Eleusis in 401/0, these had an extremely limited field of application in contrast with the practices of the Thirty, who had made suspending laws their mode of government. Then, with the exception of the *paragraphē*, these emergency measures had no institutional posterity in Athens after 403. Much more than a continued state of exception, the Athenian reconciliation can be described as the elaboration of a transitional form of justice seeking to ensure the return to democracy through a skillful mix of targeted convictions, selective forgetting and exceptional measures.[77]

In the end, we must come to terms with complexity and stand firmly in the middle of the fray. On the one hand, we cannot accept without debate the chronological divisions of certain key players in the conflict who tried to reduce the civil war to no more than the period that the Thirty were in power, or even to a few weeks of their reign. On the other hand, it is no more appropriate to make the civil war overflow upstream or downstream, as if the difference between democracy and oligarchy was only a question of degree, and not of nature. Today, like yesterday, determining the extension of the *stasis* is not only a historiographical choice, but an ethical and political one, since when someone proclaims that they are in a state of civil war while they are still living in a democracy, they risk bringing about the exact thing they claim to be fighting ...

Let us then propose a final definition of civil war. It occurs when a bloody fight concerns the definition of the very foundations of the

---

[76] Pseudo-Aristotle, *Athenian Constitution*, 39.6. The oligarchs jumped at this opportunity: Although he had been a member of the Ten, Rhinon emerged from his *euthynai* without being damaged, while Eratosthenes, one of the Thirty, may well have been acquitted by the popular court, despite the fierce attacks of Lysias. See *supra*, Chapter 3, pp. 108–10. On the difficult-to-determine outcome of *Against Eratosthenes*, see Todd 2000, p. 115.

[77] See also Buis 2015, pp. 59–60.

community; in this case, in 404, when a small, determined group wanted to put a brutal end to the plurality of the democratic collective life in favor of a binary distinction between the 'included' and the 'excluded.' Such a traumatic experience delivers in this respect one ultimate lesson: In spite of all their efforts, the Thirty failed in their Manichean enterprise. If some choruses disappeared or merged together, others appeared because of the crisis. To reread the civil war from a choral point of view means, in the end, leaving behind a sterile alternative that imagines no middle ground between perfect union and tragic destruction; it means giving full scope to forms of dissent that do not necessarily oppose enemies (*hostis*), but 'nonfriends' (*inimicus*). For it is one thing to consider politics as inseparable from conflict; it is another to affirm that the essence of politics lies in hostility and radical discord, whether this is assumed or repressed.[78] Neither of the two is accurate: At the end of the civil war, the city was neither cacophonous, nor monophonous, but rife with plural and sometimes dissonant harmonics.

A Change of Pace? Athens after 403

At the end of our investigation, one final danger looms. Does our analysis not risk dissolving the events we have described? To put this differently, might the civil war actually have changed nothing about Athenian political life, which was multifaceted both before and after it happened? This would, of course, be an exaggeration. The city emerged from its trials transfigured, and it falls to us, at the very end of our journey, to identify the exact nature of these changes. In short, it is a question of passing from a conception of the event as a *historical* sequence – of which it is necessary to define, with accuracy, the chronological limits – to the event as a *historical turning point* – that is to say, as 'what comes out of what has come to pass.'[79]

First of all, while the civil war never erased the plural nature of Athenian community life, it did succeed in limiting its expression within an institutional framework accepted by all. For Isocrates is right to affirm that the insane cruelty of the Thirty made the Athenians 'all democrats.'[80] Let us specify our meaning: After 403, the democratic regime did not have any

---

[78] See Loraux 2006, p. 70, who speaks nicely of the 'vertigo of the One.'
[79] Goetschel and Granger 2011.
[80] Isocrates, *On the Peace* (8), 108: 'And have not we, all of us (*hapantes*), because of the madness of the Thirty, become greater enthusiasts for democracy than those who occupied Phyle?'

alternatives that could be admitted to as such, except within the walls of philosophical schools.[81] This political consensus was conveyed by the resurgence of a potent anti-tyranny discourse, which we can see in the extraordinary popularity of the Tyrannicides after 403.[82]

More generally, the civil war brought about a change of pace in Athenian political life. The reconciliation indeed brought to a close a decade of unbridled political experiments, whether these were democratic (like the self-organized fleet of Samos, where Thrasybulus had started to make a name for himself) or oligarchic (like the closed community of the 'best,' dreamed up by Critias). Symptomatically, the *Athenian Constitution*, written in the 330s, ends its review of the different (r)evolutions (*metabolai*) that the city had experienced since its foundation in 403, as if political time had come to a stop in the aftermath of the reconciliation. Institutional upheavals certainly slowed down due to a series of well-known changes. Initiated as early as 410, a procedure for the revision of the Athenian laws led, after many vicissitudes, to the republication of all the laws in 400/399. Laws (*nomoi*) were henceforth clearly distinguished from simple decrees (*psēphismata*): No decree could contradict an existing law, while the introduction of new laws was made more complex and formal, slowing down the rhythm of legislative changes.[83]

This phenomenon of hierarchization also affected the statutory organization of the community and, in particular, served to increase the distance between citizens and noncitizens. In 403, the Athenians put an end to the (relative) fluidity of status created by the disruption of the Peloponnesian War: Having fallen into disuse, Pericles' law on citizenship was reinstated, and, soon, marriages between Athenians and foreigners were prohibited, which had never been the case in the fifth century. Naturalizations were now carried out on an individual basis (and after a formal vote of the Assembly requiring a certain quorum) and not collectively, as in the previous century.

This process of stabilization is particularly perceptible in the intellectual field. In the fifth century, intellectual life functioned in an intermittent

---

[81] Cohen 2001, p. 349: 'Paradoxically, one might well be justified in attributing part of the political stability of 4th-century Athens to the Thirty and their aftermath. Oligarchy in any extreme form was lastingly discredited and the democrats could represent themselves as the restorers of Athenian unity who had brought the divided political community back together through their moderation and respect for their oaths and the laws. One might make the same kind of argument about post-war Germany and France.'

[82] Azoulay 2017, pp. 71–89.

[83] Cf. e.g. Andocides, *On the Mysteries* (1), 87. See Ostwald 1986, pp. 497–524. On the *nomothesia* procedure itself, see Canevaro 2013b.

A Change of Pace? Athens after 403

way; it took place in very diverse spaces – in the Agora, in shops or in private houses – and gathered groups of listeners around wandering 'masters of truth,' who were paid handsomely for their lessons.[84] The sophists or *sophoi* were, as a result, a nebulous group, mixing tragedians, sophists, doctors and even soothsayers, to quote Aristophanes' strange enumeration in the *Clouds*.[85] However, after 403, these temporary groupings gradually gave way to real intellectual schools, located in very specific places (concentrated around the gymnasia)[86] and henceforth operating on a long-term basis, with teaching cycles lasting several years.[87] Isocrates was the first to start a school, barely ten years after the reconciliation, soon followed by Plato in 387/6. This stabilization of the intellectual field was further accentuated by the development of writing, which helped to establish teaching traditions over the long term.

But let's be clear: This change of pace should not be taken as a dulling of democratic life. To put it another way, a slower pace is not necessarily a languid pace! In fact, the apparent consensus around the democratic regime did not prevent very diverse political options – of which some were only democratic in name – from continuing to clash in the city. Within the walls of his school, Isocrates thus became the champion of a 'democracy' so moderate that it resembled a real oligarchy, since the people were only meant to have supervisory powers over rulers who were selected on merit.[88] It was, in name, a democracy, but in fact the 'best' were to hold all real power.

Moreover, the supposed 'moderate democracy' of the fourth century is largely a historiographical fiction.[89] For while the reconciliation was indeed orchestrated by the 'moderates' from each of the two sides, it did not result in the demise of popular hegemony. Let us take the example of the supposed passage from popular sovereignty (in the fifth century) to the 'sovereignty of laws' (after 403). First of all, the distinction between laws and decrees had hardly any concrete influence on Athenian political life: The cumbersome procedure of the *nomothesia* was rarely implemented,[90] whereas, through texts and inscriptions, we know of more than 500 decrees

---

[84] Plato, *Lysis*, 203a ff; *Republic*, 1.327a ff; *Protagoras*, 309a–311a.
[85] Aristophanes, *Clouds*, v. 331–4. See on this subject Loraux 2000, p. 254.
[86] See Lynch 1972, pp. 32–67, Delorme 1960, pp. 52–9, 317–8, and Baslez 1998, pp. 431–2.
[87] Isocrates, *Antidosis* (15), 87: 'In fact, although I have had so many pupils, and they have studied with me in some cases *three, and in some cases four years*, yet not one of them will be found to have uttered a word of complaint about his sojourn with me' (our emphasis).
[88] Cf. Isocrates, *Areopagiticus* (7), 23–7. Azoulay 2010, pp. 29–30.   [89] Millett 2000.
[90] Nine proven occurrences of the procedure have been documented: see Canevaro 2011, p. 57 n.7.

voted by the Assembly in the fourth century. Secondly, there is no evidence that the *nomothetai* were less democratic than the people gathered in the Assembly: Drawn by lot from among the members of the courts, they were a faithful representation of Athenian sociology.[91] The opposition between *nomothetai*, supposedly thoughtful and moderate, and an Assembly, quick to make hasty and radical decisions, is based on debatable prejudices. What ultimately changed was the *pace* at which decisions of a general nature could be taken, not their more or less democratic nature.

In the same way, the rigidification of status barriers does not imply the implementation of a more moderate policy. In the previous century, it was the advocates of a radical democracy, starting with Pericles, who had tightened access to citizenship in order to better regulate the redistribution of wealth and advantages of all kinds linked to the city's growing imperialism.[92] Symmetrically, some Athenians, who were not very democratic, defended a more open approach to citizenship, willingly stigmatizing the city's withdrawal into its autochthonous core.[93]

More generally, one could argue that the city was never as democratic as in the fourth century. The *Constitution of the Athenians* says so explicitly: '[After 403] the people has made itself master of everything, and administers everything by decrees and by jury courts in which the people is the ruling power, for even the cases tried by the Council have come to the people.'[94] The rapid increase in the fees received for participating in the Assembly (*misthos ekklēsiastikos*) between 403 and 392 also testifies to this form of democratization. If the measure was initially symbolic in scope, given how little money it provided, it took on an undoubtedly democratic connotation over time, and Plato is not mistaken in targeting the *misthos* as the very symbol of popular hegemony.[95]

However, the introduction of the *misthos* at the Assembly has left very few written traces: It is only through the passing allusions of Aristophanes that one learns, almost fortuitously, of its existence.[96] And when the ancient sources mention institutional changes after 403, it is in general to relativize their novelty. The distinction between laws and decrees – a radical innovation if ever there was one – was linked to Draco and Solon, the two great legislators of archaic times, as the Athenians boasted that they had left their ancestral laws in force.[97] It was the same a few years later, in

---

[91] See Christ 1998, pp. 20–1.   [92] See Azoulay 2014a, p. 83.   [93] Irwin 2015, p. 77.
[94] Pseudo-Aristotle, *Athenian Constitution*, 41.2.   [95] Plato, *Gorgias*, 515e.
[96] Aristophanes, *Assembly Women*, v. 182–8, 289–93 (392 BC).
[97] Andocides, *On the Mysteries* (1), 81.

394, when the Athenians erected their first statue in honor of the victorious general Conon. While this marked an innovation, introducing a new (and ambiguous) way for the *demos* to control the elites, the Athenians felt the need to connect it to a (false) precedent – the statuary group of the Tyrannicides – to conceal the break with tradition they were in fact accomplishing.[98]

This is the real change brought about by the civil war: The trauma of the *stasis* accentuated the denial by democracy of its own historicity.[99] The real novelty was precisely the denial of all novelty. In other words, reconciliation led to a radical change in the regime of historicity – that is, in the way Athenians articulated past, present and future.[100] In the previous century, Periclean democracy seemed entirely oriented toward the future: In the work of Thucydides, the speech of the Corinthians emphasizes, with a mixture of admiration and fear, the historical temporality characteristic of the Athenians, where 'the action [...] fills constantly the future and obliterates the past and almost the present.'[101] While historians tend to exaggerate the 'innovation' of Periclean democracy,[102] this nevertheless allows us to identify, by contrast, a major turning point: After 411 and, to an even greater extent, after 403, Athenian public discourse tended to valorize the past in an obsessive way, advocating a return to the constitution of the Ancestors (*patrios politeia*).[103]

Thus, the restoration of democracy is the culmination of a slow process begun a decade earlier, during which the civic archives were reorganized, Draco's and Solon's laws (now posted on the Agora for all to see) were collated and revised and the Athenian Archon list was established – a set of

---

[98] Azoulay 2017, pp. 93–4.
[99] *Contra* Loraux 2006, pp. 63–4. The author makes a point of equating three denials that, in reality, do not function in concert: 'democracy's denial of its historicity [...]; the Athenian city's denial of the role women played in the reproduction of Athens [...]; the denial of conflict as a constitutive principle, in order to construct the generality "city".'
[100] Hartog 2015.
[101] Castoriadis 2011, pp. 132, 172–3 (commenting on Thucydides, 1.70). See the earlier text Castoriadis 1998, pp. 208–9. Cf. also Thucydides, 2.41.4: 'We have no need of a Homer to sing our praises, or of any encomiast whose poetic version may have immediate appeal but then fall foul of the actual truth.'
[102] Dunn 2007 shows the clash of different regimes of historicity as early as the fifth century, as represented in Aristophanes' *The Clouds* (v. 1365–76), which depicts the tension between attraction for novelty and respect for one's ancestors. Cf. Euripides, *Suppliant Women*, 195ff, 238ff. See the earlier texts Edelstein 1967 and Meier 1990, pp. 186–221, which show how the assertion of a prodigious form of human agency (*auxēsis*) and, in parallel, very weak expectations of political and social change are combined in fifth-century Athens.
[103] Finley 1975, pp. 34–59 ('The Ancestral Constitution'). Even the sophist Hippias says he gives more credit to the ancients than to his contemporaries, 'for while I take care to avoid the envy of the living, I fear the wrath of the dead' (Plato, *Hippias Major*, 282a).

measures that aimed to streamline the management of official documents and also to reflect the establishment of this new relationship with the past.[104] It was also shortly after the reconciliation that the Athenians began to reenact theatrical works composed in the fifth century. If certain particularly appreciated plays had already been revived before the outbreak of the civil war, such as Aristophanes' *Frogs*, the practice now took root and soon became institutionalized. From this point of view, the performance of *Oedipus at Colonus* was a breakthrough. Written before the death of Sophocles in 406, it was put on stage posthumously in March 401 during the Dionysia thanks to the poet's grandson. Playfully echoing the recent past,[105] it showed the deadly consequences of the *stasis*, or, to borrow the words of Oedipus, of the discord's 'breath':

> Dearest son of Aegeus, it is the gods alone
> who do not have to age and die.
> Everything else is overcome by the power of time.
> The earth decays, the body wastes away,
> trust dies while bad faith flourishes
> and the same breath (*pneuma*) never remains
> between the closest friends and neighboring cities.[106]

Beyond its topical theme, this posthumous performance was the first step in embalming Athenian theater. For as early as 386, it became habit for an ancient tragedy to be reenacted during the Dionysia, probably every year, until the orator Lycurgus set the practice in stone in the 330s, transforming theater into a literary art passed down from one generation to the next.[107]

This impression of stagnation was further accentuated by two factors, one urban, the other historiographic. First of all, the completion of the Erechtheion in 406 marked the end of a sequence of major architectural projects initiated at the time of Cimon and Pericles. During the first half of the fourth century, the Athenians had lived in the intimidating shadow of the monuments built during the previous century, without making their own mark on the city. More profoundly, the citizens remained orphans of their past greatness[108]: In 378, when they founded the second maritime confederation, the Athenians undoubtedly felt they were playing second

---

[104] Pébarthe 2005 proposes the date of 410, but, in fact, the inscription could just as well have been engraved in 403. See *supra*, Chapter 3, p. 106.
[105] Jouanna 2007, pp. 59–60, on the implicit references to the oligarchic revolution of 411.
[106] Sophocles, *Oedipus at Colonus*, v. 607–13 (transl. Loeb modified). See Herrenschmidt 1996, p. 178, and, more generally, Vidal-Naquet 1990.
[107] See Scodel 2007, p. 150.   [108] Badian 1995.

fiddle to their glorious elders. It is necessary to acknowledge the historical disorder in which they found themselves for a good part of the fourth century. While their ancestors' experience had been dictated by the ups and downs of their politico-military hegemony, they themselves had no such coherent narrative thread to hang on to. Be it Sparta, Thebes or Athens, no city was now powerful enough to dominate the Greek world in the long term and, consequently, to organize the succession of events into an intelligible historical sequence. Xenophon testifies to this disarray at the very end of *Hellenica*, when he concludes his account of the Battle of Mantinea in 362 with this disillusioned observation: 'neither was found to be any better off, as regards either additional territory, or city, or sway, than before the battle took place; but there was even *more confusion and disorder* in Greece after the battle than before.'[109]

Disoriented and haunted by their fall from power, the Athenians long took refuge in the unconditional praise of their past, even when this meant masking the political innovations that they had introduced under the uniform varnish of the ancestral constitution. It is precisely this singular regime of historicity that has resulted in the cliché of a languishing, even decadent fourth-century democracy in contemporary historiography. For all that, this perception of historical time did not imply any weakening of democratic vitality, but rather another modulation of the relations between instituting moments and instituted functioning. Far from being diluted, the choral city had a bright future ahead of it.

Aristion's Last Dance

For the history of Athenian chorality does not end in 403, nor even at the end of the classical era. It took several more centuries for democracy to breathe its last – not in 322, with the establishment of a (short-lived) system based on a property qualification, but on the 1st of March, 86 BC, when Roman legions entered the city. Like the Spartans in 404, the soldiers of Sulla destroyed the city's walls, but contrary to the Lacedemonians, they did not stop there. The city was given over to the soldiers, and Plutarch made a chilling account of the acts of violence committed: 'For without mention of those who were killed in the rest of the city, the blood that was shed in the agora covered all the Ceramicus inside the Dipylon gate; nay, many say that it flowed through the gate and

---

[109] Xenophon, *Hellenica*, 7.5.27: *akrisia de kai tarachē* (our emphasis). See Darbo-Peschanski 2000, p. 111.

deluged the suburb.'[110] The most recognizable emblems of the Athenian culture of the classical age – the Academy of Plato, the Lyceum of Aristotle and the sanctuary of Eleusis – were sacked. In the face of such disaster, many Athenians even chose to kill themselves: 'But although those who were thus slain were so many, there were yet more who slew themselves, out of yearning pity for their native city, which they thought was going to be destroyed.'[111] Contrary to the route taken by Thrasybulus when he restored the democratic regime, the Roman general, after having taken the city, moved toward Piraeus to seal the fate of its harbor for good. In the port of Athens, he made sure the warehouses and the arsenal were burnt and had most of the public buildings destroyed.

A few days before, while the besieged city was reduced to starvation, one man had, however, indulged in one final act of provocation against the Romans. He had danced…

> Aristion was himself continually indulging in drinking-bouts and revels by daylight, was dancing in armor and making jokes to deride the enemy.[112]

By dancing the pyrrhic dance, Aristion and his companions made fun of the invader. Similar to the dithyramb but gathering together armed men, this choral dance was far from innocent: Foreshadowing the defeat to come, it mimicked the ultimate confrontation against the Roman legions while also celebrating Athenian choral culture. While Plutarch, as the Greco-Roman dignitary that he was, may have recognized in this the derisory gesticulations of a tyrant, Aristion's dance expressed one of the most singular features of Athenian political identity. In a distant echo of Cleocritus' words on the battlefield of Piraeus, it commemorated by an aesthetic gesture as fleeting as it is brilliant Athenian chorality and the democratic regime in the vain hope of warding off their imminent disappearance.

---

[110] Plutarch, *Life of Sulla*, 14.4.   [111] Plutarch, *Life of Sulla*, 14.7.
[112] Plutarch, *Life of Sulla*, 13.3. Cf. 13.1: Aristion, 'who always danced in mockery as he scoffed,' infuriates Metella. The arrival of Aristion/Athenion, moreover, mirrors Thrasybulus' entry into Athens: On returning from Piraeus, he is welcomed at the gates of Athens by the *Technitai* of Dionysus, who lead him in great pomp into the city; he then makes a sacrifice, like Thrasybulus, although this ritual is held not on the Acropolis but on a plot of land belonging to the *Technitai*; finally, he leaves to address the Assembly, which elects him as a *stratēgos*. Cf. Poseidonios of Apamea, fr. 253 Edelstein-Kidd (= Athenaeus, 5.211d–215b).

Bibliography

Acton, P. 2015. *Poiesis. Manufacturing in Classical Athens*. Oxford University Press.
Agamben, G. 2005. *State of Exception (Homo Sacer II, 1)*. University of Chicago Press.
  2015. *Stasis: Civil War as a Political Paradigm (Homo Sacer II, 2)*. Edinburgh University Press.
Akrigg, B. 2007. 'The Nature and Implications of Athens' Changed Social Structure and Economy', in R. Osborne (ed.), *Debating the Athenian Cultural Revolution. Art, Literature, Philosophy and Politics*. Cambridge University Press, pp. 27–43.
  2015. 'Metics in Athens', in C. Taylor and K. Vlassopoulos (eds.), *Communities and Networks in the Ancient Greek World*. Oxford University Press, pp. 155–76.
Allan, A. 2012. 'Turning Remorse to Good Effect? Arginusae, Theramenes and Aristophanes' Frogs', in C. W. Marshall and G. Kovacs (eds.), *No Laughing Matter. Studies in Athenian Comedy*. Bloomsbury, pp. 101–14.
Ameling, W. 1998. 'Landwirtschaft und *Sklaverei* im klassischen Attika', *HZ* 266: 281–315.
Amouretti, M.-C. 1986. *Le Pain et l'huile dans la Grèce antique. De l'araire au moulin*. Les Belles Lettres.
Andrieu, K. 2012. *La justice transitionnelle. De l'Afrique du Sud au Rwanda*. Gallimard.
Arthur-Katz, M. 1989. 'Sexuality and the Body in Ancient Greece', *Métis* 4: 155–79.
Asheri, D. 1989. 'Formes et procédures de réconciliation dans les cités grecques: le décret de Nakoné', in H. J. Wolff (ed.), *Symposion 1982. Akten der Gesellschaft für griechische und hellenistische Rechtsgeschichte*. Böhlau, pp. 135–45.
Avezzù, G. 1991. *Lisia. Contro i Tiranni (Contro Eratostene)*. Marsilio.
Azoulay, V. 2007a. 'Champ intellectuel athénien et stratégies de distinction dans la première moitié du IVe siècle: de Socrate à Isocrate', in J.-C. Couvenhes and S. Milanezi (eds.), *Individus, groupes et politique à Athènes de Solon à Mithridate*. Presses universitaires François-Rabelais, pp. 171–99.

2007b. 'Panthée, Mania et quelques autres: les jeux du genre dans l'œuvre de Xénophon', in V. Cuchet-Sébillotte (ed.), *Problèmes du genre en Grèce ancienne*. Publications de la Sorbonne, pp. 277–87.

2009. 'Une éloquence de combat: querelles intellectuelles et appel à la violence chez Isocrate', in V. Azoulay and P. Boucheron (eds.), *Le Mot qui tue. Les violences intellectuelles de l'antiquité à nos jours*. Champ Vallon, pp. 303–21.

2010. 'Isocrate et les élites: cultiver la distinction', in L. Capdetrey and Y. Lafond (eds.), *Pratiques et représentations des formes de domination et de contrôle social dans les cités grecques (viiie av.-i^{er} ap. J.-C.)*. Ausonius, pp. 19–48.

2011. 'L'*Espace public* et la cité grecque: d'un malentendu structurel à une clarification conceptuelle', in P. Boucheron and N. Offenstadt (eds.), *L'Espace public au Moyen Âge*. Presses Universitaires de France, pp. 63–76.

2014a. *Pericles of Athens*. Princeton University Press (French original 2010).

2014b. 'Repoliticizing the Ancient Greek City, Thirty Years Later', *Annales HSS* 69(3): 471–501.

2017. *The Tyrant Slayers of Ancient Athens: A Tale of Two Statues*. Oxford University Press (French original 2014).

2018. *Xenophon and the Graces of Power. A Greek Guide to Political Manipulation*. Classical Press of Wales (French original 2004).

Azoulay, V. and P. Ismard 2018. 'The City in Chorus. For a Choral History of Athenian Society', in M. Canevaro, A. Erskine, B. Gray and J. Ober (eds.), *Ancient Greek History and Contemporary Social Science*. Edinburgh University Press, pp. 47–67.

Badian, E. 1995. 'The Ghost of Empire: Reflections on Athenian Foreign Policy in the Fourth Century BC', in W. Eder (ed.), *Die athenische Demokratie im 4. Jh. v. Chr: Vollendung oder Verfall einer Verfassungsform?* F. Steiner, pp. 79–106.

Bailly, J.-C. 2005. *Le Champ mimétique*. Ed. du Seuil.

Bakewell, G. W. 1999. 'Lysias 12 and Lysias 31: Metics and Athenian Citizenship in the Aftermath of the Thirty', *GRBS* 40: 5–22.

2008. 'Trierarch's Records and the Athenian Naval Catalogue (*IG* I^3 1032)', in E. A. Mackay (ed.), *Orality, Literacy, Memory in the Ancient Greek and Roman World*. Brill, pp. 143–62.

Bakola, E. 2010. *Cratinus and the Art of Comedy*. Oxford University Press.

Baslez, M.-F. 1998. 'Les associations dans la cité et l'apprentissage du collectif', *Ktèma* 23: 431–40.

2003. *Les sources littéraires de l'histoire grecque*. Armand Colin.

2008. *L'étranger dans la Grèce antique*. Les Belles Lettres (1st edition 1984).

Bearzot, C. 1979. 'Teramene tra storia e propaganda', *Rendiconti dell'Istituto Lombardo* 113: 195–219.

2007. *Vivere da democratici. Studi su Lisia e la democrazia ateniese*. 'L'Erma' di Bretschneider.

2010. 'Sull'orientamento politico di Androzione', in C. Bearzot and F. Landucci (eds.), *Storie di Atene, storia dei Greci: studi e ricerche di attidografia*. Vita e Pensiero, pp. 113–28.

2014. 'L'image "noire" de Thrasybule dans le *Contre Ergoclès* de Lysias', in A. Queyrel Bottineau (ed.), *La Représentation négative de l'autre dans l'Antiquité. Hostilité, réprobation, dépréciation*. Ed. universitaires de Dijon, pp. 299–312.
Bekker, I. 1814. *Anecdota Graeca*, vol. 1. G. Nauck.
Belis, A. 1991. 'Le chant des Grenouilles, Aristophane, *Grenouilles*, v. 1249–1364: Eschyle et Euripide μελοποιοί', *Revue des Etudes Grecques* 104: 31–51.
Bers, V. 1975. 'Solon's Law Forbidding Neutrality and Lysias 31', *Historia* 25: 493–8.
Bertoli, M. 2003. 'Archino tra oratoria e politica: l'epitafio', *Rendiconti dell'Istituto Lombardo* 137: 339–66.
Bielman, A. 2002. *Femmes en public dans le monde hellénistique, ive–i^{er} s. av. J.-C.* SEDES.
Bizos, M. and L. Gernet 1924. *Lysias. Discours, I–XV*. Les Belles Lettres [CUF].
Blanchot, M. 1988. *The Unavowable Community*. Station Hill Press (French original 1983).
Blanshard, A. 2007. 'The Problems with Honouring Samos: An Athenian Document Relief and Its Interpretation', in Z. Newby and R. Leader-Newby (eds.), *Art and Inscriptions in the Ancient World*. Cambridge University Press, pp. 19–37.
Blok, J. 2009. 'Gentrifying Genealogy: On the Genesis of the Athenian Autochthony Myth', in C. Walde and U. Dill (eds.), *Antike Mythen. Medien, Transformationen, Konstruktionen. Festschrift für Fritz Graf*. De Gruyter, pp. 251–75.
  2014. 'The Priestess of Athena Nike – A New Reading of *IG* I^3 35 and 36', *Kernos* 27: 99–126.
  2015. 'The *diōbelia*: On the Political Economy of an Athenian State Fund', *ZPE* 193: 87–102.
Blok, J. and S. Lambert 2009. 'The Appointment of Priest in Attic *gene*', *ZPE* 169: 95–121.
Blumenberg, H. 2010. *Paradigms for a Metaphorology*. Cornell University Press (German original 1960).
  2022. *The Readability of the World*. Cornell University Press.
Blundell, M. W. 1989. *Helping Friends and Harming Enemies. A Study in Sophocles and Greek Ethics*. Cambridge University Press.
Bodei, R. 2004. '*Navigatio Vitae*. Métaphore et concept dans l'œuvre de Hans Blumenberg', *Archives de Philosophie* 67: 211–25.
Boucheron, P. and C. Robin 2015. *L'Exercice de la peur. Usages politiques d'une émotion*. Presses universitaires de Lyon.
Bourdet, C. 1975. *L'Aventure incertaine. De la Résistance à la Restauration*. Stock.
Bourdieu, P. 1972. 'Les doxosophes', *Minuit* 1: 26–45.
  1982. 'Les rites comme actes d'institution', *Actes de la recherche en sciences sociales* 43: 58–63.
  2000. *Pascalian Meditations*. Stanford University Press (French original 1997).
  2016. *Sociologie générale, vol. 2. Cours au Collège de France (1983–1986)*. Ed. du Seuil.
  2017. *Anthropologie économique. Cours au Collège de France (1992–1993)*. Ed. du Seuil.

Braudel, F. 1980. *On History*. University of Chicago Press (French original 1969).
Breder, J. 2013. *Attische Grabbezirke klassischer Zeit*. Harrassowitz.
Breitenbach, L. 1873. *Xenophons Hellenika*, vol. 1. Weidmann.
Bremmer, J. N. 2006. 'Atheism in Antiquity', in M. Martin (ed.), *The Cambridge Companion to Atheism*. Cambridge University Press, pp. 11–26.
Bresson, A. 2015. *The Making of the Ancient Greek Economy: Institutions, Markets, and Growth in the City-States*. Princeton University Press (French original 2007–2008).
Bretin-Chabrol, M. 2012. *L'Arbre et la lignée. Métaphores végétales de la filiation et de l'alliance en latin classique*. J. Millon.
Brisson, L. 1987. *Platon, Lettres*. Garnier-Flammarion.
　2009. 'Critias d'Athènes', in J.-F. Pradeau (ed.), *Les Sophistes I*. Flammarion, pp. 419–20.
Brown, P. 1990. 'Bodies and Minds: Sexuality and Renunciation in Early Christianity', in D. Halperin (ed.), *Before Sexuality: The Construction of Erotic Experience in the Ancient Greek World*. Princeton University Press, pp. 479–93.
Brown Ferrario, S. 2014. *Historical Agency and the 'Great Man' in Classical Greece*. Cambridge University Press.
Brulé, P. 1987. *La Fille d'Athènes. La religion des filles à Athènes à l'époque classique. Mythes, cultes et société*. Les Belles Lettres.
Brulé, P. and J. Wilgaux 2018. '*Hoi peri Kritian*: solidarités et appartenances dans la vie politique athénienne à la fin du Ve s. a.C.', in J. Yvonneau (ed.), *La Muse au long couteau. Critias, de la création littéraire au terrorisme d'État*. Ausonius, pp. 139–58.
Buck, R. J. 1998. *Thrasybulus and the Athenian Democracy: The Life of an Athenian Statesman*. F. Steiner.
Budelmann, F. 2018. 'Group Minds in Classical Athens? Chorus and *Dēmos* as Case Studies of Collective Cognition', in M. Anderson, D. L. Cairns and M. Sprevak (eds.), *The History of Distributed Cognition*, vol. 1. Edinburgh University Press, pp. 190–208.
Budelmann, F. and T. Power 2015. 'Another Look at Female Choruses in Classical Athens', *Classical Antiquity* 34(2): 252–95.
Buis, E. 2015. 'Between *Isonomia* and *Hegemonia*: Political Complexities of Transitional Justice in Ancient Greece', in M. Bergsmo, W. L. Cheah, T. Song and P. Yi (eds.), *Historical Origins of International Criminal Law*, vol. 3, Torkel Opsahl Academic Publisher, pp. 27–61.
Bultrighini, U. 1999. '*Maledetta democrazia*'. *Studi su Crizia*. Edizioni dell'Orso.
Burford, A. 1993. *Land and Labor in the Greek World*. Johns Hopkins University Press.
Burkert, W. 1985. *Greek Religion: Archaic and Classical*. Wiley-Blackwell.
Caire, E. 1998. *Critias d'Athènes, sophiste et tyran*. Atelier national de reproduction des thèses (Thèse Lettres, Aix-Marseille).
　2002. 'L'homme qui inventa la divinité. Le *Sisyphe* de Critias (fr. D.K. 88 B25)', in G. Dorival and D. Pralon (eds.), *Nier les dieux, nier Dieu*. Publications de l'Université de Provence, pp. 37–49.

2015. 'Jouer de *'aulos* à Athènes était-il politiquement correct?', *Pallas* 98: 57–72.
2016. *Penser l'oligarchie à Athènes aux ve et ive siècles. Aspects d'une idéologie.* Les Belles Lettres.
2018. 'Du superlatif au comparatif: l'excellence selon Critias', in J. Yvonneau (ed.), *Critias, de la création littéraire au terrorisme d'État.* Ausonius, pp. 117–35.
forthcoming. 'Le langage de la terreur: autour de l'affrontement de Critias et de Théramène dans les Helléniques de Xénophon', in M.-P. Noël (ed.), *Le Geste et la Parole.*
Calame, C. 1977. *Les Chœurs de jeunes filles en Grèce archaïque, 1. Morphologie, fonction religieuse et sociale.* Ed. dell'Ateneo & Bizzarri.
2011. 'Sacrifice des filles d'Érechthée et autochtonie. Fondations étiologiques dans l'Athènes classique', *Classics@* 7 [online]: https://classics-at.chs.harvard.edu/classics7-claude-calame-sacrifice-des-filles-derechthee-et-autochtonie/
2013a. 'De la pratique culturelle dominante à la philologie classique: le rôle du chœur dans la tragédie attique', *Lexis* 31: 16–28.
2013b. 'Le chant choral des jeunes filles à Sparte: cadences poétiques, rythmes rituels, arts musicaux et identité sexuée', in S. Bornand and M. Manca (eds.), *D'un rythme à l'autre [Cahiers de Littérature Orale 73–74].* MSH Paris, pp. 19–40.
2015. *Qu'est-ce que la mythologie grecque?* Gallimard.
2017. *La Tragédie chorale. Poésie grecque et rituel musical.* Les Belles Lettres.
Calder III, W. M., B. Huss, M. Mastrangelo, R. S. Smith and S. M. Trzaskoma 2002. *The Unknown Socrates. Translations, with Introductions and Notes, of Four Important Documents in the Late Antique Reception of Socrates the Athenian.* Bolchazy Carducci Publishers.
Calero, L. 2018. 'El coro dramático y la falange de los hoplitas', in *Philos hetaîros. Homenaje al profesor Luis M. Macia.* UAM Ediciones, pp. 37–44.
Calhoun, G. M. 1918. 'Διαμαρτυρία, παραγραφή and the Law of Archinus', *Classical Philology* 13: 169–85.
Campbell, D. A. 1991. *Stesichorus, Ibycus, Simonides and Others. Greek Lyric*, vol. III. Harvard University Press [Loeb].
Canevaro, M. 2010. 'The Decree Awarding Citizenship to the Plataeans ([Dem.] 59.104)', *GRBS* 50: 337–69.
2011. 'The twilight of *nomothesia*: Legislation in Early-Hellenistic Athens (322–301)', *Dike* 14: 55–85.
2013a. *The Documents in the Attic Orators: Laws and Decrees in the Public Speeches of the Demosthenic Corpus.* Oxford University Press.
2013b. '*Nomothesia* in Classical Athens: What Sources Should We Believe?', *The Classical Quarterly* 63: 139–60.
2019. 'La délibération démocratique à l'Assemblée athénienne. Procédures et stratégies de légitimation', *Annales HSS* 74: 339–81.
Canevaro, M. and D. M. Lewis 2014. '*Khoris oikountes* and the obligations of freedmen in late classical and early hellenistic Athens', *Incidenza dell'antico* 12: 91–121.

Canfora, L. 1989. *La Démocratie comme violence*. Desjonquères (Italian original 1982).
  1994. *Histoire de la littérature grecque d'Homère à Aristote*. Desjonquères (Italian original 1986).
  2001. *Une profession dangereuse. Les penseurs grecs dans la cité*. Desjonquères (Italian original 2000).
  2013. *La Guerra civile ateniese*. Rizzoli.
  2017. *Cleofonte deve morire: Teatro e politica in Aristofane*. Laterza.
Carastro, M. 2009. 'Les liens de l'écriture. *Katadesmoi* et instances de l'enchaînement', in M. Cartry, J.-L. Durand and R. K. Piettre (eds.) *Architecturer l'invisible. Autels, ligatures, écritures*. Brepols, pp. 263–91.
Carawan, E. 2002. 'The Athenian Amnesty and the "Scrutiny of the Laws"', *Journal of Hellenic Studies* 122: 1–23.
  2011. '*Paragraphê* and the Merits', *GRBS* 51: 254–95.
  2013. *The Athenian Amnesty and Reconstructing the Law*. Oxford University Press.
Carey, C. 2007. *Lysiae Orationes cum Fragmentis*. Oxford University Press.
Cassin, B. 1995. *L'effet sophistique*. Gallimard.
Castel, R. 2002. *From Manual Workers to Wage Laborers: Transformation of the Social Question*. Transaction Publishers (French original 1995).
Castoriadis, C. 1986. 'L'imaginaire: la création dans le domaine social-historique', in *Domaines de l'homme, Carrefour du Labyrinthe 2*. Ed. du Seuil, pp. 272–95.
  1991. *Philosophy, Politics, Autonomy. Essays in Political Philosophy*. Oxford University Press.
  1998. *The Imaginary Institution of Society*. MIT Press (French original 1975).
  2011. *Ce qui fait la Grèce, 3. Thucydide, La force et le droit*. Ed. du Seuil.
Centanni, M. 1997. *Atene assoluta. Crizia dalla tragedia alla storia*. Esedra.
Chabod, A. forthcoming. *Lois, normes et performance en Grèce ancienne (viiie–ve siècle av. J.-C.)*. Kernos.
Chiron, P. 2015. *Lysias. Discours I, XII, XXIV et XXXII*. Les Belles Lettres.
Christ, M. R. 1998. *The Litigious Athenian*. Johns Hopkins University Press.
Chroust, A. H. 1957. *Socrates, Man and Myth. The Two Socratic apologies of Xenophon*. Routledge and Kegan Paul.
Clairmont, C. W. 1970. *Gravestone and Epigram. Greek Memorials from the archaic and classical period*. P. von Zabern.
  1979. 'The Lekythos of Myrrhine', in G. Köpcke and M. Moore (eds.), *Studies in Classical Art and Archaeology*. Locust Valley, pp. 103–10.
  1993. *Classical Attic Tombstones* (8 vols.), vol. 2. Akanthus.
  2001. 'Bilan historiographique sur les monuments funéraires attiques (1951–1997)', in G. Hoffmann (ed.), *Les Pierres de l'offrande. Autour de l'œuvre de Christoph W. Clairmont*, vol. 1. Akanthus, pp. 15–8.
Clarke, K. 2008. *Making Time for the Past. Local History and the Polis*. Oxford University Press.
Classen, C. J. 1984. 'Xenophons Darstellung der Sophistik und der Sophisten', *Hermes* 112: 154–67.

Clerc, M. 1893. *Les métèques athéniens*. Thorin.
Clinton, K. 2008. *Eleusis. The Inscriptions on Stone*, 2 vols. Archaeological Society at Athens.
Cloché, P. 1915. *La Restauration démocratique à Athènes en 403 av.* J.-C. Leroux.
　1921. 'Le discours de Lysias contre Hippothersès', *Revue des Études Anciennes* 23: 28–36.
Cobetto Ghiggia, P. 1999. *L'adozione ad Atene in epoca classica*. Edizioni dell'Orso.
　2002. *Iseo. Contro Leocare (Sulla Successione di Diceogene). Introduzione, testo critico, traduzione e comment*. ETS.
Cohen, D. 2001. 'The Rhetoric of Justice: Strategies of Reconciliation and Revenge in the Restoration of Athenian Democracy in 403 BC', *European Journal of Sociology/Archives européennes de sociologie* 42: 335–56.
Cohen, E. 2000. *The Athenian Nation*. Princeton University Press.
Collard, C. and M. Cropp 2009. *Euripides. Fragments: Oedipus-Chrysippus. Other Fragments*. Harvard University Press [Loeb].
Collins, R. 1998. *The Sociology of Philosophies. A Global Theory of Intellectual Change*. Harvard University Press.
Connelly, J. B. 2007. *Portrait of a Priestess: Women and Ritual in Ancient Greece*. Princeton University Press.
Cooper, J. M. and D. S. Hutchinson 1997. *Plato. Complete Works*. Hackett Publishing Company.
Corbel-Morana, C. 2012. *Le Bestiaire d'Aristophane*. Les Belles Lettres.
Costabile, F. 2000. 'Defixiones dal Kerameikòs di Atene II', *Minima epigraphica et papyrologica* III: 37–122.
Cousseau, V. 2013. *Prendre nom aux Antilles. Individu et appartenances (xviie–xixe siècles)*. Éd. du CTHS.
Cox, C. A. 1998. *Household Interests. Property, marriage strategies and family dynamics in Ancient Athens*. Princeton University Press.
Cropp, M. J. and G. Fick 1985. *Resolutions and Chronology in Euripides. The Fragmentary Tragedies*. Institute of Classical Studies.
Csapo, E. 2008. 'Star Choruses: Eleusis, Orphism, and New Musical Imagery and Dance', in M. Revermann and P. Wilson (eds.), *Performance, Iconography, Reception: Studies in Honour of Oliver Taplin*. Oxford University Press, pp. 262–90.
D'Angour, A. J. 1999. 'Archinus, Eucleides and the Reform of the Athenian Alphabet', *BICS* 43: 109–30.
　2013. 'Music and movement in the dithyramb', in B. Kowalzig and P. Wilson (eds.), *Dithyramb in Context*. Oxford University Press, pp. 198–209.
Damet, A. 2012. *La septième porte. Les conflits familiaux de l'Athènes classique*. Publications de la Sorbonne.
Damet, A. and P. Moreau 2018. *Famille et société dans le monde grec et en Italie (ve s. av. J.-C.-iie s. av. J.-C.)*. Armand Colin.
Danzig, G. 2014. 'The use and abuse of Critias: Conflicting portraits in Plato and Xenophon', *Classical Quarterly* 64: 507–24.

Darbo-Peschanski, C. 2000. '*Historia* et historiographie grecque: "le temps des hommes"', in C. Darbo-Pechanski (ed.), *Constructions du temps* dans le monde grec ancien. CNRS Éditions, pp. 89–114.

Darmezin, L. 1999. *Les Affranchissements par consécration en Béotie et dans le monde hellénistique*. Association pour la diffusion de la recherche sur l'Antiquité.

David, J.-M. 2019. *Au service de l'honneur. Les appariteurs des magistrats romains*. Les Belles Lettres.

Davidson, J. 1998. *Courtesans and Fishcakes. The Consuming Passions of Classical Athens*. St. Martin's Press.

Davies, J. K. 1971. *Athenian Propertied Families*. Clarendon Press.

  1981. *Wealth and the Power of Wealth in Classical Athens*. Arno Press.

de Baecque, A. 2008. *L'histoire-caméra*. Gallimard.

Degand, M. 2011. 'L'Antiquité à l'épreuve des sciences sociales, Les liturgies athéniennes', *AC* 80: 95–106.

DeLanda, M. 2006. *A New Philosophy of Society: Assemblage Theory and Social Complexity*. Bloomsbury.

Delavaud-Roux, M. H. 1994. *Les danses pacifiques en Grèce antique*, Publications de l'Université de Provence.

Deleuze, G. 2006. 'What Is a *Dispositif*?', in *Two Regimes of Madness: Texts and Interviews 1975-1995*. Semiotext(e), pp. 338–48.

Deleuze, G. and C. Parnet 1977. *Dialogues*. Columbia University Press (French original 1977).

Delorme, J. 1960. *Gymnasion. Étude sur les monuments consacrés à l'éducation en Grèce des origines à l'Empire romain*. De Boccard.

Demont, P. 2009. *La Cité grecque archaïque et classique et l'idéal de tranquillité*. Les Belles Lettres (1st edition 1990).

Denis, P. 2009. Les Services religieux féminins en Grèce de l'époque classique à l'époque impériale. PhD thesis, University Lyon-3.

Derrida, J. 1981. 'Plato's Pharmacy', in *Dissemination*, The Athlone Press (French original 1972), pp. 61–171.

Descat, R. 1987. 'L'économie d'une cité grecque au IVe s. av. J.-C.: l'exemple athénien', *Revue des Études Anciennes* 89: 239–52.

  1995. 'L'économie antique et la cité grecque. Un modèle en question', *Annales HSS* 50: 961–89.

Desrousseaux, A. M. and M. Egger 1890. *Denys d'Halicarnasse. Jugement sur Lysias. Texte et traduction française, avec commentaire*. Hachette.

Dihle, A. 1977. 'Das Satyrspiel "*Sisyphos*"', *Hermes* 105: 28–42.

Dillery, J. 1995. *Xenophon and the History of his Times*. Routledge.

Dilts, M. R. (ed.) 1971. *Heraclides Lembi, Excerpta Politiarum*. Duke University.

Dorandi, T. 2012. 'Phèdre', *Dictionnaire des philosophes antiques*, t. 5a. CNRS Editions, p. 286.

Dorion, L.-A. 2000. *Xénophon. Mémorables*, t. 1. Les Belles Lettres [CUF].

  2013. *L'Autre Socrate. Études sur les écrits socratiques de Xénophon*. Les Belles Lettres.

Dover, K. J. 1968. *Lysias and the 'Corpus Lysiacum'* (Sather Classical Lectures, vol. 39). University of California Press.

1993. *Aristophanes Frogs. Edited with an Introduction and Commentary*. Clarendon Press.
Dow, S. 1960. 'The Athenian Calendar of Sacrifices: The Chronology of Nikomachos' Second Term', *Historia* 9: 270–93.
  1961. 'The Walls Inscribed with Nikomakhos' Law Code', *Hesperia* 30: 58–73.
Dubois, L. 1989. *Inscriptions grecques dialectales de Sicile*, t. I: *Contribution à l'étude du vocabulaire grec colonial*. École Française de Rome.
Duby, G. 1992. 'Foreword to a History of Private Life', in P. Ariès and G. Duby (eds.), *A History of Private Life, Vol. 1: From Pagan Rome to Byzantium*. Belknap Press/Harvard University Press (French original 1985), pp. vii–ix.
Dunn, F. M. 2007. *Present Shock in Late Fifth-Century Greece*. University of Michigan Press.
Dupont, F. 1994. *L'invention de la littérature. De l'ivresse grecque au livre latin*. La Découverte.
  2007. *Aristote ou le vampire du théâtre occidental*. Aubier.
  2015. *Eschyle*. Ides et Calendes.
Eck, B. 2011. 'Le *pharmakos* et le meurtrier', in V. Liard (ed.), *Histoires de crimes et société*. Ed. universitaires de Dijon, pp. 15–29.
Edelstein, L. 1967. *The Idea of Progress in Classical Antiquity*. Johns Hopkins Press.
Edwards, M. 1999. *Lysias. Five Speeches (I, XII, XIX, XXII, XXX)*. Bristol Classical Press.
Edwards, M. and S. Usher 1985. *Antiphon and Lysias*, transl., notes et commentaries. Aris and Phillips.
Eernstman, J. P. A. 1932. *Oikeios, Etairos, Epitedeios, Philos. Bijdrage tot de kennis van de terminologie der vriendschap bij de Grieken*. Wolters.
Eidinow, E. 2007. *Oracles, Curses and Risks among the Ancient Greeks*. Oxford University Press.
Ellinger, P. 2005. 'En marge des lois chantées: la peste et le trouble', in P. Sineux (ed.), *Le législateur et la loi dans l'Antiquité. Hommage à Françoise Ruzé*. Presses Universitaires de Caen, pp. 49–61.
Elsner, J. 2015. 'Visual Culture and Ancient History: Issues of Empiricism and Ideology in the Samos Stele at Athens', *Classical Antiquity* 34: 33–73.
Elster, J. 2004. *Closing the Books: Transitional Justice in Historical Perspective*. Cambridge University Press.
Evans-Pritchard, E. 1928. 'The Dance', *Africa* 1: 446–62.
Faraone, C. A. 1989. 'An Accusation of Magic in Classical Athens (Ar. *Wasps* 946–48)', *TAPhA* 119: 149–60.
  1991. 'Binding and Burying the Forces of Evil: The Defensive Use of "Voodoo Dolls" in Ancient Greece', *CA* 10: 165–220.
Ferckel, F. 1937. *Lysias und Athen*. Triltsch.
Ferrandini Troisi, F. 2003. 'La cosiddetta "riforma euclidea"', *Epigraphica* 65: 19–26.
Ferrari, G. 2008. *Alcman and the Cosmos of Sparta*. University of Chicago Press.
Feyel, C. 2006. *Les artisans dans les sanctuaires grecs aux époques classique et hellénistique à travers la documentation financière en Grèce*. École française d'Athènes.

Finley, M. I. 1971. *The Ancestral Constitution*. Cambridge University Press. Reprinted in Finley 1975.
  1975. *The Use and Abuse of History*. Chatto & Windus.
Fisher, N. 2003. '"Let Envy Be Absent". Envy, Liturgies and Reciprocity in Athens', in D. Konstan and N. K. Rutter (eds.), *Envy, Spite and Jealousy. The Rivalrous Emotions in Ancient Greece*. Edinburgh University Press, pp. 181–215.
Forsdyke, S. 2005. *Exile, Ostracism and Democracy*. Princeton University Press.
Fortenbaugh, W. W. and E. Schütrumpf (eds.) 2000. *Demetrius of Phalerum. Text, Translation and Discussion*. Routledge.
Fowler, H. N. 1969. *Plutarch's Moralia*, t. X, Harvard University Press [Loeb].
Freedman, M. 1975. 'Granet sociologue et sinologue', *Critique* 337: 624–48.
Fröhlich, P. 2004. *Les Cités grecques et le contrôle des magistrats, ive–i^{er} s. av. J.-C.* Droz.
Fuks, A. 1951. '*Kolonos misthios*: Labour Exchange in Classical Athens', *Eranos* 49: 171–3.
Funke, P. 1983. 'Konons Rückkehr nach Athen im Spiegel epigraphischer Zeugnisse', *ZPE* 53: 149–89.
Gagné, R. and M. Govers Hopman (eds.) 2013. *Choral Mediations in Greek Tragedy*. Cambridge University Press.
Gallavotti, M. 1979. 'Appunti di filologia epigrafica', *QUCC*, n.s. 2: 143–54.
Gantz, T. 1993. *Early Greek Myth: A Guide to Literary and Artistic Sources*. Johns Hopkins University Press.
García Quintela, M. V. 2002. 'Protagoras et le panthéon de Thourioi', *Revue de l'histoire des religions* 219: 131–9.
Garlan, Y. 2007. 'Le travail libre en Grèce ancienne' in P. Brulé, J. Oulhen and F. Prost (eds.), *Économie et Société en Grèce antique (478–88 av. J.-C.)*. Presses universitaires de Rennes, pp. 245–58 (1st edition 1980).
Gauthier, P. 1972. *Symbola. Les étrangers et la justice dans les cités grecques*. Annales de l'Est publiées par l'Université de Nancy II.
  1976a. *Un commentaire historique des Poroi de Xénophon*. Droz.
  1976b. 'À propos des clérouquies athéniennes du ve siècle', in M. I. Finley (ed.), *Problèmes de la terre en Grèce ancienne*. Mouton, pp. 163–78.
  1986. 'L'octroi du droit de cité à Athènes', *Revue des Etudes Grecques* 99: 119–33.
  1990. 'Quorum et participation civique dans les démocraties grecques', in C. Nicolet (ed.), *Cahiers du centre Glotz, 1. Du pouvoir dans l'Antiquité: mots et réalités*. Droz, pp. 73–99.
  1993. 'Sur l'institution du *misthos* de l'assemblée à Athènes (*Ath. Pol.* 41, 3)', in M. Piérart (ed.), *Aristote et Athènes*. De Boccard, pp. 231–50.
Gallavotti, M. 1979. 'Appunti di filologia epigrafica', *QUCC*, n.s. 2: 143–54.
Georgoudi, S. 1993. 'Lysimachè la prêtresse', in N. Loraux (ed.), *La Grèce au féminin*. Les Belles Lettres, pp. 167–214.
Gernet, L. 1920. 'La création du testament', *Revue des Etudes Grecques* 33: 123–68.
  1926. *Lysias. Discours (XVI–XXXV)*, t. II. Les Belles Lettres [CUF].
  1981. *The Anthropology of the Ancient Greece*. Johns Hopkins University Press.

Gherchanoc, F. 2012. *L'oikos en fête. Célébrations familiales et sociabilité en Grèce ancienne*. Publications de la Sorbonne.

Ginzburg, C. 2003. '"L'historien et l'avocat du diable." Entretien avec Charles Illouz et Laurent Vidal. Première partie', *Genèses* 53: 1113–38.

Goetschel, P. and C. Granger 2011. '"L'événement, c'est ce qui advient à ce qui est advenu...". Entretien avec Pierre Laborie', *Sociétés & Représentations* 32: 167–81.

González González, M. 2019. *Funerary Epigrams of Ancient Greece. Reflections on Literature, Society and Religion*. Bloomsbury.

Gotteland, S. 2018. 'Critias dans la Seconde Sophistique et les traités des rhéteurs', in J. Yvonneau (ed.), *La Muse au long couteau. Critias, de la création littéraire au terrorisme d'État*. Ausonius, pp. 179–96.

Goukowsky, P. and C. Feyel 2019. *Le Profil d'une ombre. Études sur les Helléniques d'Oxyrhynchos*. Association pour la diffusion de la recherche sur l'Antiquité.

Goulet, R. 2012. 'Polémarque', in R. Goulet (ed.), *Dictionnaire des philosophes antiques*, t. 5b. CNRS Éditions, pp. 1186–8.

Goulet-Cazé, M.-O. 1989. 'Aischinès de Sphettos', in R. Goulet (ed.), *Dictionnaire des philosophes antiques*, t. 1. CNRS Éditions, pp. 89–94.

Goupy, M. 2016. *L'État d'exception ou l'impuissance autoritaire de l'État à l'époque du libéralisme*. CNRS Éditions.

Graf, F. 1996. '*Pompai* in Greece', in R. Hägg (ed.), *The Role of Religion in the Early Greek Polis*. Aström, pp. 55–65.

Graham, A. J. 1992. 'Thucydides 7.13.2 and the crews of Athenian triremes', *TAPhA* 122: 257–70.

Granet, M. 1959. *Danses et légendes de la Chine ancienne*. Presses Universitaires de France (1st edition 1926).

1982. *Fêtes et chansons anciennes de la Chine*. Albin Michel (1st edition 1919)

Grangé, N. 2015. *Oublier la guerre civile? Stasis, chronique d'une disparition*, Vrin/ Éd. de l'EHESS,

Gray, B. 2015. *Stasis and Stability. Exile, the Polis, and Political Thought, c. 404–146 BC*. Oxford University Press.

Gray, V. 1989. *The Character of Xenophon's Hellenica*. Duckworth.

2004. 'Le Socrate de Xénophon et la démocratie', *Études philosophiques* 69: 141–76.

Green, P. 2010. *Diodorus Siculus. The Persian Wars to the Fall of Athens. Books 11–14.34 (480–401 BC)*. University of Texas Press.

Grendi, E. 1977. 'Microanalisi e storia sociale', *Quaderni di Storia* 35: 506–20.

Grenfell, B. P. and A. S. Hunt (eds.) 1919. *The Oxyrhynchus Papyri, Part XIII*. Oxford University Press.

Griffin, M. 2016. *Olympiodorus. On Plato. First Alcibiades 10–28*. Bloomsbury.

Griffith, M. 2013. *Aristophanes' Frogs [Oxford Approaches to Classical Literature]*. Oxford University Press.

Guerreau, A. 2001. 'Avant le marché, les marchés: en Europe, XIIIe–XVIIIe siècle (note critique)', *Annales HSS* 56: 1129–75.

Guicharrousse, R. 2023. *Athènes en partage. Les étrangers au sein de la cité (v^e–iiie siècles avant notre ère)*. Ed. de la Sorbonne.

Habermas, J. 1989. *The Structural Transformation of the Public Sphere. An Inquiry into a Category of Bourgeois Society*. MIT Press (German original 1962).

Hall, E. 2006. 'Lawcourts Dramas: Acting and Performance in Legal Oratory', in E. Hall (ed.), *The Theatrical Cast of Athens*. Oxford University Press, pp. 353–92.

Hamel, D. 2003. *Trying Neaira. The True Story of a Courtesan's Life in Ancient Greece*. Yale University Press.

Hammond, M. and P. J. Rhodes 2009. *Thucydides. The Peloponnesian War*. Oxford University Press.

Hansen, M. H. 1975. *Eisangelia: The Sovereignty of the People's Court in Athens in the Fourth Century B.C. and the Impeachment of Generals and Politicians*. Odense University Press.

   1983. *The Athenian Ecclesia: A Collection of Articles 1976–83*. Museum Tusculanum Press.

   1988. 'Athenian Population Losses 431–403 BC and the Number of Athenian Citizens in 431 BC', in *Three Studies in Athenian Demography*. Munksgaard, pp. 14–28.

   1991. *The Athenian Democracy in the Age of Demosthenes: Structure, Principles and Ideology*. Blackwell.

   2019. 'A Note on Paulin Ismard's *Democracy's Slaves: A Political History of Ancient Greece*', *Polis* 36: 337–45.

Hansen, P. A. 1989. *Carmina Epigraphica Graeca, seculi IV a.chr.n*, t. 2. W. de Gruyter.

Harding, P. 1994. 'Comedy and Rhetoric', in I. Worthington (ed.), *Persuasion. Greek Rhetoric in Action*. Routledge, pp. 196–221.

Harris, E. M. 2016. 'From Democracy to the Rule of Law? Constitutional Change in Athens during the Fifth and Fourth Centuries BCE', in C. Tiersch (ed.), *Die Athenische Demokratie im 4. Jahrhundert. Zwischen Modernisierung und Tradition*. F. Steiner, pp. 71–84.

Hartog, F. 2015. *Regimes of Historicity: Presentism and Experiences of Time*. Columbia University Press (French original 2003).

Hatzfeld, J. 1940. 'Socrate au procès des Arginuses', *REA* 42: 165–71.

Hauck, M. 2018. *Dynamis eis soterian. Eine Untersuchung zum semantischen Hintergrund eines neutestamentlichen Syntagmas*. Vandenhoeck & Ruprecht.

Hébrard, J. 2003. 'Esclavage et dénomination: imposition et appropriation d'un nom chez les esclaves de la Bahia au XIXe siècle', *Cahiers du Brésil contemporain* 53-4: 31–92.

Heinrichs, A. 2003. 'Writing Religion: Inscribed Texts, Ritual Authority, and the Religious Discourse of the Polis', in H. Yunis (ed.), *Written Texts and the Rise of Literate Culture in Ancient Greece*. Cambridge University Press, pp. 38–58.

Helly, B. 1997. 'Arithmétique et Histoire (II): sur les *fratrai* de Camarina', *Parola del Passato*. 52: 365–406.

Herington, J. 1985. *Poetry into Drama: Early Tragedy and the Greek Poetic Tradition*. University of California Press.

Herrenschmidt, C. 1996. 'L'écriture et quelques questions juives et grecques', in J. Bottéro, C. Herrenschmidt and J.-P. Vernant (eds.), *L'Orient ancien et nous. L'écriture, la raison, les dieux*. Albin Michel, pp. 93–188.

Herrmann, F.-G. 2017. 'Hat Kritias nach Spartas Pfeife getanzt?', in V. Pothou and A. Powell (eds.), *Das antike Sparta*. F. Steiner, pp. 133–56.

Hignett, C. 1952. *A History of the Athenian Constitution to the End of the Fifth Century B.C.* Clarendon Press.

Hildebrandt, F. 2006. *Die attischen Namenstelen. Untersuchungen zu Stelen des 5. Und 4. Jahrhunderts v. Chr.* Frank & Timme.

Hirsch, T. 2011. 'Historiographie et histoire disciplinaire. Marcel Granet et les sciences sociales', *L'Atelier du Centre de recherches historiques* 7 [online]: http://acrh.revues.org/3579.

Hoffmann, G. 1993. 'Le portrait de groupe avec Dame: étude sociologique des monuments', in C. W. Clairmont (ed.), *Classical Attic Tombstones*, Introductory volume. Akanthus, pp. 160–79.

Holtzmann, B. 2003. *L'Acropole d'Athènes, Monuments, cultes et histoire du sanctuaire d'Athéna Polias*. Picard.

Hornblower, S. 2011. *The Greek World 479–323 B.C.* Routledge.

Hubert, H. and M. Mauss 1903. 'Esquisses d'une théorie générale de la magie', *L'Année sociologique* 7: 1–146.

Humbert, J. 1930. *Polycratès. L'Accusation de Socrate et le Gorgias*. Klincksieck.

Humphreys, S. C. 1971. 'The Work of Louis Gernet', *History and Theory* 10: 172–96.

2004. *The Strangeness of Gods. Historical Perspectives on the Interpretation of Athenian Religion*. Oxford University Press.

2018. *Kinship in Ancient Athens. An Anthropological Analysis*. Oxford University Press.

Hunt, P. 1998. *Slaves, Warfare and Ideologies in the Greek Historians*, Cambridge University Press.

Hurni, F. 2010. *Théramène ne plaidera pas coupable. Un homme politique engagé dans les révolutions athéniennes de la fin du ve siècle av. J.-C.* Schwabe.

Iannucci, A. 2002. *La parola e l'azione. I frammenti simposiali di Crizia*. Nautilus.

Ingold, T. 2011. *Being Alive: Essays on Movement, Knowledge and Description*. Routledge.

Iogna-Prat, D. 1998. *Ordonner et exclure. Cluny et la société chrétienne face à l'hérésie, au judaïsme et à l'islam*. Flammarion.

Irwin, E. 2015. 'The *nothoi* Come of Age? Illegitimate Sons and Political Unrest in Late Fifth-Century Athens', in P. Sänger (ed.), *Minderheiten und Migration in der griechisch-römischen Welt: Politische, rechtliche, religiöse und kulturelle Aspekte*. Ferdinand Schöningh, pp. 75–122.

Isaac, J. 1946. *Les Oligarques. Essai d'histoire partiale*. Ed. de Minuit.

Ismard, P. 2010. *La Cité des réseaux. Athènes et ses associations (vi^e–i^{er} siècle av. J.-C.)*. Publications de la Sorbonne.

2012. 'Le public et le civique dans la cité grecque: hypothèses à partir d'une hypothèse', in V. Azoulay, F. Gherchanoc and S. Lalanne (eds.), *Le banquet* de Pauline Schmitt Pantel. *Genre, mœurs et politique dans l'Antiquité grecque et romaine*. Publications de la Sorbonne, pp. 317–29.

2013. *L'Evénement Socrate*. Flammarion.

2017. *Democracy's Slaves: A Political History of Ancient Greece*. Harvard University Press (French original 2015).

2018. "Phormion l'Athénien", *Dike*, 21 : 183–200.

2019. *La Cité et ses esclaves. Institution, fictions, expériences*. Ed. du Seuil.

Jameson, M. H. 1977–1978. 'Agriculture and Slavery in Classical Athens', *Classical Journal* 73: 122–45.

Jordan, D. R. 2000. 'New Greek Curse Tablets (1985–2000)', *GRBS* 41: 5–46.

Jouan, F. and H. Van Looy (eds.) 2000. *Euripide. Fragments, tome VIII. Bellérophon-Protésilas*. Les Belles Lettres [CUF].

Jouanna, J. 2007. *Sophocle*. Fayard.

Joyce, C. 2008. 'The Athenian Amnesty and Scrutiny of 403', *Classical Quarterly* 58: 507–18.

2014. 'μή μνησικακεῖν and "All the Laws" (*On the Mysteries* 81–2): A Reply to E. Carawan', *Antichthon* 48: 37–54.

2015. 'Oaths (ὅρκοι), Covenants (συνθῆκαι) and Laws (νόμοι) in the Athenian Reconciliation Agreement of 403 BC', *Antichthon* 49: 24–49.

Judet de La Combe, P. 2012. *Aristophane. Les Grenouilles. Introduction, commentaires et notes*. Les Belles Lettres.

Kamen, D. 2020. *Insults in Classical Athens*. University of Wisconsin Press.

Kapellos, A. 2009. 'Adeimantus at Aegospotami: Innocent or Guilty?', *Historia* 58: 257–75.

2014. *Lysias 21: A Commentary*. De Gruyter.

Kapparis, K. A. 1999. *Apollodoros' Against Neaira*. W. de Gruyter.

Karabélias, E. 2005. 'La fabrique d'armement dans l'Athènes classique', *Études d'histoire juridique et sociale de la Grèce ancienne: recueil d'études*. Académie d'Athènes, pp. 333–43.

Karamoutsou-Teza, S. 1988. *Ο Θρασύβουλος και ο Πελοποννησιακός Πόλεμος*. PhD thesis. University of Ioannina.

Karila-Cohen, K. 2018. 'Le graphe, la trace et les fragments. L'apport des méthodes quantitatives et des outils numériques à l'étude des élites civiques athéniennes', *Annales HSS* 73: 785–815.

Kasimis, D. 2018. *The Perpetual Immigrant and the Limits of Athenian Democracy*. Cambridge University Press.

Kavoulaki, A. 1999. 'Processional Performance and the Democratic *Polis*', in S. Goldhill and R. Osborne (eds.), *Performance Culture and Athenian Democracy*. Cambridge University Press, pp. 293–320.

Keesling, C. 2012. 'Syeris, Diakonos of the Priestess Lysimache on the Athenian Acropolis', *Hesperia* 81: 467–505.

Kennedy, G. A. 1959. 'The Earliest Rhetorical Handbooks', *AJPh* 80: 169–78.

1963. *The Art of Persuasion in Greece*. Princeton University Press.

Kirchner, J. 1901. *Prosopographia Attica*, vol. 1. Reimer.

Klapisch-Zuber, C. 2000. *L'Ombre des ancêtres. Essai sur l'imaginaire médiéval de la parenté*. Fayard.

Kowalzig, B. 2007. *Singing for the Gods. Performance of Myth and Ritual in Archaic and Classical Greece*. Oxford University Press.
   2013a. 'Broken Rhythms in Plato's *Laws*: Materialising Social Time in the *Khoros*', in A.-E. Peponi (ed.), *Performance and Culture in Plato's Laws*. Cambridge University Press, pp. 171–211.
   2013b. 'Dancing Dolphins on the Wine-Dark Sea: Dithyramb and Social Change in the Archaic Mediterranean', in B. Kowalzig and P. Wilson (eds.), *Dithyramb in Context*. Oxford University Press, pp. 31–58.
Kowerski, L. M. 2005. *Simonides on the Persian Ward. A Study of the Elegiac Verses of the 'New Simonides'*. Routledge.
Krentz, P. 1980. 'Foreigners against the Thirties. *IG* II² 10 Again', *Phoenix* 34: 298–306.
   1982. *The Thirty at Athens*. Cornell University Press.
   1986. 'The rewards for Thrasyboulos' Supporters', *ZPE* 62: 201–4.
   (ed.) 1989. *Xenophon: Hellenika I–II.3.10*. Aris & Phillips.
Kurke, L. 2007. 'Visualizing the Choral: Epichoric Poetry, Ritual, and Elite Negotiation in Fifth Century Thebes', in C. Kraus, S. Goldhill, H. P. Foley and J. Elsner (eds.), *Visualizing the Tragic. Drama, Myth, and Ritual in Greek Art and Literature*. Oxford University Press, pp. 63–101.
   2013. 'Imagining Chorality: Wonder, Plato's Puppets, and Moving Statues', in A.-E. Peponi (ed.), *Performance and Culture in Plato's Laws*. Cambridge University Press, pp. 123–70.
Lafargue, P. 2013. *Cléon, le guerrier d'Athéna*. Ausonius Éditions.
Lahire, B. 2005. *L'esprit sociologique*. La Découverte.
Lambert, S. D. 1993. *The Phratries of Attica*. University of Michigan Press.
   2000. 'The Greek Inscriptions on Stone in the Collection of the British School at Athens', *Annual of the British School at Athens* 95: 485–516.
   2002. 'The Sacrificial Calendar of Athens', *ABSA* 97: 353–99.
   2010. 'A Polis and Its Priests: Athenian Priesthoods before and after Pericles' Citizenship Law', *Historia* 59: 143–75.
Lanni, A. 2010. 'Transitional Justice in Ancient Athens: A Case Study', *University of Pennsylvania Journal of International Law* 32: 551–94.
Lateiner, D. 1971. *Lysias and Athenian Politics*. PhD thesis. Stanford University.
   1981a. 'An Analysis of Lysias' Political Defense Speeches', *RSA* 11: 147–60.
   1981b. 'Lysias 25 and the Intractable Democratic Abuses', *AJPh* 113: 543–58.
Latour, B. 1999. 'On recalling ANT', in J. Law and J. Hassard (eds.), *Actor Network Theory and After*. Blackwell, pp. 15–25.
   2005. *Reassembling the Social: An Introduction to Actor-Network-Theory*. Oxford University Press.
Lauffer, S. 1979. *Die Bergwerkssklaven von Laureion*. F. Steiner (1st edition 1955–1956).
Leader, R. E. 1997. 'In Death Not Divided: Gender, Family, and State on Classical Athenian Grave Stelae', *AJA* 101: 683–99.
Leduc, C. 2011. 'L'adoption dans la cité des Athéniens, vi^e–ive siècle av. J.-C.', *Pallas* 85: 175–201.

Lenfant, D. 2016. 'Anytos et la corruption massive de juges dans l'Athènes démocratique', *Historia* 65: 258–74.
Lévi-Strauss, C. 1963. *Structural Anthropology I*. Basic Books (French original 1958).
Lévy, E. 2001. 'Critias ou l'intellectuel au pouvoir', in P.-M. Morel and J.-F. Pradeau (eds.), *Les anciens savants: études sur les philosophes préplatoniciennes [Les Cahiers Philosophiques de Strasbourg, t. 12]*. Presses Universitaires de Strasbourg, pp. 231–51.
Lewis, D. M. 1955. 'Who Was Lysistrata?', *BSA* 50: 1–12.
Lind, H. 1990. *Der Gerber Kleon in den 'Rittern' des Aristophanes. Studien zur Demagogenkomödie*. Peter Lang, pp. 239–41.
Lipka, M. 2002. *Xenophon's Spartan Constitution*. W. De Gruyter.
Lissarrague, F. 2000. 'Figures of Women', in P. Schmitt Pantel (ed.), *History of Women in the West, Volume I: From Ancient Goddesses to Christian Saints*. Belknap Press (French and Italian originals 1991), pp. 139–229.
Livingstone, N. 2001. *A Commentary on Isocrates' Busiris*. Brill.
Loening, T. C. 1987. *The Reconciliation Agreement of 403/402 B.C. in Athens: Its Contents and Application*. F. Steiner.
Loraux, N. 1986. *The Invention of Athens: The Funeral Oration in the Classical City*. Harvard University Press (French original 1981).
  1994. 'La cité grecque pense l'Un et le Deux', in *Mélanges Pierre Lévêque. Tome 8: Religion, anthropologie et société*. Les Belles Lettres, pp. 275–91.
  1997. *The Experiences of Tiresias: The Feminine and the Greek Man*. Princeton University Press (French original 1989).
  2000. *Born of the Earth: Myth and Politics in Athens*. Cornell University Press (French original 1996).
  2002. *The Mourning Voice. An Essay on Greek Tragedy*. Cornell University Press (French original 1999).
  2005. *La tragédie d'Athènes. La politique entre l'ombre et l'utopie*. Éd. du Seuil.
  2006. *The Divided City: On Memory and Forgetting in Ancient Athens*. Zone Books (French original 1997).
Loraux, P. 2000. 'Le pragmaticien', in N. Loraux and C. Mirales (eds.), *Figures de l'intellectuel en Grèce ancienne*. Belin, pp. 223–60.
Low, P. 2011. 'Athenian Foreign Policy and the Quest for Stability', in G. Herman (ed.), *Stability and Crisis in the Athenian Democracy*. F. Steiner, pp. 67–86.
Luce, J.-M. 1998. 'Thésée, le synoecisme et l'agora d'Athènes', *Revue archéologique* n.s. 1: 3–31.
Luraghi, N. 2014. 'Stratokles of Diomeia and Party Politics in Early Hellenistic Athens', *C&M* 65: 191–226.
Lynch, J. P. 1972. *Aristotle's School. A Study of a Greek Educationnal Institution*. University of California Press.
Ma, J. 1994. 'Black Hunter Variations', *Proceedings of the Cambridge Philological Society* 40: 49–80.
MacDowell, D. M. 1985. 'Athenian Laws about Choruses', in *Symposion 1982. Akten der Gesellschaft für griechische und hellenistische Rechtsgeschichte*. Böhlau, pp. 65–77.

1995. *Aristophanes and Athens. An Introduction to the Plays.* Oxford University Press.
2000. *Demosthenes. On the False Embassy (Oration 19). Edited with Introduction and Commentary.* Oxford University Press.
2009. *Demosthenes. The Orator.* Oxford University Press.

Macé, A. 2009. 'Publicité politique et publicité sensible: l'extravagance politique du Socrate platonicien', *Études platoniciennes* 6: 83–103.
    2014. 'Deux formes du commun en Grèce ancienne', *Annales HSS* 69: 659–88.
    2019. 'Citoyenneté politique et vie sociale. Sur la guerre civile des Athéniens, 404-403 av. J.-C.', in G. Labarre (ed.), *Citoyenneté et éducation par la société*. Presses de l'Université de Franche-Comté, pp. 21–40.

Mactoux, M.-M. 1986. 'Les pratiques discursives comme stratégie de reconnaissance (Lysias XXX, *Contre Nicomachos*)', in *L'Aveu. Antiquité et Moyen Âge. Actes de la table ronde de Rome (28–30 mars 1984)*. École française de Rome, pp. 27–51.
    1993. 'Phobos à Sparte', *Revue de l'Histoire des Religions* 210: 259–304.

Malouchou, G. E. 2014. 'Τὸ ἐνεπίγραφο τῶν ἀπὸ Φυλῆς τὸν δῆμον καταγαγόντων (*SEG* 28, 45)', *Horos* 22–25: 115–44.
    2015. 'The Restoration of Athenian Democracy in 403 BC: New Epigraphic Evidence', *Grammateion* 4: 89–98.

Mansouri, S. 2010. *La Démocratie athénienne, une affaire d'oisifs? Travail et participation politique à Athènes au i^{ve} siècle av. J.-C.* André Versaille.
    2011. *Athènes vue par ses métèques (Ve–IVe siècle av. J.-C.).* André Versaille.

Marchiandi, D. 2011a. *I periboli funerari nell'Attica classica. Lo specchio di una 'borghesia'.* Pandemos.
    2011b. 'Les périboles funéraires familiaux à l'époque de Lycurgue: entre aspirations "bourgeoises" et tendances nouvelles', in V. Azoulay and P. Ismard (eds.), *Clisthène et Lycurgue d'Athènes. Autour du politique dans la cité classique.* Publications de la Sorbonne, pp. 133–62.

Martin, G. 2014. 'Interpreting Instability: Considerations of the *Lives of the Ten Orators*', *Classical Quarterly* 64: 321–36.

Masson, O. 1988. 'Les noms théophores de Bendis en Grèce et en Thrace', *MH* 45: 6–12.

Matthaiou, A. P. 2011. 'The Theozotides Decree on the Sons of those murdered in the Oligarchy', in A. P. Matthaiou (ed.), *Τὰ ἐν τῆι στήληι γεγραμμένα. Six Greek Historical Inscriptions of the Fifth Century B.C.* Hellenikē Epigraphikē Hetaireia, pp. 71–81.

Mauss, M. 1903. 'Les débuts de la poésie selon Gummere', *L'Année sociologique* 6: 560–5.
    2001. *A General Theory of Magic.* Routledge (French original 1902).

Mauvignier, L. 2014. *Autour du monde.* Ed. de Minuit.

McCoy, J. 1975. 'The Identity of Leon', *American Journal of Philology* 96: 187–99.

McHugh, M. 2019. 'To Reap a Rich Harvest: Experiencing Agricultural Labour in Ancient Greece', *World Archaeology* 51: 208–25.

Meier, C. 1990. *The Greek Discovery of Politics*. Harvard University Press (German original 1980).
Mellet, P.-A. and J. Foa 2016. 'Une "politique de l'oubliance"? Mémoire et oubli pendant les guerres de Religion (1550–1600)', *Astérion* 15: 10.4000/asterion.2829.
Meritt, B. D. 1933. 'The Inscriptions', *Hesperia: The Journal of the American School of Classical Studies at Athens* 2: 149–69.
Message, V. 2013. *Romanciers pluralistes*. Ed. du Seuil.
Miccolis, E. R. 2017. *Archippos. Einleitung, Übersetzung, Kommentar*. Verlag Antike.
Middleton, D. 1982. 'Thrasyboulos' Thracian Support', *Classical Quarterly* 32: 298–303.
Mikalson, J. D. 1998. *Religion of Hellenistic Athens*. University of California Press.
Millett, P. 2000. 'Mogens Hansen and the Labelling of Athenian Democracy', in P. Flensted-Jensen, T. H. Nielsen and L. Rubinstein (eds.), *Polis & Politics. Studies in Ancient Greek History, Presented to Mogens Herman Hansen on his 60th Birthday*. Museum Tusculanum Press, pp. 339–60.
Mirhady, D. C. and Y. L. Too 2000. *Isocrates I. Oratory of Classical Greece*. University of Texas Press.
Mitchell, L. G. 2006. 'Tyrannical Oligarchs at Athens', in S. Lewis (ed.), *Ancient Tyranny*. Edinburgh University Press, pp. 178–87.
Monod, J.-C. 2006. 'La patience de l'image. Éléments pour une localisation de la métaphorologie' [Postface], in H. Blumenberg (ed.), *Paradigmes pour une métaphorologie*. Vrin, pp. 171–95.
Moretti, J.-C. 2001. *Théâtre et société dans la Grèce antique*. Librairie Générale Française.
Mossé, C. 1976. 'Les salariés à Athènes au IVe siècle', *DHA* 2: 97–101.
   1979. 'Citoyens actifs et citoyens "passifs" dans les cités grecques: une approche théorique du problème', *Revue des Etudes Anciennes* 81: 241–9.
Müller, C. 2018. 'Itinéraires d'une prostituée: Néaira et les espaces de la cité au IVe siècle av. J.-C.', in C. Moatti and C. Müller (eds.), *Statuts personnels et espaces sociaux. Questions grecques et romaines*. De Boccard, pp. 243–70.
Munn, M. 2000. *The School of History: Athens in the Age of Socrates*. University of California Press.
Murray, O. 1990. 'The Affair of the Mysteries: Democracy and the Drinking Group', in O. Murray (ed.), *Sympotica: A Symposium on the Symposion*. Oxford University Press, pp. 149–61.
Nails, D. 1998. 'The Dramatic Date of Plato's *Republic*', *Classical Journal* 93: 383–96.
   2002. *The People of Plato. A Prosopography of Plato and Other Socratics*. Hackett.
Nancy, J.-L. 2013. *Être singulier pluriel*. Galilée.
Németh, G. 2006. *Kritias und die Dreissig Tyrannen. Untersuchungen zur Politik und Prosopographie der Führungselite in Athen 404/403 v. Chr*. F. Steiner.
Norwood, G. 1931. *Greek Comedy*. Methuen & Company.
Ober, J. 2008. *Democracy and Knowledge: Innovation and Learning in Classical Athens*. Princeton University Press.

2013. 'Democracy's Wisdom: An Aristotelian Middle Way for Collective Judgment', *American Political Science Review* 107: 104–22.
Offredi, C. 1998. 'La précarité des années 80 ou un phénomène social en gestation dans la société', *Revue internationale d'action communautaire* 19: 21–32.
Olivetti, P. 2011. *Uses and Interpretations of Ritual Terminology: Goos, Oimoge, Threnos and Linos in Ancient Greek Literature*. PhD thesis. University of Birmingham.
Oranges, A. 2013. 'La concessione dell'epigamia agli Eubei', in C. Bearzot and F. Landucci (eds.), *Tra mare e continente: l'isola di Eubea*. Vita e Pensiero, pp. 173–89.
Orfanos, C. 2003. 'Ecclésia vs Banquet', *Pallas* 61: 203–18.
Osborne, M. J. 1981–1983. *Naturalization in Athens*, 4 vols. Paleis der Academiën.
  2012. 'Secretaries, Psephismata and Stelai in Athens', *Ancient Society* 42: 33–59.
Osborne, R. 1997. 'Law, the Democratic Citizen and the Representation of Women in Classical Athens', *Past and Present* 155: 3–33; reprinted in Osborne, R. 2010. *Athens and Athenian Democracy*. Cambridge University Press, pp. 244–66.
  2004. *The Old Oligarch: Pseudo-Xenophon's Constitution of the Athenians*. London Association of Classical Teachers (LACTOR).
Osborne, R. and P. J. Rhodes 2003. *Greek Historical Inscriptions, 404–323 BC*. Oxford University Press.
Ostwald, M. 1986. *From Popular Sovereignty to the Sovereignty of Law: Law, Society, and Politics in Fifth-Century Athens*. University of California Press.
Pakaluk, M. 1998. 'The Egalitarianism of the *Eudemian ethics*', *Classical Quarterly* 48: 411–32.
Papazarkadas, N. 2011. *Sacred and Public Land in Ancient Athens*. Oxford University Press.
Parker, R. 1996. *Athenian Religion: A History*. Oxford University Press.
  2005. *Polytheism and Society at Athens*. Oxford University Press.
Patera, I. 2013. 'Reflections on the discourse of fear in Greek sources', in A. Chaniotis and P. Ducrey (eds.), *Unveiling Emotions II*. F. Steiner, pp. 109–34.
Patillon, M. 2009. 'Alcidamas d'Élée', in J.-F. Pradeau (ed.), *Les Sophistes*, vol. 2. Flammarion, pp. 95–101.
Paugam, G. 2004. 'L'état d'exception: sur un paradoxe d'Agamben', *Labyrinthe* 19: 43–58.
Payen, P. 2010. 'Les historiens grecs entre la cité et l'exil', *Incidenza dell'antico* 8: 11–37.
  2012. *Les revers de la guerre en Grèce ancienne. Histoire et historiographie*. Belin.
Pébarthe, C. 2005. 'La liste des archontes athéniens (*IG* I³ 1031). Réflexions sur la datation d'une inscription', *Revue des Etudes Anciennes* 107: 11–28.
  2006. *Cité, démocratie et écriture. Histoire de l'alphabétisation d'Athènes à l'époque classique*. De Boccard.

2014a. 'Les sandales de Socrate. Les sophistes, les philosophes et la pauvreté', in E. Galbois and S. Rougier-Blanc (eds.), *La Pauvreté en Grèce ancienne*. Ausonius, pp. 223–36.

2014b. '*Oikonomia*, entre champ économique, champ politique et champ philosophique en Grèce ancienne. Méditations bourdieusiennes sur l'*Économique* de Xénophon', *Revue Française de Socio-Économie* 13: 67–84.

Pellegrin, P. 2017. *L'Excellence menacée. Sur la philosophie politique d'Aristote*. Classiques Garnier.

Peponi, A.-E. 2013a. 'Theorizing the Chorus in Greece', in J. Billings, F. Budelmann and F. Macintosh (eds.). *Choruses, Ancient and Modern*. Oxford University Press, pp. 15–34.

2013b. 'Choral Anti-Aesthetics', in A.-E. Peponi (ed.), *Performance and Culture in Plato's Laws*. Cambridge University Press, pp. 212–39.

Pérec, G. 2010. *La Vie mode d'emploi*. Hachette (1st edition 1978).

Pernin, I. 2014. *Les baux ruraux en Grèce ancienne. Corpus épigraphique et étude*. MOM Éditions.

Phillips, D. 2009. 'Hypereides 3 and the Athenian Law of Contracts', *TAPhA* 139: 89–122.

Piccirilli, L. 1981. '*Nomoi* cantati e *nomoi* scritti', *CCC* 2: 7–14.

Piovan, D. 2011. *Memoria e oblio della guerra civile: strategie giudiziarie e racconto del passato in Lisia*. Edizioni ETS.

Pirenne-Delforge, V. 2005. 'La cité, les *dèmotelè hiera* et les prêtres', in V. Dasen and M. Piérart (eds.), *Idiai kai dêmosiai. Les cadres 'privés' et 'publics' de la religion grecque antique*. Presses universitaires de Liège, pp. 55–68.

Pirrotta, S. 2009. *Plato comicus. Die fragmentarischen Komödien. Ein Kommentar*. Verlag Antike.

Planeaux, C. 2001. 'The Date of Bendis' Entry into Attica', *CJ* 96: 165–92.

Pontier, P. 2006. *Trouble et ordre chez Platon et Xénophon*. Vrin.

Potts, S. 2008. *The Athenian Navy: An Investigation into the Operations, Politics and Ideology of the Athenian Fleet between 480 and 322 BC*. PhD thesis. Cardiff University.

Powell, A. 2018. 'Athens as New Sparta? Lakonism and the Athenian Revolution of 404–3 BC', in P. Cartledge and A. Powell (eds.), *The Greek Superpower: Sparta in the Self-Definitions of Athenians*. Classical Press of Wales, pp. 61–85.

Pownall, F. 2008a. 'Critias on the Aetiology of the Kottabos Game', in M. Chassignet (ed.), *L'étiologie dans la pensée antique*. Brepols, pp. 17–33.

2008b. 'Critias' commemoration of Athens', *Mouseion*, Series III, 8: 333–54.

Pradeau, J.-F. 1997. *Le monde de la politique. Sur le récit atlante de Platon, Timée (17–27) et Critias*. Academia Verlag.

Prauscello, L. 2014. *Performing Citizenship in Plato's Laws*. Cambridge University Press.

Pritchett, W. K. 1985. *The Greek State at War, Part IV*. University of California Press.

Psilakis, C. 2014. *Dynamiques et mutations d'une figure d'autorité: la réception de Solon aux IVe et Ve siècles avant J.-C*. PhD thesis. Université Lille 3.

Radcliffe-Brown, A. 1922. *The Andaman Islanders. A Study in Social Anthropology.* Cambridge University Press.
Rambourg, C. 2015. *Topos. Les premières méthodes d'argumentation dans la rhétorique grecque des ve–ive siècles.* Vrin.
Rancière, J. 1994. *The Names of History: On the Poetics of Knowledge.* University of Minnesota Press (French original 1992).
Rankin, D. I. 1987. 'Socrates an Oligarch?', *L'Antiquité classique* 56: 68–87.
  1988. 'The Mining Lobby at Athens', *Ancient Society* 19: 189–205.
Raubitschek, A. E. 1941. 'The Heroes of *Phyle*', *Hesperia* 10: 284–95.
  1943. 'Greek Inscriptions', *Hesperia* 12: 12–88.
Reed, C. M. 2003. *Maritime Traders in the Ancient Greek World.* Cambridge University Press.
Reinach, T. 1919. 'Le plaidoyer de Lysias contre Hippothersès', *Revue des Etudes Grecques* 32: 443–50.
Rhodes, P. J. 1972. *The Athenian Boule.* Oxford University Press.
  1981. *A Commentary on the Aristotelian Athenaion Politeia.* Clarendon Press.
  2000. 'Oligarchs in Athens', in R. Brock and S. Hodkinson (eds.), *Alternatives to Athens: Varieties of Political Organization and Community in Ancient Greece.* Oxford University Press, pp. 119–36.
  2003. 'Nothing to Do with Democracy: Athenian Drama and the *Polis*', *Journal of Hellenic Studies* 123: 104–19.
  2011. 'Appeals to the Past in Classical Athens', in G. Herman (ed.), *Stability and Crisis in the Athenian Democracy.* F. Steiner, pp. 13–30.
Richer, N. 1998. *Les éphores. Études sur l'histoire et sur l'image de Sparte (viiie-iiie siècles av. J.-C.).* Publications de la Sorbonne.
Rihll, T. S. 2008. 'Slavery and Technology in Pre-Industrial Contexts', in E. Dal Lago and C. Katsari (eds.), *Slave Systems, Ancient and Modern.* Cambridge University Press, pp. 127–47.
Robertson, B. 2008. 'The Slave-Names of *IG* I^3 1032 and the Ideology of Slavery at Athens', in C. Cooper (ed.), *Epigraphy and the Greek Historian.* University of Toronto Press, pp. 79–116.
Roisman, J. and I. Worthington (eds.) 2015. *Lives of the Attic Orators: Texts from Pseudo-Plutarch, Photius, and the Suda.* Oxford University Press.
Romeyer-Dherbey, G. 2005. 'L'Un et l'Autre dans la cité d'Aristote', *Revue philosophique de la France et de l'étranger* 130: 191–202.
Romilly, J. de 1980. *Précis de littérature grecque.* Presses Universitaires de France.
Rosenbloom, D. 2002. 'From *Ponêros* to *Pharmakos*: Theater, Social Drama, and Revolution in Athens, 428–404 BCE', *Classical Antiquity* 21: 283–346.
Rosenmeyer, T. G. 1949. 'The Family of Critias', *American Journal of Philology* 70: 404–10.
Rossetti, L. and C. Lausdei 1981. '*P. Oxy.* 2889 e il *Milziade* di Eschine Socratico', *RhM* 124: 154–65.
Roubineau, J.-M. 2007. 'La fiscalité des cités grecques aux époques classique et hellénistique', *Pallas* 74: 179–200.
Rousseau, J.-J. 1960 [1758]. *Politics and the Arts: Letter to M. d'Alembert on the Theatre.* The Free Press.

Roussel, P. (ed.) 1926. *Isée. Discours*. Les Belles Lettres [CUF] (1st edition 1922).
Rubinstein, L. 1993. *Adoption in IV. Century Athens*. Museum Tusculanum Press.
Ruschenbuch, E. 1966. *Solonos Nomoi: die Fragmente des Solonischen Gesetzeswerkes*. F. Steiner.
Rutherford, I. 2004. '*Khoros heis ek tesde tes poleos*: State-Pilgrimage and Song-Dance in Athens', in P. Murray and P. Wilson (eds.), *Music and the Muses: The Culture of 'Mousike' in the Classical Athenian City*. Oxford University Press, pp. 67–90.
  2013. 'Chorus, Song and Anthropology', in J. Billings, F. Budelmann and F. Macintosh (eds.), *Choruses, Ancient and Modern*. Oxford University Press, pp. 67–77.
Ruzé, F. 2001. 'La Loi et le chant', in J.-P. Brun and P. Jockey (eds.), *Techniques et sociétés en Méditerrannée. Hommage à M.-Cl. Amouretti*. Maisonneuve et Larose, pp. 708–19.
  2007. '"Laconiser" à Athènes: à propos des *Guêpes* d'Aristophane', in P. Schmitt Pantel and F. de Polignac (eds.), *Athènes et le politique. Dans le sillage de Claude Mossé*. Albin Michel, pp. 249–70.
Ryan, P. 2012. *Plato's Phaedrus: A Commentary for Greek Readers*. University of Oklahoma Press.
Saetta Cottone, R. 2005. *Aristofane e la poetica dell'ingiuria*. Carocci.
Salmon, P. 1969. 'L'établissement des Trente à Athènes', *Antiquité Classique* 38: 497–500.
Salviat, F. 1989. 'La deuxième représentation des *Grenouilles*. La faute d'Adeimantos, Cléophon et le seuil de l'hirondelle', in R. Etienne, M.-T. Le Dinahet and M. Yon (eds.), *Architecture et poésie dans le monde grec. Hommage à Georges Roux*. MOM, pp. 171–83.
Sartori, F. 1983. 'Aristofane e Agirrio nel 405 av. J.-C.', *Festschrift für Hermann Bengtson zum 70. Geburtstag*. F. Steiner, pp. 56–77.
Saunders, T. J. and T. A. Sinclair 1992. *Aristotle. Politics*. Penguin Books.
Schaps, D. 1977. 'The Woman Least Mentioned: Etiquette and Women's Names', *Classical Quarterly* 27: 323–30.
Scheid, J. and J. Svenbro 1996. *The Craft of Zeus: Myths of Weaving and Fabric*. Harvard University Press (French original 1994).
Schindel, U. 1967. 'Untersuchungen zur Biographie des Redners Lysias', *RhM* 110: 44.
Schmaltz, B. 2002. 'Griechische Grabreliefs klassischer Zeit: Beobachtungen zum Menschenbild des 4. Jhs', in J. M. Højte (ed.), *Images of Ancestors*. Aarhus University Press, pp. 49–58.
Schmitt, C. 1985. *Political Theology: Four Chapters on the Concept of Sovereignty*. MIT Press (German original 1922).
  1996. *The Concept of the Political*. University of Chicago Press (German original 1932).
Schmitt Pantel, P. 1994–1995. 'Autour d'une anthropologie des sexes. À propos de la femme sans nom d'Ischomaque', *Métis* 9–10: 299–305.

2009. *Aithra et Pandora. Femmes, genre et cité dans la Grèce antique*. L'Harmattan.
Schmitz, W. 2004. *Nachbarschaft und Dorfgemeinschaft im archaischen und klassischen Griechenland*. Akademie Verlag.
Schneider, J. 1999. 'Une centauromachie littéraire: Grenouilles, v. 902–904', *Kentron* 15: 67–74.
Schofield, M. 1998. 'Political Friendship and the Ideology of Reciprocity', in P. Cartledge, P. Millett and S. von Reden (eds.), *Kosmos. Essays in Order, Conflict and Community in Classical Athens*. Cambridge University Press, pp. 37–51.
Scodel, R. 2007. 'Lycurgus and the State Text of Tragedy', in C. Cooper (ed.), *Politics of Orality: Orality and Literacy in Ancient Greece*. Brill, pp. 129–54.
Sealey, R. 1955. 'Athens after the Social War', *JHS* 75: 74–81.
Sébillotte, V. 2006. *Libérez la patrie ! Patriotisme et politique en Grèce ancienne*. Belin.
Serna, P. 2005. *La République des girouettes. 1789–1815, et au-delà: une anomalie politique, la France de l'extrême centre*. Champ Vallon.
Shear, J. L. 2011. *Polis and Revolution. Responding to Oligarchy in Classical Athens*. Cambridge University Press.
Sickinger, J. P. 1999. *Public Records and Archives in Classical Athens*. University of North Carolina Press.
Simmonton, M. 2012. 'Review of J. L. Shear, *Polis and Revolution. Responding to Oligarchy in classical Athens*', *Bryn Mawr Classical Review* [online]. https://bmcr.brynmawr.edu/2012/2012-02-12.html.
Sommerstein, A. H. 1993. 'Kleophon and the restaging of *Frogs*', in A. H. Sommerstein, S. Halliwell, J. Henderson and B. Zimmermann (eds.), *Tragedy, Comedy and the Polis*. Levante editori, pp. 461–76.
  2002a. *Lysistrata and Other Plays*. Penguin Books.
  2002b. 'Platon, Eupolis and the "Demagogue-Comedy"', in D. Harvey and J. Wilkins (eds.), *The Rivals of Aristophanes. Studies in Athenian Old Comedy*. Classical Press of Wales, pp. 437–51.
Sommerstein, A. H. and A. J. Bayliss 2013. *Oath and State in Ancient Greece*. De Gruyter.
Stanton, G. R. 1996. 'Some Inscription in Attic Demes', *ABSA* 91: 341–64.
Stark, I. 2004. *Die Hämische Muse. Spott als soziale und mentale Kontrolle in der griechischen Komödie*. C. H. Beck.
Ste Croix, G. de 1981. *The Class Struggle in the Ancient Greek World: From the Archaic Age to the Arab Conquests*. Duckworth.
Stem, R. 2003. 'The Thirty at Athens in the summer of 404', *Phoenix* 57: 18–34.
Storey, I. C. 2003. *Eupolis. Poet of Old Comedy*. Oxford University Press.
  2011. *Fragments of Old Comedy, Volume III: Philonicus to Xenophon. Adespota* [Loeb Classical Library]. Harvard University Press.
Strauss, B. S. 1987. *Athens after the Peloponnesian War: Class, Faction and Policy 403–386 B.C.* Cornell University Press.

Stroud, R. S. 1998. *The Athenian Grain-Tax Law of 374/3 B.C.* American School of Classical Studies at Athens.
Svenbro, J. 1993. *Phrasikleia. An Anthropology of Reading in Ancient Greece.* Cornell University Press.
Tackett, T. 2015. *The Coming of the Terror in the French Revolution.* Belknap Press.
Taylor, C. 2007. 'A new political world', in R. Osborne (ed.), *Debating the Athenian Cultural Revolution.* Cambridge University Press, pp. 72–90.
  2017. *Poverty, Wealth, and Well-Being. Experiencing Penia in Democratic Athens.* Oxford University Press.
Taylor, C. and K. Vlassopoulos 2015. *Communities and Networks.* Oxford University Press.
Taylor, M. C. 2002. 'One Hundred Heroes of Phyle?', *Hesperia* 71: 377–97.
Teitel, R. G. 2002. *Transitional Justice.* Oxford University Press (1st edition 2000).
Thomas, R. 2019. *Polis Histories, Collective Memories and the Greek World.* Cambridge University Press.
Thomas, Y. 1999. 'L'usage et les fruits de l'esclave. Opérations juridiques romaines sur le travail', *Enquête* 7: 203–30.
Todd, S. C. 1990. 'The Use and Abuse of the Attic Orators', *Greece & Rome* 37: 159–78.
  1996. 'Lysias against Nicomachos. The Fate of the Expert in Athenian Law', in L. Foxhall and A. Lewis (eds.), *Greek Law in Its Political Setting. Justifications Not Justice.* Clarendon Press, pp. 101–31.
  2000. *Lysias.* University of Texas Press.
  2007. *A Commentary on Lysias, Speeches 1–11.* Oxford University Press.
Toole, H. 1975. 'The Social Status of Socrates as Inferred from His Military Service and Other Informations', *Platôn* 27: 147–53.
Traill, J. S. 1968. 'The Bouleutic List of 303/2 B.C.', *Hesperia* 37: 1–24.
  1969. 'The Bouleutic List of 281/0 B.C.', *Hesperia* 38: 459–94.
Tran, N. 2013. 'The Work Statuses of Slaves and Freedmen in the Great Ports of the Roman World (First Century BCE–Second Century CE)', *Annales HSS* 68: 659–84.
Trédé-Boulmer, M. 2002. 'Le théâtre comme métaphore au IIe s. ap. J.–C.: survivances et métamorphoses', *CRAI* 146: 581–605.
Tribulato, O. 2014. 'Compound Nouns', in G. K. Giannakis (ed.), *Encyclopedia of Ancient Greek Language and Linguistics*, vol. 1. Brill, pp. 344–7.
Tsagalis, C. 2008. *Inscribing Sorrow: Fourth-Century Attic Funerary Epigrams.* De Gruyter.
Tsing, A. L. 2015. *The Mushroom at the End of the World: On the Possibility of Life in Capitalist Ruins.* Princeton University Press.
Usher, S. 1968. 'Xenophon, Critias and Theramenes', *Journal of Hellenic Studies* 88: 128–35.
  1976. 'Lysias and His Clients', *Greek, Roman and Byzantine Studies* 17: 31–40.
  1979. 'This to the Fair Critias', *Eranos* 77: 39–42.
  1999. *Greek Oratory. Tradition and Originality.* Oxford University Press.

Usher, S. and D. Najock 1982. 'A Statistical Study of Authorship in the *Corpus Lysiacum*', *Computers and the Humanities* 16: 85–105.
Van Effenterre, H. and M. Van Effenterre 1988. 'L'acte de fraternisation de Nakone', *Mélanges de l'École française de Rome–Antiquité* 100: 687–700.
Van't Wout, P. E. 2010. 'Solon's Law on *Stasis*: Promoting Active Neutrality', *Classical Quarterly* 60: 289–301.
Vérilhac, A.-M. and C. Vial 1998. *Le Mariage grec du VIe siècle avant J.-C. à l'époque d'Auguste*. École française d'Athènes.
Vernant, J.-P. 1983. *Myth and Thought Among the Greeks*. Zone Books (French original 1965).
Vidal-Naquet, P. 1990. 'Oedipus between Two Cities: An Essay on *Oedipus at Colonus*', in J.-P. Vernant and P. Vidal-Naquet, *Myth and Tragedy in Ancient Greece*. Zone Book, pp. 329–360 (French original 1972 and 1986).
  2002. *Le miroir brisé. Tragédie athénienne et politique*. Les Belles Lettres.
  2007. *The Atlantis Story: A Short History of Plato's Myth*. Liverpool University Press (French original 2005).
Visvardi, E. 2015. *Emotion in Action. Thucydides and the Tragic Chorus*. Brill.
Viveiros de Castro, E. 2014. *Cannibals Metaphysics*. Univocal Publishing.
Vlassopoulos, K. 2007. 'Free Spaces: Identity, Experience and Democracy in Classical Athens', *Classical Quarterly* 57: 33–52.
  2015. 'Plotting Strategies, Networks and Communities in Classical Athens: The Evidence of Slave Names', in K. Vlassopoulos and C. Taylor (eds.), *Communities and Networks in the Ancient Greek World*. Oxford University Press, pp. 101–27.
Volonaki, E. 2001. 'The Re-Publication of the Athenian Laws in the Last Decade of the Fifth Century BC', *Dike* 4: 137–67.
Walbank, M. B. 1982. 'The Confication and Sale by the *Poletai* in 402/1 of the Property of the Thirty Tyrants', *Hesperia* 51: 74–98.
Wallace, R. W. 2015. *Reconstructing Damon. Music, Wisdom Teaching, and Politics in Perikles' Athens*. Oxford University Press.
Weber, M. 1978. *Economy and Society: An Outline of Interpretive Sociology*. University of California Press (German original 1922).
  2001. 'Koroibos, ein Architekt des Perikles, und der Grabbezirk XVIII seiner Familie im Kerameikos', *Thetis* 8: 77–96.
Westermann, A. 1833. *Plutarchi Vitae Decem Oratorum*. J. Becker.
Whitehead, D. 1977. *The Ideology of the Athenian Metic*. Cambridge Philological Society.
  1982–1983. 'Sparta and the Thirty Tyrants', *Ancient Society* 13–4: 105–30.
  1986. 'The Political Career of Aristophon', *Classical Philology* 81: 313–9.
  2002. 'Athenian Laws and Lawsuits in the Late Fifth Century B.C.', *Museum Helveticum* 59: 71–96.
Wijma, S. 2014. *Embracing the Immigrant. The Participation of Metics in Athenian Polis Religion (5th–4th century BC)*. F. Steiner.
Wilamowitz-Moellendorff, U. von 1875. *Analecta Euripidea*. Borntraeger.
  1887. 'Demotika der Attischen Metoeken. II', *Hermes* 22: 211–59.

1893. *Aristoteles und Athen*, t. II. Weidmann.

1924. *Die griechische Literatur des Altertums*. Die Kultur der Gegenwart, t. I, vol. VIII. B. G. Teubner.

Will, É. 1975. 'Notes sur *Misthos*', in J. Bingen (ed.), *Le monde grec: pensée, littérature, histoire, documents. Hommages à Claire Préaux*. Ed. de l'Université de Bruxelles, pp. 426–38.

1995. '*Syngeneia, oikeiotès, philia*', *RPh* 69: 299–325.

Williamson, M. 2017. 'Africa or Old Rome? Jamaican Slave Naming Revisited', *Slavery & Abolition* 38: 117–34.

Wilson, P. 2000. *The Athenian Institution of the Khoregia. The Chorus, The City and the Stage*. Cambridge University Press.

2003a. 'The Sound of Cultural Conflict. Kritias and the Culture of *Mousikê* in Athens', in C. Dougherty and L. Kurke (eds.), *The Cultures within Ancient Greek Culture. Contact, Conflict, Collaboration*. Cambridge University Press, pp. 181–206.

2003b. 'The Politics of Dance: Dithyrambic Contest and Social Order in Ancient Greece', in D. Phillips and D. Pritchard (eds.), *Sport and Festival in the Ancient Greek World*. Classical Press of Wales, pp. 163–96.

2011. 'The Glue of Democracy? Tragedy, Structure, and Finance', in D. Carter (ed.), *Why Athens? A Reappraisal of Tragic Politics*. Oxford University Press, pp. 19–43.

Witt, M. 2013. *Jean-Luc Godard. Cinema Historian*. Indiana University Press.

Wolff, F. 1997. 'Être disciple de Socrate', in G. Giannantoni and M. Narcy (eds.), *Lezioni socratiche*. Bibliopolis, pp. 29–79.

Wolpert, A. 2001. *Remembering Defeat: Civil War and Civic Memory in Ancient Athens*. Johns Hopkins University Press.

Wood, E. M. 1983. 'Agricultural Slavery in Classical Athens', *AJAH* 8: 1–47.

Woodhead, A. G. 1997. *The Athenian Agora: Results of Excavations Conducted by the American School of Classical Studies at Athens, Vol. XVI, Inscriptions: The Decrees*. American School of Classical Studies at Athens.

Yunis, H. 2011. *Plato: Phaedrus*. Cambridge University Press.

Yvonneau, J. 2018. 'Critias: l'invention et l'inventaire', in J. Yvonneau (ed.), *La muse au long couteau, Critias, de la création littéraire au terrorisme d'État*. Ausonius, pp. 13–32.

Zimmermann, H.-D. 1974. 'Die freie Arbeit in Griechenland während des 5. und des 4. Jahrhunderts v. u. Z.', *Klio* 56: 337–52.

Zurbach, J. 2014. 'Entre libres et esclaves dans l'Athènes classique', in C. Apicella, M.-L. Haack and F. Lerouxel (eds.), *Les Affaires de Monsieur Andreau. Économie et société dans le monde romain*. Ausonius, pp. 273–85.

Index

This Index distinguishes between different categories of names according to the following conventions: Names of deities, heroes and fictional characters are capitalized; modern and contemporary individuals are in small capitals; names of ancient Greek individuals are in normal characters; among the ancient authors, only those who were in some way involved in the events of 404/3 are indexed; we have specified the demotic of Athenian citizens (if known), and for noncitizens their status.

Adeimantus (of Skambonidai), 238
Aeschines (of Kothokidai, orator), 82–4, 85, 98, 116, 122–3, 196, 246–7
Aeschines (of Sphettos), 132–3, 279
Aeschylus (of Eleusis, tragic poet), 26, 52, 236–7, 238, 240
AGAMBEN, Giorgio, 63, 96, 105, 308, 318
Agathon (status unknown), 229
Agoratus (demotic unknown), 290
Agyrrhius (of Collytos), 71, 99, 113, 118–19
Aisimus (demotic unknown), 85
Alcamenes (demotic unknown, sculptor), 81
Alcias (freedman), 191
Alcibiades (of Kollytos), 133
Alcibiades (of Skambonidai), 18, 39, 42, 48, 78, 81, 238
Alexander the Great (macedonian king), 10
ALTMANN, Robert, 22
Amphilochus (demotic unknown), 131, 280
Andocides (of Kydantidai), 34, 41–3, 111, 113, 127, 151–4, 160, 291
Anthemion (of Euonymon), 84, 120
Anticles (demotic unknown), 188
Anticles (origin unknown), 190
Anticles (demotic unknown, secretary of the *epistatai* of the Parthenon), 246
Antisthenes (demotic unknown), 191
Anytus (of Euonymon), 81, 84–5, 86, 100, 119–21, 128, 138, 152
Aphobetus (of Kothokidai), 246
APOLLO, 11, 16, 58, 223, 238
Apollodorus (demotic unknown, orator), 259, 275, 294
Apollodorus (of Megara), 190
Arcesilaus (of Sparta), 36

Archeneus (demotic unknown, shipowner), 279
Archenomus (demotic unknown), 238, 240
Archinus (of Koile), 29, 82–4, 92, 93, 95, 96–108, 113, 115–32, 134, 137, 138, 203, 221, 289, 300, 318
Archippus (demotic unknown, comic poet), 134
Arethousius (demotic unknown), 199
Aristandros (of Eleusis), 229
Aristarchus (demotic unknown), 149–51, 163, 164, 202
Aristogeiton (of Aphidn, tyrannicide), 6
Aristophanes (of Kydathenaion), 24, 35, 36, 59, 73, 99–100, 118, 119, 133, 154, 157, 159, 167, 171–4, 230, 235–40, 242, 243–4, 301, 316, 323, 324, 326
Aristophon (of Azenia), 116, 122
Aristoteles (of Thorai), 34, 42
ARTEMIS, 25, 58, 231, 233
Aspasia (of Miletus), 23, 317
Astyages (metic), 196–8
ATHENA, 6, 29, 81, 113, 166–87, 188
 Athena Nike, 176–80, 214
 Athena Polias, 166, 167, 173, 175, 179–80
Atrometus (of Kothokidai), 85, 116

BAILLY, Jean-Christophe, 12
Bendiphanes (metic), 232
BENDIS, 232–4
Blepon (metic), 232
Blepyrus (of Paiania), 248
BOURDIEU, Pierre, 297–8
Brachyllus (of Erchia), 275–6, 277
Brasidas (of Sparta), 36

355

Index

Callaischros (demotic unknown), 35, 39, 68
Calliades (demotic unknown), 59
Callias (eponymous archon), 235, 264, 267
Callias (of Skambonidai), 157
Callias (status unknown), 229
Callicrates (demotic unknown), 176
Callimachus (demotic unknown, litigant), 126, 129–31, 144–5
Callimachus (demotic unknown, Myrrhine's father), 177
Callimachus (demotic unknown, sculptor), 214
Callistratus (demotic unknown), 191
CANFORA, Luciano, 40, 310–14
Carpos (status unknown), 229–30
CARVER, Raymond, 22
Cephalus (metic, father of Lysias), 251, 255, 258, 259, 262, 273
Cephisophon (of Paiania), 110–14, 124–5, 211
Cephisophon (slave), 244
Chabrias (of Aixone), 80
Chaerephon (of Sphettos), 156
Charicles (demotic unknown), 3, 34, 38–9, 41–2, 108, 153
Charmides (demotic unknown), 69, 159
Cimon (of Lakiadai), xiv, 36, 80, 107, 326
Cittos, 228–30
Cephisophon (of Paiania), 211
Cleanthes (metic, philosopher), 196
Cleidemides (of Melite), 214–19
Cleidemos (of Melite), 214–18
Cleisthenes (of Athens), 3, 18, 91
Cleitophon (demotic unknown), 100
Cleocritus (demotic unknown, eponymous archon of 413/2), 258, 264
Cleocritus (demotic unknown, herald of the mysteries of Eleusis), 7–9, 31, 310, 314, 328
Cleon (of Kydathenaion), 35, 120, 134, 289
Cleophon (of Acharnai), 42, 58, 84, 133, 235, 238–40, 241, 291, 316–17, 319
Conon (of Anaphlystos), 73, 325
Coroibos I (of Melite), 216–19
CREON, 41
Critias (demotic unknown), 3, 7, 28, 31–71, 77, 87, 92, 114, 123, 136, 186, 221, 299, 322
Crito (of Alopeke), 156, 202

Damnippus (demotic unknown), 281–2, 294
DE GAULLE, Charles, 83, 87
Demaretus (demotic unknown), 69, 102
DEMETER, 7
Demetrius (origin unknow, sculptor), 167
Demetrius (status unknown, farmer), 191
Dexios (metic), 232

Dicaeogenes (II) (of Kydathenaion), 207–12, 220
Dicaeogenes (III) (of Kydathenaion), 207–12, 214, 220
Dio (demotic unknown), 101
Dioclides (demotic unknown), 41
Diodoros (status unknown), 124
Diognetus (of Kydantidai), 145
Dionysia (festival), 25, 133, 235, 293–4, 306, 326
Dionysius (tyrant of Syracuse), 71
Dionysodorus (of Chios), 85
DIONYSUS, 99, 196, 235–8, 244
Diophanes (demotic unknown), 124
DÖBLIN, Aldred, 21
DOS PASSOS, John, 21
Draco (of Athens, legislator), 106, 324–5
Dracontides (of Bate, Lysimache's father), 167
Dropides (demotic unkown), 35, 136

Egersis (metic), 232
Ephialtes (demotic unknown, orator), xxii
Epicrates (of Kephisia), 278
Epictas (metic), 232
Eratosthenes (member of the Thirty tyrants), 70, 284–5, 286, 314, 320
Eratosthenes (of Oe), 292
ERECHTHEUS, 169–70, 182, 183
Ergocles (demotic unknown), 71, 77, 79, 85, 265, 288, 290
Eryximachus (demotic unknown), 211, 287, 290
Euandros (of Euonymon?), 109–10, 129
Eucleides (demotic unknown, eponymous archon of 403/2 BC), 160
Eucleides (demotic unknown, socratic philosopher), 154
Eucrates (of Kydantidai), 289
Eucolion (metic), 196–9
Euphiletus (demotic unknown), 292
Euripides (of Plya, tragic poet), 51, 169–71, 235–7, 243–4
Eutherus (demotic unknown), 192–4, 195, 196–8, 201–3
Euthydemos (of Eitea), 214–18
Euthydemus (metic, Lysias' brother), 274
Euthydemus (of Chios), 33, 157

Gerys (*isotelēs*), xix, 29, 196, 224–8, 230–4, 260, 295, 300
Glaucon (of Kollytos), 255, 258
Glycanthis (status unknown), 229
GRANET, Marcel, 20–1

HADES, 49, 54, 196
Hagnon (of Steiria), 34, 196

Index 357

Harmodius (of Aphidna, fourth century BCE), 211, 218
Harmodius (of Aphidna, tyrannicide), 6, 211
Hegeso (of Athens), 29, 207, 214, 218–20, 300
HERA, 49
HERACLES, 50–1, 81, 232, 236
Herman (or Hermon, demotic unknown), 267, 281
HERMES, 177, 220, 229
Herms (pillars), 41, 66
HESTIA, 65, 220
Hipparchus (son of Peisistratus), 6
Hippias (son of Peisistratus), 182
HIPPODAMIA, 49
Hippodamus (of Miletus), 283
Hippotherses (demotic unknown), 276–7, 286
HUBERT, Henri, 19
Hyperbolus (of Perithoidai), 84

Iphicrates (of Rhamnous, general), 211
Isaeus (metic, orator), 207–8
Isagoras (of Athens), 18
Ischomachus (demotic unknown), 205–7, 219
Ismenias (of Thebes), 81
Isocrates (of Erchia, orator), 115, 120, 126, 127, 129, 130–1, 144–5, 195, 266, 313, 321–3

Lampon (demotic unknown), 283
Leodamas (of Acharnai), 287
Leon (of Salamis), 59, 159–61, 286
LORAUX, Nicole, 96, 98, 104, 123, 134–6, 138, 141, 163–4, 307, 319
Lycurgus (of Boutadai), 80, 173, 326
Lysander (of Sparta), 34, 38, 129, 146, 311, 315
Lysiades (demotic unknown), 88
Lysias (metic, citizen, *isoteles*), 34, 39, 42, 56, 57, 60, 70, 73, 85, 87, 90, 91, 94, 97, 101, 109–10, 117, 121, 122, 125, 128–9, 130, 134, 139, 141–4, 146–9, 152–3, 189–91, 211, 240–2, 251–96, 300, 315, 317
Lysimache (of Athens), 29, 166–87, 300
LYSISTRATA, 59, 171–6, 179–80, 183, 184–5, 187

Malthake (status unknown), 229
Mania (status unknown), 229
Mantitheus (demotic unknown), 146–7, 163, 287, 312
MAUSS, Marcel, 19–20
MAUVIGNER, Laurent, 22
Medeus (of Larissa), 10
Melas the Egyptian, 208
Meletus (demotic unknown, accuser of Socrates), 110, 152, 160, 286, 290, 298
Meletus (demotic unknown, negotiator), 110

Melobius (demotic unknown), 42
Menander (of Kephisia), 195–6
Menexenus (of Kydathenaion), 207, 211
MESSAGE, Vincent, 22
Metaneira (hetaira), 254, 255, 259, 294
Metrodorus (public slave), 248
Miltiades (of Lakiadai, general), 72
Miltiades (of Lakiadai, son of Stesagoras), 133
Mnesilochus (of Phya), 42
Morychos (of Thria), 278
Myrmex (demotic unknown), 238, 240
Myrrhine (of Athens, priestess of Athena Nike), 176–80, 182

Nicias (of Kydantidai), 73, 80, 289, 291
Nicomachus (demotic unknown, *anagrapheus* of the laws), 29, 238, 240–5, 249–50, 288, 295, 300, 312, 317
Nicomachus (demotic unknown, farmer), 190
Nicomachus (origin unknown, sculptor), 180–1
Niceratus (of Kydantidai), 59
Nico (*isotelēs?*), 226–7

OEDIPUS, 326
OFFREDI, Claudine, 198

Pancleon (status unknown), 198, 260
Pasion (of Acharnai), 196, 226
Patrocleides (demotic unknown), 235, 237
Patrocles (demotic unknown), 131, 145
Pausanias (of Sparta), 79, 108, 129, 135, 145
Peisistratus (of Athens), 6, 182
Peison (demotic unknown), 252, 279–80
PÉREC, Georges, 22
Pericles (of Cholargos), 47, 72, 80, 93, 114, 136, 138, 139, 184, 218, 261, 263, 307, 324, 326
Pericles' law, 90, 93, 116, 122, 184, 212, 322
PERSEPHONE, 7, 49
Phaedrus (of Myrrhinous), 155, 256, 264, 265, 270–2, 278
Phayllus (of Acherdous), 108
Philip II (king of Macedonia), 16, 196,
Philon (of Acharnai), 142–4
Philon (status unknown), 229
Philostratus (of Colonos), 259, 294
Phormion (of Erythrae), 232
Phormisius (demotic unknown), 87, 100, 119, 121–2, 128, 135, 194
Phrynichus (of Deiradiotai), 39–40, 41, 86, 190, 281, 316
PIRITHOOS, 49–52, 62, 63
Pisander (of Acharnai), 40, 190
Pistos (slave), 222
Pithias (status unknown), 196

Plato (demotic unknown, comic poet), 239
Plato (of Kollytos, philosopher), 2, 9, 11–12, 14,
    15, 23, 26, 28, 31, 43, 46–7, 54, 57, 120,
    154, 158–61, 193, 223, 231, 242–3, 249,
    255–6, 258, 264, 265, 268–71, 273,
    278–9, 297–300, 302, 323, 324, 328
PLUTO, 236, 238–9
Polemarchus (metic, brother of Lysias), 70,
    251–2, 255, 256, 263, 273–5, 279
Poliochus (demotic unknown), 291
Polyaratus (of Cholargos), 211
POLYNICES, 41
Polystratus (of Deiradiotai), 292
PRAXITHEA, 170–1
Procleides (of Xypete), 248
Protagoras (of Abdera), 10, 283, 306
Proteas (status unknown), 191
Proxenos (of Aphidna), 207, 208–11, 214,
    218–19, 220
Pseudo-Xenophon (demotic unknown), 17, 40,
    44, 60, 199
PYNCHON, Thomas, 22
Pythocles/Pythocleides (demotic unknown), 47
Pythodoros (demotic unknown, eponymous
    archon), 311

Rhinon (of Paiania), 97, 108–10, 111, 130–4,
    138, 211
ROUSSEAU, Jean-Jacques, 13
RUSHDIE, Salman, 22

Satyrus (of Kephisia), 34, 65, 239, 317
SCHMITT, Carl, 104, 105, 163
Seuthes (Thracian king), 79
Simon (demotic unknown, shoemaker), 300
Simonides (of Ceos), 226
SISYPHUS, 52–5
Socrates (of Alopeke), 14, 29, 31, 33, 84, 110,
    120, 123, 127, 132–3, 140, 147, 152,
    154–63, 251, 279, 286, 292, 295, 300, 315
  Socrates of Plato, 16, 46, 101, 256, 259, 271,
    298–9
  Socrates of Xenophon, 14, 32, 43, 149–51,
    192–3, 201–3
Solon (of Athens, legislator), 35, 46, 93, 106,
    109, 136, 138–9, 172, 210, 242, 300, 301,
    309, 324–6

Sosicles (of Eitea), 214–18
Sosimenes (status unknown), 229–30
Strombichides (of Euonymon), 59
Sulla (roman general), 327
Syeris (status unknown), 180–2, 185–6

Telecleides (demotic unknown,
    comic poet), 39
Telemachos (demotic unknown), 173
Themistocles (of Phrearrhioi), 173
Theodoros (of Byzantium), 268
Theodorus (demotic unknown), 298
Theocles (of Sounion), 84
Theophilos (*isotelēs*), 226–7
Theozotides (of Athmonon), 116–18, 122,
    124–5
Theramenes (of Steiria), xx, 31, 34, 39, 41–2, 45,
    49, 56, 60–6, 69, 78, 81, 85, 87, 91–2, 93,
    100, 114–15, 119–21, 128–9, 133, 138,
    160, 221–2, 281, 313
Therippides (of Paiania), 199
THESEUS, 49–52, 62–3
Thraitta (slave), 223, 229
Thrasybulus (of Collytos), 85, 287
Thrasybulus (of Steiria), 3–7, 29, 67, 69, 70,
    71–82, 86–95, 98, 100, 106–8, 115, 121,
    125, 132, 141–2, 144–5, 147, 149, 166,
    180, 185–7, 196, 203, 211, 221, 224–6,
    230, 232–3, 234, 257, 258, 264–5, 286,
    290, 292, 295, 300, 311, 314, 318, 322, 328
Thrasydaeus (of Elis), 267, 280
Thrasyllus (demotic unknown), 74
Thucydides (of Halimous), 2–3, 74–7, 101, 189,
    205, 272, 307, 325
Timotheus (of Anaphlystos), 80

XANTHIAS (slave), 196
Xenaenetus (demotic unknown), 88, 127
Xenophon (of Erchia), 6–9, 14–16, 18, 33–4, 43,
    45, 53, 56, 61–7, 71, 73, 82, 88, 92, 93, 98,
    101, 110, 120, 126, 128–9, 130, 149–51,
    154, 158, 160–3, 164, 189, 192–4, 198,
    201, 203, 206, 219, 221, 232, 251–2,
    311–13, 316, 317, 327
Xerxes (Persian king), 188

ZEUS, 49, 152, 220